Readings
in the History
of Anthropology

READINGS IN THE HISTORY OF ANTHROPOLOGY

Regna Darnell
University of Alberta

HARPER & ROW, PUBLISHERS
NEW YORK, EVANSTON, SAN FRANCISCO, LONDON

Sponsoring Editor: Walter H. Lippincott, Jr.
Project Editor: Carol E. W. Edwards
Designer: June Negrycz
Production Supervisor: Valerie Klima

Readings in the History of Anthropology

Library of Congress Cataloging in Publication Data
Darnell, Regna, comp.
Readings in the history of anthropology.

Bibliography: p.
1. Ethnology–History. I. Title.
GN17.D35 301.2′09 73-14107
ISBN 0-06-041499-5

Contents

Part Two Voyagers and Philosophers 79

Part Three Professionalization of Anthropology 169

Part Four History from Within the Discipline 289

Preface

Virtually by definition, the compilation of a volume of readings is an autobiographical exercise. My own conviction that the history of anthropology must be part of the discipline, both as a specialization for some scholars and as part of the consciousness of every practicing anthropologist, is closely intermeshed with my experience of anthropology. When I was an undergraduate at Bryn Mawr College, I studied the history of anthropology with Frederica de Laguna and A. Irving Hallowell. Later, as a graduate student at the University of Pennsylvania, I became aware of the rich documentary sources for the history of anthropology in Philadelphia, especially at the Library of the American Philosophical Society. The Department of Anthropology at the University of Pennsylvania had already had a long-standing commitment to the history of the discipline, with Loren Eiseley and A. Irving Hallowell setting the tone.

I was fortunate to acquire at the University of Pennsylvania a broad interdisciplinary background for this sort of study. My dissertation on the history of American anthropology from 1890 to 1920 is still virtually unique as an acceptable topic for a Ph.D. degree in cultural anthropology (Darnell 1969). I was strongly encouraged by my major advisor, Dell

Hymes, to believe that I could be an anthropologist without doing fieldwork for my dissertation. Although I have since done considerable fieldwork, I still do not see it as the only route to professional identity as as anthropologist.

Historian George Stocking, Jr., was on leave at the University of Pennsylvania while I was preparing my dissertation proposal. He has continued to work with me and served as outside reader for my dissertation. I learned more about the historian's view of anthropology through course work in American history with Charles Rosenberg. Further interdisciplinary perspective came from Dan Ben-Amos in the Department of Folklore, where he was then just beginning to develop a serious research program in the history of folklore. Throughout, I have received encouragement and aid from A. Irving Hallowell.

I have also profited greatly from long-standing discussions with a number of colleagues. I would particularly like to thank Keith Basso, Raymond De Mallie, William Fenton, John Rowe, Joel Sherzer, William Sturtevant, and Kurt Wolff. Of course, I have also learned much from my students, graduate and undergraduate, in the history of anthropology at the University of Alberta. Walter Lippincott of Harper & Row has been of great help, particularly through his assurance that a book such as this is needed in anthropology. Elizabeth Kerr, my research assistant, has borne the brunt of much of the technical preparation of the manuscript.

Finally, I would like to thank my husband, Anthony L. Vanek, who, although he does not type, has contributed in innumerable ways to the completion of this manuscript.

Regna Darnell
University of Alberta

Readings
in the History
of Anthropology

Introduction

Why is there a history of anthropology? It is a question that has often been asked by both students and professionals within the discipline. Traditionally, history of anthropology has been a required course offered for graduate students to inculcate respect for the elders of their field. The instructor, until quite recently, has tended to be the most elderly member of the department, apparently on the logic that he knows more about the disciplinary history because he has lived it (or perhaps even made it). Certainly, several prominent anthropologists have turned to recording their participation in the history of the discipline during the later portions of their professional careers, notably, A. L. Kroeber, Robert Lowie, A. Irving Hallowell, and Margaret Mead. However, the relevance of such a course to students eager to make their own contribution to the forefront of the discipline has too often been minimal or nonexistent. This will continue to be so as long as the history of anthropology is seen as irrelevant to its practice by the majority of practitioners. If the only reason for taking a course in the history of anthropology is that it is required (and it is required because it has always been required), then we as teachers of anthropology have failed.

Anthropology is more thoroughly interdisciplinary than most other fields, even those in the social sciences. Most anthropologists have training or research competence in disciplines adjacent to their field of specialization. Most read and contribute to journals in other disciplines. In this profession, we have learned that existence in isolation is undesirable, if not impossible. The resulting diversity of subject matter, professional discourse, and theoretical stance has made self-examination a necessary preoccupation.

Every introductory course begins with the question, "What is anthropology?" Answers certainly differ, because each individual will place himself slightly differently in relation to the whole of anthropology as a discipline. At its most general, anthropology is the study of man, a label that can include virtually all of the social sciences and humanities. Another frequent definition stresses the remarkably varied activities of anthropologists. From the historical point of view, anthropology is that which anthropologists do because they are members of an historically constituted cultural tradition that we call anthropology.

Such a perspective requires concern with the history of the discipline as a prelude to its intelligent practice, whether by student or teacher-researcher. If there are historical reasons for the prevalence of particular research methods or theories, then the anthropologist must decide whether the original reasons for the perspective still apply. Too often, we take over a theory without examining its philosophical underpinnings as they relate to an earlier stage of the science. History of anthropology can provide an evaluation matrix for past work in which what is still useful can be separated from what is now outdated.

Moreover, studying the history of anthropology can give anthropologists needed distance from their own theoretical and methodological preoccupations. The science of anthropology as understood today is almost certainly *not* the ultimate science of man. Our commitment as anthropologists to the premise that cultures change through time assures us that the novelties of our time will themselves be superseded, presumably by more sophisticated and generalized theories.

This point of view, however, has been taken as a threat to the validity of present research strategies by many anthropologists in recent years. Just as those scholars in some disciplinary traditions have ignored the diachronic dimension of cultural life, anthropologists looking at the history of their own speciality have attempted to ignore the possibility of future development and change. Like practitioners of any discipline, we exist in a social milieu that cannot, by definition, be static. Sensitivity to the changing character of this social milieu, which extends far beyond the boundaries of anthropology itself, is an important, if not the only, means to place ourselves within the developing mainstream of the discipline. To feel threatened by change, or to legislate for the eternal legitimacy of a single research strategy, is to take the position of an ostrich intellectually. The historian of anthropology might well predict that history will pass the ostrich by, except perhaps as a quaint and amusing curiosity of his time.

There are a number of book-length treatments of the history of anthropology, none of which is entirely satisfactory, with none standing as a definitive history of the discipline. The perspective that history casts light on the practice of anthropology and the identity of anthropologists has been little considered. Therefore, the compilation of a new collection of readings designed for teaching the history of anthropology constitutes a challenge; indeed, an adequate history must deal with the problems of how the past development of the discipline is to be conceived by anthropologists.

The first history of American anthropology appeared in 1933 and celebrated the new synthesis created by the descriptive labors of Boasian anthropology (Mitra 1933). The author, a native of Calcutta, failed to appreciate the complexity of the discipline's history in America; instead, he recorded simply a catalog of dates and facts that Mitra believed to herald the approach of a new synthesis between East and West. Robert Lowie's *The History of Ethnological Theory* provides a far solider base (Lowie 1937). Lowie was a member of the so-called Boasian school, but he treated broadly the intellectual currents that had contributed to his theoretical stance as an anthropologist. The book tends, however, to be limited to factual accounts and to ignore schools of thought not felt important by Lowie personally.

There have been several collections of papers purporting to cover the current scope of anthropology. In 1960, Margaret Mead and Ruth Bunzel edited a volume on the "golden age" of anthropology. It consists largely of examples of the kinds of data presented by anthropologists until about 1920. The final articles deal with the future of anthropology from the point of view of Boas' students in North America. Also in 1960, Frederica deLaguna edited a selection of papers from the first thirty years of the *American Anthropologist.* These articles strike a sanguine balance between description, method, and theory. The volume begins with an excellent introduction by A. Irving Hallowell and includes an extensive bibliography. Its limitations are primarily in the realm of what it does not attempt; it is strictly American in focus and makes no effort to evaluate the anthropology of the period from a more recent vantage point.

In 1965, T. K. Penniman published a history of the past century of anthropological studies, with an emphasis on British and European anthropology. J. O. Brew edited in 1968 a collection of papers on the subdisciplines of anthropology. Both studies are restricted to consideration of facts and dates chosen according to their relevance for what now passes for anthropology. None of the preceding four works deals seriously with the epistemological questions of anthropological identity.

Two additional serious contributions to the history of anthropology are little used in North America because they are not in English (Erasmus 1953; Mercier 1966).

The two major works to date in the history of anthropology both appeared in 1968; they are by anthropologist Marvin Harris and historian George Stocking. These two books define the poles of possible approaches to the meaning and practice of the study of history of anthropology. Harris takes the view that the history of the discipline is a mere handmaiden to present theoretical and methodological concerns. His history, encompassing vast scope and including an extensive bibliography, is integrated by the author's preference for techno-environmental determinism as the organizing principle of all valid anthropology. That which does not conform to this research strategy is, by definition, not part of the mainstream of anthropology. Stocking, in contrast, argues that the history of anthropology must stress the historian's traditional stance of historicism, in which past controversies of method and theory are placed within the social context of their times to make understanding possible. Stocking is, however, not an anthropologist and candidly admits that he is not enthralled by the factual data collected by anthropologists. Rather, he does fieldwork among anthropologists and reports their version of the disciplinary culture from the stance of an intellectual historian.

The publication of these two books has given considerable impetus to the status of the history of anthropology within the discipline itself. Indeed, given the history of historical studies, a rather small body of recent literature constitutes a drastic increase of interest (Stocking 1966). Yet the problem of teaching the history of the discipline has not yet been resolved. This collection of readings, and my own work in general, has attempted to steer a middle course between these opposing positions. On the one hand, the anthropologist studying the history of his own profession cannot avoid commitments to his own version of the present discipline, and he will define his research problems in terms of them. On the other hand, the standards of historical interpretation must be applied in order to distinguish between the present relevance and culturally constituted meaning of events in the past. It is in terms of a reconstructed social context that present evaluation of past history must take place. Neither the thoroughly objective historian nor the thoroughly committed anthropological theoretician, whatever their disciplinary training, provides such a perspective, although both may contribute to it in important ways.

Any selection of readings in the history of anthropology is bound to be arbitrary. One may defend the inclusion or exclusion of particular figures, or even whole schools, but there is no right or wrong answer. In the last analysis, it is the definition of what constitutes anthropology that will determine the content and organization of selections. This volume is liberally supplied with bibliographies for the student who wants to follow up issues and topics covered in its various sections. The intent has been, not to exhaust the potential subject matter, but to provide an integrated perspective toward it that will extend beyond the confines of a single textbook or course.

Part One, following the Introduction, deals with the nature and definition of anthropology as a subject of inquiry. The assumption is that all men everywhere have had theories about their fellowmen, but that something new occurs when these observations are systematized and recorded in the manner we associate with science. Western Europe has been the source of the major traditions of anthropological study existing today, but comparable phenomena have developed in other cultural contexts in the past. The Greeks, the Romans, the Arabs, perhaps the Chinese, have studied cultural similarities and differences of human populations and attempted to provide explanations for them. Not all of these developments have had a direct influence on the anthropology we know today. However, the anthropologist's traditional comparative method leads to a statement of the social-structural features in which anthropological inquiry can be pursued. Through such typological comparison, the uniqueness of our own tradition can be delineated.

Part Two deals with the results of the Age of Discovery in Western Europe. Anthropologists have long recognized that one important starting point for their discipline was the knowledge of new peoples that followed the European Renaissance. There were two major trends in the anthropology of this period: on the one hand, toward detailed reports by first-hand observers of savage peoples; and on the other hand, toward philosophical integration of the information brought home from the voyages with the existing philosophical structure of European thought. For the most part, these two trends remained separate until the professionalization of anthropology in the mid-nineteenth century (although there were, of course, exceptions).

Part Two is somewhat brief, simply because much of the material that could have been included is easily available elsewhere. The role of the eighteenth-century Scottish philosophers or the French rationalists of the same period is already well known to the history of social science. These men laid the foundations not only of anthropology as a discipline, but also of other fields of inquiry. Many of the philosophical contributions to anthropological theory were largely incidental to concerns that are now the province of other disciplines. The quantity of ethnographic reporting that ultimately resulted from the voyages of discovery is immense and any selections from it would have to be arbitrary. Therefore, throughout this section, the intent is to provide perspective toward the broad history of the discipline. Additional materials can be added according to the interests, areal or theoretical, of the student or researcher.

Part Three deals with the professionalization of anthropology in the second half of the nineteenth century. At this time, of course, it became much easier to identify unambiguously a piece of work as "anthropological." Professionalization involved the establishment of institutional frameworks for anthropology, along with the other sciences, in which individuals could earn a living studying their discipline and were in frequent interaction with fellow anthropologists. Standards were set up for the identification of an individual as an anthropologist (stressing museum or university training). During the late nineteenth century, major works in anthropology, using the term itself, were published in America, England, and on the Continent by the individuals we now hail as the "fathers" of anthropology: Tylor, Morgan, Powell, Fraser, and Boas. Their efforts were devoted as much to developing the institutional framework of anthropology as to the substance of the discipline.

Part Four deals with the writing of the history of anthropology by anthropologists. Contributions range from factual treatment of topics related to the individual's anthropological specialty to comments on why the history of the discipline is important. There are, of course, additional works that could have been included. An effort has been made to avoid polemical works, although some examples are cited in the bibliography and discussion. This section concentrates on the epistemological issues to teaching and studying the history of anthropology, using the statements of anthropologists themselves for documentation (in line with the anthropologist's traditional bias toward letting his subjects speak for themselves).

A glance at the Contents will make it clear that the focus is almost entirely American. It would be impossible to record in detail the disparate development of anthropological traditions in North America, Britain, France, and Germany within the compass of a single volume. In the interests of brevity and coherence, this volume stresses the historical context of the North American tradition, with brief contrasts to other developments. A welcome supplement to this volume, then, will be the one now in press edited by Stanley Diamond on national traditions of anthropology, written largely by major figures in the anthropological sciences of other nations.

In a number of respects, North American anthropology is unique. For example, the focus upon the American Indian has encouraged an interdisciplinary perspective. The traditional American subdisciplines of socio-cultural anthropology, physical anthropology, prehistoric archaeology, and linguistics are virtually unknown in the rest of the world. Study of the American Indian forced recognition of different races, languages, and cultures, all of which had to be taken into account to explain the role of the Indian in world history. In contrast, European anthropology tended to begin with folklore and folk life, that is, with the study of the European cultural past as still represented by peasants. Such a definition of anthropology did not require attention to race and language as variables; thus, anthropology could remain essentially ethnology.

The geographical isolation of North America encouraged American students to confine their attention to the continent. Because the American Indians seemed to be indigenous and the question of their origin persisted until the mid-nineteenth century, there was little motivation to relate North America to world ethnology. Indeed, efforts to do so were discouraged. For example, nineteenth-century anthropologist Daniel Brinton staunchly maintained that the American Indians were unique in their physical, racial, and linguistic typology from all other human beings. Moreover, until the 1920s, there was no archaeological sequence in North America parallel to that of the European Paleolithic, Mesolithic, and Neolithic periods. Thus, American anthropologists were not able to correlate the shallower time depth of their own studies with the longer developments abroad. Again, the trend was toward isolation and internally sufficient studies of the American Indians from all possible perspectives.

Study of the Indians in North America was also encouraged by practical necessity. From the founding of the first colonies, settlers had to deal with the Indians' cultural, racial, and linguistic diversity. For the most part, their dealings depended on the positive or negative character of settler–Indian relations (Pearce 1953). The Bureau of Indian Affairs remained under the Department of War from its founding in 1819 until it was transferred to the Department of the Interior in 1849. The transfer reflected not a softening attitude toward the Indians, but a vision of continental political domination that was the manifest destiny of the United States. The Indians became enemy aliens rather than foreign enemies. Anthropologists aided in setting the terms of the peace. One of the major functions of the Bureau of American Ethnology, founded by John Wesley Powell in 1879, was to provide census information to aid in settling the Indians on appropriate reservations.

Finally, we must raise the question of whether anthropology really exists as a unified discipline. A number of anthropologists in recent years have become intrigued by the literature of the history of science and have worried, perhaps excessively, about whether anthropology has a "paradigm." The term is taken from a currently popular treatment, Thomas Kuhn's *The Structure of Scientific Revolutions,* although similar concepts have been advanced by others (Kuhn 1962; Bernal 1954; Nagel 1961). Kuhn's claim, devastating to the egos of many theoretically oriented anthropologists, is that the social sciences are "pre-paradigmatic"; that is, they have not yet reached that stage of their growth at which a single theory or paradigm provides direction to research.

In fact, however, anthropologists who protest their impoverishment in the absence of a paradigm are actually behaving according to Kuhn's predictions. He contends that scientists stressing the claims of a new perspective or theory necessarily force polarities until they emerge as the dominant school of thought within their field. The convert or adherent to a minority position is the one who is most concerned with his paradigmatic status. "New archaeology," "new ethnography," "theoretical linguistics," "neo-evolutionism," and other labels illustrate the tendency to cite *evolution,* or gradual development, as *revolution,* which is entirely cut off from the past. In fact, scientific revolutions are always gradual (Darnell 1969).

Kuhn's notion of paradigm may be useful in stressing that anthropology, like other disciplines, has at any given moment a set of accepted postulates and a body of recognized practitioners. The most legitimate question is not whether or not anthropology has a paradigm but how does paradigmatic organization of scientific research affect the ongoing practice of anthropology. In this context, we may wish to speak, not of *a* paradigm, but of *several* paradigms, or perhaps even of several *levels* of paradigms. A paradigm is, in Kuhn's view, social and institutional organization as well as theoretical methods and concepts. Therefore, it may be useful to conceive contexts in which the anthropologist is a university scholar, a social scientist, an anthropologist, a historian of anthropology, at least by courtesy a historian, and a specialist in a particular area or group (in the extreme case, "his" people as a result of fieldwork). Each of these titles has some of the elements of Kuhn's paradigm, and all pertain to a single individual in terms of his practice of his discipline and his sense of identity.

Current anthropologists express considerable anxiety about whether present subdisciplines continue to have relevance to one another. Many graduate programs are changing their long-established stress on research competence in all four traditional subdisciplines for a Ph.D. candidate. Where the requirement is maintained, it has often become more an index of fortitude than a measure of intellectual stature. There are even those who maintain that the unity of anthropology is only historical and that the conditions of the modern world, especially the disappearance of the so-called primitive society, render anthropology anachronistic. Moreover, many of the basic premises of anthropological research, like cultural relativism, have been largely adopted as intellectual premises by the larger society. In its most extreme form, the argument is that anthropology retains as its identifying attribute only its commitment to imperialist conquest of the Third World (Fried 1972; Harris 1968; Diamond, in press). This position is incongruent with the positive identity felt by many anthropologists, who see themselves as mediators between primitive societies and the world outside. Again, it is to the history of the discipline and to the continuity of present concerns with past ones in a historicist tradition that the anthropologist must look for answers to these and related questions regarding his identity.

PART ONE
The Nature of Anthropology

Attention is too often wasted deciding when the history of anthropology begins. Proponents can be found for three major views, each of which stresses a particular facet of anthropology as we know it today and seeks its origin in the past. First, the history of anthropology is traced to the Greeks, with Herodotus as the "father" of anthropology as well as of history. Classical scholarship that we now classify as anthropological is considered the baseline for a continuous development toward professional anthropology within the Western intellectual tradition. A second view is that anthropology developed out of the Renaissance and the concurrent voyages of discovery, which made available more information about human cultural, racial, and linguistic diversity. Thirdly, there are those who prefer to restrict the label "anthropology" to developments beginning with the founding of professional societies in the mid-nineteenth century.

Each of these views is, in some sense, correct. Herodotus did perform some of the tasks of an anthropologist in the course of his observations and travels. The voyages of discovery did result in consideration of anthropological issues as Europe turned more and more to studying the world around it. And certainly, professionalization of the discipline did provide direct continuity to the discipline we now know and did introduce a new factor in anthropological inquiries. Yet none of these so-called starting points is sufficient alone. The features we now associate with the discipline have multiple and complex origins within the history of Western thought. It is the interrelationship of starting points and the way in which diverse traditions came to be associated in what we now call "anthropology" that must be the predominant concern of disciplinary historians. Consideration must be given to each of the putative origins. "For anthropology, unlike Athena, did not spring in full panoply from the brow of some Jovian 'father' of the science and does not come to us, therefore, with a convenient date to mark its birth" (Shapiro 1964: 339).

The history of a discipline such as anthropology may be conceived in two ways. The first approach is chronological and depends on the succession and interrelationship of events from some more or less arbitrary starting point in the past to the present. From such a perspective, Herodotus belongs in a history of anthropology if, and only if, his works influenced later anthropologists in a direct continuity to the present time. An alternative approach suggests that anthropological inquiry, whatever its position in time, has a structure that is of concern to the discipline we now label as anthropology. The inquiry is typological rather than chronological. Anthropology is known to us as a complex discipline whose particular course developed within a single intellectual tradition, but in fact its habitual activities have been more widespread in the history of the world.

There is, of course, a sense in which anthropology is a universal of human culture. Members of every society known to us have some forms of tradition that interpret cultural diversity and national or tribal history. A. Irving Hallowell has characterized this tradition as the stage of "folk anthropology" (1965; reprinted in Part Five). Such folk knowledge relates to the science of anthropology in its goals in a way that is independent of professional science. Anthropology, perhaps more than its sister academic disciplines, is a layman's paradise; whoever is human can have opinions about the science of man.

One example of folk anthropology is presented here, the creation myth of the Maidu Indians of California. The myth, having obvious parallels to the account in the Book of Genesis within our own cultural tradition, tells how different peoples were given their lands, how the things in the world were named, and how the gods and men found themselves in position for the beginning of the known world. The flood element, although superficially similar to the Biblical story of Noah, is widely found in tribal mythologies and should not be interpreted as a mere product of acculturation. The myth is validated as a social charter by the prophecy incorporated within it that in future times men shall tell of these events of creation in their myths.

Folk anthropology reflects the curiosity of man about himself and his neighbors. All societies no doubt have their characteristic ways of handling these universal questions. Some societies, for example Classical Greece or Medieval Europe, have tended to look inward to understand human nature. Others, for example Renaissance Europe, have turned to cross-cultural comparison for perspective on human nature and human achievement. Whatever the strategy or combination of strategies regarding the description and explanation of cultural similarities and differences, the subject matter of anthropology necessarily exists within a specific cultural context. Individual students of the nature of man may or may not establish a tradition that has continuity with later developments. Failure to do so does not, in itself, invalidate the relevance of their work to the history of the discipline.

The putative father of anthropology, Herodotus, is a case in point. His direct influence on the development of Western anthropology was minimal, yet his activities are worthy of note as theoretical and methodological concomitants of ethnographic investigations. During the Middle Ages, Herodotus was renowned for his style but considered a liar. Only in the fifteenth century was a Latin translation of *The Histories* produced. In the course of describing the war between the Greeks and the Persians in the sixth century B.C., Herodotus intended to record everything worthy of preservation about all human history. His accounts of his readings and travels described in greater or lesser detail nearly fifty groups of people. Importance assigned to particular groups was relative to their political status in the Greek world of the time.

Histories of anthropology frequently stress that Herodotus had an implicit list of ethnographic categories for the description of little-known peoples. Primarily, he classified peoples according to descent, language, religion, and culture. For some groups, he also discussed geography, clothing, food practices, house types, marriage forms, self-defense, and prestige as judges (Hodgen 1964:22–23). In line with the psychology of his day, Herodotus believed that a man's eating habits were integrally related to his character (Myres 1908:163). Herodotus recorded family types ranging from promiscuity to patriarchal monogamy (Myres 1908:155). The status of women was a crucial issue in Greek civilization itself, and Herodotus concerned himself extensively with questions of patriarchal and matriarchal descent; additional examples of diverse rules of descent only confirmed the impression that customs of descent must be arbitrary (Myres 1908: 153).

The other major congruence between Herodotus' practice and modern anthropological methodology was in his evaluation of what he was told. The primary data for *The Histories* came from talking to people on his travels. In his account of the Libyan tribes, reproduced here, Herodotus was careful to point out when his materials seemed strange. Thus, the headless men with eyes in their breasts strained his credulity, and he claimed only to repeat what the Libyans said. On the other hand, he recognized that many apparently fabulous things were true; for example, he accepted the report of Egyptian hole-men who ate snakes, lizards, and reptiles and had a language that sounded like screeching bats. Whereas Thucydides took the view, as a point of methodology, that only immediate history was possible because of the inherent fallibility of the human memory, Herodotus faithfully recorded what he was told as long as he believed that someone could have known what was reported. Herodotus was a better observer of human behavior than a theoretician; Thucydides, for example, provided more sophisticated explanations for the causes of historical events.

In some of its social structures, the environment in which Herodotus lived was similar to the Renaissance world that produced the voyages of discovery. Herodotus had the distance and perspective necessary to subject the Greek world to cross-cultural scrutiny because he was a Greek only by courtesy and education. His birth in Asia Minor also gave him access to the greater cultural tolerance of the Persian Empire, in which inscriptions were automatically translated into the languages of all the subjects. The age in which Herodotus made his journeys came toward the end of a period of geographical exploration, particularly in India and the Mediterranean. The Greek time perspective was suddenly lengthened by discovery of the relatively ancient culture of Egypt. In Athens, criticism of received philosophies was the order of the day. The search was on for a rationalist and materialist philosophy, for a social science alongside the natural sciences, and for a theory of progress and evolution (albeit cyclical rather than unilineal).

In such an environment, it is not surprising that Herodotus could have carried out his inquiries. In spite of the auspicious beginning, however, Herodotus did not establish a lasting tradition of ethnographic reporting. In the next century, Greek philosophy turned inward upon itself. Socrates argued that patriarchy was unnatural and inexpedient, but he did so on a priori grounds, not on the basis of cross-cultural variability of custom, as reported by Herodotus.

The Romans also failed to establish a persisting tradition of anthropological inquiry. But *De Rerum Naturae* (*On the Nature of the Universe*), which appeared in 55 B.C., included anthropological speculations about the nature and history of man. In it, Lucretius set forth the philosophical basis of Epicureanism in honor of his patron, a Roman statesman named Gaius Memmius. The body of the long poem is devoted to explicating a materialist atomic structure of the universe. Lucretius believed that knowledge was derived from the senses, that superstition (including much of religion) must be avoided, and that the sciences provided the solution to the disillusionment of Roman society with its luxury and lassitude (Sarton 1959).

In his discussion of sociology, presented here, Lucretius set forth a philosophy of progress or evolution, in contrast to the usual Classical emphasis on degeneration from a primitive golden age. Lucretius saw the childhood of the earth as benign. Early men were tougher than their modern equivalents and lived with no need of social contracts. Inventions of fire, family life, language, kingship, property, gold, religion, metals, clothing, agriculture, and music all came into being gradually. Lucretius delineated the three Ages of Stone, Bronze, and Iron nineteen centuries before the Danish archaeologist, Christian Jurgensen Thomsen. Because each step in human evolution followed logically, according to the practices of the previous stage, there was nothing inexplicable about human development. Experience was the causal factor in movement from one stage to another, an argument similar to that employed by Lewis Henry Morgan in the nineteenth century. Both saw the stages as defined by material progress but motivated by human mental effort.

The historian of anthropology might legitimately wonder if something resembling the modern concept of anthropology arose in the long Chinese bureaucratic tradition. For the most part, it did not, perhaps because the Chinese lacked a rival civilization that could be compared favorably to their own. In the histories of the Han era, there is considerable information about Roman civilization, which was respected by Chinese scholars of the time (Fitzgerald 1964:8–9). The Roman reports of the same contacts are less impressive as anthropological data. However, the inward-looking tone of the Chinese empire was already set, and trade did not have serious intercultural consequences.

Ethnographic reports of the customs of barbarians were made over two thousand years of Chinese history but generally were framed in actively pejorative terms. Ideographs for ethnic groups varied directly with the quality of political relations, ranging from human to dog to insect in their base (Fried 1972:59). In contrast to the Greek civilization of Herodotus, the Chinese were secure and self-sufficient. There was, then, little motivation for ethnography. During the conflict between two equally or almost equally great civilizations—the Greek and the Persian—self-examination and reliance on allies with different traditions were viable and, indeed, necessary virtues.

Like Herodotus, Islam historian Ibn Khaldûn was a cultural outsider, born of Spanish-Arabic descent in northwest Africa. During his early efforts at a political career, he learned to switch political allegiance readily and to place local historical events in larger perspective. Ibn Khaldûn spent the last twenty-five years of his life in Cairo, where he held offices of judge and religious teacher. Most of this time was devoted to preparation of his universal history, based partly on his travels throughout the known world in his earlier years and partly on his conviction that history and politics could be understood only in a generalized framework that he called "the science of culture." It was clear to him that the Islamic Empire was in a period of decline, but the causes had to be sought in political philosophy and universal history. Although events differed in detail, causes of events were limited and could be studied through reason to produce general laws of history (Mahdi 1957; Daniel 1966).

Ibn Khaldûn's description of the Arabs or Bedouins, included here, stressed that they were a "natural" group whose character was determined by their means of making a living. The Bedouins were idealized as having greater personal virtues of strength and courage than the sedentary peoples who developed civilization in cities. The Bedouins were also historically "prior"; that is, they provided a reservoir from which civilization could develop. Ibn Khaldûn stressed that men in the desert were held together by feelings based on blood relationship rather than by laws. In effect, this is the nineteenth-century notion that social ties may be based either on kinship or on the state.

Ibn Khaldûn was clearly ambivalent toward the Bedouins. He admired their warlike spirit and primitive virtues of courage and simplicity. Yet he also realized that study of the sciences required the leisure provided by cities and states. Civilization could not be rejected simply because maintenance of moral fiber was difficult. Ibn Khaldûn tried to record objectively the contrasts between civilization as he knew it and cross-cultural diversity. He praised the Indian and Greek monotheisms, in spite of their contradiction to the tenets of Islam, and reported other customs not congenial to his Islam audience (Nasr 1968:233). In addition to his efforts at relativism, however, Ibn Khaldûn was also an evolutionist. Man's needs for leisure, power, and riches led him through a series of natural stages to civilization. Economic restrictions on primitive culture motivated men to seek greater political strength. There were five developmental stages that led to Islamic civilization (Mahdi 1957).

Ibn Khaldûn, like Herodotus, has been hailed as a link between intellectual periods. Although he forms a bridge between Classical Antiquity and the European Renaissance, the actual influence of Islamic scholarship appears to have been minimal. The modernity of Ibn Khaldûn was not rediscovered until the early nineteenth century, over four centuries after his death. As in the case of Herodotus and Lucretius, it is the anthropological quality of Ibn Khaldûn's work, carried out in a cultural context independent of our own, that constitutes his importance to the history of anthropology.

In sum, therefore, traditions of anthropological inquiry have developed, albeit abortively, in traditions other than our own. The Greeks, the Romans, and the Arabs, at least, produced individual thinkers or climates of thought congenial to the study of cross-cultural diversity. In each of these cases, the social milieu permitted criticism of the highest civilization existing at the time and an effort to understand that civilization by contrasting other lifeways. In each case, it had been assumed that human cultures differ in time and space and that these diverse societies have an integrity of their own. This perspective may be a prelude to political domination; it is perhaps necessarily pragmatically oriented. The basic contrast of "us" and "them" is probably again a cultural universal, but the study of "them" depends on a sense of identity as members of the human species. Sometimes, this may come about through concern for the past history of one's own society; in others, it is the sense that differing customs cannot be ignored because of the exigencies of existing social interactions.

In this context, it is possible to turn to the direct origins of Western anthropology in the European Renaissance. Taken in detail, the notion of "the Renaissance" is an abstraction; there were many holes in the medieval worldview and many partial renaissances before the one we now honor with that name (Bolgar 1954). The Renaissance that was important for anthropology resulted from the voyages of discovery through which European society came to examine the diversity of human customs. The discovery of African and American Indian peoples forced reexamination of basic values, particularly in relation to the tenets of Christianity. The Christian tradition was universalistic, meaning that anyone who was human had to be led into the Church. Thus, the early explorers and their armchair counterparts in Europe had to classify newly discovered peoples and recommend them for salvation. The Biblical account of human races had to be reconciled with newfound cultural diversity. The problem occupied Europe for several centuries and ultimately made it impossible for Europe to retreat again into confident isolationism.

Anthropology as a field of professional study developed only at the end of the Age of Exploration, but the tone of the inquiry had been set much earlier (Shapiro 1964:338). Already by the fifteenth century, travel reports filtering back from the expeditions had whetted the curiosity of Europe. Details of exotic customs could be evaluated in light of greater information, and greater commitment to further exploration, than had even been possible in the Classical world of Herodotus or Lucretius, or even Ibn Khaldûn.

The philosophers were interested in travel reports not because they were anthropologists but because European philosophy had to be modified to correspond to new knowledge challenging its very premises (Shapiro 1964:341). In the process, a pattern of inquiry was established that would later be performed for its own sake.

John Rowe's paper, presented here, on the background of the

Renaissance attitude toward cultural diversity, draws on literature not usually considered by anthropologists, unless they are also Classicists. Rowe argues that the Renaissance discovered the early history of its own civilization before it discovered primitive man. Realization that the past was distant and different made it possible for spatial distance and concomitant cultural diversity to be incorporated into the European world view as new information became available. Western man had to expand the perspective of human history if he were to understand himself.

The anthropology that grew out of the Renaissance change in attitude toward spatial and temporal diversity has been longer lived than the other traditions discussed in this section. It contains, of course, the particular set of postulates on which our present-day discipline is based. But the explanation of its uniqueness, and, consequently, the uniqueness of anthropology as a science, must be sought in comparing the social structures that produce inquiries resembling the present-day science of anthropology. The sources of the Renaissance change in worldview were part of the history of Western Europe and did not draw directly on the other anthropological writings that preceded them chronologically. But these developments aid understanding at a different level because they are both the same and different. That there are similarities between the worlds of Herodotus, Ibn Khaldûn, and the Renaissance voyagers suggests that anthropological inquiry has some identity independent of particular historical circumstances.

1. Maidu Creation Myth
Roland Dixon

When this world was filled with water, Earth-Maker floated upon it, kept floating about. Nowhere in the world could he see even a tiny bit of earth. No persons of any kind flew about. He went about in this world, the world itself being invisible, transparent like the sky.

He was troubled. "I wonder how, I wonder where, I wonder in what place, in what country, we shall find a world!" he said. "You are a very strong man, to be thinking of this world," said Coyote. "I am guessing in what direction the world is, then to that distant land let us float!" said Earth-Maker.

In this world they kept floating along, kept floating along, hungry, having nothing to eat. "You will die of hunger," said Coyote. Then he thought. "No, I cannot think of anything," he said. "Well," said Earth-Maker, "the world is large, a great world. If somewhere I find a tiny world, I can fix it up."

Then he sang, "Where, little world, art thou?" It is said he sang, kept singing, sang all the time. "Enough!" he said, and stopped singing. "Well! I don't know many songs (?)," he said. Then Coyote sang again, kept singing, asking for the world, singing, "Where, O world, art thou?" He sang, kept singing; then "Enough!" he said, "I am tired. You try again."

So Earth-Maker sang. "Where are you, my great mountains, my world mountains?" he said. He sang, and all the time kept saying, "Where are you?" He stopped singing. "Enough!" he said. "You try also." Coyote tried, kept singing. "My foggy mountains, where one goes about," he said. "Well, we shall see nothing at all. I guess there never was a world anywhere," said he. "I think if we find a little world, I can fix it very well," said Earth-Maker.

As they floated along, they saw something like a bird's-nest. "Well! That is very small," said Earth-Maker. "It is small. If it were larger, I could fix it. But it is too small," he said. "I wonder how I can stretch it a little!" He kept saying, "What is the best way! How shall I make it larger!" So saying, he prepared it. He extended a rope to the east, to the south he extended a rope, to the west, to the northwest, and to the north he extended ropes.

From Roland Dixon, *Maidu Texts.* Reprinted from American Ethnological Society Publication 4 (1912): pp. 4–27.

When all were stretched, he said, "Well, sing, you who were the finder of this earth, this mud! 'In the long, long ago, Robin-Man made the world, stuck earth together, making this world.' Thus mortal men shall say of you, in myth-telling." Then Robin sang, and his world-making song sounded sweet. After the ropes were all stretched, he kept singing; then, after a time, he ceased.

Then Earth-Maker spoke to Coyote also. "Do you sing too," he said. So he sang, singing, "My world, where one travels by the valley-edge; my world of many foggy mountains; my world where one goes zigzagging hither and thither; range after range," he said, "I sing of the country I shall travel in. In such a world I shall wander," he said.

Then Earth-Maker sang—sang of the world he had made, kept singing, until by and by he ceased. "Now," he said, "it would be well if the world were a little larger. Let us stretch it!"—"Stop!" said Coyote. "I speak wisely. This world ought to be painted with something, so that it may look pretty. What do ye two think?"

Then Robin-Man said, "I am one who knows nothing. Ye two are clever men, making this world, talking it over; if ye find anything evil, ye will make it good."—"Very well," said Coyote, "I will paint it with blood. There shall be blood in the world; and people shall be born there, having blood. There shall be birds born who shall have blood. Everything—deer, all kinds of game, all sorts of men without any exception—all things shall have blood that are to be created in this world. And in another place, making it red, there shall be red rocks. It will be as if blood were mixed up with the world, and thus the world will be beautiful," he said. "What do you think about it?"—"Your words are good," he said, "I know nothing." So Robin-Man went off. As he went, he said, "I shall be a person who travels only in this way," and he flew away.

Earth-Maker spoke: "You had better lie down here on your face."—"All right!" said Coyote, and, kneeling down, he lay on his face. Then Earth-Maker stretched the world with his foot. Stretching it once, he extended it towards the east, extended it on that side; then to the south, then to the west, he stretched it; then to the northwest and to the north he stretched it. Having extended it only a little ways, he said, "All right!"

Coyote stood up and looked around. "Well, I think it would be better if this world were just large enough to go around it." By and by Earth-Maker said, "You had better kneel down again, and lie flat on your belly. Do not look up. You must not!"—"Very well," said Coyote, "I will not look up." He lay down; and Earth-Maker, stretching the earth with his foot eastward, stretched it as far as it would go. He extended it fully toward the south, toward the west, toward the northwest, toward the north. "All right!" said he.

Coyote stood up, and, having risen, started to walk hither eastward.

Earth-Maker, when he was left alone, stood for a time, then, departing, he went toward the south. In the direction of the sunset he went far around, going over to the northwest, going around to the north, going all the way around to the east. And having gone around, having returned to the spot where he had first turned off, he prepared things.

He made two white men; then he made others, white, but a little different. As he made them, he counted them. He kept on making them—made one black, then another almost black. Two of each only he made. Then he counted all the countries, and, as he counted, assigned them, gave them to the countries. "You are a country having this name, you shall have this people," he said. "This sort of people, naming you, shall own the country. These people shall grow, shall keep on growing through many winters, through many dawns. They shall continue to grow until, their appointed winters being past, their dawns being over, this people having finished growing, shall be born," he said. "Very many winters will have passed before they shall be born. And they shall have children, girls and boys; and these children, growing up, shall have children in their turn," he said. "When several winters have passed, there will be very many people."

Then again, to another sort of people, he gave another country, saying, "This people, I leave you in this country, and ye shall be the owners of this land. Ye shall be a people with a name." And they also were a different sort of people, a people with a name; and their country also was named, it is said. "Your country also shall have a name," he said. "Ye too shall have a name, and your children shall fill the land, and every single child shall have a name," he said. "There, growing steadily, many winters, many days, shall pass before ye are fully grown. Then ye shall possess this country," he said.

Thereafter he spoke to another, again he gave a different kind of country to a different kind of people. He said, "Ye shall be a different-speaking and a different-looking people. Ye also shall possess a country," he said. "Your children, if they weary of this land, going from this country to one with another name, to a country that is good to live in, shall remain there. There every country shall be full of people, who will continue to be born," he said. And then he divided the world among many. To one he gave one sort, to another he gave another. "Ye shall all have different names," he said. Finally he finished giving, he distributed all.

Then after a while, continuing on his way, he came hither, kept travelling; and after arriving in the middle of the world, he made other people. "Ye shall be mortal men like this," he said; and, having made two, he left them. "Ye here, growing steadily, when so many winters shall have passed, very many winters, many days, ye shall be fully grown," he said.

"Then ye shall be mortal men, ye shall be born full-grown. This country shall have a name. Beyond these mountains there shall be another country, which also shall have a name. Ye shall not be born soon," he said. Then he named everything, and, having left the people here in the middle of the world, he went away.

Continuing on his way, he went to all countries that were of the proper sort, and when he had gone as far as mortal men were to live, he stopped. Then there again he created two—two more, it is said, he laid down, and again two more. He kept counting them; and when he had counted them all, he spoke. "Ye shall remain here," he said, "and your country shall have a name. Although living in a small country, in one that is not large, it shall be sufficient for you. This I leave; and growing continually, so many winters passing, very many winters passing, many days passing, ye shall be fully grown. And then ye, being fully grown, shall be born," he said. "Then your food will grow,—different sorts of food, all kinds of food; and ye, being born with sufficient intelligence, will survive," he said. Then he pushed them down under a gopher-hill.

He spoke again. "Ye, too, shall possess a small country. 'Come, now! leave this country!' (this ye must not say to others, wishing to take their land.) Ye shall be people who will not drive others away, driving them off to another country. Ye shall be different, ye shall name your country. Ye also shall be a differently named people. There, growing continually, many days being passed, many winters having passed, ye shall be born, when your birthday has passed," he said. "Living there and having children, when other winters are passed, they will become a little larger, and will keep on thus, growing all the time, until, when enough winters shall have passed, always becoming more numerous, ye shall have enough people. Your children, all without exception, shall have names. This country also, in the same way is named; all countries shall have names, just as yourselves. If ye are going to look at the country over there, then, when ye go, (ye shall say) 'I am going to that place,' naming it; then all people will understand where ye are going," he said.

Then, counting the people on this side (in this direction), he left them; and, speaking to those on this side, he said, "Ye also shall be mortal men. So many winters passing over, (?) ye shall be born. All the time growing, each winter ye shall grow a little, a very little. Again, when the winter is over, continually growing, when many winters are passed, ye will have finished growing; then ye shall be born, full-grown. There ye also shall have a country, and your country shall be one bearing a name, and ye too shall be named," he said. "Ye shall have children; and when your children have grown larger, then, looking all over this country, ye must tell them about it, teach them about it, naming the country and places, showing them and naming them to your children. 'That is such and such a place, and that is such and such a mountain.' So, when ye have caused them to learn this, teaching them, they shall understand even as ye do yourselves." Then, placing them between his thumb and finger, he snapped them away.

And when he had given countries thus to all that he had counted out, there was one pair left. "Ye also, ye shall be a people speaking differently. There will be a little too many of you for you to have the same sort of a country also. So ye shall have that kind of a country, a great country," he said. "Now, wherever I have passed along, there shall never be a lack of anything," he said, and made motions in all directions. "The country where I have been shall be one where nothing is ever lacking. I have finished talking to you, and I say to you that ye shall remain where ye are to be born. Ye are the last people; and while ye are to remain where ye are created, I shall return, and stay there. When this world becomes bad, I will make it over again; and after I make it, ye shall be born," he said. Long ago Coyote suspected this, they say.

"This world will shake," he said. "This world is spread out flat, the world is not stable. After this world is all made, by and by, after a long time, I will pull this rope a little, then the world shall be firm. I, pulling on my rope, shall make it shake. And now," he said, "there shall be songs, they shall not be lacking, ye shall have them." And he sang, and kept on singing until he ceased singing. "Ye mortal men shall have this song," he said, and then he sang another; and singing many different songs, he walked along, kept walking until he reached the middle of the world; and there, sitting down over across from it, he remained.

But, in making the world, Robin-Man sang that which was pleasant to hear. He, they say, was the first created person—a man whose song passed across the valleys, a man who found the world, a man who in the olden time sang very beautifully-sounding songs. And Earth-Maker, going along, and having passed by the middle of the world, made a house for himself, and remained there. That is as far as he went. That is all, they say.

2. The Libyan Tribes
Herodotus

The following is a description of the Libyan tribes in their order: starting from Egypt, the first are the Adyrmachidae, whose way of living is more or less Egyptian in character. They dress like the rest of the Libyans. Their women wear a bronze ring on each leg, and grow their hair long; when they catch a bug on their persons, they give it bite for bite before throwing it away. They are the only Libyan tribe to follow this practice, as also that of taking girls who are about to be married to see the king. Any girl who catches his fancy, leaves him a maid no longer. This tribe extends from the Egyptian border as far as the port called Plynus.

Next come the Giligamae, whose territory runs westward as far as the island of Aphrodisias. In between lies Platea, the island off the coast where the Cyrenaeans first settled, and on the mainland is the Harbour of Menelaus, and Aziris where the Cyrenaeans also lived for a time. It is in this part of the country that silphium begins to be found, and extends all the way from Platea to the mouth of the Syrtis. The Giligamae live in much the same sort of way as the other tribes. Next to the westward are the Asbystae; their territory lies further inland than Cyrene, and does not extend to the coast, which is occupied by the Cyrenaeans. This tribe is conspicuous amongst the Libyans for its use of four-horse chariots, and in its general way of life does its best to imitate that of Cyrene. Westward, again, are the Auschisae, who live south of Barca and touch the sea near Euesperides. Within their territory is the small tribe of the Bacales, who reach the coast near Tauchira, a town belonging to Barca; they live in the same sort of way as the people south of Cyrene. Still proceeding in a westerly direction, one comes next to the Nasamones, a numerous tribe, who in the summer leave their cattle on the coast and go up country to a place called Augila for the date harvest. The date-palms here grow in large numbers and to a great size, and are all of the fruit-bearing kind. These people also catch locusts, which they dry in the sun and grind up fine; then they sprinkle the powder on milk and drink it. Each of them has a number of wives, which they use in common, like the Massagetae—when a man wants to lie with a woman, he puts up a pole to indicate his intention. It is the custom, at a man's first marriage, to give a party, at which the bride is enjoyed by each of the guests in turn; they take her one after another, and then give her a present—something or other they have brought with them from home. In the matter of oaths, their practice is to swear by those of their countrymen who had the best reputation for integrity and valour, laying their hands upon their tombs; and for purposes of divination they go to sleep, after praying, on the graves of their forebears, and take as significant any dream they may have. When two men make a solemn compact, each drinks from the other's hand, and if there is no liquor available, they take some dust from the ground and lick it up.

The neighbours of the Nasamones are the Psylli—though they no longer exist. There is a story which the Libyans tell (and I repeat it here) that the south wind dried up the water in their storage tanks, so that they were left with none whatever, as their territory lies wholly within the Syrtis. Upon this they held a council, and having unanimously decided to declare war on the south wind, they marched out to the desert, where the wind blew and buried them in sand. The whole tribe was wiped out, and the Nasamones occupied their former domain.

Further inland to the southward, in the part of Libya where wild beasts are found, live the Garamantes, who avoid all intercourse with men, possess no weapons of war, and do not know how to defend themselves. Along the coast to the westward the neighbours of the Nasamones are the Macae. These people wear their hair in the form of a crest, shaving it close on either side of the head and letting it grow long in the middle; in war they carry ostrich skins for shields. The river Cinyps, which rises on a hill called the Hill of the Graces, runs through their territory to the sea. The Hill of the Graces is about twenty-five miles inland, and is densely wooded, unlike the rest of Libya so far described, which is bare of trees.

Next come the Gindanes. The women of this tribe wear leather bands round their ankles, which are supposed to indicate the number of their lovers: each woman puts on one band for every man she has gone to bed with, so that whoever has the greatest number enjoys the greatest reputation for success in love. Within the territory of the Gindanes a headland runs out into the sea, and it is here that the Lotophagi live, a tribe which lives exclusively on the fruit of the lotus. The lotus fruit is about as big as a mastic-berry, and as sweet as a date. The Lotophagi also make wine from it.

Next along the coast are the Machlyes, who also make use of the lotus, but to a lesser extent than the Lotophagi. Their territory reaches to a large river called Triton, which flows into the great lagoon of Tritonis. In the lagoon there is an island named Phla, and there is said to have been an oracle to the effect that the Lacedaemonians should send settlers there. The story is also told of how Jason, when he had finished building the *Argo* under Mount Pelium, put on board, in addition to the usual offerings, a bronze tripod, and set sail to round the Peloponnese on his way to Delphi. Off Cape Malea he was caught by a northerly blow and carried to Libya, where, before he could get his bearings, he found himself in the shoal water off the lagoon of Tritonis. How to get clear was a problem; but at that moment Triton appeared and told Jason to give him the tripod, in return for which he would show him the channel and let them all get away in safety. Jason did as he was asked, whereupon Triton showed him the course to steer in order to clear the shallows. He then placed the tripod in his own temple, after uttering over it in full detail, for the benefit of Jason's crew, the prophecy that when a descendant of the *Argo*'s company should carry off the tripod, it was unavoidably decreed by fate that a hundred Grecian cities should then be built on the shores of Lake Tritonis. The Libyans in the neighbourhood got to know of this prophecy, and hid the tripod.

The people next to the Machlyes are the Auses; both these tribes live on the shores of the lagoon, and the river Triton forms the boundary between them. The Machlyes let the hair grow on the back of their heads, the Auses on the front. They hold an annual festival in honour of Athene, at which the girls divide themselves into two groups and fight each other with stones and sticks; they say this rite has come down to them from time immemorial, and by its performance they pay honour to their native deity—which is the same as our Greek Athene. If any girl, during the course of the battle, is fatally injured and dies, they say it is a proof that she is no maiden. Before setting them to fight, they pick out the best-looking girl and dress her up publicly in a full suit of Greek armour and a Corinthian helmet; then they put her in a chariot and drive her round the lagoon. How they dressed these girls before there were Greeks settled in the neighbourhood, I cannot say; presumably the armour they used was Egyptian—for I am perpared to maintain that both shields and helmets were introduced into Greece from Egypt. There is a belief amongst these people that Athene is the daughter of Poseidon and the lake, but that having some quarrel with her father she put herself at the disposal of Zeus, who made her his own daughter. The women of the tribe are common property; there are no married couples living together, and intercourse is casual—like that of animals. When a child is fully grown, the men hold a meeting, and it is considered to belong to the one it most closely resembles.

I have now mentioned all the pastoral tribes along the Libyan coast. Up country further to the south lies the region where wild beasts are found, and beyond that there is a great belt of sand, stretching from Thebes in Egypt to the Pillars of Heracles. Along this belt, separated from one another by about ten days' journey, are little hills formed of lumps of salt, and from the top of each gushes a spring of cold, sweet water. Men live in the neighbourhood of these springs—beyond the wild beasts' region, they are the furthest south, towards the desert, of any human beings. The first of them, ten days' journey from Thebes, are the Ammonians, with their temple derived from that of the Theban Zeus—I have already pointed out how the image of Zeus in both temples has a ram's face. They have another spring there, of which the water is tepid in the early morning and cools down towards the time when townspeople begin to go out; by noon it is very cold, and that is the moment when they water their gardens; then, as the day draws toward evening, the chill gradually goes off it, until by sunset it is tepid again; after that it gets hotter and hotter as the night advances, and at midnight it boils furiously. Then, after midnight, the process is reversed, and it steadily cools off until dawn. The spring is known as the Fountain of the Sun.

Ten days' journey west of the Ammonians, along the belt of sand, there is another similar salt-hill and spring. This place, called Augila, is also inhabited, and it is here that the Nasamonians come for their date harvest. Again at the same distance to the west is a salt-hill and spring, just as before, with date-palms of the fruit-bearing kind, as in the other oases; and here live the Garamantes, a very numerous tribe of people, who spread soil over the salt to sow their seed in. From these people is the shortest route—thirty days' journey—to the Lotophagi; and it is amongst them that the cattle are found which walk backwards as they graze. The reason for this curious habit is provided by the formation of their horns, which bend forwards and downwards; this prevents them from moving forwards in the ordinary way, for, if they tried to do so, their horns would stick in the ground. In other respects they are just like ordinary cattle—except for the thickness and toughness of their hide. The Garamantes hunt the Ethiopian hole-men, or troglodytes, in four-horse chariots, for these troglodytes are exceedingly swift of foot—more so than any people of whom we have any information. They eat snakes and lizards and other reptiles and speak a language like nothing upon earth—it might be bats screeching.

Ten days' journey from the Garamantes is yet another hill and spring—this time the home of the Atarantes, the only people in the world, so far as our knowledge goes, to do without names. Atarantes is the collective name—but individually they have none. They curse the sun as it rises and call it by all sorts of opprobrious names, because it wastes and burns both themselves and their land. Once more at a distance of ten days' journey there is a salt-hill, a spring, and a tract of inhabited country, and adjoining it rises Mount Atlas. In shape the mountain is a slender cone, and it is so high that according to report the top cannot be seen, because summer and winter it is never free of cloud. The natives (who are known as the Atlantes, after the mountain) call it the Pillar of the Sky. They are said to eat no living creature, and never to dream.

Thus far I am able to give the names of the tribes who inhabit the sand-belt, but beyond this point my knowledge fails. I can affirm, however, that the belt continues to the Pillars of Heracles and beyond, and that at regular intervals of ten days' journey are salt-hills and springs, with people living in the neighbourhood. The houses are all built of salt-blocks—an indication that there is no rain in this part of Libya; for if there were, salt walls would collapse. The salt which is mined there is of two colours, white and purple. South of the sand-belt, in the interior, lies a waterless desert, without rain or trees or animal life, or a drop of moisture of any kind.

The coast of Libya, then, between Egypt and Lake Tritonis is occupied by nomads living on meat and milk—though they do not breed pigs, and abstain from cows' meat for the same reason as the Egyptians. Even at Cyrene women think it is wrong to eat cows' meat, out of respect for the Egyptian Isis, in whose honour they celebrate both fasts and festivals. At Barca the women avoid eating pigs' flesh, as well as cows'. West of Tritonis, nomad tribes are no longer found; the people are quite different, not only in their general way of life, but in the treatment of their children. Many of the nomads—perhaps all, but I cannot be certain about this—when their children are four years old, burn the veins on their heads, and sometimes on their temples, with a bit of greasy wool, as a permanent cure for catarrh. For this reason they are said to be the healthiest people in the world—indeed, it is true enough that they are healthier than any other race we know of, though I should not care to be too certain that this is the reason. Anyway, about the fact of their health there is no doubt. Should the cauterizing of the veins bring on convulsions, they have discovered that the effective remedy is to sprinkle goat's urine on the child—I only repeat in all this what is said by the Libyans. When the nomad tribes sacrifice, the process is to begin by cutting off the victim's ear, which they throw over the house as a preliminary offering, and then to wring the animal's neck. They sacrifice to the sun and moon, the worship of which is common to all the Libyans, though those who live round Lake Tritonis sacrifice chiefly to Athene, and, after her, to Triton and Poseidon. It is evident, I think, that the Greeks took the 'aegis' with which they adorn statues of Athene from the dress of the Libyan women; for except that the latter is of leather and has fringes of leather thongs instead of snakes, there is no other point of difference. Moreover, the word 'aegis' itself shows that the dress represented in statues of Athene is derived from Libya; for Libyan women wear goatskins with the hair stripped off, dyed red and fringed at the edges, and it was from these skins that we took our word 'aegis'. I think too that the crying of women at religious ceremonies also originated in Libya—for the Libyan women are much addicted to this practice, and they do it very beautifully. Another thing the Greeks learnt from Libya was to harness four horses to a chariot. The nomad Libyans—except the Nasamonians—bury their dead just as we do in Greece; the Nasamonians, however, bury them in a sitting position, and take care when anyone is dying to make him sit up, and not to let him die flat on his back. Their houses, which are portable, are made of the dry haulms of some plant, knit together with rush ropes.

West of the Triton, and beyond the Auses, Libya is inhabited by tribes who live in ordinary houses and practise agriculture. First come the Maxyes, a people who grow their hair on the right side of their heads and shave it off on the left. They stain their bodies red and claim to be descended from the men of Troy. The country round here, and the rest of Libya to the westward, has more forest and a greater number of wild animals than the region which the nomads occupy. The latter—that is, eastern Libya—is low-lying and sandy as far as the river Triton, whereas the agricultural region to the west is very hilly, and abounds with forest and animal life. It is here that the huge snakes are found—and lions, elephants, bears, asps, and horned asses, not to mention dog-headed men, headless men with eyes in their breasts (I don't vouch for this, but merely repeat what the Libyans say), wild men and wild women, and a great many other creatures by no means of a fabulous kind. In the nomads' country none of these occur; instead, one finds white-rump antelopes, gazelles, deer, asses—not the horned sort but a different species which can do without water; it is a fact that they do not drink—another kind of antelope, about as big as an ox, the horns of which are used for making the curved sides of lyres, foxes, hyaenas, hedgehogs, wild rams, jackals, panthers, and others, including landcrocodiles like huge lizards, four and a half feet long, ostriches and small snakes with a single horn. All these are found, together with other animals common elsewhere, with the exception of the stag and the wild boar, of which there are none at all in Libya. There are however, three kinds of mice, called respectively *dipodes, zegeries,* and *echines*—also weasels, which are found amongst the silphium, and resemble those at Tartessus. So much, then, for the animal life in that part of Libya where the nomads are: I have made it as full and accurate as my extensive inquiries permit.

Continuing westward from the Maxyes, one comes next to the Zaueces: amongst this people the drivers of the war-chariots are the women. Their neighbours are the Gyzantes, whose country is very well supplied with honey—much of it made by bees, but even more by some process which the people have discovered. Everybody here paints himself red and eats monkeys, of which there is an abundant supply in the hills. Off the coast, according to the Carthaginian account, is an island called Cyrauis, about twenty-five miles long, but narrow, which can be reached on foot from the mainland and is full of olive-trees and vines. In the island is a lake, and the native girls dip feathers smeared with pitch into the mud at the bottom of it, and bring up gold dust—again, I merely record the current story, without guaranteeing the truth of it. It may, however, be true enough; for I have myself seen something similar in Zacynthus, where pitch is fetched up from the water in a lake. There are a number of lakes—or ponds—in Zacynthus, of which the largest measures seventy feet each way and has a depth of two fathoms. The process is to tie a branch of myrtle on to the end of a pole, which is then thrust down to the bottom of this pond; the pitch sticks to the myrtle, and is thus brought to the surface. It smells like bitumen, but in all other respects it is better than the pitch of Pieria. It is then poured into a trench near the pond, and when a good quantity has been collected, it is removed from the trench and transferred to jars. Anything that falls into this pond, passes underground and comes up again in the sea, a good half mile distant. In view of all this, the account of what happens in the island off Libya may quite possibly be true.

The Carthaginians also tell us that they trade with a race of men who live in a part of Libya beyond the Pillars of Heracles. On reaching this country, they unload their goods, arrange them tidily along the beach, and then, returning to their boats, raise a smoke. Seeing the smoke, the natives come down to the beach, place on the ground a certain quantity of gold in exchange for the goods, and go off again to a distance. The Carthaginians then come ashore and take a look at the gold; and if they think it represents a fair price for their wares, they collect it and go away; if, on the other hand, it seems too little, they go back aboard and wait, and the natives come and add to the gold until they are satisfied. There is perfect honesty on both sides; the Carthaginians never touch the gold until it equals in value what they have offered for sale, and the natives never touch the goods until the gold has been taken away.

I have now mentioned all the Libyans whose names I am acquainted with; most of them, at the time of which I write, cared nothing for the king of Persia, any more than they do to-day. One other thing I can add about this country: so far as one knows, it is inhabited by four races, and four only, of which two are indigenous and two not. The indigenous peoples are the Libyans and Ethiopians, the former occupying the northerly, the latter the more southerly, parts; the immigrants are the Phoenicians and Greeks. I do not think the country can be compared for the fertility of its soil with either Asia or Europe, with the single exception of the region called Cinyps—so named after the river which waters it. This region, however, is quite different from the rest of Libya, and is as good for cereal crops as any land in the world. The soil here, unlike the soil elsewhere, is black and irrigated by springs; it has no fear of drought on the one hand, or of damage, on the other, from excessive rain (it does, by the way, rain in that part of Libya). The yield of the harvests is equal to the yield in Babylonia. There is also good soil at Euesperides—in the best years it will yield a hundred-fold—but the yield in Cinyps is three times as great. The land of Cyrene, the highest of that part of Libya which is inhabited by nomads, has the remarkable peculiarity of three separate harvest-seasons: first, the crops near the coast ripen and are ready for cutting or picking; then, when these are in, the crops in what they call the hill-country—the middle region above the coastal belt—are ready for harvesting; and lastly, when this second harvest is over, the crops in the highest tract of country are ripe and ready, so that by the time the first harvest is all eaten or drunk, the last comes in—making, for the fortunate people of Cyrene, a continuous autumn of eight months on end. I must now leave this subject.

3. Sociology
Lucretius

I have explained the processes by which the various phenomena may be brought about in the blue expanses of the firmament. I have made intelligible the forces that may actuate the movements of the sun and the moon's wanderings. I have shown how both may suffer eclipse through the obscuration of their light and plunge the unexpecting earth in gloom, as though they blinked and then with reopened eye surveyed the world, aglow with limpid radiance. I return now to the childhood of the world, to consider what fruits the tender fields of earth in youthful parturition first ventured to fling up into the light of day and entrust to the fickle breezes.

First of all, the earth girdled its hills with a green glow of herbage, and over every plain the meadows gleamed with verdure and with bloom. Then trees of every sort were given free rein to join in an eager race for growth into the gusty air. As feathers, fur and bristles are generated at the outset from the bodies of winged and four-footed creatures, so then *the new-born earth first flung up herbs and shrubs. Next in order it engendered the various breeds of mortal creatures,* manifold in mode of origin as in form. The animals cannot have fallen from the sky, and those that live on land cannot have emerged from the briny gulfs. We are left with the conclusion that the name of mother has rightly been bestowed on the earth, since out of the earth everything is born.

Even now multitudes of animals are formed out of the earth with the aid of showers and the sun's genial warmth. So it is not surprising if more and bigger ones took shape and developed in those days, when earth and ether were young. First, the various breeds of winged birds were hatched out of eggs in the spring season, just as now the cicadas in summer crawl out spontaneously from their tubular integuments in quest of sustenance and life. Then it was that the earth brought forth the first mammals. There was a great superfluity of heat and moisture in the soil. So, wherever a suitable spot occurred, there grew up wombs, clinging to the earth by roots. These, when the time was ripe, were burst open by the maturation of the embryos, rejecting moisture now and struggling for air. Then nature directed towards that spot the pores of the earth, making it open its veins and exude a juice resembling milk, just as nowadays every female when she has given birth is filled with sweet milk because all the flow of nourishment within her is directed into the breasts. The young were fed by the earth, clothed by the warmth and bedded by the herbage, which was then covered with abundance of soft down. The childhood of the world provoked no hard frosts or excessive heats or winds of boisterous violence. For all things keep pace in their growth and the attainment of their full strength. Here then, is further proof that the name of mother has rightly been bestowed on the earth, since it brought forth the human race and gave birth at the appointed season to every beast that runs wild among the high hills and at the same time to the birds of the air in all their rich variety.

Then, because there must be an end to such parturition, the earth ceased to bear, like a woman worn out with age. For the nature of the world as a whole is altered by age. Everything must pass through successive phases. Nothing remains for ever what it was. Everything is on the move. Everything is transformed by nature and forced into new paths. One thing, withered by time, decays and dwindles. Another emerges from ignominy, and waxes strong. So the nature of the world as a whole is altered by age. The earth passes through successive phases, so that it can no longer bear what it could, and it can now what it could not before.

In those days the earth attempted also to produce a host of monsters, grotesque in build and aspect—hermaphrodites, halfway between the sexes yet cut off from either, creatures bereft of feet or dispossessed of hands, dumb, mouthless brutes, or eyeless and blind, or disabled by the adhesion of their limbs to the trunk, so that they could neither do anything nor go anywhere nor keep out of harm's way nor take what they needed. These and other such *monstrous and misshapen births were created. But all in vain.* Nature debarred them from increase. They could not gain the coveted flower of maturity nor procure food nor be coupled by the arts of Venus. For it is evident that many contributory factors are essential to the reproduction of a species. First, it must have a food-supply. Then it must have some channel by which the procreative seeds can travel outward through the body when the limbs are relaxed. Then, in order that male and female may couple, they must have some means of interchanging their mutual delight.

In those days, again, *many species must have died out altogether* and failed to reproduce their kind. Every species that you now see drawing the breath of life has been protected and preserved from the beginning of the world either by cunning or by prowess or by speed. In addition, there are many that survive under human protection because their usefulness has commended them to our care. The surly breed of lions, for instance, in their native ferocity have been preserved by prowess, the fox by cunning and the stag by flight. The dog, whose loyal heart is alert even in sleep, all beasts of burden of whatever breed, fleecy sheep and horned cattle, over all these, my Memmius, man has established his protectorate. They have gladly escaped from predatory beasts and sought peace and the lavish meals, procured by no effort of theirs, with which we recompense their service. But those that were gifted with none of these natural assets, unable either to live on their own resources or to make any contribution to human welfare, in return for which we might let their race feed in safety under our guardianship—all these, trapped in the toils of their own destiny, were fair game and an easy prey for others, till nature brought their race to extinction.

But *there never were,* nor ever can be, Centaurs—*creatures with a double nature,* combining organs of different origin in a single body so that there may be a balance of power between attributes drawn from two distinct sources. This can be inferred by the dullest wit from these facts. First, a horse reaches its vigorous prime in about three years, a boy far from it: for often even at that age he will fumble in sleep for his mother's suckling breasts. Then, when the horse's limbs are flagging and his mettle is fading with the onset of age and the ebbing of life, then is the very time when the boy is crowned with the flower of youth and his cheeks are clothed with a downy bloom. You need not suppose, therefore, that there can ever be a Centaur, compounded of man and draught-horse, or a Scylla, half sea-monster, with a girdle of mad dogs, or any other such monstrous hybrid between species whose bodies are obviously incompatible. They do not match in their maturing, in gaining strength or in losing it with advancing years. They respond diversely to the flame of Venus. Their habits are discordant. Their senses are not gratified by the same stimuli. You may even see bearded goats battening on hemlock, which to man is deadly poison. Since flame sears and burns the tawny frames of lions no less than any other form of flesh and blood that exists on earth, how could there be a Chimaera with three bodies rolled into one, in front a lion, at the rear a serpent, in the middle the she-goat that her name implies, belching from her jaws a dire flame born of her body? If anyone pretends that such monsters could have been begotten when earth was young and the sky new, pinning his faith merely on that empty word 'young,' he is welcome to trot out a string of fairy tales of the same stamp. Let him declare that rivers of gold in those days flowed in profusion over the earth; that the trees bore gems for blossoms, or that a man was born with such a stretch of limbs that he could bestride the high seas and spin the whole firmament around him with his hands. The fact that there were abundant seeds of things in the earth at the time when it first gave birth to living creatures is no indication that beasts could have been created of intermingled shapes with limbs compounded from different species. The growths that even now spring profusely from the soil—the varieties of herbs and cereals and lusty trees—cannot be produced in this composite fashion; each species develops according to its own kind, and they all guard their specific characters in obedience to the laws of nature.

The *human beings* that peopled these fields were far tougher than the men of to-day, as became the offspring of tough earth. They were built on a framework of bigger and solider bones, fastened through their flesh to stout sinews. They were relatively insensitive to heat and cold, to unaccustomed diet and bodily ailments in general. Through many decades of the sun's cyclic course they lived out their lives in the fashion of wild beasts roaming at large. No one spent his strength in guiding the curved plough. No one knew how to cleave the earth with iron, or to plant young saplings in the soil or lop the old branches from tall trees with pruning hooks. Their hearts were well content to accept as a free gift what the sun and showers had given and the earth had produced unsolicited. Often they stayed their hunger among the acorn-laden oaks. Arbutus berries, whose scarlet tint now betrays their winter ripening, were then produced by the earth in plenty and of a larger size. In addition the lusty childhood of the earth yielded a great variety of tough foods, ample for afflicted mortals. Rivers and springs called to them to slake their thirst, as nowadays a clamorous cataract of water, tumbling out of the high hills, summons from far away the thirsty creatures of the wild. They resorted to those woodland sanctuaries of the nymphs, familiar to them in their wandering, from which they knew that trickling streams of water issued to bathe the dripping rocks in a bountiful shower, sprinkled over green moss, and gushed out here and there over the open plain.

They did not know as yet how to enlist the aid of fire, or to make use of skins, or to clothe their bodies with trophies of the chase. They lived in thickets and hillside caves and forests and stowed their rugged limbs among bushes when driven to seek shelter from the lash of wind and rain.

They could have no thought of the common good, no notion of the mutual restraint of morals and laws. The individual, taught only to live and fend for himself, carried off on his own account such prey as fortune brought him. Venus coupled the bodies of lovers in the greenwood. Mutual desire brought them together, or the male's mastering might and overriding lust, or a payment of acorns or arbutus berries or choice pears. Thanks to their surpassing strength of hand and foot, they hunted the woodland beasts by hurling stones and wielding ponderous clubs. They were more than a match for many of them; from a few they took refuge in hiding-places.

When night overtook them, they flung their jungle-bred limbs naked on the earth like bristly boars, and wrapped themselves round with a coverlet of leaves and branches. It is not true that they wandered panic-stricken over the countryside through the darkness of night, searching with loud lamentations for the daylight and the sun. In fact they waited, sunk in quiet sleep, till the sun with his rose-red torch should bring back radiance to the sky. Accustomed as they were from infancy to seeing the alternate birth of darkness and light, they could never have been struck with amazement or misgiving whether the withdrawal of the sunlight might not plunge the earth in everlasting night. They were more worried by the peril to which unlucky sleepers were often exposed from predatory beasts. Turned out of house and home by the intrusion of a slavering boar or a burly lion, they would abandon their rocky roofs at dead of night and yield up their leaf-strewn beds in terror to the savage visitor.

The proportion of mortal men that relinquished the dear light of life before it was all spent was not appreciably higher then than now. Then it more often happened that an individual victim would furnish living food to a beast of prey: engulfed in its jaws, he would fill thicket and mountainside and forest with his shrieks, at the sight of his living flesh entombed in a living sepulchre. Those who saved their mangled bodies by flight would press trembling palms over ghastly sores, calling upon death in heart-rending voices, till life was wrenched from them by racking spasms. In their ignorance of the treatment that wounds demand, they could not help themselves. But it never happened then that many thousands of men following the standards were led to death on a single day. Never did the ocean levels, lashed into tumult, hurl ships and men together upon the reefs. Here, time after time, the sea would rise and vainly vent its fruitless ineffectual fury, then lightly lay aside its idle threats. The crafty blandishment of the unruffled deep could not tempt any man to his undoing with its rippling laughter. Then, when the mariner's presumptuous art lay still unguessed, it was lack of food that brought failing limbs at last to death. Now it is superfluity that proves too much for them. The men of old, in their ignorance, often served poison to themselves. Now, with greater skill, they administer it to others.

As time went by, men began to build huts and to use skins and fire. Male and female learnt to live together in a stable union and to watch over their joint progeny. Then it was that humanity first began to mellow. Thanks to fire, their chilly bodies could no longer so easily endure the cold under the canopy of heaven. Venus subdued brute strength. Children by their wheedling easily broke down their parents' stubborn temper. Then neighbours began to form *mutual alliances,* wishing neither to do nor to suffer violence among themselves. They appealed on behalf of their children and womenfolk, pointing out with gestures and inarticulate cries that it is right for everyone to pity the weak. It was not possible to achieve perfect unity of purpose. Yet a substantial majority kept faith honestly. Otherwise the entire human race would have been wiped out there and then instead of being propagated, generation after generation, down to the present day.

As for the various sounds of *spoken language*, it was nature that drove men to utter these, and practical convenience that gave a form to the names of objects. We see a similar process at work when babies are led by their speechless plight to employ gestures, such as pointing with a finger at objects in view. For every creature has a sense of the purposes for which he can use his own powers. A bull-calf, before ever his horns have grown and sprouted from his forehead, butts and thrusts with them aggressively when his temper is roused. Panther and lion cubs tussle with paws and jaws when their claws and teeth are scarcely yet in existence. We see every species of winged bird trust in its wings and seek faint-hearted aid from flight. To suppose that someone on some particular occasion allotted names to objects, and that by this means men learnt their first words, is stark madness. Why should we suppose that one man had this power of indicating everything by vocal utterances and emitting the various sounds of speech when others could not do it? Besides, if others had not used such utterances among themselves, from what source was the mental image of its use implanted in him? Whence did this one man derive the power in the first instance of seeing with his mind what he wanted to do? One man could not subdue a greater number and induce them by force to learn his names for things. It is far from easy to convince deaf listeners by any demonstration what needs to be done. They would not endure it or submit for long on any terms to have incomprehensible noises senselessly dinned into their ears.

And what, after all, is so surprising in the notion that the human race, possessed of a vigorous voice and tongue, should indicate objects by various vocal utterances expressive of various feelings? Even dumb cattle and wild beasts utter distinct and various sounds when they are gripped by fear or pain or when joy wells up within them. Indeed we have direct evidence of such distinctions. Molossian hounds, for instance, when first their gaping flabby jowls are drawn back in a grim snarl that bares their hard teeth, give vent to a gruff growl. Very different is the sound when the growl has grown to a loud-mouthed reverberating bay. Different again is the soft crooning with which they fondle their pups when they fall to licking them lovingly with their tongues or toss them with their paws, snapping with open jaws in a playful pretence of gobbling them up with teeth that never close. And different from all these are their howls when left alone in the house, or the whimpering with which they shrink and cringe to avoid the whip. In the same way, when a stallion in the prime of his youth is let loose among the mares, smarting from the prick of winged Cupid's darts, and snorts defiance to his rivals through distended nostrils, his neigh is surely not the same that shakes his limbs on other occasions. So also with the various species of winged birds. The hawks and ospreys and gulls that seek a livelihood among the salt sea-waves all have distinctive cries that show when they are squabbling over their booty or struggling to master a quarry. Some birds even vary their note according to the weather. So the hoarse-throated cawing of long-lived ravens and gregarious rooks varies from time to time according as they are clamouring for showers of rain, as it is said, or summoning wind and storm. If the animals, dumb though they be, are impelled by different feelings to utter different cries, how much the more reason to suppose that men in those days had the power of distinguishing between one thing and another by distinctive utterances!

Here is the answer to another question that you may be putting to yourself. *The agent by which fire was first brought down to earth* and made available to mortal man was lightning. To this source every hearth owes its flames. Think how many things we see ablaze with heaven-sent flame, when a stroke from heaven has endowed them with heat. There is also, however, another possible source. When a branching tree, tossed by the wind, is swaying and surging to and fro and stooping to touch the branches of another tree, the violent friction squeezes out seeds of fire, till sometimes from the rubbing of bough against bough, trunk against trunk, there flashes out a blazing burst of flame. Either of these occurrences may have given fire to mortals. Later it was the sun that taught them to cook food and soften it by heating on the flames, since they noticed in roaming through the fields how many things were subdued and mellowed by the impact of its ardent rays.

As time went by, men learnt to change their old way of life by means of fire and other new inventions, instructed by those of outstanding ability and mental energy. *Kings began to found cities* and establish citadels for their own safeguard and refuge. They parcelled out cattle and lands, giving to each according to his looks, his strength and his ability; for good looks were highly prized and strength counted for much. Later came the invention of property and the discovery of gold, which speedily robbed the strong and the handsome of their pre-eminence. The man of greater riches finds no lack of stalwart frames and comely faces to follow in his train. And yet, if a man would guide his life by true philosophy, he will find ample riches in a modest livelihood enjoyed with a tranquil mind. Of that little he need never be beggared. Men craved for fame and power so that their fortune might rest on a firm foundation and they might live out a peaceful life in the enjoyment of plenty. An idle dream. In struggling to gain the pinnacle of power they beset their own road with perils. And then from the very peak, as though by a thunderbolt, they are cast down by envy into a foul abyss of ignominy. For envy, like the thunderbolt, most often strikes the highest and all that stands out above the common level. Far better to lead a quiet life in subjection than to long for sovereign authority and lordship over kingdoms. So leave them to the blood and sweat of their wearisome unprofitable struggle along the narrow pathway of ambition. Since they savour life through another's mouth and choose their target rather by hearsay than by the evidence of their own senses, it avails them now, and will avail them, no more than it has ever done.

So the kings were killed. Down in the dust lay the ancient majesty of thrones, the haughty sceptres. The illustrious emblem of the sovereign head, dabbled in gore and trampled under the feet of the rabble, mourned its high estate. What once was feared too much is now as passionately downtrodden. So the conduct of affairs sank back into the turbid depths of mob-rule, with each man struggling to win dominance and supremacy for himself. Then some men showed how to form a constitution, based on fixed rights and recognized laws. Mankind, worn out by a life of violence and enfeebled by feuds, was the more ready to submit of its own free will to the bondage of laws and institutions. This distaste for a life of violence came naturally to a society in which every individual was ready to gratify his anger by a harsher vengeance than is now tolerated by equitable laws. Ever since then the enjoyment of life's prizes has been tempered by the fear of punishment. A man is enmeshed by his own violence and wrong-doing, which commonly recoil upon their author. It is not easy for one who breaks by his acts the mutual compact of social peace to lead a peaceful and untroubled life. Even if he hides his guilt from gods and men, he must feel a secret misgiving that it will not rest hidden for ever. He cannot forget those oft-told tales of men betraying themselves by words spoken in dreams or delirium that drag out long-buried crimes into the daylight.

Let us now consider why *reverence for the gods* is widespread among the nations. What has crowded their cities with altars and inaugurated those solemn rites that are in vogue to-day in powerful states and busy resorts? What has implanted in mortal hearts that chill of dread which even now rears new temples of the gods the wide world over and packs them on holy days with pious multitudes? The explanation is not far to seek. Already in those early days men had visions when their minds were awake, and more clearly in sleep, of divine figures, dignified in mien and impressive in stature. To these figures they attributed sentience, because they were seen to move their limbs and give voice to lordly utterances appropriate to their stately features and stalwart frames. They further credited them with eternal life, because the substance of their shapes was perpetually renewed and their appearance unchanging and in general because they thought that beings of such strength could not lightly be subdued by any force. They pictured their lot as far superior to that of mortals, because none of them was tormented by the fear of death, and also because in dreams they saw them perform all sorts of miracles without the slightest effort.

Again, men noticed the orderly succession of celestial phenomona and the round of the seasons and were at a loss to account for them. So they took refuge in handing over everything to the gods and making everything dependent on their whim. They chose the sky to be the home and headquarters of the gods because it is through the sky that the moon is seen to tread its cyclic course with day and night and night's ominous constellations and the night-flying torches and soaring flames of the firmament, clouds and sun and rain, snow and wind, lightning and hail, the sudden thunder-crash and the long-drawn intimidating rumble.

Poor humanity, to saddle the gods with such responsibilities and throw in a vindictive temper! What griefs they hatched then for themselves, what festering sores for us, what tears for our posterity! This is not piety, this oftrepeated show of bowing a veiled head before a graven image; this bustling to every altar; this kow-towing and prostration on the ground with palms outspread before the shrines of the gods; this deluging of altars with the blood of beasts; this heaping of vow on vow. True piety lies rather in the power to contemplate the universe with a quiet mind.

When we gaze up at the supernal regions of this mighty world, at the ether poised above, studded with flashing stars, and there comes into our minds the thought of the sun and moon and their migrations, then in hearts already racked by other woes a new anxiety begins to waken and rear up its head. We fall to wondering whether we may not be subject to some unfathomable divine power, which speeds the shining stars along their various tracks. It comes as a shock to our faltering minds to realize how little they know about the world. Had it a birth and a beginning? Is there some limit in time, beyond which its bastions will be unable to endure the strain of jarring motion? Or are they divinely gifted with everlasting surety, so that in their journey through the termless tract of time they can mock the stubborn strength of illimitable age?

Again, who does not feel his mind quailing and his limbs unnerved with shuddering dread of the gods when the parched earth reels at the dire stroke of the thunderbolt and tumult rolls across the breadth of heaven? Do not multitudes quake and nations tremble? Do not proud monarchs flinch, stricken in every limb by terror of the gods and the thought that the time has come when some foul deed or arrogant word must pay its heavy price?

Or picture a storm at sea, the wind scouring the water with hurricane force and some high admiral of the fleet swept before the blast with all his lavish complement of troops and battle elephants. How he importunes the peace of the gods with vows! How fervently he prays in his terror that the winds, too, may be at peace and favouring breezes blow! But, for all his prayers, the tornado does not relax its grip, and all too often he is dashed upon the reefs of death. So irresistibly is human power ground to dust by some unseen force, which seems to mock at the majestic rods and ruthless axes of authority and trample on them for its sport.

Lastly, when the whole earth quakes beneath their feet, when shaken cities fall in ruins or hang hesitantly tottering, what wonder if mortal men despise themselves and find a place in nature for superhuman forces and miraculous divine powers with supreme control over the universe?

We come next to *the discovery of copper, gold and iron, weighty silver and serviceable lead.* This occurred when fire among the high hills had consumed huge forests in its blaze. The blaze may have been started by a stroke of lightning, or by men who had employed fire to scare their enemies in some woodland war, or were tempted by the fertility of the country to enlarge their rich ploughlands and turn the wilds into pasturage. Or they may have wished to kill the forest beasts and profit by their spoils; for hunting by means of pitfall and fire developed earlier than fencing round a glade with nets and driving the game with dogs. Let us take it, then, that for one reason or another, no matter what, a fierce conflagration, roaring balefully, has devoured a forest down to the roots and roasted the earth with penetrative fire. Out of the melted veins there would flow into hollows on the earth's surface a convergent stream of silver and gold, copper and lead. Afterwards, when men saw these lying solidified on the earth and flashing with resplendent colour, they would be tempted by their attractive lustre and polish to pick them up. They would notice that each lump was moulded into a shape like that of the bed from which it had been lifted. Then it would enter their minds that these substances, when liquefied by heat, could run into any mould or the shape of any object they might desire, and could also be drawn out by hammering into pointed tips of any slenderness and sharpness. Here was a means by which they could equip themselves with weapons, chop down forests, rough-hew timber and plane it into smooth planks and pierce holes in it by boring, punching or drilling. At the outset they would try to do this with silver and gold no less than with tough and stubborn copper. But this would not work. These metals would give under the strain, lacking strength to stand up to such exacting tasks. So copper was more highly prized, and gold with its quickly blunted edge was despised as useless. Now it is copper that is despised, while gold has succeeded to the highest honours. So the circling years bring round reversals of fortune. What once was prized is afterwards held cheap. In its place, something else emerges from ignominy, is daily more and more coveted and, as its merits are detected, blossoms into glory and is acclaimed by mankind with extravagant praises.

At this point, Memmius, you should find it easy to puzzle out for yourself how men discovered the properties of iron. The earliest weapons were hands, nails and teeth. Next came stones and branches wrenched from trees, and fire and flame as soon as these were discovered. Then men learnt to use tough iron and copper Actually the use of copper was discovered before that of iron, because it is more easily handled and in more plentiful supply. With copper they tilled the soil. With copper they whipped up the clashing waves of war, scattered a withering seed of wounds and made a spoil of flocks and fields. Before their armaments all else, naked and unarmed, fell an easy prey. Then by slow degrees the iron sword came to the fore; the bronze sickle fell into disrepute; the ploughman began to cleave the earth with iron, and on the darkling field of battle the odds were made even.

The art of mounting armed on horseback, guiding the steed with reins and keeping the right hand free for action, came earlier than braving the hazards of war in a two-horsed chariot. This again preceded the yoking of two pairs in one harness and the charge of armed warriors in chariots set with scythes. Later the redoubtable snake-handed elephant, its body crowned by a tower, was taught by the men of Carthage to endure the wounds of war and embroil the long-drawn ranks of Mars. So tragic discord gave birth to one invention after another for the intimidation of the nations' fighting men and added daily increments to the horrors of war.

Bulls, too, were enlisted in the service of war, and the experiment was made of launching savage boars against the enemy. Some even tried an advance guard of doughty lions with armed trainers and harsh masters to discipline them and keep them on the lead. But these experiments failed. The savage brutes, enflamed by promiscuous carnage, spread indiscriminate confusion among the cavaliers, as they tossed the terrifying manes upon their heads this way and that. The riders failed to soothe the breasts of their steeds, panic-stricken by the uproar, and direct them with the reins against the enemy. The lionesses hurled their frenzied bodies in a random spring, now leaping full in the face of oncomers, now snatching down unsuspecting victims from behind and dragging them to the gound, mortally wounded in the embrace and gripped fast by tenacious jaws and crooked claws. The bulls tossed their own employers and trampled them underfoot and with their horns gored the flanks and bellies of horses from below and hacked up the very earth with defiant forehead. The infuriated boars with their stout tusks slashed their allies. They reddened with their own blood the weapons broken in their bodies. They mowed down horse and foot pell-mell. The horses would shy away, or rear up and paw the air in a vain attempt to escape the savage onslaught of those tusks. But down you would see them tumble hamstrung, and bury the earth beneath their fallen mass. Even such beasts as their masters had once thought tame enough at home were seen to boil over in the stir of action—wounds, yells, stampedes, panic and turmoil; and none of them would obey the recall. Brutes of every breed were rushing wildly about. The sight must have been just such as is sometimes seen in our own times when elephants, badly wounded by the steel, run wild after turning savagely upon their own associates. If, indeed, the experiment was ever tried. For my part, I find it hard to believe that men had no mental apprehension and prevision of this mutual disaster and disgrace before it could happen. It would be safer to assert that this has happened somewhere in the universe, somewhere in the multiplicity of diversely formed worlds, than in any one specific globe. In any event it must have been undertaken more to spite the enemy than with any hope of victory, by men mistrustful of their own numbers and armaments but not afraid to die.

As to *costume,* plaited clothes came before woven ones. Woven fabrics came after iron, because iron is needed for making a loom. Apart from it no material can be made smooth enough for treadles and spindles and shuttles and clattering heddles. Nature ordained that this should be men's work before it was women's. For the male sex as a whole is by far the more skilful and gifted in the arts. But eventually it was damned as effeminate by a censorious peasantry, so that they chose rather to leave it to women's hands while they joined in the endurance of hard labour and by the hardness of their toil hardened hands and thews.

For the *sowing and grafting of plants* the first model was provided by creative nature herself. Berries and acorns, lying below the trees from which they had fallen, were seen to put forth a swarm of shoots in due season. From the same source men learnt to engraft slips in branches and to plant young saplings in the soil of their fields. After that they tried one type of cultivation after another in their treasured plot. They saw the wild fruits grow mild in the ground with cosseting and humouring. Day by day they kept forcing the woodland to creep further up the hillside, surrendering the lower reaches to tillage. Over hill and plain they extended meadowland and cornland, reservoirs and water-courses and laughing vineyards, with the distinctive strip of blue-grey olives running between, rippling over hump and hollow and along the level ground. So the countryside assumed its present aspect of variegated beauty, gaily interspersed with luscious orchards and marked out by encircling hedges of luxuriant trees.

Men learnt to mimic with their mouths the trilling notes of birds long before they were able to enchant the ear by joining together in *tuneful song*. It was the whistling of the breeze through hollow reeds that first taught countryfolk to blow through hollow stalks. After that, by slow degrees, they learnt those plaintive melodies that flow from the flute at the touch of the player's fingers, melodies that took shape far from the busy highways, amid groves and glades and thickets in the solitudes where the shepherd spends his sunlit leisure. These are the tunes that soothed and cheered their hearts after a full meal: for at such times everything is enjoyable. So they would often recline in company on the soft grass by a running stream under the branches of a tall tree and refresh their bodies pleasurably at small expense. Better still if the weather smiled upon them and the season of the year emblazoned the green herbage with flowers. Then was the time for joking and talking and merry laughter. Then was the heyday of the rustic muse. Then light-hearted jollity prompted them to wreathe head and shoulders with garlands twisted of flowers and leaves and dance out of step, moving their limbs clumsily and with clumsy foot stamping on mother earth. This was matter enough for mirth and boisterous laughter. For these arts were still in their youth, with all the charm of novelty.

In the same occupation the wakeful found a means to while away their sleepless hours, pitching their voices high or low through the twisted intricacies of song and running over the pipes with curving lips. This remains a recognized tradition among watchmen to this day, and they have now learnt to keep in tune. But this does not mean that they derive any greater enjoyment from it than did the woodland race sprung from the soil. For what we have here and now, unless we have known something more pleasing in the past, gives the greatest satisfaction and is reckoned the best of its kind. Afterwards the discovery of something new and better blunts and vitiates our enjoyment of the old. So it is that we have lost our taste for acorns. So we have abandoned those couches littered with herbage and heaped with leaves. So the wearing of wild beasts' skins has gone out of fashion. And yet I daresay that the invention of this costume provoked such envy that its first wearer met his death in an ambush and the costume itself was so daubed with blood and torn to shreds by rival claimants that it could not be used by anyone. Skins yesterday, purple and gold to-day—such are the baubles that embitter human life with resentment and waste it with war. In this, I do not doubt, the greater blame rests with us. To the earth-born generation in their naked state the lack of skins meant real discomfort through cold; but we are in no way discommoded by going without robes of purple, brocaded with gold and gorgeously emblazoned, so long as we have some plebeian wrap to throw around us. So mankind is perpetually the victim of a pointless and futile martyrdom, fretting life away in fruitless worries through failure to realize what limit is set to acquisition and to the growth of genuine pleasure. It is this discontent that has driven life steadily onward, out to the high seas, and has stirred up from the depths the surging tumultuous tides of war.

It was the sun and moon, the watchmen of the world, encircling with their light that vast rotating vault, who taught men that the seasons of the year revolve and that there is a constant pattern in things and a constant sequence.

By this time men were living their lives fenced by fortifications and tilling an earth already parcelled out and allotted. The sea was aflutter with flying sails. Societies were bound together by compacts and alliances. Poets were beginning to record history in song. But letters were still a recent invention. Therefore our age cannot look back to see what happened before this stage, except in so far as its traces can be uncovered by reason.

So we find that not only such arts as sea-faring and agriculture, city walls and laws, weapons, roads and clothing, but also without exception the amenities and refinements of life, songs, pictures, and statues, artfully carved and polished, *all were taught gradually by usage* and the active mind's experience as men groped their way forward step by step. So each particular development is brought gradually to the fore by the advance of time, and reason lifts it into the light of day. Men saw one notion after another take shape within their minds until by their arts they scaled the topmost peak.

4. The Bedouins
Ibn Khaldûn

1 Both Bedouins and sedentary people are natural groups

It[1] should be known that differences of condition among people are the result of the different ways in which they make their living. Social organization enables them to co-operate toward that end and to start with the simple necessities of life, before they get to conveniences and luxuries.[2]

Some people adopt agriculture, the cultivation of vegetables and grains, (as their way of making a living). Others adopt animal husbandry, the use of sheep, cattle, goats, bees, and silkworms, for breeding and for their products. Those who live by agriculture or animal husbandry cannot avoid the call of the desert, because it alone offers the wide fields, acres, pastures for animals, and other things that the settled areas do not offer.[3] It is therefore necessary for them to restrict themselves to the desert. Their social organization and co-operation for the needs of life and civilization, such as food, shelter, and warmth, do not take them beyond the bare subsistence level, because of their inability (to provide) for anything beyond those (things). Subsequent improvement of their conditions and acquisition of more wealth and comfort than they need, cause them to rest and take it easy. Then, they co-operate for things beyond the (bare) necessities. They use more food and clothes, and take pride in them. They build large houses, and lay out towns and cities for protection. This is followed by an increase in comfort and ease, which leads to formation of the most developed luxury customs. They take the greatest pride in the preparation of food and a fine cuisine, in the use of varied splendid clothes of silk and brocade and other (fine materials), in the construction of ever higher buildings and towers, in elaborate furnishings for the buildings, and the most intensive cultivation of crafts in actuality. They build castles and mansions, provide them with running water,[4] build their towers higher and higher, and compete in furnishing them (most elaborately). They differ in the quality of the clothes, the beds, the vessels, and the utensils they employ for their purposes. Here, now, (we have) sedentary people. "Sedentary people" means the inhabitants of cities and countries, some of whom adopt the

From Ibn Khaldûn, *The Muqaddimah*, trans. Franz Rosenthal, Bollingen Series XLIII, © 1958, Bollingen Foundation. Reprinted by permission of Princeton University Press: vol. 1, pp. 249–268.

crafts as their way of making a living, while others adopt commerce. They earn more and live more comfortably than Bedouins, because they live on a level beyond the level of (bare) necessity, and their way of making a living corresponds to their wealth.

It has thus become clear that Bedouins and sedentary people are natural groups which exist by necessity, as we have stated.

2 The Arabs[5] are a natural group in the world

We have mentioned in the previous section that the inhabitants of the desert adopt the natural manner of making a living, namely, agriculture and animal husbandry. They restrict themselves to the necessary in food, clothing, and mode of dwelling, and to the other necessary conditions and customs. They do not possess conveniences and luxuries beyond (these bare necessities). They use tents of hair and wool, or houses of wood, or of clay and stone, which are not furnished (elaborately). The purpose is to have shade and shelter, and nothing beyond that. They also take shelter in caverns and caves. The food they take is either little prepared or not prepared at all, save that it may have been touched by fire.[6]

For those who make their living through the cultivation of grain and through agriculture, it is better to be stationary than to travel around. Such, therefore, are the inhabitants of small communities, villages, and mountain regions. These people make up the large mass of the Berbers and non-Arabs.

Those who make their living from animals requiring pasturage, such as sheep and cattle, usually travel around in order to find pasture and water for their animals, since it is better for them to move around in the land. They are called "sheepmen" (*shâwîyah*), that is, men who live on sheep and cattle. They do not go deep into the desert, because they would not find good pastures there. Such people include the Berbers, the Turks and their relatives, the Turkomans and the Slavs,[7] for instance.

Those who make their living by raising camels move around more. They wander deeper into the desert, because the hilly[8] pastures with their plants and shrubs do not furnish enough subsistence for camels. They must feed on the desert shrubs and drink the salty desert water. They must move around the desert regions during the winter, in flight from the harmful cold to the warm desert air. In the desert sands, camels can find places to give birth to their young ones. Of all animals, camels have the hardest delivery and the greatest need for warmth in connection with it.[9] (Camel nomads) are therefore forced to make excursions deep (into the desert). Frequently, too, they are driven from the hills by the militia, and they penetrate farther into the desert, because they do not want the militia[10] to mete out justice to them or to punish them for their hostile acts. As a result, they are the most savage human beings that exist. Compared with sedentary people, they are on a level with wild, untamable (animals) and dumb beasts of prey. Such people are the Arabs. In the West, the nomadic Berbers and the Zanâtah are their counterparts, and in the East, the Kurds, the Turkomans, and the Turks. The Arabs, however, make deeper excursions into the desert and are more rooted in desert life (than the other groups), because they live exclusively on camels, while the other groups live on sheep and cattle, as well as camels.

It has thus become clear that the Arabs are a natural group which by necessity exists in civilization.

God is "the Creator, the Knowing One."[11]

3 Bedouins are prior to sedentary people. The desert is the basis and reservoir of civilization and cities

We[12] have mentioned that the Bedouins restrict themselves to the (bare) necessities in their conditions (of life) and are unable to go beyond them, while sedentary people concern themselves with conveniences and luxuries in their conditions and customs. The (bare) necessities are no doubt prior to the conveniences and luxuries. (Bare) necessities, in a way, are basic, and luxuries secondary and an outgrowth (of the necessities). Bedouins, thus, are the basis of, and prior to, cities and sedentary people. Man seeks first the (bare) necessities. Only after he has obtained the (bare) necessities, does he get to comforts and luxuries. The toughness of desert life precedes the softness of sedentary life. Therefore, urbanization is found to be the goal of the Bedouin. He aspires to (that goal).[13] Through his own efforts, he achieves what he proposes to achieve in this respect. When he has obtained enough to be ready for the conditions and customs of luxury, he enters upon a life of ease and submits himself to the yoke of the city. This is the case with all Bedouin tribes. Sedentary people, on the other hand, have no desire for desert conditions, unless they are motivated by some urgent necessity[14] or they cannot keep up with their fellow city dwellers.

Evidence for the fact that Bedouins are the basis of, and prior to, sedentary people is furnished by investigating the inhabitants of any given city. We shall find that most of its inhabitants originated among Bedouins dwelling in the country and villages of the vicinity. Such Bedouins became wealthy, settled in the city, and adopted a life of ease and luxury, such as exists in the sedentary environment. This proves that sedentary conditions are secondary to desert conditions and that they are the basis of them.[15] This should be understood.

All Bedouins and sedentary people differ also among themselves in their conditions (of life). Many a clan is greater than another, many a tribe greater than another, many a city larger than another, and many a town more populous (*'umrân*) than another.

It has thus become clear that the existence of Bedouins is prior to, and the basis of, the existence of towns and cities. Likewise, the existence of towns and cities results from luxury customs pertaining to luxury and ease, which are posterior to the customs that go with the bare necessities of life.

4 Bedouins are closer to being good than sedentary people

The[16] reason for it is that the soul in its first natural state of creation is ready to accept whatever good or evil may arrive and leave an imprint upon it. Muḥammad said: "Every infant is born in the natural state. It is his parents who make him a Jew or a Christian or a Magian."[17] To the degree the soul is first affected by one of the two qualities, it moves away from the other and finds it difficult to acquire it. When customs proper to goodness have been first to enter the soul of a good person and his (soul) has thus acquired the habit of (goodness, that person) moves away from evil and finds it difficult to do anything evil. The same applies to the evil person when customs (proper to evil) have been first to affect him.

Sedentary people are much concerned with all kinds of pleasures. They are accustomed to luxury and success in worldly occupations and to indulgence in worldly desires. Therefore, their souls are colored with all kinds of blameworthy and evil qualities. The more of them they possess, the more remote do the ways and means of goodness become to them. Eventually they lose all sense of restraint. Many of them are found to use improper language in their gatherings as well as in the presence of their superiors and womenfolk. They are not deterred by any sense of restraint, because the bad custom of behaving openly in an improper manner in both words and deeds has taken hold of them. Bedouins may be as concerned with worldly affairs as (sedentary people are). However, such concern would touch only the necessities of life and not luxuries or anything causing, or calling for, desires and pleasures. The customs they follow in their mutual dealings are, therefore, appropriate. As compared with those of sedentary people, their evil ways and blameworthy qualities are much less numerous. They are closer to the first natural state and more remote from the evil habits that have been impressed upon the souls (of sedentary people) through numerous and ugly, blameworthy customs. Thus, they can more easily be cured than sedentary people. This is obvious. It will later on[18] become clear that sedentary life constitutes the last stage of civilization and the point where it begins to decay. It also constitutes the last stage of evil and of remoteness from goodness. It has thus become clear that Bedouins are closer to being good than sedentary people. "God loves those who fear God."[19]

This is not contradicted by the statement of al-Ḥajjâj to Salamah b. al-Akwaʿ, which is included among the traditions of al-Bukhârî. When al-Ḥajjâj learned that Salamah was going to live in the desert, he asked him, "You have turned back and become an Arab?" Salamah replied, "No, but the Messenger of God permitted me to go (back) to the desert."[20]

It should be known that at the beginning of Islam, the inhabitants of Mecca were enjoined to emigrate, so as to be with the Prophet wherever he might settle, in order to help him and to aid him in his affairs and to guard him. The Arab Bedouins of the desert were not enjoined to emigrate, because the Meccans were possessed of a strong group feeling for the Prophet to aid and guard him, such as did not exist among the desert Arabs. The emigrants, therefore, used to express an aversion to "becoming Arabs," that is, (to becoming) inhabitants of the desert upon whom emigration was not obligatory. According to the tradition of Saʿd b. Abî Waqqâṣ, Muḥammad said, when (Saʿd) was ill in Mecca: "O God, give success to the emigration of my companions and do not cause them to turn back."[21] That means, God should enable them to stay in Medina and not to have to leave it, so that they would not have to discontinue the emigration they had begun, and return. It is the same meaning as is implied in the expression "turning back" in connection with any enterprise.

It is (also) said that the (prohibition against "turning back") was restricted to the time before the conquest of Mecca, when there was a need for emigration because of the small number of Muslims. After the conquest, when the Muslims had become numerous and strong, and God had guaranteed His Prophet inviolability (*ʿiṣmah*), emigration was no longer necessary. Muḥammad said: "There is no emigration after the conquest."[22] This has been interpreted as meaning that the injunction to emigrate was no longer valid for those who became Muslims after the conquest. It has also been interpreted (to mean) that emigration was no longer obligatory upon those who had become Muslims and had emigrated before the conquest. (At any rate,) all agree that emigration was no longer necessary after the Prophet's death, because the men around Muḥammad had by then dispersed and spread in all directions. The only thing that remained was the merit of living in Medina, which constituted emigration.

Thus, al-Ḥajjâj's statement to Salamah, who went to live in the desert: "You have turned back and become an Arab?" is a reproach to Salamah for giving up his residence in Medina. It contains an allusion to the words of the afore-mentioned prayer of the Prophet: "Do not cause them to turn back." The words, "You have become an Arab?" are a reproach, as they imply that Salamah had become one of the Arabs who did not emigrate. In his reply, Salamah denied both insinuations. He said that the Prophet had permitted him to go to the desert. This was a special (permission) in Salamah's case, exactly as, for instance, the testimony of Khuzaymah[23] and Abû Burdah's[24] lamb were special to the cases of Khuzaymah and Abû Burdah. Or, (it may be) al-Ḥajjâj reproached Salamah only because he was giving up his residence in Medina, as he was aware that emigration was no longer necessary after the Prophet's death. Salamah's reply was that it was more proper and better to avail himself of the Prophet's permission, who had distinguished him by this special permission only because (the Prophet) had some motive known to him(self) when he gave it.

In any event, the story does not imply that censure of desert (life) is meant by the expression "to become an Arab." It is known that the legal obligation to emigrate served the purposes of aiding and guarding the Prophet. It did not have the purpose of censuring desert (life). Use of the expression "to become an Arab," to condemn non-fulfillment of the duty (of emigration), is no indication that "becoming an Arab" is something blameworthy. And God knows better.

5 Bedouins are more disposed to courage than sedentary people

The[25] reason for this is that sedentary people have become used to laziness and ease. They are sunk in well-being and luxury. They have entrusted defense of their property and their lives to the governor and ruler who rules them, and to the militia which has the task of guarding them. They find full assurance of safety in the walls that surround them, and the fortifications that protect them. No noise disturbs them, and no hunting occupies them. They are carefree and trusting, and have ceased to carry weapons. Successive generations have grown up in this way of life. They have become like women and children, who depend upon the master of the house. Eventually, this has come to be a quality of character that replaces natural (disposition).

The Bedouins, on the other hand, live separate from the community. They are alone in the country and remote from militias. They have no walls and gates. Therefore, they provide their own defense and do not entrust it to, or rely upon others for it. They always carry weapons. They watch carefully all sides of the road. They take hurried naps only when they are together in company or when they are in the saddle. They pay attention to every faint barking and noise. They go alone into the desert, guided by their fortitude, putting their trust in themselves. Fortitude has become a character quality of theirs, and courage their nature. They use it whenever they are called upon or an alarm stirs them. When sedentary people mix with them in the desert or associate with them on a journey, they depend on them. They cannot do anything for themselves without them. This is an observed fact. (Their dependence extends) even to knowledge of the country, the (right) directions, watering places, and crossroads. The reason for this is the thing we have explained. At the base of it is the fact that man is a child of the customs and the things he has become used to. He is not the product of his natural disposition and temperament.[26] The conditions to which he has become accustomed, until they have become for him a quality of character and matters of habit and custom, have replaced his natural disposition. If one studies this in human beings, one will find much of it, and it will be found to be a correct (observation).

"God creates whatever He wishes."[27]

6 The reliance of sedentary people upon laws destroys their fortitude and power of resistance

Not everyone is master of his own affairs. Chiefs and leaders who are masters of the affairs of men are few in comparison with the rest. As a rule, man must by necessity be dominated by someone else. If the domination is kind and just and the people under it are not oppressed by its laws and restrictions, they are guided by the courage or cowardice that they possess in themselves. They are satisfied with the absence of any restraining power. Self-reliance eventually becomes a quality natural to them. They would not know anything else. If, however, the domination with its laws is one of brute force and intimidation, it breaks their fortitude and deprives them of their power of resistance as a result of the inertness that develops in the souls of the oppressed, as we shall explain.

'Umar forbade Sa'd (b. Abî Waqqâṣ) to exercise such (arbitrary power) when Zuhrah b. Ḥawîyah took the spoils of al-Jâlinûs. The value of the spoils was 75,000 gold pieces. (Zuhrah) had followed al-Jâlinûs on the day of al-Qâdisîyah, killed him, and taken his spoils. Sa'd took them away from him and said, "Why did you not wait for my permission to follow him?" He wrote to 'Umar and asked 'Umar for permission (to confiscate the spoils). But 'Umar replied, "Would you want to proceed against a man like Zuhrah, who already has borne so much of the brunt (of battle),[28] and while there still remains so much of the war for you (to finish)? Would you want to break his strength and morale?" Thus, 'Umar confirmed (Zuhrah) in possession of the spoils.[29]

When laws are (enforced) by means of punishment, they completely destroy fortitude, because the use of punishment against someone who cannot defend himself generates in that person a feeling of humiliation that, no doubt, must break his fortitude.

When laws are (intended to serve the purposes of) education and instruction and are applied from childhood on, they have to some degree the same effect, because people then grow up in fear and docility and consequently do not rely on their own fortitude.

For this (reason), greater fortitude is found among the savage Arab Bedouins than among people who are subject to laws. Furthermore, those who rely on laws and are dominated by them from the very beginning of their education and instruction in the crafts, sciences, and religious matters, are thereby deprived of much of their own fortitude. They can scarcely defend themselves at all against hostile acts. This is the case with students, whose occupation it is to study and to learn from teachers and religious leaders, and who constantly apply themselves to instruction and education in very dignified gatherings. This situation and the fact that it destroys the power of resistance and fortitude must be understood.

It is no argument against the (statement just made) that the men around Muḥammad observed the religious laws, and yet did not experience any diminution of their fortitude, but possessed the greatest possible fortitude. When the Muslims got their religion from the Lawgiver (Muḥammad), the restraining influence came from themselves, as a result of the encouragement and discouragement he gave them in the Qur'ân.[30] It was not a result of technical instruction or scientific education. (The laws) were the laws and precepts of the religion, which they received orally and which their firmly rooted (belief in) the truth of the articles of faith caused them to observe. Their fortitude remained unabated, and it was not corroded by education or authority. 'Umar said, "Those who are not educated (disciplined) by the religious law are not educated (disciplined) by God."[31] (This statement expresses) 'Umar's desire that everyone should have his restraining influence in himself. It also expresses his certainty that the Lawgiver (Muḥammad) knew best what is good for mankind.

(The influence of) religion, then, decreased among men, and they came to use restraining laws. The religious law became a branch of learning and a craft to be acquired through instruction and education. People turned to sedentary life and assumed the character trait of submissiveness to law. This led to a decrease in their fortitude.

It has thus become clear that governmental and educational laws destroy fortitude, because their restraining influence is something that comes from outside. The religious laws, on the other hand, do not destroy fortitude, because their restraining influence is something inherent. Therefore, governmental and educational laws influence sedentary people, in that they weaken their souls and diminish their stamina, because they have to suffer (their authority) both as children and as adults. The Bedouins, on the other hand, are not in the same position, because they live far away from the laws of government, instruction, and education. Therefore, Abû Muḥammad b. Abî Zayd,[32] in his book on the laws governing teachers and students (*Aḥkâm al-mu'allimîn wa-lmuta'a-l-limîn*), said: "The educator must not strike a boy more than three times (in one punishment) as an educational measure."[33] (Ibn Abî Zayd) reported this remark on the authority of Judge Sharayḥ.[34] Certain scholar(s) argued in favor of the procedure mentioned, by referring to the threefold choking mentioned in the tradition concerned with the beginning of revelation.[35] This, however, is a weak argument. (The tradition about the) choking is not suitable proof, because it has nothing to do with ordinary instruction. God "is wise and knowing."[36]

7 Only tribes held together by group feeling can live in the desert

It should be known that God put good and evil into the nature of man. Thus, He said in the Qur'ân: "We led him along the two paths."[37] He further said: "And inspired (the soul) with its wickedness as well as its fear of God."[38]

Evil is the quality that is closest to man when he fails to improve his customs and (when) religion is not used as the model to improve him. The great mass of mankind is in that condition, with the exception of those to whom God gives success. Evil[39] qualities in man are injustice and mutual aggression. He who casts his eye upon the property of his brother will lay his hand upon it to take it, unless there is a restraining influence to hold him back. The poet thus said:

> Injustice is a human characteristic. If you find
> A moral man,[40] there is some reason why he is not unjust.

Mutual aggression of people in towns and cities is averted by the authorities and the government, which hold back the masses under their control from attacks and aggression upon each other. They are thus prevented by the influence of force and governmental authority from mutual injustice, save such injustice as comes from the ruler himself.

Aggression against a city from outside may be averted by walls, in the event of negligence,[41] a surprise attack at night, or inability (of the inhabitants) to withstand the enemy during the day. (Or,) it may be averted with the help of a militia of government auxiliary troops, if (the inhabitants are otherwise) prepared and ready to offer resistance.

The[42] restraining influence among Bedouin tribes comes from their *shaykhs* and leaders. It results from the great respect and veneration they generally enjoy among the people. The hamlets of the Bedouins are defended against outside enemies by a tribal militia composed of noble youths of the tribe who are known for their courage. Their defense and protection are successful only if they are a closely-knit group[43] of common descent. This strengthens their stamina and makes them feared, since everybody's affection for his family and his group is more important (than anything else). Compassion and affection for one's blood relations and relatives exist in human nature as something God put into the hearts of men. It makes for mutual support and aid, and increases the fear felt by the enemy.

This may be exemplified by the story in the Qur'ân about Joseph's brothers. They said to their father: "If the wolf eats him, while we are a group, then, indeed, we have lost out."[44] This means that one cannot imagine any hostile act being undertaken against anyone who has his group feeling to support him.

Those who have no one of their own lineage (to care for) rarely feel affection for their fellows. If danger is in the air on the day of battle, such a one slinks away and seeks to save himself, because he is afraid of being left without support[45] and dreads (that prospect). Such people, therefore, cannot live in the desert, because they would fall prey to any nation that might want to swallow them up.

If this is true with regard to the place where one lives, which is in constant need of defense and military protection, it is equally true with regard to every other human activity, such as prophecy, the establishment of royal authority, or propaganda (for a cause). Nothing can be achieved in these matters without fighting for it, since man has the natural urge to offer resistance. And for fighting one cannot do without group feeling, as we mentioned at the beginning. This should be taken as the guiding principle of our later exposition.

God gives success.

8 Group feeling results only from (blood) relationship or something corresponding to it

(Respect for) blood[46] ties is something natural among men, with the rarest exceptions. It leads to affection for one's relations and blood relatives, (the feeling that) no harm ought to befall them nor any destruction come upon them. One feels shame when one's relatives are treated unjustly or attacked, and one wishes to intervene between them and whatever peril or destruction threatens them. This is a natural urge in man, for as long as there have been human beings. If the direct relationship between persons who help each other is very close, so that it leads to close contact and unity, the ties are obvious and clearly require the (existence of a feeling of solidarity) without any outside (prodding). If, however, the relationship is somewhat distant, it is often forgotten in part. However, some knowledge of it remains and this causes a person to help his relatives for the known motive, in order to escape the shame he would feel in his soul were a person to whom he is somehow related treated unjustly.[47]

Clients and allies belong in the same category. The affection everybody has for his clients and allies results from the feeling of shame that comes to a person when one of his neighbors, relatives, or a blood relation in any degree (of kinship) is humiliated. The reason for it is that a client (-master) relationship leads to close contact exactly, or approximately in the same way, as does common descent. It is in that sense that one must understand Muḥammad's remark, "Learn as much of your pedigrees as is necessary to establish your ties of blood relationship."[48] It means that pedigrees are useful only in so far as they imply the close contact that is a consequence of blood ties and that eventually leads to mutual help and affection. Anything beyond that is superfluous.[49] For a pedigree is something imaginary and devoid of reality.[50] Its usefulness consists only in the resulting connection and close contact. If the fact of (common descent) is obvious and clear, it evokes in man a natural affection, as we have said. If, however, its existence is known only from remote history, it moves the imagination but faintly. Its usefulness is gone, and preoccupation with it becomes gratuitous, a kind of game, and as such is not permissible. In this sense, one must understand the remark, "Genealogy is something that is of no use to know and that it does no harm not to know."[51] This means that when common descent is no longer clear and has become a matter of scientific knowledge, it can no longer move the imagination and is denied the affection caused by group feeling. It has become useless.

And God knows better.

9 Purity of lineage is found only among the savage Arabs of the desert and other such people

This[52] is on account of the poor life, hard conditions, and bad habitats that are peculiar to the Arabs. They are the result of necessity that destined (these conditions) for (the Arabs), in as much as their subsistence depends on camels and camel breeding and pasturage. The camels are the cause of (the Arabs') savage life in the desert, since they feed on the shrubs of the desert and give birth (to their young ones) in the desert sands, as has been mentioned before.[53] The desert is a place of hardship and starvation, but to them it has become familiar and accustomed. Generations of (Arabs) grew up in the desert. Eventually, they become confirmed in their character and natural qualities. No member of any other nation was disposed to share their conditions. No member of any other race felt attracted to them. But if one of them were to find ways and means of fleeing from these conditions, he would not (do so or) give them up.[54] Therefore, their pedigrees can be trusted not to have been mixed up and corrupted. They have been preserved pure in unbroken lines. This is the case, for instance, with Muḍar tribes such as the Quraysh, the Kinânah, the Thaqîf, the Banû Asad, the Hudhayl, and their Khuzâ'ah neighbors. They lived a hard life in places where there was no agriculture or animal husbandry. They lived far from the fertile fields of Syria and the 'Irâq, far from the sources of seasonings and grains. How pure have they kept their lineages! These are unmixed in every way, and are known to be unsullied.

Other Arabs lived in the hills and at the sources of fertile pastures and plentiful living. Among these Arabs were the Ḥimyar and the Kahlân, such as the Lakhm, the Judhâm, the Ghassân, the Ṭayy, the Quḍâ'ah, and the Iyâd. Their lineages were mixed up, and their groups intermingled. It is known that people (genealogists) differ with respect to each one of these families. This came about as the result of intermixture with non-Arabs. They did not pay any attention to preserving the (purity of) lineage of their families and groups. This[55] was done only by (true) Arabs. 'Umar said: "Study genealogy, and be not like the Nabataeans of the Mesopotamian lowlands. When one of them is asked about his origin he says: 'From such and such a village.'"[56] Furthermore, the Arabs of the fertile fields were affected by the general human trend toward competition for the fat soil and the good pastures. This resulted in intermingling and much mixture of lineages. Even at the beginning of Islam, people occasionally referred to themselves by their places of residence. They referred to the Districts of Qinnasrîn, of Damascus, or of the 'Awâṣim (the border region of northern Syria). This custom was then transferred to Spain. It happened not because the Arabs rejected genealogical considerations, but because they acquired particular places of residence after the conquest. They eventually became known by their places of residence. These became a distinguishing mark, in addition to the pedigree, used by (the Arabs) to identify themselves in the presence of their amirs. Later on, sedentary (Arabs) mixed with Persians and other non-Arabs. Purity of lineage was completely lost, and its fruit, the group feeling, was lost and rejected. The tribes, then, disappeared and were wiped out, and with them, the group feeling was wiped out. But the (earlier situation) remained unchanged among the Bedouins.

God inherits the earth and whomever is upon it.

10 How lineages become confused

It is clear that a person of a certain descent may become attached to people of another descent, either because he feels well-disposed toward them, or because there exists an (old) alliance or client(-master) relationship, or yet because he had to flee from his own people by reason of some crime he committed. Such a person comes to be known as having the same descent as those (to whom he has attached himself) and is counted one of them with respect to the things that result from (common descent), such as affection, the rights and obligations concerning talion and blood money, and so on. When the things which result from (common) descent are there, it is as if (common descent) itself were there, because the only meaning of belonging to one or another group is that one is subject to its laws and conditions, as if one had come into close contact with it. In the course of time, the original descent is almost forgotten. Those who knew about it have passed away, and it is no longer known to most people. Family lines in this manner continually changed from one tribal group to another, and some people developed close contact with others (of a different descent). This happened both in pre-Islamic and in Islamic times, and between both Arabs and non-Arabs. If one studies the different opinions concerning the pedigree of the family of al-Mundhir[57] and others, the matter will become somewhat clearer.

The affair of the Bajîlah and 'Arfajah b. Harthamah is an(other) illustration. When 'Umar appointed 'Arfajah their governor, (the Bajîlah) asked ('Umar) to withdraw him, saying that he was a *nazîf*[58] among them, that is, one who had come to them from outside and attached himself to them. They asked that he appoint Jarîr (instead). 'Umar asked 'Arfajah about this, and he replied: "They are right, O Commander of the Faithful. I am from the Azd. I shed blood among my people, and joined (the Bajîlah)."[59] This shows how 'Arfajah had come to mix with the Bajîlah, had become of their skin, and was known as one having the same descent as they, to the extent that he could eventually become a candidate for leadership over them, (and would have) had someone not remembered the genealogical ramifications. Had they overlooked it and had (still) more time elapsed, (his foreign origin) would have been forgotten, and he would have been considered one of them in every respect.

This should be understood and pondered as one of God's ways with His creatures. Similar things occur frequently in our own times, and have always been frequent in former times.

Notes (Page references within *Notes* throughout refer to respective volumes from which readings were extracted.)

[1] Cf. Issawi, pp. 80 f.

[2] Cf. pp. lxxxi and 85.

[3] Cf. G. E. von Grunebaum, "as-Sakkâkî on Milieu and Thought," *Journal of the American Oriental Society*, LXV (1945), 62.

[4] Cf. also p. 339.

[5] As a sociological term, "Arab" is always synonymous with "Bedouin, nomad" to Ibn Khaldûn, regardless of racial, national, or linguistic distinctions.

[6] Ibn Khaldûn was familiar with this phrase for "preparing food in the open

fire" through the *ḥadîth* literature. Cf. F. Rosenthal, *A History of Muslim Historiography,* p. 206.

[7] Though the Arabic text need not be understood as saying that there exists a relationship between the Slavs and the Turks, it is the most natural construction to understand it that way. It has been shown that Muslim geographers did not always mean precisely Slavs when they spoke about the *Ṣaqâlibah.* (Cf. A. Zeki Validi Togan, *Ibn Faḍlân's Reisebericht,* pp. 295 ff.) However, the above statement should not be taken too literally, and the term used for "relatives" (*ikhwân* "brethren") may perhaps be translated as "companions" or the like, implying no real relationship.

[8] *Tall,* pl. *tulûl* "hills." The expression reflects the situation in northwestern Africa rather than in Arabia.

[9] Cf. p. 265 and 2:353 and *'Ibar,* II, 336 f.

[10] Bulaq, apparently by mistake, has "to humiliate them" for the rest of the sentence.

[11] Qur'ân 15.86 (86); 36.81 (81).

[12] Cf. Issawi, pp. 81 f.

[13] But contrast p. 266.

[14] Ibn Khaldûn is probably thinking of political exile and retirement in the country such as he experienced himself when writing the *Muqaddimah.*

[15] The pronouns are as ambiguous in Arabic as they are in English, and, were it not for the context, would be understood to mean the opposite of what they are intended to mean.

[16] Cf. Issawi, pp. 66 f.

[17] Cf., for instance, al-Bukhârî, *Ṣaḥîḥ,* I, 341; *Concordance,* I, 7*b,* ll. 5 f. Cf. also p. 306.

[18] Cf. 2:291 ff.

[19] Qur'ân 3.76 (70); 9.4 (4), 7 (7).

[20] Cf. al-Bukhârî, *Ṣaḥîḥ,* IV, 373; *Concordance,* II, 247*a,* ll. 32 f.; Ibn Ḥajar, *Tahdhîb,* IV, 150 ff.

[21] Cf. al-Bukhârî, *Ṣaḥîḥ,* I, 326; *Concordance,* I, 245*b,* ll. 25 ff.

[22] Cf. the references in *Handbook,* p. 98*b.*

[23] Khuzaymah b. Thâbit's testimony was counted by the Prophet as that of two men. Cf. *Concordance,* III, 198*b,* l. 4; al-Bukhârî, *Ta'rîkh,* II[1], 188; Ibn Sa'd, *Ṭabaqât,* ed. E. Sachau *et al.* (Leiden, 1905–40), IV[2], 90 ff.; Ibn Ḥajar, *Tahdhîb,* III, 140.

[24] The sacrificial animal should be slaughtered after prayer, but in the case of Abû Burdah Hâni' b. Niyâr, the animal he had slaughtered previously was accounted a valid sacrifice by the Prophet. This, however, is stated not to be a precedent. Cf. al-Bukhârî, *Ṣaḥîḥ,* IV, 21; *Concordance,* I, 329*b,* ll. 32 ff.

[25] Cf. Issawi, pp. 67 f.

[26] Cf. n. 21 to Ch. v.

[27] Qur'ân 3.47 (42); 5.17 (20); 24.45 (44); 28.68 (68); 30.54 (53); 39.4 (6); 42.49 (48).

[28] Or, more generally, "who has shown himself so courageous."

[29] Cf. aṭ-Ṭabarî, *Annales,* I, 2346.

[30] *Talâ* "he recited." Cf. the term *matlûw,* p. 192 (n. 261), above, and p. 437 and 3:113, 284.

[31] Cf. 3:306.

[32] Cf. p. 223.

[33] Cf. also 3:206. In the city of Ibn Khaldûn's ancestors, it was prescribed *ca.* 1100 that "an older child should not be struck more than five times, nor a small one more than three, and the severity of the blows should be according to the strength of the individual children to stand them." Cf. E. Lévi-Provençal, "Le Traité d'Ibn

'Abdûn," *Journal asiatique*, CCXXIV (1934), 214; tr. by the same, *Séville musulmane au début du XIIe siècle* (Islam d'hier et d'aujourd'hui, No. 2) (Paris, 1947), pp. 53 f.

[34] Shurayḥ lived in the seventh century and is said to have been appointed judge of al-Kûfah by 'Umar. Cf. J. Schacht, *The Origins of Muhammadan Jurisprudence* (Oxford, 1950), pp. 228 f.

[35] Cf. pp. 201 f. The story of the threefold choking is here understood as an educational measure, serving the purpose of teaching Muḥammad how to read the writing revealed to him by Gabriel.

[36] Qur'ân 6.18 (18), 73 (73); 34.1 (1).

[37] Qur'ân 90.10 (10).

[38] Qur'ân 91.8 (8).

[39] Cf. Issawi, pp. 105 f.

[40] *'Iffah* is the term picked by translators of Greek texts into Arabic for *σωφροσύνη*.

The verse is by al-Mutanabbi'; cf. the appendix to the edition of his *Dîwân* (Beirut, 1882), II, 630, and ar-Râghib al-Iṣfahânî, *Muḥâḍarât*, I, 140.

[41] That is, a general state of unpreparedness.

[42] The remainder of this section was translated by R. A. Nicholson, *Translations of Eastern Poetry and Prose*, pp. 181 f.

[43] Here the text has *'aṣabîyah* "group feeling," though *'uṣbah* "group" would seem better.

[44] Qur'ân 12.14 (14).

[45] Cf. R. Dozy in *Journal asiatique*, XIV[6] (1869), 152 f.

[46] Cf. Issawi, pp. 103 f.

[47] Cf. Bombaci, pp. 446 f.

[48] Cf. *Concordance*, II, 238*b*; Ibn Abî Zayd, *Risâlah*, ed. L. Bercher (3d ed.), p. 326, where 'Umar is credited with the saying; F. Rosenthal, *A History of Muslim Historiography*, p. 27 (n. 3). The phrase *waṣala ar-raḥim* (*al-arḥâm*) has been understood to mean "to be kind and give presents to one's blood relatives." In the context where it occurs below, 2:145 (n. 761), one might think of such a translation, though it does not seem to be correct there. Here it would be impossible.

[49] The correct vocalization *mustaghnân* is indicated in C and D.

[50] Cf. p. 374.

[51] Cf. F. Rosenthal, *op. cit.*, p. 242.

[52] Cf. Issawi, pp. 104 f.

[53] Cf. p. 251.

[54] But see p. 252.

[55] Cf. Issawi, pp. 106 f.

[56] Cf. Ibn 'Abdrabbih, *'Iqd*, II, 37; Ibn 'Abd-al-Barr, *al-Inbâh 'alâ qabâ'il ar-ruwâh* (Cairo, 1350/1931–32), p. 43.

[57] The Lakhmids of al-Ḥîrah on the Euphrates.

[58] Bulaq has the freehand correction *lazîq*. *Nazîf* has no meaning that would be suitable here, according to the Arabic dictionaries. R. Dozy, *op. cit.* (n. 44, above), and also in *Supplément aux dictionnaires arabes*, II, 658*a*, called attention to the fact that aṭ-Ṭabarî has *nazî'* in reporting this story. Cf. aṭ-Ṭabarî, *Annales*, I, 2186, l. 14, and glossary, p. DIX. It seems that Ibn Khaldûn misread the word in aṭ-Ṭabarî or an intermediary source. The accusative *nazî'an* that appears in aṭ-Ṭabarî could easily be misread *nazîfan*.

[59] The story was referred to on p. 55. Cf. also 2:39.

5. The Renaissance Foundations of Anthropology

John Howland Rowe

The comparative point of view of anthropology rests on a recognition that there are physical and cultural differences among human populations which must be taken into account in any attempt to generalize about mankind. It is anthropology's recognition of the scientific importance of such differences which chiefly distinguishes it from other disciplines concerned with man and human behavior. The history of this idea is therefore a particularly important part of the history of anthropology.[1]

It is the thesis of this paper that the anthropological tradition of interest in differences among men had its beginnings in the Italian Renaissance of the 14th and 15th centuries and specifically in Renaissance archaeology. The first differences which were recognized as significant to a general understanding of mankind were the cultural and linguistic differences between Classical antiquity and what was then the present. It was only after the beginnings of an archaeological perspective had been established that the interest in differences was extended to contemporary contrasts.

Renaissance studies of Classical antiquity not only stimulated a general interest in differences among men, they also provided models for describing such differences. When the problem of describing contemporary non-Western cultures arose, there were Renaissance studies of Roman customs and institutions to serve as precedents. Similarly, Renaissance grammars and dictionaries of Classical Latin and Greek became models for the description of spoken languages in all parts of the world, and the study of the ancient monuments of Italy and Greece became the basis for archaeological reporting elsewhere. The beginnings of physical anthropology were delayed, because the study of Classical antiquity in this case offered little precedent.

In order to demonstrate the Renaissance origin of the comparative point of view of anthropology, it is necessary to show first that there was

From the *American Anthropologist*, vol. 67, no. 1 (1965): pp. 1–20. Reprinted by permission of the American Anthropological Association.

no continuous anthropological tradition of comparative studies stretching back through the Middle Ages to Classical antiquity, and second that the interest in differences of custom and language and in local antiquities, characteristic of some writers of the period of the voyages of discovery, was related to a fundamental change in men's attitude toward Classical antiquity which was the essence of the Italian Renaissance.

I

It is a fact that there was no continuous anthropological tradition of comparative studies in Classical antiquity and the Middle Ages. There were, however, a number of individual writers in both periods who displayed some interest in cultural differences. The number of such writers was not large, and their anthropological interests made little impression on their contemporaries; if they were respected it was for other qualities. Such ancient writings of an anthropological nature as still survived were discovered with great enthusiasm by Renaissance scholars and only then began to influence effectively the development of anthropology.

The essence of the anthropological point of view is that in order to understand ourselves we need to study others. In contrast, the ancient Greeks for the most part held that the way to understand ourselves is to study ourselves, while what others do is irrelevant. This was the view taken by such influential thinkers as Thucydides and Socrates, for example. It was congenial to Greek ethnocentrism and contributed to the lack of any sustained interest in the customs and languages of "the barbarians," i.e., all non-Greeks. The Romans acknowledged the natural superiority which the Greeks liked to claim and therefore endeavored to identify themselves with the Greeks as far as possible. Instead of studying the differences between the Greeks and themselves, a procedure which would have implied an acceptance of their barbarian status, the Romans traced their ancestry to the heroes of Greek legend, identified their gods with Greek ones, imitated Greek manners, and used the grammatical categories of Greek to describe the Latin language.

In this context of general indifference the few writers of Classical antiquity who took an interest in anthropological comparison are conspicuous exceptions. The earliest and most important of such writers was Herodotus, whose *History* was written about the middle of the 5th century B.C. Herodotus displays as much interest in the customs of the Egyptians, Scythians, and other "barbarian" peoples as he does in Greek and Persian political history, and it has been said on this account that he is "the father of anthropology" as well as "the father of history."[2] The epithet is misleading, as will be seen from the discussion which follows.

How did Herodotus happen to develop an interest so foreign to the main current of Greek thought? A good case can be made that he learned it from Persian sources. There is no question that Herodotus had access to such sources. He was born a Persian subject in Halicarnassus, a cosmopolitan Greek city on the coast of Asia Minor. In his youth he travelled extensively in the western provinces of the Persian Empire, collecting information which he later used in his *History* (1921–38). Some of the Persian historical traditions which he incorporated in the *History* were evidently derived from sources in the Persian nobility.[3]

The Persians had no less national pride than the Greeks did, but they managed to combine it with a respect for the customs and languages of others which was unique in the ancient world.[4] Herodotus illustrates the Persian attitude by telling how the Persian king, Darius the Great, rebuked the Greeks who were present at his court for their intolerance toward "barbarian" customs. Herodotus says:

> If it were proposed to all nations to choose which of all customs seemed best, each, after examination, would place its own first, so strongly is each persuaded that its own are by far the best. . . . That all men have this feeling about their customs may be concluded from many proofs, among them this. When Darius was king he summoned the Greeks who were with him and asked them for how much money they would be willing to eat the dead bodies of their fathers. They answered that there was no price for which they would do it. Then he summoned those Indians who are called Callatians, who eat their parents, and asked them, with the Greeks present and understanding what was said through an interpreter, what price they would accept to burn their dead at death [i.e., follow the Greek custom]. The Indians cried aloud and begged him to avoid such sacrilegious speech. Such is the nature of custom, and I think it is rightly said in Pindar's poem that custom is lord of all (Bk 3 ch. 38; 1921–38, 2:50).

Darius had evidently taken the trouble to inform himself about some of the differences in custom among his subjects.

It was this same Darius who had his deeds recorded on the cliff at Bisitun in Old Persian, Babylonian, and Elamite, the three languages most likely to be understood by educated travellers in this area. The Bisitun inscriptions are famous today because they provided the basis for the decipherment of the cuneiform script, but the cultural significance of the repetition of the king's message in three languages is rarely noted. Earlier ancient rulers simply expected any subject who was interested in reading royal inscriptions to learn the official language.

The Jews, who benefited greatly from the Persian policy of toleration, preserved its memory long after the Persian Empire had fallen. The Book of Esther in the Old Testament, written in the second half of the 2nd century B.C., is a historical romance laid at the court of the Persian king Xerxes, the son of Darius, who ruled from 485 to 465 B.C. Part of the local color which is provided to authenticate the story is a statement that royal dispatches were issued "to every province in its own script and to every people in its own language." This phraseology is repeated each time the issue of a royal order is mentioned.[5]

The Persian royal tradition appeared again in the 1st century B.C. exemplified by Mithridates the Great, king of Pontus, who claimed descent from one of the companions of Darius. Mithridates is said to have spoken fluently the languages of the 25 peoples who were under his rule: "quinque et viginti gentium quas sub dicione habuit linguas percalluit."[6]

If the ancient Persian interest in differences of culture and language led to the formation of a body of written literature of a more or less anthropological character, however, the *History* of Herodotus is its principal and perhaps only surviving document. Almost the whole of Old Persian literature perished after the conquest of the Persian Empire by Alexander the Great in the 4th century B.C.

No tradition of comparative cultural study developed in antiquity out of Herodotus' work. On the contrary, Herodotus was attacked time and again as a liar, and it was his statements about the unfamiliar customs of the "barbarians" which his Greek and Roman readers found particularly difficult to believe. As Arnaldo Momigliano has pointed out, Herodotus had many admirers in antiquity who praised his work as a model of literary style and an inspiring account of the heroic deeds of the Persian war, but none of them ever went so far as to defend him from the charge of being a liar. Herodotus' credit for veracity was not restored until 1566, when Henri Estienne argued that the information on differences in custom available in his day demonstrated the credibility of Herodotus' data on cultural variation (Momigliano 1960; Estienne 1566:xxix–xxxii; see also Legrand 1932; Spiegelberg 1927; Burn 1962: 1–17).

The only lasting effect which Herodotus' ethnographic information had on Greek and Roman thought was that it inspired a tenuous thread of interest among philosophers in the fact that customs are different in different areas. As early as the end of the 5th century B.C. some of the teachers of rhetoric and ethics were asking whether there was in fact any absolute standard by which to distinguish between what is honorable and what is shameful, since the same act may be honorable in one place and shameful in another (Diels 1959:405–416; Taylor 1911:102–105; Untersteiner 1954:304–310). This debating problem became part of the standard repertory of Greek philosophers, and every teacher needed a few handy examples of contrasts in custom to which he could refer. As a very minor part of his comprehensive effort to organize knowledge and provide materials for teaching, Aristotle made a collection of examples of odd customs, only a few fragments of which have come down to us (Heitz 1869:297–299; Moraux 1951:130–131). A similar collection was made in the 1st century B.C. by Nicholas of Damascus, a later member of

Aristotle's school (Jacoby 1926–30, A:384–390, C:255–261; Reimann 1895; Wacholder 1962:70–88). The examples in these collections were compiled from the works of earlier writers on history and geography, including Herodotus. The philosophers did not make fresh ethnographic observations of their own.

The closest approach to an anthropological study in Greek after Herodotus appears to have been the description of India and its peoples by Megasthenes, written in the 3rd century B.C. (Müller 1874–83, 2:397–429; McCrindle 1877; Stein 1931). Megasthenes was ambassador of the Greek ruler of western Asia, Seleucus Nicator, at the court of Chandragupta, where he had excellent opportunities to see Indian life at first hand and to question informants. He was active only about 20 years after the Persian monarchy had been overthrown, and he represented the state which had inherited the lion's share of the former Persian territory. It is not unlikely that the Persian tradition of tolerant awareness of cultural differences influenced him, as it had influenced Herodotus. Only fragments of Megasthenes' work have been preserved, but it evidently contained substantial sections on Indian customs and beliefs as well as descriptions of the country and of Indian plants and animals. Like Herodotus, Megasthenes was branded as a liar by later Classical writers. The charge was inaccurate; Megasthenes' weakness was not mendacity but an innocent inability to distinguish the circumstantial narratives of Indian mythology from factual reports of areas he had not visited personally.

In Latin literature the only work of Classical antiquity which resembles an ethnographic report is a treatise entitled *On the origin, location, customs and peoples of the Germans,* written by Cornelius Tacitus in A.D. 98 (Tacitus 1938; Norden 1922; Walser 1951; Syme 1958:46–48; 126–128). This work is better known by the short title *Germania,* but the longer one gives a clearer idea of its contents. The whole treatise is not much longer than a modern journal article, and it conveys rather less ethnographic information than does Herodotus' description of the Scythians. Nevertheless, the fact that a Roman should write any separate work on a foreign people is notable in itself.

Tacitus was a Roman lawyer and civil servant, and it is not at all certain that he was ever in Germany. At the time he wrote his essay on the Germans, the Roman emperor Trajan was on the left bank of the Rhine, and the timing suggests that Tacitus was motivated by a desire to persuade the emperor to undertake an invasion of Germany. The *Germania* certainly reads like an article of the sort written by the political commentators of today to explain the background of current events and perhaps influence public policy at the same time. The author took advantage of the opportunity to read his fellow citizens a moral lesson by praising the Germans for maintaining certain values which Tacitus identified as part of the older Roman tradition and which he felt that his contemporaries were neglecting. In discussing those German customs which conflicted with Roman values, however, Tacitus' attitude was one of marked disapproval.

The *Germania* failed to influence Trajan's foreign policy, and it inspired no interest among the Romans in making more detailed studies of the Germans or of other foreign peoples. In fact, it had little effect on anyone's thinking until after its rediscovery in the Renaissance, when a new tradition of interest in cultural differences had developed on a different basis. In this new context the Germania was read with enthusiasm and attention for the ethnographic information it contained. It was hailed as a "golden book," and it had a considerable influence on pioneer ethnographic writings.

There is a certain amount of information on human differences scattered through the rest of ancient literature, particularly in works on geography, such as that of Strabo, and in more encyclopaedic works, of which the *Natural History* of the elder Pliny is the chief example that has come down to us (Strabo 1917–32; Plinius Secundus 1938–63). The information provided by the geographers consists of brief references to foreign customs which the author considered sufficiently peculiar to amuse his readers. It is present only as incidental detail, the main emphasis being on physical geography, the location of cities, and varieties of animals and plants. The complete lack of an anthropological perspective is particularly striking in Pliny's *Natural History,* a work which includes four books on geography (Books III–VI) and one on man (Book VII). There is a section at the beginning of the book on man in which Pliny provides a catalogue of the fabulous anatomical freaks with which the imagination of the ancients peopled the more remote parts of the earth; thereafter, he discusses human variation only in terms of Greek and Roman examples.

Such information on foreign customs as we find in ancient literature is greatly reduced in value by the tendency of ancient writers to copy well-turned phrases from one another and show greater concern with form than with content. In discussing barbarians, men felt free to transfer an interesting statement of a peculiar custom from one people to another. Thus, statements made by Greek writers about Scythian customs were applied by Tacitus to the Germans. Evidently differences among barbarians were not considered important enough to require accurate reporting by historians and encyclopaedists. The result was the development of a series of ethnographic commonplaces such as that barbarians use neither images nor temples in their worship; that they live by war and pillage; that they do not appreciate the value of precious metals; and so forth.[7]

During the Middle Ages some Arabic writers showed more interest in cultural differences than was common in Classical antiquity, but their work failed to influence the European tradition of the time. A certain number of Arabic works were translated into Latin and circulated in Mediaeval Europe, but these were chiefly mathematical and medical works. No significant influence of Moslem interest in cultural differences can be traced in Europe until the time of Giovanni Leone Granatino ("Leo the African") who completed the Italian version of his *Description of Africa* in 1526 (Granatino 1957). Renaissance scholars of the 14th and 15th centuries were, on the whole, hostile to Arabic learning, which they compared unfavorably with that of the ancient Greeks.

The intellectual climate of Mediaeval Europe was not favorable to comparative studies. European Christians were much concerned about religious differences but only for the purpose of suppressing them. Other cultural differences were assigned little importance; it was differences in character and morality among individuals which were considered significant. At the same time, there was a literary interest in monsters and marvels, derived from the Classical literary tradition represented by the elder Pliny, which biased the expectations of travellers to distant lands. Thus, Mediaeval writers added little new information on differences among men to the stock which they had inherited from the geographical compilations of Classical antiquity.

In the 13th century, however, the Europeans had their attention forcibly attracted to the Mongols, a strange people from the eastern end of the world about whom the European literary tradition provided no information. Jenghiz Khan defeated the Russians at the Kalka River in 1223; Batu overran Russia between 1237 and 1240, and in 1241 he destroyed the armies of Poland and Hungary, supported by French and German contingents. In 1259 Berke invaded Poland again and defeated a crusade sent against him from the west. Here were "barbarians" whom the Europeans obviously could not afford to ignore. Many emissaries were sent to the new rulers of Asia with orders to collect information while conducting their official business. Respect for the military power of the Mongols led to some sober and factual reporting.

The most informative of the European envoys to the Mongol courts were the Franciscan friars Giovanni da Pian del Carpini, who travelled in Asia between 1245 and 1247, and Willem van Rubroek, who made his trip in 1253 and 1254. These men wrote accounts of their experiences among the Mongols which were intended primarily as military intelligence reports but included a certain amount of information on Mongol customs. Pian del Carpini's *History of the Mongols* fills 68 small pages in English translation; a little over one quarter of it is devoted to presenting ethnographic information. Rubroek's *Itinerary* is nearly twice as long (130 of the same size pages) and about one fifth of it deals with Mongol customs (Wyngaert 1929:1–130, 145–332; Dawson 1955).

A few years later (1275–1292) Marco Polo, the son of a Venetian merchant, spent 17 years in the service of Kublai Khan as an official of his imperial administration, eventually returning to Italy with many marvellous tales to tell. He was taken prisoner by the Genoese in a sea fight in 1296 and spent two or three years in a Genoese prison. There, in 1298, his story was written down in rough French by a fellow prisoner, Rusticiano of Pisa. Marco Polo's narrative is very different in tone from the earlier Franciscan reports. It is, in a sense, propaganda for Kublai Khan, whom Marco served loyally and greatly admired; it also reflects a personal interest in cultural differences which Marco says he learned from the Great Khan himself (Polo, ch. 16; 1938, 1:86). However, the ethnographic information in Marco Polo's book is neither very extensive nor very accurate. It is intermingled with much fabulous material on the "wonders of the east" which reflects a characteristically Mediaeval attitude (Polo 1938; Olschki 1960:138–146).

The influence of the works of Giovanni da Pian del Carpini, Willem van Rubroek, and Marco Polo on European thought was not proportional to the value of the information they provided. Pian del Carpini's brief account of the Mongols was reproduced in the *Speculum historiale* of Vincent of Beauvais, compiled between 1256 and 1259 as part of Vincent's great encyclopaedia, the *Speculum maius*, a popular Mediaeval work of reference. Marco Polo's picturesque narrative was also widely read. The more detailed and informative work of Willem van Rubroek was used by Roger Bacon, who met the author, and through Bacon's influence it had a modest circulation in England. It was unknown to continental scholars, however, until it was printed in the 16th century (Dawson 1955:2, 88; Bacon 1900, 1:305).

Roger Bacon, who lived from about 1214 to about 1292, was one of the most original thinkers of his time. He had a vision of a comprehensive science in the service of religion which he expounded to Pope Clement IV in his *Opus maius* of 1267 (Easton 1952). Part Four of this work contains a description of the world, occupying more than 70 pages, in which the reports of Pian del Carpini and Rubroek are both utilized. Here, if anywhere in Mediaeval literature, we might expect to find a foreshadowing of the comparative point of view of anthropology. Bacon does, indeed, stress the fact that the customs of men are different in different regions, but he goes on to explain that the differences are determined by the astrological influence of the planets, so that the way to study them is to determine the precise latitude and longitude of every place. There is no suggestion that direct observation of human behavior might be useful.[8] Bacon derived this theory of astrological determination from the pseudo-Aristotelian *Secret of secrets*, a work which profoundly influenced his thinking (Easton 1952:73).

Our review of pre-Renaissance writings by Europeans concerned with cultural differences can be summed up by saying that works of this sort were not numerous, and that the best ones were neglected or disbelieved. The intellectual climate of Europe was not favorable to a native development of anthropology either in Classical antiquity or in the Middle Ages, and the European tradition successfully resisted Persian and Mongol influence in this direction.

II

When a broader perspective was finally developed, it did not originate with observations of contemporary differences but with the study of Greek and Roman antiquity. The first cultural contrast to be recognized was that between the present and the past. This recognition was an achievement of the Italian Renaissance and, in fact, was the new idea which generated the greater part of the Renaissance movement. Only when men had learned to see differences by studying the past were they able to observe contemporary differences in the world around them in any systematic fashion.[9]

Before the Renaissance, Europeans were no more sensitive to differences in time than they were to differences in space. The only remote past which the Greeks and Romans recognized as different enough to form a contrast with the present was a realm of mythological fantasy, and when the myths ceased to be acceptable in their literal sense they were reinterpreted as allegories. The Christians transferred the allegorical method to the interpretation of biblical texts, thus destroying the documentary value of these texts as records of a non-Classical culture.

In the Middle Ages Europeans recognized no significant difference between themselves and the ancients. The distinction between a Classical and a Mediaeval period was an invention of the Renaissance which would have been incomprehensible to the people of earlier times. The fact is that the cultural tradition of Greece and Rome continued unbroken into the Middle Ages. Latin was everywhere the language of education and continued to be the common written language of Europe. Educated people were therefore not entirely cut off from ancient literature, although books became very scarce. Some ancient writers continued to be read, chiefly the later ones of Christian Rome. Stories from ancient literature and history were retold and illustrated in art. The fact that some changes had taken place was recognized, but the changes were regarded as isolated discrepancies, not sufficiently significant to establish a systematic contrast between antiquity and the present. Where their attention was not called to a specific difference, people simply assumed that the ancients behaved in familiar ways; thus Alexander the Great appeared in Mediaeval romances as a feudal monarch, and the heroes of ancient Rome were depicted in Mediaeval dress in paintings and book illustrations. As Erwin Panofsky puts it, "For want of a 'perspective distance' classical civilization could not be viewed as a coherent cultural system within which all things belonged together" (1960:111). The Renaissance has done its work so well that it now requires some effort to understand this Mediaeval point of view.

In the 13th century, with the rise of scholasticism and the High Gothic style in art, there was a general abandonment of the Classical tradition in philosophy, literary style, architecture and sculpture, the change being particularly marked in France. In architecture, for example, Classical ornament was almost systematically eliminated. The Latin language was not abandoned, but it was modified in syntax and vocabulary to fit the new patterns of scholastic thinking, and Classical writers were no longer taken as models of literary style.[10]

The Renaissance began in the 14th century as a reaction against the new ideals of the 13th. The founders of the Renaissance wanted to turn again to Classical models and restore the old tradition. Their attack on the work of their immediate predecessors, however, led them to emphasize the differences between current practice and Classical values, so that the cultural contrast between antiquity and the present gradually came to be recognized. The Renaissance learned to see antiquity at the "perspective distance" stipulated by Panofsky.

The man who was most influential in starting the Renaissance movement was Petrarch (Francesco Petrarca, 1304–1374), and his interests shaped its development.[11] Petrarch was a poet and essayist, an artist with language who was more concerned with literary form than with content. He collected the works of ancient writers, particularly the Roman poets and orators, modelled his Latin style after theirs, imitated their literary forms, and wrote on subjects which they suggested to him. Antiquity for Petrarch represented an ideal of perfection in every department of life, an ideal to be imitated as faithfully as possible. In order to imitate Classical antiquity, however, it was first necessary to study it. Petrarch's own studies of Roman literature were too personal and unsystematic to initiate a tradition of scholarship, and for this step we must look to his friend and admirer, Giovanni Boccaccio (1313–1375), who wrote treatises on Classical mythology and topography as well as the prose stories for which he is now more famous (Voigt 1894:159–180; Hortis 1879; Wilkins 1927). The first systematic observations of archaeological monuments were made about 1375 by another friend of Petrarch's, the physician and mechanical engineer Giovanni Dondi (1318–1389) [Sarton 1948:1676–1677; Rossi 1871 and 1888:330–334; Bormann and Henzen 1876:xxvii–xxviii; Panofsky 1960:208–210].

Petrarch particularly admired the poetry of Virgil and Cicero's prose, but he knew also the works of perhaps 15 to 20 other ancient Roman writers from manuscripts which were more or less readily accessible in northern Italy. He studied Greek, though only with limited success, and owned a manuscript of Homer and several of the works of Plato. The selection of ancient literature available gradually increased as Petrarch's followers became more numerous and began to exchange copies of the manuscripts they found. The search for manuscripts was carried on chiefly in Italy at first, but shortly after 1400 Italian scholars discovered the riches of the monastery libraries north of the Alps and began purchasing manuscripts in Greece and at Constantinople. The greater part of ancient Greek and Latin literature which has survived was known in Italy by about 1430.[12] By this time also a tradition of teaching ancient literature was well established. The effective beginning of Greek studies in Italy dates from the appointment in 1396 of the Byzantine scholar Manuel Chrysoloras to teach Greek at Florence (Symonds 1888:108–113; Voigt 1894:219–228).

The discovery, reproduction, and teaching of ancient literature occupied the energy of Renaissance intellectual leaders until well into the 15th century, allowing little opportunity for the development of systematic study. Then, with many new resources available, the foundations of modern scholarship were laid by three remarkable men, Ciriaco de' Pizzicolli of Ancona (1391–1452), Lorenzo Valla (1406–1457), and Biondo Flavio of Forlì (1392–1463).

Ciriaco de' Pizzicolli founded the discipline of archaeology.[13] In 1421 he had occasion to study the Latin inscription on the triumphal arch of Trajan at Ancona and was inspired by the idea that archaeological monuments could provide a more direct testimony of antiquity than the literary tradition. He devoted the rest of his life to studying ancient monuments in the field, copying inscriptions and recording ancient sculpture and architecture in Italy, Dalmatia, Greece, Turkey, and even Egypt. Once, at Vercelli in northern Italy, an ignorant priest asked Ciriaco his business, and the archaeologist replied, "Restoring the dead to life" (Pizzicolli 1742:55). The remark is still a good statement of the business of archaeology.

Ciriaco's concern with ancient monuments implied no rejection of the literary tradition of antiquity; he regarded the two kinds of evidence as complementing one another. He was himself an enthusiastic student of ancient literature and collected many important Greek manuscripts on his eastern travels. Some of his field notes were made in the margins of a copy of Strabo's *Geography* which was his guide to the identification of many ancient sites.

Little of Ciriaco's work has come down to us in the form it left his hands. Only a few pages of his voluminous original field notes (*Commentaria*) have survived, and we know his work chiefly from copies of extracts made by contemporaries who were interested in the evidence he provided. He wrote no work of synthesis of his own. Nevertheless, his influence on posterity was considerable.

Lorenzo Valla was the founder of the Renaissance tradition of linguistics (Mancini 1891; Gaeta 1955; Valla 1962). His major linguistic work was a manual of literary style entitled *Elegances of the Latin language* which was begun before 1435 and finished in 1444 (Valla 1962, 1:1–235; Mancini 1891:261–275). It is a descriptive study of Classical usage based on specific examples from ancient texts. Valla's perspective view of ancient Latin enabled him to recognize that linguistic change had occurred, and his descriptive method made study of such change possible. The *Elegances* was first printed in 1471 and went through 26 editions before 1500.

Valla also stimulated Renaissance interest in cultural differences by translating Herodotus into Latin. He is probably best known, however, as the founder of historical criticism. He earned this title by an attack, written in 1440, on the authenticity of the so-called "Donation of Constantine," a forgery of the time of Charlemagne on which the popes had, for several centuries, based their claims to temporal power (Valla 1922 and 1962, 1:761–795). Valla's attack on the "Donation" includes such explicit criticism of abuses in the church that he has been hailed as a forerunner of Luther. He had the further audacity to criticize St. Jerome's Latin translation of the New Testament, which he proposed to correct by comparison with the original Greek. A comparable degree of intellectual independence had brought Jan Hus to the stake only a few years earlier, but the triumph of the Renaissance in Italy introduced an interlude of toleration which not only saved Valla from persecution but made it possible for him to be appointed a papal secretary.

Valla was a versatile scholar who wrote philosophical and devotional essays, current history, polemics, and verse as well as the linguistic and critical works mentioned. In addition, he was one of the discoverers of manuscripts of ancient literature.

Biondo Flavio also made important contributions to Renaissance linguistics and archaeology, and he was the first to undertake a systematic study of ancient Roman culture.[14] His first work was an essay on the language spoken by the ancient Romans, written in 1435.[15] Leonardo Bruni and others had suggested that Latin was only the literary language of ancient Rome, while the spoken language was like the Italian of their own day. This theory in effect projected the 15th century situation into the past, in Mediaeval fashion, and blurred the new perspective view of antiquity. Biondo defended the Renaissance position by presenting evidence that the spoken language of the ancient Romans was a form of Latin. In doing so, he displayed an essentially modern view of dialect differences.

Between 1444 and 1446 Biondo wrote the first archaeological monograph intended for publication. It was entitled *Rome restored* and was a study of the topography and monuments of the ancient city based on a combination of literary evidence and observations of surviving remains. Printing was introduced into Italy in 1464, and Biondo's *Rome restored* became the first archaeological work to be published by the new process, appearing in 1471. It had a profound influence on later work. Biondo followed up his study of ancient Rome with another one which provided similar topographic treatment of the antiquities of other parts of Italy. *Italy illustrated,* as this work was called, was written between 1448 and 1453 and printed in 1474.

Biondo's study of ancient Roman culture was written between 1457 and 1459 and was first printed about 1473. It was entitled *Rome triumphant* and included sections on religion, government, military organization, life and customs, dwellings and transportation, and public honors. There were also frequent comparisons with customs and institutions of the author's own time which reflect the beginnings of an anthropological point of view.

Biondo was also a historian concerned with more recent events. His *Decades of history from the decline of the Romans,* written between 1438 and 1453, is a general history of Italy from the end of the 4th century to the year 1441, the first survey of the Middle Ages from the Renaissance point of view and a work which had a great influence on later scholarship in the Mediaeval field. It ends with an account of the arrival of envoys from Ethiopia at the papal court.

The Renaissance scholars whose work we have discussed treated antiquity as a different world from the one they knew, remote but accessible to all through its literature and its monuments. The Renaissance education of their time spread the view that the ancients were both different and worthy of study. Men trained in this tradition were better prepared than any of their predecessors to observe and record contemporary cultural differences when the opportunity presented itself.

The importance of the Renaissance point of view in making men sensitive to cultural differences is clearly seen in the records of early Portuguese and Spanish explorations in Africa and the Atlantic. The accounts of most of the early explorers are limited to relating their own adventures, discussing problems of navigation, and indicating the physical characteristics of the new lands and the opportunities for trade which they presented. The rare writers who devoted some attention to the natives and their customs in the early days of the great voyages of discovery were all either educated Italians or men who had been exposed to Italian Renaissance influence.

The first great program of western voyages, that of Prince Henry the Navigator of Portugal, took place in the 15th century and was contemporary with the first flowering of Renaissance scholarship in Italy. After sending ships to explore Madeira and the Azores, Prince Henry turned his attention in 1434 to the west coast of Africa, looking for slaves and gold. In 1441 his captains reached the Senegal at the northern edge of black Africa, and Europeans stood at the threshold of their first contemporary new world. Thereafter, voyages along the West African coast for trade and further exploration were frequent. Although a number of the captains who participated in these voyages wrote reports which have come down to us, only one made a systematic attempt to provide some ethnographic information on the peoples he visited. He was an Italian merchant, Alvise Ca' da Mosto (1432–1483), member of the Venetian nobility, who made two voyages to West Africa for Prince Henry, one in 1455 and the other in 1456. His account of what he saw in Rio de Oro, the Canary Islands, Senegal and Gambia was printed in 1507 (Ca' da Mosto 1937:1–84).

The Renaissance tradition of scholarship was taken to Spain in the late 15th century by Elio Antonio de Lebrija (1444–1522), an Andalusian educated at Bologna, and Pietro Martire d'Anghiera (1457–1526), an Italian scholar attached to the court of Ferdinand and Isabella. Lebrija was a notable pioneer in linguistics. His Latin-Spanish and Spanish-Latin dictionary, published in 1492–95, was the first bilingual dictionary to include a modern spoken language, and his Spanish grammar, published in 1492, was the first grammar of a spoken language inspired by Renaissance scholarship (Lebrija 1926, 1946, 1951). While based on a Latin grammar which Lebrija had written earlier, the Spanish grammar is by no means a mechanical application of the rules of Latin to Spanish. Where differences between Latin and Spanish struck his attention, Lebrija attempted to describe the Spanish constructions in their own terms. He was especially interested in pronunciation and proposed a reform of Spanish spelling to bring it more into line with the results of his analysis of the sounds of the language. Lebrija's work set a precedent for the later efforts of missionaries, many of them Spanish or Spanish trained, to describe the native languages of America.

Pietro Martire considered the discovery of America to be the most interesting event of his time. Although he never visited the New World himself, he became its first systematic reporter, beginning at once, with the return of Columbus in 1493, to collect information on American explorations from the men who were participating in them. His position at court enabled him to keep in close touch with events, and he entertained and questioned many of the explorers on their return to Spain. He saw the objects they brought with them and examined the captives they exhibited to the king. The information he collected was communicated immediately in elegant Latin to the popes and the community of Renaissance scholarship. A small volume in Italian based on his letters was published in Venice without the author's name in 1505. Pietro Martire's own Latin version of his reports was published in parts, the first in 1511, the first three in 1516, and the entire work in eight parts in 1530, after the author's death. It was entitled *New World decades* (Salas 1959:13–60 and references; Wagner 1947; Anghiera 1892 and 1912).

Pietro Martire took a special interest in ethnographic and linguistic information about the natives of the newly discovered lands. His letter of November, 1493, to Cardinal Ascanio Sforza, which became Book 1 of the first *Decade,* includes a brief vocabulary of Taino words recorded from the natives of Hispaniola whom Columbus brought back from his first voyage. This vocabulary is our earliest European record of any New World language. Pietro Martire's ethnographic information is relatively abundant and is presented in a notably objective fashion, the only American customs which he feels called upon to condemn outright being cannibalism and human sacrifice. The fairness of his attitude toward both cultural and physical differences is well illustrated by a passage in which he gives his reactions to the sight of the lip plugs worn by some Mexicans whom Cortés had sent to the Spanish court:

> I do not remember ever having seen anything more repulsive; they, however, consider that there is nothing more elegant under the orb of the moon, an example which teaches us how absurdly the human race is sunk in its own blindness, and how much we are all mistaken. The Ethiopian considers that black is a more beautiful color than white, while the white man thinks otherwise. The hairless man thinks he looks better than the hairy one, and the bearded man better than the beardless. It is clearly a reaction of the emotions and not a reasoned conclusion that leads the human race into such absurdities, and every district is swayed by its own taste (*Decade* 4, bk. 7; Anghiera 1892, 2:41–42).

Darius the Great would have approved this statement.

The anthropological importance of Pietro Martire rests on more than his own objective reports on American ethnography, however. It was he who inspired the actual explorers of the New World to make notes on native customs. He provided a focus of interest in such matters at the Spanish court, questioning returning travellers, demanding reports, distributing information, and over the years creating a public interest which stimulated others to publish the information they had collected in far countries. To give only one specific example of his influence, a good case can be made on circumstantial evidence that Gonzalo Fernández de Oviedo y Valdés was stimulated to write his *General and natural history of the Indies* by the visit he paid to Pietro Martire in January, 1516, and by reading the first three *Decades* published in the same year. There is no doubt that Fernández de Oviedo came to regard himself as Pietro Martire's great rival as an expert on New World matters. Once started on his American research, however, Fernández de Oviedo drew on a Renaissance background of his own. He had travelled in Italy between 1497 and 1502 and had read extensively in Classical literature. He utilized this background to compare New World customs with those of antiquity in a much more systematic fashion than Pietro Martire had done (Salas 1959: 122–125).

No one who makes a general survey of the literature bearing on historical ethnology which has come down to us from 16th century Europe can fail to be struck by the fact that it provides better and more detailed information on New World cultures than on those of the other parts of the world which the Europeans were exploring at the same time. The difference can be credited very largely to Pietro Martire's influence.

III

The significance of the Renaissance to the history of anthropology is that it created a "perspective distance" at which antiquity or any more recent culture might be seen whole and observed with a respect that would make it an acceptable object of study. The perspective of anthropology owes much to the experience of Europeans in the great voyages of discovery, but it did not originate in the observation of contemporary differences. Travellers see only what they are prepared to see, and men's eyes had first to be opened by the study of Classical antiquity in a framework which contrasted it with their own times.

It is paradoxical in a sense that Renaissance admiration for Classical antiquity should have made men more ready to study linguistic and cultural differences in the world around them. Why did they not concentrate exclusively on the study of Classical antiquity? Many, of course, were content to do so. But the Renaissance movement was more than a nostalgic return to the past. It was a dynamic reform movement which asked the advice of the past in order to handle the problems of the present, and it was born in comparison. There were always many Renaissance thinkers for whom the present had to be part of the equation.

The enthusiasm of the Renaissance for Classical antiquity had the further effect of cracking the shell of ethnocentric prejudice which had traditionally isolated the men of the west. If the Greeks and Romans were the great masters, never rivalled since, it was ridiculous for any modern people to claim an exclusive excellence. A touch of humility toward the great past made possible the impartial curiosity of men like Pietro Martire d'Anghiera.

Notes

[1] This paper is a by-product of research on the early history of archaeology. Its central idea is the result of thinking about the history of anthropology in the framework provided by Arnaldo Momigliano's Sather Lectures of 1962, "The Classical foundations of modern historiography," and Erwin Panofsky's work on the significance of the Renaissance (Panofsky 1960, 1962). Momigliano's Sather Lectures have not yet been published, but key portions of his argument are available in earlier articles (Momigliano 1955, 1960).

My argument, inspired by Momigliano, that there was no continuous anthropological tradition in Classical antiquity, is intended to challenge the notion common among anthropologists interested in the history of their discipline that anthropology begins with Herodotus and has had a more or less continuous development since. This notion is derived from such earlier studies as Myres 1908, Sikes 1914, and Trüdinger 1918, where its presence reflects the influence of the idea of progress.

A shorter version of this paper was read at the Seventh Annual Meeting of the Kroeber Anthropological Society, Berkeley, April 6, 1963. It is a pleasure to express my appreciation to William C. Sturtevant, John F. Freeman, Dell H. Hymes, Luís Monguió, Gene M. Schramm, Dorothy Menzel, and Margaret T. J. Rowe for encouragement and suggestions. Except as specifically noted, all translations were made by me from the original texts.

[2] It was Cicero who called Herodotus "the father of history" (see Momigliano 1960:29) and J. L. Myres (1908:125) who called him "the father of anthropology." Momigliano (1960:44) concludes that "Herodotus has really become the father of history only in modern times."

[3] Wells 1923; Glover 1924:60–61; Myres 1953:159–160.

[4] The best general account of Persian imperial policy is still that of Eduard Meyer (1953–56, 4, Band, 1:20–89). Meyer contributed a summary of this account in English to the eleventh edition of the *Encyclopaedia Britannica* (article Persia). A detailed study of Persian toleration is badly needed.

[5] Esther 1:22, 3:12, 8:9, quoted from the Revised Standard Version.

[6] Gellius (mid 2nd century A.D.), *Noctes Atticae,* Bk. XVII, ch. xvii; 1927–28, 3:262–263.

[7] Schroeder 1921; compare John George Clark Anderson's review of the influence of commonplaces in the *Germania* in Tacitus 1938:xxvii–xxxvii.

[8] Bacon 1900,1:300–301. Bacon took most of his geographical and ethnological information from Pliny.

[9] There is an immense literature on the Italian Renaissance. For present purposes the most useful research guides to this literature are Stark 1880 and Cosenza 1962. Novices in the Renaissance field should be warned that there has been much controversy among historians in recent years regarding the differences between the Renaissance and the Middle Ages (see Ferguson 1948 and Helton 1961). In this controversy I follow Panofsky, because I find his arguments convincing. The neo-Burckhardtian approach of this paper therefore represents a deliberate and reasoned choice among the alternatives.

[10] This paragraph is based on Panofsky 1960:101–103.

[11] On Petrarch see especially Voigt 1894; Essling and Müntz 1902; Nolhac 1907; Venturi 1929; and Mommsen 1957.

[12] On the recovery of Latin and Greek manuscripts see Symonds 1888:127–142; Voigt 1894:229–259; and Sabbadini 1905–14.

[13] Bodnar 1960:8–15 gives an extensive bibliography of works relating to Ciriaco; to it should be added Essen 1958. The basic source on Ciriaco's life is Scalamonti 1792. On the value of his field records see Lehmann-Hartleben 1943 and Ashmole 1956.

[14] Biondo Flavio 1927:xix–cxciii (by Bartolomeo Nogara), and notes kindly provided by Margaret T. J. Rowe. Biondo, of course, wrote in Latin, although the titles of his works are given in English in the text of this paper.

[15] *De verbis Romanae locutionis;* Biondo Flavio 1927:115–130.

PART TWO
Voyagers and Philosophers

Although the results were not immediate, the increased cultural contacts that followed the Age of Discovery ultimately resulted in a revision of the traditional European view of human nature. Existing conceptions of nature and culture had to be reexamined, especially in the case of the American continents. During the Middle Ages men had depended on stereotypes handed down from the ancients in which imaginary reports of travels were not easy to distinguish from real reports, such as those of Herodotus. As voyages became more and more common, the European public became sensitive to the emergence of cross-cultural insight. The early explorers had sufficient practical motivation to observe accurately because of their commitment to developing trade and commerce. Indeed, the realities of small exploring parties often meant that the supposedly superior Europeans were, in fact, utterly dependent on the mercy and goodwill of natives in all parts of the world.

Travel literature was extremely popular in Europe and was translated into various vernacular languages. Although Renaissance scientific works were still almost inevitably written in Latin, the travel narratives were read by men who were not scholars. The travel reports were the fare on which young men grew up; they longed to become adventurers themselves. And part and parcel of the adventures were the vastly different and surprising aboriginal peoples. They were human, according to most estimates, and therefore subject to understanding and conversion to Christianity, but their differences provided a challenge to the previously isolated European intellectual climate. There were, of course, still occasional forgeries of travel narratives, using the commonplaces of a genre that developed over several centuries of exploration and colonization; but now they were closer to ethnographic reality. Between the discovery of the New World and the end of the eighteenth century, Europeans gradually realized that the stereotypes of the past regarding biologically deformed and culturally deficient human groups would not be found among real societies. The real ethnographic diversity was realized concomitantly to be fascinating and worthy of report.

For the most part, the observers were not the same individuals who integrated the results of the explorations with European philosophy. Scholars devised questions to be answered by firsthand observation, but rarely did they themselves venture out to seek such information. Questionnaires were a favorite method of such anthropological scholars. For example, Catherine the Great of Russia circulated linguistic questionnaires; several French learned societies prepared questions for the La-Perouse expedition, which sailed on the eve of the French Revolution; and Thomas Jefferson provided detailed instructions for the Lewis and Clark expedition. In each case, there was an implicit set of categories to classify any group in relation to human society as a whole. Many of the preoccupations of Renaissance scholars overlapped those of Herodotus. There is a remarkable similarity, whether they were designed by philosophers, practical statesmen, or agents of contact.

In each area of the world, the process of gaining and utilizing information about cultural similarities and differences proceeded slightly differently. Always, attitudes toward native peoples depended simultaneously on the character of the people contacted and on the motives and political fortunes of the contact. For example, Curtin has described British attitudes toward India; Bearce, British attitudes toward India; and Pearce and Smith, American attitudes toward the American Indian (Curtin 1964; Bearce 1961; Pearce 1953; Smith 1950). In each case, the history of anthropological discussion was thoroughly dependent on the larger intellectual context within which contact was pursued, maintained, and rationalized.

The emphasis in this volume will be on the Americas. It would be virtually impossible to sample completely the travel literature that emerged as a result of the Age of Discovery. Some discussions of its contents are available (for example, Rowe 1964, Cornelius 1965; Hanzeli 1969). Each of these works attempts to catalog and evaluate assorted contributions of the early observers to later anthropological knowledge and theory.

Acosta, in the sixteenth century, was the first to combine personal observation with theoretical claims about the nature of the New World aborigines. He believed that the American Indians had come from Asia and were, therefore, entirely separate in their development from the European tradition. There had been an evolutionary development of human culture, with the Europeans as the highest level. Below them were the Chinese with their literacy and civilization, the Mexicans and Peruvians who lived in stable settlements but lacked writing systems, and the real savages (divided according to whether or not they were peaceful). Acosta's categories were effectively based on European stereotypes about the validity of their own culture, but they also served as a framework for description of the actual customs of people at different stages of development.

As students of man provided additional data about the realities of cultural diversity, the European mind moved away from the abstractions of the noble savage, the wise Egyptian, or the Chinese sage, which had been used as a means of getting outside one's own society sufficiently to criticize it with impunity (otherwise difficult within the Christian tradition) (Myres 1906). In the same period that voyagers were reporting on strange savages, European human sciences were turning to self-examination. European acculturation and local folklore were particularly important. For example, William Camden compared the Irish to the American Indians and used the travel literature as an ethnographic model for describing their way of life. (Compare with the observations in Part One by Rowe who argues that self-examination of its own tradition operated to motivate early Renaissance description of cultural diversity.)

Problems arose in describing the New World because of the greater internal cultural diversity among American Indians. Early explorers in Middle America discovered peoples whose civilizations had to be compared to those of Europe. European man might have been surprised to find such peoples in distant places and who existed apparently independently of his own history, but he was still more or less at home with the cultures. In contrast, the early explorers in the northern portions of the continent found savages as Hobbes had conceived them, living in rude conditions without the formal social and political institutions that constituted culture in the eyes of Europe. Two contrasting examples are presented here of the resulting styles of reporting, contrasts that have continued to affect the rationale whereby anthropologists incorporate different kinds of American Indian cultures within a general perspective of human cultural diversity.

Samuel Hearne was a sailor who came to work for the Hudson's Bay Company out of Churchill, Manitoba. Hearne's writings about his explorations in northern Canada were popular, partly because of the British need for a Northwest Passage, which would open a trade route in the northern part of the continent through to the Far East. The more reasonable routes through Panama and the Strait of Magellan were, of course, controlled by the Spanish, thus restricting British trade opportunities in the direction of the Orient.

Hearne dealt carefully with the Indians, partially because he was almost totally dependent on his guides. He also believed that the natives had to be kept in line. His overall assessment of their character was negative, and he stressed that the generosity and kindness of white men was not always returned by the Indians. On the other hand, Hearne's portrayal of the difficulties of life in this environment and the extreme poverty of the people was sympathetic. Although he found some of their customs "unnatural" and upsetting, he attempted to set down the rationale behind customs as well as the facts, otherwise inexplicable to European readers. The Indians were described as fully human, but the question of favorable comparison to European culture could simply not arise. Philosophers back home were welcome to conclude that the benefits of civilization could be brought with profit to the Indian peoples of the northern continent.

The contrast in tone when we turn to the Aztec and Inca cultures further south is remarkable. Bernal Díaz was a member of the Cortez expedition, which conquered Mexico City. Although Díaz was entirely committed to the aims of the conquest, he was still forced to recognize the sophistication of the Aztec kingdom. He did not devote great attention to the customs or character of the people, but what he did was in terms that would have been easily comprehensible in Europe. His description of the court of Montezuma recorded impressive elegance both in social and material terms. Cortez and his men often acted like sightseers, marveling at the wonders of the hospitality offered them. Díaz was negative in his description of sacrifices and other religious rites, but he still tried to report openly the complexity and luxury of the royal city. These were no abject savages, living in misery.

However, opinions differed as to how American Indians, including the relatively sophisticated peoples of Middle America, related to the Old World. Gonzalo Fernandez de Oviedo wrote the official Spanish history of the New World, published in 1526. His primary concern was the realistic one that some of the aborigines were warlike and needed to be approached with caution. His difficulties in publishing his manuscript seem to have been related to the antithetical belief of his contemporary, Bartolome de las Casas, who believed that the Indians were mild and docile and should be immediately converted to Christianity (at considerable expense to the Spanish crown). As happened among the French and

British colonists farther to the north, political questions and anthropological ones were not isolated from one another. The Spanish were dealing with more civilized savages, but the contrast between savage and civilized man was not lost. Europe still had to make up its mind what to think about the American Indians.

The third selection from the literature of the exploration is found in the writings of Alexander von Humboldt, whose voyages took place between 1799 and 1804. In describing the Guanches of the island of Teneriffe, he praised their gentle character and noted their contrast to the decadence of European civilization. On the other hand, he was appalled that they did not respect work. Anthropological description and observer's values proved to be closely related. Humboldt stressed that the presence of mummies did not guarantee connection to the Egyptians, because such similarities might arise independently.

Humboldt was particularly concerned with linguistic evidence about the past history of these people. He noted that grammatical information would be most useful but that the brief lexical lists available showed similarities to Berberic. He did not commit himself as to proof of common origin but was certain that some ancient connection between the two peoples must have taken place. Humboldt was surprised to learn that Spanish settlers who had been in the area for three hundred years still had white skin. European philosophy at the time leaned toward environmental determinism, which claimed that climate directly affected physical traits. The time perspective for biological differentiation of human populations was, however, not yet available. Thus, Humboldt had to conclude that the correlation was false if three hundred years had been insufficient to bring about a change.

American anthropology has devoted considerable attention to more recent reports about the various tribes, much of the material seen as part of the current, not merely the historical, literature. The history of anthropology in America is summarized in a long essay by Hallowell in which inquiries are organized according to the traditional four subdisciplines (Hallowell in deLaguna, ed., 1960). The assorted literature on which Hallowell draws includes discussion of the reports of Columbus' voyages (Browne 1906), Hallowell's own study of the influence of the Indians on American culture (Hallowell 1957), the Wilkes Exploring Expedition (Tyler 1968), Indian captivity narratives (Barbeau 1950), the Lewis and Clark expedition (Ray and Lurie 1954), the American Indian studies of the American Philosophical Society (Wissler 1942), the contributions of Duponceau to American linguistics (Pratt 1971), and the early history of American Indian linguistics (Wolfart 1967; Edgerton 1943).

It is not always possible to distinguish clearly between voyagers (reporters who had direct contact with native peoples) and philosophers (who developed theories to explain the observations). Among those who combined both roles was Thomas Jefferson, better remembered as a statesman than as an anthropologist. As a scholar, Jefferson was thoroughly immersed in the European rationalist tradition; as an American, he was closely involved with the American Indian. Jefferson believed that language was the key to placing the aborigines in the general history of human culture, and he collected numerous vocabularies (unfortunately lost). Along with Duponceau, Gallatin, and others, he was active in founding a committee on American Indian studies at the American Philosophical Society in Philadelphia. Its circulars were concerned primarily with natural history, but the history of the Indians was included within this framework. The Committee on Antiquities was interested in the "customs, manners, languages, and character of the Indian nations, ancient and modern, and their migration."

Jefferson's most extensive description of the Indians is found in his *Notes on the State of Virginia*, written in answer to a questionnaire for the information of Europeans curious about the New World. Jefferson was initially hesitant to publish this work because it criticized many of the political footballs of its time, including slavery. The chapter on aborigines, presented here, noted that the Indians might be better than civilized men because they live peacefully in small societies and have no need for laws.

Jefferson concerned himself extensively with studying the origin of the American Indians, particularly on the basis of linguistic evidence. The Indians appeared to be older in America than in Asia because of the extreme differentiation among their languages. Jefferson noted almost parenthetically that the traditional Mosaic chronology for the age of the earth might not be sufficient for the development of such extreme diversity. Problems of classifying the cultural and linguistic diversity of the continent were stressed.

Jefferson is also remembered as an archaeological fieldworker, because he satisfied his curiosity about an Indian barrow by excavating it. Although his technique did not meet modern standards, he was able to conclude that Indians still revered the place, that it had been used as a burial ground over a considerable period of time, and that people of all ages were buried there.

Americans, however, were not the only ones who were interested in descriptions of the American savages. In France, Michel de Montaigne went down to the docks and to the courts to interview Indians brought back by the voyagers. His *Essays*, devoted to self-improvement through setting down his opinions and testing them one against the other, frequently referred to data from the voyagers' reports. He preferred informants who were uneducated, because they would not falsify their testimony in light of pet theories.

Montaigne's comments about customs such as cannibalism, presented here, and the wearing of clothes are remarkably relativistic, given his lack of firsthand acquaintance with the functioning cultures in which these customs were practiced. As a European scholar of his time, Montaigne moved easily between Classical examples and ethnographic ones to demonstrate that the morality and customs of his own age were not the only possible ones and perhaps not the ultimately correct ones. Montaigne did not believe that Western man was necessarily the center of the universe; he did believe that Western man could understand the universe by studying cultural diversity. On the basis of the cross-cultural contrasts that he observed, he came to question the postulates of his society. "Barbarous" was seen to mean primarily unfamiliar. Montaigne lauded the simplicity of the savages and their adherence to natural law, although he realized that many of their customs were indeed horrible. But he pointed out that the faults of our own society have not been subjected to similar scrutiny. The implication is that barbarism exists in every society when assessed from the standards of pure reason and, therefore, that the ways of all societies are worthy of respect.

The philosophical period that has received the most attention as a forerunner of the science of anthropology is the Scottish Enlightenment of the eighteenth century. A number of general treatments are available, many of which stress the interdisciplinary roots of all the social sciences (for example, Schneider, ed., 1967; Baker 1947; Glacken 1967; Wells 1959; Gay 1966; Manuel 1959, 1962; Bryson 1945). Most of the men described in these books were influenced by the data of explorers; generally, they applied the anthropological material to philosophical problems defined in the European context. One might cite as particularly interesting examples: Lord Kames, on national character; Adam Ferguson, on the institution of property among savages; and John Millar, on rank and sexual roles; in addition to the more directly anthropological works of Lord Monboddo and William Robertson that are presented here.

Anthropologists have also considered the relevance of the Enlightenment to their discipline; for example: Voget, on the eighteenth century as it influenced the early period of professionalism (1960, 1967, 1968); Hoebel, on the anthropological contributions of William Robertson (1960); Cunningham, on the eighteenth-century anthropology as a direct contribution to the present discipline (1908). Slotkin's *Readings in Early Anthropology*, although it provides virtually no commentary on brief selections from 237 different social thinkers, includes extensive examples from the eighteenth-century Enlightenment as a baseline for more recent theory (Slotkin 1965).

William Robertson divided his history of the American continent into sections, including Columbus in the West Indies, the conquests of Mexico and Peru, and the anthropology of the American Indians. Later he added discussions of the British colonies in Virginia and New England. Most of North America was in a stage of savagery because of the absence of writing, metallurgy, and animal domestication; the civilizations of Middle and South America, however, had reached advanced barbarism, again reinforcing the contrast in reports and attitudes between the northern and so-called civilized Indians. Robertson was concerned primarily, not with the differences among tribal groups, but with what they shared. The problem was to fit the aborigines into the European picture of human history, rather than to describe the particular customs and lifeways of the Indians.

Robertson's discussion of the aborigines was based largely on questionnaires. He aimed to complete European knowledge of the human species, but this task was impossible in face of contradictory theories about the Indians. Not only was Robertson interested in using American data to clarify the origins of panhuman institutions, but he was careful to evaluate his sources, noting particularly that travelers' reports have presented much information that we now know to be absurd. We have, in effect, learned what kind of human diversity to expect in relation to different cultural conditions. Robertson believed that savages lacked abstract ideas, that they perceived directly only through their senses, and that European ideas of morality, love, and religion required leisure and civilization to develop. His overall evaluation of the Indian character was not particularly positive.

James Burnet, Lord Monboddo, was firmly committed to the wisdom of the classics, and opposed much of the secular and scientific current of his time (Darnell, in press). Many of his anthropological ideas were unusual, to say the least, in light of later understanding. But his reasons were not always equally absurd. For example, he was ridiculed in his own time and later for his belief that the orangutan was human. However, his criteria—family life, modesty, and burial of the dead—are reasonable in light of more recent studies. It was his failure to evaluate critically travelers' reports that was, in retrospect, most culpable.

The Scots' elaboration of the primitivism lauded by Jean Jacques Rousseau can be traced largely to Monboddo. He accepted Rousseau's postulates of human perfectibility and progress from an original animal condition that was ideal only in physical terms (Lovejoy 1933). Both Rousseau and Monboddo believed that the new science of history must include a study of savages in order to document an important step of man's progress toward civilization. Rousseau defined four stages, the first of which, the state of nature, was negative. It was the third stage, with culture but not yet property or the state, that constituted the ideal youth of the world. The fourth stage was civilization, which had lost these primitive virtues. There was, therefore, need for an additional stage in which simplicity could be regained without loss of the benefits of civilization. This progressivism was new in the Enlightenment and contrasted sharply with the Classical and Biblical notions of degeneration from an original Golden Age.

Monboddo differed from Rousseau primarily in believing that the chicken-and-egg dilemma of whether society preceded language or language preceded society could be solved. His extensive discussion of animal social organization outlined precedents for considering that language, rather than society, is unique to man. Language was part of the mental superiority that caused civilization to develop. Progress came about because the human arts grew gradually out of societies through the aid of linguistic symbolism.

Baron de Montesquieu was another seminal figure of the eighteenth century; his stress on political institutions and the influence of climate on culture has passed, with modifications, into the mainstream of anthropology. Montesquieu believed that laws were not universal and that no legal system could ever be abstractly correct or permanent. Justice in the widest philosophical sense could not be realized in civil society. But a science of laws has to devise, on the basis of known human experience, the best legal system for the time and place. It is by this route that anthropological data got into *The Spirit of Laws.*

Customs were not immutable, according to Montesquieu, but were dependent on climate. He cataloged the natural faults of each nation in some detail without suggestion as to remedy. Each nation must devise a legal system to control its faults without restricting the expression of its virtues. Although the explanations offered appear dogmatic in retrospect, Montesquieu helped to focus the attention of comparative jurisprudence on the range of known legal institutions, both in the Classical world and among primitive peoples. This trend reappeared in nineteenth-century anthropology in the works of Lewis Henry Morgan, John McLennan, Henry Maine, Edward B. Tylor, and others.

As a result of the voyages of discovery and the reports back to Europe, the lifeways of primitive men became known. Given the changes in worldview that began in the Renaissance, incorporation of information from the voyages was almost bound to be widely diffused. During the period between the discovery of the New World and the beginnings of professional anthropology in the mid-nineteenth century, human history was redefined in Western Europe from a decidedly anthropological perspective. What the Scots called "moral philosophy" was human history in all its possible manifestations, in which the origins of the customs and institutions of the observer's own society were compared to those of different peoples. As yet, however, the observers and philosophers had not come to consider themselves anthropologists; they were still observers of the human condition from the premises of philosophy, history, and letters. A scholar did not identify himself as an anthropologist, although his writings might have dealt extensively with anthropological subjects and might have had considerable influence on the early professionalism of the nineteenth century.

6. The Northern Indians
Samuel Hearne

As to the persons of the Northern Indians, they are in general above the middle size; well-proportioned, strong, and robust, but not corpulent. They do not possess that activity of body, and liveliness of disposition, which are so commonly met with among the other tribes of Indians who inhabit the West coast of Hudson's Bay.

Their complexion is somewhat of the copper cast, inclining rather toward a dingy brown; and their hair, like all the other tribes in India, is black, strong, and straight.[1] Few of the men have any beard; this seldom makes its appearance till they are arrived at middle-age, and then is by no means equal in quantity to what is observed on the faces of the generality of Europeans; the little they have, however, is exceedingly strong and bristly. Some of them take but little pains to eradicate their beards, though it is considered as very unbecoming; and those who do, have no other method than that of pulling it out by the roots between their fingers and the edge of a blunt knife. Neither sex have any hair under their armpits, and very little on any other part of the body, particularly the women; but on the place where Nature plants the hair, I never knew them attempt to eradicate it.

Their features are peculiar, and different from any other tribe in those parts; for they have very low foreheads, small eyes, high cheekbones, Roman noses, full cheeks, and in general long broad chins. Though few of either sex are exempt from this national set of features, yet Nature seems to be more strict in her observance of it among the females, as they seldom vary so much as the men. Their skins are soft, smooth, and polished; and when they are dressed in clean clothing, they are as free from an offensive smell as any of the human race.

Every tribe of Northern Indians, as well as the Copper and Dog-ribbed Indians, have three or four parallel black strokes marked on each cheek, which is performed by entering an awl or needle under the skin, and, on drawing it out again, immediately rubbing powdered charcoal into the wound.

Their dispositions are in general morose and covetous, and they seem to be entirely unacquainted even with the name of gratitude. They are for ever pleading poverty, even among themselves; and when they visit the Factory, there is not one of them who has not a thousand wants.

When any real distressed objects present themselves at the Company's Factory, they are always relieved with victuals, clothes, medicines, and every other necessary, *gratis;* and in return, they instruct every one of their countrymen how to behave, in order to obtain the same charity. Thus it is very common to see both men and women come to the Fort half-naked, when either the severe cold in Winter, or the extreme troublesomeness of the flies in Summer, make it necessary for every part to be covered. On those occasions they are seldom at a loss for a plausible story, which they relate as the occasion of their distress (whether real or pretended), and never fail to interlard their history with plenty of sighs, groans, and tears, sometimes affecting to be lame, and even blind, in order to excite pity. Indeed, I know of no people that have more command of their passions on such occasions; and in this respect the women exceed the men, as I can affirm with truth I have seen some of them with one side of the face bathed in tears, while the other has exhibited a significant smile. False pretences for obtaining charity are so common among those people, and so often detected that the Governor is frequently obliged to turn a deaf ear to many who apply for relief; for if he did not, he might give away the whole of the Company's goods, and by degrees all the Northern tribe would make a trade of begging, instead of bringing furs, to purchase what they want. It may truly be said, that they possess a considerable degree of deceit, and are very complete adepts in the art of flattery, which they never spare as long as they find that it conduces to their interest, but not a moment longer. They take care always to seem attached to a new Governor, and flatter his pride, by telling him that they look up to him as the father of their tribe, on whom they can safely place their dependence; and they never fail to depreciate the generosity of his predecessor, however extensive that might have been, however humane or disinterested his conduct; and if aspersing the old, and flattering the new Governor, has not the desired effect in a reasonable time, they represent him as the worst of characters, and tell him to his face that he is one of the most cruel of men; that he has no feeling for the distresses of their tribe, and that many have perished for want of proper assistance (which, if it be true, is only owing to want of humanity among themselves,) and then they boast of having received ten times the favours and presents from his predecessor. It is remarkable that those are most lavish in their praises, who have never either deserved or received any favours from him. In time, however, this language also ceases, and they are perfectly reconciled to the man whom they would willingly have made a fool, and say, "he is no child, and not to be deceived by them."

They differ so much from the rest of mankind, that harsh uncourteous usage seems to agree better with the generality of them, particularly the lower class, than mild treatment; for if the least respect be shown them, it makes them intolerably insolent; and though some of their leaders may be exempt from this imputation, yet there are but few even of them who have sense enough to set a proper value on the favours and indulgences which are granted to them while they remain at the Company's Factories, or elsewhere within their territories. Experience has convinced me, that by keeping a Northern Indian at a distance, he may be made serviceable both to himself and the Company; but by giving him the least indulgence at the Factory, he will grow indolent, inactive, and troublesome, and only contrive methods to tax the generosity of an European.

The greatest part of these people never fail to defraud Europeans whenever it is in their power, and take every method to over-reach them in the way of trade. They will disguise their persons and change their names, in order to defraud them of their lawful debts, which they are sometimes permitted to contract at the Company's Factory; and all debts that are outstanding at the succession of a new Governor are entirely lost, as they always declare, and bring plenty of witnesses to prove, that they were paid long before, but that their names had been forgotten to be struck out of the book.

Notwithstanding all those bad qualities, they are the mildest tribe of Indians that trade at any of the Company's settlements; and as the greatest part of them are never heated with liquor, are always in their senses, and never proceed to riot, or any violence beyond bad language.

The men are in general very jealous of their wives, and I make no doubt but the same spirit reigns among the women; but they are kept so much in awe of their husbands, that the liberty of thinking is the greatest privilege they enjoy. The presence of a Northern Indian man strikes a peculiar awe into his wives, as he always assumes the same authority over them that the master of a family in Europe usually does over his domestic servants.

Their marriages are not attended with any ceremony; all matches are made by the parents, or next of kin. On those occasions the women seem to have no choice, but implicitly obey the will of their parents, who always endeavour to marry their daughters to those that seem most likely to be capable of maintaining them, let their age, person, or disposition be ever so despicable.

The girls are always betrothed when children, but never to those of equal age, which is doubtless sound policy with people in their situation, where the existence of a family depends entirely on the abilities and industry of a single man. Children, as they justly observe, are so liable to alter in their manners and disposition, that it is impossible to judge from the actions of early youth what abilities they may possess when they arrive at puberty. For this reason the girls are often so disproportionably matched for age, that it is very common to see men of thirty-five or forty years old have young girls of no more than ten or twelve, and sometimes much younger. From the early age of eight or nine years, they are prohibited by custom from joining in the most innocent amusements with children of the opposite sex; so that when sitting in their tents, or even when travelling, they are watched and guarded with such an unremitting attention as cannot be exceeded by the most rigid discipline of an English boarding-school. Custom, however, and constant example, make such uncommon restraint and confinement sit light and easy even on children, whose tender ages seem better adapted to innocent and cheerful amusements, than to be cooped up by the side of old women, and constantly employed in scraping skins, mending shoes, and learning other domestic duties necessary in the care of a family.

Notwithstanding those uncommon restraints on the young girls, the conduct of their parents is by no means uniform or consistent with this plan; as they set no bounds to their conversation, but talk before them, and even to them, on the most indelicate subjects. As their ears are accustomed to such language from their earliest youth, this has by no means the same effect on them, it would have on girls born and educated in a civilized country, where every care is taken to prevent their morals from being contaminated by obscene conversation. The Southern Indians are still less delicate in conversation, in the presence of their children.

The women among the Northern Indians are in general more backward than the Southern Indian women; and though it is well known that neither tribe lose any time, those early connections are seldom productive of children for some years.

Divorces are pretty common among the Northern Indians; sometimes for incontinency, but more frequently for want of what they deem necessary accomplishments or for bad behaviour. This ceremony, in either case, consists of neither more nor less than a good drubbing, and turning the woman out of doors; telling her to go to her paramour, or relations, according to the nature of her crime.

Providence is very kind in causing these people to be less prolific than the inhabitants of civilized nations; it is very uncommon to see one woman have more than five or six children; and these are always born at such a distance from one another, that the youngest is generally two or three years old before another is brought into the world. Their easy births, and the ceremonies which take place on those occasions, have already been mentioned; I shall therefore only observe here, that they make no use of cradles, like the Southern Indians, but only tie a lump of moss between their legs, and always carry their children at their backs, next the skin, till they are able to walk. Though their method of treating young children is in this respect the most uncouth and awkward I ever saw, there are few among them that can be called deformed, and not one in fifty who is not bow-legged.

There are certain periods at which they never permit the women to abide in the same tent with their husbands. At such times they are obliged to make a small hovel for themselves at some distance from the other tents. As this is an universal custom among all the tribes, it is also a piece of policy with the women, upon any difference with their husbands, to make that an excuse for a temporary separation, when, without any ceremony, they creep out (as is their usual custom on those occasions) under the eves of that side of the tent at which they happen to be sitting; for at those times they are not permitted to go in or out through the door. This custom is so generally prevalent among the women, that I have frequently known some of the sulky dames leave their husbands and tent for four or five days at a time, and repeat the farce twice or thrice in a month, while the poor men have never suspected the deceit, or if they have, delicacy on their part has not permitted them to enquire into the matter. I have known Matonabbee's handsome wife, who eloped from him in May one thousand seven hundred and seventy-one, live thun-nardy, as they call it, (that is, alone,) for several weeks together, under this pretence; but as a proof he had some suspicion, she was always carefully watched, to prevent her from giving her company to any other man. The Southern Indians are also very delicate in this point; for though they do not force their wives to build a separate tent, they never lie under the same clothes during this period. It is, however, equally true, that the young girls, when those symptoms make their first appearance, generally go a little distance from the other tents for four or five days, and at their return wear a kind of veil or curtain, made of beads, for some time after, as a mark of modesty; as they are then considered marriageable, and of course are called women, though some of those periods are not more than thirteen, while others at the age of fifteen or sixteen have been reckoned as children, though apparently arrived at nearly their full growth.

On those occasions a remarkable piece of superstition prevails among them; women in this situation are never permitted to walk on the ice of rivers or lakes, or near the part where the men are hunting beaver, or where a fishingnet is set, for fear of averting their success. They are also prohibited at those times from partaking of the head of any animal, and even from walking in, or crossing the track where the head of a deer, moose, beaver, and many other animals, have lately been carried, either on a sledge or on the back. To be guilty of a violation of this custom is considered as of the greatest importance; because they firmly believe that it would be a means of preventing the hunter from having an equal success in his future excursions.

Those poor people live in such an inhospitable part of the globe, that for want of firing, they are frequently obliged to eat their victuals quite raw, particularly in the Summer season, while on the barren ground; but early custom and frequent necessity make this practice so familiar to them, that so far from finding any inconvenience arise from it, or having the least dislike to it, they frequently do it by choice, and particularly in the article of fish; for when they do make a pretence of dressing it, they seldom warm it through. I have frequently made one of a party who has sat round a fresh-killed deer, and assisted in picking the bones quite clean, when I thought that the raw brains and many other parts were exceedingly good; and, however strange it may appear, I must bestow the same epithet on half-raw fish: even to this day, I give the preference to trout, salmon, and the brown tittemeg, when they are not warm at the bone.

The extreme poverty of those Indians in general will not permit one half of them to purchase brass kettles from the Company; so that they are still under the necessity of continuing their original mode of boiling their victuals in large upright vessels made of birch-rind. As those vessels will not admit of being exposed to the fire, the Indians, to supply the defect, heat stones red-hot and put them into the water, which soon occasions it to boil; and by having a constant succession of hot stones, they may continue the process as long as it is necessary. This method of cooking, though very expeditious, is attended with one great evil; the victuals which are thus prepared are full of sand: for the stones thus heated, and then immerged in the water, are not only liable to shiver to pieces, but many of them being of a coarse gritty nature, fall to a mass of gravel in the kettle, which cannot be prevented from mixing with the victuals which are boiled in it. Besides this, they have several other methods of preparing their food, such as roasting it by a string, broiling it, &c.; but these need no farther description.

The most remarkable dish among them, as well as all the other tribes of Indians in those parts, both Northern and Southern, is blood mixed with the half-digested food which is found in the deer's stomach or paunch, and boiled up with a sufficient quantity of water, to make it of the consistence of pease-pottage. Some fat and scraps of tender flesh are also shred small and boiled with it. To render this dish more palatable, they have a method of mixing the blood with the contents of the stomach in the paunch itself, and hanging it up in the heat and smoke of the fire for several days; which puts the whole mass into a state of fermentation, and gives it such an agreeable acid taste, that were it not for prejudice, it might be eaten by those who have the nicest palates. It is true, some people with delicate stomachs would not be easily persuaded to partake of this dish, especially if they saw it dressed; for most of the fat which is boiled in it is first chewed by the men and boys, in order to break the globules that contain the fat; by which means it all boils out, and mixes with the broth: whereas, if it were permitted to remain as it came from the knife, it would still be in lumps, like suet. To do justice, however, to their cleanliness in this particular, I must observe, that they are very careful that neither old people with bad teeth, nor young children, have any hand in preparing this dish. At first, I must acknowledge that I was rather shy in partaking of this mess, but when I was sufficiently convinced of the truth of the above remark, I no longer made any scruple, but always thought it exceedingly good.

The stomach of no other large animal beside the deer is eaten by any of the Indians that border on Hudson's Bay. In Winter, when the deer feed on fine white moss, the contents of the stomach is so much esteemed by them, that I have often seen them sit round a deer where it was killed, and eat it warm out of the paunch. In Summer the deer feed more coarsely, and therefore this dish, if it deserve that appellation, is then not so much in favour.

The young calves, fawns, beaver, &c. taken out of the bellies of their mothers, are reckoned most delicate food; and I am not the only European who heartily joins in pronouncing them the greatest dainties that can be eaten. Many gentlemen who have served with me at Churchill, as well as at York Fort, and the inland settlements, will readily agree with me in asserting, that no one who ever got the better of prejudice so far as to taste of those young animals, but has immediately become excessively fond of them; and the same may be said of young geese, ducks, &c. in the shell. In fact, it is almost become a proverb in the Northern settlements, that whoever wishes to know what is good, must live with the Indians.

The parts of generation belonging to any beast they kill, both male and female, are always eaten by the men and boys; and though those parts, particularly in the males, are generally very tough, they are not, on any account, to be cut with an edge-tool, but torn to pieces with the teeth; and when any part of them proves too tough to be masticated, it is thrown into the fire and burnt. For the Indians believe firmly, that if a dog should eat any part of them, it would have the same effect on their success in hunting, that a woman crossing their hunting-track at an improper period would have. The same ill-success is supposed also to attend them if a woman eat any of those parts.

They are also remarkably fond of the womb of the buffalo, elk, deer, &c. which they eagerly devour without washing, or any other process but barely stroking out the contents. This, in some of the larger animals, and especially when they are some time gone with young, needs no description to make it sufficiently disgusting; and yet I have known some in the

Company's service remarkably fond of the dish, though I am not one of the number. The womb of the beaver and deer is well enough, but that of the moose and buffalo is very rank, and truly disgusting.[2]

Our Northern Indians who trade at the Factory, as well as all the Copper tribe, pass their whole Summer on the barren ground, where they generally find plenty of deer; and in some of the rivers and lakes, a great abundance of fine fish.

Their bows and arrows, though their original weapons, are, since the introduction of fire-arms among them, become of little use, except in killing deer as they walk or run through a narrow pass prepared for their reception, where several Indians lie concealed for that purpose. This method of hunting is only practicable in Summer, and on the barren ground, where they have an intensive prospect, and can see the herds of deer at a great distance, as well as discover the nature of the country, and make every necessary arrangement for driving them through the narrow defiles. This method of hunting is performed in the following manner:

When the Indians see a herd of deer, and intend to hunt them with bows and arrows, they observe which way the wind blows, and always get to leeward, for fear of being smelled by the deer. The next thing to which they attend, is to search for a convenient place to conceal those who are appointed to shoot. This being done, a large bundle of sticks, like large ramrods, (which they carry with them the whole Summer for the purpose,) and ranged in two ranks, so as to form the two sides of a very acute angle, and the sticks placed at the distance of fifteen or twenty yards from each other. When those necessary arrangements are completed, the women and boys separate into two parties, and go round on both sides, till they form a crescent at the back of the deer, which are drove right forward; and as each of the sticks has a small flag, or more properly a pendant, fastened to it, which is easily waved to and fro by the wind, and a lump of moss stuck on each of their tops, the poor timorous deer, probably taking them for ranks of people, generally run straight forward between the two ranges of sticks, till they get among the Indians, who lie concealed in small circular fences, made with loose stones, moss, &c. When the deer approach very near, the Indians who are thus concealed start up and shoot: but as the deer generally pass along at full speed, few Indians have time to shoot more than one or two arrows, unless the herd be very large.

This method of hunting is not always attended with equal success; for sometimes after the Indians have been at the trouble of making places of shelter, and arranging the flag-sticks, &c. the deer will make off another way, before the women and children can surround them. At other times I have seen eleven or twelve of them killed with one volley of arrows; and if any gun-men attend on those occasions, they are always placed behind the other Indians, in order to pick up the deer that escape the bow-men.

By these means I have seen upwards of twenty fine deer killed at one broadside, as it may be termed.

Though the Northern Indians may be said to kill a great number of deer in this manner during the Summer, yet they have so far lost the art of shooting with bows and arrows, that I never knew any of them who could take those weapons only, and kill either deer, moose, or buffalo, in the common, wandering, and promiscuous method of hunting. The Southern Indians, though they have been much longer used to fire-arms, are far more expert with the bow and arrow, their original weapons.

The tents made use of by those Indians, both in Summer and Winter, are generally composed of deer-skins in the hair; and for convenience of carriage, are always made in small pieces, seldom exceeding five buck-skins in one piece. These tents, as also their kettles, and some other lumber, are always carried by dogs, which are trained to that service, and are very docile and tractable. Those animals are of various sizes and colours, but all of the fox and wolf breed, with sharp noses, full brushy tails, and sharp ears standing erect. They are of great courage when attacked, and bite so sharp, that the smallest cur among them will keep several of our largest English dogs at bay, if he can get up in a corner. These dogs are equally willing to haul in a sledge, but as few of the men will be at the trouble of making sledges for them, the poor women are obliged to content themselves with lessening the bulk of their load, more than the weight, by making the dogs carry these articles only, which are always lashed on their backs, much after the same manner as packs are, or used formerly to be, on packhorses.

In the fall of the year, and as the Winter advances, those people sew the skins of the deer's legs together in the shape of long portmanteaus, which, when hauled on the snow as the hair lies, are as slippery as an otter, and serve them as temporary sledges while on the barren ground; but when they arrive at any woods, they then make proper sledges, with thin boards of the larch-tree, generally known in Hudson's Bay by the name of Juniper.

Those sledges are of various sizes, according to the strength of the persons who are to haul them: some I have seen were not less than twelve or fourteen feet long, and fifteen or sixteen inches wide, but in general they do not exceed eight or nine feet in length, and twelve or fourteen inches in breadth.

The boards of which those sledges are composed are not more than a quarter of an inch thick, and seldom exceed five or six inches in width; as broader would be very unhandy for the Indians to work, who have no other tools than an ordinary knife, turned up a little at the point, from which it acquires the name of Bafe-hoth among the Northern Indians,[3] but among the Southern tribes it is called Mo-co-toggan. The boards are sewed together with thongs of parchment deer-skin, and several cross bars of wood are sewed on the upper side, which serves both to strengthen the sledge and secure the ground-lashing, to which the load is always fastened by other smaller thongs, or stripes of leather. The head or forepart of the sledge is turned up so as to form a semi-circle, of at least fifteen or twenty inches diameter. This prevents the carriage from diving into light snow, and enables it to slide over the inequalities and hard drifts of snow which are constantly met with on the open plains and barren grounds. The trace or draught-line to those sledges is a double string, or slip of leather, made fast to the head; and the bight is put across the shoulders of the person who hauls the sledge, so as to rest against the breast. This contrivance, though so simple, cannot be improved by the most ingenious collar-maker in the world.

Their snow-shoes differ from all others made use of in those parts; for though they are of the galley kind, that is, sharp-pointed before, yet they are always to be worn on one foot, and cannot be shifted from side to side, like other snow-shoes; for this reason the inner-side of the frames are almost straight, and the outer-side has a very large sweep. The frames are generally made of birch-wood, and the netting is composed of thongs of deer-skin; but their mode of filling that compartment where the foot rests, is quite different from that used among the Southern Indians.

Their clothing, which chiefly consists of deer-skins in the hair, makes them very subject to be lousy; but that is so far from being thought a disgrace, that the best among them amuse themselves with catching and eating these vermin; of which they are so fond, that the produce of a lousy head or garment affords them not only pleasing amusement, but a delicious repast. My old guide, Matonabbee, was so remarkably fond of those little vermin, that he frequently set five or six of his strapping wives to work to louse their hairy deer-skin shifts, the produce of which being always very considerable, he eagerly received with both hands, and licked them in as fast, and with as good a grace, as any European epicure would the mites in a cheese.[4] He often assured me that such amusement was not only very pleasing, but that the objects of the search were very good; for which I gave him credit, telling him at the same time, that though I endeavoured to habituate myself to every other part of their diet, yet as I was but a sojourner among them, I had no inclination to accustom myself to such dainties as I could not procure in that part of the world where I was most inclined to reside.

The Southern Indians and Esquimaux are equally fond of those vermin, which are so detestable in the eyes of an European; nay, the latter have many other dainties of a similar kind, for beside making use of train-oil as a cordial and as sauce to their meat, I have frequently seen them eat a whole handful of maggots that were produced in meat by fly-blows. It is their constant custom to eat the filth that comes from the nose; and when their noses bleed by accident, they always lick the blood into their mouths, and swallow it.

The track of land inhabited by the Northern Indians is very extensive, reaching from the fifty-ninth to the sixty-eighth degree of North latitude; and from East to West is upward of five hundred miles wide. It is bounded by Churchill River on the South; the Athapuscow Indians' Country on the West; the Dog-ribbed and Copper Indians' Country on the North; and by Hudson's Bay on the East. The land throughout that whole track of country is scarcely anything but one solid mass of rocks and stones, and in most parts very hilly, particularly to the Westward among the woods. The surface, it is very true, is in most places covered with a thin sod of moss, intermixed with the roots of the Wee-sa-ca-pucca, cranberries, and a few other insignificant shrubs and herbage; but under it there is in general a total want of soil, capable of producing anything except what is peculiar to the climate. Some of the marshes, indeed, produce several kinds of grass, the growth of which is amazingly rapid; but this is dealt out with so sparing a hand as to be barely sufficient to serve the geese, swans, and other birds of passage, during their migrations in the Spring and Fall, while they remain in a moulting state.

The many lakes and rivers with which this part of the country abounds, though they do not furnish the natives with water-carriage, are yet of infinite advantage to them; as they afford great numbers of fish, both in Summer and Winter. The only species caught in those parts are trout, tittameg, (or tickomeg,) tench, two sorts of barble, (called by the Southern Indians Na-may-pith,) burbot, pike, and a few perch. The four former are caught in all parts of this country, as well the woody as the barren; but the three latter are only caught to the Westward, in such lakes and rivers as are situated among the woods; and though some of those rivers lead to the barren ground, yet the three last mentioned species of fish are seldom caught beyond the edge of the woods, not even in the Summer season.

There is a black, hard, crumply moss, that grows on the rocks and large stones in those parts, which is of infinite service to the natives, as it sometimes furnishes them with a temporary subsistence, when no animal food can be procured. This moss, when boiled, turns to a gummy consistence, and is more clammy in the mouth than sago; it may, by adding either moss or water, be made to almost any consistence. It is so palatable, that all who taste it generally grow fond of it. It is remarkably good and pleasing when used to thicken any kind of broth, but it is generally most esteemed when boiled in fish-liquor.

The only method practised by those people to catch fish either in Winter or Summer, is by angling and setting nets; both of which methods is attended with much superstition, ceremony, and unnecessary trouble;

but I will endeavour to describe them in as plain and brief a manner as possible.

When they make a new fishing-net, which is always composed of small thongs cut from raw deer-skins, they take a number of birds bills and feet, and tie them, a little apart from each other, to the head and foot rope of the net, and at the four corners generally fasten some of the toes and jaws of the otters and jackashes. The birds feet and bills made choice of on such occasions are generally those of the laughing goose, wavey, (or white goose,) gulls, loons, and black-heads; and unless some or all of these be fastened to the net, they will not attempt to put it into the water, as they firmly believe it would not catch a single fish.

A net thus accoutred is fit for setting whenever occasion requires, and opportunity offers; but the first fish of whatever species caught in it, are not to be sodden in the water, but broiled whole on the fire, and the flesh carefully taken from the bones without dislocating one joint; after which the bones are laid on the fire at full length and burnt. A strict observance of these rules is supposed to be of the utmost importance in promoting the future success of the new net; and a neglect of them would render it not worth a farthing.[5]

When they fish in rivers, or narrow channels that join two lakes together, they could frequently, by tying two, three, or more nets together, spread over the whole breadth of the channel, and intercept every sizable fish that passed; but instead of that, they scatter the nets at a considerable distance from each other, from a superstitious notion, that were they kept close together, one net would be jealous of its neighbour, and by that means not one of them would catch a single fish.

The methods used, and strictly observed, when angling, are equally absurd as those I have mentioned; for when they bait a hook, a composition of four, five, or six articles, by way of charm, is concealed under the bait, which is always sewed round the hook. In fact, the only bait used by those people is in their opinion a composition of charms, inclosed within a bit of fish skin, so as in some measure to resemble a small fish. The things used by way of charm, are bits of beavers tails and fat, otter's vents and teeth, musk-rat's guts and tails, loon's vents, squirrel's testicles, and curdled milk taken out of the stomach of sucking fawns and calves, human hair, and numberless other articles equally absurd.

Every master of a family, and indeed almost every other person, particularly the men, have a small bundle of such trash, which they always carry with them, both in Summer and Winter; and without some of those articles to put under their bait, few of them could be prevailed upon to put a hook into the water, being fully persuaded that they may as well sit in the tent, as attempt to angle without such assistance. They have also a notion that fish of the same species inhabiting different parts of the country, are fond of different things; so that almost every lake and river they arrive at, obliges them to alter the composition of the charm. The same rule is observed on broiling the first fruits of a new hook that is used for a new net; an old hook that has already been successful in catching large fish is esteemed of more value, than a handful of new ones which have never been tried.

Deer also, as well as fish, are very numerous in many parts of this country; particularly to the North of the sixtieth degree of latitude. Alpine hares are in some parts of the barren ground pretty plentiful, where also some herds of musk-oxen are to be met with; and to the Westward, among the woods, there are some rabbits and partridges. With all those seeming sources of plenty, however, one half of the inhabitants, and perhaps the other half also, are frequently in danger of being starved to death, owing partly to their want of economy; and most of these scenes of distress happen during their journies to and from Prince of Wales's Fort, the only place at which they trade.

When Northern Indians are at the Factory, they are very liable to steal any thing they think will be serviceable; particularly iron hoops, small bolts, spikes, carpenters tools, and, in short, all small pieces of iron-work which they can turn to advantage, either for their own use, or for the purpose of trading with such of their countrymen as seldom visit the Company's Settlement: among themselves, however, the crime of theft is seldom heard of.

When two parties of those Indians meet, the ceremonies which pass between them are quite different from those made use of in Europe on similar occasions; for when they advance within twenty or thirty yards of each other, they make a full halt, and in general sit or lie down on the ground, and do not speak for some minutes. At length one of them, generally an elderly man, if any be in company, breaks silence, by acquainting the other party with every misfortune that has befallen him and his companions from the last time they had seen or heard of each other; and also of all deaths and other calamities that have befallen any other Indians during the same period, at least as many particulars as have come to his knowledge.

When the first has finished his oration, another aged orator, (if there be any) belonging to the other party relates, in like manner, all the bad news that has come to his knowledge; and both parties never fail to plead poverty and famine on all occasions. If those orations contain any news that in the least affect the other party, it is not long before some of them begin to sigh and sob, and soon after break out into a loud cry, which is generally accompanied by most of the grown persons of both sexes; and sometimes it is common to see them all, men, women, and children, in one universal howl. The young girls, in particular, are often very obliging on those occasions; for I never remember to have seen a crying match (as I called it) but the greatest part of the company assisted, although some of them had no other reason for it, but that of seeing their companions do the same. When the first transports of grief subside, they advance by degrees, and both parties mix with each other, the men always associating with the men, and the women with the women. If they have any tobacco among them, the pipes are passed round pretty freely, and the conversation soon becomes general. As they are on their first meeting acquainted with all the bad news, they have by this time nothing left but good, which in general has so far the predominance over the former, that in less than half an hour nothing but smiles and cheerfulness are to be seen in every face; and if they be not really in want, small presents of provisions, ammunition, and other articles, often take place; sometimes merely as a gift, but more frequently by way of trying whether they cannot get a greater present.

They have but few diversions; the chief is shooting at a mark with bow and arrows; and another out-door game, called Holl, which in some measure resembles playing with quoits; only it is done with short clubs sharp at one end. They also amuse themselves at times with dancing, which is always performed in the night. It is remarkable that those people, though a distinct nation, have never adopted any mode of dancing of their own, or any songs to which they can dance; so that when anything of this kind is attempted, which is but seldom, they always endeavour to imitate either the Dog-ribbed or Southern Indians, but more commonly the former, as few of them are sufficiently acquainted either with the Southern Indian language, or their manner of dancing. The Dog-ribbed method is not very difficult to learn, as it only consists in lifting the feet alternately from the ground in a very quick succession, and as high as possible, without moving the body, which should be kept quite still and motionless; the hands at the same time being closed, and held close to the breast, and the head inclining forward. This diversion is always performed quite naked, except the breech-cloth, and at times that is also thrown off; and the dancers, who seldom exceed three or four at a time, always stand close to the music. The music may, by straining a point, be called both vocal and instrumental, though both are sufficiently humble. The former is no more than a frequent repetition of the words, hee, hee, hee, ho, ho, ho, &c. which, by a more or less frequent repetition, dwelling longer on one word and shorter on another, and raising and lowering the voice, produce something like a tune, and has the desired effect. This is always accompanied by a drum or tabor; and sometimes a kind of rattle is added, made with a piece of dried buffalo skin, in shape exactly like an oil-flask, into which they put a few shot or pebbles, which, when shook about, produces music little inferior to the drum, though not so loud.

This mode of dancing naked is performed only by the men; for when the women are ordered to dance, they always exhibit without the tent, to music which is played within it; and though their method of dancing is perfectly decent, yet it has still less meaning and action than that of the men: for a whole heap of them crowd together in a straight line, and just shuffle themselves a little from right to left, and back again in the same line, without lifting their feet from the ground; and when the music stops, they all give a little bend of the body and knee, somewhat like an awkward curtsey, and pronounce, in a shrill tone, h-e-e, h-o-o-o-e.

Beside these diversions, they have another simple in-door game, which is that of taking a bit of wood, a button, or any other small thing, and after shifting it from hand to hand several times, asking their antagonist, which hand it is in? When playing at this game, which only admits of two persons, each of them have ten, fifteen, or twenty small chips of wood, like matches; and when one of the players guesses right, he takes one of his antagonist's sticks, and lays it to his own; and he that first gets all the sticks from the other in that manner, is said to win the game, which is generally for a single load of powder and shot, an arrow, or some other thing of inconsiderable value.

The women never mix in any of their diversions, not even in dancing; for when that is required of them, they always exhibit without the tent, as has been already observed; nor are they allowed to be present at a feast. Indeed, the whole course of their lives is one continued scene of drudgery, *viz.* carrying and hauling heavy loads, dressing skins for clothing, curing their provisions, and practising other necessary domestic duties which are required in a family, without enjoying the least diversion of any kind, or relaxation, on any occasion whatever; and except in the execution of those homely duties, in which they are always instructed from their infancy, their senses seem almost as dull and frigid as the zone they inhabit. There are indeed some exceptions to be met with among them, and I suppose it only requires indulgence and precept to make some of them as lofty and insolent as any women in the world. Though they wear their hair at full length, and never tie it up, like the Southern Indians; and though not one in fifty of them is ever possessed of a comb, yet by a wonderful dexterity of the fingers, and a good deal of patience, they make shift to stroke it out so as not to leave two hairs entangled; but when their heads are infested with vermin, from which very few of either sex are free, they mutually assist each other in keeping them under.

A scorbutic disorder, resembling the worst stage of the itch, consumptions, and fluxes, are their chief disorders. The first of these, though very troublesome, is never known to prove fatal, unless it be accompanied with some inward complaint; but the two latter, with a few accidents, carries off great numbers of both sexes and all ages; indeed few of them live to any great age, probably owing to the great fatigue they undergo from their youth up, in procuring a subsistence for themselves and their offspring.

Though the scorbutic disorder above mentioned does appear to be infectious, it is rare to see one have it without the whole tent's crew being more or less affected with it; but this is by no means a proof of its being contagious; I rather attribute it to the effects of some bad water, or the unwholesomeness of some fish they may catch in particular places, in the course of their wandering manner of life. Were it otherwise, a single family would in a short time communicate it to the whole tribe; but, on the contrary, the disease is never known to spread. In the younger sort it always attacks the hands and feet, not even sparing the palms and soles. Those of riper years generally have it about the wrists, insteps, and posteriors; and in the latter particularly, the blotches, or boils as they may justly be called, are often as large as the top of a man's thumb. This disorder most frequently makes its appearance in the Summer, while the Indians are out on the barren ground; and though it is by no means reckoned dangerous, yet it is so obstinate, as not to yield to any medicine that has ever been applied to it while at the Company's Factory. And as the natives themselves never make use of any medicines of their own preparing, Nature alone works the cure, which is never performed in less than twelve or eighteen months; and some of them are troubled with this disagreeable and loathsome disorder for years before they are perfectly cured, and then a dark livid mark remains on those parts of the skin which have been affected, for many years afterwards, and in some during life.

When any of the principal Northern Indians die, it is generally believed that they are conjured to death, either by some of their own countrymen, by some of the Southern Indians, or by some of the Esquimaux: too frequently the suspicion falls on the latter tribe, which is the grand reason of their never being at peace with those poor and distressed people. For some time past, however, those Esquimaux who trade with our sloops at Knapp's Bay, Navel's Bay, and Whale Cove, are in perfect peace and friendship with the Northern Indians; which is entirely owing to the protection they have for several years past received from the Chiefs at the Company's Fort at Churchill River.[6] But those of that tribe who live so far to the North, as not to have any intercourse with our vessels, very often fall a sacrifice to the fury and superstition of the Northern Indians; who are by no means a bold or warlike people; nor can I think from experience, that they are particularly guilty of committing acts of wanton cruelty on any other part of the human race beside the Esquimaux. Their hearts, however, are in general so unsusceptible of tenderness, that they can view the deepest distress in those who are not immediately related to them, without the least emotion; not even half so much as the generality of mankind feel for the sufferings of the meanest of the brute creation. I have been present when one of them, imitating the groans, distorted features, and contracted position, of a man who had died in the most excruciating pain, put the whole company, except myself, into the most violent fit of laughter.

The Northern Indians never bury their dead, but always leave the bodies where they die, so that they are supposed to be devoured by beasts and birds of prey; for which reason they will not eat foxes, wolves, ravens, &c. unless it be through mere necessity.

The death of a near relation affects them so sensibly, that they rend all their cloths from their backs, and go naked, till some persons less afflicted relieve them. After the death of a father, mother, husband, wife, son, or brother, they mourn, as it may be called, for a whole year, which they measure by the moons and seasons. Those mournful periods are not distinguished by any particular dress, except that of cutting off the hair; and the ceremony consists in almost perpetually crying. Even when walking, as well as at all other intervals from sleep, eating, and conversation, they make an odd howling noise, often repeating the relationship of the deceased. But as this is in a great measure mere form and custom, some of them have a method of softening the harshness of the notes, and bringing them out in a more musical tone than that in which they sing their songs. When they reflect seriously on the loss of a good friend, however, it has such an effect on them for the present, that they give an uncommon loose to their grief. At those times they seem to sympathise (through custom) with each other's afflictions so much, that I have often seen several scores of them crying in concert, when at the same time not above half a dozen of them had any more reason for so doing than I had, unless it was to preserve the old custom, and keep the others in countenance. The women are remarkably obliging on such occasions; and as no restriction is laid on them, they may with truth be said to cry with all their might and main; but in common conversation they are obliged to be very moderate.

They have a tradition among them, that the first person upon earth was a woman, who, after having been some time alone, in her researches for berries, which was then her only food, found an animal like a dog, which followed her to the cave where she lived, and soon grew fond and domestic. This dog, they say, had the art of transforming itself into the shape of a handsome young man, which it frequently did at night, but as the day approached, always resumed its former shape; so that the woman looked on all that passed on those occasions as dreams and delusions. These transformations were soon productive of the consequences which at present generally follow such intimate connexions between the two sexes, and the mother of the world began to advance in her pregnancy.

Not long after this happened, a man of such a surprising height that his head reached up to the clouds, came to level the land, which at that time was a very rude mass; and after he had done this, by the help of his walking-stick he marked out all the lakes, ponds, and rivers, and immediately caused them to be filled with water. He then took the dog, and tore it to pieces; the guts he threw into the lakes and rivers, commanding them to become the different kinds of fish; the flesh he dispersed over the land, commanding it to become different kinds of beasts and land-animals; the skin he also tore in small pieces, and threw it into the air, commanding it to become all kinds of birds; after which he gave the woman and her offspring full power to kill, eat, and never spare, for that he had commanded them to multiply for her use in abundance. After this injunction, he returned to the place whence he came, and has not been heard of since.

Religion has not as yet begun to dawn among the Northern Indians; for though their conjurors do indeed sing songs, and make long speeches, to some beasts and birds of prey, as also to imaginary beings, which they say assist them in performing cures on the sick, yet they, as well as their credulous neighbours, are utterly destitute of every idea of practical religion. It is true, some of them will reprimand their youth for talking disrespectfully of particular beasts and birds; but it is done with so little energy, as to be often retorted back in derision. Neither is this, nor their custom of not killing wolves and quiquehatches, universally observed, and those who do it can only be viewed with more pity and contempt than the others; for I always found it arose merely from the greater degree of confidence which they had in the supernatural power of their conjurors, which induced them to believe, that talking lightly or disrespectfully of any thing they seemed to approve, would materially affect their health and happiness in this world: and I never found any of them that had the least idea of futurity. Matonabbee, without one exception, was a man of as clear ideas in other matters as any that I ever saw:[7] he was not only a perfect master of the Southern Indian language, and their belief, but could tell a better story of our Saviour's birth and life, than one half of those who call themselves Christians; yet he always declared to me, that neither he, nor any of his countrymen, had an idea of a future state. Though he had been taught to look on things of this kind as useless, his own good sense had taught him to be an advocate for universal toleration; and I have seen him several times assist at some of the most sacred rites performed by the Southern Indians, apparently with as much zeal, as if he had given as much credit to them as they did: and with the same liberality of sentiment he would, I am persuaded, have assisted at the altar of a Christian church, or in a Jewish synagogue; not with a view to reap any advantage himself, but merely, as he observed, to assist others who believed in such ceremonies.

Being thus destitute of all religious control, these people have, to use Matonabbee's own words, "nothing to do but consult their own interest, inclinations, and passions; and to pass through this world with as much ease and contentment as possible, without any hopes of reward, or painful fear of punishment, in the next." In this state of mind they are, when in prosperity, the happiest of mortals; for nothing but personal or family calamities can disturb their tranquillity, while misfortunes of the lesser kind sit light on them. Like most other uncivilized people, they bear bodily pain with great fortitude, though in that respect I cannot think them equal to the Southern Indians.

Old age is the greatest calamity that can befall a Northern Indian; for when he is past labour, he is neglected, and treated with great disrespect, even by his own children. They not only serve him last at meals, but generally give him the coarsest and worst of the victuals: and such of the skins as they do not choose to wear, are made up in the clumsiest manner into clothing for their aged parents; who, as they had, in all probability, treated their fathers and mothers with the same neglect, in their turns, submitted patiently to their lot, even without a murmur, knowing it to be the common misfortune attendant on old age; so that they may be said to wait patiently for the melancholy hour when, being no longer capable of walking, they are to be left alone, to starve, and perish for want. This, however shocking and unnatural it may appear, is nevertheless so common, that, among those people, one half at least of the aged persons of both sexes absolutely die in this miserable condition.

The Northern Indians call the *Aurora Borealis,* Ed-thin: that is, Deer: and when that meteor is very bright, they say that deer is plentiful in that part of the atmosphere; but they have never yet extended their ideas so far as to entertain hopes of tasting those celestial animals.

Beside this silly notion, they are very superstitious with respect to the existence of several kinds of fairies, called by them Nant-e-na, whom they frequently say they see, and who are supposed by them to inhabit the different elements of earth, sea, and air, according to their several qualities. To one or other of those fairies they usually attribute any change in their circumstances, either for the better or worse; and as they are led into this way of thinking entirely by the art of the conjurors, there is no such thing as any general mode of belief; for those jugglers differ so much from each other in their accounts of these beings, that those who believe any thing they say, have little to do but change their opinions according to the will and caprice of the conjuror, who is almost daily relating some new whim, or extraordinary event, which, he says, has been revealed to him in a dream, or by some of his favourite fairies, when on a hunting excursion.

Notes

[1] I have seen several of the Southern Indian men who were near six feet high, preserve a single lock of their hair, that, when let down, would trail on the ground as they walked. This, however, is but seldom seen; and some have suspected it to be false: but I have examined the hair of several of them, and found it to be real.

[2] The Indian method of preparing this unaccountable dish is by throwing the filthy bag across a pole directly over the fire, the smoke of which, they say, much improves it, by taking off the original flavour; and when any of it is to be cooked, a large flake, like as much tripe, is cut off and boiled for a few minutes; but the many large nodes with which the inside of the womb is studded, make it abominable. These nodes are as incapable of being divested of moisture as the skin of a live eel; but when boiled, much resemble, both in shape and colour, the yolk of an egg, and are so called by the natives, and as eagerly devoured by them.

The tripe of the buffalo is exceedingly good, and the Indian method of cooking it infinitely superior to that practised in Europe. When opportunity will permit, they wash it tolerably clean in cold water, strip off all the honey-comb, and only boil it about half, or three-quarters of an hour: in that time it is sufficiently done for eating; and though rather tougher than what is prepared in England, yet is exceedingly pleasant to the taste, and must be much more nourishing than tripe that has been soaked and scrubbed in many hot waters, and then boiled for ten or twelve hours.

The lesser stomach, or, as some call it, the many-folds, either of buffalo, moose, or deer, are usually eat raw, and are very good; but that of the moose, unless great care be taken in washing it, is rather bitter, owing to the nature of their food.

The kidneys of both the moose and buffalo are usually eat raw by the Southern Indians; for no sooner is one of those beasts killed, than the hunter rips up its belly, thrusts in his arm, snatches out the kidneys, and eats them warm, before the animal is quite dead. They also at times put their mouths to the wound the ball has made, and suck the blood; which they say quenches thirst, and is very nourishing.

[[3] "Bess-hath" is a modern spelling of the Chipewyan name for a curved knife. Here Hearne's compositor has substituted an "f" for the old-fashioned long "s".]

[[4] The past tense indicates that this was written after Matonabbee's death in 1782.]

[5] They frequently sell new nets, which have not been wet more than once or twice, because they have not been successful. Those nets, when soaked in water, are easily opened, and then make most excellent heel and toe netting for snow-shoes. In general it is far superior to the netting cut by the Southern Indian women, and is not larger than common net-twine.

[6] In the Summer of 1756, a party of Northern Indians lay in wait at Knapp's Bay till the sloop had sailed out of the harbour, when they fell on the poor Esquimaux, and killed every soul. Mr. John Bean, then Master of the sloop, and since Master of the Trinity yacht, with all his crew, heard the guns very plain; but did not know the meaning or reason of it till the Summer following, when he found the shocking remains of more than forty Esquimaux, who had been murdered in that cowardly manner; and for no other reason but because two principal Northern Indians had died in the preceding Winter.

No Esquimaux were seen at Knapp's Bay for several years after; and those who trade there at present have undoubtedly been drawn from the Northward, since the above unhappy transaction; for the convenience of being nearer the woods, as well as being in the way of trading with the sloop that calls there annually. It is to be hoped that the measures taken by the Governors at Prince of Wales's Fort of late years, will effectually prevent any such calamities happening in future, and by degrees be the means of bringing about a lasting friendly, and reciprocal interest between the two nations.

Notwithstanding the pacific and friendly terms which begin to dawn between those two tribes at Knapp's Bay, Navel's Bay, and Whale Cove, farther North hostilities continue, and most barbarous murders are perpetrated: and the only protection the Esquimaux have from the fury of their enemies, is their remote situation in the

Winter, and their residing chiefly on islands and pensinsulas in Summer, which renders them less liable to be surprised during that Season. But even this secluded life does not prevent the Northern Indians from harassing them greatly, and at times they are so closely pursued as to be obliged to leave most of their goods and utensils to be destroyed by their enemy; which must be a great loss, as these cannot be replaced but at the expence of much time and labour; and the want of them in the meantime must create much distress both to themselves and their families, as they can seldom procure any part of their livelihood without the assistance of a considerable apparatus.

In 1756, the Esquimaux at Knapp's Bay sent two of their youths to Prince of Wales's Fort in the sloop, and the Summer following they were carried back to their friends, loaded with presents, and much pleased with the treatment they received while at the Fort. In 1767, they again sent one from Knapp's Bay and one from Whale Cove; and though during their stay at the Fort they made a considerable progress both in the Southern Indian and the English languages, yet those intercourses have not been any ways advantageous to the Company, by increasing the trade from that quarter. In fact, the only satisfaction they have found for the great expense they have from time to time incurred, by introducing those strangers, is, that through the good conduct of their upper servants at Churchill River, they have at length so far humanized the hearts of those two tribes, that at present they can meet each other in a friendly manner; whereas, a few years since, whenever they met, each party premeditated the destruction of the other; and what made their war more shocking was, they never gave quarter: so that the strongest party always killed the weakest, without sparing either man, woman, or child.

It is but a few years ago that the sloop's crew who annually carried them all their wants, durst not venture on shore among the Esquimaux unarmed, for fear of being murdered; but latterly they are so civilized, that the Company's servants visit their tents with the greatest freedom and safety, are always welcome, and desired to partake of such provisions as they have: and knowing now our aversion from train-oil, they take every means in their power to convince our people that the victuals prepared for them is entirely free from it. But the smell of their tents, cooking-utensils, and other furniture, is scarcely less offensive than Greenland Dock. However, I have eaten both fish and venison cooked by them in so cleanly a manner, that I have relished them very much, and partaken of them with a good appetite.

[[7] Again the tense indicates that Matonabbee was dead when this was written.]

7. The Aztecs
Bernal Díaz

The great Montezuma was about forty years old, of good height, well proportioned, spare and slight, and not very dark, though of the usual Indian complexion. He did not wear his hair long but just over his ears, and he had a short black beard, well-shaped and thin. His face was rather long and cheerful, he had fine eyes, and in his appearance and manner could express geniality or, when necessary, a serious composure. He was very neat and clean, and took a bath every afternoon. He had many women as his mistresses, the daughters of chieftains, but two legitimate wives who were *Caciques* in their own right, and when he had intercourse with any of them it was so secret that only some of his servants knew of it. He was quite free from sodomy. The clothes he wore one day he did not wear again till three or four days later. He had a guard of two hundred chieftains lodged in rooms beside his own, only some of whom were permitted to speak to him. When they entered his presence they were compelled to take off their rich cloaks and put on others of little value. They had to be clean and walk barefoot, with their eyes downcast, for they were not allowed to look him in the face, and as they approached they had to make three obeisances, saying as they did so, 'Lord, my lord, my great lord!' Then, when they had said what they had come to say, he would dismiss them with a few words. They did not turn their backs on him as they went out, but kept their faces towards him and their eyes downcast, only turning round when they had left the room. Another thing I noticed was that when other great chiefs came from distant lands about disputes or on business, they too had to take off their shoes and put on poor cloaks before entering Montezuma's apartments; and they were not allowed to enter the palace immediately but had to linger for a while near the door, since to enter hurriedly was considered disrespectful.

For each meal his servants prepared him more than thirty dishes cooked in their native style, which they put over small earthenware braziers to prevent them from getting cold. They cooked more than three hundred plates of the food the great Montezuma was going to eat, and more than a thousand more for the guard. I have heard that they used to cook him the flesh of young boys. But as he had such a variety of dishes, made of so many different ingredients, we could not tell whether a dish

From Bernal Díaz, *The Conquest of New Spain,* trans. J. M. Cohen, © 1963, J. M. Cohen. Reprinted by permission of Penguin Books Ltd.: pp. 224–231.

was of human flesh or anything else, since every day they cooked fowls, turkeys, pheasants, local partridges, quail, tame and wild duck, venison, wild boar, marsh birds, pigeons, hares and rabbits, also many other kinds of birds and beasts native to their country, so numerous that I cannot quickly name them all. I know for certain, however, that after our Captain spoke against the sacrifice of human beings and the eating of their flesh, Montezuma ordered that it should no longer be served to him.

Let us now turn to the way his meals were served, which was like this. If it was cold, they built a large fire of live coals made by burning the bark of a tree which gave off no smoke. The smell of the bark from which they made these coals was very sweet. In order that he should get no more heat than he wanted, they placed a sort of screen in front of it adorned with the figures of idols worked in gold. He would sit on a soft low stool, which was richly worked. His table, which was also low and decorated in the same way, was covered with white tablecloths and rather long napkins of the same material. Then four very clean and beautiful girls brought water for his hands in one of those deep basins that they call *xicales*.[1] They held others like plates beneath it to catch the water, and brought him towels. Two other women brought him maize-cakes.

When he began his meal they placed in front of him a sort of wooden screen, richly decorated with gold, so that no one should see him eat. Then the four women retired, and four great chieftains, all old men, stood beside him. He talked with them every now and then and asked them questions, and as a great favour he would sometimes offer one of them a dish of whatever tasted best. They say that these were his closest relations and advisers and judges of lawsuits, and if he gave them anything to eat they ate it standing, with deep reverence and without looking in his face.

Montezuma's food was served on Cholula ware, some red and some black. While he was dining, the guards in the adjoining rooms did not dare to speak or make a noise above a whisper. His servants brought him some of every kind of fruit that grew in the country, but he ate very little of it. Sometimes they brought him in cups of pure gold a drink made from the cocoaplant, which they said he took before visiting his wives. We did not take much notice of this at the time, though I saw them bring in a good fifty large jugs of this chocolate, all frothed up, of which he would drink a little. They always served it with great reverence. Sometimes some little humpbacked dwarfs would be present at his meals, whose bodies seemed almost to be broken in the middle. These were his jesters. There were other Indians who told him jokes and must have been his clowns, and others who sang and danced, for Montezuma was very fond of music and entertainment and would reward his entertainers with the leavings of the food and chocolate. The same four women removed the tablecloths and again most reverently brought him water for his hands. Then Montezuma would talk to these four old chieftains about matters that interested him, and they would take their leave with great ceremony. He stayed behind to rest.

As soon as the great Montezuma had dined, all the guards and many more of his household servants ate in their turn. I think more than a thousand plates of food must have been brought in for them, and more than two thousand jugs of chocolate frothed up in the Mexican style, and infinite quantities of fruit, so that with his women and serving-maids and bread-makers and chocolate-makers his expenses must have been considerable.

One thing I had forgotten to say is that two more very handsome women served Montezuma when he was at table with maize-cakes kneaded with eggs and other nourishing ingredients. These maize-cakes were very white, and were brought in on plates covered with clean napkins. They brought him a different kind of bread also, in a long ball kneaded with other kinds of nourishing food, and *pachol* cake, as they call it in that country, which is a kind of wafer. They also placed on the table three tubes, much painted and gilded, in which they put liquidamber[2] mixed with some herbs which are called tobacco. When Montezuma had finished his dinner, and the singing and dancing were over and the cloths had been removed, he would inhale the smoke from one of these tubes. He took very little of it, and then fell asleep.

I remember that at that time his steward was a great *Cacique* whom we nicknamed Tapia, and he kept an account of all the revenue that was brought to Montezuma in his books, which were made of paper—their name for which is *amal*—and he had a great house full of these books. But they have nothing to do with our story.

Montezuma had two houses stocked with every sort of weapon; many of them were richly adorned with gold and precious stones. There were shields large and small, and a sort of broadsword, and two-handed swords set with flint blades that cut much better than our swords, and lances longer than ours, with five-foot blades consisting of many knives. Even when these are driven at a buckler or a shield they are not deflected. In fact they cut like razors, and the Indians can shave their heads with them. They had very good bows and arrows, and double and single-pointed javelins as well as their throwing sticks and many slings and round stones shaped by hand, and another sort of shield that can be rolled up when they are not fighting, so that it does not get in the way, but which can be opened when they need it in battle and covers their bodies from head to foot. There was also a great deal of cotton armour richly worked on the outside with different coloured feathers, which they used as devices and distinguishing marks, and they had casques and helmets made of wood and bone which were also highly decorated with feathers on the outside. They had other arms of different kinds which I will not mention through fear of prolixity, and workmen skilled in the manufacture of such things, and stewards who were in charge of these arms.

Let us pass on to the aviary. I cannot possibly enumerate every kind of bird that was in it or describe its characteristics. There was everything from the royal eagle, smaller kinds of eagles, and other large birds, down to multi-coloured little birds, and those from which they take the fine green feathers they use in their feather-work. These last birds are about the size of our magpies, and here they are called *quetzals.* There were other birds too which have feathers of five colours: green, red, white, yellow, and blue, but I do not know what they are called. Then there were parrots with different coloured plumage, so many of them that I have forgotten their names. There were also beautifully marked ducks, and bigger ones like them. At the proper season they plucked the feathers of all these birds, which then grew again. All of them were bred in this aviary, and at hatching time the men and women who looked after them would place them on their eggs and clean their nests and feed them, giving each breed of birds its proper food.

In the aviary there was a large tank of fresh water, and in it was another type of bird on long stilt-like legs with a red body, wings, and tail. I do not know its name, but in Cuba birds rather like them are called *ypiris.* Also in this tank there were many other kinds of water birds.

Let us go on to another large house where they kept many idols whom they called their fierce gods, and with them all kinds of beasts of prey, tigers and two sorts of lion, and beasts rather like wolves which they call *adives,*[3] and foxes and other small animals, all of them carnivores, and most of them bred there. They were fed on deer, fowls, little dogs, and other creatures which they hunt and also on the bodies of the Indians they sacrificed, as I was told.

I have already described the manner of their sacrifices. They strike open the wretched Indian's chest with flint knives and hastily tear out the palpitating heart which, with the blood, they present to the idols in whose name they have performed the sacrifice. Then they cut off the arms, thighs, and head, eating the arms and thighs at their ceremonial banquets. The head they hang up on a beam, and the body of the sacrificed man is not eaten but given to the beasts of prey. They also had many vipers in this accursed house, and poisonous snakes which have something that sounds like a bell in their tails. These, which are the deadliest snakes of all, they kept in jars and great pottery vessels full of feathers, in which they laid their eggs and reared their young. They were fed on the bodies of sacrificed Indians and the flesh of the dogs that they bred. We know for certain, too, that when they drove us out of Mexico and killed over eight hundred and fifty of our soldiers, they fed those beasts and snakes on their bodies for many days, as I shall relate in due course. These snakes and wild beasts were dedicated to their fierce idols, and kept them company. As for the horrible noise when the lions and tigers roared, and the jackals and foxes howled, and the serpents hissed, it was so appalling that one seemed to be in hell.

I must now speak of the skilled workmen whom Montezuma employed in all the crafts they practised, beginning with the jewellers and workers in silver and gold and various kinds of hollowed objects, which excited the admiration of our great silversmiths at home. Many of the best of them lived in a town called Atzcapotzalco, three miles from Mexico. There were other skilled craftsmen who worked with precious stones and *chalchihuites*, and specialists in feather-work, and very fine painters and carvers. We can form some judgement of what they did then from what we can see of their work today. There are three Indians now living in the city of Mexico, named Marcos de Aquino, Juan de la Cruz, and El Crespillo, who are such magnificent painters and carvers that, had they lived in the age of the Apelles of old, or of Michael Angelo, or Berruguete in our own day, they would be counted in the same rank.

Let us go on to the women, the weavers and seamstresses, who made such a huge quantity of fine robes with very elaborate feather designs. These things were generally brought from some towns in the province of Cotaxtla, which is on the north coast, quite near San Juan de Ulua. In Montezuma's own palaces very fine cloths were woven by those chieftains' daughters whom he kept as mistresses; and the daughters of other dignitaries, who lived in a kind of retirement like nuns in some houses close to the great *cue* of Huichilobos, wore robes entirely of featherwork. Out of devotion for that god and a female deity who was said to preside over marriage, their fathers would place them in religious retirement until they found husbands. They would then take them out to be married.

Now to speak of the great number of performers whom Montezuma kept to entertain him. There were dancers and stilt-walkers, and some who seemed to fly as they leapt through the air, and men rather like clowns to make him laugh. There was a whole quarter full of these people who had no other occupation. He had as many workmen as he needed, too, stonecutters, masons, and carpenters, to keep his houses in repair.

We must not forget the gardens with their many varieties of flowers and sweet-scented trees planted in order and their ponds and tanks of fresh water into which a stream flowed at one end and out of which it flowed at the other, and the baths he had there, and the variety of small birds that nested in the branches, and the medicinal and useful herbs that grew there. His gardens were a wonderful sight, and required many gardeners to take care of them. Everything was built of stone and plastered; baths and walks and closets and rooms like summerhouses where they danced and sang. There was so much to see in these gardens, as everywhere else, that we could not tire of contemplating his great riches and the large number of skilled Indians employed in the many crafts they practised.

When we had already been in Mexico for four days, and neither our Captain nor anyone else had left our quarters except to visit these houses and gardens, Cortes said it would be a good thing to visit the large square of Tlatelolco and see the great *cue* of Huichilobos. So he sent Aguilar, Doña Marina, and his own young page Orteguilla, who by now knew something of the language, to ask for Montezuma's approval of this plan. On receiving his request, the prince replied that we were welcome to go, but for fear that we might offer some offence to his idols he would himself accompany us with many of his chieftains. Leaving the palace in his fine litter, when he had gone about half way, he dismounted beside some shrines, since he considered it an insult to his gods to visit their dwelling in a litter. Some of the great chieftains then supported him by the arms, and his principal vassals walked before him, carrying two staves, like sceptres raised on high as a sign that the great Montezuma was approaching. When riding in his litter he had carried a rod, partly of gold and partly of wood, held up like a wand of justice. The prince now climbed the steps of the great *cue,* escorted by many *papas,* and began to burn incense and perform other ceremonies for Huichilobos.

Notes

[1] Gourds.

[2] The gum of a native tree.

[3] Bernal Díaz is mistaken here. This is an Arabic word for jackal, quite commonly used in Spain.

8. The Guanches
Alexander von Humboldt

A short time after the discovery of America, when Spain was at the highest degree of its splendor, the gentle character of the Guanches was the fashionable topic, as we chaunt in our times the Arcadian innocence of the inhabitants of Otaheite. In both these pictures, the coloring is more gaudy than appropriate. When nations, wearied with mental enjoyments, behold nothing in the refinement of manners but the germe of depravity, they are flattered with the idea, that in some distant region, in the first dawn of civilization, infant societies enjoy pure and perpetual felicity. To this sentiment Tacitus owed a part of his success, when he sketched for the Romans, subjects of the Caesars, the picture of the manners of the inhabitants of Germany. The same sentiment gives an ineffable charm to the narrative of those travellers, who, at the close of the last century, visited the islands of the Pacific Ocean.

The inhabitants of those islands, too much vaunted, though heretofore anthropophagi, resemble, under more than one point of view, the Guanches of Teneriffe. We see both nations groaning under the yoke of feudal government. Among the Guanches this institution, which facilitates and renders a state of warfare perpetual, was sanctioned by religion. The priests declared to the people, "The great Spirit, Achaman, created first the nobles, the *achimenceys,* to whom he distributed all the goats, that exist on the face of the Earth. After the nobles, Achaman created the plebeians, *achicaxnas.* This younger race had the boldness to petition also for goats; but the supreme being answered, that this race was destined to serve the nobles, and that they had need of no property." This tradition was made, no doubt, to please the rich vassals of the shepherd kings. Thus the *faycan,* or high priest, exercised the right of conferring nobility; and the law of the Guanches expressed, that every achimencey, who degraded himself by milking a goat with his own hands, lost his title to nobility. This law does not remind us of the simplicity of the Homeric age. We are astonished to see the useful labours of agriculture, and of a pastoral life, exposed to contempt at the very dawn of civilization.

From Alexander von Humboldt and Aime Bonpland, *Personal Narrative of Travels to the Equinoctial Regions of the New Continent During 1799–1804,* trans. Helen Maria Williams, 1966. Reprinted by permission of AMS Press, Inc.: vol. 2, pp. 175–183.

The Guanches, famed for their tall stature, were the Patagonians of the old world; and historians exaggerated the muscular force of the Guanches, as, previous to the voyage of Bougainville and Cordoba, a colossal form was conferred on the tribe, that inhabited the southern extremity of America. I never saw Guanche mummies but in the cabinets of Europe; at the period of my journey, they were very scarce; a considerable number, however, might be found, if miners were employed to open the sepulchral caverns, which are cut in the rock on the eastern slope of the Peak, between Arico and Guimar. These mummies are in a state of desiccation so singular, that whole bodies, with their integuments, frequently do not weigh above six or seven pounds; or a third less than the skeleton of an individual of the same size, recently striped of the muscular flesh. The conformation of the scull has some slight resemblance to that of the white race of the ancient Egyptians; and the incisive teeth of the Guanches are blunted, like those in the mummies found on the banks of the Nile. But this form of the teeth is owing to art alone; and on examining more carefully the physiognomy of the ancient Canarians, able anatomists[1] have recognised in the cheek bones, and the lower jaw, perceptible differences from the Egyptian mummies. On opening those of the Guanches, remains of aromatic plants are discovered, among which the chenopodium ambrosioïdes is constantly perceived: the corpses are often decorated with small laces, to which are hung little discs of baked earth, that appear to have served as numerical signs, and resemble the *quippoes* of the Peruvians, the Mexicans, and the Chinese.

As the population of islands is in general less exposed to the effect of migrations than that of continents, we may presume, that, in the time of the Carthaginians and the Greeks, the Archipelago of the Canaries was inhabited by the same race of men, as were found by the Norman and Spanish conquerors. The only monument that can throw some light on the origin of the Guanches is their language; but unhappily there are not above a hundred and fifty words remaining, several of which express the same object, according to the dialect of the different islanders. Independent of these words, which have been carefully noted, there are still some valuable fragments existing in the names of a great number of hamlets, hills, and valleys. The Guanches, like the Biscayans, the Hindoos, the Peruvians, and all the primitive nations, had named the places after the quality of the soil they cultivated, the shape of the rocks, the caverns that gave them shelter, and the nature of the tree that overshadowed the springs.

It has been long imagined, that the language of the Guanches had no analogy with the living tongues: but since the travels of Hornemann, and the ingenious researches of Marsden and Venturi, have drawn the attention of the learned to the Berbers, who like the Sarmatic tribes, occupy an immense extent of country in the north of Africa, we find, that several Guanche words have common roots with words of the Chilha and Gebali dialects.[2] We shall cite for instance the words:

Heaven,	*in Guanche* —	Tigo;	*in Berberic,*		Tigot.
Milk	·	· Aho;	·	·	Acho.
Barley	·	· Temasen	·	·	Tomzeen.
Basket	·	· Carianas	·	·	Carin.
Water	·	· Aenum	·	·	Anan.

I doubt whether this analogy is a proof of a common origin; but it is an indication of the ancient connexion between the Guanches and Berbers, a tribe of mountaineers, in which the Numidians, the Getuli, and the Garamanti are confounded, and who extend themselves from the eastern extremity of Atlas by Harutsch and Fezzan, as far as the Oasis of Siwah and Augela. The natives of the Canary Islands called themselves Guanches from *guan*, man; as the Tonguese call themselves *bye* and *donki*, which have the same signification as *guan*. Besides, the nations who speak the Berberic language are not all of the same race; and the description, which Scylax gives in his Periplus of the inhabitants of Cerne, a shepherd people of a tall stature and long hair, reminds us of the features which characterise the Canary Guanches.

The greater attention we give to the study of languages in a philosophical point of view, the more we must observe, that no one of them is entirely distinct; the language of the Guanches[3] would appear still less so, had we any data respecting its mechanism and grammatical construction; two elements more important than the form of words, and the identity of sounds. It is the same with certain idioms, as with those organized beings, that seem to shrink from all classification in the series of natural families. Their isolated state is only so in appearance; for it ceases, when, on embracing a greater number of objects, we come to discover the intermediate links. The learned, who find Egyptians wherever there are mummies, hieroglyphics, or pyramids, will imagine, perhaps, that the race of Typhon was united to the Guanches by the Berbers, real Atlantics, to whom belong the Tibboes and the Tuarycks of the Desert[4]; but it is sufficient here to observe, that this hypothesis is supported by no analogy[5] between the Berberic and Coptic languages, which are justly considered as a remnant of the ancient Egyptian.

The people who succeeded the Guanches descended from the Spaniards, and in a less degree from the Normans. Though these two races have been exposed during three centuries past to the same climate, the latter is distinguished by a whiter skin. The descendants of the Normans inhabit the valley of Teganana, between Punta de Naga and Punta de Hidalgo. The names of Grandville and Dampierre are still pretty common in this district. The Canarians are a moral, sober, and religious people; of a less industrious character at home, than in foreign countries. A roving and enterprising disposition leads these islanders, like the Biscayans and Catalonians, to the Philippines, to the Marian islands, to America, and wherever there are Spanish settlements, from Chili and la Plata to New-Mexico. To them we are in a great measure indebted for the progress of agriculture in those colonies. The whole Archipelago does not contain 160,000 inhabitants, and the *Islennos* are perhaps more numerous in the new continent, than in their own country.

Notes

[1] *Blumenbach, Decas quinta Collect. suc Craniorum diversarum Gentium illustr.* 1808, p. 7.

[2] Adelung und Vater, Mithridates, t. iii, p. 60.

[3] According to the researches of Mr. Vater, the Guanche language offers the following analogies with the languages of nations very remote from each other: *dog* among the American Hurons, *aguienon;* among the Guanches *aguyan; man,* among the Puruvians, *cari;* among the Guanches, *coran; king,* among the African Mandingoes, *monso;* among the Guanches, *monsey.* The name of the island of Gomera is found in that of Gomer, which designates a tribe of Berbers (*Vater, Untersuch. ueber Amerika,* p. 170). The Guanche words *Alcorac, God,* and *almogaron, temple,* seem to be of Arabic origin; at least in the latter tongue *almoharram* signifies *sacred.*

[4] Voyage de Hornemann du Cairo à Mourzouk, t. ii, p. 406.

[5] Mithridates, t. iii. p. 77.

9. The Aborigines
Thomas Jefferson

When the first effectual settlement of our colony was made, which was in 1607, the country from the sea-coast to the mountains, and from the Potomac to the most southern waters of James' river, was occupied by upwards of forty different tribes of Indians. Of these the *Powhatans,* the *Mannahoacs,* and *Monacans,* were the most powerful. Those between the seacoast and falls of the rivers, were in amity with one another, and attached to the *Powhatans* as their link of union. Those between the falls of the rivers and the mountains, were divided into two confederacies; the tribes inhabiting the head waters of Potomac and Rappahannock, being attached to the *Mannahoacs;* and those on the upper parts of James' river to the *Monacans.* But the *Monacans* and their friends were in amity with the *Mannahoacs* and their friends, and waged joint and perpetual war against the *Powhatans.* We are told that the *Powhatans, Mannahoacs,* and *Monacans,* spoke languages so radically different, that interpreters were necessary when they transacted business. Hence we may conjecture, that this was not the case between all the tribes, and, probably, that each spoke the language of the nation to which it was attached; which we know to have been the case in many particular instances. Very possibly there may have been anciently three different stocks, each of which multiplying in a long course of time, had separated into so many little societies. This practice results from the circumstance of their having never submitted themselves to any laws, any coercive power, any shadow of government. Their only controls are their manners, and that moral sense of right and wrong, which, like the sense of tasting and feeling in every man, makes a part of his nature. An offence against these is punished by contempt, by exclusion from society, or, where the case is serious, as that of murder, by the individuals whom it concerns. Imperfect as this species of coercion may seem, crimes are very rare among them; insomuch that were it made a question, whether no law, as among the savage Americans, or too much law, as among the civilized Europeans, submits man to the greatest evil, one who has seen both conditions of existence would pronounce it to be the last; and that the sheep are happier of themselves, than under care of the wolves. It will be said, that

From Thomas Jefferson, *Notes on the State of Virginia,* introduction by T. P. Abernethy, Harper Torchbooks, 1964. Reprinted by permission of Harper & Row, Publishers: pp. 92–97.

great societies cannot exist without government. The savages, therefore, break them into small ones.

The territories of the *Powhatan* confederacy, south of the Potomac, comprehended about eight thousand square miles, thirty tribes, and two thousand four hundred warriors. Captain Smith tells us, that within sixty miles of Jamestown were five thousand people, of whom one thousand five hundred were warriors. From this we find the proportion of their warriors to their whole inhabitants, was as three to ten. The *Powhatan* confederacy, then, would consist of about eight thousand inhabitants, which was one for every square mile; being about the twentieth part of our present population in the same territory, and the hundredth of that of the British islands.

Besides these were the *Nottoways,* living on Nottoway river, the *Meherrins* and *Tuteloes* on Meherrin river, who were connected with the Indians of Carolina, probably with the Chowanocs.

The preceding table contains a state of these several tribes, according to their confederacies and geographical situation, with their numbers when we first became acquainted with them, where these numbers are known. The numbers of some of them are again stated as they were in the year 1669, when an attempt was made by assembly to enumerate them. Probably the enumeration is imperfect, and in some measure conjectural, and that a farther search into the records would furnish many more particulars. What would be the melancholy sequel of their history, may, however, be argued from the census of 1669; by which we discover that the tribes therein enumerated were, in the space of sixty-two years, reduced to about one-third of their former numbers. Spirituous liquors, the small-pox, war, and an abridgement of territory to a people who lived principally on the spontaneous productions of nature, had committed terrible havoc among them, which generation, under the obstacles opposed to it among them, was not likely to make good. That the lands of this country were taken from them by conquest, is not so general a truth as is supposed. I find in our historians and records, repeated proofs of purchase, which cover a considerable part of the lower country; and many more would doubtless be found on further search. The upper country, we know, has been acquired altogether by purchases made in the most unexceptionable form.

Westward of all these tribes, beyond the mountains, and extending to the great lakes, were the *Maffawomees,* a most powerful confederacy, who harassed unremittingly the *Powhatans* and *Manahoacs.* These were probably the ancestors of tribes known at present by the name of the *Six Nations.*

Very little can now be discovered of the subsequent history of these tribes severally. The *Chickahominies* removed about the year 1661, to Mattapony river. Their chief, with one from each of the Pamunkies and

Table 1. The Indians Established

North

	Mannahoacs				*Powhatans*					
			Cf.	Warr's				Warriors		
	Tribes	Country	Towns	1669	Tribes	Country	Chief Towns	1607	1669	
					Tauxenents	Fairfax	About Gen. Washing- [ton's	40		By the name of Mat- chotics, U. Matchodic, Nanzaticos, Nanzatico, Appoma- tox, Matox
					Patówomekes	Stafford, King George	Pawtomac cr.	200		
Between Patowmac and Rappahannoc	Whonkenties	Fauquier			Cuttatawomans	King George	About Lamb creek	20	60	
	Tegninaties	Culpepper			Pissasecs	King George, Richmond	Above Leeds Town	. .		
	Ontponies	Orange			Onaumanients	Westmoreland	Nomony river	100		
	Tauxitanians	Fauquier			Rappahànocs	Richmond co.	Rappahanoc creek	100	30	
	Hassinungaes	Culpepper			Moàughtacunds	Lancaster, Richmond	Moratico river	80	40	
					Secacaconies	Northumberland	Coan river	30		By the name of Totus- keys
					Wighcocòmicoes	Northumberland	Wicocomico river	130	70	
					Cuttatawomans	Lancaster	Corotoman	30		
					Nantaughtacunds	Essex. Caroline	Port Tobacco creek	150	60	
Between Rappahannoc & York	Stegarakies	Orange			Màttapoments	Mattapony river	. . . .	30	20	
	Shackakonies	Spotsylvania			Pamùnkies	King William	Romuncock	300	50	
	Manahoacs	Stafford			Wérowocòmicos	Gloucester	About Rosewell [by.	40		
		Spotsylvania			Payànkatonks	Piankatank river	Turk's Ferry. Grimes-	55		
					Youghtanunds	Pamunkey river	. . . .	60		
	Monacans				Chickahòminies	Chickahominy r.	Orapaks	250	60	
					Powhatàns	Henrico	Powhatan Mayo's	40	10	
	Monacans	James river above the falls	Fork of James river		Arrowhàtocs	Henrico	Arrohatocs	30		
					Wèanocs	Charles city	Weynoke	100	15	
Between York and James				30	Paspahèghes	Charles city, James city	Sandy-Point	40		
	Monasiccapan- oes	Louisa			Chiskiacs	York	Chiskiac	45	15	1699
		Fluvanna			Kecoughtáns	Elizabeth city	Roscows	20		
					Appamàttocs	Chesterfield	Bermuda Hundred	60	50	Nottoways . .
	Monahassanoes	Bedford			Quiocohànoes	Surry	About Upp. Chipoak	25	3 Po- hics	Meherrics 90
Between James & Carolina		Buckingham			Wàrrasqueaks	Isle of Wight	Warrasqueoc	. .		Tuteloes 50
	Massinacacs	Cumberland			Nasamónds	Nansamond	A't mouth W. branch	200	45	
	Mohemenchoes	Powhatan			Chèsapeaks	Princess Anne	About Lynhaven riv.	100		
Eastern shore					Accohanocs	Accom, Northhampton	Occohanoc river	40		
					Accomàcks	Northhampton	About Cheriton's	80		

West

East

South

Mattaponies, attended the treaty of Albany in 1685. This seems to have been the last chapter in their history. They retained, however, their separate name so late as 1705, and were at length blended with the Pamunkies and Mattaponies, and exist at present only under their names. There remain of the *Mattaponies* three or four men only, and have more negro than Indian blood in them. They have lost their language, have reduced themselves, by voluntary sales, to about fifty acres of land, which lie on the river of their own name, and have from time to time, been joining the Pamunkies, from whom they are distant but ten miles. The *Pamunkies* are reduced to about ten or twelve men, tolerably pure from mixture with other colors. The older ones among them preserve their language in a small degree, which are the last vestiges on earth, as far as we know, of the Powhatan language. They have about three hundred acres of very fertile land, on Pamunkey river, so encompassed by water that a gate shuts in the whole. Of the *Nottoways,* not a male is left. A few women constitute the remains of that tribe. They are seated on Nottoway river, in Southampton country, on very fertile lands. At a very early period, certain lands were marked out and appropriated to these tribes, and were kept from encroachment by the authority of the laws. They have usually had trustees appointed, whose duty was to watch over their interests, and guard them from insult and injury.

The *Monacans* and their friends, better known latterly by the name of *Tuscaroras,* were probably connected with the Massawomecs, or Five Nations. For though we are[1] told their languages were so different that the intervention of interpreters was necessary between them, yet do we also[2] learn that the Erigas, a nation formerly inhabiting on the Ohio, were of the same original stock with the Five Nations, and that they partook also of the Tuscarora language. Their dialects might, by long separation, have become so unlike as to be unintelligible to one another. We know that in 1712, the Five Nations received the Tuscaroras into their confederacy, and made them the Sixth Nation. They received the Meherrins and Tuteloes also into their protection; and it is most probable, that the remains of many other of the tribes, of whom we find no particular account, retired westwardly in like manner, and were incorporated with one or the other of the western tribes.

I know of no such thing existing as an Indian monument; for I would not honor with that name arrow points, stone hatchets, stone pipes, and half-shapen images. Of labor on the large scale, I think there is no remain as respectable as would be a common ditch for the draining of lands; unless indeed it would be the barrows, of which many are to be found all over this country. These are of different sizes, some of them constructed of earth, and some of loose stones. That they were repositories of the dead, has been obvious to all; but on what particular occasion constructed, was a matter of doubt. Some have thought they covered the bones of those who have fallen in battles fought on the spot of interment. Some ascribed them to the custom, said to prevail among the Indians, of collecting, at certain periods, the bones of all their dead, wheresoever deposited at the time of death. Others again supposed them the general sepulchres for towns, conjectured to have been on or near these grounds; and this opinion was supported by the quality of the lands in which they are found, (those constructed of earth being generally in the softest and most fertile meadow-grounds on river sides,) and by a tradition, said to be handed down from the aboriginal Indians, that, when they settled in a town, the first person who died was placed erect, and earth put about him, so as to cover and support him; that when another died, a narrow passage was dug to the first, the second reclined against him, and the cover of earth replaced, and so on. There being one of these in my neighborhood, I wished to satisfy myself whether any, and which of these opinions were just. For this purpose I determined to open and examine it thoroughly. It was situated on the low grounds of the Rivanna, about two miles above its principal fork, and opposite to some hills, on which had been an Indian town. It was of a spheroidical form, of about forty feet diameter at the base, and had been of about twelve feet altitude, though now reduced by the plough to seven and a half, having been under cultivation about a dozen years. Before this it was covered with trees of twelve inches diameter, and round the base was an excavation of five feet depth and width, from whence the earth had been taken of which the hillock was formed. I first dug superficially in several parts of it, and came to collections of human bones, at different depths, from six inches to three feet below the surface. These were lying in the utmost confusion, some vertical, some oblique, some horizontal, and directed to every point of the compass, entangled and held together in clusters by the earth. Bones of the most distant parts were found together, as, for instance, the small bones of the foot in the hollow of a scull; many sculls would sometimes be in contact, lying on the face, on the side, on the back, top or bottom, so as, on the whole, to give the idea of bones emptied promiscuously from a bag or a basket, and covered over with earth, without any attention to their order. The bones of which the greatest numbers remained, were sculls, jaw-bones, teeth, the bones of the arms, thighs, legs, feet and hands. A few ribs remained, some vertebrae of the neck and spine, without their processes, and one instance only of the[3] bone which serves as a base to the vertebral column. The sculls were so tender, that they generally fell to pieces on being touched. The other bones were stronger. There were some teeth which were judged to be smaller than those of an adult; a scull, which on a slight view, appeared to be that of an infant, but it fell to pieces on being taken out, so as to prevent satisfactory examination; a rib, and a fragment of the underjaw of a person about half grown; another rib of an infant; and a part of the jaw of a child, which had not cut its teeth. This last furnishing the most decisive proof of the burial of children here, I was particular in my attention to it. It was part of the right half of the under-jaw. The processes, by which it was attenuated to the temporal bones, were entire, and the bone itself firm to where it had been broken off, which, as nearly as I could judge, was about the place of the eye-tooth. Its upper edge, wherein would have been the sockets of the teeth, was perfectly smooth. Measuring it with that of an adult, by placing their hinder processes together, its broken end extended to the penultimate grinder of the adult. This bone was white, all the others of a sand color. The bones of infants being soft, they probably decay sooner, which might be the cause so few were found here. I proceeded then to make a perpendicular cut through the body of the barrow, that I might examine its internal structure. This passed about three feet from its centre, was opened to the former surface of the earth, and was wide enough for a man to walk through and examine its sides. At the bottom, that is, on the level of the circumjacent plain, I found bones; above these a few stones, brought from a cliff a quarter of a mile off, and from the river one-eighth of a mile off; then a large interval of earth, then a stratum of bones, and so on. At one end of the section were four strata of bones plainly distinguishable; at the other, three; the strata in one part not ranging with those in another. The bones nearest the surface were least decayed. No holes were discovered in any of them, as if made with bullets, arrows, or other weapons. I conjectured that in this barrow might have been a thousand skeletons. Every one will readily seize the circumstances above related, which militate against the opinion, that it covered the bones only of persons fallen in battle; and against the tradition also, which would make it the common sepulchre of a town, in which the bodies were placed upright, and touching each other. Appearances certainly indicate that it has derived both origin and growth from the accustomary collection of bones, and deposition of them together; that the first collection had been deposited on the common surface of the earth, a few stones put over it, and then a covering of earth, that the second had been laid on this, had covered more or less of it in proportion to the number of bones, and was then also covered with earth; and so on. The following are the particular circumstances which give it this aspect. 1. The number of bones. 2. Their confused position. 3. Their being in different strata. 4. The strata in one part having no correspondence with those in another. 5. The different states of decay in these strata, which seem to indicate a difference in the time of inhumation. 6. The existence of infant bones among them.

But on whatever occasion they may have been made, they are of considerable notoriety among the Indians; for a party passing, about thirty years ago, through the part of the country where this barrow is, went through the woods directly to it, without any instructions or inquiry, and having staid about it for some time, with expressions which were construed to be those of sorrow, they returned to the high road, which they had left about half a dozen miles to pay this visit, and pursued their journey. There is another barrow much resembling this, in the low grounds of the south branch of Shenandoah, where it is crossed by the road leading from the Rockfish gap to Staunton. Both of these have, within these dozen years, been cleared of their trees and put under cultivation, are much reduced in their height, and spread in width, by the plough, and will probably disappear in time. Ther is another on a hill in the Blue Ridge of mountains, a few miles north of Wood's gap, which is made up of small stones thrown together. This has been opened and found to contain human bones, as the others do. There are also many others in other parts of the country.

Great question has arisen from whence came those aboriginals of America? Discoveries, long ago made, were sufficient to show that the passage from Europe to America was always practicable, even to the imperfect navigation of ancient times. In going from Norway to Iceland, from Iceland to Greenland, from Greenland to Labrador, the first traject is the widest; and this having been practised from the earliest times of which we have any account of that part of the earth, it is not difficult to suppose that the subsequent trajects may have been sometimes passed. Again, the late discoveries of Captain Cook, coasting from Kamschatka to California, have proved that if the two continents of Asia and America be separated at all, it is only by a narrow strait. So that from this side also, inhabitants may have passed into America; and the resemblance between the Indians of America and the eastern inhabitants of Asia, would induce us to conjecture, that the former are the descendants of the latter, or the latter of the former; excepting indeed the Esquimaux, who, from the same circumstance of resemblance, and from identity of language must be derived from the Greenlanders, and these probably from some of the northern parts of the old continent. A knowledge of their several languages would be the most certain evidence of their derivation which could be produced. In fact, it is the best proof of the affinity of nations which ever can be referred to. How many ages have elapsed since the English, the Dutch, the Germans, the Swiss, the Norwegians, Danes and Swedes have separated from their common stock? Yet how many more must elapse before the proofs of their common origin, which exist in their several languages, will disappear? It is to be lamented then, very much to be lamented, that we have suffered so many of the Indian tribes already to extinguish, without our having previously collected and deposited in the records of literature, the general rudiments at least of the languages they spoke. Were vocabularies formed of all the languages spoken in North and South America, preserving their appellations of the most common objects in nature, of those which must be present to every nation barbarous or civilized, with the inflections of their nouns and verbs, their principles of regimen and concord, and these deposited in all the public libraries, it would furnish opportunities to those skilled in the languages of the old world to compare them with these, now, or at any future time, and hence to construct the best evidence of the derivation of this part of the human race.

But imperfect as is our knowledge of the tongues spoken in America, it suffices to discover the following remarkable fact: Arranging them under the radical ones to which they may be palpably traced, and doing the same by those of the red men of Asia, there will be found probably twenty in America, for one in Asia, of those radical languages, so called because if they were ever the same they have lost all resemblance to one another. A separation into dialects may be the work of a few ages only, but for two dialects to recede from one another till they have lost all vestiges of their common origin, must require an immense course of time; perhaps not less than many people give to the age of the earth. A greater number of those radical changes of language having taken place among the red men of America, proves them of greater antiquity than those of Asia.

I will now proceed to state the nations and numbers of the Aborigines which still exist in a respectable and independent form. And as their undefined boundaries would render it difficult to specify those only which may be within any certain limits, and it may not be unacceptable to present a more general view of them, I will reduce within the form of a catalogue all those within, and circumjacent to, the United States, whose names and numbers have come to my notice. These are taken from four different lists, the first of which was given in the year 1759 to General Stanwix by George Croghan, deputy agent for Indian affairs under Sir William Johnson; the second was drawn up by a French trader of considerable note, resident among the Indians many years, and annexed to Colonel Bouquet's printed account of his expedition in 1764. The third was made out by Captain Hutchins, who visited most of the tribes, by order, for the purpose of learning their numbers, in 1768; and the fourth by John Dodge, an Indian trader, in 1779, except the numbers marked, which are from other information.

Notes

[1] Smith.
[2] Evans.
[3] The os sacrum.

10. On Cannibals
Michel de Montaigne*

Having surveyed, during his invasion of Italy, the marshalling of the army that the Romans had set out against him, King Pyrrhus remarked: 'I do not know what barbarians these are'—for so the Greeks called all foreign nations—'but the ordering of the army before me has nothing barbarous about it.' The Greeks said the same of the forces with which Flaminius invaded their country; and Philip also, when from a little hill he saw the orderly arrangement of the Roman camp, set up in his kingdom under Publius Sulpicius Galba. We see from this how chary we must be of subscribing to vulgar opinions; we should judge them by the test of reason and not by common report.

I had with me for a long time a man who had lived ten or twelve years in that other world which has been discovered in our time, in the place where Villegaignon landed,[1] and which he called Antarctic France. This discovery of so vast a country seems to me worth reflecting on. I should not care to pledge myself that another may not be discovered in the future, since so many greater men than we have been wrong about this one. I am afraid that our eyes are bigger than our stomachs, and that we have more curiosity than understanding. We grasp at everything, but catch nothing except wind.

Plato interpolates a story told by Solon, and learnt by him from the priests of Sais in Egypt, to the effect that there was, long ago before the Deluge, a great island called Atlantis, right at the mouth of the Straits of Gibraltar, which contained more land than Asia and Africa put together. The kings of that country not only possessed the island, but had extended so far on to the mainland that they held the whole breadth of Africa as far as Egypt, and the length of Europe as far as Tuscany. They proposed to push on into Asia, and conquer all the nations on the Mediterranean shores as far as the Black Sea, and therefore crossed Spain, Gaul, and Italy, on their way to Greece, where they were halted by the Athenians.

* Montaigne originally intended, as already noted, to print la Boétie's treatise on Voluntary Servitude. But this, as he says, had already appeared in a collection of Huguenot pamphlets. He therefore substituted, in the editions of the *Essays* published in his lifetime, 29 Sonnets by la Boétie. But when these were printed in 1588 in a collection of la Boétie's works, Montaigne crossed them out in his own copy. They once formed the greater part of Chapter 27.

But some time later both the Athenians, and they and their island, were swallowed up by the Deluge.

It is very probable that this immense inundation made strange alterations in the inhabited earth, by which it is thought that the sea cut Sicily off from Italy.

Haec loca, vi quondam et vasta convulsa ruina,
dissiluisse ferunt, cum protinus utraque tellus
una foret;[2]

Cyprus from Syria, and the isle of Euboea from the mainland of Boeotia; and that elsewhere it united lands that were once separate, filling the straits between them with sand and mud,

sterilisque diu palus aptaque remis
vicinas urbes alit, et grave sentit aratrum.[3]

But it is not very probable that the new world we have lately discovered is, in fact, that island. For it almost touched Spain, and it would have been an incredible effect of an inundation to have pushed it back where it is, more than twelve hundred leagues away. Besides, recent voyages have made it almost certain that it is not an island, but a mainland, which connects with the East Indies on one side, and with the lands that lie beneath the two poles on the others; or, if it is divided from them, it is by so narrow a strait or distance that it is not entitled to be called an island.

It would seem that there are movements, some natural and some feverish, in these great bodies, as in our own. When I consider the encroachment that my own river, the Dordogne, is making at present on its right bank, and that in twenty years it had gained so much, undermining the foundations of several buildings, I clearly see that this disturbance is no ordinary one. For if it had always done so at this rate or were always to do so, the face of the world would be totally transformed. But rivers are subject to changes; sometimes they overflow one bank, and sometimes the other; and sometimes they keep to their channels. I am not speaking of sudden floods, of which the causes are clear to us. In Médoc, beside the sea, my brother, the Sieur d'Arsac, sees one of his estates being swallowed up by the sand that the sea is throwing up on it. The roofs of some buildings are still visible, but his rents and property have been transformed into very poor pasture. The inhabitants say that for some time the sea has been advancing on them so hard that they have lost four leagues of land. These sands are her outriders; we see great piles of moving dunes marching half a league before her, and occupying the land.

The other testimony from antiquity with which some would connect this discovery is in Aristotle—at least if the little book *On Unheard-of*

Wonders is his. He there relates that certain Carthaginians, after sailing for a very long time through the Straits of Gibraltar out into the Atlantic Sea, finally discovered a large fertile island, well covered with woods and watered by broad deep rivers. It was very far from any mainland, but they, and others after them, attracted by the goodness and fertility of the soil, went there with their wives and children, and there settled. When the rulers of Carthage saw their country being gradually depopulated, they expressly forbade any more of their people to go there, under pain of death; and they drove the new inhabitants out, fearing, it is said, that in course of time they might so multiply as to supplant themselves and ruin the state of Carthage. This tale of Aristotle's relates no more closely to our new lands than Plato's.

This man who stayed with me was a plain, simple fellow, and men of this sort are likely to give true testimony. Men of intelligence notice more things and view them more carefully, but they comment on them; and to establish and substantiate their interpretation, they cannot refrain from altering the facts a little. They never present things just as they are but twist and disguise them to conform to the point of view from which they have seen them; and to gain credence for their opinion and make it attractive, they do not mind adding something of their own, or extending and amplifying. We need either a very truthful man, or one so ignorant that he has no material with which to construct false theories and make them credible: a man wedded to no idea. My man was like that; and besides he has on various occasions brought me seamen and merchants whom he met on his voyage. Therefore I am satisfied with his information, and do not inquire what the cosmographers say about it.

We need topographers to give us exact descriptions of the places where they have been. But because they have this advantage over us, that they have seen the Holy Land, they claim the additional privilege of telling us news about all the rest of the world. I would have everyone write about what he knows and no more than he knows, not only on this, but on all other subjects. One man may have some special knowledge at first-hand about the character of a river or a spring, who otherwise knows only what everyone else knows. Yet to give currency to this shred of information, he will undertake to write on the whole science of physics. From this fault many great troubles spring.

Now, to return to my argument, I do not believe, from what I have been told about this people, that there is anything barbarous or savage about them, except that we all call barbarous anything that is contrary to our own habits. Indeed we seem to have no other criterion of truth and reason than the type and kind of opinions and customs current in the land where we live. There we always see the perfect religion, the perfect political system, the perfect and most accomplished way of doing everything. These people are wild in the same way as we say that fruits are wild, when nature has produced them by herself and in her ordinary way; whereas, in fact, it is those that we have artificially modified, and removed from the common order, that we ought to call wild. In the former, the true, most useful, and natural virtues and properties are alive and vigorous; in the latter we have bastardized them, and adapted them only to the gratification of our corrupt taste. Nevertheless, there is a special savour and delicacy in some of the uncultivated fruits of those regions that is excellent even to our taste, and rivals our own. It is not reasonable that art should win the honours from our great and mighty mother nature. We have so loaded the riches and beauty of her works with our inventions that we have altogether stifled her. Yet, wherever she shines forth in her purity, she makes our vain and trivial enterprises marvellously shameful.

> *Et veniunt ederae sponte sua melius,*
> *surgit et in solis formosior arbutus antris,*
> *et volucres nulla dulcius arte canunt.*[4]

With all our efforts we cannot imitate the nest of the very smallest bird, its structure, its beauty, or the suitability of its form, nor even the web of the lowly spider. All things, said Plato, are produced either by nature, or by chance, or by art; the greatest and most beautiful by one or other of the first two, the least and most imperfect by the last.

These nations, then, seem to me barbarous in the sense that they have received very little moulding from the human intelligence, and are still very close to their original simplicity. They are still governed by natural laws and very little corrupted by our own. They are in such a state of purity that it sometimes saddens me to think we did not learn of them earlier, at a time when there were men who were better able to appreciate them than we. I am sorry that Lycurgus and Plato did not know them, for I think that what we have seen of these people with our own eyes surpasses not only the pictures with which poets have illustrated the golden age, and all their attempts to draw mankind in the state of happiness, but the ideas and the very aspirations of philosophers as well. They could not imagine an innocence as pure and simple as we have actually seen; nor could they believe that our society might be maintained with so little artificiality and human organization.

This is a nation, I should say to Plato, in which there is no kind of commerce, no knowledge of letters, no science of numbers, no title of magistrate or of political superior, no habit of service, riches or poverty, no contracts, no inheritance, no divisions of property, only leisurely occupations, no respect for any kinship but the common ties, no clothes, no agriculture, no metals, no use of corn or wine. The very words denoting lying, treason, deceit, greed, envy, slander, and forgiveness have never been heard. How far from such perfection would he find the republic that he imagined: 'men fresh from the hands of the gods.'[5]

Hos natura modos primum dedit.[6]

For the rest, they live in a land with a very pleasant and temperate climate, and consequently, as my witnesses inform me, a sick person is a rare sight; and they assure me that they never saw anyone palsied or blear-eyed, toothless or bent with age These people inhabit the seashore, and are shut in on the landward side by a range of high mountains, which leave a strip about a hundred leagues in depth between them and the sea. They have a great abundance of fish and meat which bear no resemblance to ours, and they eat them plainly cooked, without any other preparation. The first man who brought a horse there, although he had made friends with them on some earlier voyages, so terrified them when in the saddle that they shot him to death with arrows before recognizing him.

Their buildings are very long and capable of holding two or three hundred people. They are covered with strips of bark from tall trees, tethered at one end of the ground and attached at the other for mutual support to the roof beam, after the manner of some of our barns whose roofing comes down to the ground and serves for side walls. They have a wood so hard that they can cut with it, and make it into swords and grills to roast their meat. Their beds are of woven cotton, hung from the roof like those on our ships; and each has his own, for the women sleep apart from their husbands. They get up with the sun, and immediately after rising they eat for the whole day, for they have no other meal. They do not drink at the same time, but like some Eastern peoples described by Suidas, always apart from their meals. They drink several times a day, and a great deal. Their beverage is made of some root, and is of the colour of our red wine. They drink it only warm, and it will not keep for more than two or three days. It is rather sharp in taste, not at all heady, good for the stomach, and laxative to those who are not used to it; it is a very pleasant drink to those who are. Instead of bread they use a white stuff like preserved coriander, which I have tasted; the flavour is sweetish and rather insipid.

They spend the whole day dancing. Their young men go hunting after wild beasts with bows and arrows. Some of their women employ themselves in the meantime with the warming of their drink, which is their principal duty. In the morning, before they begin to eat, one of their old men preaches to the whole barnful, walking from one end to the other, and repeating the same phrase many times, until he has completed the round—for the buildings are quite a hundred yards long. He enjoins only two things upon them: valour against the enemy and love for their wives. And he never fails to stress this obligation with the refrain that it is they who keep their drink warm and well-seasoned for them.

There may be seen in a number of places, including my own house, examples of their beds, of their ropes, of their wooden swords, of the wooden bracelets with which they protect their wrists in battle, and of the great canes, open at one end, which they sound to beat time for their dancing. They are close-shaven all over, and perform the operation much more cleanly than we, with only a razor of wood or stone. They believe in the immortality of the soul, and that those who have deserved well of the gods have their abode in that part of the sky where the sun rises; and those who are damned in the West.

They have some sort of priests and prophets, who very seldom appear among the people, but have their dwelling in the mountains. When they come, a great festival and solemn assembly of several villages is held. Each of these barns which I have decribed forms a village, and they are about one French league apart. The prophet speaks to them in public, exhorting them to virtue and to do their duty. But their whole ethical teaching contains only two articles; resolution in battle and affection for their wives. He prophesies things to come, and tells them what outcome to expect from their enterprises; he encourages them to war, or dissuades them from it; but all this with the proviso that should he make a false prophecy, or should things not turn out for them according to his predictions, they will cut him into a thousand pieces if he is caught, and condemn him as a false prophet. For this reason, one of them who has made a miscalculation is never seen again.

Divination is a gift of God. Therefore its abuse should be treated as a punishable imposture. Among the Scythians, when diviners failed in their predictions, they were laid, bound hand and foot, in a little ox-drawn cart filled with brushwood, and there burned. Those who undertake matters that depend only on the human capacities for guidance, are to be excused if they merely do their best. But these others who come deluding us with pretensions to some extraordinary faculty beyond our understanding should surely be punished for their bold impostures, when they fail to carry out their promises.

They have their wars against the people who live further inland, on the other side of the mountains; and they go to them quite naked, with no other arms but their bows or their wooden swords, pointed at one end like the heads of our boar-spears. It is remarkable with what obstinacy they fight their battles, which never end without great slaughter and bloodshed. As for flight and terror, they do not know what they are. Every man brings home for a trophy the head of an enemy he has killed, and hangs it over the entrance of his dwelling. After treating a prisoner well for a long time, and giving him every attention he can think of, his captor assembles a great company of his acquaintances. He then ties a rope to one of the prisoner's arms, holding him by the other end, at some yards' distance for fear of being hit, and gives his best friend the man's other arm, to be held in the same way; and these two, in front of the whole assembly, despatch him with their swords. This done, they roast him, eat him all together, and send portions to their absent friends. They do not do this, as might be supposed, for nourishment as the ancient Scythians did, but as a measure of extreme vengeance. The proof of this is that when they saw the Portuguese, who had allied themselves with their enemies, inflicting a different sort of death on their prisoners—which was to bury them to the waist, to shoot the rest of their bodies full of arrows, and then to hang them—they concluded that these people from another world who had spread the knowledge of so many wickednesses among their neighbours, and were much more skilled than they in all sorts of evil, did not choose this form of revenge without a reason. So, thinking that it must be more painful than their own, they began to give up their old practice and follow this new one.

I am not so anxious that we should note the horrible savagery of these acts as concerned that, whilst judging their faults so correctly, we should be so blind to our own. I consider it more barbarous to eat a man alive than to eat him dead; to tear by rack and torture a body still full of feeling, to roast it by degrees, and then give it to be trampled and eaten by dogs and swine—a practice which we have not only read about but seen within recent memory, not between ancient enemies, but between neighbours and fellow-citizens and, what is worse, under the cloak of piety and religion—than to roast and eat a man after he is dead. Chrysippus and Zeno, the heads of the Stoic sect, did indeed consider that there was no harm in using a dead body for any need of our own, or in consuming it either, as our own ancestors did during Caesar's blockade of the city of Alexia, when they resolved to relieve the hunger of the siege with the bodies of the old men, women, and other persons who were incapable of fighting.

Vascones, fama est, alimentis talibus usi
produxere animas.[7]

Physicians, too, are not afraid to use a corpse in any way that serves our health, and will apply it either internally or externally. But no man's brain has yet been found so disordered as to excuse treachery, disloyalty, tyranny, and cruelty, which are our common faults.

We are justified therefore in calling these people barbarians by reference to the laws of reason, but not in comparison with ourselves, who surpass them in every kind of barbarity. Their fighting is entirely noble and disinterested. It is as excusable, and beautiful too, as is compatible with this disease of humanity, their only motive for war being the desire to display their valour. They do not strive for conquest of new territories since their own still possess such natural fertility as to yield them all their necessities without labour or trouble, in such abundance that they have no need to extend their borders. They are still at the happy stage of desiring no more than their simple appetites demand; everything beyond that is to them a superfluity.

If of the same age they generally call one another brothers; those who are younger are called children, and the old men are fathers to all the rest. They leave to their heirs the undivided possession of their property, to be held in common, with no other title than the plain one which nature bestows on her creatures when she brings them into the world. If their neighbours cross the mountains to attack them and win a victory over them, the victors gain nothing but glory, and the advantage of a proved superiority in valour and virtue. For the rest, they have no use for the possessions of the conquered, and so return to their country, where they are not short of any necessity, nor yet of that great gift of knowing how to enjoy their happy condition in perfect content. The seaboard peoples do the same. They ask no ransom of their prisoners but only the confession and acknowledgement that they have been beaten: but there has never been one, in a whole century, who has not chosen death rather than yield, either by word or behaviour, one single jot of their magnificent and invincible courage; not one of them has ever been known who has not preferred to be killed and eaten rather than beg to be spared. Prisoners are treated with all liberality so that their lives may be the more dear to them, and are usually plied with threats of their imminent death. They are reminded of the tortures that they are to suffer, of the preparations then being made to that end, of the lopping off of their limbs, and of the feast that will be held at their expense. All this is done solely in order to extort from their lips some weak or despondent word, or to rouse in them a desire to escape; its only purpose is to gain the advantage of having frightened them and shaken their constancy. For, properly understood, a true victory rests on that point alone,

victoria nulla est
quam quae confessos animo quoque subjugat hostes.[8]

The Hungarians of old, who were very bellicose fighters, never pursued their advantage further once they had brought their enemy to ask for mercy. Having once extorted this admission from them, they let them go unhurt and without any ransom, compelling them, at the most, to give their word never to bear arms against them again.

Many of the advantages that we gain over our enemies are only borrowed advantages, not truly ours. To have stouter legs and arms is the quality of a porter, not a sign of valour; skill is a dead and physical possession; it is a stroke of luck that causes our enemy to stumble or his eyes to be dazzled by the sunlight; it is a trick of art and science that makes one who may easily be cowardly and worthless into a nimbler fencer. A man's value and reputation depend on his heart and his resolution; there his true honour lies. Valour is strength, not of leg or arm, but of the heart and soul; it lies not in the goodness of our horse or our weapons, but in our own. He who falls with a firm courage, 'will, though fallen, fight on his knees.'[9] The man who yields no jot to his steadfastness for any threat of imminent death, who, as he yields up his soul, still gazes on his enemy with a firm and disdainful eye, is beaten not by us but by fortune; he is killed but he is not vanquished. The most valiant are sometimes the most unfortunate.

There are defeats, therefore, that are as splendid as victories. Never did those four sister triumphs of Salamis, Plataea, Mycale, and Sicily—the fairest on which the sun ever gazed—dare to oppose all their combined glories to the glorious defeat of King Leonidas and his men at the pass of Thermopylae.

What captain ever rushed with a more glorious and ambitious desire to win a battle than did Ischolas to lose one?[10] Who in all the world took more ingenious pains to ensure his safety than he for his own destruction? He was instructed to defend a certain Peloponnesian pass against the Arcadians. Finding that the nature of the place and the inferior numbers of his forces made it quite impossible for him to do so, he concluded that all who confronted the enemy must inevitably fall where they stood. On the other hand, he thought it unworthy of his own courage and noble spirit, and of the Lacedaemonian name, to fail in his charge. So between these two extremes he took a middle course, which was this: the youngest and most active of his troops he reserved for the defence and service of their country, and sent them back. Then, with those whose loss would be least felt, he decided to defend the pass, and by their death to make the enemy purchase his passage at the highest possible price. Thus it fell out. For soon they were hedged in on every side by the Arcadians; and after making a great slaughter he and his men were all put to the sword. Is there any trophy which is a victor's due that was not more truly earned by these men in their defeat? The true victory lies in battle rather than in survival; the prize of valour in fighting, not in winning.

To return to our narrative, these prisoners are so far from giving in, whatever their treatment, that all through these two or three months of their captivity they show a cheerful face, and urge their masters to be quick in putting them to the test. They defy them, insult them, and reproach them with cowardice, counting over the number of battles in which their own people have defeated them. I have a ballad made by one prisoner in which he tauntingly invites his captors to come boldly forward, every one of them, and dine off him, for they will then be eating their own fathers and grandfathers, who have served as food and nourishment to his body. 'These muscles,' he says, 'this flesh, and these veins are yours, poor fools that you are! Can you not see that the substance of your ancestors' limbs is still in them? Taste them carefully, and you will find the flavour is that of your own flesh.' A shaft of wit that by no means savours of barbarism. Those who tell us how they die, and describe their executions, depict the prisoner spitting in the faces of his killers and grimacing defiantly. In fact, up to their last gasp they never cease to brave and defy them with word and gesture. Here are men who compared with us are savages indeed. They must be so, indubitably, if we are not, for there is an amazing difference between their characters and ours.

Their men have many wives; the higher their reputation for valour the larger the number; and one very beautiful thing about their marriages is that whereas our wives anxiously keep us from enjoying the friendship and kindliness of other women, their wives are equally anxious to procure just those favours for their husbands. Being more concerned for the honour of their men than for anything else, they take pains to find and keep as many companions as they can, in as much as this is a testimony to their husband's worth.

Our wives will exclaim that this is a miracle. It is not. It is a proper marital virtue, but of the highest order. And in the Bible Leah, Rachel, Sarah, and Jacob's wives[11] gave their beautiful handmaidens to their husbands; Livia too aided Augustus in his passions, to her own disadvantage; and Stratonice, the wife of King Deiotarus, not only lent her husband a very beautiful young servant-maid of hers as a concubine, but carefully brought up the children he had by her, and supported them in their claim to their father's estates.

It should not be supposed that all this is done out of simple and servile bondage to common usage, or under weight of the authority of their ancient customs, without reflection or judgement. The minds of this people are not so dull that they cannot take another course; and to prove this I will give some examples of their capabilities. In addition to the verse I have just quoted from one of their war-songs, I have another, a love-song, which begins like this: 'Adder, stay. Stay, adder, so that my sister may follow the pattern of your markings, to make and embroider a fine girdle for me to give to my beloved. So shall your beauty and markings be preferred for ever above all other serpents.' This first verse forms the refrain of the song. Now I have enough acquaintance with poetry to form this judgement: that far from there being anything barbaric in its conception, it is quite Anacreontic. Their language, moreover, is a soft one, and has a pleasant sound; it is much like Greek in its terminations.

Not knowing how costly a knowledge of this country's corruptions will one day be to their happiness and repose, and that from intercourse with us will come their ruin—which, I suppose, is far advanced already—three men of their nation—poor fellows to allow themselves to be deluded by the desire for things unknown, and to leave the softness of their own skies to come and gaze at ours—were at Rouen at the time when the late King Charles the Ninth visited the place. The King talked with them for some time; they were shown our way of living, our magnificence, and the sights of a fine city. Then someone[12] asked them what they thought about all this, and what they had found most remarkable. They mentioned three things, of which I am sorry to say I have forgotten the third. But I still remember the other two. They said that in the first place they found it very strange that so many tall, bearded men, all strong and well armed, who were around the King—they probably meant the Swiss of his guard—should be willing to obey a child, rather than choose one of their own number to command them. Secondly—they have a way in their language of speaking of men as halves of one another—that they had noticed among us some men gorged to the full with things of every sort while their other halves were beggars at their doors, emaciated with hunger and poverty. They found it strange that these poverty-stricken halves should suffer such injustice, and that they did not take the others by the throat or set fire to their houses.

I talked to one of them for some time; but I had an interpreter who followed my meaning so badly, and was so hindered by stupidity from grasping my ideas, that I could hardly get any satisfaction from him. When I asked the visitor what advantage he gained by his superior position among his own people—for he was a captain and our sailors called him the king—he said, the privilege of marching first into battle. And by how many men was he followed? He pointed to a piece of ground, to indicate that they were as many as would fill a space of that size. It might have been four or five thousand. And when there was no war, did all his authority cease? He answered that it remained, and that when he visited the villages that depended upon him, paths were cleared for him through their thickets, so that he could travel at his ease. All this does not seem too bad. But then, they do not wear breeches.

Notes

[1] Brazil.

[2] 'They say that these lands were once violently rent by a great convulsion. Until then the two lands were one.' Virgil, *Aeneid,* III, 414.

[3] 'Long a sterile marsh, on which men rowed, it now feeds the neighbouring towns and feels the weight of the plough.' Horace, *Ars Poetica,* 65.

[4] 'The ivy grows best when it grow wild, and the arbutus is most lovely when it grows in some solitary cleft; birds sing most sweetly untaught.' Propertius, I, ii, 10.

[5] Seneca, *Letters,* XC.

[6] 'These are the first laws that nature gave.' Virgil, *Georgics,* II, 20.

[7] 'They say that the Gascons prolonged their lives with such food.' Juvenal, xv, 93.

[8] 'There is no victory, except when the enemy in his own mind acknowledges himself beaten.' Claudian, *On the Sixth Consulate of Honorius,* 248 (adapted).

[9] Seneca, *On Providence,* II.

[10] See Diodorus Siculus, xv, 64.

[11] Jacob's wives were Leah and Rachel; Montaigne seems to be confused.

[12] Montaigne himself.

11. The American Aborigines

William Robertson

Almost two centuries elapsed after the discovery of America, before the manners of its inhabitants attracted, in any considerable degree, the attention of philosophers. At length they discovered, that the contemplation of the condition and character of the Americans in their original state, tended to complete our knowledge of the human species, might enable us to fill up a considerable chasm in the history of its progress, and lead to speculations no less curious than important. They entered upon this new field of study with great ardour; but, instead of throwing light upon the subject, they have contributed, in some degree, to involve it in additional obscurity. Too impatient to inquire, they hastened to decide; and began to erect systems, when they should have been searching for facts on which to establish their foundations. Struck with the appearance of degeneracy in the human species throughout the New World, and astonished at beholding a vast continent occupied by a naked, feeble, and ignorant race of men, some authors of great name have maintained, that this part of the globe had but lately emerged from the sea, and become fit for the residence of man; that every thing in it bore marks of a recent original; and that its inhabitants, lately called into existence, and still at the beginning of their career, were unworthy to be compared with the people of a more ancient and improved continent.[1] Others have imagined, that, under the influence of an unkindly climate, which checks and enervates the principle of life, man never attained in America the perfection which belongs to his nature, but remained an animal of an inferior order, defective in the vigour of his bodily frame, and destitute of sensibility, as well as of force, in the operations of his mind.[2] In opposition to both these, other philosophers have supposed that man arrives at his highest dignity and excellence long before he reaches a state of refinement; and, in the rude simplicity of savage life, displays an elevation of sentiment, and independence of mind, and a warmth of attachment, for which it is vain to search among the members of polished societies.[3] They seem to consider that as the most perfect state of man which is the least civilized. They describe the manners of the rude Americans with such rapture, as if they proposed them for models to the rest of

From William Robertson, *The History of America*, 1777, pp. 1–21.

the species. These contradictory theories have been proposed with equal confidence, and uncommon powers of genius and eloquence have been exerted, in order to clothe them with an appearance of truth.

As all those circumstances concur in rendering an inquiry into the state of the rude nations in America intricate and obscure, it is necessary to carry it on with caution. When guided in our researches by the intelligent observations of the few philosophers who have visited this part of the globe, we may venture to decide. When obliged to have recourse to the superficial remarks of vulgar travellers, of sailors, traders, buccaneers, and missionaries, we must often pause, and, comparing detached facts, endeavour to discover what they wanted sagacity to observe. Without indulging conjecture, or betraying a propensity to either system, we must study with equal care to avoid the extremes of extravagant admiration, or of supercilious contempt, for those manners which we describe.

In order to conduct this inquiry with greater accuracy, it should be rendered as simple as possible. Man existed as an individual before he became the member of a community; and the qualities which belong to him under his former capacity should be known, before we proceed to examine those which arise from the latter relation. This is peculiarly necessary in investigating the manners of rude nations. Their political union is so incomplete, their civil institutions and regulations so few, so simple, and of such slender authority, that men in this state ought to be viewed rather as independent agents, than as members of a regular society. The character of a savage results almost entirely from his sentiments or feelings as an individual, and is but little influenced by his imperfect subjection to government and order. I shall conduct my researches concerning the manners of the Americans in this natural order, proceeding gradually from what is simple to what is more complicated.

I shall consider, I. The bodily constitution of the Americans in those regions now under review. II. The qualities of their minds. III. Their domestic state. IV. Their political state and institutions. V. Their system of war, and public security. VI. The arts with which they were acquainted. VII. Their religious ideas and institutions. VIII. Such singular detached customs as are not reducible to any of the former heads. IX. I shall conclude with a general review and estimate of their virtues and defects.

I. The bodily constitution of the Americans.—The human body is less affected by climate than that of any other animal. Some animals are confined to a particular region of the globe, and cannot exist beyond it; others, though they may be brought to bear the injuries of a climate foreign to them, cease to multiply when carried out of that district which Nature destined to be their mansion. Even such as seem capable of being naturalized in various climates, feel the effect of every remove from their proper station, and gradually dwindle and degenerate from the vigor and perfection peculiar to their species. Man is the only living creature whose frame is at once so hardy and so flexible, that he can spread over the whole earth, become the inhabitant of every region, and thrive and multiply under every climate. Subject, however, to the general law of nature, the human body is not entirely exempt from the operation of climate; and when exposed to the extremes either of heat or cold, its size or vigour diminishes.

The first appearance of the inhabitants of the New World, filled the discoverers with such astonishment, that they were apt to imagine them a race of men different from those of the other hemisphere. Their complexion is of a reddish brown, nearly resembling the colour of copper.[4] The hair of their heads is always black, long, coarse, and uncurled. They have no beard, and every part of their body is perfectly smooth. Their persons are of a full size, extremely straight and well proportioned[5]. Their features are regular, though often distorted by absurd endeavours to improve the beauty of their natural form, or to render their aspect more dreadful to their enemies. In the islands, where four-footed animals were both few and small, and the earth yielded her productions almost spontaneously, the constitution of the natives, neither braced by the active exercises of the chase, nor invigorated by the labour of cultivation, was extremely feeble and languid. On the continent, where the forests abound with game of various kinds, and the chief occupation of many tribes was to pursue it, the human frame acquired greater firmness. Still, however, the Americans were more remarkable for agility than strength. They resembled beasts of prey, rather than animals formed for labour.[6] They were not only averse to toil, but incapable of it; and when roused by force from their native indolence, and compelled to work, they sunk under tasks which the people of the other continent would have performed with ease.[7] This feebleness of constitution was universal among the inhabitants of those regions in America which we are surveying, and may be considered as characteristic of the species there.[8]

The beardless countenance and smooth skin of the American, seems to indicate a defect of vigour, occasioned by some vice in his frame. He is destitute of one sign of manhood and of strength. This peculiarity, by which the inhabitants of the New World are distinguished from the people of all other nations, cannot be attributed, as some travellers have supposed, to their mode of subsistence.[9] For though the food of many Americans be extremely insipid, as they are altogether unacquainted with the use of salt, rude tribes in other parts of the earth have subsisted on aliments equally simple, with out this mark of degradation, or any apparent symptom of a diminution in their vigour.

As the external form of the Americans leads us to suspect that there is some natural debility in their frame, the smallness of their appetite for food has been mentioned by many authors as a confirmation of this suspicion. The quantity of food which men consume varies according to the temperature of the climate in which they live, the degree of activity which they exert, and the natural vigour of their constitutions. Under the enervating heat of the torrid zone, and when men pass their days in indolence and ease, they require less nourishment than the active inhabitants of temperate or cold countries. But neither the warmth of their climate, nor their extreme laziness, will account for the uncommon defect of appetite among the Americans. The Spaniards were astonished with observing this, not only in the islands, but in several parts of the continent. The constitutional temperance of the natives far exceeded, in their opinion, the abstinence of the most mortified hermits[10]; while, on the other hand, the appetite of the Spaniards appeared to the Americans insatiably voracious; and they affirmed, that one Spaniard devoured more food in a day than was sufficient for ten Americans.[11]

A proof of some feebleness in their frame, still more striking, is the insensibility of the Americans to the charms of beauty, and the power of love. That passion, which was destined to perpetuate life, to be the bond of social union, and the source of tenderness and joy, is the most ardent in the human breast. Though the perils and hardships of the savage state, though excessive fatigue, on some occasions, and the difficulty at all times of procuring subsistence, may seem to be adverse to this passion, and to have a tendency to abate its vigour, yet the rudest nations in every other part of the globe seem to feel its influence more powerfully than the inhabitants of the New World. The negro glows with all the warmth of desire natural to his climate; and the most uncultivated Asiatics discover that sensibility, which, from their situation on the globe, we should expect them to have felt. But the Americans are, in an amazing degree, strangers to the force of this first instinct of nature. In every part of the New World the natives treat their women with coldness and indifference. They are neither the objects of that tender attachment which takes place in civilized society, nor of that ardent desire conspicuous among rude nations. Even in climates where this passion usually acquires its greatest vigour, the savage of America views his female with disdain, as an animal of a less noble species. He is at no pains to win her favour by the assiduity of courtship, and still less solicitous to preserve it by indulgence and gentleness.[12] Missionaries themselves, notwithstanding the austerity of monastic ideas, cannot refrain from expressing their astonishment at the dispassionate coldness of the American young men in their intercourse with the other sex.[13] Nor is this reserve to be ascribed to any opinion which they entertain with respect to the merit of female chastity. That is an idea too refined for a savage, and suggested by a delicacy of sentiment and affection to which he is a stranger.

But in inquiries concerning either the bodily or mental qualities of particular races of men, there is not a more common or more seducing error, than that of ascribing to a single cause, those characteristic peculiarities which are the effect of the combined operation of many causes. The climate and soil of America differ, in so many respects, from those of the other hemisphere, and this difference is so obvious and striking, that philosophers of great eminence have laid hold on this as sufficient to account for what is peculiar in the constitution of its inhabitants. They rest on physical causes alone, and consider the feeble frame and languid desire of the Americans, as consequences of the temperament of that portion of the globe which they occupy. But the influences of political and moral causes ought not to have been overlooked. These operate with no less effect than that on which many philosophers rest as a full explanation of the singular appearances which have been mentioned. Wherever the state of society is such as to create many wants and desires, which cannot be satisfied without regular exertions of industry, the body, accustomed to labour, becomes robust, and patient of fatigue. In a more simple state, where the demands of men are so few and so moderate, that they may be gratified, almost without any effort, by the spontaneous productions of nature, the powers of the body are not called forth, nor can they attain their proper strength. The natives of Chili and of North-America, the two temperate regions in the New World, who live by hunting, may be deemed an active and vigorous race, when compared with the inhabitants of the isles, or of those parts of the continent where hardly any labour is requisite to procure subsistence. The exertions of a hunter are not, however, so regular, or so continued, as those of persons employed in the culture of the earth, or in the various arts of civilized life, and though his agility may be greater than theirs, his strength is on the whole inferior. If another direction were given to the active powers of man in the New World, and his force augmented by exercise, he might acquire a degree of vigour which he does not in his present state possess. The truth of this is confirmed by experience. Wherever the Americans have been gradually accustomed to hard labour, their constitutions become robust, and they have been found capable of performing such tasks, as seemed not only to exceed the powers of such a feeble frame as has been deemed peculiar to their country, but to equal any effort of the natives, either of Africa or of Europe.[14]

The same reasoning will apply to what has been observed concerning their slender demand for food. As a proof that this should be ascribed as much to their extreme indolence, and often total want of occupation, as to any thing peculiar in the physical structure of their bodies, it has been observed, that in those districts, where the people of America are obliged to exert any unusual effort of activity in order to procure subsistence, or wherever they are employed in severe labour, their appetite is not inferior to that of other men, and, in some places, it has struck observers as remarkably voracious.[15]

The operation of political and moral causes is still more conspicuous, in modifying the degree of attachment between the sexes. In a state of high civilization, this passion, inflamed by restraint, refined by delicacy, and cherished by fashion, occupies and engrosses the heart. It is no longer a simple instinct of nature; sentiment heightens the ardour of desire, and the most tender emotions of which our frame is susceptible, sooth and agitate the soul. This description, however, applies only to those, who, by their situation, are exempted from the cares and labours of life. Among persons of inferior order, who are doomed by their condition to incessant toil, the dominion of this passion is less violent; their solicitude to procure subsistence, and to provide for the first demand of nature, leaves little leisure for attending to its second call. But if the nature of the intercourse between the sexes varies so much in persons of different rank in polished societies, the condition of man, while he remains uncivilized, must occasion a variation still more apparent. We may well suppose, that amidst the hardships, the dangers, and the simplicity of savage life, where subsistence is always precarious, and often scanty, where men are almost continually engaged in the pursuit of their enemies, or in guarding against their attacks, and where neither dress nor reserve are employed as arts of female allurement, that the attention of the Americans to their women would be extremely feeble, without imputing this solely to any physical defect or degradation in their frame.

It is accordingly observed, that in those countries of America, where, from the fertility of the soil, the mildness of the climate, or some farther advances which the natives have made in improvement, the means of subsistence are more abundant, and the hardships of savage life are less severely felt, the animal passion of the sexes becomes more ardent. Striking examples of this occur among some tribes seated on the banks of great rivers well stored with food, among others who are masters of hunting-grounds abounding so much with game, that they have a regular and plentiful supply of nourishment with little labour. The superior degree of security and affluence which these tribes enjoy, is followed by their natural effects. The passions implanted in the human frame by the hand of Nature acquire additional force; new taste and desires are formed; the women, as they are more valued and admired, become more attentive to dress and ornament; the men, beginning to feel how much of their own happiness depends upon them, no longer disdain the arts of winning their favour and affection. The intercourse of the sexes becomes very different from that which takes place among their ruder countrymen; and as hardly any restraint is imposed on the gratification of desire, either by religion, or laws, or decency, the dissolution of their manners is excessive.[16]

Notwithstanding the feeble make of the Americans, hardly any of them are deformed, or mutilated, or defective in any of their senses. All travellers have been struck with their circumstance, and have celebrated the uniform symmetry and perfection of their external figure. Some authors search for the cause of this appearance in their physical condition. As the parents are not exhausted or over-fatigued with hard labour, they suppose that their children are born vigorous and sound. They imagine, that, in the liberty of savage life, the human body, naked and unconfined from its earliest age, preserves its natural form; and that all its limbs and members acquire a juster proportion, than when fettered with artificial restraints, which stint its growth, and distort its shape.[17] Something, without doubt, may be ascribed to the operation of these causes; but the true reasons of this apparent advantage, which is common to all savage nations, lie deeper, and are closely interwoven with the nature and genius of that state. The infancy of man is so long and so helpless, that it is extremely difficult to rear children among rude nations. Their means of subsistence are not only scanty, but precarious. Such as live by hunting must range over extensive countries, and shift often from place to place. The care of children, as well as every other laborious task, is devolved upon the women. The distresses and hardships of the savage life, which are often such as can hardly be supported by persons in full vigour, must be fatal to those of more tender age. Afraid of undertaking a task so laborious, and of such long duration, as that of rearing their offspring, the women, in some parts of America, procure frequent abortions by the use of certain herbs, and extinguish the first sparks of that life which they are unable to cherish.[18] Sensible that only stout and well-formed children have force of constitution to struggle through such an hard infancy, other nations abandon or destroy such of their progeny as appear feeble or defective, as unworthy of attention.[19] Even when they endeavour to rear all their children without distinction, so great a proportion of the whole number perishes under the rigorous treatment which must be their lot in the savage state, that few of those who laboured under any original frailty attain the age of manhood.[20] Thus, in polished societies, where the means of subsistence are secured with certainty, and acquired with ease; where the talents of the mind are often of more importance than the powers of the body; children are preserved notwithstanding their defects or deformity, and grow up to be useful citizens. In rude nations, such persons are either cut off as soon as they are born, or, becoming a burden to themselves and to the community, cannot long protract their lives. But in those provinces of the New World, where, by the establishment of the Europeans, more regular provision has been made for the subsistence of its inhabitants, and they are restrained from laying violent hands on their children, the Americans are so far from being eminent for any superior perfection in their form, that one should rather suspect some peculiar imbecility in the race, from the extraordinary number of individuals who are deformed, dwarfish, mutilated, blind, or deaf.[21]

How feeble soever the constitution of the Americans may be, it is remarkable, that there is less variety in the human form throughout the New World, than in the ancient continent. When Columbus and the other discoverers first visited the different countries in America which lie within the torrid zone, they naturally expected to find people of the same complexion with those in the corresponding regions of the other hemisphere. To their amazement, however, they discovered that America contained no negroes[22]; and the cause of this singular appearance became as much the object of curiosity, as the fact itself was of wonder. In what part or membrane of the body that humour resides which tinges the complexion of the negro with a deep black, it is the business of anatomists to inquire and describe. The powerful operation of heat appears manifestly to be the cause which produces this striking variety in the human species. All Europe, a great part of Asia, and the temperate countries of Africa, are inhabited by men of a white complexion. All the torrid zone in Africa, some of the warmer regions adjacent to it, and several countries in Asia, are filled with people of a deep black colour. If we survey the nations of our continent, making our progress from cold and temperate countries towards those parts which are exposed to the influence of vehement and unremitting heat, we shall find, that the extreme whiteness of their skin soon begins to diminish; that its colour deepens gradually as we advance; and after passing through all the successive gradations of shade, terminates in an uniform unvarying black. But in America, where the agency of heat is checked and abated by various causes, which I have already explained, the climate seems to be destitute of that force which produces such wonderful effects on the human frame. The colour of the natives of the torrid zone, in America, is hardly of a deeper hue than that of the people in the more temperate parts of their continent. Accurate observers, who had an opportunity of viewing the Americans in very different climates, and in provinces far removed from each other, have been struck with the amazing similarity of their figure and aspect.[23]

But though the hand of nature has deviated so little from one standard in fashioning the human form in America, the creation of fancy hath been various and extravagant. The same fables that were current in the ancient continent, have been revived with respect to the New World, and America too has been peopled with human beings of monstrous and fantastic appearance. The inhabitants of certain provinces were described to be pigmies of three feet high; those of others to be giants of an enormous size. Some travellers published accounts of people with only one eye, others pretended to have discovered men without heads, whose eyes and mouths were planted in their breasts. The variety of Nature in her productions is indeed so great, that it is presumptuous to set bounds to her fertility, and to reject indiscriminately every relation that does not perfectly accord with our own limited observation and experience. But the other extreme, of yielding a hasty assent, on the slightest evidence, to whatever has the appearance of being strange and marvellous, is still more unbecoming a philosophical inquirer, as, in every period, men are more apt to be betrayed into error, by their weakness in believing too much, than by their arrogance in believing too little. In proportion as science extends, and nature is examined with a discerning eye, the wonders which amused ages of ignorance disappear. The tales of credulous travellers concerning America are forgotten; the monsters which they describe have been searched for in vain; and those provinces where they pretend to have found inhabitants of singular forms, are now known to be possessed by people nowise different from the other Americans.

Though those relations may, without discussion, be rejected as fabulous, there are other accounts of varieties in the human species in some parts of the New World, which rest upon better evidence, and merit more attentive examination. This variety has been particularly observed in three different districts. The first of these is situated in the isthmus of Darien, near the centre of America. Lionel Wafer, a traveller possessed of more curiosity and intelligence than we should have expected to find in an associate of Buccaneers, discovered there a race of men, few in number, but of a singular make. They are of low stature, according to his description, of a feeble frame, incapable of enduring fatigue. Their colour is a dead milk white; not resembling that of fair people among Europeans, but without any tincture of a blush or sanguine complexion. Their skin is covered with a fine hairy down of a chalky white, the hair of their heads, their eye brows, and eye-lashes, are of the same hue. Their eyes are of a singular form, and so weak, that they can hardly bear the light of the sun; but they see clearly by moon-light, and are most active and gay in the night.[24] No race similar to this has been discovered in any other part of America. Cortes, indeed, found some persons exactly resembling the white people of Darien, among the rare and monstrous animals which Montezuma had collected.[25] But as the power of the Mexican empire extended to the provinces bordering on the isthmus of Darien, they were probably brought thence. Singular as the appearance of those people may be, they cannot be considered as constituting a distinct species. Among the negroes of Africa, as well as the natives of the Indian islands, nature sometimes produces a small number of individuals, with all the characteristic features and qualities of the white people of Darien. The former are called *Albinos* by the Portuguese, the latter *Kackerlakes* by the Dutch. In Darien, the parents of those *Whites* are of the same colour with the other natives of the country; and this observation applies equally to the anomalous progeny of the negroes and Indians. The same mother who produces some children of a colour that does not belong to the race, brings forth the rest with the complexion peculiar to her country.[26] One conclusion may then be formed with respect to the people described by Wafer, the *Albinos* and the *Kackerlakes;* they are a degenerated breed, not a separate class of men; and from some disease or defect of their parents, the peculiar colour and debility which mark their degradation are transmitted to them. As a decisive proof of this, it has been observed, that neither the white people of Darien, nor the Albinos of Africa, propagate their race; their children are of the colour and temperament peculiar to the natives of their respective countries.[27]

The second district that is occupied by inhabitants differing in appearance from the other people of America, is situated in a high northern latitude, extending from the coast of Labradore towards the pole, as far as the country is habitable. The people scattered over those dreary regions, are known to the Europeans by the name of *Esquimaux.* They themselves, with that idea of their own superiority, which consoles the rudest and most wretched nations, assume the name of *Keralit* or *Men.* They are of a middle size, and robust, with heads of a disproportioned bulk, and feet as remarkably small. Their complexion, though swarthy, by being continually exposed to the rigour of a cold climate, inclines to the European white, rather than to the copper colour of America, and the men have beards which are sometimes bushy and long.[28] From these marks of distinction, as well as from one still less equivocal, the affinity of their language to that of the Greenlanders, which I have already mentioned, we may conclude, with some degree of confidence, that the Esquimaux are a race different from the rest of the Americans.

We cannot decide with equal certainty concerning the inhabitants of the third district, situated at the southern extremity of America. These are the famous *Patagonians,* who, during two centuries and a half, have afforded a subject of controversy to the learned, and an object of wonder to the vulgar. They are supposed to be one of the wandering tribes, which occupy that vast, but least known region of America, which extends from the river De la Plata to the Straits of Magellan. Their proper station is in that part of the interior country which lies on the banks of the river Negro; but in the hunting season they often roam as far as the straits which separate Tierra del Fuego from the main land. The first accounts of this people were brought to Europe by the companions of Magellan,[29] who described them as a gigantic race, above eight feet high, and of strength in proportion to their enormous size. Among several tribes of animals, a disparity in bulk as considerable may be observed. Some large breeds of horses and dogs exceed the more diminutive races in stature and strength, as far as the Patagonian is supposed to rise above the usual standard of the human body. But animals attain the highest perfection of their species only in mild climates, or where they find the most nutritive food in greatest abundance. It is not then in the uncultivated waste of the Magellanic regions, and among a tribe of improvident savages, that we should expect to find man possessing the highest honours of his race, and distinguished by a superiority of size and vigour, far beyond what he has reached in any other part of the earth. The most explicit and unexceptionable evidence is requisite, in order to establish a fact repugnant to those general principles and laws, which seem to affect the human frame in every other instance, and to decide with respect to its nature and qualities. Such evidence has not hitherto been produced. Though several persons to whose testimony great respect is due, have visited this part of America since the time of Magellan, and have had interviews with the natives; though some have affirmed, that such as they saw were of gigantic stature, and others have formed the same conclusion from measuring their footsteps, or from viewing the skeletons of their dead; yet their accounts vary from each other in so many essential points, and are mingled with so many circumstances manifestly false or fabulous, as detract much from their credit. On the other hand, some navigators, and those among the most eminent of their order for discernment and accuracy, have asserted that the natives of Patagonia, with whom they had intercourse, though stout and well-made, are not of such extraordinary size as to be distinguished from the rest of the human species.[30] The existence of this gigantic race of men seems, then, to be one of those points in natural history, with respect to which a cautious inquirer will hesitate, and will choose to suspend his assent until more complete evidence shall decide, whether he ought to admit a fact, seemingly inconsistent with what reason and experience have discovered concerning the structure and condition of man, in all the various situations in which he has been observed.

Notes

[1] M. de Buffon Hist. Nat. iii. 484, &c. ix. 103. 114.

[2] M. de P. Recherches Philos. sur les Ameri. passim.

[3] M. Rousseau.

[4] Oviedo Somario, p. 46, D. Life of Columbus, c. 24.

[5] See Note XLIV.

[6] See Note XLV.

[7] Oviedo Som. p. 51, C. Voy. de Correal, ii, 138. Wafer's Description, p. 131.

[8] Be Las Casas Brev. Relac. p. 4. Torquem, Monar. i. 580. Oviedo Somario, p. 41. Histor. lib. iii. c. 6. Herrera, dec. 1. lib. ix. c. 5. Simon, p. 41.

[9] Charlev. Hist. de Nouv. Fr. iii. 310.

[10] Ramusio, iii. 304, F. 306, A. Simon Conquista, &c. p. 39. Hakluyt, iii. 408, 508.

[11] Herrera, dec. 1. lib. ii. c. 16.

[12] Hennepin Moeurs des Sauvages, 32, &c. Rochefort Hist. des Isles Antilles, p. 461. Voyage de Coreal, ii. 141. Ramusio, iii. 309. F. Lozano Descr. des Gran Chaco,

71. Falkner's Descr. of Patagon. p. 125. Lettere di P. Cataneo ap. Muratori Il Christian. Felice, i. 305.

[13] Chanvalon, p. 51. Lettr. Edif. tom. xxiv. 318. Tertre. p. 377 Venegas, i, 81. Ribas Hist. de los Triumf. p. 11.

[14] See Note XLVI.

[15] Gamilla, ii. 12. 70. 247. Lafitau, i. 515. Ovalle Church, ii. 81. Muratori, i. 295.

[16] Biet. 389. Charlev. iii. 423. Dumont Mem. sur Louisiane, i. 155.

[17] Piso, p. 6.

[18] Ellis's Voyage to Hudson's Bay, 198. Herrera, dec. 7. lib. ix. c. 4.

[19] Gumilla Hist. ii. 234. Techo's Hist. of Paraguay. &c. Churchill's Collect. vi. 108.

[20] Creuxii Hist. Canad. p. 57.

[21] Voyage de Ulloa, i. 232.

[22] P. Martyr, dec. p. 71.

[23] See Note XLVII.

[24] Wafer Descript. of Isth. ap. Dampier, iii. p. 346.

[25] Cortes ap. Ramus. iii. p. 241, E.

[26] Margrav. Hist. Rer. Nat. Bras. lib. viii. c. 4.

[27] Wafer, p. 348. Demaner Hist. de l'Afrique, ii, 234. Recherch Philos. sur les Amer. ii. 1, &c. Note XLVIII.

[28] Ellis Voy. to Huds. Bay, p. 131. 139. De la Potherie, tom. i. p. 79. Wales' Journ. of a Voy. to Churchill River. Phil. Trans. vol. lx. 109.

[29] Falkner's Description of Patagonia, p. 102.

[30] See Note XLIX.

12. The Origin of Language and Society

James Burnet (Lord Monboddo)

In the preceding book, we have placed man in a state of society and of political union, carrying on of common consent, and with joint labour, some work necessary for defence, or the support of life. In this situation, and this only, could language have been invented. But more was necessary for the invention of so difficult an art. And, in the *first* place, the proper organs of pronunciation were indispensably required. These are given to some few animals besides man; but I believe they are in none so perfect.

2dly, They must have been a very long time in this political state; so long at least as to have improved into an art the business they were carrying on; by which I do not mean to require, that they should have been regular artists, knowing the causes and principles of their art, and operating by certain rules which they could demonstrate from those principles; but my meaning is, that they must have improved their rude practice at first into a better practice by observation and experience; and, in that way, have fixed a certain method of doing the thing, which, when it is done by degrees, and from observation and experience, may not improperly be called an art. For, as I have already observed, one of the great differences betwixt instinct and art is, that what is done by instinct, is performed as well at first as at last; whereas art is necessarily formed by gradual improvements. In short, before man could have invented a language, he must have been perhaps for many ages in the same state the beaver is in, as I have described it above. For the beaver, of all the animals we know, that are not, like the Ouran Outangs, of our species, comes the nearest to us in sagacity, and, as I have already observed, appears to have some other principle of action beside instinct; of which there is a proof that I have not mentioned, arising from the form of their

From James Burnet (Lord Monboddo), *On the Origin and Progress of Language.* Facsimile printed by Scolar Press Limited, 1967: pp. 300–312.

huts or cabanes; which, as Mons. Buffon tells us, is not always the same; so that it would appear they have different opinions of things as well as we: whereas instinct performs every thing in the same invariable manner. I am therefore persuaded, that the beaver did, from experience and observation, the old teaching the young, learn the architecture of his dike and his hut, as we have learned our architecture and other arts.

3dly, Another thing absolutely required, as preparatory to the invention of a language, is, that men should previously have formed ideas to be expressed by language: for it is impossible to conceive a language of proper names only without general terms. Now, ideas must have been formed by an animal, such as man, carrying on any common business, and operating, not by instinct, but learning by observation and experience. For such an animal must have an idea of the end for which he acts, and of the means for attaining that end. For, as I have shown, every animal that does not act from instinct, like the bee or the spider, must act with knowledge of the end. Besides, man, in the state in which I have described him, must necessarily have had ideas, however imperfect, of trees and animals, and other objects, with which he was conversant: and he must have had more perfect ideas of the instruments of art which he used; especially if they were of his own invention.

Lastly, It appears to me to have required an extraordinary degree of sagacity, to invent so artificial a thing as speech; nor do I think that there is any animal other than man yet discovered, unless perhaps it be the beaver, that has sagacity enough to have invented it: for however easy the invention may seem, now that it is discovered, and so commonly practised; yet it was truly far from being obvious, but, on the contrary, very far removed from common apprehension. For, in the *first* place, Man, as we have seen, does not naturally form articulate sounds; but, on the contrary, it is a great work of art, difficult to be learned even after it is invented, but infinitely more difficult to be invented. *2dly,* Suppose this first difficulty got over, and articulate sounds invented, it was by no means an obvious thought, to apply them to the expression of ideas, with the greater part of which they have no connection, at least that is easily discovered; for though there be words expressing certain sounds, which are imitations of those sounds, it is certain that by far the greater part of words are not natural signs of ideas. And how is it possible they should? for what natural connection is there betwixt the idea of a tree, *ex. gr.* the earth, the sun, the moon, and any articulation of sound? And indeed the making ideas in this way *audible,* appears to me to have been full as great a refinement of art, as the so-much-boasted discovery of making sounds *visible,* I mean the invention of alphabetical characters; and so much the more wonderful, that it was invented in a much earlier age of mankind. And it must appear still more wonderful when we consider, that it is not the only method of communication, and therefore not absolutely necessary for the purposes of political life; but that there are other methods, as we have seen, which in great part answer those purposes, and with which, accordingly, other animals that live in the political state, as well as man, remained satisfied. Of these other methods we are now to speak more particularly, in order to try whether from these we cannot trace the progress to the invention of language.

The only ways that I can think of by which men could communicate together, before the invention of speech, are four: *first, Inarticulate cries,* expressive of sentiments and passions; *2dly, Gestures,* and the expression of the countenance; *3dly, Imitative sounds,* by which audible things may be expressed; and, *lastly, Painting,* by which visible objects may be represented. The two first are common to us with the brutes; the two last are peculiar to man; and all the four may be said to be *natural* signs of what they express; for even the connection betwixt inarticulate cries and the things expressed by them, though it appear to be the most remote, is so established in nature, that it is understood by every animal, without any previous compact or agreement.

Of those inarticulate cries there is a very great variety; and it is really surprising how many different passions, such as love, joy, anger, grief, fear, the brutes express by them; and I am persuaded the nearer the economy of any of them comes to ours, the greater variety will be found in their cries, because they have the more to express by them. The Russian academicians say, that the *sea-cat* above mentioned, which has so much of human nature in it, can low like a cow, growl like a bear, and chirp like a cricket, which last is a song of triumph after he has vanquished his enemy[1]; and if the beaver living in a social state was accurately observed, there would be found a great variety of this kind of language among them! When the brutes are tamed, and become familiar with us, they acquire voices and tones that they had not before. Thus Porphyry the philosopher tells us, that his partridge learned to converse with him in a voice very different from what she used in communication with her fellows[2]; and some of them, as it is well known, may be taught to articulate. But it is evident, that all this variety of cries, though it were much greater than it really is, would not answer the purposes of human life, when it came to be enlarged and extended to many different arts and occupations, which the growing wants of men render necessary.

The *next* kind of expression I mentioned was that of *looks* and *gestures,* which is also very strong, and various among the brutes, and it is a language which they perfectly well understand. The only use they make of it is to express their passions and feelings; but we know certainly, from the example of dumb persons among us, that it may be used to express ideas; and we learn from history, that they may be expressed in this language with the utmost accuracy and precision; for in Rome there was an art of this kind formed, called the *pantomime* art, which was brought to the utmost perfection about the time of Augustus Caesar.[3] An artist of this kind could express by signs, not only every sentiment and passion of the human mind, but every idea, with as great accuracy; and as great variety too, as any orator could do by words; and it is a noted story of Roscius the player in Rome, that he used to contend with Cicero, which of them could express the same thing, he by looks and gestures, or Cicero by words, with the greatest variety and copiousness.

There can be no doubt but that, before the invention of language, this kind of expression, as well as the other by inarticulate cries, would be much used. That savage nation which Diodorus Siculus, in the passage I quoted before, calls the *Insensibles,* conversed in no other way; and the savages in North America do at this day supply the defects of their language by a great deal of action and gesticulation. But it is impossible to suppose, that this art of speaking to the eyes could be brought to such perfection among savages as it was by Roscius at Rome, or by the pantomimes in after times, who *danced* whole theatrical pieces, according to the expression in ancient language; that is, represented them by gestures and movements performed to music, without one word being uttered.[4] Even in Greece, where all the other arts of pleasure and entertainment were cultivated, and brought to the highest degree of perfection, the art of the pantomime was not carried so far as in Rome. For although their players did no doubt express a great deal by their action, particularly in the movements of their choruses, and their monodies, there was no such thing, so far as I can learn, practised among them as dancing a whole piece, or even acting a single monody, without speaking; at least not in the better days of Greece. For in the later times it is not improbable that they may have adopted the pantomimes of the Romans; and Lucian appears to me to speak of it as an entertainment among the Greeks in his time.[5]

So far from being brought to this state of perfection among savages in the first stage of humanity, I am persuaded it would not go the length of serving the purposes of common intercourse, where there was any number of wants to be supplied by mutual assistance: or if we could make so wild a supposition, as that it would be carried to the same degree of perfection as in the polite age of Augustus, still it is in sundry respects far inferior to the method of communication by speech; for, first, it speaks only to the eyes, so that it can be of no use but in the light; and then we cannot converse in that way at such a distance as by words, which alone makes it a very improper vehicle of our thoughts in carrying on any business without doors, such as fishing and hunting, which are the chief occupations of savages.

The *third* method of communication I mentioned was by *imitative* or *mimic sounds,* which, I doubt not, was practised before the invention of language, as it has been since; but the expression of it could not go any great length; no farther than to denote sounds, or objects which were distinguished by particular sounds, such as beasts and birds of different kinds.

As to the *last* method I mentioned, *painting,* or delineating any object by drawing the figure of it, it may have been used before the invention of language; but it could go no farther than to communicate the notion of visible objects; and, besides, it is of slow and difficult practice, and not at all of so ready use as language.

Of these four ways of communication, it is plain, that only two have any connection with language, viz. inarticulate cries and imitative sounds, which are both modifications of the human voice, as well as language, and could alone lead the way to the invention of language. And we are now to inquire, whether, from one or other, or both of these, that invention can be traced.

Notes

1 *History of Kamschatka,* p. 128.

2 See before, *book* I. p. 136.

3 *See Lucian,* πєρὶ ὀρχωσεως.

4 Before the Romans had pantomimes, their actors, such as Roscius, played certain parts in dumb show. Those parts were the monodies, or *cantica,* as the Latins call them, which were soliloquies spoken *in recitativo* to music. In such parts of the play the actor among the Romans only gesticulated, and expressed the sense by his action, that is, *danced,* as they called it, while another *sung,* or pronounced the words to music: so that it was only in the *diverbium* or dialogue that the Roman actor used his voice. How this strange custom of dividing the acting and speaking, such as never was practised in any other nation, so far I as know, came to be introduced among the Romans, Livy has informed us, *lib.* 7. p. 2.

5 I have often wondered, that Horace, in his epistle to Augustus, where he flatters that prince so much as to compare the arts of Rome in his time to the arts of Greece, in these lines,

Venimus ad summum fortuna; pingimus, atoue
Psallimus, et luctamur Achivis doctius unctis

does not mention this *pantomime* art, which I believe was the only one in which the Romans of those days excelled the Greeks. And this perhaps was one of the reasons which made the people of Rome so passionately fond of it: for as to painting and music, mentioned by Horace, I cannot believe that there was the least degree of comparison betwixt those arts, as practised in Rome, and as practised in Greece, and particularly painting; for, so far as I know, the Romans never produced one good painter or statuary. And with respect to wrestling; as the first *palastra* in Rome was, as I remember, no earlier than the days of Augustus Caesar, I think it is hardly possible that the Romans should all of a sudden have become such expert wrestlers. As therefore he flatters Augustus so much at the expense of truth, I can assign no reason why he omitted this pantomime art, in which he might have truly said the Romans excelled the Greeks, except that he did not esteem it, either as a useful art, which it certainly is not among persons who can understand one another by language, or of any natural grace and beauty. And indeed it appears from what Lucian says in his dialogue upon dancing, that the men of gravity and correct taste condemned this mimical representation, as fit only for the lower sort of people.

13. Of Laws in Relation to the Nature of the Climate

Baron de Montesquieu

1 General Idea

If it be true that the temper of the mind and the passions of the heart are extremely different in different climates, the laws ought to be in relation both to the variety of those passions and to the variety of those tempers.

2 Of the Difference of Men in different Climates

Cold air constringes the extremities of the external fibres of the body[1]; this increases their elasticity, and favors the return of the blood from the extreme parts to the heart. It contracts[2] those very fibres; consequently it increases also their force. On the contrary, warm air relaxes and lengthens the extremes of the fibres; of course it diminishes their force and elasticity.

People are, therefore, more vigorous in cold climates. Here the action of the heart and the reaction of the extremities of the fibres are better performed, the temperature of the humors is greater, the blood moves more freely towards the heart, and reciprocally the heart has more power. This superiority of strength must produce various effects; for instance, a greater boldness, that is, more courage; a greater sense of superiority, that is, less desire of revenge; a greater opinion of security, that is, more frankness, less suspicion, policy, and cunning. In short, this must be productive of very different tempers. Put a man into a close, warm place, and for the reasons above given he will feel a great faintness. If under this circumstance you propose a bold enterprise to him, I believe

From Baron de Montesquieu, *The Spirit of the Laws*, translated by Thomas Nugent. Reprinted by permission of Hafner Press, Macmillan Publishing Co., Inc., 1949: pp. 221–234.

you will find him very little disposed towards it; his present weakness will throw him into despondency; he will be afraid of everything, being in a state of total incapacity. The inhabitants of warm countries are, like old men, timorous; the people in cold countries are, like young men, brave. If we reflect on the late wars,[3] which are more recent in our memory, and in which we can better distinguish some particular effects that escape us at a greater distance of time, we shall find that the northern people, transplanted into southern regions,[4] did not perform such exploits as their countrymen, who, fighting in their own climate, possessed their full vigor and courage.

This strength of the fibres in northern nations is the cause that the coarser juices are extracted from their ailments. Hence two things result: one, that the parts of the chyle or lymph are more proper, by reason of their large surface, to be applied to and to nourish the fibres; the other, that they are less proper, from their coarseness, to give a certain subtility to the nervous juice. Those people have, therefore, large bodies and but little vivacity.

The nerves that terminate from all parts in the cutis form each a nervous bundle; generally speaking, the whole nerve is not moved, but a very minute part. In warm climates, where the cutis is relaxed, the ends of the nerves are expanded and laid open to the weakest action of the smallest objects. In cold countries the cutis is constringed and the papillæ compressed: the miliary glands are in some measure paralytic; and the sensation does not reach the brain, except when it is very strong and proceeds from the whole nerve at once. Now, imagination, taste, sensibility, and vivacity depend on an infinite number of small sensations.

I have observed the outermost part of a sheep's tongue, where, to the naked eye, it seems covered with papillæ. On those papillæ I have discerned through a microscope small hairs, or a kind of down; between the papillæ were pyramids shaped towards the ends like pincers. Very likely these pyramids are the principal organ of taste.

I caused the half of this tongue to be frozen, and observing it with the naked eye I found the papillæ considerably diminished: even some rows of them were sunk into their sheath. The outermost part I examined with the microscope, and perceived no pyramids. In proportion as the frost went off, the papillæ seemed to the naked eye to rise, and with the microscope the miliary glands began to appear.

This observation confirms what I have been saying, that in cold countries the nervous glands are less expanded: they sink deeper into their sheaths, or they are sheltered from the action of external objects; consequently they have not such lively sensations.

In cold countries they have very little sensibility for pleasure; in temperate countries, they have more; in warm countries, their sensibility is exquisite. As climates are distinguished by degrees of latitude, we might distinguish them also in some measure by those of sensibility. I have been at the opera in England and in Italy, where I have seen the same pieces and the same performers; and yet the same music produces such different effects on the two nations: one is so cold and phlegmatic, and the other so lively and enraptured, that it seems almost inconceivable.

It is the same with regard to pain, which is excited by the laceration of some fibre of the body. The Author of nature has made it an established rule that this pain should be more acute in proportion as the laceration is greater: now it is evident that the large bodies and coarse fibres of the people of the North are less capable of laceration than the delicate fibres of the inhabitants of warm countries; consequently the soul is there less sensible of pain. You must flay a Muscovite alive to make him feel.

From this delicacy of organs peculiar to warm climates it follows that the soul is most sensibly moved by whatever relates to the union of the two sexes: here everything leads to this object.

In northern climates scarcely has the animal part of love a power of making itself felt. In temperate climates, love, attended by a thousand appendages, endeavors to please by things that have at first the appearance, though not the reality, of this passion. In warmer climates it is liked for its own sake, it is the only cause of happiness, it is life itself.

In southern countries a machine of a delicate frame but strong sensibility resigns itself either to a love which rises and is incessantly laid in a seraglio, or to a passion which leaves women in a greater independence, and is consequently exposed to a thousand inquietudes. In northern regions a machine robust and heavy finds pleasure in whatever is apt to throw the spirits into motion, such as hunting, travelling, war, and wine. If we travel towards the North, we meet with people who have few vices, many virtues, and a great share of frankness and sincerity. If we draw near the South, we fancy ourselves entirely removed from the verge of morality; here the strongest passions are productive of all manner of crimes, each man endeavoring, let the means be what they will, to indulge his inordinate desires. In temperate climates we find the inhabitants inconstant in their manners, as well as in their vices and virtues: the climate has not a quality determinate enough to fix them.

The heat of the climate may be so excessive as to deprive the body of all vigor and strength. Then the faintness is communicated to the mind; there is no curiosity, no enterprise, no generosity of sentiment; the inclinations are all passive; indolence constitutes the utmost happiness; scarcely any punishment is so severe as mental employment; and slavery is more supportable than the force and vigor of mind necessary for human conduct.

3 Contradiction in the Tempers of some Southern Nations

The Indians[5] are naturally a pusillanimous people; even the children[6] of Europeans born in India lose the courage peculiar to their own climate. But how shall we reconcile this with their customs and penances so full of barbarity? The men voluntarily undergo the greatest hardships, and the women burn themselves: here we find a very odd compound of fortitude and weakness.

Nature, having framed those people of a texture so weak as to fill them with timidity, has formed them at the same time of an imagination so lively that every object makes the strongest impression upon them. That delicacy of organs which renders them apprehensive of death contributes likewise to make them dread a thousand things more than death: the very same sensibility induces them to fly and dare all dangers.

As a good education is more necessary to children than to such as have arrived at maturity of understanding, so the inhabitants of those countries have much greater need than the European nations of a wiser legislator. The greater their sensibility, the more it behooves them to receive proper impressions, to imbibe no prejudices, and to let themselves be directed by reason.

At the time of the Romans the inhabitants of the north of Europe were destitute of arts, education, and almost of laws; and yet the good sense annexed to the gross fibres of those climates enabled them to make an admirable stand against the power of Rome, till the memorable period in which they quitted their woods to subvert that great empire.

4 Cause of the Immutability of Religion, Manners, Customs, and Laws in the Eastern Countries

If to that delicacy of organs which renders the eastern nations so susceptible of every impression you add likewise a sort of indolence of mind, naturally connected with that of the body, by means of which they grow incapable of any exertion or effort, it is easy to comprehend that when once the soul has received an impression is cannot change it. This is the reason that the laws, manners, and customs,[7] even those which seem quite indifferent, such as their mode of dress, are the same to this very day in eastern countries as they were a thousand years ago.

5 That those are bad Legislators who favor the Vices of the Climate, and good Legislators who oppose those Vices

The Indians believe that repose and non-existence are the foundation of all things, and the end in which they terminate. Hence they consider entire inaction as the most perfect of all states, and the object of their desires. To the Supreme Being they give the title of immovable.[8] The inhabitants of Siam believe that their utmost happiness[9] consists in not being obliged to animate a machine or to give motion to a body.

In those countries where the excess of heat enervates and exhausts the body, rest is so delicious, and motion so painful, that this system of metaphysics seems natural; and Foe,[10] the legislator of the Indies, was directed by his own sensations when he placed mankind in a state extremely passive; but his doctrine arising from the laziness of the climate favored it also in its turn; which has been the source of an infinite deal of mischief.

The legislators of China were more rational when, considering men not in the peaceful state which they are to enjoy hereafter, but in the situation proper for discharging the several duties of life, they made their religion, philosophy, and laws all practical. The more the physical causes incline mankind to inaction, the more the moral causes should estrange them from it.

6 Of Agriculture in warm Climates

Agriculture is the principal labor of man. The more the climate inclines him to shun this labor, the more the religion and laws of the country ought to incite him to it. Thus the Indian laws, which give the lands to the prince, and destroy the spirit of property among the subjects, increase the bad effects of the climate, that is, their natural indolence.

7 Of Monkery

The very same mischiefs result from monkery: it had its rise in the warm countries of the East, where they are less inclined to action than to speculation.

In Asia the number of dervishes or monks seems to increase together with the warmth of the climate. The Indies, where the heat is excessive, are full of them; and the same difference is found in Europe.

In order to surmount the laziness of the climate, the laws ought to endeavor to remove all means of subsisting without labor: but in the southern parts of Europe they act quite the reverse. To those who want to live in a state of indolence, they afford retreats the most proper for a speculative life, and endow them with immense revenues. These men who live in the midst of plenty which they know not how to enjoy, are in the right to give their superfluities away to the common people. The poor are bereft of property; and these men indemnify them by supporting them in idleness, so as to make them even grow fond of their misery.

8 An excellent Custom of China

The historical relations[11] of China mention a ceremony[12] of opening the ground which the emperor performs every year. The design of this public and solemn act is to excite the people to tillage.[13]

Further, the emperor is every year informed of the husbandman who has distinguished himself most in his profession; and he makes him a mandarin of the eighth order.

Among the ancient Persians[14] the kings quitted their grandeur and pomp on the eighth day of the month, called *Chorrem-ruz,* to eat with the husbandmen. These institutions were admirably calculated for the encouragement of agriculture.

9 Means of encouraging Industry

We shall show, in the nineteenth book, that lazy nations are generally proud. Now the effect might well be turned against the cause, and laziness be destroyed by pride. In the south of Europe, where people have such a high notion of the point of honor, it would be right to give prizes to husbandmen who had excelled in agriculture; or to artists who had made the greatest improvements in their several professions. This practice has succeeded in our days in Ireland, where it has established one of the most considerable linen manufactures in Europe

10 Of the Laws in relation to the Sobriety of the People

In warm countries the aqueous part of the blood loses itself greatly by perspiration[15]; it must, therefore, be supplied by a like liquid. Water is there of admirable use; strong liquors would congeal the globules[16] of blood that remain after the transuding of the aqueous humor.

In cold countries the aqueous part of the blood is very little evacuated by perspiration. They may, therefore, make use of spirituous liquors, without which the blood would congeal. They are full of humors; consequently strong liquors, which give a motion to the blood, are proper for those countries.

The law of Mohammed, which prohibits the drinking of wine, is, therefore, fitted to the climate of Arabia: and, indeed, before Mohammed's time, water was the common drink of the Arabs. The law[17] which forbade the Carthaginians to drink wine was a law of the climate; and, indeed, the climate of those two countries is pretty nearly the same.

Such a law would be improper for cold countries, where the climate seems to force them to a kind of national intemperance, very different from personal ebriety. Drunkenness predominates throughout the world, in proportion to the coldness and humidity of the climate. Go from the equator to the north pole, and you will find this vice increasing together with the degree of latitude. Go from the equator again to the south pole, and you will find the same vice travelling south,[18] exactly in the same proportion.

It is very natural that where wine is contrary to the climate, and consequently to health, the excess of it should be more severely punished than in countries where intoxication produces very few bad effects to the person, fewer to the society, and where it does not make people frantic and wild, but only stupid and heavy. Hence those laws[19] which inflicted a double punishment for crimes committed in drunkenness were applicable only to a personal, and not to a national, ebriety. A German drinks through custom, and a Spaniard by choice.

In warm countries the relaxing of the fibres produces a great evacuation of the liquids, but the solid parts are less transpired. The fibres, which act but faintly, and have very little elasticity, are not much impaired; and a small quantity of nutritious juice is sufficient to repair them; for which reason they eat very little.

It is the variety of wants in different climates that first occasioned a difference in the manner of living, and this gave rise to a variety of laws. Where people are very communicative there must be particular laws, and others where there is but little communication.

11 Of the Laws in relation to the Distempers of the Climate

Herodotus[20] informs us that the Jewish laws concerning the leprosy were borrowed from the practice of the Egyptians. And, indeed, the same distemper required the same remedies. The Greeks and the primitive Romans were strangers to these laws, as well as to the disease. The climate of Egypt and Palestine rendered them necessary; and the facility with which this disease is spread is sufficient to make us sensible of the wisdom and sagacity of those laws.

Even we ourselves have felt the effects of them. The Crusades brought the leprosy amongst us; but the wise regulations made at that time hindered it from infecting the mass of the people.

We find by the law of the Lombards[21] that this disease was spread in Italy before the Crusades, and merited the attention of the legislature. Rotharis ordained that a leper should be expelled from his house, banished to a particular place, and rendered incapable of disposing of his property; because from the very moment he had been turned out of his house he was reckoned dead in the eye of the law. In order to prevent all communication with lepers, they were rendered incapable of civil acts.

I am apt to think that this disease was brought into Italy by the conquests of the Greek emperors, in whose armies there might be some soldiers from Palestine or Egypt. Be that as it may, the progress of it was stopped till the time of the Crusades.

It is related that Pompey's soldiers returning from Syria brought a distemper home with them not unlike the leprosy. We have no account of any regulation made at that time; but it is highly probable that some such step was taken, since the distemper was checked till the time of the Lombards.

It is now two centuries since a disease unknown to our ancestors was first transplanted from the new world to ours, and came to attack human nature even in the very source of life and pleasure. Most of the principal families in the south of Europe were seen to perish by a distemper that had grown too common to be ignominious, and was considered in no other light than in that of its being fatal. It was the thirst of gold that propagated this disease; the Europeans went continually to America, and always brought back a new leaven of it.[22]

Reasons drawn from religion seemed to require that this punishment of guilt should be permitted to continue; but the infection had reached the bosom of matrimony, and given the vicious taint even to guiltless infants.

As it is the business of legislators to watch over the health of the citizens, it would have been a wise part in them to have stopped this communication by laws made on the plan of those of Moses.

The plague is a disease whose infectious progress is much more rapid. Egypt is its principal seat, whence it spreads over the whole globe. Most countries in Europe have made exceedingly good regulations to prevent this infection, and in our times an admirable method has been contrived to stop it; this is by forming a line of troops round the infected country, which cuts off all manner of communication.

The Turks,[23] who have no such regulations, see the Christians escape this infection in the same town, and none but themselves perish; they buy the clothes of the infected, wear them, and proceed in their old way, as if nothing had happened. The doctrine of a rigid fate, which directs their whole conduct, renders the magistrate a quiet spectator; he thinks that everything comes from the hand of God, and that man has nothing more to do than to submit.

12 Of the Laws against Suicides

We do not find in history that the Romans ever killed themselves without a cause; but the English are apt to commit suicide most unaccountably; they destroy themselves even in the bosom of happiness. This action among the Romans was the effect of education, being connected with their principles and customs; among the English it is the consequence of a distemper,[24] being connected with the physical state of the machine, and independent of every other cause.

In all probability it is a defect of the filtration of the nervous juice: the machine, whose motive faculties are often unexerted, is weary of itself; the soul feels no pain, but a certain uneasiness in existing. Pain is a local sensation, which leads us to the desire of seeing an end of it; the burden of life, which prompts us to the desire of ceasing to exist, is an evil confined to no particular part.

It is evident that the civil laws of some countries may have reasons for branding suicide with infamy: but in England it cannot be punished without punishing the effects of madness.

13 Effects arising from the Climate of England

In a nation so distempered by the climate as to have a disrelish of everything, nay, even of life, it is plain that the government most suitable to the inhabitants is that in which they cannot lay their uneasiness to any single person's charge, and in which, being under the direction rather of the laws than of the prince, it is impossible for them to change the government without subverting the laws themselves.

And if this nation has likewise derived from the climate a certain impatience of temper, which renders them incapable of bearing the same train of things for any long continuance, it is obvious that the government above mentioned is the fittest for them.

This impatience of temper is not very considerable of itself; but it may become so when joined with courage.

It is quite a different thing from levity, which makes people undertake or drop a project without cause; it borders more upon obstinacy, because it proceeds from so lively a sense of misery that it is not weakened even by the habit of suffering.

This temper in a free nation is extremely proper for disconcerting the projects of tyranny,[25] which is always slow and feeble in its commencement, as in the end it is active and lively; which at first only stretches out a hand to assist, and exerts afterwards a multitude of arms to oppress.

Slavery is ever preceded by sleep. But a people who find no rest in any situation, who continually explore every part, and feel nothing but pain, can hardly be lulled to sleep.

Politics are a smooth file, which cuts gradually, and attains its end by a slow progression. Now the people of whom we have been speaking are incapable of bearing the delays, the details, and the coolness of negotiations: in these they are more unlikely to succeed than other nations; hence they are apt to lose by treaties what they obtain by their arms.

14 Other Effects of the Climate

Our ancestors, the ancient Germans, lived in a climate where the passions were extremely calm. Their laws decided only in such cases where the injury was visible to the eye, and went no farther. And as they judged of the outrages done to men from the greatness of the wound, they acted with no other delicacy in respect to the injuries done to women. The law of the Alemansi[26] on this subject is very extraordinary. If a person uncovers a woman's head, he pays a fine of fifty sous; if he uncovers her leg up to the knee, he pays the same; and double from the knee upwards. One would think that the law measured the insults offered to women as we measure a figure in geometry; it did not punish the crime of the imagination, but that of the eye. But upon the migration of a German nation into Spain, the climate soon found a necessity for different laws. The law of the Visigoths inhibited the surgeons to bleed a free woman, except either her father, mother, brother, son, or uncle was present. As the imagination of the people grew warm, so did that of the legislators; the law suspected everything when the people had become suspicious.

These laws had, therefore, a particular regard for the two sexes. But in their punishments they seem rather to humor the revengeful temper of private persons than to administer public justice. Thus, in most cases, they reduced both the criminals to be slaves to the offended relatives or to the injured husband; a free-born woman[27] who had yielded to the embraces of a married man was delivered up to his wife to dispose of her as she pleased. They obliged the slaves,[28] if they found their master's wife in adultery, to bind her and carry her to her husband; they even permitted her children[29] to be her accusers, and her slaves to be tortured in order to convict her. Thus their laws were far better adapted to refine, even to excess, a certain point of honor than to form a good civil administration. We must not, therefore, be surprised if Count Julian was of opinion that an affront of that kind ought to be expiated by the ruin of his king and country: we must not be surprised if the Moors, with such a conformity of manners, found it so easy to settle and to maintain themselves in Spain, and to regard the fall of their empire.

15 Of the different Confidence which the Laws have in the People, according to the Difference of Climates

The people of Japan are of so stubborn and perverse a temper that neither their legislators nor magistrates can put any confidence in them: they set nothing before their eyes but judgments, menaces, and chastisements; every step they take is subject to the inquisition of the civil magistrate. Those laws which out of five heads of families establish one as a magistrate over the other four; those laws which punish a family or a whole ward for a single crime; those laws, in fine, which find nobody innocent where one may happen to be guilty, are made with a design to implant in the people a mutual distrust, and to make every man the inspector, witness, and judge of his neighbor's conduct.

On the contrary, the people of India are mild,[30] tender, and compassionate. Hence their legislators repose great confidence in them. They have established[31] very few punishments; these are not severe, nor are they rigorously executed. They have subjected nephews to their uncles, and orphans to their guardians, as in other countries they are subjected to their fathers; they have regulated the succession by the acknowledged merit of the successor. They seem to think that every individual ought to place entire confidence in the good nature of his fellow-subjects.[32]

They enfranchise their slaves without difficulty, they marry them, they treat them as their children.[33] Happy climate which gives birth to innocence, and produces a lenity in the laws!

Notes

[1] This appears even in the countenance: in cold weather people look thinner.

[2] We know that it shortens iron.

[3] Those for the succession to the Spanish monarchy.

[4] For instance, in Spain.

[5] "One hundred European soldiers," says Tavernier, "would without any great difficulty beat a thousand Indian soldiers."

[6] Even the Persians who settle in the Indies contract in the third generation the indolence and cowardice of the Indians. See Bernier on the "Mogul," tom. i. p. 182.

[7] We find by a fragment of Nicolaus Damascenus, collected by Constantine Porphyrogenitus, that it was an ancient custom in the East to send to strangle a Governor who had given any displeasure; it was in the time of Medes.

[8] Panamanack: See Kircher.

[9] La Loubiere, "Relation of Siam," p. 446.

[10] Foe endeavored to reduce the heart to a mere vacuum: "We have eyes and ears, but perfection consists in neither seeing nor hearing; a mouth, hands, etc., but perfection requires that these members should be inactive." This is taken from the dialogue of a Chinese philosopher, quoted by Father Du Halde, tom. iii.

[11] Father Du Halde, "History of China," tom. i. p. 72.

[12] Several of the kings of India do the same. "Relation of the Kingdom of Siam," by La Loubiere, p. 69.

[13] Venty, the third Emperor of the third dynasty, tilled the lands himself, and made the Empress and his wives employ their time in the silkworks in his palace. "History of China."

[14] Hyde, "Religion of the Persians."

[15] Monsieur Bernier, travelling from Lahore to Cashmere, wrote thus: "My body is a sieve; scarcely have I swallowed a pint of water, but I see it transude like dew out of all my limbs, even to my fingers' ends. I drink ten pints a day, and it does me no manner of harm."—Bernier's "Travels," tom. ii. p. 261.

[16] In the blood there are red globules, fibrous parts, white globules, and water, in which the whole swims.

[17] Plato, book II. of "Laws"; Aristotle, of the care of domestic affairs; Eusebius's "Evangelical Preparation," book XII. chap. xvii.

[18] This is seen in the Hottentots, and the inhabitants of the most southern part of Chili.

[19] As Pittacus did, according to Aristotle, "Polit." lib. I. cap. iii. He lived in a climate where drunkenness is not a national vice.

[20] Book II.

[21] Book II. tit. 1, sec. 3, and tit. 18, sec. 1.

[22] It has been thought that this malady has a still more ancient origin, and that it is probable the Spaniards carried it to America at the start.—Ed.

[23] Ricaut on the "Ottoman Empire," p. 284.

[24] It may be complicated with the scurvy, which, in some countries especially, renders a man whimsical and unsupportable to himself. See Pirard's "Voyages," part II. chap. xxi.

[25] Here I take this word for the design of subverting the established power, and especially that of democracy; this is the signification in which it was understood by the Greeks and Romans.

[26] Chap. lviii. secs. 1 and 2.

[27] "Law of the Visigoths," book III. tit. 4, sec. 9.

[28] Ibid. book III. tit. 4, sec. 6.

[29] Ibid. book III. tit. 4, sec. 13.

[30] See Bernier, tom. ii. p. 140.

[31] See in the 14th collection of the "Edifying Letters," p. 403, the principal laws or customs of the inhabitants of the peninsula on this side the Ganges.

[32] See "Edifying Letters," IX. 378. Great exception has been taken to Montesquieu's abuse upon the effects of climate physically; it is Servan who avers that the weakness attributed to organisms under the equator is erroneous.—Ed.

[33] I had one thought that the lenity of slavery in India had made Diodorus say that there was neither master nor slave in that country; but Diodorus has attributed to the whole continent of India what, according to Stabo, lib. XV., belonged only to a particular nation.

PART THREE
Professionalization of Anthropology

By about the middle of the nineteenth century, anthropology had developed into a discrete subject of inquiry. Previously there had been a number of *traditions* of anthropological study but no *profession* per se. The factors that changed gradually at about this time were multiple. Disciplinary boundaries were set more firmly, so that the different social sciences began to go their separate ways. Institutions for the study of human cultural diversity were established; for the first time, an individual scholar could earn his living by the practice of anthropology. A community of scholars was emerging in which individuals were in constant communication with one another through publication, correspondence, or personal contacts. At the same time, standards for membership in the scientific community were being established, either by formal educational credentials or by research results that met consensual standards among practitioners. The pace of scientific investigation within anthropology was substantially increased by these developments, because nonprofessional work could be ignored with impunity and valid research results could be more easily transmitted to interested colleagues.

In one sense, the professionalization of anthropology was unique.

But all of the sciences were moving in the same direction during the last half of the nineteenth century; anthropology was no exception to the trend, although details of its developing institutional structure were specific to it. There is no single date at which the science of anthropology can be said to have become professional. There were amateur anthropologists long after the establishment of anthropological societies and formal training programs. Over a long period, individual anthropologists devoted their energies to bringing about the state of the discipline they envisioned. From the perspective of practitioners, the outcome may have often seemed far from inevitable. It is only from the historical hindsight of professionalized science, as a process that has occurred only once in the history of the world, that the trend appears unilinear.

The process of legislating the goals of professional science is in part dependent on the way the history of the discipline is perceived by its practitioners. Those who have an axe to grind choose what they see as the relevant trends and encourage those trends by selecting their own intellectual paternity. At a period when professionalization is a major issue, it is not surprising to find many reviews and historical discussions concerning the appropriate foundations of the sciences. In the case of anthropology, the early professional developments involved simultaneous burgeoning of societies for its study and programmatic statements based on the tenuous traditions, at least by modern standards, of past anthropological works.

The first society devoted specifically to the study of anthropology was the short-lived Society of the Observers of Man, established in Paris in 1800 (Stocking 1968; Degerando 1969). This was a group of scientists who prepared, for a voyage of discovery, a set of inquiries in the area of anthropology (among other concerns). Although the scientific results were minimal, the increasing professionalism involved in the establishment of the Society was a forerunner of things to come.

Other groups followed quickly in a number of countries, indicating that anthropology (or ethnology) was a popular subject of scholarly inquiry throughout the Western world. The Ethnological Society of Paris appeared in 1839, the American Ethnological Society in 1842, and the Ethnological Society of London in 1843 (Dieserud 1908; Smith 1943). The British and American Associations for the Advancement of Science were established in 1846 and 1851, respectively. Although these two associations covered far more extensive subjects than anthropology, they did provide a public forum for anthropological debate and strengthened the claim of the new discipline to recognition as a science (Putnam 1895). By 1870, anthropological societies also existed in Moscow, Madrid, Berlin, and Vienna. There were approximately forty societies, most of which are still in existence, when the American Anthropological Association was founded in 1902 (Dieserud 1908).

As a result of the activities of the new societies, there were publication outlets for anthropologists and channels of personal communication open among individuals. Some of the splintering of societies during the early period related to differences in definition of the scope and content of anthropology: There were those who saw that it had major ties to biology, social work, ethnology or archaeology (Stocking 1972). Stocking, for example, has explored the conflicting identities within the Royal Anthropological Institute in Britain in 1871 to illustrate how factions attempted to enforce their own ideas about the nature of the discipline.

Because anthropology was a relatively new field to be represented in the traditional curriculum of school or university, questions as to its appropriate scope or focus could be entertained. The history of the discipline had to be written so that it would reflect the identity wished by practitioners at the time. There were a number of such efforts. In England, T. Hodgkin in 1848 and R. Cull in 1852 wrote in the publications of the Ethnological Society of London; J. Hunt in 1863 and T. Bendyshe in 1865 published through the Anthropological Society of London. In America, John Russell Bartlett described the progress of ethnology for the American Ethnological Society. In France, Armand de Quatrefages wrote in 1867 on the development of anthropology; only two years later Paul Broca cataloged the progress of the Anthropological Society of Paris since its founding in 1859 (compare Bender 1965). In the early years of professional science, the entire face of anthropology seemed to participants to change almost overnight as a result of new institutional frameworks. In Germany, the developments were slightly later but still connected to the rise of professional societies and the effect on the individual anthropologist's sense of identity. In 1881, Adolph Bastian described the early history of ethnology; in 1889, T. Achelis cataloged the development of modern ethnology. Although this list is far from exhaustive, it suffices to demonstrate that similar changes were taking place at about the same time in the nascent anthropological disciplines of several countries.

Before the establishment of the first anthropological societies, most scholars were informally attached to local learned societies, of which in America the most distinguished was probably the American Philosophical Society in Philadelphia (Freeman 1967). Within its framework, Thomas Jefferson pursued his inquiries, as did many other early American statesmen and scholars. Anthropology was peripheral to the scope of such a society, and most of the members were not professionals in any specific discipline. They were gentlemen with sufficient income to indulge their scholarly interests, which often had remarkably wide scope when viewed from the perspective of a more specialized concept of science that has since developed. Integration of what were becoming the separate disciplines came primarily through the "moral philosophy" of the Enlightenment, which remained the basis of American education until near the end of the nineteenth century.

In America, much of the early professional activity was sponsored by the federal government, because it was important to pacify the aborigines and settle them on reservations. This type of anthropology gradually developed impetus in the years before the establishment of the Bureau of American Ethnology in 1879 (Lyon 1960). Much of the labor was performed by the use of questionnaires, as shown particularly by the work of Henry Schoolcraft, Albert Gallatin, and others (Freeman 1965). The Smithsonian Institution had been founded in 1846 to act as a clearinghouse and resource center for all types of scientific research. In the field of anthropology, as in many other disciplines, this governmental support preceded other institutional supports for science.

During this period, the most important task was to classify the languages and tribes of North America. Even a basic map of groups and their distributions could not be drawn accurately. The 1863 guide provided by George Gibbs for ethnology and philology (culture and language) of the American aborigines was one important Smithsonian effort to rectify the lack of knowledge. Like many others, Gibbs' questionnaire was designed for the traveler or untrained observer, whose comments could then be used for cross-cultural comparison. Ethnological questions included: tribal designation, geographical locale, demography, physical condition, writing systems (including picture writing), clothes, food, houses, art, trade, religion, government, social life, war, medicine, literature, calendar and astronomy, the group's view of its own history, and antiquities. Such a list was formidable for the untrained traveler, and most of the schedules are incomplete. But it provided a guideline, a statement of what there was to be known, in as much detail as possible.

In the realm of philology, reproduced here, Gibbs wanted to amass as much material as possible that might aid in tracing the genetic relationships of the different tribes. To this end, he included long word lists for comparative philology. He also commented extensively on how to write down the sounds of Indian languages, so that the results from different questionnaires would be easily comparable. Gibbs realized that only the "more obvious" linguistic relationships would emerge from the direct comparison of limited word lists. He looked forward to the day when observations would be carried out by trained personnel in more extensive contact with the aborigines; as a result, more "remote" affinities would be discovered. Gibbs believed that unwritten languages changed very quickly, because they had no written tradition to stabilize them. The Indians were clearly modifying, if not losing, their languages rapidly, so his work has the urgency of salvage.

The Gibbs' questionnaire was a precursor of John Wesley Powell's *Introduction to the Study of Indian Languages*, which appeared in 1877, and to the linguistic classification of North American languages, published under Powell's name by the Bureau of American Ethnology in 1891 (Darnell 1971b, 1971c). The government-sponsored anthropology, however, was never able to meet Gibbs' desire for detailed study of particular groups so that remote culture history might be reconstructed. This work was done instead during the early twentieth century by the students of Franz Boas, particularly Edward Sapir, who reduced the number of units in the linguistic classification from fifty-eight to only six. The Boasian fieldworkers were not subject to the same restrictions as the government anthropologists, because they did not have to produce practical results for Congress in order to continue their work. This was a function as much of changes in institutional structure of anthropology during the period as it was of differences in data that were collected and analyzed.

Another Smithsonian production that set the tone for an emerging professionalism in American anthropology was Samuel Haven's 1856 treatment of the longstanding problem of the origin of the Mound Builders. Students during the early nineteenth century had made a romantic mystery out of the Mound Builders; they postulated a mysterious superrace previously living in the same area, because the present Indians could never have produced such complex structures. Haven, a librarian, concluded that the mystery had been quietly laid to rest and presented extensive evidence from natural history and anthropology to support his claim. He could not use geology because it was not sufficiently developed in America. Although travel between the Old and New Worlds was possible "in very rude ages," he concluded that this could only have been an occasional and accidental source of population. A native population must have developed in the Americas essentially independently of the Old World. Haven favored the Bering Strait hypothesis because of similarities in physical type and the mythological "recollections" of various tribes that they came from the Northwest. However, the American Indians were racially and linguistically unique, and so the time span required for developing this uniqueness would have to have been immense. Haven claimed that there was no question of the great antiquity of the aborigines; they were contemporary with the earliest human developments.

It is interesting to note that, at this period, the archaeological question of the origin of the Mound Builders could not be answered on the basis of existing evidence. Sequences for the shallow time depth of North American archaeological sites (in contrast to those of Europe) had not yet been developed. Therefore, the student of the Indian mounds had to depend on other evidence and to be a holistic anthropologist (although he always had Jefferson's option of excavating a mound himself). Yet the problem was also one of public opinion that the present-day Indians were savages and could not have produced the archaeologically attested art and architecture of the Mississippi Valley. Of course, there continued to be protests from lunatic fringes favoring explanations of lost tribes, sunken continents, disappearing civilizations, etc., but reputable anthropological science in America assumed after 1857 that the Indians had built in situ whatever monuments were found to exist.

Daniel G. Brinton was among the last of the preprofessional anthropologists of major stature in America. Throughout his life, his major institutional affiliation was with the American Philosophical Society. Although he was named in 1887 the first university professor of anthropology at the University of Pennsylvania, he had no students and taught no courses (Darnell 1967, 1970). His major contribution was keeping public attention focused on anthropology as a serious field of study. His paper, reproduced here, on reasons for studying Indian languages explicated his conviction that the history of the world would not be complete until all of its peoples had been described. Brinton argued that language was the major clue to prehistory and that the "evolution" of the human mind was reflected in primitive languages. All languages had once had a structure like that of the American Indian ones, but some had progressed to another stage.

Brinton sharply criticized Powell's 1877 *Introduction to the Study of Indian Languages,* because it began with a lecture on the superiority of Indo-European languages. Brinton took a more relativistic view, arguing that any language can be put to any use, although differences do exist. It was not fair to compare Indian languages to present-day English, which had many abstract and scientific terms that were quite recent developments. Brinton's defense of the existence of serious oral literature among the unwritten languages of the American Indians is impassioned. He published at his own expense eight volumes of American Indian texts, *Brinton's Library of Aboriginal American Literature.* Although Brinton was an evolutionist, his insistence on the racial, cultural, and linguistic uniqueness of the North American Indians made him avoid direct comparison between the products of the American Indian mind and those elsewhere in the world. Instead, he idealized the American aborigines.

Brinton himself was never a professional anthropologist, but he envisioned the future directions of the discipline. In 1892, he wrote a programmatic article on the organization of university resources for the teaching of anthropology; this work was ostensibly a prospectus for a program at the University of Pennsylvania. Brinton called for professional training programs through universities and for a holistic scope of the discipline. In a sense, Brinton stood at the crossroads. His program was realized only by Boas and his students in the first two decades of the twentieth century. Brinton's contribution has rarely been recognized, partially because he himself did not participate in the professionalization and partly because his theoretical views conflicted with the developing Boasian anthropology.

Edward B. Tylor has been called the father of modern anthropology, apparently on the logic that he is the first anthropologist whose works form part of the literature of the present discipline. Certainly, Tylor's books on primitive culture and anthropology provided a rallying point for the growing identity of professional anthropologists in Britain and elsewhere. Like Brinton, however, Tylor was not a fieldworker and was not trained in anthropology. His method was comparative, and he drew examples from the existing literature on exotic peoples all over the globe.

Tylor's paper on the contribution of American workers to the development of anthropology as a science gives a British view of the New World. The British Association for the Advancement of Science had provided an institutional framework for Canadian study of American Indians (Gruber 1967; Trigger 1966a, 1966b). When Tylor came to America in 1884 to deliver his address, he wanted both to relate the nascent disciplines in North America and Britain and to encourage North American developments.

Tylor noted that the American aborigines offered possibilities of archaeological continuity to present-day peoples; this continuity had long since been impossible in Europe. The antiquity of man emerged as a problem that would have to be solved outside the discipline of anthropology. However, in the meantime, anthropologists would have to go on building their hypotheses about migration and history. In other words, America was the place where many of the pressing questions concerning European anthropological theory would be answered.

Anthropological theory in America during the late nineteenth century was predominantly evolutionary. The work of Lewis Henry Morgan on the evolution of kinship terminologies is still a matter of controversy within the discipline (Engels 1884; Stern 1931; Lowie 1936; Tolstoy 1952; Resek 1960; Tax 1955; Fortes 1969). Morgan's work was taken as God's truth by John Wesley Powell, founder of the Bureau of American Ethnology. Powell controlled most of the government research on the Indians, and his Bureau was the most powerful institution for anthropological research in America throughout the rest of the nineteenth century. The theoretical work of the Bureau has been neglected, because, from present perspectives, it blatantly argued for evolutionism. Rather, the stress of folk histories of the discipline has been on factual ethnographic work of the Bureau. The outdatedness of the theoretical writings is largely due to the success of Franz Boas' revolt against evolutionism in the early twentieth century.

W J [sic] McGee, whose major claim to fame in the annals of

anthropology is that he objected to using periods after his initials, showed how sundry members of the Bureau staff worked out many of Powell's ideas. McGee thought that a new stage had been reached, a synthesis in which the origins of human activities could be placed in their proper evolutionary perspectives. He called for a "natural history" of human arts and inventions. Anthropology had the same intellectual roots as biology and was just as scientific. Human mental development was seen as an additional factor in the evolution of man.

Throughout the works of the Bureau of American Ethnology, the achievements of the American aborigines are contrasted, implicitly or explicitly, to the pinnacle of civilization reached by the culture that developed the science of anthropology. Again, the perspective is one that was effectively demolished by Boas and his students; they insisted on the need for cultural relativism and analysis of a culture in its own terms. There are a considerable number of works describing the Bureau, but they are not well known (for example, Dupree 1957; Darnell 1971a; Judd 1967; Lamb 1906; McGee 1897; Stegner 1954; Sturtevant 1958).

John Swanton was an ambiguous figure in the professionalization of American anthropology. He was employed by the Bureau of American Ethnology but was trained by Franz Boas. Thus, he spanned two successive "paradigms" in American anthropology. His comments here on the reevaluation of a forgery of an American Indian language are instructive as illustrating how new standards for evaluation of past work were becoming accepted. He was only partially interested in settling the factual question of whether the Taënsa really were distinct from the Natchez. More importantly, he was concerned that all ethnographic reporting should be subject to scrutiny on the kinds of grounds that he recommended in this particular case.

The details of the Taënsa case seem absurd now; but at least for a few years, it was taken seriously. The consequences were potentially significant, because at this time professional standards for evaluating scholarship were just being established. Swanton noted with some humor that Brinton, who originally accepted the materials and later criticized them in two long papers, had compared the poetry to that of Ossian for its lyricism; this work was also later unmasked as a forgery. When Swanton reanalyzes Brinton's critique, he leaves the reader with the impression that Brinton alone was not sufficient authority; that is, Brinton was right about the forgery but for all the wrong reasons. The conclusion, dated 1911, is that Boasian anthropology is writing its own history.

Franz Boas wrote his address on "The History of Anthropology" in 1904 as an explicit attempt to legislate the future development of the discipline by a major figure in that history. In 1904, Boas' status as the major figure of the discipline was far from secure. He was just beginning to train students at Columbia University. Even ten years later, the history of the discipline would have looked entirely different, because Boas would have had results to show instead of programmatic statements. At the earlier time, neither the personnel nor the institutional framework had emerged.

There were two major routes to professional anthropology outside of the government in the late nineteenth century: the university department and the museum (Darnell 1969, 1971a). At first, the museum seemed more promising; it permitted fieldwork, and public support, especially for archaeology, was considerable (Dexter 1966; Hellman 1968). University programs were slower to get started (Freeman 1965). The first effective one was at Harvard University under the direction of Frederick Ward Putnam, whose primary commitment always remained to the associated Peabody Museum of American Archaeology and Ethnology. Efforts by Boas to develop a joint program between the American Museum of Natural History and Columbia University were abortive, as were efforts at collaboration in Chicago and Philadelphia. By about 1900, it was clear that academia was the institutional framework of the future.

As early as 1892, Frederick Starr of the University of Chicago summarized developments in the field at American universities. In 1896, George Dorsey cataloged progress at Harvard (see also Dixon 1930). Between 1899 and 1902, George Grant MacCurdy wrote three articles in *Science,* the journal of the American Association for the Advancement of Science, on developing professional resources for anthropology, particularly in the universities. In Britain, parallel beginnings were under way at about the same time (Read 1906). Anthropologists of both countries were trying to maximize the resources potentially available to them.

Of course, the universities themselves were changing, under the influence of the German university system, which inspired the establishment of numerous graduate programs during the late nineteenth and early twentieth centuries. As the traditional curriculum was being drastically revised, anthropologists saw a niche for themselves among the new and more practically oriented studies, especially the social sciences. Boas, of course, was a German scholar, and a product of the very system that was giving new impetus to American education.

According to Boas' influential history, anthropology was a new discipline. He claimed that no one had had appropriate training until ten years before. Previous students had been mere observers who had failed to contribute to needed theory. The intellectual roots of anthropology were stressed in preference to the specific achievements of people calling themselves anthropologists. Anthropology straddled the line between the biological and the mental sciences, because it studied all aspects of man. It thus provided, in one sense, a methodological model for the mental sciences generally.

Boas stressed that history was a major intellectual trend but that evolutionary theories in anthropology had been vastly premature and overly ambitious. His own more cautious studies of particular cases of diffusion would build an empirical base for the new level of theory yet to come. Indeed, Boas claimed that theories always preceded the empirical data that substantiated them. Thus, the outdated evolutionary theories were wrong, but they were still a necessary stepping-stone to the new empirical stage that anthropology was about to enter. The major remaining questions were (1) independent invention versus diffusion and (2) the status of race, language, and culture as independent variables. In the case of the first question, Boas argued that the two were equally likely on logical grounds and that only empirical data would answer the question. In the case of the latter, counterexamples to the earlier unilinear theories demonstrated that a new formulation was needed. This was, indeed, Boas' program for the future. Although he had begun to develop it in 1904, the results had not yet become available. From a longer time perspective, of course, the day went almost entirely to Boas, partly because he was so good at rewriting the history of the discipline. He devoted one sentence to Brinton, his chief opponent among American evolutionists; the major positive references were to German scholars, Steinthal and Bastian. For Boas' students, the earlier evolutionary theories were so thoroughly buried that they never seemed real. The portion of the history of anthropology that took them seriously had been virtually lost.

Turning now to the professionalization of British anthropology, we find that anthropology had a slightly different though overlapping set of culture heroes: E. B. Tylor, Sir James Frazer, and Bronislaw Malinowski. William Robertson-Smith collaborated extensively with Sir James Frazer, who is now, of course, far in anthropological disrepute. He represents a tradition, important in British anthropology, that has retained ties to the Classics. Robertson-Smith was the most explicitly anthropological of a group of scholars that also includes Gilbert Murray, Francis Cornford, Jane Harrison, and Jessie Weston. Following difficulties tied to his lack of theoretical orthodoxy, Robertson-Smith became Professor of Arabic at Cambridge in 1883, where he applied an anthropological perspective to the study of Semitic ritual tradition (Leach 1966).

Robertson-Smith shared with Tylor an interest in the "life history of religious institutions." His contemporaries, A. Lang, R. Marett, and Frazer, are considered more traditional anthropologists, because they studied primitive peoples. But Robertson-Smith made his contribution to the theory of anthropology by not stressing theology in primitive religion. Theology is simply a secondary rationalization of the actually prior rite or performance. Religion is also presented as a political phenomenon, again de-emphasizing theology.

Edmund Leach has recently argued that Frazer was important in his own time but that British anthropology had moved beyond his influence by 1910 (a date comparable to the developments in America). Frazer's prestige was mainly based on his writings; he was not responsible for any university programs. Indeed, he taught for only one year, in 1908, while a program at Cambridge University, begun in 1898, grew up under the leadership of Alfred Haddon and W. H. R. Rivers. As in the United States, the new developments were closely tied up with fieldwork (Leach 1966; Wallis 1957).

The fieldwork tradition developed largely through Malinowski, a Pole who was interned in Australia during the First World War and who consequently devoted considerable time to studying the inhabitants of the Trobriand Islands. His later influence on the discipline was primarily through his students, who were liberally infused with functionalism and fieldwork. He gained widespread notoriety, because his writings on the sex life of savages were titillating to Victorian readers. As happened in American anthropology under the leadership of Boas, it was the combination of personality, theoretical postulates, and institutional resources that made Malinowski the major figure of the British tradition (Leach 1966; Firth, ed., 1957).

The publication of Malinowski's field diaries in 1967 touched off a new rash of controversy. Like the field diaries of Boas (Rohner, ed., 1969), they indicated that the early heroes of the discipline in many ways did not meet present standards of fieldwork. Stocking's review of the Malinowski diaries, included here, attempts to get outside the problem of the anthropologist looking at himself and his heroes to the social context of what fieldwork actually meant to Malinowski professionally and psychologically. The context is not entirely specific to anthropology. Malinowski is compared directly to another exiled Pole, Joseph Conrad, whose literary portrayal of the plight of the civilized European in contact with the primitive world parallels the anthropologist's field experience. Such an analysis helps to separate what is still useful to fieldworkers about Malinowski's experience and what is bound to his particular situation.

This section has stressed the relatively brief period in which anthropology became the discipline we know today. Since this period, in great part through the deliberate efforts of the early professionals, we can speak of *a discipline and a tradition* rather than merely of a tradition. The identity of some men as anthropologists has been decisively established; their reputation will continue under the assumption that anthropology is a separate field of study, worthy of attention from educated men.

14. Instructions for Philology
George Gibbs

In view of the importance of a uniform system in collecting words of the various Indian languages of North America, adapted to the use of officers of the government, travellers, and others, the following is recommended as a STANDARD VOCABULARY. It is mainly the one prepared by the late Hon. Albert Gallatin, with a few changes made by Mr. Hale, the Ethnologist of the United States Exploring Expedition, and is adopted as that upon which nearly all the collections hitherto made for the purpose of comparison have been based. For the purpose of ascertaining the more obvious relations between the various members of existing families, this number is deemed sufficient. The remote affinities must be sought in a wider research, demanding a degree of acquaintance with their languages beyond the reach of transient visitors.

The languages spoken within the limits of the United States, in which the greatest deficiencies exist, are those of the tribes comprised in the States of California and Texas, and the Territories of Utah, Nevada, and New Mexico, and to these attention is particularly directed. It is not intended, however, to confine the collection to the languages of the United States. Those of British and Russian America and of Mexico, particularly the western coast, fall within the purpose of this circular; and the alphabet may, in fact, with certain local adaptations, be used in any region.

Some of the words contained in it will of course be found inapplicable in particular sections of the country; as, for example, ice, salmon, and sturgeon among the southern tribes, buffalo among the coast tribes of the Pacific, and such should at once be omitted.

Where several languages are obtained by the same person in one district, the inquirer may substitute for these the names of familiar things, taking care that the same are carried through them all, and that they are those of native and not imported objects. Such words as coat, hat, etc., are of course useless for purposes of comparison, unless it is

From George Gibbs, *Instructions for Research Relative to the Ethnology and Philology of America,* Smithsonian Miscellaneous Collections 160 (1863). Reprinted by permission of Smithsonian Institution Press: pp. 13–17.

explained that they refer to the dress of deer-skin, the hat of basket-work used by the natives, and of their own primitive manufacture.

As the languages of savage nations, being unwritten and without fixed standard, are subject to constant change, the number of dialects is everywhere considerable. The collector is therefore recommended to obtain vocabularies in each dialect; and for the greater certainty, to employ one of those already collected, on the correctness of which reliance can be placed, as the medium of obtaining others.

Whenever leisure and opportunity offer for the collection of larger vocabularies than that here given, it will of course be desirable to procure them; as also information concerning the grammatical structure of the language, such as the modes of forming the plurals in nouns and adjectives, their declension, the conjugation of verbs, the character and use of pronouns, the number and employment of adverbs, prepositions, &c. Grammars and dictionaries, never yet published, were made of many of the languages of Upper and Lower California and the Mexican States by the Spanish missionaries, and the Smithsonian Institution has been favored with the loan of several manuscripts which are in the course of publication. It is desired to procure others, or copies of them, whenever it is possible, from all parts of both the American continents, or of printed works on the same subject. The present form is issued for the use of travellers or merely transient residents among tribes where no such records are procurable.

In making collections, the utmost care is requisite to represent accurately the sounds of unfamiliar languages, particularly those which to us appear uncouth; and the inquirer should satisfy himself, by repetition of the words to other individuals, that he has correctly acquired their pronunciation. While the assistance of interpreters conversant with the language is desirable to insure a correct understanding, the words themselves should be taken down from the lips of an Indian of the tribe. A great difference indeed exists among Indians in the purity with which they speak their own language, chiefs and men of note and women of good standing, as a general thing, speaking more correctly than common persons. Great patience is necessary to secure accuracy, as their attention soon becomes fatigued by being kept on the stretch. Whenever this is observed to be the case, it is best to postpone the subject for a time, if possible.

The character of the Indian mind is so essentially different from that of the white man, they think in so different a matter, that many precautions are necessary to avoid giving them wrong impressions of our meaning, and of course obtaining incorrect replies.

Indians not only distinguish by different names the degrees and modifications of relationship, such as the elder from the younger brother and sister, but women use different words from men in addressing their relations; as, for instance, a man employs one word in saying "my father," and a woman another. Again, different words are, at least in some languages, used in speaking *of* one's parents from those used in speaking *to* them. It is, therefore, necessary either to give each form, or to specify by what sex and in what sense the words are used. Further to prevent uncertainty, it is preferable to enploy the possessive pronoun in connection with the word, as given in the vocabulary, *e.g.*, "my father," &c.; and this is, in fact, in consonance with Indian practice.

Their languages are deficient in *generic* terms, or those representing classes of objects. Thus very few possess words equivalent to "tree," "bird," "fish," &c., though names will be found for every particular species, as each kind of oak and pine, of duck or salmon; and of certain animals, such as deer, there will be found, besides the specific name, black or white-tailed deer, as the case may be, separate words signifying buck, doe, and fawn, as with us. It is, therefore, essential in obtaining such names, to ascertain definitively the object intended, and to note this in the vocabulary.

This tendency to particularize extends to almost every class of objects. In regard to parts of the body, it has been found that in many languages there is no one word for arm or leg, but separate ones for the upper arm, and that below the elbow; for the thigh, and that part below the knee. Even of the hands and feet there are often no names embracing the whole. So, too, the words "leaf," "bark," are represented by distinct names, according to their character, as broad and needle-shaped leaves, the woody and fibrous barks. Sheath and pocket knives and the various forms of canoes have in like manner each their specific names.

In respect to particular words, the following points may be noted:

Man. This must be carefully distinguished from the word "person," the collective of which is "people," *i. e.*, Indians.

Boy, Girl, Infant. The answer often given for these is simply "little man," "little woman," "little one."

Husband and *wife.* Distinct words exist in most languages for these relationships; in others, it would seem as if there was only "my man," "my woman."

Indians, people. Care must be taken that the name of the tribe is not given unless really so designated.

Head. A very common mistake to be guarded against is the substitution of hair or scalp.

Face. The name for the forehead or eyes is, in some cases, employed for the whole face.

Neck. Throat is apt to be given instead of neck.

In naming parts of the body, as well as relationship, it will be found a very common practice with Indians to prefix the pronoun "my" to each one, as "my head," &c. The recurrence of the same syllable at the beginning of each word will indicate this.

Town, village. Generally speaking, the same word is given as for house, or it is rendered "many houses." In New Mexico, *pueblo* would have a different meaning from the habitations of the wild tribes.

Warrior. Among the tribes of the Pacific coast, where there is no distinctive class of warriors, this is frequently rendered "strong man," "quarrelsome," &c.

Friend is a word of very indefinite meaning. Instead of it, "cousin," or "one liked," will often be given.

Sun and *moon.* Curiously enough, these, among several tribes, bear the same name and are actually supposed to be the same. Others use for moon "night sun."

The Seasons. These words have been retained, though it is questionable if they have a very definite signification with Indians. The names of particular months, or "moons," warm or cold weather, or the periods in which particular occupations are followed probably, in most cases, replace them.

River, lake. For these simply the word "water" will often be given, as, among tribes of limited range, their own river or lake is "the water" which they best know.

Mountain. "Rock" is frequently the translation. Some tribes, again, apply a special name to snow peaks.

The colors. The idea of color seems to be indistinct, dark blue and dark green having, in many languages, the same name as black, and yellow the same as light green.

Old and *young.* Care should be taken that the words for "old man," "young man," are not supplied; or, on the other hand, "worn out," and "new," as is often the case.

Alive is frequently rendered "not dead."

Cold, warm. Here, again, caution is requisite, as cold or warm *weather* may be given instead.

Yesterday and *to-morrow.* In some languages, a single word is used for both, the distinction being made only by the connection.

Numerals. Many tribes go no farther in counting than ten, and among those of California, it is said, some have no names for numbers beyond five. Others, on the contrary, have different sets of numerals, or rather their numerals have different terminations, one class being used in ordinary counting, the other applying to men, money, &c.

Pronouns. The personal pronouns are of two classes, one simple or absolute, the other variously called fragmentary and copulative. These last are used only in composition, as in the form of prefixes and suffixes to the verbs.

Verbs. It is a matter of dispute whether the Indian verb has any true infinitive mood, as "to go," "to eat," &c., and its simplest form appears to be, in all cases, the third person singular present, "he goes," "he eats." It will be better, therefore, to obtain either this form or that of the first person, "I go," &c. The last will be found often to be combined with the copulative pronoun.

15. The Origin of the Mound Builders

Samuel Haven

In the preceding pages we have endeavored to select and condense, from a mass of miscellaneous notes, such materials as would illustrate the views entertained at different periods, and by various writers, upon subjects relating to the archaeology of the United States.

This has been done under whatever disadvantages are incident to the circumstance of having portions of the text printed before other portions were written. Had opportunity and leisure been afforded for revision of the entire paper, changes and additions might have been made that would have been likely to improve the consistency as well as the completeness of the narrative.

After a consideration of statements and speculations that have failed to present a harmonious result, the mind naturally craves the satisfaction of being able to distinguish acknowledged verities from data that are problematical, if it is only for the sake of some solid basis on which to build new theories, or some fixed point from which future investigations may take their departure. The reader will doubtless expect to be assisted in an effort to separate matters of fact from inferences and hypotheses, by a recapitulation of the principal points that have been with reasonable certainty established.

We shall endeavor, while glancing rapidly along the course of inquiry, to ascertain in what direction, and to what extent, the way is tolerably clear and the path tolerably firm.

The comparative geological antiquity of the two hemispheres is accounted by some an element of weight in estimating the probabilities of an indigenous population on this continent. It is a point, however, that cannot be determined in the present stage of geological observations. If we admit that portions of the western continent exhibit appearances of an earlier emergence than is known to be indicated elsewhere, it might still be true that the mass of the eastern hemisphere was sooner developed, and sooner prepared for the habitation of man. But until it is generally

From Samuel F. Haven, *Archaeology of the United States, or Sketches, Historical and Bibliographical, of Information and Opinion Respecting Vestiges of Antiquity in the United States,* Smithsonian Contribution to Knowledge VIII (1856). Reprinted by permission of Smithsonian Institution Press: pp. 140–159.

accepted as a fact by scientific men that America really has claims to priority of age, the assertion is, at any rate, entitled to no more than the rank of an hypothesis.[1]

The discovery of human skeletons in a fossilized state, might, under the first impression, be received as conclusive evidence of the presence of mankind in what are called the geological periods. The petrified condition of remains whose place in the rocky tablet of the earth's chronology is not beyond the reach of question, is, however, often to be explained by the rapid growth, under certain circumstances, of calcareous, silicious, and other mineral formations; while the great and sudden changes of level, produced by terrestrial convulsions and elemental influences, afford a solution of the mystery of many deep deposits beneath the soil.

The association of human bones with those of extinct species of animals, observed by Dr. Lund in the caves of Brazil, has been attributed to accidental causes. A comparatively modern date has also been assigned for the disappearance of many species of animals that have ceased to exist. The remains of the megatherium and the mastodon are found near the surface of the earth, in the United States, and do not exhibit signs of having been rolled by floods, or seriously disturbed by commotions. From the stomach of a mastodon, disinterred, at no great depth, from the mud of a small pond in Warren County, New Jersey, were taken seven bushels of the vegetable substances on which it fed, resembling the young shoots of the white cedar, still a common tree in our forests. The bones of the nearly complete specimen from Newburg, New York, purchased by the late Dr. John C. Warren, contain a considerable portion of their original gelatine, and are firm in texture. A megatherium, exhumed while digging the Brunswick Canal, was so near the surface that the roots of a pine tree penetrated its bones. Sir Charles Lyell has shown that the fresh-water and land shells, lying, in some cases, *beneath* such remains, are of the species now living in the same region; so that their climate could scarcely have differed very materially from that now prevailing in the same latitudes. In another passage, speaking of extinct quadrupeds, he says: "That they were exterminated by the arrows of the Indian hunter, is the first idea presented to the mind of almost every naturalist."[2]

An account is given of a mastodon found in Gasconade County, Missouri, which had apparently been stoned to death by the Indians, and then partially consumed by fire. The pieces of rock, weighing from two to twenty-five pounds each, which must have been brought from the distance of four or five hundred yards, "were," says the narrator, "evidently thrown with the intention of hitting some object." Intermixed with burned wood, and burned bones, were broken spears, axes, knives, &c., of stone. "The fire appeared to have been largest on the head and neck of the animal, as the ashes and coals were much deeper there than on the rest of the body." "It appeared, by the situation of the skeleton, that the animal had sunk with its hind feet in the mud and water, and, being unable to extricate itself, had fallen on its right side, and in that situation was found and killed, as above described; consequently, the hind and fore-feet, on the right side, were sunk deeper in the mud, and thereby saved from the effects of the fire." "Between the rocks that had sunk through the ashes were found large pieces of skin, that appeared like fresh tanned soleleather strongly impregnated with the lye of the ashes, and a great many of the sinews and arteries were plain to be seen on the earth and rocks, but in such a state as not to be moved, excepting in small pieces, the size of the hand, which are now preserved in spirits."[3]

In a chapter on "Traditions respecting Extinct Species," Col. Smith remarks, that the bones of the megatherium, in Brazil, are on or near the surface, in a recent state. "Now," he continues, "could they have resisted disintegration during four or five thousand years, considering these to have lain exposed to, or at least within, the influence of a tropical sun and the periodical rains? Yet they often occur on the surface, and the bones of the pelvis have been used for temporary fire-places by the aborigines, wandering on the pampas, beyond the memory of man. In North America, there are native legends which indicate traditional knowledge of more than one species. Such is that of the great Elk or Buffalo, which, besides its enormous horns, had an arm protruding from its shoulder, with a hand at the extremity (a proboscis). Another, the *Tagesho,* or *Yagesho,* was a giant bear, long bodied, broad down the shoulders, thin and narrow about the hind quarters, with a large head, powerful teeth, short and thick legs, paws with very long claws, body almost destitute of hair, except about the hind legs; and therefore called 'the Naked Bear.' Further details are furnished by the Indians, which, allowing for inadequate terminology, incorrectness in tradition and translation from the native dialects to English, leave a surprisingly applicable picture to a species of *megatheridae,* perhaps the *Jeffersonian megalonyx.* The colossal Elk, another name for the mastodon, or *Père aux Boeufs,* points out, that with designations of existing species, the Indians describe extinct animals with a precision which, in their state of information, nothing but traditionary recollections of their real structure could have furnished."[4]

Thus the bones of men and non-existent species of animals may be admitted to be contemporary without supposing that either perished previous to the chronological period.

So great advances have recently been made in Physical Geography, that we are able to determine, with reasonable accuracy, not only the probability of arrivals on the American coasts from the eastern continent, before the age of Columbus, but the points to which vessels would be driven, and the regions from whence they would be most likely to come.

To present in a few words a general idea of the currents and prevalent winds of the ocean, let us suppose the earth at rest, and the equatorial regions continually heated by the sun in his diurnal revolutions. In this condition, a continuous current of air from the north, and another directly opposite from the south, would blow towards the equator, there ascend and flow backward above toward the poles. If we next suppose the earth to be in motion on its axis from east to west and compound the effects of this motion with that of the winds towards the equator on either side, they will not meet directly opposite each other, as in the previous supposition, but in an acute angle, and produce a belt of wind from east to west entirely around the earth in the region of the equator. The continued action of this wind on the surface of the water would evidently give rise to a current of the ocean in the belt over which the wind passed. If, now, instead of considering the earth entirely covered with water, we suppose the existence of two continents extending from north to south, so as to form two separate oceans similar to the Atlantic and Pacific, then the continuous current to the west we have described would be deflected right and left at the western shore of each ocean, and would form four immense whirlpools, viz: two in the Atlantic, one north and the other south of the equator, and two in the Pacific similar in situation and direction of motion. The regularity of the outline of these whirls will be disturbed by the configuration of the deflecting coasts, the form of the bottom of the sea, as well as by islands and irregular winds. Such is a very general view of the tendencies in the direction of motion of the principal currents of the ocean.[5]

The great whirl in the north Atlantic, the western and northern portions of which are known as the Gulf Stream, passes southward down the coast of Africa, crosses the ocean in the region of the equator, is deflected from the northern portion of South America and the coast of Mexico along the United States, and recrosses the Atlantic to return into itself at the place where it started. A portion, however, of this current, probably owing to the configuration of the bottom, passes off in a tangent to the circumference of the great whirl, and flows northward along the coast of Ireland and Norway. The great whirl of the south Atlantic may also be considered as starting from the coast of Africa, crossing the Atlantic, passing down the coast of Brazil, and again recrossing the ocean at the south to near the Cape of Good Hope, and then returning to the place of original departure.

In like manner, the primary currents of the north Pacific Ocean may be described as an immense irregular whirl, the longer axis of which is in an easterly and westerly direction. Starting from the west side of Central America, it passes along the tropical region, across the ocean, then flows northerly past Japan, returns in the vicinity of the Aleutian Islands, and down the coast of Oregon and California to the place of starting. A similar, but perhaps less perfectly defined, current may be traced in the south Pacific.

The winds follow the same general law. Their prevailing direction, as we have before stated, is from the east toward the west in a belt of several degrees in width on either side of the equator, while in the northern and southern latitudes, between 40° and 60° the tendency of the wind is easterly.

A slight consideration of the foregoing views of the currents and winds of the ocean will render the fact evident, that bodies floating on the eastern shore of the Atlantic, near the equator, will tend to move in a westerly direction towards the American continent, and that bodies in higher northern and southern latitudes will move in an easterly direction, towards the coasts of Europe and Africa; that in the Pacific the currents near the equator tend to carry floating masses from the continent of America, and, in higher north and south latitudes, to bring them to its shores. For example, if a body be cast into the axis of the Gulf Stream, it will tend to move along the curve of the current towards the Cape De Verd Islands, or to be deflected by the tangential current we have mentioned to the coast of Ireland or Norway.

Besides the parallel currents we have mentioned, there is a narrow polar current from Baffin's Bay passing in part between the Gulf Stream and the American coast, and which probably bore the Icelandic navigators to Labrador and to New England.

"From present knowledge of currents, we can hardly be justified in the supposition that South America was peopled from Asia by vessels being driven south of the Equator to the American shores. The distance by that route (west-wind region south of the S. E. Trades) is not less than 10,000 miles without any islands, except New Zealand, for a resting place. The route by the Aleutian Islands, with the North Pacific 'Gulf Stream' is a much more probable route."[6]

From the foregoing view, it appears that both the winds and the currents favor an approach to this continent; and there seems to be no reason in the nature of things why both oceans may not from time to time have poured their casual and perhaps irreclaimable contributions on our shores.

Not many instances have been recorded of chance arrivals upon the European coasts from the western hemisphere. Some however may be mentioned in connection with a few illustrations of the general tendencies of the ocean currents.

Humboldt says: "There are well authenticated proofs, however much the facts may have been called in question, that natives of America (probably Eskimaux from Greenland or Labrador) were carried by currents or streams from the northwest to our own (the eastern) continent. James Wallace relates that in the year 1682 a Greenlander in his canoe was seen on the southern extremity of the Island of Eda by many persons, who could not, however, succeed in reaching him. In 1684, a

Greenland fisherman appeared near the Island of Westram. In the church at Burra, there was suspended an Eskimaux boat which had been driven on the shore." "In Cardinal Bembo's *History of Venice* I find it stated, that in the year 1508 a small boat manned by seven persons of a foreign aspect was captured near the English coast by a French ship. The description given of them applies perfectly to the form of the Eskimaux. Six of these men perished during the voyage and the seventh, a youth, was presented to the king of France."[7]

The men called *Indians* that appeared on the coasts of Germany in the tenth and twelfth centuries, and the stranded dark-colored men given to Metellus Celer by the king of the Suevi (see ante, p. 7) are supposed to have been natives of Labrador. The corpses of men of a peculiar race, having very broad faces, are said to have confirmed Columbus in his belief of the existence of countries situated in the west.

The mainmast of the English ship of war, the Tilbury, which was destroyed by fire near St. Domingo, was carried by the Gulf Stream to the northern coasts of Scotland; and casks of palm oil from the wreck of an English ship on a rock off Cape Lopez, in Africa, were carried to Scotland, having followed the equinoxial current from east to west between 2° and 12° north latitude, and the Gulf Stream from west to east between the latitudes 45° and 50°, north. Of two bottles, cast out together, in south latitude, on the coast of Africa, one was found on the Island of Trinidad; the other on Guernsey in the English channel. Another bottle, thrown over off Cape Horn by an American master, in 1837, was picked up within a few years on the coast of Ireland.

In A.D. 1500, Pedro Cabral, while on his way from Portugal to the East Indies, was driven to the coast of Brazil, which he thus accidentally discovered. In 1731, a batteau from Teneriffe came ashore near the mouth of the Orinoco. In 1797, the slaves in a ship from Africa rose upon the crew, who leaped into a boat and cut it adrift. At the end of thirty-eight days the survivors were cast upon Barbadoes. In 1799, six men in a boat from St. Helena lost their course, and after being a month at sea, and resorting to cannibalism, as was the case in the previous instance, four of them reached the South American coast alive.

To account for the population of the islands of the Pacific, Sir Charles Lyell has collected examples of the drifting of parties of savages to very great distances in their frail canoes. In one case, eight months are reported to have been passed on the broad ocean, with no other sustenance than the fishes they caught, and the rain water they found means to secure. It is remarked, in the same connection, that "the space traversed, in some instances was so great, that similar accidents might suffice to transport canoes from various parts of Africa to South America, or from Spain to the Azores, and from thence to North America."[8]

It seems necessary to concede that casual passages from the eastern to the western continents have been possible in very rude ages; and at whatever periods human enterprise has ventured to leave the immediate proximity of the land, before the arts of navigation were assisted by the compass, the probability of their occurrence must have been great.

There is within the American continent no deficiency of evidence tending to confirm the presumptions that rest on maritime facts and principles. The natives of Hispaniola are said to have intimated to Columbus that a *black people* lived south and southeast of them.[9] According to Peter Martyr, Balboa, in 1511, found *"blackamoors"* on the isthmus of Darien.[10] Torquemada says the Californians signified to Viscaino, in 1602, that there was a village of negroes not far from their neighborhood.[11] A race of very *white* Indians was said to exist in Brazil.[12] Humboldt speaks of "several tribes of a whitish complexion" in the forests of Guiana.[13] Legendary references to bearded men, with a white skin, arriving from the sea, are common to both the northern and the southern continents. Diversities of color and of physical conformation, and traces of foreign influence supposed to be detected in arts, customs, language, religion, and astronomical science, too numerous to mention, are often cited in proof of intercourse with inhabitants of the other hemisphere before the arrival of Columbus.

But all these evidences fall short of sustaining the probability of intentional colonization. They do not even suggest the arrival of men in any considerable numbers, or by other than accidental means. They imply the previous presence in the country of a native population, in whose language, arts, and physical attributes, all foreign traits have been merged almost to extinction. However frequent foreign accessions may have been, they have not had power to affect materially the structural uniformity of speech and physical conformation, and the homogeneous mental type, of the aboriginal inhabitants.

It may be inferred, from observations upon the land, as well as from the phenomena of the sea, that the casual voyagers who, in ancient times, have crossed the breadth of either ocean to our shores, were in small and feeble parties, last survivors of tempest and famine, and without women to perpetuate their race. They appear to have brought no agricultural productions from their native regions, and to have taught none of the useful arts of civilized industry. According to the laws that determine the transmission of hereditary qualities in the crossing of breeds, all traces of foreign ancestry might, under these circumstances, disappear in a few generations.

These remarks are applicable to arrivals that may be supposed to have taken place from the western shores of the eastern hemisphere, and across the middle and southern latitudes of the Pacific; but in the northern regions, where the two continents are brought almost into contact, there are other circumstances to be considered.

The practicability of voluntary passages to America, at an early period, by way of Iceland and Greenland, has been demonstrated by the Northmen; but we are unable to produce any well-established facts going to show that this practicability has ever been followed by results affecting the population of the country. We are, indeed, justified by the present aspect of the question in assuming that the Scandinavians have left no marks of residence, linguistic, physical, or monumental, to prove that they have, primarily or secondarily, been important contributors to the peopling of the New World.

The probability of permanent settlements from the Pacific side of the eastern hemisphere, near Behring's Strait, has the support of more positive indications.

The Aleutian Islands, about fifteen degrees south of the Strait, appearing on the map like stepping-stones from one continent to the other, are admirably adapted to facilitate communication between the two countries. The diminished space to be traversed, the protective proximity of the islands, a climate mild for the latitude, and a plentiful supply of fish and game, are favorable, not to change passages merely, but to intentional and continuous transits. The opposing shores are in fact occupied by divisions of the same tribe[14]; and the neighboring regions of Asia are held by that variety of mankind whose physical characters are nearly identical with those of the American race. These are circumstances that, of themselves, give plausibility to the theories which point to that quarter as the place where inhabitants were originally, and have been consecutively, transported to this continent. Those theories also derive some confirmation from the traditions and pictorial records of the southern nations, referring to a pilgrimage of their ancestors from the northwest.[15]

There are also some striking ethnological analogies which seem to connect these distant sections. The Peruvian practice of flattening the skull by compression, as a mark of nobility, is a prominent peculiarity of the tribes on Columbia River. There, too, prevails the singular and inconvenient custom of inserting disks of wood in the lips and ears, found again in Brazil;[16] and, in the dialects of the Columbians and Nootkas, may be observed that distinguishing characteristic of Mexican words, the terminal *tl*.[17]

But beyond a few such coincidences, the evidence of connection does not extend. Though often imagined, vestiges of migration from the north to the south have not been satisfactorily traced. Mr. Bartlett, while at the head of the United States Boundary Commission, gave much attention to this subject; an inquiry for which his previous ethnological studies had given him interest and preparation. "I have been unable," he says, "to learn from what source the prevailing idea has arisen of the migration of the Aztecs, or ancient Mexicans, from the north into the valley of Mexico, and of the three halts they made in the journey thither. I confess I have seen no satisfactory evidence of its truth."

"The traditions which gave rise to this notion are extremely vague, and were not seriously entertained until Torquemada, Boturini, and Clavigero gave them currency. But they must now give way to the more reliable results of linguistic comparisons. No analogy has yet been traced between the language of the old Mexicans and any tribe at the North in the district from which they are supposed to have come; nor in any relics, ornaments, or works of art, do we observe a resemblance between them."[18]

There are no antiquities in Oregon.[19] On the route from thence, there are no monuments or other works of art, such as the southern nations have left in their ancient seats, until the northern limits of a reflux influence are attained. And it is equally true that there are none of the traits of Chinese, or Japanese, or Tartarian semi-civilization, which emigrants from those nations might be expected to have brought with them.[20]

Affinities which have no *united* reference to any particular nation, but point now to one people, and then to another totally distinct from the first, and, in a third case, to others equally disconnected, however numerous they may be in the aggregate, tend, by their diversity, to weaken the force of each individual analogy as an evidence of origin, and can only serve to illustrate the possibility of accidental and partial communications. If congruous affinities, of a positive character, should be found in some detached locality, they might seem to indicate descent from a special stock; but claims to distinctive derivation, founded on such evidence, are opposed by the linguistic and physical proofs of a general unity of race throughout the entire continent.

If a feature in the customs, institutions, or dialect, of a particular tribe, or of many tribes, has a resemblance to some feature in the customs, institutions, or language, of any well-known historical people (the Jews for example), before receiving it as a proof of connection, or as an inheritance, a reason may be required why other features, more likely to be retained, are wanting; and even if many such features are adduced, unless a decided national impress accompanies them, adventitious causes may afford an explanation, which, if not entirely satisfactory, will often correspond to the real importance of the problem.[21]

Thus, if able philologists have shown the existence of certain general principles or phenomena in the languages of America, which are peculiar and characteristic, uniting them together, and distinguishing them from other languages; and if able anatomists have become assured of physical traits in the American aborigines which justify their classification as a separate variety of man; exceptions which may be pointed out in either case do not necessarily impair the soundness of their general conclusions. For exceptions may, with plausibility, be attributed to causes that are accidental, and applicable only to particular instances; and although philological and physiological affinities with other races should be equally well established, the argument drawn from radical peculiarities and idiosyncrasies may still remain unsubverted, so long as the latter are paramount.

If, in the process of reasoning, a lapse of time, whose duration cannot be defined, and an isolation without material interruption, are admitted as probabilities, the comprehensive deductions of leading European ethnologists need not of necessity conflict with those of investigators in this country, which, while claiming that the American aborigines are a distinct and peculiar people, do not deny the primitive unity of the human race.

The Chevalier Bunsen, in his recent *Philosophy of Universal History*, remarks: "It is not yet proved in detail, but it appears highly probable, in conformity with our general principles, that the native language of the northern continent of America, comprising tribes and nations of very different degrees of civilization, from the Eskimaux of the polar regions to the Aztecs of Mexico, are of one origin, and a scion of the Turanian tribe. The similarity in the configuration of the skull renders this affinity highly probable."

Having subsequently to writing the above seen the first three volumes of Mr. Schoolcraft's national work, he adds: "But the linguistic data before us, combined with the traditions and customs, and particularly with the system of pictorial or mnemonic writing (first revealed in that work) enable me to say, that the Asiatic origin of all these tribes is as fully proved as the unity of the family among themselves. According to our system, the Indian languages can only be a deposit of a north Turanian idiom. The Mongolian peculiarity of the skull, the type of the hunter, the Shamanic excitement, which leads by means of fasting and dreams into a visionary or clairvoyant state, and the fundamental religious views, and symbols, among which the tortoise is not to be forgotten, (II. 390.) bring us back to primitive Turanism. As to the languages themselves, there is no one peculiarity in them which may not easily be explained by our theory of the secondary formation and the consequences of isolation. The verity of the grammatical type was long ago acknowledged, but we have now (as I think) the evidence of the material, historical, physical unity. The Indian mind has not only worked in one type but with one material, and that a Turanian one." (Vol. II. pp. 111–13.)

"We thus see that a very considerable part of the inhabitants of America, and the Polynesian Islands, belong to that one great family which we call the Turanian race, and that the former travelled off from the Mongolian, and the latter from Malay tribes." (Ibid., p. 115.)

"The first, however, to trace with a bold hand the broad outlines of the Turanian, or as he called it, the Scythian philology, was Rask. He proved that the Finnic had once been spoken in the northern extremities of Europe, and that allied languages extended like a girdle over the north of Asia, Europe, and America. In his inquiries into the origin of the Old Norse, he endeavors to link the idioms of Asia and America by means of the Grönland language, which he maintains is a scion of the Scythian or Turanian stock, spreading its branches over the north of America, and thus indicating the antediluvian bridge between the continent of Europe and America. According to Rask, therefore, the Scythian would form a layer of language extending in Asia from the White Sea to the valleys of Caucasus, in America from Grönland southward, and in Europe (as Rask accepts Arndt's views) from Finland as far as Britain, Gaul, and Spain. This original substratum was broken up first by Celtic inroads; secondly by Gothic; and thirdly by Sclavonic immigrations; so that traces appear like the peaks of mountains and promontories out of a general inundation." (Vol. I. pp. 272–3.)[22]

As the affinities claimed in the above extracts are not those of verbal signification but grammatical construction, the classification of American languages with those comprehended in the term *Turanian* amounts simply to this; that the structure of the former exhibits that stage of advancement from an inorganic, or monosyllabic dialect, which is indicated by the system of *agglutination;* in other words, it belongs to the oldest *organic* stage.[23]

The admitted order of development in forms of speech appears to be 1st, the *monosyllabic, or inorganic,* of which the Chinese and the "so called Original People," in the Malayan Peninsula, furnish examples;[24] 2d, the *agglutinated;* 3d, the *inflected,* or highest form. But while this division corresponds with the relative antiquity of the three forms, ethnologists do not agree in supposing the last to have necessarily, in all cases, passed through the two previous stages.[25]

According to Prof. Müller's translation of grammatical conclusions into historical language, the first migration from the common centre of mankind proceeded eastward, where the Asiatic language was arrested at the first stage of its growth, and where the Chinese, as a broken link, presents a reflection of the earliest consolidation of human speech. The second dispersion was that of the Turanian tribes, who went in two divisions, Northern and Southern. In the first division are comprehended the Tungusic, Mongolic, Tartaric, and Finnic branches. In the second the Taic, Malaic, Bhotiya, and Tamulic branches. He supposes that these divisions had not attained to any social or political consolidation before they were broken up into different colonies; that they broke up, carrying away each a portion of their common language—and hence their similarity; but they possessed as yet nothing traditional, nothing like a common inheritance in language or thought, and hence their differences.

In secluded districts these differences would ultimately "change the whole surface of grammar and dictionary." The American dialects are adduced as an exemplification of the principle that if the work of agglutination has once commenced, without any literature to keep it within limits, the languages of tribes separated only for a few generations will become mutually unintelligible. (Bunsen, Phil. of Un. Hist., I. 480, *et seq.*)[26]

It thus appears that a common element required by philological theories, whether European or American, respecting the origin of population in this country, is *time*—no less than all the time that history can grant; and while they go back nearly to the most primitive form of human utterance for a matrix in which the American system of speech might have been cast, they demand for the special development of that system, and the peculiar phenomena it exhibits, a protracted term of isolation. (See ante, pp. 63–4.)

A like duration of separate existence would go far to explain the *physical* peculiarities and idiosyncrasies of the American race. A divergence from their kindred types would seem to be the inevitable result of disconnection for ages, under different influences, moral and material; and while changes of conformation might be philosophically anticipated, the fact that a wild and savage life tends to promote physical uniformity, as domestication and civilization tend to produce variety, may suffice to account for the common direction those changes have taken.

And having the element of *time* granted, we may go behind the commencement of Chinese, Japanese, and other forms of Mongolian culture, and imagine the ancestors of our aborigines to have been still mere wanderers, without arts, and with no religious faith save the primitive oriental worship of the Sun. While the parent stock upon the eastern continent would attain to whatever development it might reach under circumstances not entirely excluding it from being acted upon and instructed by other races, the offshoot in America would experience no external influences but those of Nature, and would possess as a basis of advancement only the native instincts, and possibly a few traditions, of its race.

In this manner time and isolation, which are regarded as indispensable to one division of the problem, may be made to answer the exigencies of other divisions; and whatever is wanting to account for exceptional facts or circumstances may be supplied by the supposition of waifs from other nations, occasionally cast upon these shores.

Leaving the question of origin where the latest opinions place it, among the enigmas of immemorial time, we turn to a brief summary of the archaeological facts that have been disclosed by investigation within the United States.

The characteristic antiquities of the United States are confined within certain limits. They are scanty through the entire range of the Atlantic States. A mount of some elevation on the Kennebec, in Maine, and vestiges of enclosures at Sanbornton, and near Concord, New Hampshire, are all that can be named in New England, and few of any importance are in the eastern portions of the country elsewhere. In New York they are more numerous, especially towards its western borders. Beyond the Alleghanies, and east of the Mississippi, they extend from the Great Lakes to the Gulf of Mexico; and occupy in greater or less numbers the southern regions towards the Atlantic as far as the Carolinas. They are also found on the promontory of Florida. West of the Mississippi they have been seen on the Missouri 1300 miles from its mouth; and are said to exist on the rivers Kansas and Platte. They are also known to be on some of the principal streams in Louisiana. In Texas they have not attracted attention as prominent features of the country.[27]

The earthworks are of two classes, viz: *enclosures* and *tumuli.* The enclosures are of various sizes and forms. Some are of no greater dimensions than the ordinary circumference of an Indian Council House; others are sufficiently extended to include a village. Some are evidently defensive, occupying positions of natural strength, and adapted to the nature of the ground in a manner to promote security from attack; but, in most cases, requiring the additional protection of palisades, or parapets of timber. Others have the appearance of being intended for ceremonial or religious purposes, or designed for sports and games.

The tumuli are of various forms, conical, pyramidal, dome-shaped, and pictorial, or symbolic.

The largest and loftiest of the conical tumuli are apparently monumental, covering at the base the remains of one person, or in rare instances two; and are sometimes increased in altitude by a second interment on the summit of the original mound. Their inconsiderable numbers indicate that they are special and extraordinary memorials, whose growth may be due to the tributes of generations.

The pyramidal tumuli, usually of moderate elevation, but with a broad base and truncated summit, are without remains, and are generally connected with the ceremonial class of enclosures. At the South, temples and the dwellings of chiefs were placed upon them.

Dome-shaped mounds, or *barrows,* tending more or less to a conical form, are very numerous. They may contain a single skeleton, or may be nearly composed of human bones, or they may not have been used for sepulchral purposes. A class of them, within or near enclosures such as have been termed *sacred,* cover altars and sacrificial relics.

The pictorial or symbolic mounds are almost exclusively local, and are nearly confined to the single State of Wisconsin.

All the *relics* which the seats of ancient habitation have yielded are similar in kind to the utensils, ornaments, and implements of existing races.

We may regard it as established, that there are not in the valley of the Mississippi any remains of edifices from which can be inferred a knowledge of the art of working solid materials into permanent and ornamental buildings for religious or secular purposes. There are no ruins of temples or other structures of stone, wrought by the hammer or the chisel, such as abound in Central America. There are no traces of roads and bridges to connect territorial divisions, or facilitate the commerce of an organized state, such as are found in Peru. There are no distinct evidences of arts and manufactures employing separate classes of population, or conducted as regular branches of industry. There are no proofs of the practice of reducing metals from their ores, and melting and casting them for use and ornament—none of a knowledge of chemistry or astronomy. There are no sculptured memorials exhibiting national manners and customs, the religious ideas, or the physical characteristics of the people. In a word, tokens of civil institutions, of mechanical employments, and the cultivation of science and literature however humbly, such as appear among the remains of Mexican and Peruvian civilization, have no positive counterpart in the regions of which we are speaking. Whatever may have been the kind or degree of social advancement attained to by the ancient dwellers in the valleys of the Ohio and Mississippi, those domestic arts and habits of luxury which attend the division of labor and the accumulation of private wealth, had not been sufficiently developed to leave any symbols behind them.

Yet the great enclosures at Newark, at Marietta, at or near Chillicothe, and in many other localities, with their systems of minor embankments, mounds, and excavations, manifest a unity of design, expressive of concentrated authority and combined physical effort. If those structures were produced by a sudden exertion of these agencies, they would require the presence of large bodies of disciplined men, having experience in such labors, and some regular means of subsistence. If they were gradually formed, or brought to completion by labors at various intervals of time, they imply, in addition to unity of power and action, permanent relations to the soil, and habits inconsistent with a nomadic life.

Many of these works are also such as we should expect to see appropriated to the religious ceremonials of a populous community accustomed to meet for the common observance of solemn and pompous rites. Their arrangements correspond to those which are known to be applied elsewhere to that use. The consecrated enclosures, the mounts of adoration or sacrifice, the sacred avenues approaching guarded places of entrance, are recognized as common features of semi-civilized worship, or rather as exemplifications of the manner in which the instinct of religious reverence has everywhere a tendency to display itself.

The number of works of this character, and the scale on which they are constructed, suggest irresistibly the idea of an organized multitude fond of spectacles, and habituated to public displays of an imposing nature.

It is a circumstance of great significancy that the intelligent Spanish and French adventurers and missionaries who first explored (and that pretty thoroughly), the regions where some of the most remarkable of these remains are situated, observed no want of harmony between the social condition of the natives and whatever works of art came to their notice. They evidently regarded the tribes among whom they sojourned as fully capable of producing every form of structure that they saw. It is true they might not have looked with the eyes of antiquaries, or have estimated the age of works overgrown by venerable forests, and therefore their accounts included no archaeological problems.

If we proceed according to logical propriety, from the known to the unknown, and compare the historical habits, customs, and arts, of the aborigines, with the vestiges of a more ancient era, we shall at least determine what residuum of mystery is left for future solution.

It has been a common opinion, that articles of ornament and use taken from the mounds manifest a much higher grade of mechanical proficiency than those known to have been made by modern Indians. There is, however, reason to believe that the former are the choicest specimens of art belonging to their period; and because these are found in the tombs of chiefs and upon altars of sacrifice, it does not follow that such were in common use among the people. They do not necessarily indicate any general condition of mechanical or artistic dexterity; but are likely to be the best of their kind, from whatever source they may have been obtained.

In order to estimate correctly the degree of skill in similar handicrafts possessed by the people who were found in occupation of the soil, we must go back to a time antecedent to the decline in all domestic arts which resulted immediately from intercourse with the whites. So soon as more effective implements, more serviceable and durable utensils, and finer ornaments, could be obtained in exchange for the products of the chase, their own laborious and imperfect manufactures were abandoned; and not only their industrial but their military habits underwent essential modifications from the same influence.

All articles of metal wrought or compounded with the aid of fire, whether iron, copper, or silver, and all enamelled or glass ornaments, are now equally regarded as of extraneous if not of recent origin. The highest archaeological position assigned to any of them, is that of *"intrusive antiquities,*" which may or may not have preceded European settlements in the country.

If from the relics of the mounds are separated those finer sculptures in hard materials, representing tropical quadrupeds, birds, fishes, &c., which, with some mineral substances, must have come from a different latitude, the residue might have belonged to any savage chief of any savage tribe that the first European invaders encountered.

Mr. Schoolcraft has recorded his *matured* opinion that the antiquities of the United States preserve a general parallelism with the condition of manners, customs, and arts of the later tribes, and seldom or never rise above it (Hist. and Prosp., V. p. 115); and, so far at least as minor works of art are concerned, his conclusion appears to be well sustained. The stone axes, hatchets, gouges, chisels, arrowheads, and other implements from the mounds, cannot be distinguished from the same articles that everywhere through the country have proved to be almost identical in kind and in form. In pipes there is more variety, yet without much departure from a few established patterns. It was upon these that the aborigines expended their greatest ingenuity. From an Indian burial-place in Canada (where there are no earthworks), have been taken shell-beads, pipes, and copper bracelets, precisely like those from the Grave Creek mound, in connection with articles of European manufacture. (Schoolcraft, Hist. and Prosp., I. pp. 103–5.)[28] From whatever source or sources derived, copper seems to have been in use throughout all America. On the Atlantic coasts it was noticed by all the early navigators from Nova Scotia to Patagonia. (McCulloh's Researches, p. 85.) In New France, copper ornaments, pipes, sea-shells, mica, and flint-stones, were objects of traffic. (Schoolcraft, Hist. and Prosp., V. p. 108.) The excellence of the vases and terra-cottas of the Iroquois is attested to by Mr. Squier in his work on the antiquities of New York, even as compared with the best antique specimens. The Natchez are known to have made fine earthenware of various composition and much elegance of shape, which is described by the Portuguese historian of De Soto's expedition, as differing little from that of Portugal.[29] Indeed, the art of pottery, with unequal degrees of excellence, was practised by almost every tribe. Very large vessels were made by the Natchez Indians for the collection of salt by evaporation from saline springs. (McCulloh, p. 153.) There is nearly, if not quite, as much of spirit and power of imitation to be seen in the carvings and mouldings in clay of recent native workmanship as in the specimens collected from the sacrificial mounds of the Scioto Valley; and the origin of those ancient deposits is satisfactorily illustrated by modern examples.

Thus the Chippewas were accustomed, after the shedding of blood, to perform a sacrifice of expiation, by throwing all their ornaments, pipes, &c., into a fire kindled at some distance from their huts. (Hearne's

Journey, pp. 204–6.) Winslow, in his "Good News from New England," says, "The Nanohiggansets have a great spacious house wherein only some few (that are, as we may term them, priests) come; thither at certain known times, resort all their people, and offer almost all the riches they have to their gods, as kettles, skins, hatchets, beads, knives, &c., all which are cast by the priests into a great fire that they make in the midst of the house." They attributed their freedom from the plague, which had prevailed in other places, to this custom. (Mass. Hist. Col., 2d series, vol. IX, p. 94.)

The later aborigines have not unfrequently erected mounds and other earthworks. Those formed by collecting the bones of ancestors at certain periods have been in some instances traced to modern tribes. (Jefferson's "Notes on Virginia," pp. 139–43.) A mound was erected over the body of a chief of the Omahas on the Missouri, who died of smallpox in 1800. (Lewis and Clarke, Exp., I. p. 43.) Another was raised, about twenty years since, at Coteau des Prairies, in honor of a young Sioux chief who perished while attempting an exploit of much daring. (Catlin's N. A. Indians, II. p. 170.) In Beck's Gazetteer of Missouri, a large mound is described as having been formed by the Osages within the last half century. It is said to have been gradually enlarged at intervals. (Appendix to Squier's Ab. Mon. of N. Y., p. 107.) The Natchez Indians, after they were driven from their original seats, built a large mound near Nachitoches. (Ibid., p. 108.)

It is among these retreating tribes that we might expect to find the last traces of hereditary customs. Lewis and Clarke mention seeing repeatedly, on the upper waters of the Missouri, villages either occupied at the time, or recently deserted, that were surrounded by earthen embankments, sometimes in the form of a circle. (Exp., I. pp. 54, 92, 94, 97, 112; II. 380, &c.)

Brackenridge, while travelling in the same region, "observed the ruins of several villages which had been abandoned twenty or thirty years, and which, in every respect, resembled the vestiges on the Ohio and Mississippi." (Views of Louisiana, p. 183.) All the numerous and extensive earthworks of New York have been decided by Mr. Squier to be due to the Iroquois. The process of erecting the mounds and enclosures at the South, and the uses to which they were applied, are fully described in the narratives of the early adventurers into that region. The places constructed for the performance of games, or used for such purposes, though the work of earlier generations, are noticed as among the features characteristic of modern habits and practices; and processions, and other public ceremonies, are described as occurring on a scale hardly less imposing than such as we may imagine to have filled the stately avenues and sacred enclosures of the Scioto Valley. (Du Pratz, Hist. of Louisiana, and Bartram's travels in E. and W. Florida.)

We may narrow the circle of unexplained antiquities by tracing the cordon of less mysterious vestiges surrounding that great centre of ancient habitation which is composed of States bordering on the Ohio.

East of the Alleghanies, from the Carolinas to New York, the country is nearly destitute of such remains. In New York they assume a character so nearly resembling those on the Ohio as to have been classed with them, until Mr. Squier decided by exploration that both relics of art and traces of occupancy were "absolutely *identical* with those which mark the sites of towns and forts known to have been occupied by the Indians within the historical period." The earthworks of northern Ohio are described by the same writer as corresponding with those of New York. No higher claim can be asserted for the remains north of the same line (omitting for the present the emblematic mounds of Wisconsin) and east of the Mississippi. Beyond the Mississippi the works on the Missouri, the Platte, and the Kansas, do not differ from the character of Indian structures. Further south, where such remains occur, they are comprehended in the class to which the accounts of early adventurers apply. The same may be said of those in the entire region south of Tennessee. In fact the Natchez, according to Du Pratz, maintained that their nation once extended as far north as the Ohio.[30]

Within the boundaries thus described lies a region from which no voice has come to tell when, why, and by whom, its structures were reared. They differ less in kind than in degree from other remains respecting which history has not been entirely silent. They are more numerous, more concentrated, and, in some particulars, on a larger scale of labor, than the works which approach them on their several borders, and with whose various characters they are blended. Their numbers may be the result of frequent changes of residence by a comparatively limited population, in accordance with a superstitious trait of the Indian nature, leading to the abandonment of places where any great calamity has been suffered; but they appear rather to indicate a country thickly inhabited for a period long enough to admit of the progressive enlargement and extension of its monuments.

What mighty cause of destruction anticipated by a few centuries the mission of the whites it is not easy to conjecture. That the people perished by plague or war is not more improbable than that they transferred themselves and their institutions to some yet undiscovered locality. The terrible appellation of "The Dark and Bloody Ground" applied to Kentucky, may relate to these distant events; and the fact stated by President Harrison, that the attractive banks of the Ohio, on either side, were without permanent occupants at the advent of European settlers, may have been owing to a lingering instinct of apprehension on the part of the native race.[31]

There are two other classes of remains whose origin is involved in equal obscurity—the emblematic earthworks of Wisconsin, and the so called "Garden Beds," found in the same State, and also in Michigan and Indiana. The last have hitherto been but incidentally noticed in this paper.

It is known that the culture of maize, tobacco, and a few kinds of vegetables, was practised by the aborigines throughout the United States, wherever the climate and soil were propitious, though in a careless and irregular manner; but the garden beds referred to are laid out with all the neatness and symmetry of modern husbandry. They cover large surfaces of prairie land, and as they sometimes cross the low mounds and pictorial embankments, they are supposed to have been formed after these had ceased to be objects of reverence. Mr. Schoolcraft and Mr. Lapham have fully described them.

We desire to stop where evidence ceases; and offer no speculations as to the direction from which the authors of the vestiges of antiquity in the United States entered the country, or from whence their arts were derived. The deductions from scientific investigations, philological and physiological, tend to prove that the American races are of great antiquity. Their religious doctrines, their superstitions, both in their nature and in their modes of practice, and their arts, accord with those of the most primitive age of mankind. With all their characteristics affinities are found in the early condition of Asiatic races; and a channel of communication is pointed out through which they might have poured into this continent before the existing institutions and national divisions of the parent country were developed. Fortuitous arrivals, too inconsiderable in numbers and influence to leave decided impressions, may at intervals have taken place from other lands; and geographical facts, and atmospherical phenomena, may serve to explain why the New World remained so long a sealed book to the cultivated nations of Europe, or was only known through the vague intimations and rumors alluded to in history, such as the chances of the sea, and indefinite reports from barbarous regions and peoples would be likely to bring to their ears.

Notes

[1] "There exists no reason for assuming that one side of our planet is older or more recent than the other." Humboldt, "Views of Nature," p. 106.

[2] "A Second Visit to the United States," II. pp. 270, 271; I. pp. 234, 258–9.

[3] American Journal of Science and Arts, Vol. XXXVI. pp. 199, 200.

[4] Nat. Hist. of the Human Species, pp. 104–5.

[5] This sketch of the currents of the ocean we give on the authority of the Secretary of the Smithsonian Institution.

[6] Schoolcraft's Hist. and Prosp., &c. I. pp. 23–6.

[7] "Views of Nature," p. 123.

[8] Principles of Geology, II. pp. 57–58. Mr. Gallatin was accustomed to assert that the Pacific Islands were populated at a far more recent period than the American

continent, as evinced by their languages, and hence could not have contributed to the primitive occupation of this country. In one place, he says, "Their colonization is of a date so comparatively recent that the Malay origin of the inhabitants of Otahiti and the Sandwich Islands was immediately recognized when their vocabularies were first brought to Europe. It seems probable that some of these people may have reached the main land of America; but they found the country inhabited, and either were killed or became mixed with the ancient inhabitants. No trace of the Malay language is found on the western shores of America."—*Trans. of Am. Ethnol. Soc.*, I. p. 176.

[9] Herrera, I. 374.

[10] Third Decade, p. 97.

[11] Venega's Hist. of California, p. 239.

[12] Southey's Hist. of Brazil, I. 389.

[13] Political Essay, I. 144.

[14] The Sedentary Tchuktchi.

[15] Mr. Prescott, in his treatise on the origin of Mexican civilization, after considering the weight due to various affinities of arts, customs and dialects, remarks: "The theory of an Asiatic origin for Aztec civilization derives stronger confirmation from the light of *tradition*, which, shining steadily from the far northwest, pierces through the dark shadows that history and mythology have alike thrown around the antiquities of the country. Traditions of a western or northwestern origin were found among the more barbarous tribes, and by the Mexicans were preserved both orally and in their hieroglyphic maps, where the different stages of their migration are carefully noted. But who at this day shall read them? They are admitted to agree however in representing the populous North as the prolific hive of the American races."—*Conquest of Mexico*. Appendix, p. 397.

[16] Mr. Ewbank suggests that the term Oregon or Orejones was bestowed by the Spaniards on account of the custom of preternaturally enlarging the ears.—*Life in Brazil*. Appendix, p. 459.

[17] Vater though he detected words of common origin in the vocabularies of these widely separated peoples.—*Mithridates,* theil III. abtheil. 3. p. 312.

[18] Personal narrative of Explorations, &c., II. p. 283.

[19] Letter from George Gibbs, Esq., Indian Agent, to Mr. Schoolcraft.—*Hist. and Prosp.*, &c., Vol. V. Appendix, p. 662.

[20] Some minor arts, or handicrafts, may be traced to Asiatic sources. A letter from the "Alta Californian," quoted by Dr. Bachman, states that the writer brought from Queen Charlotte's Island some specimens of native sculpture, which struck him as resembling the sculptures of the Japanese; and on taking them to Japan, they were claimed at once as Japanese articles, without any remark directing attention to them. (Charleston Med. Journal of July, 1855, p. 527.) As Japanese junks have sometimes been cast on the coast of California, articles derived from thence may have been imitated by the natives.

[21] No practice less likely to have a natural origin can be produced than one that has prevailed among some tribes in Brazil and Guiana. At the birth of a child, the husband is put to bed, and nursed with great care for a certain period, while the mother goes about her ordinary concerns. Yet the custom is alluded to as having existed among the ancient Cantabrians, the people of Congo, certain Tartars visited by Marco Paulo, the ancient Corsicans, and in the southern French provinces.—*McCulloh's Researches*, p. 99.

[22] Prof. Müller, in his "*Last Results of Turanian Researches,*" Bunsen, I. p. 484, says:—

"The Greenland language has been pointed out as showing a transition into American dialects; and the researches of physical science have already indicated the islands east of Siberia as the only bridge on which the seeds of Asia could have been carried to the New World."

Yet neither Rask nor Müller intend to imply that Greenland is to be considered a route of migration from Europe, as the islands referred to were from Asia. The mixed character of the Greenland language is otherwise explained.

[23] The Turanian dialects share one thing in common—they all represent a state of language before its individualization by the Arian and Semitic types.—Max Müller in Bunsen's *Phil. of Un. Hist.*, II. 476.

[24] Pickering's Races of Men, Bohn's edition, p. 305.

[25] Bunsen, Phil. of Un. Hist., I. p. 283.

[26] The anonymous author of a recent treatise possessing a high degree of literary and scholastic merit, draws the following conclusions from his studies and observations.

"That the first stock of man was created in the equatorial region of Africa; * * or in other words, that the true negro, the aboriginal inhabitant of Nigritia, is the primary variety of our species.

"That from the Nigritian stock, in regions equi-distant from the equator, sprang the Hottentots and the Chinese; whose striking mutual resemblance has been remarked by the accurate Barrow. And that from the Chinese sprang all the Mongolian, or Turanian races, extending from the limits of the Malayan region, through Asia and Europe to the coldest limits of the habitable earth, and through the *American continents,* pervading every zone of climate.

"That the Malayan variety, judging from physical and philological evidences together, sprang from a branch of the Mongolian or Turanian Stock nearly allied to the Chinese.

"That the Caucasian variety was brought into existence after all the other varieties mentioned above had become developed; commencing with Adam, the man created in the image of God." (*The Genesis of the Earth and Man:* A critical examination of passages in the Hebrew and Greek Scriptures, chiefly with a view to the solution of the question whether the varieties of the human species be of more than one origin; &c. &c. Edited by Reginald Stuart Poole, Edin., 1856.)

"Dr. Prichard, Mr. Pickering, and Hamilton Smith, are of opinion that the African was the primitive form and race of man, and that all the others are divergences from this earliest type; while Dr. Bachman thinks the probability in favor of the supposition that the primitive form and color was intermediate between the African and white races; and that these are therefore variations equally removed from the original." (Smyth's "Unity of the Human Races," p. 264.)

[27] Mr. Schoolcraft says that Texas is entirely without aboriginal monuments of any kind; and that neither tumuli, or remains of ancient ditches, nor attempts at rude castrametation, occur, from the plains of that State and New Mexico, east of the foot of the Rocky Mountains, till the prairie country embraces both banks of the Missouri, and reaches to the plains of Red River, and the Sascatchawine, west of the sources of the Mississippi. (Hist. and Prosp., II. 70, IV. 115. See also respecting the absence of antiquities in Oregon, Washington, and California, Ibid., V. 101.)

[28] Some of the copper implements delineated by Messrs. Squier and Davis were from Canada. Smith. Cont., I. p. 201.

[29] Conquest of Florida, Paris ed. 1685, p. 242.

[30] London ed., 1774, p. 313.

[31] The region in which Kentucky is embraced was known to the Indians by the name of the Dark and Bloody Ground. (Filson's Disc. and Settl. of Ky., p. 4.)

16. American Languages and Why We Should Study Them

Daniel G. Brinton

I appear before you this evening to enter a plea for one of the most neglected branches of learning, for a study usually considered hopelessly dry and unproductive—that of American aboriginal languages.[1]

It might be thought that such a topic, in America and among Americans, would attract a reasonably large number of students. The interest which attaches to our native soil and to the homes of our ancestors might be supposed to extend to the languages of those nations who for uncounted generations possessed the land which we have occupied relatively so short a time.

This supposition would seem the more reasonable in view of the fact that in one sense these languages have not died out among us. True, they are no longer media of intercourse, but they survive in thousands of geographical names all over our land. In the state of Connecticut alone there are over six hundred, and even more in Pennsylvania.

Certainly it would be a most legitimate anxiety which should direct itself to the preservation of the correct forms and precise meanings of these numerous and peculiarly national designations. One would think that this alone would not fail to excite something more than a languid curiosity in American linguistics, at least in our institutions of learning and societies for historical research.

That this subject has received so slight attention I attribute to the comparatively recent understanding of the value of the study of languages in general, and more particularly to the fact that no one, so far as I know, has set forth the purposes for which we should investigate these tongues, and the results which we expect to reach by means of them. This it is my present purpose to attempt, so far as it can be accomplished in the scope of an evening address.

The time has not long passed when the only good reasons for studying a language were held to be either that we might thereby acquaint

From Daniel Brinton, *Essays of an Americanist*. New York: Johnson Reprint Corporation, Publishers, In Press, pp. 308–327.

ourselves with its literature; or that certain business, trading, or political interests might be subserved; or that the nation speaking it might be made acquainted with the blessings of civilization and Christianity. These were all good and sufficient reasons, but I cannot adduce any one of them in support of my plea to-night: for the languages I shall speak of have no literature; all transactions with their people can be carried on as well or better in European tongues; and, in fact, many of these peoples are no longer in existence—they have died out or amalgamated with others. What I have to argue for is the study of the dead languages of extinct and barbarous tribes.

You will readily see that my arguments must be drawn from other considerations than those of immediate utility. I must seek them in the broader fields of ethnology and philosophy; I must appeal to your interest in man as a race, as a member of a common species, as possessing in all his families and tribes the same mind, the same soul. Language is almost our only clue to discover the kinship of those countless scattered hordes who roamed the forests of this broad continent. Their traditions are vague or lost, written records they had none, their customs and arts are misleading, their religions misunderstood; their languages alone remain to testify to a oneness of blood often seemingly repudiated by an internecine hostility.

I am well aware of the limits which a wise caution assigns to the employment of linguistics in ethnology, and I am only too familiar with the many foolish, unscientific attempts to employ it with reference to the American race. But in spite of all this, I repeat that it is the surest and almost our only means to trace the ancient connection and migrations of nations in America.

Through its aid alone we have reached a positive knowledge that most of the area of South America, including the whole of the West Indies, was occupied by three great families of nations, not one of which had formed any important settlement on the northern continent. By similar evidence we know that the tribe which greeted Penn, when he landed on the site of this city where I now speak, was a member of the one vast family—the great Algonkin stock—whose various clans extended from the palmetto swamps of Carolina to the snow-clad hills of Labrador, and from the easternmost cape of Newfoundland to the peaks of the Rocky Mountains, over 20° of latitude and 50° of longitude. We also know that the general trend of migration in the northern continent has been from north to south, and that this is true not only of the more savage tribes, as the Algonkins, Iroquois, and Athapascas, but also of those who, in the favored southern lands, approached a form of civilization, the Aztecs, the Mayas, and the Quiches. These and many minor ethnologic facts have already been obtained by the study of American languages.

But such external information is only a small part of what they are capable of disclosing. We can turn them, like the reflector of a microscope, on the secret and hidden mysteries of the aboriginal man, and discover his inmost motives, his impulses, his concealed hopes and fears, those that gave rise to his customs and laws, his schemes of social life, his superstitions and his religions.

Personal names, family names, titles, forms of salutation, methods of address, terms of endearment, respect, and reproach, words expressing the emotions, these are what infallibly reveal the daily social family life of a community, and the way in which its members regard one another. They are precisely as correct when applied to the investigation of the American race as elsewhere, and they are the more valuable just there, because his deep-seated distrust of the white invaders—for which, let us acknowledge, he had abundant cause—led the Indian to practice concealment and equivocation on these personal topics.

In no other way can the history of the development of his arts be reached. You are doubtless aware that diligent students of the Aryan languages have succeeded in faithfully depicting the arts and habits of that ancient community in which the common ancestors of Greek and Roman, Persian and Dane, Brahmin and Irishman, dwelt together as of one blood and one speech. This has been done by ascertaining what household words are common to all these tongues, and therefore must have been in use among the primeval horde from which they are all descended. The method is conclusive, and yields positive results. There is no reason why it should not be addressed to American languages, and we may be sure that it would be most fruitful. How valuable it would be to take even a few words, as maize, tobacco, pipe, bow, arrow, and the like, each representing a widespread art or custom, and trace their derivations and affinities through the languages of the whole continent! We may be sure that striking and unexpected results would be obtained.

These languages also offer an entertaining field to the psychologist.

On account of their transparency, as I may call it, the clearness with which they retain the primitive forms of their radicals, they allow us to trace out the growth of words, and thus reveal the operations of the native mind by a series of witnesses whose testimony cannot be questioned. Often curious associations of ideas are thus disclosed, very instructive to the student of mankind. Many illustrations of this could be given, but I do not wish to assail your ears by a host of unknown sounds, so I shall content myself with one, and that taken from the language of the Lenâpé, or Delaware Indians.

I shall endeavor to trace out one single radical in that language, and show you how many, and how strangely diverse ideas were built up upon it.

The radical which I select is the personal pronoun of the first person, *I*, Latin *Ego*. In Delaware this is a single syllable, a slight nasal, *Nĕ*, or *Ni*.

Let me premise by informing you that this is both a personal and a possessive pronoun; it means both *I* and *mine*. It is both singular and plural, both *I* and *we*, *mine* and *our*.

The changes of the application of this root are made by adding suffixes to it.

I begin with *ni'hillan*, literally, "mine, it is so," or "she, it, is truly mine," the accent being on the first syllable, *ni'*, mine. But the common meaning of this verb in Delaware is more significant of ownership than this tame expression. It is an active, animate verb, and means, "I beat, or strike, somebody." To the rude minds of the framers of that tongue, ownership meant the right to beat what one owned.

We might hope this sense was confined to the lower animals; but not so. Change the accent from the first to the second syllable, *ni'hillan*, to *nihil'lan*, and you have the animate active verb with an intensive force, which signifies "to beat to death," "to kill some person;" and from this, by another suffix, you have *nihil'lowen*, to murder, and *nihil'lowet*, murderer. The bad sense of the root is here pushed to its uttermost.

But the root also developed in a nobler direction. Add to *ni'hillan* the termination *ape*, which means a male, and you have *nihillape*, literally, "I, it is true, a man," which, as an adjective, means free, independent, one's own master, "I am my own man." From this are derived the noun, *nihillapewit*, a freeman; the verb *nihillapewin*, to be free; and the abstract, *nihillasowagan*, freedom, liberty, independence. These are glorious words; but I can go even farther. From this same theme is derived the verb *nihillape-wheu*, to set free, to liberate, to redeem; and from this the missionaries framed the word *nihillape-whoalid*, the Redeemer, the Saviour.

Here is an unexpected antithesis, the words for a murderer and the Saviour both from one root! It illustrates how strange is the concatenation of human thoughts.

These are by no means all the derivatives from the root *ni*, I.

When reduplicated as *nĕnĕ*, it has a plural and strengthened form, like "our own." With a pardonable and well-nigh universal weakness, which we share with them, the nation who spoke the language believed themselves the first created of mortals and the most favored by the Creator. Hence whatever they designated as "ours" was both older and better than others of its kind. Hence *nenni* came to mean ancient, primordial, indigenous, and as such it is a frequent prefix in the Delaware language. Again, as they considered themselves the first and only true men, others being barbarians, enemies, or strangers, *nenno* was understood to be one of us, a man like ourselves, of our nation.

In their different dialects the sounds of *n*, *l*, and *r* were alternated, so that while Thomas Campanius, who translated the Catechism into Delaware about 1645, wrote that word *rhennus,* later writers have given it *lenno,* and translate it "man." This is the word which we find in the name Lenni Lenape, which, by its derivation, means "we, we men." The antecedent *lenni* is superfluous. The proper name of the Delaware nation was and still is *Len âpé,* "we men," or "our men," and those critics who have maintained that this was a misnomer, introduced by Mr. Heckewelder, have been mistaken in their facts.[2]

I have not done with the root *nĕ*. I might go on and show you how it is at the base of the demonstrative pronouns, this, that, those, in Delaware; how it is the radical of the words for thinking, reflecting, and meditating; how it also gives rise to words expressing similarity and identity; how it means to be foremost, to stand ahead of others; and finally, how it signifies to come to me, to unify or congregate together. But doubtless I have trespassed on your ears long enough with unfamiliar words.

Such suggestions as these will give you some idea of the value of American languages to American ethnology. But I should be doing injustice to my subject were I to confine my arguments in favor of their study to this horizon. If they are essential to a comprehension of the red race, not less so are they to the science of linguistics in general. This science deals not with languages, but with *language*. It looks at the idiom of a nation, not as a dry catalogue of words and grammatical rules, but as the living expression of the thinking power of man, as the highest manifestation of that spiritual energy which has lifted him from the level of the brute, the complete definition of which, in its origin and evolution, is the loftiest aim of universal history. As the intention of all speech is the expression of thought, and as the final purpose of all thinking is the discovery of truth, so the ideal of language, the point toward which it strives, is the absolute form for the realization of intellectual function.

In this high quest no tongue can be overlooked, none can be left out of account. One is just as important as another. Gœthe once said that he who knows but one language knows none; we may extend the apothegm, and say that so long as there is a single language on the globe not understood and analyzed, the science of language will be incomplete and illusory. It has often proved the case that the investigation of a single, narrow, obscure dialect has changed the most important theories of history. What has done more than anything else to overthrow, or, at least, seriously to shake, the time-honored notion that the White Race first came from Central Asia? It was the study of the Lithuanian dialect on the Baltic Sea, a language of peasants, without literature or culture, but which displays forms more archaic than the Sanscrit. What has led to a complete change of views as to the prehistoric population of Southern

Europe? The study of the Basque, a language unknown out of a few secluded valleys in the Pyrenees.

There are many reasons why unwritten languages, like those of America, are more interesting, more promising in results, to the student of linguistics, than those which for generations have been cast in the conventional moulds of written speech.

Their structure is more direct, simple, transparent; they reveal more clearly the laws of the linguistic powers in their daily exercise; they are less tied down to hereditary formulæ and meaningless repetitions.

Would we explain the complicated structure of highly-organized tongues like our own, would we learn the laws which have assigned to it its material and formal elements, we must turn to the naïve speech of savages, there to see in their nakedness those processes which are too obscure in our own.

If the much-debated question of the origin of language engages us, we must seek its solution in the simple radicals of savage idioms; and if we wish to institute a comparison between the relative powers of languages, we can by no means omit them from our list. They offer to us the raw material, the essential and indispensable requisites of articulate communication.

As the structure of a language reflects in a measure, and as, on the other hand, it in a measure controls and directs the mental workings of those who speak it, the student of psychology must occupy himself with the speech of the most illiterate races in order to understand their theory of things, their notions of what is about them. They teach him the undisturbed evolution of the untrained mind.

As the biologist in pursuit of that marvellous something which we call "the vital principle" turns from the complex organisms of the higher animals and plants to life in its simplest expression in microbes and single cells, so in the future will the linguist find that he is nearest the solution of the most weighty problems of his science when he directs his attention to the least cultivated languages.

Convinced as I am of the correctness of this analogy, I venture to predict that in the future the analysis of the American languages will be regarded as one of the most important fields, in linguistic study, and will modify most materially the findings of that science. And I make this prediction the more confidently, as I am supported in it by the great authority of Wilhelm von Humboldt, who for twenty years devoted himself to their investigation.

As I am advocating so warmly that more attention should be devoted to these languages, it is but fair that you should require me to say something descriptive about them, to explain some of their peculiarities of structure. To do this properly I should require not the fag end of one lecture, but a whole course of lectures. Yet perhaps I can say enough now to show you how much there is in them worth studying.

Before I turn to this, however, I should like to combat a prejudice which I fear you may entertain. It is that same ancient prejudice which led the old Greeks to call all those who did not speak their sonorous idioms *barbarians;* for that word meant nothing more nor less than babblers (βαλβαλοι), people who spoke an unintelligible tongue. Modern civilized nations hold that prejudice yet, in the sense that each insists that his own language is the best one extant, the highest in the scale, and that wherein others differ from it in structure they are inferior.

So unfortunately placed is this prejudice with reference to my subject, that in the very volume issued by our government at Washington to encourage the study of the Indian languages, there is a long essay to prove that English is the noblest, most perfect language in the world, while all the native languages are, in comparison, of a very low grade indeed![3]

The essayist draws his arguments chiefly from the absence of inflections in English. Yet many of the profoundest linguists of this century have maintained that a fully inflected language, like the Greek or Latin, is for that very reason ahead of all others. We may suspect that when a writer lauds his native tongue at the expense of others, he is influenced by a prejudice in its favor and an absence of facility in the others.

Those best acquainted with American tongues praise them most highly for flexibility, accuracy, and resources of expression. They place some of them above any Aryan language. But what is this to those who do not know them? To him who cannot bend the bow of Ulysses it naturally seems a useless and awkward weapon.

I do not ask you to accept this opinion either; but I do ask that you rid your minds of bias, and that you do not condemn a tongue because it differs widely from that which you speak.

American tongues do, indeed, differ very widely from those familiar to Aryan ears. Not that they are all alike in structure. That was a hasty generalization, dating from a time when they were less known. Yet the great majority of them have certain characteristics in common, sufficient to place them in a linguistic class by themselves. I shall name and explain some of these.

As of the first importance I would mention the prominence they assign to pronouns and pronominal forms. Indeed, an eminent linguist has been so impressed with this feature that he has proposed to classify them distinctively as "pronominal languages." They have many classes of pronouns, sometimes as many as eighteen, which is more than twice as many as the Greek. There is often no distinction between a noun and a verb other than the pronoun which governs it. That is, if a word is employed with one form of the pronoun it becomes a noun, if with another pronoun, it becomes a verb.

We have something of the same kind in English. In the phrase, "I love," love is a verb; but in "my love," it is a noun. It is noteworthy that this treatment of words as either nouns or verbs, as we please to employ them, was carried further by Shakespeare than by any other English writer. He seemed to divine in such a trait of language vast resources for varied and pointed expression. If I may venture a suggestion as to how it does confer peculiar strength to expressions, it is that it brings into especial prominence the idea of Personality; it directs all subjects of discourse by the notion of an individual, a living, personal unit. This imparts vividness to narratives, and directness and life to propositions.

Of these pronouns, that of the first person is usually the most developed. From it, in many dialects, are derived the demonstratives and relatives, which in Aryan languages were taken from the third person. This prominence of the *Ego,* this confidence in self, is a trait of the race as well as of their speech. It forms part of that savage independence of character which prevented them coalescing into great nations, and led them to prefer death to servitude.

Another characteristic, which at one time was supposed to be universal on this continent, is what Mr. Peter Du Ponceau named *polysynthesis.* He meant by this a power of running several words into one, dropping parts of them and retaining only the significant syllables. Long descriptive names of all objects of civilized life new to the Indians were thus coined with the greatest ease. Some of these are curious enough. The Pavant Indians call a school house by one word, which means "a stopping-place where sorcery is practiced"; their notion of book-learning being that it belongs to the uncanny arts. The Delaware word for horse means "the four-footed animal which carries on his back."

This method of coining words is, however, by no means universal in American languages. It prevails in most of those in British America and the United States, in Aztec and various South American idioms; but in others, as the dialects found in Yucatan and Guatemala, and in the Tupi of Brazil, the Otomi of Mexico, and the Klamath of the Pacific coast, it is scarcely or not at all present.

Another trait, however, which was confounded with this by Mr. Du Ponceau, but really belongs in a different category of grammatical structure, is truly distinctive of the languages of the continent, and I am not sure that any one of them has been shown to be wholly devoid of it. This is what is called *incorporation.* It includes in the verb, or in the verbal expression, the object and manner of the action.

This is effected by making the subject of the verb an inseparable prefix, and by inserting between it and the verb itself, or sometimes directly in the latter, between its syllables, the object, direct or remote, and the particles indicating mode. The time or tense particles, on the other hand, will be placed at one end of this compound, either as prefixes or suffixes, thus placing the whole expression strictly within the limits of a verbal form of speech.

Both the above characteristics, I mean Polysynthesis and Incorporation, are unconscious efforts to carry out a certain theory of speech which has aptly enough been termed *holophrasis,* or the putting the whole of a phrase into a single word. This is the aim of each of them, though each endeavors to accomplish it by different means. Incorporation confines itself exclusively to verbal forms, while polysynthesis embraces both nouns and verbs.

Suppose we carry the analysis further, and see if we can obtain an answer to the query,—Why did this effort at blending forms of speech obtain so widely? Such an inquiry will indicate how valuable to linguistic search would prove the study of this group of languages.

I think there is no doubt but that it points unmistakably to that very ancient, to that primordial period of human utterance when men had not yet learned to connect words into sentences, when their utmost efforts at articulate speech did not go beyond single words, which, aided by gestures and signs, served to convey their limited intellectual converse. Such single vocables did not belong to any particular part of speech. There was no grammar to that antique tongue. Its disconnected exclamations mean whole sentences in themselves.

A large part of the human race, notably, but not exclusively, the aborigines of this continent, continued the tradition of this mode of expression in the structure of their tongues, long after the union of thought and sound in audible speech had been brought to a high degree of perfection.

Although I thus regard one of the most prominent peculiarities of American languages as a survival from an exceedingly low stage of human development, it by no means follows that this is an evidence of their inferiority.

The Chinese, who made no effort to combine the primitive vocables into one, but range them nakedly side by side, succeeded no better than the American Indians; and there is not much beyond assertion to prove that the Aryans, who, through their inflections, marked the relation of each word in the sentence by numerous tags of case, gender, number, etc., got any nearer the ideal perfection of language.

If we apply what is certainly a very fair test, to wit: the uses to which a language is and can be put, I cannot see that a well-developed American tongue, such as the Aztec or the Algonkin, in any way falls short of, say French or English.

It is true that in many of these tongues there is no distinction made between expressions, which with us are carefully separated, and are so in thought. Thus, in the Tupi of Brazil and elsewhere, there is but one word for the three expressions, "his father," "he is a father," and "he has a father;" in many, the simple form of the verb may convey three different ideas, as in Ute, where the word for "he seizes" means also "the seizer," and as a descriptive noun, "a bear," the animal which seizes.

This has been charged against these languages as a lack of "differentiation." Grammatically, this is so; but the same charge applies with almost equal force to the English language, where the same word may belong to any of four, five, even six parts of speech, dependent entirely on the connection in which it is used.

As a set-off, the American languages avoid confusions of expression which prevail in European tongues.

Thus in none of these latter, when I say "the love of God," "l'amour de Dieu," "amor Dei," can you understand what I mean. You do not know whether I intend the love which we have or should have toward God, or God's love toward us. Yet in the Mexican language (and many other American tongues) these two quite opposite ideas are so clearly distinguished that, as Father Carochi warns the readers of his *Mexican Grammar*, to confound them would not merely be a grievous solecism in speech, but a formidable heresy as well.

Another example. What can you make out of this sentence, which is strictly correct by English grammar: "John told Robert's son that he must help him?" You can make nothing out of it. It may have any one of six different meanings, depending on the persons referred to by the pronouns "he" and "him." No such lamentable confusion could occur in any American tongue known to me. The Chippeway, for instance, has three pronouns of the third person, which designate the near and the remote antecedents with the most lucid accuracy.

There is another point that I must mention in this connection, because I find that it has almost always been overlooked or misunderstood by critics of these languages. These have been free in condemning the synthetic forms of construction. But they seem to be ignorant that their use is largely optional. Thus, in Mexican, one can arrange the same sentence in an analytic or a synthetic form, and this is also the case, in a less degree, in the Algonkin. By this means a remarkable richness is added to the language. The higher the grade of synthesis employed, the more striking, elevated, and pointed becomes the expression. In common life long compounds are rare, while in the native Mexican poetry each line is often but one word.

Turning now from the structure of these languages to their vocabularies, I must correct a widespread notion that they are scanty in extent and deficient in the means to express lofty or abstract ideas.

Of course, there are many tracts of thought and learning familiar to us now which were utterly unknown to the American aborigines, and not less so to our own forefathers a few centuries ago. It would be very unfair to compare the dictionary of an Indian language with the last edition of Webster's Unabridged. But take the English dictionaries of the latter half of the sixteenth century, before Spenser and Shakespeare wrote, and compare them with the Mexican vocabulary of Molina, which contains about 13,000 words, or with the Maya vocabulary of the convent of Motul, which presents over 20,000 both prepared at that date, and your procedure will be just, and you will find it not disadvantageous to the American side of the question.

The deficiency in abstract terms is generally true of these languages. They did not have them, because they had no use for them—and the more blessed was their condition. European languages have been loaded with several thousand such by metaphysics and mysticism, and it has required many generations to discover that they are empty windbags, full of sound and signifying nothing.

Yet it is well known to students that the power of forming abstracts is possessed in a remarkable degree by many native languages. The most recondite formulæ of dogmatic religion, such as the definition of the Trinity and the difference between consubstantiation and transubstantiation, have been translated into many of them without introducing foreign words, and in entire conformity with their grammatical structure. Indeed, Dr. Augustin de la Rosa, of the University of Guadalajara, says the Mexican is peculiarly adapted to render these metaphysical subtleties.

I have been astonished that some writers should bring up the primary meaning of a word in an American language in order to infer the coarseness of its secondary meaning. This is a strangely unfair proceeding, and could be directed with equal effect against our own tongues. Thus, I read lately a traveler who spoke hardly of an Indian tribe because their word for "to love" was a derivative from that meaning "to buy," and thence "to prize." But what did the Latin *amare,* and the English *to love,* first mean? Carnally living together is what they first meant, and this is not a nobler derivation than that of the Indian. Even yet, when the most polished of European nations, that one which most exalts *la grande passion,* does not distinguish in language between loving their wives and liking their dinners, but uses the same word for both emotions, it is scarcely wise for us to indulge in much latitude of inference from such etymologies.

Such is the general character of American languages, and such are the reasons why they should be preserved and studied. The field is vast and demands many laborers to reap all the fruit that it promises. It is believed at present that there are about two hundred wholly independent stocks of languages among the aborigines of this continent. They vary most widely in vocabulary, and seemingly scarcely less so in grammar.

Besides this, each of these stocks is subdivided into dialects, each distinguished by its own series of phonetic changes, and its own new words. What an opportunity is thus offered for the study of the natural evolution of language, unfettered by the petrifying art of writing!

This is the case which I present to you, and for which I earnestly solicit your consideration. And that I may add weight to my appeal, I close by quoting the words of one of America's most distinguished scientists, Professor William Dwight Whitney, of Yale College, who writes to this effect:

"The study of American languages is the most fruitful and the most important branch of American Archæology."

Notes

[1] An Address delivered by request before the Historical Societies of Pennsylvania and New York, in 1885. It was printed in the *Pennsylvania Magazine of History and Biography* for that year.

[2] For another derivation, see *ante*, p. 182.

[3] *Introduction to the Study of Indian Languages*. By J. W. Powell (second edition, Washington, 1880).

17. American Aspects of Anthropology

Edward B. Tylor

Our newly-constituted Section of Anthropology, now promoted from the lower rank of a Department of Biology, holds its first meeting under remarkable circumstances.[1] Here in America one of the great problems of race and civilization comes into closer view than in Europe. In England anthropologists infer from stone arrow-heads and hatchet-blades, laid up in burial-mounds or scattered over the sites of vanished villages, that Stone age tribes once dwelt in the land; but what they were like in feature and complexion, what languages they spoke, what social laws and religion they lived under, are questions where speculation has but little guidance from fact. It is very different when under our feet in Montreal are found relics of a people who formerly dwelt here, Stone age people, as their implements show, though not unskilled in barbaric arts, as is seen by the ornamentation of their earthen pots and tobacco-pipes, made familiar by the publications of Principal Dawson. As we all know, the record of Jacques Cartier, published in the sixteenth-century collection of Ramusio, proves by text and drawing that here stood the famous palisaded town of Hochelaga. Its inhabitants, as his vocabulary shows, belonged to the group of tribes whose word for five is *wisk*—that is to say, they were of the Iroquois stock. Much as Canada has changed since then, we can still study among the settled Iroquois the type of a race lately in the Stone age, still trace remnants and records of their peculiar social institutions, and still hear spoken their language of strange vocabulary and unfamiliar structure. Peculiar importance is given to Canadian anthropology by the presence of such local American types of man, representatives of a stage of culture long passed away in Europe. Nor does this by any means oust from the Canadian mind the interest of the ordinary problems of European anthropology. The complex succession of races which makes up the pedigree of the modern Englishman and Frenchman, where the descendants perhaps of palæolithic, and certainly of neolithic, man have blended with invading Keltic, Roman, Teutonic-Scandinavian peoples—all this is the inheritance of settlers in America as

From *Popular Science Monthly*, 26 (1884), pp. 152–168. Reprinted by permission of Popular Science Publishing Company.

much as of their kinsfolk who have staid in Europe. In the present scientific visit of the Old to the New World, I propose to touch on some prominent questions of anthropology with special reference to their American aspects. Inasmuch as in an introductory address the practice of the Association tends to make arguments unanswerable, it will be desirable for me to suggest rather than to dogmatize, leaving the detailed treatment of the topics raised to come in the more specialized papers and discussions which form the current business of the section.

The term *prehistoric*, invaluable to anthropologists since Professor Daniel Wilson introduced it more than thirty years ago, stretches back from times just outside the range of written history into the remotest ages where human remains or relics, or other more indirect evidence, justifies the opinion that man existed. Far back in these prehistoric periods, the problem of Quaternary man turns on the presence of his rude stone implements in the drift gravels and in caves, associated with the remains of what may be called for shortness of mammothfauna. Not to recapitulate details which have been set down in a hundred books, the point to be insisted on is how, in the experience of those who, like myself, have followed them since the time of Boucher de Perthes, the effect of a quarter of a century's research and criticism has been to give Quaternary man a more and more real position. The clumsy flint pick and its contemporary mammoth-tooth have become stock articles in museums, and every year adds new localities where palæolithic implements are found of the types catalogued years ago by Evans, and in beds agreeing with the sections drawn years ago by Prestwich. It is generally admitted that about the close of the Glacial period savage man killed the huge maned elephants, or fled from the great lions and tigers on what was then forest-clad valley-bottom, in ages before the later water-flow had cut out the present wide valleys fifty or one hundred feet or more lower, leaving the remains of the ancient drift-beds exposed high on what are now the slopes. To fix our ideas on the picture of an actual locality, we may fancy ourselves standing with Mr. Spurrell on the old sandy beach of the Thames near Crayford, thirty-five feet above where the river now flows two miles away in the valley. Here we are on the very workshop-floor where palæolithic man sat chipping at the blocks of flint which had fallen out of the chalk-cliff above his head. There lie the broken remains of his blocks, the flint-chips he knocked off, and which can be fitted back into their places, the striking-stones with which the flaking was done; and with these the splintered bones of mammoth and tichorhine rhinoceros, possibly remains of meals. Moreover, as if to point the contrast between the rude palæolithic man who worked these coarse blocks, and apparently never troubled himself to seek for better material, the modern visitor sees within fifty yards of the spot the bottle-shaped pits dug out in later ages by neolithic man through the soil to a depth in the chalk where a layer of good workable flint supplied him with the material for his neat flakes and trimly-chipped arrowheads. The evidence of caverns such as those of Devonshire and Périgord, with their revelations of early European life and art, has been supplemented by many new explorations, without shaking the conclusion arrived at as to the age known as the reindeer period of the northern half of Europe, when the mammoth and cave-bear and their contemporary mammals had not yet disappeared, but the close of the Glacial period was merging into the times when in England and France savages hunted the reindeer for food as the Arctic tribe of America do still. Human remains of these early periods are still scarce and unsatisfactory for determining race-types. Among the latest finds is part of a skull from the loess at Potbaba, near Prague, with prominent brow-ridges, though less remarkable in this way than the celebrated Neanderthal skull. It remains the prevailing opinion of anatomists that these very ancient skulls are not apt to show extreme lowness of type, but to be higher in the scale than, for instance, the Tasmanian. The evidence increases as to the wide range of palæolithic man. He extended far into Asia, where his characteristic rude stone implements are plentifully found in the caves of Syria and the foot-hills of Madras. The question which this section may have especially means of dealing with is whether man likewise inhabited America with the great extinct animals of the Quaternary period, if not even earlier.

Among the statements brought forward as to this subject, a few are mere fictions, while others, though entirely genuine, are surrounded with doubts, making it difficult to use them for anthropological purposes. We shall not discuss the sandaled human giants, whose footprints, twenty inches long, are declared to have been found with the foot-prints of mammoths, among whom they walked, at Carson, Nevada. There is something picturesque in the idea of a man in a past geological period finding on the Pampas the body of a glyptodon, scooping out its flesh, setting up its carapace on the ground like a monstrous dish-cover, and digging himself a burrow to live in underneath this animal roof; but geologists have not accepted the account. Even in the case of so well-known an explorer as the late Dr. Lund, opinions are still divided as to whether his human skulls from the caves of Brazil are really contemporary with the bones of megatherium and fossil horse. One of the latest judgments has been favorable: Quatrefages not only looks upon the cave-skulls as of high antiquity, but regards their owners as representing the ancestors of the living Indians. The high and narrow dimensions of the ancient and modern skulls are given in the "Crania Ethnica," and, whatever a similarity of proportions between them may prove, it certainly exists. Dr. Koch's celebrated flint arrow-head, recorded to have been found under the legbones of a mastodon in Missouri, is still to be seen, and has all the appearance of a modern Indian weapon, which raises doubt of its being really of the mastodon period. This antecedent improbability of remote geological age is felt still more strongly to attach to the stone pestles and mortars, etc., brought forward by Mr. J. D. Whitney, of the California Geological Survey, as found by miners in the gold-bearing gravels. On the one hand, these elaborate articles of stone-work are the very characteristic objects of the Indian graves of the district, and on the other the theory that the auriferous gravels capped by lavaflows are of Tertiary age is absolutely denied by geologists such as M. Jules Marcou in his article on "The Geology of California" ("Bull. Soc. Géol. de France," 1883). It is to be hoped that the section may have the opportunity of discussing Dr. C. C. Abbott's implements from Trenton, New Jersey. The turtle-back celts, as they are called from their flat and convex sides, are rudely chipped from pebbles of the hard argillite out of the bowlder-bed, but the question is as to the position of the sand and gravel in which they are found in the bluffs high above the present Delaware River. The first opinion come to, that the makers of the implements inhabited America not merely after but during the great Ice age, has been modified by further examination, especially by the report of Mr. H. Carvill Lewis, who considers the implement-bearing bed not to have been deposited by a river which flowed over the top of the bowlder-bed, but that, at a later period than this would involve, the Delaware had cut a channel through the bowlder-bed, and that a subsequent glacier-flood threw down sand and gravel in this cutting at a considerable height above the existing river, burying therein the rude stone implements of an Esquimau race then inhabiting the country. Belt, Wilson, and Putnam have written on this question, which I will not pursue further, except by pointing out that the evidence from the bluffs of the Delaware must not be taken by itself, but in connection with that from the terraces high above the James River, near Richmond, where Mr. C. M. Wallace has likewise reported the finding of rude stone instruments, to which must be added other finds from Guanajuato, Rio Juchipila, and other Mexican localities.

This leads at once into the interesting argument how far any existing people are the descendants and representatives of man of the post-Glacial period. The problem whether the present Esquimaux are such a remnant of an early race is one which Professor Boyd Dawkins has long worked at, and will, I trust, bring forward with full detail in this appropriate place. Since he stated this view in his work on "Cave Hunting" it has continually been cited, whether by way of affirmation or denial, but always with that gain to the subject which arises from a theory based on distinct facts. May I take occasion here to mention as preliminary the question, were the natives met with by the Scandinavian seafarers of the eleventh century Esquimaux, and whereabout on the coast were they actually found? It may be to Canadians a curious subject of contemplation how about that time of history Scandinavia stretched out its hands at once to their old and their new home. When the race of bold sea-rovers who ruled Normandy and invaded England turned their prows into the northern and western sea, they passed from Iceland to yet more inclement Greenland, and thence, according to Icelandic records, which are too consistent to be refused belief as to main facts, they sailed some way down the American coast. But where are we to look for the most southerly points which the sagas mention as reached in Vineland? Where was Keel-ness, where Thorvald's ship ran aground, and Cross-ness, where he was buried, when he died by the *skräling's* arrow? Rafn, in the "Antiquitates Americanæ," confidently maps out these places about the promontory of Cape Cod, in Massachusetts, and this has been repeated since from book to book. I must plead guilty to having cited Rafn's map before now, but when with reference to the present meeting I consulted our learned editor of Scandinavian records at Oxford, Mr. Gudbrand Vigfusson, and afterward went through the original passages in the sagas with Mr. York Powell, I am bound to say that the voyages of the Northmen ought to be reduced to more moderate limits. It appears that they crossed from Greenland to Labrador (Helluland), and thence sailing more or less south and west, in two stretches of two days each they came to a place near where wild grapes grew, whence they called the country Vineland. This would, therefore, seem to have been somewhere about the Gulf of St. Lawrence, and it would be an interesting object for a yachting-cruise to try down from the east coast of Labrador a fair four days' sail of a viking-ship, and identify, if possible, the sound between the island and the *ness*, the river running out of the lake into the sea, the long stretches of sand, and the other local features mentioned in the sagas. While this is in the printer's hands, I hear that a paper somewhat to this same effect may come before the Geographical Section, but the matter concerns us here as bearing on the southern limit of the Esquimaux. The *skrälings* who came on the sea in skin canoes (*hudhkeipr*), and hurled their spears with slings (*valslöngva*), seem by these very facts to have been probably Esquimaux, and the mention of their being swarthy, with great eyes and broad cheeks, agrees tolerably with this. The statement usually made that the word *skräling* meant "dwarf" would, if correct, have settled the question; but, unfortunately, there is no real warrant for this etymology. If we may take it that Esquimaux eight hundred years ago, before they had ever found their way to Greenland, were hunting seals on the coast of Newfoundland, and caribou in the forest, their life need not have been very unlike what it is now in their Arctic home. Some day, perhaps, the St. Lawrence and Newfoundland shores will be searched for relics of Esquimau life, as has been done with such success in the Aleutian Islands by Mr. W. H. Dall, though on this side of the continent we can hardly expect to find, as he does, traces of long residence and rise from a still lower condition.

Surveying now the vast series of so-called native, or indigenous, tribes of North and South America, we may admit that the fundamental notion on which American anthropology has to be treated is its relation to Asiatic. This kind of research is, as we know, quite old, but the recent advances of zoölogy and geology have given it new breadth as well as facility. The theories which account for the wide-lying American tribes, disconnected by language as they are, as all descended from ancestors who come by sea in boats, or across Behring Strait on the ice, may be felt somewhat to strain the probabilities of migration, and are likely to be remodeled under the information now supplied by geology as to the distribution of animals. It has become a familiar fact that the *Equidœ,* or horse-like animals, belong even more remarkably to the New than to the Old World. There was plainly land-connection-between America and Asia, for the horses whose remains are fossil in America to have been genetically connected with the horses reintroduced from Europe. The deer may have passed from the Old World into North America in the Pliocene period; and the opinion is strongly held that the camels came the other way, originating in America and spreading thence into Asia and Africa. The mammoth and the reindeer did not cross over a few thousand years ago by Behring Strait, for they had been since Pleistocene times spread over the north of what was then one continent. To realize this ancient land-junction of Asia and America, this "Tertiary bridge," to use Professor Marsh's expression, it is instructive to look at Mr. Wallace's chart of the present soundings, observing that an elevation of under two hundred feet would make Behring Strait land, while moderately shallow sea extends southward to about the line of the Aleutian Islands, below which comes the plunge into the ocean-depths. If, then, we are to consider America as having received its human population by ordinary migration of successive tribes along this highway, the importance is obvious of deciding how old man is in America, and how long the continent remained united with Asia, as well as how these two difficult questions are bound up together in their bearing on anthropology. Leaving them to be settled by more competent judges, I will only point out that the theory of northern migration on dry land is, after all, only a revival of an old opinion, which came naturally to Acosta in the sixteenth century, because Behring Strait was not yet known of, and was held by Buffon in the eighteenth because the zoölogical conditions compelled him to suppose that Behring Strait had not always been there. Such a theory, whatever the exact shape it may take, seems wanted for the explanation of that most obvious fact of anthropology, the analogy of the indigenes of America with Asiatics, and more specifically with East and North Asiatics or Mongoloids. This broad race-generalization has thrust itself on every observer, and each has an instance to mention. My own particular instance is derived from inspection of a party of Botocudo Indians lately exhibited in London, who in proper clothing could have passed without question as Thibetans or Siamese. Now, when ethnologists like Dr. Pickering remark on the South Asiatic appearance of Californian tribes, it is open to them to argue that Japanese sailors of junks wrecked on the coast may have founded families there. But the Botocudos are far south and on the other side of the Andes, rude dwellers in the forests of Brazil, and yet they exhibit in an extreme form the Mongoloid character which makes America to the anthropologist part and parcel of Asia. Looked at in this light, there is something suggestive in our still giving to the natives of America the name of Indians; the idea of Columbus that the Caribs were Asiatics was not so absurd, after all.

It is perhaps hardly needful now to protest against stretching the generalization of American uniformity too far, and taking literally Humboldt's saying that he who has seen one American has seen all. The common character of American tribes, from Hudson's Bay to Tierra del Fuego, though more homogeneous than on any other tract of the world of similar extent, admits of wide sub-variation. How to distinguish and measure this sub-variation is a problem in which anthropology has only reached unsatisfactory results. The broad distinctions which are plainly seen are also those which are readily defined, such as the shape of the nose, curve of the lips, or the projection of the cheek-bones. But all who have compared such American races as Aztecs and Ojibways must be sensible of extreme difficulty in measuring the proportions of an average facial type. The attempt to give in a single pair of portraits a generalized national type has been tried—for instance, in the St. Petersburg set of models of races at the Exhibition of 1862. But done merely by eye, as they were, they were not so good as well-chosen individual portraits. It would be most desirable that Mr. Francis Galton's method of photographs, superposed so as to combine a group of individuals into one generalized portrait, should have a thorough trial on groups of Iroquois, Aztecs, Caribs, and other tribes who are so far homogeneous in feature as to lend themselves to form an abstract portrait. A set of American races thus "Galtonized" (if I may coin the term) would very likely be so distinctive as to be accepted in anthropology. Craniological measurement has been largely applied in America, but unfortunately it was set wrong for years by the same misleading tendency to find a uniformity not really existent. Those who wish to judge Morton's dictum applied to the Scioto mound skull, "the perfect type of Indian conformation, to which the skulls of all the tribes from Cape Horn to Canada more or less approximate," will find facts to the contrary set forth in chapter xx of Wilson's "Prehistoric Man," and in Quatrefages and Hamy, "Crania Ethnica."

American crania really differ so much that the hypothesis of successive migrations has been brought in to account for the brachycephalic skulls of the mound-builders as compared with living Indians of the district. Among minor race-divisions, as one of the best extablished may be mentioned that which in this district brings the Algonquin and Iroquois together into the dolichocephalic division; yet even here some divide the Algonquins into two groups by their varying breadth of skull. What may be the interpretation of the cranial evidence as bearing on the American problem it would be premature to say; at present all that can be done is to systematize facts. It is undisputed that the Esquimaux in their complexion, hair, and features approximate to the Mongoloid type of North Asia; but when it comes to cranial measurement the Esquimaux with their narrower skulls, whose proportion of breadth to length is only seventy-five to eighty, are far from conforming to the broad-skulled type of North Asiatic Mongoloids, whose average index is toward eighty-five. Of this divergence I have no explanation to offer; it illustrates the difficulties which have to be met by a young and imperfect science.

To clear the obscurity of race-problems, as viewed from the anatomical standing-point, we naturally seek the help of language. Of late years the anthropology of the Old World has had ever-increasing help from comparative philology. In such investigations, when the philologist seeks a connection between the languages of distant regions, he endeavors to establish both a common stock of words and a common grammatical structure. For instance, this most perfect proof of connection has been lately adduced by Mr. R. H. Codrington in support of the view that the Melanesians and Polynesians, much as they differ in skin and hair, speak languages which belong to a common stock. A more adventurous theory is that of Lenormant and Sayce, that the old Chaldean language is connected with the Tartar group; yet even here there is an *a priori* case based at once on analogies of dictionary and grammar. The comparative method becomes much weaker when few or no words can be claimed as similar, and the whole burden of proof has to be borne by similar modes of word formation and syntax, as, for example, in the researches of Aymonier and Keane tending to trace the Malay group of languages into connection with the Khmer or Cambodian. Within America the philologist uses with success the strong method of combined dictionary and grammar in order to define his great language-groups, such as the Algonquin extending from Hudosn's Bay to Virginia, the Athapascan from Hudson's Bay to New Mexico, both crossing Canada in their vast range. But attempts to trace analogies between lists of words in Asiatic and American languages, though they may have shown some similarities deserving further inquiry, have hardly proved an amount of correspondence beyond what chance coincidence would be capable of producing. Thus, when it comes to judging of affinities between the great

American language-families, or of any of them with the Asiatic, there is only the weaker method of structure to fall back on. Here the Esquimau analogy seems to be with North Asiatic languages. It would be defined as agglutinative-suffixing, or, to put the definition practically, an Esquimau word of however portentous length is treated by looking out in the dictionary the first syllable or two, which will be the root, the rest being a string of modifying suffixes. The Esquimau thus presents in an exaggerated form the characteristic structure of the vast Ural-Altaic or Turanian group of Asiatic languages. In studying American languages as a whole, the first step is to discard the generalization of Duponceau as to the American languages from Greenland to Cape Horn being united together, and distinguished from those of other parts of the world, by a common character of polysynthetism, or combining whole sentences into words. The real divergences of structure in American language-families are brought clearly into view in the two dissertations of M. Lucien Adam, which are the most valuable papers of the Congrès International des Americanistes. Making special examination of sixteen languages of North and South America, Adam considers these to belong to a number of independent or irreducible families, as they would have been, he says, "had there been primitively several human couples." It may be worth suggesting, however, that the task of the philologer is to exhaust every possibility of discovering connections between languages before falling back on the extreme hypothesis of independent origins. These American language-families have grammatical tendencies in common, which suggest original relationship, and in some of these even correspond with languages of other regions in a way which may indicate connection rather than chance. For instance, the distinction of gender, not by sex as male and female, but by life as animate and inanimate, is familiar in the Algonquin group; in Cree *muskesin*=shoe (*moccasin*) makes its plural *muskesină*, while *eskwayŭ*=woman (squaw) makes its plural *eskwaywuk*. Now, this kind of gender is not peculiar to America, but appears in Southeast Asia, as for instance in the Kol languages of Bengal. In that Asiatic district also appears the habit of infixing, that is, of modifying roots or words by the insertion of a letter or syllable, somewhat as the Dakota language inserts a pronoun within the verb-root itself, or as that remarkable language, the Choctaw, alters its verbs by insertions of a still more violent character. Again, the distinction between the inclusive and exclusive pronoun *we*, according as it means "you and I" or "they and I," etc. (the want of which is perhaps a defect in English), is as familiar to the Maori as to the Ojibway. Whether the languages of the American tribes be regarded as derived from Asia or as separate developments, their long existence on the American Continent seems unquestionable. Had they been the tongues of tribes come within a short time by Behring Strait, we should have expected them to show clear connection with the tongues of their kindred left behind in Asia, just as the Lapp in Europe, whose ancestors have been separated for thousands of years from the ancestors of the Ostiak or the Turk, still shows in his speech the traces of their remote kinship. The problem how tribes so similar in physical type and culture as the Algonquins, Iroquois, Sioux, and Athapascans, should adjoin one another, yet speaking languages so separate, is only soluble by influences which have had a long period of time to work in.

The comparison of peoples according to their social framework of family and tribe has been assuming more and more importance since it was brought forward by Bachofen, McLennan, and Morgan. One of its broadest distinctions comes into view within the Dominion of Canada. The Esquimaux are patriarchal, the father being head of the family, and descent and inheritance following the male line. But the Indian tribes farther south are largely matriarchal, reckoning descent not on the father's but the mother's side. In fact, it was through becoming an adopted Iroquois that Morgan became aware of this system, so foreign to European ideas, and which he supposed at first to be an isolated peculiarity. No less a person than Herodotus had fallen into the same mistake over two thousand years ago, when he thought the Lykians, in taking their names from their mothers, were unlike all other men. It is now, however, an accepted matter of anthropology, that in Herodotus's time nations of the civilized world had passed through this matriarchal stage, as appears from the survivals of it retained in the midst of their newer patriarchal institutions. For instance, among the Arabs to this day, strongly patriarchal as their society is in most respects, there survives that most matriarchal idea that one's nearest relative is not one's father but one's maternal uncle; he is bound to his sister's children by a "closer and holier tie" than paternity, as Tacitus says of the same conception among the ancient Germans. Obviously great interest attaches to any accounts of existing tribes which preserve for us the explanation of such social phenomena. Some of the most instructive of these are too new to have yet found their way into our treatises on early institutions; they are accounts lately published by Dutch officials among the non-Islamized clans of Sumatra and Java. G. A. Wilken, "Over de Verwantschap en het Huwelijks en Erfrecht bij de Volken van den Indischen Archipel," summarizes the account put on record by Van Hasselt as to the life of the Malays of the Padang Highlands of Mid-Sumatra, who are known to represent an early Malay population. Among these people not only kinship but habitation follows absolutely the female line, so that the numerous dwellers in one great house are all connected by descent from one mother, one generation above another, children, then mothers and maternal uncles and aunts, then grandmothers and maternal great-uncles and great-aunts, etc. There are in each district several *suku* or mother-clans, between persons born in which marriage is forbidden. Here, then, appear the two well-known rules of female descent and exogamy, but now we come into view of the remarkable state of society, that, though marriage exists, it does not form the household. The woman remains in the maternal house she was born in, and the man remains in his; his position is that of an authorized visitor; if he will, he may come over and help her in the rice-field, but he need not; over the children he has no control whatever, and were he to presume to order or chastise them, their natural guardian, the mother's brother (*mamak*), would resent it as an affront. The law of female descent and its connected rules have as yet been mostly studied among the native Americans and Australians, where they have evidently undergone much modification. Thus, one hundred and fifty years ago, Father Lafitau mentions that the husband and wife, while in fact moving into one another's hut, or setting up a new one, still kept up the matriarchal idea by the fiction that neither he nor she quitted their own maternal house. But in the Sumatra district just referred to, the matriarchal system may still be seen in actual existence, in a most extreme and probably early form. If, led by such new evidence, we look at the map of the world from this point of view, there discloses itself a remarkable fact of social geography. It is seen that matriarchal exogamous society, that is, society with female descent and prohibition of marriage within the clan, does not crop up here and there, as if it were an isolated invention, but characterizes a whole vast region of the world. If the Malay district be taken as a center, the system of intermarrying mother-clans may be followed westward into Asia, among the Garos and other hill tribes of India. Eastward from the Indian Archipelago it pervades the Melanesian Islands, with remains in Polynesia; it prevails widely in Australia, and stretches north and south in the Americas. This immense district represents an area of lower culture, where matriarchalism has only in places yielded to the patriarchal system, which develops with the idea of property, and which, in the other and more civilized half of the globe, has carried all before it, only showing in isolated spots and by relics of custom the former existence of matriarchal society. Such a geographical view of the matriarchal region makes intelligible facts which, while not thus seen together, were most puzzling. When years ago Sir George Grey studied the customs of the Australians, it seemed to him a singular coincidence that a man whose maternal family name was Kangaroo might not marry a woman of the same name, just as if he had been a Huron of the Bear or Turtle totem, prohibited accordingly from taking a wife of the same. But when we have the facts more completely before us, Australia and Canada are seen to be only the far ends of a world-district pervaded by these ideas, and the problem becomes such a one as naturalists are quite accustomed to. Though Montreal and Melbourne are far apart, it may be that in prehistoric times they were both connected with Asia by lines of social institution as real as those which in modern times connect them through Europe. Though it is only of late that this problem of ancient society has received the attention it deserves, it is but fair to mention how long ago its scientific study began in the part of the world where we are assembled. Father Lafitau, whose "Mœurs des Sauvages Amériquains" was published in 1724, carefully described among the Iroquois and Hurons the system of kinship to which Morgan has since given the name of "classificatory," where the mother's sisters are reckoned as mothers, and so on. It is remarkable to find this acute Jesuit missionary already pointing out how the idea of the husband being an intruder in his wife's house bears on the pretense of surreptitiousness in marriage among the Spartans. He even rationally interprets in this way a custom which to us seems fantastic, but which is a most serious observance among rude tribes widely spread over the world. A usual form of this custom is that the husband and his parents-in-law, especially his mother-in-law, consider it shameful to speak to or look at one another, hiding themselves or getting out of the way, at least in pretense, if they meet. The comic absurdity of these scenes, such as Tanner describes among the Assiniboins, disappears if they are to be understood as a legal ceremony, implying that the husband has nothing to do with his wife's family. To this part of the world also belongs a word which has been more effective than any treatise in bringing the matriarchal system of society into notice. This is the term *totem,* introduced by Schoolcraft to describe the mother-clans of the Algonquins, named "Wolf," "Bear," etc. Unluckily the word is wrongly made. Professor Max Müller has lately called attention to the remark of the Canadian philologist, Father Cuoq ("N. O. Ancien Missionnaire"), that the word is properly *ote,* meaning "family mark," possessive *otem,* and with the personal pronoun *nind otem,* "my family mark," *kit otem,* "thy family mark." It may be seen, in Schoolcraft's own sketch of Algonquin grammar, how he erroneously made from these a word *totem,* and the question ought perhaps to be gone into in this section, whether the term had best be kept up or amended, or a new term substituted. It is quite worth while to discuss the name, considering what an important question of anthropology is involved in the institution it expresses. In this region there were found Iroquois, Algonquins, Dakotas, separate in language, and yet whose social life was regulated by the matriarchal totem structure. May it not be inferred from such a state of things, that social institutions form a deeper-lying element in man than language or even physical racetype? This is a problem which presents itself for serious discussion, when the evidence can be brought more completely together.

It is obvious that, in this speculation, as in other problems now presenting themselves in anthropology, the question of the antiquity of man lies at the basis. Of late no great progress has been made toward fixing a scale of calculation of the human period, but the arguments as to time required for alterations in valley-levels, changes of fauna, evolution of races, languages, and culture, seem to converge more conclusively than ever toward a human period short indeed as a fraction of geological time, but long as compared with historical and chronological time. While, however, it is felt that length of time need not debar the anthropologists from hypotheses of development and migration, there is more caution as to assumptions of millions of years where no arithmetical basis exists, and less tendency to treat everything prehistoric as necessarily of extreme antiquity, such as, for instance, the Swiss lake-dwelling and the Central American temples. There are certain problems of American anthropology which are not the less interesting for involving no considerations of high antiquity; indeed, they have the advantage of being within the check of history, though not themselves belonging to it.

Humboldt's argument as to traces of Asiatic influence in Mexico is one of these. The four ages in the Aztec picture-writings, ending with catastrophes of the four elements, earth, fire, air, water, compared by him with the same scheme among the Banyans of Surat, is a strong piece of evidence which would become yet stronger if the Hindoo book could be found from which the account is declared to have been taken. Not less cogent is his comparison of the zodiacs or calendar-cycles of Mexico and Central America with those of Eastern Asia, such as that by which the Japanese reckon the sixty-year cycle by combining the elements *seriatim* with the twelve animals, Mouse, Bull, Tiger, Hare, etc.; the present year is, I suppose, the second water-ape year, and the time of day is the goat-hour. Humboldt's case may be re-enforced by the consideration of the magical employment of these zodiacs in the Old and New World. The description of a Mexican astrologer, sent for to make the arrangements for a marriage by comparing the zodiac animals of the birthdays of bride and bridegroom, might have been written almost exactly of the modern Calmucks; and in fact it seems connected in origin with similar rules in our own books of astrology. Magic is of great value in thus tracing communication, direct or indirect, between distant nations. The power of lasting and traveling which it possesses may be instanced by the rock-pictures from the sacred Roches Percées of Manitoba, sketched by Dr. Dawson, and published in his father's volume on "Fossil Man," with the proper caution that the pictures, or some of them, may be modern. Besides the rude pictures of deer and Indians and their huts, one sees with surprise a pentagram more neatly drawn than that defective one which let Mephistopheles pass Faust's threshold, though it kept the demon in when he had got there. Whether the Indians of Manitoba learned the magic figure from the white man, or whether the white man did it himself in jest, it proves a line of intercourse stretching back twenty five hundred years to the time when it was first drawn as a geometrical diagram of the school of Pythagoras. To return to Humboldt's argument, if there was communication from Asia to Mexico before the Spanish Conquest, it ought to have brought other things, and no things travel more easily than games. I noticed some years ago that the Aztecs are described by the old Spanish writers as playing a game called *patolli,* where they moved stones on the squares of a cross-shaped mat, according to the throws of beans marked on one side. The description minutely corresponds with the Hindoo game of *pachisi,* played in like manner with cowries instead of beans; this game, which is an early variety of backgammon, is well known in Asia, whence it seems to have found its way into America. From Mexico it passed into Sonora and Zacatecas, much broken down but retaining its name, and it may be traced still further into the game of plum-stones among the Iroquois and other tribes. Now, if the probability be granted that these various American notions came from Asia, their importation would not have to do with any remotely ancient connection between the two continents. The Hindoo element-catastrophes, the East Asiatic zodiac-calendars, the game of backgammon, seem none of them extremely old, and it may not be a thousand years since they reached America. These are cases in which we may reasonably suppose communication by seafarers, perhaps even in some of those junks which are brought across so often by the ocean-current and wrecked on the California coast. In connection with ideas borrowed from Asia there arises the question, How did the Mexicans and Peruvians become possessed of bronze? Seeing how imperfectly it had established itself, not even dispossessing the stone implements, I have long believed it to be an Asiatic importation of no great antiquity, and it is with great satisfaction that I find such an authority on prehistoric archæology as Professor Worsaae comparing the bronze implements in China and Japan with those of Mexico and Peru, and declaring emphatically his opinion that bronze was a modern novelty introduced into America. While these items of Asiatic culture in America are so localized as to agree best with the hypothesis of communication far south across the Pacific, there are others which agree best with the routes far north. A remarkable piece of evidence pointed out by General Pitt-Rivers is the geographical distribution of the Tartar or composite bow, which in construction is unlike the long-bow, being made of several pieces spliced together, and which is bent backward to string it. This distinctly Asiatic form may be followed across the region of Behring Strait into America among the Esquimaux and northern Indians, so that it can hardly be doubted that its coming into America was by a northern line of migration. This important movement in culture may have taken place in remotely ancient times.

A brief account may now be given of the present state of information as to movements of civilization within the double continent of America. Conspicuous among these is what may be called the northward drift of civilization, which comes well into view in the evidence of botanists as to cultivated plants. Maize, though allied to, and probably genetically connected with, an Old World graminaceous family, is distinctly American, and is believed by De Candolle to have been brought into cultivation in Peru, whence it was carried from tribe to tribe up into the North. To see how closely the two continents are connected in civilization, one need only look at the distribution on both of maize, tobacco, and cacao. It is admitted as probable that from the Mexican and Central American region agriculture traveled northward, and became extablished among the native tribes. This direction may be clearly traced in a sketch of their agriculture, such as is given in Mr. Lucien Carr's paper on the "Mounds of the Mississippi Valley." The same staple cultivation passed on from place to place—maize, haricots, pumpkins, for food, and tobacco for luxury. Agriculture among the Indians of the Great Lakes is plainly seen to have been an imported craft by the way in which it had spread to some tribes but not to others. The distribution of the potter's art is similarly partial, some tribes making good earthen vessels, while others still boiled meat in its own skin with hot stones, so that it may well be supposed that the arts of growing corn and making the earthen pot to boil the hominy came together from the more civilized nations of the south. With this northward drift of civilization other facts harmonize. The researches of Buschmann, published by the Berlin Academy, show how Aztec words have become imbedded in the languages of Sonora, New Mexico, and up the western side of the continent, which could not have spread there without Mexican intercourse extending far northwest. This, indeed, has left many traces still discernible in the industrial and decorative arts of the Pueblo Indians. Along the courses of this northward drift of culture remain two remarkable series of structures probably connected with it. The *casas grandes,* the fortified communal barracks (if I may so call them) which provided house-room for hundreds of families, excited the astonishment of the early Spanish explorers, but are only beginning to be thoroughly described now that such districts as the Taos Valley have come within reach by the railroads across to the Pacific. The accounts of these village-forts and their inhabitants, drawn up by Major J. W. Powell, of the Bureau of Ethnology, and Mr. Putnam, of the Peabody Museum, disclose the old communistic society surviving in modern times, in instructive comment on the philosophers who are seeking to return to it. It would be premature in the present state of information to decide whether Mr. J. L. Morgan, in his work on the "Houses and House-Life of the American Aborigines," had realized the conditions of the problem. It is plausible to suppose with him a connection between the communal dwellings of the American Indians, such as the Iroquois long-house with its many family hearths, with the more solid buildings inhabited on a similar social principle by tribes such as the Zuñis of New Mexico. Morgan was so much a man of genius, that his speculations, even when at variance with the general view of the facts, are always suggestive. This is the case with his attempt to account for the organization of the Aztec state as a highly developed Indian tribal community, and even to explain the many-roomed stone palaces, as they are called, of Central America, as being huge communal dwellings like those of the Pueblo Indians. I will not go further into the subject here, hoping that it may be debated in the section by those far better acquainted with the evidence. I need not, for the same reason, do much more than mention the mound-builders, nor enter largely on the literature which has grown up about them since the publication of the works of Squier and Davis. Now that the idea of their being a separate race of high antiquity has died out, and their earth-works, with the implements and ornaments found among them, are brought into comparison with those of other tribes of the country, they have settled into representatives of one of the most notable stages of the northward drift of culture among the indigenes of America.

Concluding this long survey, we come to the practical question how the stimulus of the present meeting may be used to promote anthropology in Canada. It is not as if the work were new here; indeed, some of its best evidence has been gathered on this ground from the days of the French missionaries of the seventeenth century. Naturally, in this part of the country, the rudimentary stages of thought then to be found among the Indians have mostly disappeared. For instance, in the native conceptions of souls and spirits the crudest animistic ideas were in full force. Dreams were looked on as real events, and the phantom of a living or a dead man seen in a dream was considered to be that man's personality and life, that is, his soul. Beyond this, by logical extension of the same train of thought, every animal or plant or object, inasmuch as its phantom could be seen away from its material body in dreams or visions, was held to have a soul. No one ever found this primitive conception in more perfect form than Father Lallemant, who describes, in the "Rélations des Jesuites" (1626), how, when the Indians buried kettles and furs with the dead, the bodies of these things remained, but the souls of them went to the dead men who used them. So Father La Jeune describes the souls, not only of men and animals, but of hatchets and kettles, crossing the water to the Great Village out in the sunset. The genuineness of this idea of object-souls is proved by other independent explorers finding them elsewhere in the world. Two of the accounts most closely tallying with the American come from the Rev. Dr. Mason, in Burmah, and the Rev. J. Williams, in Feejee. That is to say, the most characteristic development of early animism belongs to the same region as the most characteristic development of matriarchal society, extending from Southeast Asia into Melanesia and Polynesia, and North and South America. Every one who studies the history of human thought must see the value of such facts as these, and the importance of gathering them up among the rude tribes who preserve them, before they pass into a new stage of culture. All who have read Mr. Hale's studies on the Hiawatha legend and other Indian folk-lore must admit that the native traditions, with their fragments of real history, and their incidental touches of native religion, ought never to be left to die out unrecorded. In the Dominion, especially in its outlying districts toward the Arctic region and over the Rocky Mountains, there is an enormous mass of anthropological material of high value to be collected; but this collection must be done within the next generation, or there will be little left to collect. The small group of Canadian anthropologists, able and energetic as they are, can manage and control this work, but can not do it all themselves. What is wanted is a Canadian Anthropological Society with a stronger organization than yet exists, able to arrange explorations in promising districts, to circulate questions and requirements among the proper people in the proper places, and to lay a new burden on the shoulders of the already hardworked professional men, and other educated settlers through the newly opened country, by making them investigators of local anthropology. The Canadian Government, which has well deserved the high reputation it holds throughout the world for wisdom and liberality in dealing with the native tribes, may reasonably be asked to support more thorough exploration, and collection and publication of the results, in friendly rivalry with the United States Government, which has in this way fully acknowledged the obligation of making the colonization of new lands not only promotive of national wealth, but serviceable to science. It is not for me to do more here, and now, than to suggest practical steps toward this end. My laying before the section so diffusive a sketch of the problems of anthropology, as they present themselves in the Dominion, has been with the underlying intention of calling public notice to the important scientific work now standing ready to Canadian hands; the undertaking of which, it is to be hoped, will be one outcome of this visit of the British Association to Montreal.

Notes

[1] Vice-President's address to the Section of Anthropology of the British Association at the Montreal meeting.

18. Man's Place in Nature

W. J. McGee

In the opening paragraphs of his most memorable contribution to knowledge (*Man's Place in Nature,* 1863) Huxley made mention of certain similarities between the activities of anthropoids and those of men; and while the burden of the work was devoted to structural homologies, the initial keynote was retouched here and there throughout the discussion.[1] Huxley's classic contribution to anthropology needs no encomium; it was a pioneer's milemark of progress, erected under difficulties; and it suffices that all later travelers have found it in the direct way of experiential truth. Yet it is worth while now and then to take stock of advances subsequent to, and largely consequent on, the Huxleian declaration.

Since Huxley's pioneer work, a host of investigators have carried forward the study of structural homologies connecting the genus *Homo* with lower genera and orders; and today the physical similarities are among the commonplaces of knowledge, whatsoever the background of philosophical opinion concerning cause and sequence. During the last decade or two the investigators themselves, with scarce an exception, have gone one step further, and now include sequence of development from lower to higher forms as among the commonplaces of opinion, whatsoever the background of metaphysical notion as to cause. There the strictly biologic aspect of the question as to man's place in nature may safely be considered to rest; there has been little advance in opinion beyond that of the pioneer in 1863; but the data have been multiplied, and the knowledge and opinion have been diffused widely.

Since Huxley's epoch-marking memoir was first published, occasional contributions have been made to knowledge of the activities displayed by various sub-human animals, and during the last quarter of the nineteenth century a science (which has been called the New Ethnology) has been organized to deal with the activities of mankind; yet singularly little has been done in the way of tracing activital homologies between the genus *Homo* and lower genera. It is indeed conventional for sociologists, and customary for comprehensive writers on anthropology, to

From the *American Anthropologist,* Vol. 3, no. 1 (1901), pp. 1–13. Reprinted by permission of the American Anthropological Association.

instance the social habits of mammals and birds, and even of insects and infusoria, as analogous to human society; one naturalist has gone so far as to study various mammals and birds in their activital aspects, thereby opening a most attractive field in science as well as in literature; but no investigators have turned seriously toward the habitual activities displayed by the anthropoids—still less have comparative studies been made of the activities normal to both the higher quadrumana and the lower races of mankind, albeit this is perhaps the most inviting field now open to research. Thus far this line of inquiry grovels in the stage of travelers' tales; the gorilla-hunter tells how the family sire sleeps at the foot of a tree in which mother and young are nested, the naturalist in Liberia incidentally describes the use by monkeys of stick and stone implements, while the Bornean tourist tells of the simian servant who prefers the society of human masters to that of his kin and discriminates among the garments he is permitted to wear; but there is a woful dearth of critical observation and a lamentable lack of judicious generalization pertaining to this promising meeting-ground of zoölogy and anthropology. So this aspect, too, of the great question concerning man's place in nature remains nearly as it was left by Huxley; the data are more abundant, and opinion has been both clarified and diffused; yet definite homologies remain practically unfound, if not unsought, and the scattered facts have thrown little light on cause, less on sequence.

Since Huxley's prime, the New Ethnology has arisen; and it has opened a vista of facts and relations which apparently escaped the keen vision of the pioneer in 1863—the vista embracing thought, with all the other psychic factors pertaining to the activities, sub-human as well as human. This vista is perhaps the broadest and most attractive ever opened by science: When Galileo descried the harmonious paths of the planets in a sun-centered system, he raised the minds of men to a new plane; when Newton grasped the idea of gravitation, he gave human thought a new hold on nature; when Darwin discerned the lines of specific development, he wrought a revolution in the world of intellect; but when students still living scanned the lines of activital development and realized that thought itself is bred by the very activities over which it comes later to hold dominion, they opened a new intellectual world—a world at once so novel and so commanding that some of the students themselves are fain to sit at the gate and view the prospect as fleeting phantasm rather than veritable reality. Nor is their hesitation either unprecedented or unpardonable: When the biologists of only one long generation ago unrolled the scroll picturing the origin and perpetuation of species through natural interactions, their interpretation seemed too simple to be true; when the anthropologists of the present generation unrolled a similar scroll picturing the origin of activities (arts, industries, laws, languages, doctrines) through natural interactions and self-developed interrelations—and in this way alone—their interpretation in turn seemed too simple to be true; and when the anthropologists of the old century's end (and of this Society) unroll a scroll picturing the origin and development of thought itself through the long chain of interactions between the thinking organism and external nature—and in this way alone—, they foresee that their interpretation must seem too simple to be true—though they find comfort in the teachings of experience that in the long run simple explanations are preferred, that simple doctrines at last prevail, indeed that the progress of knowledge is best measured by its own simplification. But even after full allowance for hesitation and doubt, it must still be said that the opening of the post-Huxleian vista has had much effect: It has widened the view of nature to include the psychical as well as the physical aspects of organisms; it has correspondingly narrowed the range of extra-natural explanations of phenomena; and, specifically, it has revealed a new class of homologies among the races of men and between these and sub-human organisms. So the homologies recognized today as defining man's place in nature are of three classes: (1) structural, as wrought out by Huxley; (2) activital, as suggested by Huxley and wrought out by Powell; and (3) mental, or psychic. Expressed otherwise, man's place in nature is now defined, first by what mankind and their kindred *are,* second by what they *do,* and third by what they *think.* And the chief progress of the post-Huxleian epoch, albeit practically confined to *Homo sapiens* in various grades of development, has followed the lines of psychic homologies.

It is just to say that the foundation for modern knowledge of psychic homologies was laid by Tylor in his *Primitive Culture* (1871), and especially in the seven notable chapters on animism elaborated in successive editions; for he showed that a certain type of philosophy is of world-wide extent and is, or has been, shared by every race, every known people, whatsoever their diversities of color or condition. This foundation was gradually raised into a definite platform, partly by Tylor in later publications, partly by Powell in brief memoirs on *The Mythology of the North American Indians* (1879) and *Activital Similarities* (1881), in which it was shown that the interactions between distinct peoples and similar environments frequently produce similar activities, howsoever diverse the peoples themselves; and important additions to the platform were made by Brinton in various contributions summarized in his *Religions of Primitive Peoples* (1897), in which he showed that the human mind, even in its more complex operations, reflects environment with striking fidelity. True (as recently shown by Boas[2]), the products of interaction between peoples and environments are in some measure inconsistent, and may even at first sight seem contradictory; but, as pointed out on a previous occasion,[3] the incongruities shrink or disappear when the comparisons are confined to peoples in corresponding degrees of cultural development.

The modern platform for the study of psychic homologies may be defined briefly in terms of a few generalizations, which seem to be consistent with the sum of knowledge concerning the psychic attributes of both human and sub-human organisms, viz: (1) the mentality of animals is instinctive rather than ratiocinative, and for each species responds practically alike to like stimuli; (2) the savage mind is shaped largely by instinct, and responds nearly alike to like stimuli; (3) all barbaric minds are measurably similar in their responses to environmental stimuli; (4) civilized minds rise well above instinct, and work in fairly similar ways under like stimuli; and (5) enlightened minds are essentially ratiocinative, largely independent of instinct, and less nearly alike in their responses to external stimuli than those of lower culture. The several generalizations are mutually and significantly harmonious; they combine to outline a course of development beginning in the animal realm with organisms adapted to environment through physiologic processes, and ending in that realm of enlightened humanity in which mind molds environment through nature-conquest[4]; and they measure the gradual mergence of bestial instinct in the brightening intellect of progressive humanity. To, or at least toward, this platform those working anthropologists concerned with the broader aspects of the science have been pressed by accumulating observations and generalizations; yet the platform owes much of its character and most of its strength to the concurrent development of a scientific psychology at the hands of a notable group of experimentalists in psychic phenomena. The several generalizaions embodied in the platform have already been summarized as the latest and most comprehensive among the principles of science, i.e., the responsivity of mind[5]; and by aid of this principle, psychic homologies may be traced between higher culture-grades and lower, and from people to people and tribe to tribe down to the plane of lowest savagery—where the lines cease for lack of data, leaving the lowly mind in a state even more suggestively akin to that of the sub-human organism than is the lowest human skeleton to that of the highest anthropoids.

Especially within the last decade of the old century, anthropologists have come to recognize a course of development of the esthetic arts—a sort of natural history of esthetics, arising in symbolism, running through conventionism, and maturing in a degree of refined realism found satisfying by civilized and enlightened peoples. Now a significant feature of this development is found in the fact that the initial symbolism is zoic or animistic, putatively if not patently: The esthetic hunger of primitive artists is sated by the carving of totems on trees or rocks, by the molding of animal effigies, perhaps by the delineation and painting of zoic pictographs; as the artists rise in the scale of culture, the zoic designs are partly conventionized (eventually passing into arbitrary alphabets), partly perpetuated in more realistic forms still conceived as fraught with mystical meaning, like the asp of Egyptian sculpture, the dragon of oriental painting, the curiously vestigial unicorn of a modern nation's coat-of-arms, and even the eagles of other national insignia. So, also, when primal man first yields to the charm of music, his songs and accompaniments mimic the rhythmic footfalls of feared or venerated animals, the rustling sounds of animal movements, the inchoate melody of animal voices; when he enters the demesne of drama, his characters are beasts or uncanny monsters tricked out in zoic trappings; and it is only after long stages of development that anthropomorphic motives are introduced, and that the music and drama rise to the plane of realistic representation. In some cases, if not commonly, the germ of esthetic development quickens in painting of face or body, to grow into tattooing; in simplest form the painted devices may serve as beacon-marks for the identification of kindred (like the face-marks of various animals), as among Seri matrons,[6] or may symbolize fearsome animals, as among Sioux warriors; but in every well-known case the motive is symbolic expression of zoic attributes. From these germinal efforts of esthetic faculty to that modern stage of art in which the noblest realism and the highest idealism are wedded, the way is long; but every step is marked by the dropping of zoic motives and the substitution of motives springing from human attributes and aspirations.

Within a few years working anthropologists have come to recognize more or less clearly a natural history of industries, comparable with that of arts—a course of development also arising in symbolism, running through instinct-guided conventionism, and maturing in that sublimest product of mentality, invention. It has long been known that barbaric artisans seek omens among birds, borrow lore from beasts, and run to zoic motives in decoration[7]; it has long been known, too, that savage huntsmen not only imitate the movement of feral animals in the chase and seek to incite their weapons and strengthen their arms by zoic trophies, but even mimic the feral carnivores' blood-craze in fierce berserker rage at times of battle; and more recently it has been noted that the most primitive implements are of tooth, claw, shell, and bone, selected and used as emblems of zoic power. In a typical tribe—the Seri, most primitive of known Amerinds—the pristine implement is a sea-lion tooth, differentiated into arrow, harpoon, and firestick; the teeth themselves are classed as stones, and natural pebbles are used for tools emblematic of the zoic organs; while the methods of chase and warfare still mimic the habits of local beasts. The lines of human progress from primal savagery to enlightenment may be traced in terms of development of each or all of the great groups of activities; and while all the tracings conform so closely as to inspire confidence in each, no outline is more definite than that represented by the stages of industrial progress—stages best defined in terms of the mind-led activities of which artifacts are normal products. These stages (beginning with that typified by the Seri) are (1) Zoömimic, in which bestial organs are used as arrows and other implements, to which magical powers are imputed by dominating zoötheistic faith; (2) Protolithic, in which naturally-formed stones are used for cleavers and other implements, under the sway of mystical faith modified by experience of mechanical chance; (3) Technolithic, in which design-shaped stones are used for knives and other implements in ways revealing the germ of invention; and (4) Metallurgic, in which ores are smelted and used for tools under the influence of invention.[8] Whether the progress be traced through these stages or otherwise, the way from the simple industries of the prime to the elaborate devices of modernity is long, very long; yet a full half of the steps are marked by the dropping of zoid motives and the substitution of motives expressing man's growing consciousness of power in nature-conquest.

Since Tylor traced primitive culture, and especially since Morgan wrote on *Ancient Society* (1877), it has been recognized that all known primitive peoples are banded in consanguineal groups, while advanced peoples are bound in larger groups by laws defining proprietary and personal rights; and during the last decade or two working anthropologists have come to recognize the course of development of social organization in its several stages—i.e., the natural history of laws. Now it is significant that the most primitive social bond (found alike in America, Africa, Australia, and parts of Asia) is that fixed by the ocular blood-kinship of maternity, and that the next great stage is defined by paternal relationship; for in both stages the lines seem to be homologous with the instinctive habits of sub-human species, while the earlier the more closely approaches the low plane of brute knowledge—so far as this can be inferred from brute conduct. The researches among the aborigines of America have thrown strong light on the lowly laws of primitive peoples; for it has been ascertained that both savage clans and barbaric gentes are bound not merely by community of blood but welded into homogeneous units by community of faith in zoic tutelaries—faith so profound, so blent with fear and hope, so impressed by recurrent ceremony from birth to maturity and thence to old age and death, as to dominate every thought and regulate every action. The Amerind tribesmen are grouped by totems (or tutelaries) of Wolf, Badger, Bear, Fox, Deer, Coyote, Eagle, Bluejay, etc.; they call themselves Wolves, or Badgers, or Bears, or Eagles, and glory in the strength and magical prestige believed to be brought them by their genii; most of them recite traditions of descent from the tutelary animals, or else from fantastic monsters invested with their attributes; and every adequately studied tribe has been found to possess a traditional genesis or sacred cosmogony in which the tutelaries, and perhaps other beasts, are glorified if not deified. The exoteric bond of clan or gens is blood-kinship; but the union is reinforced by an incomparably stronger esoteric bond of animistic belief. The way from beast-clanship to free citizenship is long—so long as to afford the most striking measure of human progress; yet every step of the way is marked by the elimination of zoic concepts and by the substitution of humane concepts forced on the genus *Homo* in his ceaseless strife for nature-conquest.

During some decades past, students of aboriginal tongues have been impressed by the failure of primitive folk to discriminate clearly between men and animals in their everyday speech; and this lowly habit forms one of the phenomena which have served (as recently shown by Powell)[9] as a clue to the natural history of languages. Many Amerind tribes denote themselves by a term connoting animals, either in general or of a particular class, and when pressed to specify are compelled to employ an affix or adjective to distinguish the human kind (often considered inferior) from the rest; some, like the Papago, trace human genealogy through only a few generations forward or backward, and conceive the lines as beginning and ending in an undifferentiated magma of zoic life designated by a single term; while some groups have progressed so far in the way of human superiority as to dignify themselves by the expressions "Real Men," "True Men," etc., in contradistinction from alien tribes and other contemptible creatures. The scroll picturing the development of language is expanded about midlength by the addition of the scriptorial branch, representing the growth of graphic expression; and it is quite in accord with the growth-lines of oral expression to find that the earliest essays in ideography are pictures of zoic objects, or objects to which zoic attributes were manifestly imputed. Most of the primal features of modern alphabets have been conventionized beyond recognition; but the hieroglyphs of Mexico and Egypt and the ideographs of China are among the clearer vestiges of primitive standards, while the fancy-wrought constellations of the celestial sphere—birth-mates of pre-Cadmean characters remaining unchanged by reason of remoteness from practical affairs—still conserve the graphic zoölatry in which writing began. The way from lowly language linking men and beasts in word and sign to a discrete graphic vocabulary is long; yet the earlier steps were unquestionably marked by the dropping of instincts shared by brutes and the substitution of humanitarian concepts impressed by ever-widening human associations.

Since Tylor taught the world-wide range of animism in 1871, anthropologists have grouped the myths and faiths of mankind in a series of stages outlining a course of development—a natural history of doctrine—coming up through a slavish and despairing hylozoism, and ascending thence through higher zoötheism and broadening worship of nature powers on successive planes, each brighter and more humane than the last. The zoic factors of primitive arts, industries, laws, and languages were manifestly made potent in the olden time, as they are today among lowly folk, alike by overweening faith and ever-present custom; they were, and still are, kept alive not only by recurrent ceremony and daily taboo and hourly precept, but by tireless study of animal contemporaries whose habits huntsmen must know under pain of hunger; so that much (perhaps most) of the sentient feeling of primal man must have been—as it is today among his survivors—of animal contemporaries. In savage life men and their animal associates are compelled to consecrate their best efforts to study of each other; in affairs of feeling and faith as in matters of immediate utility, the association engenders habits of body maturing in instincts eventually ripening into action-shaping habits of mind; and the stronger mentality is naturally the more deeply influenced—until continued experience of superior faculty awakens consciousness of superior power, stirs the sleeping giant of self-confidence, and rends the shackles of zoöphobia forever.

> Lo, the poor Indian! whose untutored mind
> Sees *Beasts* in clouds, or hears *them* in the wind;

so a modern Pope would write of the American natives; and so, too, he might write of any and all other aborigines made known through the researches of the last half-century. The upward way from primal beast-faith through concurrent fetichism and shamanism and thence through mysticism and all manner of occultism is long and need not now be traced; it suffices that all of the earlier and many of the later steps were marked by the dropping of zoic motives of vestiges and the substitution of even nobler motives and imageries.

When the scrolls picturing activital development are brought together—when the natural history of doctrines is outlined over those of languages, laws, industries, and arts—the leading lines are found consistent in every essential feature; and all are seen to rise from a mentality both reflecting and approaching that of lower animals (though just how closely may not be measured until the sub-human mind is better understood) toward the highest human plane revealed in science and statecraft. The savage Seri—lowest of American tribesmen—is loathed by Caucasian neighbors as an uncanny beast, and it is a revelation to find that he reciprocates the loathing and glories in the contumely, feeling that it allies him the more closely with venerated consociates like puma and shark, and divides him the more widely from the hated white creatures of unnatural ways; and the sentiment of the Seri is measurably common to all aborigines of strong individuality. The impressive fact, learned alike through observation of a typical tribe and through analysis of the mental operations of primitive peoples in general, is that the savage stands strikingly close to sub-human species in every aspect of mentality as well as in bodily habits and bodily structure.

Since Huxley's prime, the chief advances in anthropology have related to what men *do* and what men *think;* and the progress has been such as to indicate with fairly satisfactory clearness the natural history of human thinking as well as that of human doing. Thereby man's place in nature may be defined more trenchantly than was possible in 1871: (1) As shown by Huxley, the structure of *Homo sapiens* is homologous with that of lower orders, while the morphologic differences between highest anthropoids and lowest men are less than those separating lowest men from highest men; (2) as suggested by Huxley and established by later researches, the activities of *Homo sapiens* are homologous with those of the anthropoids, while the activital range between club-using gorilla and tooth-using savage is far narrower than that separating the zoömimic savage from the engine-using inventor; (3) as shown by the latest researches, the mental workings of *Homo sapiens* are homologous with those of lower animals, while the range from the instinct and budding reason of higher animals to the thinking of lowest man seems far less than that separating the beast-fearing savage from the scientist or statesman. The resemblances and differences in doing and thinking may not yet be measured in definite units, as are cranial capacities and facial angles (though the recent progress in experimental psychology gives promise of quantitative determinations of general sort at no distant day); yet the relations are hardly less clear and tangible than those customarily measured in inches and ounces and degrees.

So in the light of the latest researches man must be placed wholly within the domain of nature, yet above all other organisms at heights varying widely with that highest product and expression of nature, mental power.

Notes

[1] Address of the retiring President of the Anthropological Society of Washington, delivered before the Washington Academy of Sciences and Affiliated Societies, February 26, 1901.

[2] "The Mind of Primitive Man," *Science,* vol. XIII, 1901, pp. 281–289.

[3] "Cardinal Principles of Science," *Proceedings of the Washington Academy of Sciences,* vol. II, 1900, p. 11.

[4] Cf. "The Seri Indians," *Seventeenth Annual Report of the Bureau of American Ethnology,* 1898, p. 269.

[5] "The cardinal principles of science may be reckoned as five: the indestructibility of matter, the contribution chiefly of Chemistry; the persistence of motion, the gift mainly of Physics; the development of species, the offering of the biotic sciences; the uniformity of nature, the guerdon of Geology and the older sciences; and the responsivity of mind, the joint gift of several sciences, though put in final form by

Anthropology."—*Proceedings of the Washington Academy of Sciences,* vol. II, 1900, pp. 11–12.

[6] The sematic and telic functions of face-painting are discussed in "The Seri Indians," op. cit., p. 167 et seq.

[7] Even the faith-guided anti-zoic motive of arabesque decoration attests the force of the zoic tendency and the effort required to divert it.

[8] The stages and transitional sub-stages are set forth in greater detail in "The Seri Indians," op. cit., pp. 249–254.

[9] "Philology, or the Science of Activities Designed for Expression," *American Anthropologist,* vol. II, 1900, pp. 603–637.

19. Exposing the Taënsa Hoax
John Swanton

The relationship of Taënsa to Natchez was affirmed by all French writers who speak of their language, and no question would probably have been raised regarding it had it not been singled out about thirty years ago by an ambitious French youth as an occasion for putting forth a fraudulent grammar and dictionary. The story of this fraud and the controversy to which it gave rise is as follows:

At the commencement of the year 1880 the publishing house of Maisonneuve et Cie. received by mail a manuscript of six leaves entitled *Fragments de Littérature Tansa,* sent by M. J. Parisot, rue Stanislas, 37, at Prombières (Vosges). This manuscript was transmitted with a request to utilize it for the *Revue de Linguistique.* It was accordingly submitted to Prof. Julien Vinson, one of the editors of that publication, who wrote M. Parisot for further particulars regarding it and received a reply at some length in which the latter explained how the manuscript had come into his possession.

The appearance of these *Fragments*, under the title *Notes sur la Langue des Taensas,* was followed in 1881 by seven supposed Taënsa songs in the original, unaccompanied by translations, printed at Épinal under the title *Cancionero Americano.* A preface in Spanish was inserted, however, in which it was claimed that the texts had been collected in 1827 or 1828. This did not bear M. Parisot's name, but on writing to the publisher M. Adam, who had received a copy of the work, was referred to Parisot, pupil of the "Grand Séminaire de Saint-Dié." M. Adam then wrote to M. Ch. Leclerc, of the Maisonneuve publishing house, and by his advice on the 8th of May, 1882, he asked M. Parisot for the manuscripts in order to publish them in the *Bibliothèque Linguistique Américaino.* M. Parisot, then aged 19 or 20, came to see M. Adam at Nancy in the course of the following July; in October he sent him the manuscript of the grammar and the printing began.

The article in the *Revue* and the pamphlet published at Épinal excited only local interest, but the grammar[1] was widely circulated and

From John Swanton, *Indian Tribes of the Lower Mississippi Valley and Adjacent Coast of the Gulf of Mexico,* Bureau of American Ethnology Bulletin 43 (1911). Reprinted by permission of Smithsonian Institution Press: pp. 9–26.

was acclaimed as a notable addition to our literature on the subject of Indian languages. The fact that Dr. A. S. Gatschet, a leading student of American languages, furnished an introduction rendered its acceptance all the more ready. In his work on Aboriginal American Authors, published the following year, Brinton speaks appreciatively of it and quotes one of the songs entire. In commenting on these songs he says: "Some of the songs of war and death are quite Ossianic in style, and yet they appear to be accurate translations. The comparatively elevated style of such poems need not cast doubt upon them" (pp. 48, 49). The comparison with Ossian was perhaps more significant than the commentator at that time realized, though even then he admitted that the Taënsa songs were unusual.

It was probably not long after this that the noted ethnologist began to change his mind regarding them, but it was not until March, 1885, that he came out against them with the direct charge of forgery. His article appeared in the *American Antiquarian* for that month and was entitled "The Taënsa grammar and dictionary; a deception exposed." This attack bore so heavily against the part of the compilation which embraced the Taënsa songs that Adam made no attempt to defend them, but in the three successive brochures which he issued in reply tried to prove that all of the material, especially the grammatical sections, had not been forged. These brochures were entitled *Le taensa a-t-il été forgé de toutes pièces? Réponse à M. Daniel Brinton; Le taensa n'a pas été forgé de toutes pièces, lettre de M. Friedrich Müller à Lucien Adam; Dom Parisot ne Produira pas le Manuscrit Taensa, lettre à M. Victor Henry.* These brought an answer from Brinton in the *American Antiquarian* for September, and in November of that year the whole controversy to date was noticed at length in *The Kansas City Review* (vol. ix, no. 4, pp. 253–254). The most thorough history of the case, however, embracing the earlier chapters, that had hardly been touched upon so far, was written by Prof. Julien Vinson under the title *La Langue Taensa*, in January, 1886, and published in the April issue of the *Revue de Linguistique et de Philologie Comparée*. Although he had first introduced Parisot to the public and was largely responsible for the publication of the grammar by Adam, Vinson now sided with Brinton, at least in the belief that the authenticity of the work had not yet been established. The *Revue* for January, 1888, contains a letter from Doctor Brinton, entitled *Linguistique Américaine*, in which he refers to several differences of opinion between himself and Doctor Gatschet, and closes with another reference to the Taënsa apropos of the introduction furnished by the latter gentleman. This brought out a *Réplique* from the noted philologist, in which he for the first time enters the Taënsa controversy in person, and a counter rejoinder in the October issue. The whole question was reviewed once more by Brinton in a special chapter in his Essays of an Americanist (pp. 452–467, 1890), and here the active controversy practically ended, apparently with neither side convinced. So much doubt was thrown upon the new material, however, that in making up his linguistic map of North America north of Mexico Powell excluded it from consideration, and it is probably regarded as fraudulent by most prominent ethnologists. At the same time, until very recently sufficient evidence had not been brought forward to absolutely discredit the grammar of Parisot and remove it from the category of possibilities. In determining the ethnological complexion of the lower Mississippi tribes and attempting so far as possible to recover their past history, it is most unpleasant to have to deal with a possibility of such radical importance, and it is therefore of the utmost consequence, if not to demonstrate the fraudulent or genuine character of the grammar, at least to properly classify the language of the Taënsa tribe itself. Rather unexpectedly material has recently come into the writer's hands which he believes to be decisive.

Having reviewed the course of the controversy in outline it will be in order, before bringing in this new evidence, to take up the points brought forward pro and con in the articles above mentioned. Those adduced by Brinton in his initial attack were that no scholar of standing had had access to the original manuscript from which the material was taken; that the language could not have been recorded by a Spaniard, as claimed, because from the time when the Taënsa tribe was first known until their destruction "as minutely recorded by Charlevoix" in 1730–1740 they were under French influences entirely; no Spanish mission was among them, and no Spaniard in civil life could have remained among them without having been noticed, owing to the national jealousies everywhere prevalent at the time.[2] Turning to the grammar itself this critic finds that the pronunciation of Taënsa sounds is explained by means of the French, English, German, and Spanish. Now, inasmuch as neither M. Haumonté, among whose papers the manuscript was supposed to have been found, nor M. Parisot could have heard the language spoken, it is conceived that the original compiler must have had a knowledge of languages quite remarkable for the early part of the eighteenth century. He also finds references to the Nahuatl, Kechua, and Algonkin tongues, which must certainly have been introduced by the translator, although no explanation of this is vouchsafed. Regarding the structure of the language itself Doctor Brinton says:

> That an American language should have a distinctively grammatical gender; that it should have a true relative pronoun; that its numeral system should be based on the nine units in the extraordinarily simple manner here proposed; that it should have three forms of the plural; that its verbs should present the singular of these—these traits are, indeed, not impossible, but they are too unusual not to demand the best of evidence.[3]

The most convincing proof "as to the humbuggery of this whole business" he finds, however, in the Taënsa songs. According to these, the sugar maple is made to flourish in the Louisiana swamps; the sugar cane was raised by the Taënsa, "although the books say it was introduced into Louisiana by the Jesuits in 1761;" potatoes, rice, apples, and bananas were familiar to them, "and the white birch and wild rice are described as flourishing around the bayous of the lower Mississippi." To the argument that these might be mistranslations of misunderstood native words he asks what sort of editing it is "which could not only commit such unpardonable blunders, but send them forth to the scientific world without a hint that they do not pretend to be anything more than guesses?" The same ignorance of climatic conditions appears in the Calendar of the Taënsa, particularly in the references to snow and ice here and in other places. The style of the songs themselves is also "utterly unlike that reported from any other native tribe. It much more closely resembles the stilted and tumid imitations of supposed savage simplicity common enough among French writers of the eighteenth century."[4] As an example of this un-Indian style and the geographical ignorance accompanying it Brinton quotes one of these songs, "The Song of the Marriage," and comments upon it as follows:

> The Choctaws are located ten days' journey up the Mississippi, in the wildrice region about the headwaters of the stream, whereas they were the immediate neighbors of the real Taënsa and dwelt when first discovered in the middle and southern parts of the present State of Mississippi. The sugar maple is made to grow in the Louisiana swamps, the broad-leaved magnolia and the ebony in Minnesota. The latter is described as the land of the myrtle and the former of the vine. The northern warrior brings feet rings and infant clothing as presents, while the southern bride knows all about boiling maple sap and is like a white birch. But the author's knowledge of aboriginal customs stands out most prominently when he has the up-river chief come with an ox cart and boast of his cows! After that passage I need say nothing more. He is, indeed, ignorant who does not know that not a single draft animal and not one kept for its milk was ever found among the natives of the Mississippi valley.[5]

In conclusion the writer recalls the grammar of a fictitious Formosa language brought forth by George Psalmanazar, and adds the statements of De Montigny, Gravier, and Du Pratz to the effect that the Taënsa spoke the Natchez language, which is known to be entirely distinct from that contained in the Taënsa Grammar. "Moreover," he says, "we have in old writers the names of the Taënsa villages furnished by the Taënsa themselves, and they also are nowise akin to the matter of this grammar, but are of Chahta-Muskoki derivation."[6]

Two of the three brochures which contain M. Adam's reply to this attack show in their titles a confession of weakness, since they merely maintain that the grammar had not been forged in all portions. In fact, M. Adam at once abandons any defense of the "texts," saying: "In my own mind I have always considered them the work of some disciple of the Jesuit fathers, who had taken a fancy to the Taënsa poetry."[7] The brochures also contain copies of correspondence between MM. Adam, Parisot, and others relative to the original manuscript which Adam demanded and Parisot declared to be no longer in his possession. It further developed that M. Haumonté, M. Parisot's maternal uncle, among whose papers the Taënsa manuscripts were supposed to have been found, was no linguist, and could have had nothing to do with the documents. Parisot furthermore admitted that the originals were not all in Spanish, and that he had written out and altered the grammar, besides augmenting the vocabulary with terms which had been translated only by conjectures. Not only was Parisot unable to produce the original, but a thorough search among the family papers on the part of his father failed to reveal anything of the sort. Nevertheless, M. Adam explained the presence of the manuscripts among M. Haumonté's papers by supposing that they had been left there by some visitor, M. Haumonté having kept a lodging house, and proceeded to defend the grammar itself by replying to the philological objections raised by Doctor Brinton. He supported his position by means of a letter from the noted German philologist, Friedrich Müller, who also gave it as his opinion that the grammar was not altogether fraudulent.

After recapitulating the various concessions and showing up the weak points developed by the defense, Brinton meets the grammatical part of the French philologist's reply by stating that he had never denied the existence of the exceptional grammatical features he had referred to in American languages, but maintained that it was unlikely they should all occur in one language. He concludes his argument by saying that "even if some substructure will be shown to have existed for this Taënsa Grammar and texts (which, individually, I still doubt), it has been presented to the scientific world under conditions which are far from adequate to the legitimate demands of students."[8]

With this view Professor Vinson, the next contributor to the discussion, entirely concurs, and in detailing his early association with Parisot is able to show further discrepancies between the claims of that individual in earlier and later years.[9]

In his letter to the *Revue de Linguistique* for January, 1888, Brinton touches upon Taënsa long enough to expose several glaring blunders in the pamphlet of texts published at Épinal in 1881. This, occurring in connection with criticisms on certain opinions expressed by Dr. A. S. Gatschet, brought forth from the latter student the best defense of the Taënsa Grammar that has appeared. Gatschet agrees with Brinton, indeed, in his criticism of the Épinal pamphlet,[10] but attempts to defend the rest, including the texts thrown over by Adam, although he allows for the possibility of their fraudulent nature by saying that "the eleven songs might be the work of a forger without the language itself being necessarily unauthentic."[11] To the statement that the Taënsa did not survive the year 1740 he produces documentary evidence of their existence as late as 1812. Nor was it necessary that a "Spanish monk" should have recorded this language, since any Spaniard straying over from Pensacola, only 10 leagues from the later location of the Taënsa near Mobile, might have performed that service. Like M. Adam, Gatschet finds the exceptional grammatical forms cited by Brinton in various other American languages, and he meets the obstacle raised by references to various American and European languages by supposing that they had been inserted by M. Adam in revision. The mention of sugar cane, rice, apples, potatoes, bananas, cattle, and a cart are to be explained on the ground that the Taënsa had existed long after the introduction of those things. The month of December was called "the white month," not on account of the snow, but on account of the frost, which the critic himself had seen in Louisiana in parishes made farther south than that in which the Taënsa lived. The sugar maple is found not only in the north, but in mountainous sections of the south.[12]

In answer Brinton states that he has "nothing to say about M. Gatschet's advocacy of the Taënsa language. If," he adds, "he desires to employ his time in bolstering up the manufacturers of that bold forgery, posterity will reward him with a pitying smile."[13] In the later work before referred to he gives a sketch of the controversy but adds no new arguments.

In this discussion the opponents of the Taënsa Grammar, namely, Messrs. Brinton and Vinson, had made the following points: They had shown that the claimed original manuscript was not in the hands of the person by whom the linguistic material had been furnished nor among the documents of his family, that it could not have been entirely in Spanish as at first claimed, and that the grammar could not have been compiled by M. Haumonté, to whom it had been ascribed. M. Parisot was also shown to have been inconsistent in the statements he gave out from time to time. Thus, though he does not claim to have made more than one discovery of Taënsa manuscripts, in 1880 he possessed "only some principles of grammar, a fairly long list of words, two songs or stories, and the translation of the *Pater*, the *Ave*, and the *Credo*," all of which occupied 11 pages in the *Revue de Linguistique*, while in 1882 his material covered 42 larger pages and the two songs had swelled to 11. In 1880 he expressed himself as unable to complete an account of the grammar of the language for lack of material, but in 1882 he did that very thing. In 1880 he was unable to find any numbers above 8 except 10 and 60, while in 1882, 9, 11, 12, 13, 20, 21, 30, 40, 50, 70, 80, 90, 100, 101, 110, 119, 200, 300, 1,000, 1,002, 1,881, 2,000, and 10,000 had made their appearance. During the same period the language had developed two dialects, five new alphabetic signs, and a dual not even hinted at in the beginning.

As suggested by Adam, the texts might have been put together by some priest or student for his own pleasure, strange as the undertaking would appear to be, but the rejection of this material as aboriginal tends to throw discredit on the rest, for if we admit that it had passed through the hands of some one willing to make such original use of it, why might not his creative faculty have been devoted to the manufacture of the whole? Gatschet's attempt to defend the climatic and other inconsistencies which these texts contain will hardly appeal to anyone who has examined them as a wise or well executed move. Admitting that the texts were collected in 1827 or 1828, as claimed for the seven published at Épinal, it is of course probable that the Taënsa were acquainted with the foreign fruits and vegetables there referred to, but it is questionable whether they would have introduced them prominently into their songs, and granted that they knew of the sugar maple, it is not conceivable that they should have treated it as a tree of every day knowledge or designated one of their months by its name. If the texts were recorded in the years mentioned, the Taënsa were then in central Louisiana not far from Red river, and were reduced to a very small band. By no possibility, therefore, could the Choctaw be represented as descending to them from the north. In fact there was but one time when the Choctaw ever did live north of them, and that was when the Taënsa were in the neighborhood of Mobile. Supposing that "The Song of the Marriage," which the writer has in mind, was composed at that period, are we to believe that the Choctaw chief came to Tensaw river for his bride, across Alabama and Tensas rivers, with an ox cart full of presents? But if this song must be placed at the period when the tribe was near Mobile "The Poisoned River" goes back to the very beginning of the eighteenth century, since it refers to wars between the Taënsa and the Yazoo, who were near neighbors at that time only. The poisoning of Tensas river, supposing that to have been possible, could, however, have had little effect on persons who did not live upon it, the home of the Taĕnsa having been on Lake St. Joseph.

The whole tone of the *Cancionero Taensa* is, however, so utterly un-Indian that no one familiar with Indians will accept for a moment songs in which one party gravely asks another whether his people know how to hunt buffalo and deer, whether there are squirrels in his country, and what plants grow there.

These being dismissed from consideration as at least subsequent compositions, we are reduced to a consideration of the grammar and vocabulary apart from the use that has been made of them in composition.

In one particular Doctor Brinton has made an egregious blunder, and that is in supposing that the Taënsa Indians had been destroyed in 1730–1740. If Charlevoix makes any such statement for the years mentioned the writer has yet to find it, and must suppose that Brinton is thinking of a reference to the Taënsa village site in Charlevoix's Journal (letter of January 10, 1722), in which the destruction is indeed affirmed.[14] Charlevoix was mistaken, however, the tribe being at that time in the neighborhood of Mobile and according to some accounts occupying 100 cabins. In 1764 they moved again to the west side of the Mississippi and settled on Red river, and about the time of the cession of Louisiana to the United States they sold their lands and moved south of Red river to Bayou Boeuf. Later still they sold their land there, but continued to live in the neighborhood for some time longer, being noted, as Gatschet states, as late as 1812. At this time they drop out of sight, but it is known that they moved farther south and settled on a small bayou at the head of Grand lake which came to be known by their name. Some afterward intermarried with the Chitimacha, and Chitimacha of Taënsa blood are still living, but the tribe, as such, has disappeared from sight, whether by death or migration being unknown. Brinton is mistaken, therefore, regarding the possibility of linguistic material having been collected from them in 1827 or 1828. The improbable part of the story is that a tribe which numbered but 25 men in 1805 should, twenty-two years later, and after all had been living together for a hundred years, retain two distinguishable dialects. There were, indeed, two tribes called Taënsa, though as yet the writer has found but one reference to the second under that name, but the statements of the grammar regarding them do not fit the facts. Gatschet, with strange inconsistency, strives to identify one division with the Tangipahoa, though at the same time admitting that these probably spoke a dialect of Choctaw.[15] The second Taënsa tribe, or "little Taënsas," spoken of by Iberville were another people who lived west of the Mississippi and were evidently identical with the Avoyel.[16] But while the languages spoken by the Taënsa proper and the Avoyel may have been two dialects of the same tongue, the tribes speaking them correspond not at all with those described by the grammar. According to that authority the northern dialect was current among those who spent most of their time in hunting and were less refined, while the southern dialect was among the more refined Taënsa living along the Mississippi. On the contrary, the more refined of these two tribes, Taënsa and Avoyel, were the former, who lived to the north but whose home was not along the Mississippi but on an oxbow cut-off west of it now known as Lake St. Joseph. The Avoyel, on the other hand, lived to the south and west on Red river. There is no evidence, however, that the Taënsa and Avoyel lived together in historic times, and in 1805 Sibley states that all that remained of the latter were 2 or 3 women on Washita river. The chance in 1827 of collecting the "more polished southern dialect," on which more stress is laid than on the other, would thus seem to have been very slight. As we have seen, it developed in the course of the controversy that all of the manuscripts could not have been in Spanish, but that even a small part of them should be in that language is surprising. During the Spanish occupation of Louisiana it is true that many Spaniards settled in the country, but the presence of a Spanish Taënsa manuscript in Europe would almost necessitate the supposition that it had been written by an intelligent Spanish traveler, and the records do not teem with instances of intellectual Spaniards burying themselves in the canebrakes of Louisiana after its cession to the United States. If, on the other hand, we consider the date given for the collection of the texts published at Épinal to be erroneous, we must argue in the face of one more inconsistency, and the change of base does not help us much, since Spanish influence over the whites of central Louisiana between 1764 and 1803 was little enough and still less over the Indians. Before that period they were always under French government, and it is not likely that a Pensacola Spaniard, lay or clerical, would have been tolerated in the tribe at that period.

The writer has not attempted a minute analysis of the language here presented, believing such an analysis not needed for a condemnation. Notwithstanding Adam's skillful reply, it must be admitted that the force of Brinton's grammatical argument is but slightly shaken. Take for instance the number nine, *vat*. This is a simple syllable and differs not at all in form in the two dialects, though smaller numbers such as three, five, and seven show such variation. Constancy in the form of this particular number is possible but unlikely, but where in North America shall we look for a word for nine composed of a simple syllable? In most of the languages with which the writer is familiar this numeral is indicated by a form meaning "ten less one," and in any case he does not recall a single instance of a simple syllable presenting no resemblance to the other numerals being used for nine. Brinton's objections to the "three forms for the plural" and the simplicity of the verbs appears to the writer not well taken, for, as Gatschet points out, the former might be only variations of one form while simplicity in verb stems is not so uncommon as Brinton seems to suppose. The existence of a pronominal form used like our relative is somewhat remarkable, but far less wonderful than the entire morphological difference between it and the forms for the interrogative and indefinite. This distinctiveness is, indeed, "hard to swallow." The existence of a distinctively grammatical gender, by which Brinton means a grammatical sex gender, is also singular, but the fact instead of being an argument against the authenticity of the material has become one of the strongest arguments in its favor through the discovery by Doctor

Gatschet of a sex gender in the Tunica language which was spoken in the immediate neighborhood. More remarkable still, and a coincidence strangely overlooked by Gatschet in arguing for the genuineness of Taënsa, is the fact that the two agree in distinguishing gender in the second persons as well as in the third. When we consider that there is no evidence that the Tunida language was recorded in any form until Gatschet visited the tribe in 1885, three years after the appearance of the Taënsa Grammar, we must admit that, if the latter is altogether a forgery, fate was very kind to the perpetrators. Looking deeper, however, we find a marked contrast between Taënsa and Tunica gender, for while gender in the latter language divides men and women and masculine and feminine animals, it also divides inanimate objects, such as sun and moon, wind, clouds, rocks, and trees, while in Taënsa the feminine includes all inanimate things, the male being confined to men and male animals. This constitutes a point of difference between the two languages as wide as if no gender existed. Although Algonquian languages distinguish between animate and inanimate and Iroquois presents analogies to Taënsa in this particular, it is natural to Indians to personify inanimate objects sometimes as masculine and sometimes as feminine, and therefore the Taënsa line of demarcation is less probable than the Tunica one which agrees in this particular very closely with the Chinook system. The method of distinguishing masculine and feminine pronominal forms is also decidedly unlike, Taënsa employing a suffix while Tunica uses entirely distinct forms. A difference not mentioned by Brinton which marks this language off from anything in its immediate vicinity is the presence of a long series of instrumental prefixes, a phenomenon common in Siouan dialects and in many others but nonexistent in those spoken along the lower Mississippi. Perhaps the strongest objection from a linguistic point of view is one that would not at first occur to most students, and that is the absolute lexical difference between this language and any of its supposed neighbors. However self-sufficient a language may be it is almost certain to have a few borrowed words, and the languages of the south are no exceptions in this particular. Several words, notably those for 'war-club,' 'buffalo,' 'opossum,' and 'fish,' are common to a number of related stocks, but in this new grammar we recognize not one of them, nor indeed more than two or three slight resemblances to any American language whatever. The only exceptions are, perhaps, in the case of the pronominal stems for the second and third persons singular, in which sounds *wi* and *s* occur prominently, agreeing closely with those appearing in Tunica. The phonetics are no less strange, not only on account of their number but from the occurrence in one language of *u*, or *f*, or *r*, which elsewhere on the lower Mississippi are confined to different stocks.

The writer has left until the last, because this is the point on which new light has recently been thrown, the direct statements of early travelers and missionaries regarding the Taënsa language of their day. Brinton, it will be remembered, adduced the testimony of three writers to the effect that the Taënsa language was the same as that of the Natchez. This testimony is by De Montigny in 1699,[17] by Gravier in 1700,[18] and by Du Pratz, whose information dates from 1718 to 1734,[19] and their meaning is plain and unqualified. Gatschet replied to this argument, however, by saying that at the time when these travelers wrote none of them was personally familiar with both tribes. Thus De Montigny had visited the Taënsa, but not the Natchez; Gravier had not visited the Taënsa or Natchez, but had evidently derived his information from St. Cosme, who had lately settled among the latter people, but was not necessarily familiar with the former; and Du Pratz was sufficiently familiar with the Natchez, but had not, so far as we know, ever seen a Taënsa, the Taënsa tribe having in his time moved to Mobile bay. It was quite possible, therefore, as argued by Gatschet, that these men had merely assumed a linguistic connection to exist on the strength of well-known resemblances between the tribes in manners and customs. Against the new evidence, however, no such objection can be made.

In order to understand the strength of this new evidence, which emanates from missionary sources, it will be necessary to review in a few words the movements of the early missionaries on the lower Mississippi. After the Recollect fathers who accompanied La Salle and Tonti, the first missionaries to descend below the country of the Quapaw were three missionary priests named De Montigny, Davion, and La Source, sent out under direction of the ecclesiastical center at Quebec. These descended the river in the summer of 1698 as far as the Tunica and the Taënsa, but returned to the Quapaw without going any farther, and it is from the letter of De Montigny, dated from the latter tribe on January 2, 1699, and published in Shea's Early Voyages Up and Down the Mississippi,[20] that the statement referred to by Brinton and Gatschet relative to the Taënsa and Natchez languages is taken. Later in the year 1699 De Montigny and Davion again visited the tribes below and began missions among the Taënsa and Tunica, respectively. In June they voyaged down the Mississippi together, accompanied by four Shawnee Indians, two Taënsa, and some Canadians, visited the Natchez and the Houma, and reached Iberville's new settlement at Biloxi July 1.[21] A few days later they returned to their charges, and Davion continued to minister to his chosen tribe for about twenty years. De Montigny, on the other hand, had determined to transfer the seat of his labors to the Natchez as being more important, and seized the opportunity presented by Iberville's visit to the Taënsa to return with him to the former tribe.[22] Later on, however, he left these also, repaired to Biloxi, and accompanied Iberville on his return to France.[23] Soon after his departure, if not indeed before it took place, St. Cosme came down from the upper Mississippi to assume his duties and remained there until December, 1706, when he was killed by a Chitimacha war party when on his way to Biloxi.[24] For one reason or another no further missionary efforts were made among the Natchez or Taënsa except incidentally in connection with white congregations, and it is evident that of all men De Montigny and St. Cosme, especially the latter, were best fitted to pass upon the relationship of Natchez to the language of its neighbors. As already noted, we have the direct or indirect opinion of both of these men on the question before us, but, what has hitherto not been known, we have their opinion expressed a second time and in a way to which the same objections can not be applied as were raised by Gatschet.

At the Fifteenth Congress of Americanists held in Quebec in 1906, M. l'abbé Amédée Gosselin, professor in Laval University, presented a paper entitled, "*Les Sauvages du Mississippi (1698–1708) d'après la Correspondance des Missionnaires des Missions Étrangères de Québec.*"[25] The information contained in this is drawn partly from the original documents published by Shea, but in greater part from letters which still remain in manuscript, as they were sent by the missionary priests to their superior, the Bishop of Quebec. From these most valuable information is adduced regarding the population, languages, religion, government, warfare, character, manners, and customs of the tribes of that region, much of which will be quoted in this paper. The only reference to the language of the Taënsa, however, is to the effect that "the Tonicas [Tunica], the Taënsa, and the Natchez spoke the same language, but it differed from that of the Chicachas [Chickasaw] and that of the Arkansas [Quapaw]."[26] As authority for this statement the letters of De Montigny of January 2 and August 25, 1699, are cited. The coupling of Tunica with the other two languages being at variance with statements in De Montigny's letter of January 2, and so far as Tunica and Natchez are concerned at variance with known facts, the writer supposed that the missionary must have expressed different views in his unpublished letter of August 25. In order to settle this question, and if possible to elicit further information regarding the linguistic position of the tribe under discussion, he addressed a letter to Professor Gosselin, calling attention to the matter and asking for any excerpts relating to the language of the Taënsa which the unpublished letters might contain. Professor Gosselin very kindly and promptly replied to his request. He explained that the erroneous statement was the result of an unfortunate confusion in his own notes and did not exist in the originals. In answer to the second query he inclosed several extracts in the original which are of the utmost value and contain the decisive information alluded to. It is to be hoped that the whole of these important manuscripts will soon be given to the public, but for the present the following rough translations will serve well enough for our purposes:

From a letter of De Montigny, written August 25, 1699, page 6

The 12th [of June] we reached the Natchez, or, as others call them, the Challaouelles, who are almost twenty leagues from the Taënsas. * * * They were warring at that time with almost all the nations which are on the Mississippi * * * and out of consideration for us, although they were at war with the Taënsas, they gave those [Taënsa] who were with us a very good reception. We told the chief that the black robes, like ourselves, were not warriors, that we had not come to see them in that spirit, and that on the contrary we exhorted every one to peace, that they would know it well one day when I should know their language, which is the same as that of the Taënsas (*qui est la méme que celle des Taënsas*) and then, after having made them some little presents, we separated very well satisfied with each other.

From a letter of St. Cosme, August 1, 1701

I have past the winter among the Natchez; I have applied myself a little to the language and I find myself in a position to compose something of the catechism and prayers. I have made a journey to the Tahensas, distant 12 leagues from the Natchez. As that village is much diminished I think no missionary will be needed there, since it now numbers only about 40 cabins, but it is necessary to try to draw them to the Natchez, the languages being the same (*n'étant que d'une même langue*) * * *

From a memoir without name of author or date, but which goes back to the first years of the eighteenth century

After the departure of Mons. Tonty, M. De Montigny and the two other missionaries pursued their way as far as the Tonicats, where they thought it well to make an establishment and to leave there Mons. Davion, and from there to the Tahensas and Natchez, which have the same language (*qui ont la même langue*), and are only a day's journey apart. * * *

The last of these may have been based on De Montigny's letters and would therefore contain only secondhand information, but the others leave little room for doubt. Before writing the former De Montigny had visited one tribe in company with members of the other, and had had abundant opportunity to hear the two peoples converse together. Had they been of alien speech they would not have employed Natchez but the Mobilian jargon, and he would hardly have failed to observe the fact. St. Cosme's evidence is yet stronger, since at the time of writing he had had the advantage of one winter's study of Natchez; nor is it probable that he would have made a recommendation to his superior to draw the two into one mission until he had fully satisfied himself that their languages were indeed identical. It should be added that in other excerpts from this unpublished correspondence, sent to the writer by Professor Gosselin, occur references to the linguistic affinities and divergences of the Chickasaw, Tunica, Houma, Quinipissa, Osage, Quapaw, Kansa, and Missouri, and in the light of all our present knowledge not a single mistake is made. The information of the priests extends even to the point of determining the closer relationship of Osage, Quapaw, and Kansa to one another than of any of them to the Missouri. If this were true of the comparatively remote tribes, why should they have blundered regarding the nearer ones?

The writer had hoped to render assurance doubly sure by discovering some living representative of the tribe in question from whom a few words in the old Taënsa language might be gathered. From the Chitimacha, at Charenton, La., he learned that the father of the oldest woman of that tribe was a Taënsa, and that she herself had formerly been able to use the language. A few days after receiving this intelligence he called upon this woman and endeavored in every way to stimulate her memory into the resurrection of at least a word of the old tongue, but in vain. All that he could learn was that *ki'pi,* which signifies 'meat' in Chitimacha, had another meaning in Taënsa, but what it was she could not say. This is indefinite enough, but perhaps it may have really been the Natchez infinitive ending *-kip, -kipi, -kup, -kupi,* which is employed very frequently, and consequently may have retained a place in the memory after everything else had gone. At any rate *ki'pi* is a combination of sounds not conspicuous, if indeed it is existent, in Parisot's Taënsa Grammar.

The writer is informed that not merely the old woman just referred to had once been familiar with Taënsa, but a number of the other Chitimacha Indians, and the old negro Baptiste himself, from whom Doctor Gatschet obtained practically all of his Chitimacha linguistic material. Thus, by a curious irony of fate, in the same year in which the grammar which occasioned so much discussion appeared, its principal American defender was in communication with a man who possessed information which would have nipped the controversy in the bud, and yet he never appears to have been aware of the fact.

Summing up, then, we find the following state of affairs: So far as is known, the original Taënsa manuscript has never been seen by any person except the gentleman who professed to copy from it. The statements made by that person regarding it in 1880 and 1882 do not agree. The "Taënsa songs" are un-Indian in tone and contain geographical, botanical, and ethnological blunders which Gatschet has not satisfactorily explained, while Adam has conceded that they are later compilations of "some disciple of the Jesuit fathers who had taken a fancy to the Taënsa poetry." The language itself is in almost every respect unlike any in the region where it is supposed to have been spoken and contains no words that may be recognized as having been borrowed from any of those tongues. That it does contain certain features found only in the neighboring but subsequently discovered Tunica, combined with a few lexical similarities with that language, is the strongest argument in its favor, but on looking closer these resemblances are found to be very superficial. Finally, the direct statements of several early French writers must be cited, including two missionaries personally acquainted with both tribes, that the Taënsa language was identical with that of the Natchez, which we know to have been quite different from the one brought out by Parisot. It may be safely set down, therefore, that if the language in the work under discussion was ever a living speech it was not that of the Taënsa, and since, in consequence, the texts containing as they do references to this tribe, must have been the work of white men, we may conclude with probability that the whole of the material had the same origin and is entirely fraudulent.

Notes

[1] Grammaire et Vocabulaire de la Langue Taensa, *Bibliothèque Linguistique Américaine,* IX, Paris, 1882.
[2] *Amer. Antiq.*, VII, 109–110.
[3] Ibid., 110.
[4] Ibid., 111.
[5] *Amer. Antiq.*, VII, 112–113.
[6] Ibid., 113.
[7] See p. 10.
[8] *Amer. Antiq.*, VII, 276.
[9] *Revue de Linguistique,* XIX, 147–169.
[10] Ibid., 207.
[11] Ibid., XXI, 203–204.
[12] Ibid., 204–207.
[13] *Revue de Linguistique,* XXI, 341.
[14] French, Hist. Coll. La., 178, 1851.
[15] La Langue Taensa, xvii–xix, Paris, 1882.
[16] See p. 26.
[17] Shea, Early Voy. Miss., 76, 1861.
[18] Ibid., 136.
[19] Du Pratz, Hist. de La Louisiane, II, 213, 225.
[20] Pp. 75–79.
[21] La Harpe, Jour. Hist., 16, 1831; Margry, Découvertes, IV, 451–452.
[22] Margry, Découvertes, IV, 417, 1880.
[23] Ibid., 430–431.
[24] La Harpe, Jour. Hist., 101, 1831.
[25] Compte Rendu Cong. Internat. des Amér., 15th sess., I, 31–51.
[26] Ibid., 38.

20. The History of Anthropology

Franz Boas

I have been asked to speak on the history of anthropology.[1] The task that has been allotted to me is so vast and the time at my disposal is so short, that it will be impossible to do justice to the work of the minds that have made anthropology what it is. It would even be futile to characterize the work of the greatest among the contributors to our science. All that I can undertake to do is to discuss the general conditions of scientific thought that have given rise to anthropology.

Viewing my task from this standpoint, you will pardon me if I do not first attempt to define what anthropology ought to be, and with what subjects it ought to deal, but if I take my cue rather from what it is, and how it has developed.

Before I enter into my subject I will say that the speculative anthropology of the 18th and of the early part of the 19th century is distinct in its scope and method from the science which is called anthropology at the present time and is not included in our discussion.

At the present time anthropologists occupy themselves with problems relating to the physical and mental life of mankind as found in varying forms of society, from the earliest times up to the present period, and in all parts of the world. Their researches bear upon the form and functions of the body as well as upon all kinds of manifestations of mental life. Accordingly, the subject matter of anthropology is partly a branch of biology, partly a branch of the mental sciences. Among the mental phenomena language, invention, art, religion, social organization and law have received particular attention. Among anthropologists of our time we find a considerable amount of specialization of the subject matter of their researches according to the divisions here given.

As in other sciences whose subject matter is the actual distribution of phenomena and their causal relation, we find in anthropology two distinct methods of research and aims of investigation: the one, the historical method, which endeavors to reconstruct the actual history of

From *Science,* Vol. 20 (21 October 1904), pp. 513–524. Reprinted by permission of the American Association for the Advancement of Science.

mankind; the other, the generalizing method, which attempts to establish the laws of its development. According to the personal inclination of the investigator, the one or the other method prevails in his researches. A considerable amount of geographical and historical specialization has also taken place among what may be called the historical school of anthropologists. Some devote their energies to the elucidation of the earliest history of mankind, while others study the inhabitants of remote regions, and still others the survivals of early times that persist in our midst.

The conditions thus outlined are the result of a long development, the beginnings of which during the second half of the 18th century may be clearly observed. The interest in the customs and appearance of the inhabitants of distant lands is, of course, much older. The descriptions of Herodotus show that even among the nations of antiquity, notwithstanding their self-centered civilization, this interest was not lacking. The travelers of the Middle Ages excited the curiosity of their contemporaries by the recital of their experiences. The literature of the Spanish conquest of America is replete with remarks on the customs of the natives of the New World. But there is hardly any indication of the thought that these observations might be made the subject of scientific treatment. They were and remained curiosities. It was only when their relation to our own civilization became the subject of inquiry that the foundations of anthropology were laid. Its germs may be discovered in the early considerations of theologists regarding the relations between pagan religions and the revelations of Christianity. They were led to the conclusion that the lower forms of culture, more particularly of religion, were due to degeneration, to a falling away from the revealed truth, of which traces are to be found in primitive beliefs.

During the second half of the eighteenth century we find the fundamental concept of anthropology well formulated by the rationalists who preceded the French Revolution. The deep-seated feeling that political and social inequality was the result of a faulty development of civilization and that originally all men were born equal, led Rousseau to the naïve assumption of an ideal natural state which we ought to try to regain. These ideas were shared by many and the relation of the culture of primitive man to our civilization remained the topic of discussion. To this period belongs Herder's 'Ideen zur Geschichte der Menschheit,' in which perhaps for the first time the fundamental thought of the development of the culture of mankind as a whole is clearly expressed.

About this time Cook made his memorable voyages and the culture of the tribes of the Pacific Islands became first known to Europe. His observations and the descriptions of Forster were eagerly taken up by students and were extensively used in support of their theories. Nevertheless even the best attempts of this period were essentially speculative and deductive, for the rigid inductive method had hardly begun to be understood in the domain of natural sciences, much less in that of the mental sciences.

While, on the whole, the study of the mental life of mankind had in its beginning decidedly a historical character, and while knowledge of the evolution of civilization was recognized as its ultimate aim, the biological side of anthropology developed in an entirely different manner. It owes its origin to the great zoologists of the eighteenth century, and in conformity with the general systematic tendencies of the times, the main efforts were directed towards a classification of the races of man and to the discovery of valid characteristics by means of which the races could be described as varieties of one species or as distinct species. The attempts at classification were numerous, but no new point of view was developed.

During the nineteenth century a certain approach between these two directions was made, which may be exemplified by the work of Klemm. The classificatory aspect was combined with the historical one and the leading discussion related to the discovery of mental differences between the zoological varieties or races of men, and to the question of polygenism and monogenism. The passions that were aroused by the practical and ethical aspects of the slavery question did much to concentrate attention on this phase of the anthropological problem.

As stated before, most of the data of anthropology had been collected by travelers whose prime object was geographical discoveries. For this reason the collected material soon demanded the attention of geographers, who viewed it from a new standpoint. To them the relations between man and nature were of prime importance and their attention was directed less to psychological questions than to those relating to the dependence of the form of culture upon geographical surroundings, and the control of natural conditions gained by man with the advance of civilization.

Thus we find about the middle of the nineteenth century the beginnings of anthropology laid from three distinct points of view: the historical, the classificatory and the geographical. About this time the historical aspect of the phenomena of nature took hold of the minds of investigators in the whole domain of science. Beginning with biology, and principally through Darwin's powerful influence, it gradually revolutionized the whole method of natural and mental science and led to a new formulation of their problems. The idea that the phenomena of the present have developed from previous forms with which they are genetically connected and which determine them, shook the foundations of the old principles of classification and knit together groups of facts that hitherto had seemed disconnected. Once clearly enunciated, the historical view of the natural sciences proved irresistible and the old problems faded away before the new attempts to discover the history of evolution. From the very beginning there has been a strong tendency to combine with the historical aspect a subjective valuation of the various phases of development, the present serving as a standard of comparison. The oft-observed change from simple forms to more complex forms, from uniformity to diversity, was interpreted as a change from the less valuable to the more valuable and thus the historical view assumed in many cases an ill-concealed teleological tinge. The grand picture of nature in which for the first time the universe appears as a unit of ever-changing form and color, each momentary aspect being determined by the past moment and determining the coming changes, is still obscured by a subjective element, emotional in its sources, which leads us to ascribe the highest value to that which is near and dear to us.

The new historical view also came into conflict with the generalizing method of science. It was imposed upon that older view of nature in which the discovery of general laws was considered the ultimate aim of investigation. According to this view laws may be exemplified by individual events, which, however, lose their specific interest once the laws are discovered. The actual event possesses no scientific value in itself, but only so far as it leads to the discovery of a general law. This view is, of course, fundamentally opposed to the purely historical view. Here the laws of nature are recognized in each individual event, and the chief interest centers in the event as an incident of the picture of the world. In a way the historic view contains a strong, esthetic element, which finds its satisfaction in the clear conception of the individual event. It is easily intelligible that the combination of these two standpoints led to the subordination of the historical fact under the concept of the law of nature. Indeed, we find all the sciences which took up the historical standpoint for the first time, soon engaged in endeavors to discover the laws according to which evolution has taken place. The regularity in the processes of evolution became the center of attraction even before the processes of evolution had been observed and understood. All sciences were equally guilty of premature theories of evolution based on observed homologies and supposed similarities. The theories had to be revised again and again, as the slow progress of empirical knowledge of the data of evolution proved their fallacy.

Anthropology also felt the quickening impulse of the historic point of view, and its development followed the same lines that may be observed in the history of the other sciences. The unity of civilization and of primitive culture that had been divined by Herder now shone forth as a certainty. The multiplicity and diversity of curious customs and beliefs appeared as early steps in the evolution of civilization from simple forms of culture. The striking similarity between the customs of remote districts was the proof of the uniform manner in which civilization had developed the world over. The laws according to which this uniform development of culture took place became the new problem which engrossed the attention of anthropologists.

This is the source from which sprang the ambitious system of Herbert Spencer and the ingenious theories of Edward Burnett Tylor. The underlying thought of the numerous attempts to systematize the whole range of social phenomena or one or the other of its features—such as religious belief, social organization, forms of marriage—has been the belief that one definite system can be found according to which all culture has developed, that there is one type of evolution from a primitive form to the highest civilization which is applicable to the whole of mankind, that notwithstanding many variations caused by local and historical conditions, the general type of evolution is the same everywhere.

This theory has been discussed most clearly by Tylor, who finds proof for it in the sameness of customs and beliefs the world over. The typical similarity and the occurrence of certain customs in definite combinations are explained by him as due to their belonging to a certain stage in the development of civilization. They do not disappear suddenly, but persist for a time in the form of survivals. These are, therefore, wherever they occur, a proof that a lower stage of culture of which these customs are characteristic has been passed through.

Anthropology owes its very existence to the stimulus given by these scholars and to the conclusions reached by them. What had been a chaos of facts appeared now marshaled in orderly array, and the great steps in the slow advance from savagery to civilization were drawn for the first time with a firm hand. We can not overestimate the influence of the bold generalizations made by these pioneers of modern anthropology. They applied with vigor and unswerving courage the new principles of historical evolution to all the phenomena of civilized life, and in doing so sowed the seeds of the anthropological spirit in the minds of historians and philosophers. Anthropology, which was hardly beginning to be a science, ceased at the same time to lose its character of being a single science, but became a method applicable to all the mental sciences and indispensable to all of them. We are still in the midst of this development. The sciences first to feel the influence of anthropological thought were those of law and religion. But it was not long before ethics, esthetics, literature and philosophy in general were led to accept the evolutionary standpoint in the particular form given to it by the early anthropologists.

The generalized view of the evolution of culture in all its different phases which is the final result of this method may be subjected to a further analysis regarding the psychic causes which bring about the regular sequence of the stages of culture. Owing to the abstract form of the results, this analysis must be deductive. It can not be an induction from empirical psychological data. In this fact lies one of the weaknesses of the method which led a number of anthropologists to a somewhat different statement of the problem. I mention here particularly Adolf Bastian and Georg Gerland. Both were impressed by the sameness of the fundamental traits of culture the world over. Bastian saw in their sameness an effect of the sameness of the human mind and terms these fundamental traits 'Elementargedanken,' declining all further consideration of their origin, since an inductive treatment of this problem is impossible. For him the essential problem of anthropology is the discovery of the elementary ideas, and in further pursuit of the inquiry, their modification under the influence of geographical environment. Gerland's views agree with those of Bastian in the emphasis laid upon the influence of geographical environment on the forms of culture. In place of the mystic elementary idea of Bastian, Gerland assumes that the elements found in many remote parts of the world are a common inheritance from an early stage of cultural development. It will be seen that in both these views the system of evolution plays a secondary part only, and that the main stress is laid on the causes which bring about modifications of the fundamental and identical traits. There is a close connection between this direction of anthropology and the old geographical school. Here the psychic and environmental relations remain amenable to inductive treatment, while, on the other hand, the fundamental hypotheses exclude the origin of the common traits from further investigation.

The subjective valuation which is characteristic of most evolutionary systems, was from the very beginning part and parcel of evolutionary anthropology. It is but natural that in the study of the history of culture our own civilization should become the standard, that the achievements of other times and other races should be measured by our own achievements. In no case is it more difficult to lay aside the 'Culturbrille'—to use Von den Steinen's apt term—than in viewing our own culture. For this reason the literature of anthropology abounds in attempts to define a number of stages of culture leading from simple forms to the present civilization, from savagery through barbarism to civilization, or from an assumed presavagery through the same stages to enlightenment.

The endeavor to establish a schematic line of evolution naturally led back to new attempts at classification in which each group bears a genetic relation to the other. Such attempts have been made from both the cultural and the biological point of view.

It is necessary to speak here of one line of anthropological research that we have hitherto disregarded. I mean the linguistic method. The origin of language was one of the much discussed problems of the nineteenth century, and owing to its relation to the development of culture, it has a direct anthropological bearing. The intimate ties between language and ethnic psychology were expressed by no one more clearly than by

Steinthal, who perceived that the form of thought is molded by the whole social environment of which language is part. Owing to the rapid change of language, the historical treatment of the linguistic problem had developed long before the historic aspect of the natural sciences was understood. The genetic relationship of languages was clearly recognized when the genetic relationship of species was hardly thought of. With the increasing knowledge of languages they were grouped according to common descent, and when no further relationship could be proved, a classification according to morphology was attempted. To the linguist whose whole attention is directed to the study of the expression of thought by language, language is the individuality of a people, and therefore a classification of languages must present itself to him as a classification of peoples. No other manifestation of the mental life of man can be classified so minutely and definitely as language. In none are the genetic relations more clearly established. It is only when no further genetic and morphological relationship can be found, that the linguist is compelled to coordinate languages and can give no further clue regarding their relationship and origin. No wonder, then, that this method was used to classify mankind, although in reality the linguist classified only languages. The result of the classification seems eminently satisfactory on account of its definiteness as compared with the results of biological and cultural classifications.

Meanwhile the methodical resources of biological or somatic anthropology had also developed and had enabled the investigator to make nicer distinctions between human types than he had been able to make. The landmark in the development of this branch of anthropology has been the introduction of the metric method, which owes its first strong development to Quetelet. A little later we shall have to refer to this subject again. For the present it may suffice to say that a clearer definition of the terms 'type' and 'variability' led to the application of the statistical method by means of which comparatively slight varieties can be distinguished satisfactorily. By the application of this method it soon became apparent that the races of man could be subdivided into types which were characteristic of definite geographical areas and of the people inhabiting them. The same misinterpretation developed here as was found among the linguists. As they identified language and people, so the anatomists identified somatic type and people and based their classifications of peoples wholly on their somatic characters.

The two principles were soon found to clash. Peoples genetically connected by language, or even the same in language, were found to be diverse in type, and people of the same type were found to be diverse in language. Furthermore, the results of classifications according to cultural groups disagreed with both the linguistic and the somatic classifications. In long and bitter controversies the representatives of these three directions of anthropological research contended for the correctness of their conclusions. This war of opinions was fought out particularly on the ground of the so-called Aryan question, and only gradually did the fact come to be understood that each of these classifications is the reflection of a certain group of facts. The linguistic classification records the historical fates of languages and indirectly of the people speaking these languages; the somatic classification records the blood relationships of groups of people and thus traces another phase of their history; while the cultural classification records historical events of still another character, the diffusion of culture from one people to another and the absorption of one culture by another. Thus it became clear that the attempted classifications were expressions of historical data bearing upon the unwritten history of races and peoples, and recorded their descent, mixture of blood, changes of language and development of culture. Attempts at generalized classifications based on these methods can claim validity only for that group of phenomena to which the method applies. An agreement of their results, that is, original association between somatic type, language and culture, must not be expected. Thus the historical view of anthropology received support from the struggles between these three methods of classification.

We remarked before that the evolutionary method was based essentially on the observation of the sameness of cultural traits the world over. On the one hand, the sameness was assumed as proof of a regular, uniform evolution of culture. On the other hand, it was assumed to represent the elementary idea which arises by necessity in the mind of man and which can not be analyzed, or as the earliest surviving form of human thought.

The significance of these elementary ideas or universal traits of culture has been brought into prominence by the long continued controversy between the theory of their independent origin and that of their transmission from one part of the world to another. This struggle began even before the birth of modern anthropology, with the contest between Grimm's theory of the origin and history of myths and Benfey's proof of transmissions, which was based on his learned investigations into the literary history of tales. It is still in progress. On the one hand, there are investigators who would exclude the consideration of transmission altogether, who believe it to be unlikely and deem the alleged proof irrelevant, and who ascribe sameness of cultural traits wholly to the psychic unity of mankind and to the uniform reaction of the human mind upon the same stimulus. An extremist in this direction was the late Daniel G. Brinton. On the other hand, Friedrich Ratzel, whose recent loss we lament, inclined decidedly to the opinion that all sameness of cultural traits must be accounted for by transmission, no matter how far distant the regions in which they are found. In comparison with these two views the third one, which was mentioned before as represented by Gerland, namely, that such cultural traits are vestiges or survivals of the earliest stages of a generalized human culture, has found few supporters.

It is evident that this fundamental question can not be settled by the continued discussion of general facts, since the various explanations are logically equally probable. It requires actual investigation into the individual history of such customs to discover the causes of their present distribution.

Here is the place to mention the studies in folklore which have excited considerable interest in recent times and which must be considered a branch of anthropological research. Beginning with records of curious superstitions and customs and of popular tales, folklore has become the science of all the manifestations of popular life. Folklorists occupy themselves primarily with the folklore of Europe and thus supplement the material collected by anthropologists in foreign lands. The theorists of folklore are also divided into the two camps of the adherents of the psychological theory and those of the historical theory. In England the former holds sway, while on the continent the historical theory seems to be gaining ground. The identity of the contents of folklore all over Europe seems to be an established fact. To the one party the occurrence of these forms of folklore seems to be due in part to psychic necessity, in part to the survival of earlier customs and beliefs. To the other party it seems to owe its origin to the spread of ideas over the whole continent which may, in part at least, be followed by literary evidence.

However this controversy, both in folklore and in anthropology, may be settled, it is clear that it must lead to detailed historical investigations, by means of which definite problems may be solved, and that it will furthermore lead to psychological researches into the conditions of transmission, adaptation and invention. Thus this controversy will carry us beyond the limits set by the theory of elementary ideas, and by that of a single system of evolution of civilization.

Another aspect of the theories here discussed deserves special mention. I mean the assumption of a 'folk psychology' (Völkerpsychologie) as distinct from individual psychology. Folk psychology deals with those psychic actions which take place in each individual as a social unit, and the psychology of the individual must be interpeted by the data of a social psychology, because each individual can think, feel and act only as a member of the social group to which he belongs. The growth of language and all ethnic phenomena have thus been treated from the point of view of a social psychology, and special attention has been given to the subconscious influences which sway crowds and masses of people, and to the processes of imitation. I mention Steinthal, Wundt, Baldwin, Tarde, Stoll, among the men who have devoted their energies to these and related problems. Notwithstanding their efforts, and those of a number of sociologists and geographers, the relation of 'folk psychology' to individual psychology has not been elucidated satisfactorily.

We will now turn to a consideration of the recent history of somatology. The historical point of view wrought deep changes also in this branch of anthropology. In place of classification the evolution of human types became the main object of investigation. The two questions of man's place in nature and of the evolution of human races and types came to the front. The morphological and embryological methods which had been developed by biologists were applied to the human species and the new endeavors were directed to the discovery of the predecessor of man, to his position in the animal series, and to evidences regarding the direction in which the species develops. I need mention only Huxley and Wiedersheim to characterize the trend of these researches.

In one respect, however, the study of the human species differs from that of the animal series. I stated before that the slight differences between types which are important to the anthropologist had led to the substitution of the metric quantitative description for the verbal or qualitative method. The study of the effects of natural selection, of environment, of heredity, as applied to man, made the elaboration of these methods a necessity. Our interest in slight differences is so much greater in man than in animals or plants, that here the needs of quantitative precision were first felt. We owe it to Francis Galton that the methods of the quantitative study of the varieties of man have been developed and that the study has been extended from the field of anatomy over that of physiology and experimental psychology. His researches were extended and systematized by Karl Pearson, in whose hands the question which was originally one of the precise treatment of the biological problem of anthropology has outgrown its original limits and has become a general biological method for the study of the characteristics and of the development of varieties.

We may now summarize the fundamental problems which give to anthropology its present character. In the biological branch we have the problem of the morphological evolution of man and that of the development of varieties. Inseparable from these questions is also that of correlation between somatic and mental characters which has a practical as well as a theoretical interest. In psychological anthropology the important questions are the discovery of a system of the evolution of culture, the study of the modifications of simple general traits under the influence of different geographical and social conditions, the question of transmission and spontaneous origin, and that of folk psychology *versus* individual psychology. It will, of course, be understood that this enumeration is not exhaustive, but includes only some of the most important points of view that occupy the minds of investigators.

The work of those students who are engaged in gathering the

material from which this history of mankind is to be built up is deeply influenced by these problems. It would be vain to attempt to give even the briefest review of what has been achieved by the modest collector of facts, how his efforts have covered the remotest paths of the world, how he has tried to uncover and interpret the remains left by the races of the past.

I think we may say, without injustice, that his work is directed principally to the explanation of special problems that derive their chief interest from a personal love for the particular question and an ardent desire to see its obscurity removed and to present its picture in clear outlines. Nevertheless the well trained and truly scientific observer will always be aware of the general relations of his special problem and will be influenced in his treatment of the special question by the general theoretical discussions of his times. It must be said with regret that the number of anthropological observers who have a sufficient understanding of the problems of the day is small. Still their number has increased considerably during the last twenty years and consequently a constant improvement in the reliability and thoroughness of the available observations may be noticed.

One or two aspects of the research work of the field anthropologist must be mentioned. The studies in prehistoric archæology have been given a lasting impulse by the discussions relating to the evolution of mankind and of human culture. Two great problems have occupied the attention of archæologists, the origin and first appearance of the human race, and the historical sequence of races and of types of culture. To the archæologist the determination of the chronological order is an important one. The determination of the geological period in which man appeared, the chronological relation of the earliest types of man to their later successors, the sequence of types of culture as determined by the artifacts of each period, and approximate determinations of the absolute time to which these remains belong are the fundamental problems with which archæology is concerned. The results obtained have the most immediate bearing upon the general question of the evolution of culture, since the ideal aim of archæology practically coincides with this general problem, the solution of which would be contained in a knowledge of the chronological development of culture. Of course, in many cases the chronological question can not be answered and then the archæological observations simply rank with ethnological observations of primitive people.

The field work of ethnologists has been influenced in several directions by the theoretical discussions of anthropologists. We do not need to dwell on the fact that the scope of ethnological research has become more extensive and exhaustive by taking into consideration more thoroughly than before the whole range of cultural phenomena. More interesting than this is the stimulus that has been given to historic and psychological observation. On the one hand, the theory of transmission has induced investigators to trace the distribution and history of customs and beliefs with care so as to ascertain empirically whether they are spontaneous creations or whether they are borrowed and adapted. On the other hand, the psychic conditions that accompany various types of culture have received more careful attention.

These detailed archæological and ethnological studies have retroacted upon the theories of anthropology. The grand system of the evolution of culture, that is valid for all humanity, is losing much of its plausibility. In place of a simple line of evolution there appear a multiplicity of converging and diverging lines which it is difficult to bring under one system. Instead of uniformity the striking feature seems to be diversity. On the other hand, certain general psychic facts seem to become discernible, which promise to connect folk psychology with individual psychology. The trend of this development is familiar to us in the history of other sciences, such as geology and biology. The brilliant theories in which the whole range of problems of a science appears simple and easily explorable have always preceded the periods of steady empirical work which make necessary a complete revision of the original theories and lead through a period of uncertainty to a more strictly inductive attack of the ultimate problems. So it is with anthropology. Later than the older sciences, it has outgrown the systematizing period and is just now entering upon the empirical revision of its theories.

Our sketch of the history of the prevailing tendencies in anthropology would be incomplete without a few remarks on the men who have made it what it is. What has been said before shows clearly that there is hardly a science that is as varied in its methods as anthropology. Its problems have been approached by biologists, linguists, geographers, psychologists, historians and philosophers. Up to ten years ago we had no trained anthropologists, but students drifted into anthropological research from all the sciences that I have mentioned here and perhaps from others. With many it was the interest aroused by a special problem, not theoretical considerations, that decided their course. Others were attracted by a general interest in the evolution of mankind. The best among them were gradually permeated by the fundamental spirit of anthropological research, which consists in the appreciation of the necessity of studying all forms of human culture, because the variety of its forms alone can throw light upon the history of its development, past and future, and which deigns even the poorest tribe, the degraded criminal and the physical degenerate worthy of attentive study because the expressions of his mental life, no less than his physical appearance, may throw light upon the history of mankind.

Even now the multifarious origin of anthropology is reflected in the multiplicity of its methods. The historian or the political economist who comes into contact with anthropological problems can not follow the methods of the biologist and of the linguist. Neither can the anthropologist of our period fill the demands for information of all those who may need anthropological data. It might almost seem that the versatility required of him will set a limit to his usefulness as a thorough scientist. However, the solution of this difficulty is not far off. We have seen that a great portion of the domain of anthropology has developed through the application of the new historical point of view to the mental sciences. To those who occupy themselves with this group of problems anthropological knowledge will be indispensable. Though the anthropological point of view may thus pervade the treatment of an older branch of science and help to develop new standpoints, the assistance that anthropology renders it does not destroy the independence of the older science which in a long history has developed its own aims and methods. Conscious of the invigorating influence of our point of view and of the grandeur of a single all-compassing science of man, enthusiastic anthropologists may proclaim the mastery of anthropology over older sciences that have achieved where we are still struggling with methods, that have built up noble structures where chaos reigns with us; the trend of development points in another direction, in the continuance of each science by itself, assisted where may be by anthropological methods. The practical demands of anthropology also demand a definition and restriction of its field of work rather than constant expansion.

The historical development of the work of anthropologists seems to single out clearly a domain of knowledge that heretofore has not been treated by any other science. It is the biological history of mankind in all its varieties; linguistics applied to people without written languages; the ethnology of people without historic records, and prehistoric archæology. It is true that these limits are constantly being overstepped, but the unbiased observer will recognize that in all other fields special knowledge is required which can not be supplied by general anthropology. The *general* problem of the evolution of mankind is being taken up now by the investigator of primitive tribes, now by the student of the history of civilization. We may still recognize in it the ultimate aim of anthropology in the wider sense of the term, but we must understand that it will be reached by cooperation between all the mental sciences and the efforts of the anthropologist.

The field of research that has been left for anthropology in the narrower sense of the term is, even as it is, almost too wide, and there are indications of its breaking up. The biological, linguistic and ethnologic-archæological methods are so distinct that on the whole the same man will not be equally proficient in all of them. The time is rapidly drawing near when the biological branch of anthropology will be finally separated from the rest and become a part of biology. This seems necessary, since all the problems relating to the effect of geographical and social environment and those relating to heredity are primarily of a biological character. Problems may be set by the general anthropologist. They will be solved by the biologist. Almost equally cogent are the reasons that urge on to a separation of the purely linguistic work from the ethnological work. I think the time is not far distant when anthropology pure and simple will deal with the customs and beliefs of the less civilized people only, and when linguistics and biology will continue and develop the work that we are doing now because no one else cares for it. Nevertheless, we must always demand that the anthropologist who carries on field research must be familiar with the principles of these three methods, since all of them are needed for the investigation of his problems. No less must we demand that he has a firm grasp of the general results of the anthropological method as applied by various sciences. It alone will give his work that historic perspective which constitutes its higher scientific value.

A last word as to the value that the anthropological method is assuming in the general system of our culture and education. I do not wish to refer to its practical value to those who have to deal with foreign races or with national questions. Of greater educational importance is its power to make us understand the roots from which our civilization has sprung, that it impresses us with the relative value of all forms of culture, and thus serves as a check to an exaggerated valuation of the standpoint of our own period, which we are only too liable to consider the ultimate goal of human evolution, thus depriving ourselves of the benefits to be gained from the teachings of other cultures and hindering an objective criticism of our own work.

Note

[1] Address at the International Congress of Arts and Science, St. Louis, September, 1904.

21. On Semitic Religion

William Robertson-Smith

Let it be understood from the outset that we have not the materials for anything like a complete comparative history of Semitic religions, and that nothing of the sort will be attempted in these Lectures. But a careful study and comparison of the various sources is sufficient to furnish a tolerably accurate view of a series of general features, which recur with striking uniformity in all parts of the Semitic field, and govern the evolution of faith and worship down to a late date. These widespread and permanent features form the real interest of Semitic religion to the philosophical student; it was in them, and not in the things that vary from place to place and from time to time, that the strength of Semitic religion lay, and it is to them therefore that we must look for help in the most important practical application of our studies, for light on the great question of the relation of the positive Semitic religions to the earlier faith of the race.

Before entering upon the particulars of our enquiry, I must still detain you with a few words about the method and order of investigation that seem to be prescribed by the nature of the subject. To get a true and well-defined picture of the type of Semitic religion, we must not only study the parts separately, but must have clear views of the place and proportion of each part in its relation to the whole. And here we shall go very far wrong if we take it for granted that what is the most important and prominent side of religion to us was equally important in the ancient society with which we are to deal. In connection with every religion, whether ancient or modern, we find on the one hand certain beliefs, and on the other certain institutions ritual practices and rules of conduct. Our modern habit is to look at religion from the side of belief rather than of practice; for, down to comparatively recent times, almost the only forms of religion seriously studied in Europe have been those of the various Christian Churches, and all parts of Christendom are agreed that ritual is important only in connection with its interpretation. Thus the study of religion has meant mainly the study of Christian beliefs, and instruction

From William Robertson-Smith, *The Religion of the Semites*, 1914. Reprinted by permission of Adam and Charles Black, Ltd.: pp. 15–27.

in religion has habitually begun with the creed, religious duties being presented to the learner as flowing from the dogmatic truths he is taught to accept. All this seems to us so much a matter of course that, when we approach some strange or antique religion, we naturally assume that here also our first business is to search for a creed, and find in it the key to ritual and practice. But the antique religions had for the most part no creed; they consisted entirely of institutions and practices. No doubt men will not habitually follow certain practices without attaching a meaning to them; but as a rule we find that while the practice was rigorously fixed, the meaning attached to it was extremely vague, and the same rite was explained by different people in different ways, without any question of orthodoxy or heterodoxy arising in consequence. In ancient Greece, for example, certain things were done at a temple, and people were agreed that it would be impious not to do them. But if you had asked why they were done, you would probably have had several mutually contradictory explanations from different persons, and no one would have thought it a matter of the least religious importance which of these you chose to adopt. Indeed, the explanations offered would not have been of a kind to stir any strong feeling; for in most cases they would have been merely different stories as to the circumstances under which the rite first came to be established, by the command or by the direct example of the god. The rite, in short, was connected not with a dogma but with a myth.

In all the antique religions, mythology takes the place of dogma; that is, the sacred lore of priests and people, so far as it does not consist of mere rules for the performance of religious acts, assumes the form of stories about the gods; and these stories afford the only explanation that is offered of the precepts of religion and the prescribed rules of ritual. But, strictly speaking, this mythology was no essential part of ancient religion, for it has no sacred sanction and no binding force on the worshippers. The myths connected with individual sanctuaries and ceremonies were merely part of the apparatus of the worship; they served to excite the fancy and sustain the interest of the worshipper; but he was often offered a choice of several accounts of the same thing, and, provided that he fulfilled the ritual with accuracy, no one cared what he believed about its origin. Belief in a certain series of myths was neither obligatory as a part of true religion, nor was it supposed that, by believing, a man acquired religious merit and conciliated the favour of the gods. What was obligatory or meritorious was the exact performance of certain sacred acts prescribed by religious tradition. This being so, it follows that mythology ought not to take the prominent place that is too often assigned to it in the scientific study of ancient faiths. So far as myths consist of explanations of ritual, their value is altogether secondary, and it may be affirmed with confidence that in almost every case the myth was derived from the ritual, and not the ritual from the myth; for the ritual was fixed and the myth was variable, the ritual was obligatory and faith in the myth was at the discretion of the worshipper. Now by far the largest part of the myths of antique religions are connected with the ritual of particular shrines, or with the religious observances of particular tribes and districts. In all such cases it is probable, in most cases it is certain, that the myth is merely the explanation of a religious usage; and ordinarily it is such an explanation as could not have arisen till the original sense of the usage had more or less fallen into oblivion. As a rule the myth is no explanation of the origin of the ritual to any one who does not believe it to be a narrative of real occurrences, and the boldest mythologist will not believe that. But if it be not true, the myth itself requires to be explained, and every principle of philosophy and common sense demands that the explanation be sought, not in arbitrary allegorical theories, but in the actual facts of ritual or religious custom to which the myth attaches. The conclusion is, that in the study of ancient religions we must begin, not with myth, but with ritual and traditional usage.

Nor can it be fairly set against this conclusion, that there are certain myths which are not mere explanations of traditional practices, but exhibit the beginnings of larger religious speculation, or of an attempt to systematise and reduce to order the motley variety of local worships and beliefs. For in this case the secondary character of the myths is still more clearly marked. They are either products of early philosophy, reflecting on the nature of the universe; or they are political in scope, being designed to supply a thread of union between the various worships of groups, originally distinct, which have been united into one social or political organism; or, finally, they are due to the free play of epic imagination. But philosophy, politics and poetry are something more, or something less, than religion pure and simple.

There can be no doubt that, in the later stages of ancient religions, mythology acquired an increased importance. In the struggle of heathenism with scepticism on the one hand and Christianity on the other, the supporters of the old traditional religion were driven to search for ideas of a modern cast, which they could represent as the true inner meaning of the traditional rites. To this end they laid hold of the old myths, and applied to them an allegorical system of interpretation. Myth interpreted by the aid of allegory became the favourite means of infusing a new significance into ancient forms. But the theories thus developed are the falsest of false guides as to the original meaning of the old religions.

On the other hand, the ancient myths taken in their natural sense, without allegorical gloss, are plainly of great importance as testimonies to the views of the nature of the gods that were prevalent when they were formed. For though the mythical details had no dogmatic value and no binding authority over faith, it is to be supposed that nothing was put into a myth which people at that time were not prepared to believe without offence. But so far as the way of thinking expressed in the myth was not already expressed in the ritual itself, it had no properly religious sanction; the myth apart from the ritual affords only a doubtful and slippery kind of evidence. Before we can handle myths with any confidence, we must have some definite hold of the ideas expressed in the ritual tradition, which embodied the only fixed and statutory elements of the religion.

All this, I hope, will become clearer to us as we proceed with our enquiry, and learn by practical example the use to be made of the different lines of evidence open to us. But it is of the first importance to realise clearly from the outset that ritual and practical usage were, strictly speaking, the sum-total of ancient religions. Religion in primitive times was not a system of belief with practical applications; it was a body of fixed traditional practices, to which every member of society conformed as a matter of course. Men would not be men if they agreed to do certain things without having a reason for their action; but in ancient religion the reason was not first formulated as a doctrine and then expressed in practice, but conversely, practice preceded doctrinal theory. Men form general rules of conduct before they begin to express general principles in words; political institutions are older than political theories, and in like manner religious institutions are older than religious theories. This analogy is not arbitrarily chosen, for in fact the parallelism in ancient society between religious and political institutions is complete. In each sphere great importance was attached to form and precedent, but the explanation why the precedent was followed consisted merely of a legend as to its first establishment. That the precedent, once established, was authoritative did not appear to require any proof. The rules of society were based on precedent, and the continued existence of the society was sufficient reason why a precedent once set should continue to be followed.

Strictly speaking, indeed, I understate the case when I say that the oldest religious and political institutions present a close analogy. It would be more correct to say that they were parts of one whole of social custom. Religion was a part of the organised social life into which a man was born, and to which he conformed through life in the same unconscious way in which men fall into any habitual practice of the society in which they live. Men took the gods and their worship for granted, just as they took the other usages of the state for granted, and if they reasoned or speculated about them, they did so on the presupposition that the traditional usages were fixed things, behind which their reasonings must not go, and which no reasoning could be allowed to overturn. To us moderns religion is above all a matter of individual conviction and reasoned belief, but to the ancients it was a part of the citizen's public life, reduced to fixed forms, which he was not bound to understand and was not at liberty to criticise or to neglect. Religious nonconformity was an offence against the state; for if sacred tradition was tampered with the bases of society were undermined, and the favour of the gods was forfeited. But so long as the prescribed forms were duly observed, a man was recognised as truly pious, and no one asked how his religion was rooted in his heart or affected his reason. Like political duty, of which indeed it was a part, religion was entirely comprehended in the observance of certain fixed rules of outward conduct.

The conclusion from all this as to the method of our investigation is obvious. When we study the political structure of an early society, we do not begin be asking what is recorded of the first legislators, or what theory men advanced as to the reason of their institutions; we try to understand what the institutions were, and how they shaped men's lives. In like manner, in the study of Semitic religion, we must not begin by asking what was told about the gods, but what the working religious institutions were, and how they shaped the lives of the worshippers. Our enquiry, therefore, will be directed to the religious institutions which governed the lives of men of Semitic race.

In following out this plan, however, we shall do well not to throw ourselves at once upon the multitudinous details of rite and ceremony, but to devote our attention to certain broad features of the sacred institutions which are sufficiently well marked to be realised at once. If we were called upon to examine the political institutions of antiquity, we should find it convenient to carry with us some general notion of the several types of government under which the multifarious institutions of ancient states arrange themselves. And in like manner it will be useful for us, when we examine the religious institutions of the Semites, to have first some general knowledge of the types of divine governance, the various ruling conceptions of the relations of the gods to man, which underlie the rites and ordinances of religion in different places and at different times. Such knowledge we can obtain in a provisional form, before entering on a mass of ritual details, mainly by considering the titles of honour by which men addressed their gods, and the language in which they expressed their dependence on them. From these we can see at once, in a broad, general way, what place the gods held in the social system of antiquity, and under what general categories their relations to their worshippers fell. The broad results thus reached must then be developed, and at the same time controlled and rendered more precise, by an examination in detail of the working institutions of religion.

The question of the metaphysical nature of the gods, as distinct from their social office and function, must be left in the background till this whole investigation is completed. It is vain to ask what the gods are in themselves till we have studied them in what I may call their public life, that is, in the stated intercourse between them and their worshippers which was kept up by means of the prescribed forms of cultus. From the antique point of view, indeed, the question what the gods are in themselves is not a religious but a speculative one; what is requisite to religion is a practical acquaintance with the rules on which the deity acts and on which he expects his worshippers to frame their conduct—what in 2 Kings xvii. 26 is called the "manner" or rather the "customary law" (*mishpat*) of the god of the land. This is true even of the religion of Israel. When the prophets speak of the knowledge of God, they always mean a practical knowledge of the laws and principles of His government in Israel,[1] and a summary expression for religion as a whole is "the knowledge and fear of Jehovah,"[2] *i.e.* the knowledge of what Jehovah prescribes, combined with a reverent obedience. An extreme scepticism towards all religious speculation is recommended in the Book of Ecclesiastes as the proper attitude of piety, for no amount of discussion can carry a man beyond the plain rule to "fear God and keep His commandments."[3] This counsel the author puts into the mouth of Solomon, and so represents it, not unjustly, as summing up the old view of religion, which in more modern days had unfortunately begun to be undermined.

The propriety of keeping back all metaphysical questions as to the nature of the gods till we have studied the practices of religion in detail, becomes very apparent if we consider for a moment what befell the later philosophers and theosophists of heathenism in their attempts to construct a theory of the traditional religion. None of these thinkers succeeded in giving an account of the nature of the gods from which all the received practices of worship could be rationally deduced, and those who had any pretensions to orthodoxy had recourse to violent allegorical interpretations in order to bring the established ritual into accordance with their theories.[4] The reason for this is obvious. The traditional usages of religion had grown up gradually in the course of many centuries, and reflected habits of thought characteristic of very diverse stages of man's intellectual and moral development. No one conception of the nature of the gods could possibly afford the clue to all parts of that motley complex of rites and ceremonies which the later paganism had received by inheritance, from a series of ancestors in every state of culture from pure savagery upwards. The record of the religious thought of mankind, as it is embodied in religious institutions, resembles the geological record of the history of the earth's crust; the new and the old are preserved side by side, or rather layer upon layer. The classification of ritual formations in their proper sequence is the first step towards their explanation, and that explanation itself must take the form, not of a speculative theory, but of a rational life-history.

I have already explained that, in attempting such a life-history of religious institutions, we must begin by forming some preliminary ideas of the practical relation in which the gods of antiquity stood to their worshippers. I have now to add, that we shall also find it necessary to have before us from the outset some elementary notions of the relations which early races of mankind conceived to subsist between gods and men on the one hand, and the material universe on the other. All acts of ancient worship have a material embodiment, the form of which is determined by the consideration that gods and men alike stand in certain fixed relations to particular parts or aspects of physical nature. Certain places, certain things, even certain animal kinds are conceived as holy, *i.e.* as standing in a near relation to the gods, and claiming special reverence from men, and this conception plays a very large part in the development of religious institutions. Here again we have a problem that cannot be solved by *à priori* methods; it is only as we move onward from step to step in the analysis of the details of ritual observance that we can hope to gain full insight into the relations of the gods to physical nature. But there are certain broad features in the ancient conception of the universe, and of the relations of its parts to one another, which can be grasped at once, upon a merely preliminary survey, and we shall find it profitable to give attention to these at an early stage of our discussion.

I propose, therefore, to devote my second lecture to the nature of the antique religious community and the relations of the gods to their worshippers. After this we will proceed to consider the relations of the gods to physical nature, not in a complete or exhaustive way, but in a manner entirely preliminary and provisional, and only so far as is necessary to enable us to understand the material basis of ancient ritual. After these preliminary enquiries have furnished us with certain necessary points of view, we shall be in a position to take up the institutions of worship in an orderly manner, and make an attempt to work out their life-history. We shall find that the history of religious institutions is the history of ancient religion itself, as a practical force in the development of the human race, and that the articulate efforts of the antique intellect to comprehend the meaning of religion, the nature of the gods, and the principles on which they deal with men, take their point of departure from the unspoken ideas embodied in the traditional forms of ritual praxis. Whether the conscious efforts of ancient religious thinkers took the shape of mythological invention or of speculative construction, the raw material of thought upon which they operated was derived from the common traditional stock of religious conceptions that was handed on from generation to generation, not in express words, but in the form of religious custom.

Notes

[1] See especially Hosea, chap. iv.

[2] Isa. xi. 2.

[3] Eccles. xii. 13.

[4] See, for example, Plutarch's *Greek* and *Roman Questions*.

22. Empathy and Antipathy in the Heart of Darkness

George W. Stocking, Jr.

Given the association we have become accustomed to make between anthropology and tolerance, it is more than a bit upsetting to discover that the diary which Bronislaw Malinowski kept in the course of his early field work in Melanesia is spotted with references to "niggers."[1] True, its editor was able to dismiss this as "the colloquial term commonly used by Europeans (at that time) . . . to denote native peoples," and it has also been suggested that the word is an artifact of translation from the Polish original. However, there is still perhaps good reason to take the matter more seriously. Field work is the central experience of modern anthropology, and it is usually thought to require not only tolerance, sympathy, and empathy, but even identification with the people studied. If, in the words of Clifford Geertz,[2] the archetypical fieldworker was in fact a "crabbed, self-preoccupied, hypochondriacal narcissist," and perhaps a racist to boot, then the discovery is certainly disturbing, if not "shattering" for "anthropology's image of itself." Geertz suggests that we must reject the "unsophisticated conception of rapport" which would "enfold the anthropologist and informant into a single moral, emotional, and intellectual universe." He goes on to explain Malinowski's undeniable virtuosity as a fieldworker as a triumph of sheer industry over inadequate empathy. According to Geertz, the pattern of Malinowski's field work moved from sexual fantasy to overwhelming guilt to expiation in ethnographic drudgery to euphoric exultation in the tropic landscape—and back again to start the cycle over. There is no doubt that the pattern is there, but before accepting a characterization of Malinowski as a kind of nasty anthropological Edison, it might be well to look a little more closely at the data.

Of course, not all of this inheres in the word "nigger," but it may still be helpful to note that the first appearance of the term is on page

Reprinted by permission of Clinical Psychology Publishing Company, Inc., Brandon, Vermont. (Originally published in a slightly different form and appeared in *Journal of the History of the Behavioral Sciences,* Volume 4, pp. 189–194 (1968).

154—i.e., that it, or its Polish equivalent, was apparently not part of Malinowski's diary vocabulary during his trip to Mailu in 1914 and 1915. Furthermore, it is worth noting that Malinowski also used a number of somewhat less charged terms ("natives," "blacks," "boys," "primitives," "savages," and "Negroes"), that he found "white superiority" "disgusting," that he was upon occasion capable of joyful indentification with "naturmenschen," and that he often spoke of individual Melanesians in very positive empathetic terms. One is inclined, therefore, to look for the factors which may account for the appearance of this particular word only at a certain point in the diary and its subsequent appearance in specific contexts. On the latter point, one notes immediately that when Malinowski referred to "niggers" it was invariably in a context of frustration, sometimes ethnographic, more often sexual. Indeed, by far the greatest number of these references occur in close association with thoughts about his Australian fiancée. All of which makes one suspect that there was something else involved than simply a crabbed and unsympathetic personality, an artifact of translation, or a widespread colloquialism.[3]

One possibility is that this usage has something to do with Malinowski's acculturation to English or Australian norms during his residence in Australia between 1916 and 1917. The theme of his cultural marginality and his ambiguous relation to things English runs through the book, and it is only with his mother's death at the end that he seems in a sense to relinquish his Polish identity. Be this as it may, there is a marked difference in style and tone between the Mailu and the Trobriand diaries. One notes in the latter a marked heightening of Malinowski's "puritanism," and also (paradoxically) a tone of Anglo-Saxon modernity—for instance, in his reference to one of the many women he "mentally" caressed as "an attractive dish." The last phrase, too, is perhaps an artifact of translation from the Polish original, but one must consider the possibility that Malinowski picked up in Australia usages more characteristic of colonial cultures than of his native Poland.

In this context, one thinks inevitably of another Pole whose life bears certain resemblances to Malinowski's. Indeed, Joseph Conrad's name crops up on several occasions in Malinowski's diaries. Conrad knew only too well what happened to Europeans who ventured into *The Heart of Darkness*. Without his being fully aware of it, it is clear that Malinowski felt in himself something of the psychology of Mistah Kurtz. He spoke disparagingly of Europeans who "have such fabulous opportunities—the sea, the ships, the jungle, power over the natives—and don't do a thing!" He imagined the plot of a novel in which a European "fights against the blacks, becomes absolute master" and then a benevolent despot. He enjoyed the "delightful feeling that now I alone am the master of this village with my 'boys.'" And at one point he even spoke of his feelings toward the natives as "decidedly tending to 'Exterminate the brutes' "—which was of course exactly the end to which Kurtz' benevolent despotism led, and almost exactly a quotation of Kurtz' barbaric footnote.

Malinowski was far from being Kurtz. But there are certain analogies of situation and perhaps of psychological dynamic in his experience in the Trobriands. During his earlier trip to Mailu, his ethnographic style was clearly still part of an older anthropological tradition. He lived among Europeans and went into the native village during the day to collect data from informants, apparently following the schedule in the 4th edition of *Notes and Queries on Anthropology*. It was only in the course of his later work in the Trobriands that the ethnographic principles he formalized in the introduction to *Argonauts of the Western Pacific* were developed in practice. There his physical and psychological situation was quite different. For long periods, he was in fact alone among the natives, almost without any contact with European culture, during a period when his personal life was undergoing an extended crisis. Like Kurtz, he was alone with his instincts in the heart of darkness.

For Malinowski, these instincts had to do with sex rather than with power. A man of strong sexual drives, he was in love with a woman whose attraction was clearly somewhat more ethereal than that of others mentioned in the diary. In this context, it is worth noting some of the sexual associations which are sprinkled throughout Malinowski's text. On the one hand, he identified woman and physical nature (which may have something to do with the euphoria of Geertz' pattern). But he also associated white women and European civilization, speaking of his "longing for civilization, for a white woman" and of the moments of "almost unbearable longing for E.R.M.—or is it for civilization?" Native women, on the other hand, were often physically attractive, and potentially available—"At moments I was sorry I was not a savage and could not possess this pretty girl." Upon occasion, he even "pawed" them, although with immediate feelings of guilt projected as aggression—"Resolve: absolutely never to touch any Kiriwina whore." Emotionally involved with a white woman far away in Australia for whom he felt "personal attraction without strong physical magnetism," he was surrounded by women for whom he felt "physical attraction and personal aversion." The result was often "sexual hysteria," which Malinowski, in a measure of the distance between his self-consciousness and ours, attributed to "lack of exercise." These themes are indeed so pervasive that his diary might well have been subtitled "Sex and Repression in Savage Society."

It is this body of sexual attitudes—attitudes perhaps especially characteristic of a particular historical context, but by no means specific to it—which provides the crucial context of Malinowski's references to primitives as "niggers." The first of these appears in the diary of his second Trobriand expedition (unfortunately there is only one brief entry for the trip of 1915–1916), after a number of entries in which his sense of isolation and his longing for "culture" and "civilization"—and for E.R.M.—have been growing sensibly stronger. More interestingly it occurs when he is virtually alone in a Trobriand village, on the page preceding this methodological aside: "Marett's comparison: *early ethnographers as prospectors*." Malinowski was quite consciously carrying ethnographic work to a level far beyond casual prospecting, to a level which in fact involved sustained immersion in the strata of native daily life, and this not as a member of a fairly large scale anthropological expedition such as Torres Straits, but as a solitary digger into the heart of darkness. And he did this in the context of an extended personal psychological crisis whose aura pervades the diaries.

Both in terms of generic situation and of the state of his own psyche, the psychological demands imposed by the new ethnographic style were very great, and it is hardly surprising that Malinowski's attitude toward natives was ambivalent and often aggressive. The darkness he penetrated, like that of Mistah Kurtz, was in large part the darkness of his own soul. Malinowski was a man whose aggressive feelings could explode in violence: on one occasion he in fact struck his cookboy, and it is clear that he would sometimes have liked to strike Trobrianders as well. Nevertheless, it may still be a mistake to assume that Malinowski was lacking in empathy. As Geertz in fact suggests, empathy may be a much more subtle psychological phenomenon than we commonly think it. It may involve passion as well as passivity; it may express itself in ambiguity and ambivalence as well as identification. Malinowski brought to the field a considerable intellectual humanism. He also brought not only his own unique personality, but much of the psychic and cultural baggage of a 19th century European. And in this repressive context he struggled with his own instinctuality.

In this light it is perhaps worth considering certain latent functions of Malinowski's diary, some of which may in fact skew its picture of his interaction with the Trobrianders. In addition to being vain, hypochondriacal and narcissistic, Malinowski was clearly a man of great passion and considerable inner honesty. His diary was explicitly an attempt to lay bare the inner dynamism of his psyche, and he quite consciously grappled with what he regarded as the darker aspects of his own being. But his diary perhaps also served functions of which he may not have been fully aware. At one point he noted that "intercourse with whites" made it impossible for him "to write the diary." If one of its functions was to create a kind of internal enclave of European culture, it may be that contact with whites made the diary less necessary. Beyond this, the diary may also have had a purgative function as an outlet for all kinds of feelings that he could not express in the day to day life of his field work.

In doing so, it may on the one hand have been a precondition of his own psychic survival in the heart of darkness. On the other hand, it may have directly facilitated his ethnographic work. When he suggested that "the Vakuta people irritate me with their insolence and cheekiness, although they are fairly helpful to my work," this effective working ethnographic relation may have depended on his having some other outlet for his irritation. Indeed, his diary may well have helped to make empathy possible even in the process of conveying the impression of its non-existence. The comments of several working anthropologists on their own field experience in fact support this interpretation.

Another bit of anecdotal data may cast further light on the whole problem. One anthropologist who studied under him assured me that Malinowski was an aggressive, authoritarian, and often rather obnoxious person. But this same individual also testified to Malinowski's unusual personal charm, which could at times endow one's relationship to him with a uniquely positive value. The interactive psychodynamics of observer and observed is a problem which bears investigation. One may assume that it varies from culture to culture, and there is evidence to suggest that it has changed over time as nonwestern populations have become more sophisticated in their understanding of the "role" of the anthropologist, and the culture he represents. But there is no *a priori* reason to assume that the combination of charm and aggressive egocentricity which men of European background later found in Malinowski could not have provided the basis for an empathetic ethnographic relationship, particularly if its negative aspects were self-consciously, and at some psychic expense, modified by ethnographic purpose.

Involved in all this is a point of considerable methodological significance to the history of anthropology. As this study proceeds beyond formal published statements of the results of anthropological inquiry to sources such as Malinowski's diary, it will be very tempting to assume that now, at last, we are getting the "real" story. But a diary is only one more perspective of an individual's life. It may in fact reveal a great deal; but one cannot assume that it tells the whole story, any more than an anthropologist can assume that the study of a people's mythology will reveal all of their culture. A diary is rather a particular form of communication, and like all forms of communication, it must be interpreted in terms of its function as well as its content. In the case of a diary "in the strict sense"—as opposed, say, to the letter diaries of Franz Boas—it is in fact a unique form of communication, in that it assumes no immediate audience save its author. Even as such a diary facilitates introspection, it may distort interpersonal relations. It must therefore be interpreted in the context of what is communicated by other modes—perhaps most importantly, in this case, by the body of Malinowski's ethnography. The amount and character of ethnographic detail which Malinowski was able to elicit and record are strong presumptive evidence for a generally positive personal interaction with the Trobrianders. It is of course possible that at certain points in the history of ethnography a good deal of data may have been elicited, as it were, under the gun of the European presence. But in view of Malinowski's isolated situation there is reason to presume at least a certain minimum of tolerance and respect for him on the part of the Trobrianders. And in the overall context of both his diary and his ethnography, one is perhaps justified in assuming that Malinowski's admittedly ambivalent and sometimes antipathetic feelings toward the Trobrianders were the basis for an interaction which, however emotionally complex, involved, in varying degrees, tolerance, sympathy, empathy and even identification.

From a broader point of view, Malinowski's diary is interesting in suggesting that the tolerance and empathy which we associate with anthropological field work is an historical phenomenon. The modern anthropological point of view was not always inherent in the study of anthropology. It was in fact quite hard-won at a particular moment in the history of Western European culture by men who carried with them many residual manifestations of the belief in Western European superiority and much of the repressive psychic structure of their culture, and who struggled, often in very trying situations, with cultural, instinctual, or idiosyncratic personality characteristics which in the past had generally produced a very different outlook. One virtue of Malinowski's diary is that it suggests, in terms of the specific psychological dynamism of a rather unique individual, something of the process by which the modern anthropological viewpoint was achieved.

Others besides Malinowski were involved in this process, and it would be illuminating to compare his field experience with that of Franz Boas. But the point I would emphasize is rather that once won—by whatever ambivalent and ambiguous processes—the anthropological viewpoint of men like Boas and Malinowski became a crucial factor in conditioning the way in which their students, and indeed modern intellectuals generally, encountered the primitive world. Despite the many differences between Boas and Malinowski, both sought to "grasp the native's point of view, his relation to life, to realize his vision of his world," as Malinowski put it in the introduction to *Argonauts.* The ethnographic realization of this goal will doubtless always be accompanied by considerable psychic strain. Laura Bohannan's fictionalized account of her life among the Tiv is ample evidence that psychological ambiguities analogous to Malinowski's have not disappeared from the field work experience. More specifically, several anthropologists have indicated to me in conversation that their own sexuality had been a gnawing problem for them in the field. From this point of view, Malinowski's diary casts valuable light on certain universal aspects of the field work situation. But in terms of the argument I have been developing here, the point is rather that this generic situation is now perceived by its anthropological actors within a cognitive framework which I have called "the modern anthropological point of view," and that we owe this way of seeing the primitive world at least in part to Malinowski's own voyage into the heart of darkness.

Notes

[1] Bronislaw Malinowski, *A Diary in the Strict Sense of the Term,* New York, Harcourt Brace Jovanovich, 1967, pp. xxii, 315. $6.95.

[2] "Under the Mosquito Net," *New York Review of Books,* 9/14/67.

[3] Since this review appeared, I have done further work on Malinowski, including research in the Malinowski papers. Although this work will lead to certain modifications of the present argument, its essential points still stand. One thing is clear: there can be no question that Malinowski did use, in English, the term "nigger."

PART FOUR
History from within the Discipline

Interest in the history of anthropology by anthropologists themselves has definitely been increasing steadily over the past decade (Stocking 1966). Existing literature varies greatly both in quality and in the methodology of writing disciplinary history. The list of papers that Dell Hymes includes in his report on the implications of the 1962 Social Science Research Council conference on the history of anthropology indicates the real extent of such scope. Some of the contributors were anthropologists having only incidental interest in the history of the discipline. Others were intellectual historians of various persuasions, whose primary disciplinary affiliation was not to anthropology. A third group consisted of anthropologists who were seriously contributing to the writing of their own discipline's history. In his report, reproduced here, Hymes considers at some length the meaning of this development for the discipline—apart from the content of the historical writings.

He suggests that anthropology is modifying its traditional identity among the social sciences. Fieldwork and cultural relativism are no longer unambiguous identifying markers of the anthropologist. The so-called primitive society is harder and harder to find. Anthropology may have to redefine drastically its role in a rapidly changing world. What we are to become in the future will depend on whether we can make such an adaptation. Under such circumstances, both individuals and the discipline itself must take stock.

Hymes stresses that the standards for historical scholarship are set by the intellectual historians, such as George Stocking, who have recorded parts of our history. Hymes' "parable" of the historian as an anthropologist studying a primitive tribe sees the history of the discipline as an analogue of other kinds of anthropological research, at which the anthropologist is already an expert. The moral of the parable is that the anthropologist can present an inside view and that his history is part of his necessary professional concern for his own discipline. The canons of historical scholarship are not mysteries to the anthropologist; he employs similar methods to different kinds of data when he carries out an ethnographic field study of a primitive tribe. Hymes' treatment of the implications is only superficially whimsical. Anthropologists already know how to write and how to evaluate disciplinary history; they have a greater interest than anyone else in seeing these tasks performed by prevailing scholarly standards. Because fieldwork has traditionally been the business of anthropologists, this is the metaphor that enables them to understand what the historian expects from his subjects; we now study ourselves as we have previously studied others. As long-standing students of oral tradition, anthropologists are fully aware that ideal culture and real culture do not always correspond and that subjects of study usually prefer to envision themselves according to the ideal or normative culture. Indeed, the ideals are part of the reality, though only part.

Hymes also raises a question that is rarely of issue to the historian per se, that is, the effect of his studies on the subjects. In recent years, ethical questions have come to the forefront in discussions of fieldwork and the role of the anthropologist. One of the processes by which the fieldworker maintains perspective on his study is to place himself mentally in the shoes of his subjects, to turn the tables on himself as it were. If he does not like what he finds in the histories written by historians, it is his option to provide an alternative account that is more acceptable to him but that also takes account of the view from the inside without sacrificing accuracy of scholarship.

One of the results of such an effort has been a fairly large quantity of recent literature that is essentially biographical; that is, individual scholars who have contributed to the discipline catalog their own experiences and those of their colleagues in order to maintain an accurate record. The responsibility to leave such a record is directly comparable to the methodology of descriptive ethnography, particularly under salvage conditions. The subtitle of one volume, "the uses of biography," has even addressed itself to the epistemological question of writing biographies

(Helm, ed., 1966). Other examples of the genre include autobiographies by Margaret Mead in 1972 and by Robert Lowie in 1959. Less formal illustrations are Stith Thompson's reminiscences (1968) and Swanton's manuscript autobiography at the Smithsonian. Article-length recollections include Kroeber (1950), Cole (1952), and Lowie (1956). The letters of Ruth Benedict have been collected for the public by Margaret Mead (1959), and the letters of Edward Sapir to Robert Lowie are available in an informal publication (1965). Theodora Kroeber has published a biography of her husband, Alfred Kroeber (1970).

Finally, Columbia University Press has initiated a new series of biographies of well-known anthropologists by scholars in the same area of anthropological specialization. To date, volumes on Linton and Lowie have appeared (Linton and Wagley 1971; Murphy 1972). Others are planned on Ruth Benedict, Franz Boas, Melville Herskovits, E. A. Hooton, A. V. Kidder, Alfred Kroeber, Bronislaw Malinowski, Robert Redfield, W. H. R. Rivers, Edward Sapir, and Benjamin Whorf. Contribution is to be evaluated by other members of the discipline, so epistemological issues of writing the history cannot be avoided.

Another important method of commenting on the profession by its own members has been through the obituary. To take a single example, when Alfred Kroeber died in 1960, four obituaries were written for different professional journals, each evaluating a different facet of Kroeber's contribution to the discipline over his long career (Hymes 1961; McCown 1961; Steward 1961; Rowe 1962). Recently, a collection of obituaries of linguists has appeared; many of these are also relevant to the history of anthropology (Sebeok, ed., 1966). A tone of evaluation is also taken by Zellig Harris in his review of the selected writings of Sapir in 1952. Hymes' obituary of Morris Swadesh goes far beyond biography into the motivating issues of a generation or more of American Indian linguists.

In still other cases, it is the need to understand the historical bases of a present theoretical position that motivates the anthropologist to turn to the history of an idea in light of his own professional concerns. Examples here are Aberle (1957) on linguistic models and culture and personality studies, Voegelin's discussion of Boas' underlying model for writing an American Indian grammar (1952), Stocking's re-analysis of the Boas' linguistic model (Hymes, ed., in press), and Swadesh's papers on the model that American anthropologists use for reconstruction of culture history through linguistic data (Swadesh 1951, 1961).

Perhaps the most important historical question in American anthropology concerns the present role of Franz Boas in the twentieth-century history of the discipline. Boas' death in 1942 did not end his influence, because most of the then-senior generation of anthropologists had been trained by him. Existing commentary ranges from extravagant eulogy to extreme depreciation, almost always with an undercurrent of ambivalence. Anthropologists on the subject of Boas often seem to lose their scholarly objectivity, a fact of interest in itself if the commentaries are taken as raw data for analysis. In 1943 and again in 1959, the American Anthropological Association devoted an entire monograph to evaluation of Boas' contribution to the discipline (Kroeber, et al., 1943; Goldschmidt, ed., 1959). Melville Herskovits, a former student, wrote a book-length biography in 1953. Briefer commentaries include: Williams (1936), Spier (1943), Kroeber (1956), Lowie (1956), Buettner-Janusch (1957), Hyman (1954), and many of the essays in Kardiner and Preble (1961).

Boas has also been criticized extensively, beginning with Murray Wax in 1956. Wax argues that Boas had restricted the claims of his anthropology until he forced himself to be critic rather than contributor, that under such circumstances creative research in anthropology was virtually impossible, and that presentation of empirical counterexamples to any theoretical claim does not constitute contribution to theory. The theme has been taken up by Leslie White (1966, 1963). Again, the critical tone justifies the importance of topics that were not studied by Boas and that, therefore, were presumably precluded from serious attention by White's colleagues. The standards of historicism as developed in history and history of science are not involved here.

White has continued this style of historical writing on other topics, particularly in his debates with Morris Opler on the present role of evolution in relation to the interpretation of past evolutionary thinkers (White 1945, 1947; Opler 1962, 1964; Harding and Leacock 1964). Much of this literature has been criticized by Stocking in his contrast between "historicism" and "presentism" in the writing of the history of anthropology (Stocking 1968). Stocking stresses the need to avoid labeling past thinkers in terms of present controversies; rather, the concern should be with the context in which past thought developed. Present concerns with the contributions of historical figures could then emerge after such study as a reevaluation of past postulates in terms of a different intellectual milieu today. White and Opler emerge from Stocking's critique as equally wrong.

Marvin Harris' *The Rise of Anthropological Theory* carries the argument of White still further; a remarkable portion of the book is devoted to a critical reevaluation of the contributions of the Boasian school. Like White, he fails to note Boas' important contributions to developing the institutional framework of anthropology. Boas' students seem to have accepted his efforts to organize the discipline and, incidentally, their research plans. This face is revealed for example, in the comments of Margaret Mead (1972:126–128).

Harris' book has been reviewed with considerable heat, both pro and con, in *Current Anthropology* (1968). Harris' abstract summarizes six stages in the history of anthropology: (1) laws of society devised during the eighteenth century, (2) revival of scientism and materialism after the French Revolution, (3) disciplinary identity forged in the midst of unproductive eclecticism, (4) cultural materialism of Marx but often without data of primitive peoples, (5) rejection of Marxist science and materialism by the twentieth-century (Boasian) rigidity of empiricism, and (6) revival of generalizing or monothetic studies beginning in the 1930s. It is clear from this statement that Harris' view of the history of anthropology is one of unilinear evolution, although his discussion of evolutionism in the discipline opts for multilinear evolution. Harris deplores the eclecticism of present anthropology, because the only productive research strategy is generalizing and materialist. For example: "Yet the basic principle of sociocultural evolution is already known" (Harris et al., 1968:520), that is, techno-environmental determinism. Harris does not comment on why it is worth studying if it is already known. Equally seriously for the epistemology of the discipline, Harris as a quasi-historian deals primarily with ideas and theories, but he calls for materialist analyses of ethnographic cultures.

The work, however, is important in that it takes a strong stance about why the history of anthropology should be written by anthropologists. Any scholar who disagrees that present theoretical concerns are the validating force of disciplinary history has a clear target for a different view. Many anthropologists find the answers to their own questions of intellectual paternity in Harris' book; others are concerned that Harris' view not stand as the history of the discipline. To some, Harris defines the mainstream of modern anthropology; to others, he himself is trapped by the same kind of particularism that he criticizes in Boas. Reactions to Harris' history tend to polarize according to whether or not the reader approves of Harris' ideas of the present status of the discipline. This attitude is far from the historicism advocated by Stocking. It is, of course, in the final analysis, anthropologists themselves who must decide whether there should be a different history of the discipline for different brands of present theoreticians, or whether history can begin with analysis of intellectual currents in the past and only then seek relationship between past and present problems of anthropology.

The article by Hallowell, included here, explicates the uniqueness of anthropology as a discipline from the context of Western intellectual thought. He defines the history of anthropology, at least in part, as the answering of questions now considered part of the profession by present practitioners; he concludes that the profession from which his judgments proceed is, indeed, a singular occurrence in the history of Western thought. He cites a level of folk anthropology in Western Europe and catalogs the a priori restrictions on its development of anthropological inquiry. For example, a question such as a typology of racial varieties could not occur unless one knew reasonably fully the range of human societies. Hallowell concludes that the voyages of discovery were the real "cause" of the development of scientific anthropology, that knowledge of human geographical diversity substantially preceded acquisition of time perspective on man's history.

The development of anthropology was encouraged by contradictions that became apparent between the folk anthropology of Western Europe and the anthropological data that developed out of the Renaissance. The roots of anthropology must be sought in the particular history of our own intellectual tradition. Hallowell does not concern himself with partially parallel developments in other cultural contexts or with the question of the universality of folk anthropologies. The assumption is that anthropology is a single discipline, not that there may be different anthropologies for different time periods and different cultural groups (see Part One, both the Introduction and papers, for further discussion).

Kroeber's paper, reprinted here, deals with the personality of anthropologists as a problem in the history of the discipline. It outlines what it means to be an anthropologist, rather than any other kind of social scientist, within the context of recent American professional anthropology. He notes that sociology and anthropology ought to be very similar, because their theoretical roots and basic assumptions are virtually coterminous. He concludes that it is in habitual activities as practitioners that sociology and anthropology actually diverge. Sociology lacks a subdisciplinary base; concomitantly, anthropology supports a holistic view of human similarities and differences. Holism, and interdisciplinary eclecticism, are related to the anthropologist's unique (in the social sciences) emphasis on fieldwork among primitive peoples. Simultaneously, the anthropologist is encouraged to stick his nose into whatever emerges from his efforts to understand native tribes and to work at a strictly empirical level. Kroeber reviews some of the current issues of the discipline as he sees it from this epistemological perspective. He concludes that, yes, Virginia, there is an anthropologist and he has something to contribute to the knowledge of man that other people do not.

Alfred Haddon, the major figure in the program in anthropology at Cambridge University, wrote two general histories of anthropology, in 1910 and 1934. In both cases, the method was factual and chronological, intending more to argue that anthropology was a discipline worthy of historical attention than to encourage a particular point of view toward its practice. The selection reproduced here is on the polygenist versus monogenist controversy. Haddon stressed that anthropologists were proud of their anarchic reputation among the sciences (part of the personality of anthropology in Kroeber's terms) and that controversies did not threaten the unity or autonomy of the discipline. Believing that the primary roots of anthropology were in biology, he noted that anthropological inquiry had a long history before anthropology became a professional discipline; these roots provided continuity to the mainstream of Western intellectual thought.

Fred Voget has written several papers on the influence of the Enlightenment on anthropology; he claims that there is intellectual continuity from earlier periods to the theories of professional anthropology (Voget 1960, 1965, 1966). In the paper reproduced here, Voget argues that the concepts of man and culture that are the core of anthropology have been defined anew in each successively dominant theory but always in relation to one another. Although each of his four stages is subject to criticism, each has contributed to the complexity of present theory. Value is placed on eclecticism and respect for work in past traditions, even when much of the detail may be outmoded theoretically and/or methodologically.

Margaret Hodgen, an intellectual historian in the tradition of Frederick Teggert, has described sixteenth- and seventeenth-century anthropological thought. Her point of view consists largely of the conviction that there is nothing new under the anthropological sun. She stresses observation of cultural similarity and diversity, not theoretical interpretations thereof, as the core of anthropology. Present-day theories appear to her insufficiently modified to represent the theoretical syntheses claimed by anthropologists. The result is a profound pessimism about the anthropologist and his failure to learn from his own history. It is an outsider's view, but one that provides a challenge to the anthropologist who disputes her conclusion. Certainly, many anthropological theories are primarily combinations and recombinations of older ideas.

The paper by Jacob Gruber concentrates, after a brief introduction on the present importance of evolution to anthropology, on the discovery of human antiquity as a problem that had to be solved before anthropology could be an autonomous discipline. The discovery of time perspective is hailed as a cultural revolution having great implications for anthropology (see Toulmin and Goodfield 1965). In Kuhn's terms, the change provided impetus for establishment of a new paradigm, out of which the present structure and organization of the discipline developed.

George Stocking's paper appears here for the first time. It is a historian's effort to sort out the tangled threads of evolution as a theoretical matrix for the development of professional anthropology. Stocking is most concerned to demonstrate that in the evolutionist positions there were differences that the Boasian critique has caused to be virtually ignored. Past treatments of evolution and race have not been specifically related to anthropology; but see also Murphree (1961), Gillespie (1951), Stocking (1960), Eiseley (1958), Greene (1959, 1961), Hofstadter (1944), Gosset (1963), and Barnes (1960). As a historian, Stocking has consulted developments beyond the confines of anthropology itself, citing issues that are otherwise almost by definition mysteries to anthropologists.

The final selection is a long extract from Meyer Fortes' inaugural address at Cambridge University in 1953. His examination of the background of British anthropology in Victorian thought between 1890 and 1930 shows that it was frequently pursued by nonanthropologists. Anthropology per se began quite late. British anthropology was precarious in its university development until the founding of a chair in social anthropology at Cambridge in 1932. Fortes looks wistfully at the stronger and earlier development of academic anthropology in North America. Social anthropology, that is, functionalism in effect, had to emerge from its evolutionary parentage in order to give British anthropology its theoretical autonomy as a discipline. Haddon, Rivers, Seligmann, and Radcliffe-Brown led this movement. To Fortes, functionalism provided a "precise and consistent" paradigm for anthropological research. He does not stress the theoretical eclecticism that is congenial to many, if not most, of his American colleagues.

Fortes cites the British colonial empire as a positive factor enabling anthropologists to put their knowledge into practice. This view sharply contrasts to what Fortes would consider the naïveté of recent American concern that anthropology is ethically unjustified because of its roots in imperialism. A corollary in much recent American controversy is that anthropologists should be on the side of the people they study.

Other treatments of British anthropology in historical perspective, many of which are factually and chronologically oriented, include Firth (1951), Murdock (1951), Radcliffe-Brown (1952), and Beattie (1955).

It is clear from the selections in this section, and secondarily in other sections, that anthropology is not, and has never been, a neatly uniform discipline. Anthropologists, partially in line with their other professional persuasions, are sharply in disagreement about the nature and role of disciplinary history. Just as the anthropologist values diversity among the world's peoples, it might be suggested that he may also want diverse contributions to the writing of his specialty's history. Each individual anthropologist would then seek his own intellectual paternity through serious self-examination. Indeed, this attitude constitutes what is perhaps the main reason why the history of the discipline should be an important specialization within anthropology.

23. On Studying the History of Anthropology

Dell Hymes

On April 13th and 14th of this year, a Conference on the History of Anthropology was held in the chambers of the Social Science Research Council in New York City, attended by a number of anthropologists, some historians of science, and a few other interested persons. A series of papers prepared for the Conference were discussed. In this brief paper I should like to inform you about the Conference, not so much in terms of its content, as in terms of its import. A list of participants and papers is appended for the interest it may have, but the main import of the Conference lies, I think, not in the intrinsic value of what occurred—like most short conferences on areas new to organized research, it was intense, varied, and confused—but in the fact that it *did* occur. The occurrence of a formal conference on the history of anthropology marks a definite shift that affects the interests and fortunes of us all.[1]

I should like first to describe the nature of the shift somewhat in the manner of a parable, then, to recommend a strategy for dealing with it.

The nature of the shift can be characterized in a preliminary way quite briefly: as a (professional) tribe, we are about to be made rather selfconscious and uncomfortable.

We can be partly gratified by the attention, by being singled out for study by historians of science. It must prove that our claims to be something of a science are being given credence. If people so close to the centers of (intellectual) prestige wish to study us, it must mean that we have been recognized as a phenomenon of some importance.

Yet it means some discomfort too. After all, we have our own accounts of our origin, nature, and destiny. Our revered elder men have often transmitted them to us in that part of the initiation known as the course on History and Theory. And who should know about these things of our past, if not ourselves, who have been initiated into the ways of the group, who are privy to its oral traditions, who can speculate retrospec-

From KASP 26:(1962), pp. 81–86. Reprinted by permission of the Kroeber Anthropological Society.

tively about our past with such authority and confidence in our identity as insiders? Others may know or obtain knowledge of the names, the dates, and the Important Theories; some of us have even led the public into thinking of such externals as the whole story, by publishing them as our history. But of course there is lacking the esoteric lore that elders sometimes impart to us, as badge of their status and sign of favor, orally in little groups—the personal detail that shows the trickster side of a culture hero, the exemplum that reveals the true hagiology of the field, etc.

It may seem at first that the historians of science visit us simply out of sincere interest in these traditions of ours, to be edified by them, as we have been, and to record them for the rest of the world and posterity, lest they be lost. Eventually, however, we may discover that our attentive visitors do not always take our accounts at face-value. They move from one campfire to another, and compare notes. We realize that they could hardly become one with us, if they have not undergone the same sort of initiation (fieldwork), been exposed to our ways early enough in their careers. But, disconcertingly, they seem untroubled, and confident in ways of their own. They even presume to decide for themselves what portion of our accounts they will believe. What for some of us is a single native category of "The (Glorious/Inglorious) Past," they divide and redistribute among several other categories of their own, such as "documented," "worth checking," "unreliable," and, even, "folklore." What for some of us is an historical black and white with all the sharp intellectual appeal of a well plotted Western, they dissemble into a motley of shadings, mostly grey. Sometimes they go so far as to impugn or dispute our ancestry, interpolating forefathers of whom we have no memory; crediting noble deeds and inventions to men who are not the culture heros about whom we tell such things; tracing lines of descent in ways that don't at all support our present segmentary oppositions.

And they seriously threaten to put all this into books, and to publish it to the world as what we are really like.

There will indeed be many such books a decade or a generation from now. How are we to respond (we cannot prevent it)? As in the cartoon in which the elders of a Pacific island forego the tribal initiation rites, and hand each youngster a copy of a book by Margaret Mead instead? Shall we simply hand our students bibliographies with exotic names, and send them off to other departments to learn who their fathers were? While the elders, demoted from their roles as arbiters of the past, shrink off into the bush and the night, muttering, "It wasn't like that at all, not like that at all"?

The situation is mildly embarrassing, especially if we wish to protest, since we have been in the business of doing the very same thing to other groups for years.

In essence, and more directly, I am saying that a good deal of the history of anthropology is going to be written by men who are not by origin, perhaps not even by aspiration or empathy, anthropologists. What should be our view, then, of the question, "Who shall write the history of anthropology"? Shall we turn the subject wholly over to historians of science and scholarship? Or shall anthropologists continue to take part?

The best solution, I believe, is one already validated in the history of science, and one for which there is ample precedent among ourselves: turn some of the informants into professional collaborators. As put by Dr. Richard Shryock, himself an eminent figure in the history of science, the important thing is not the particular origin of the scholar, but that he know enough both of the science, and of history. Historians can learn anthropology; anthropologists can learn history.

I believe that this solution is not only best, but necessary. I would add only the qualification that it should not be one-sided, that there be not only historians that learn anthropology, but also anthropologists, some of them, that learn history. In short, we must prepare to train some anthropologists as specialists in the history of anthropology. (This has already occurred in one or two cases at the University of Pennsylvania.)

But let me now proceed to say a little about the content of the Conference, and the ways in which its characteristics point to the desirability of this course. I should like to single out three characteristics that were both apparent and important: (1) how much the professionalization of our history is already under way; (2) how important our history is to us in current theory and controversy; (3) that the historian of anthropology, née historian, and the historian of anthropology, née anthropologist, converge, but do not merge entirely.

As to the first point: it is fair to say that only a portion of those participating in the Conference are, or intend to be, truly professional historians of anthropology; but the presence of that portion was unmistakable. Some of the distinctive traits, one or more of which enable one to recognize their presence, are these: use of out of the way and unfamiliar sources, including unpublished ones, such as letters; attention to textual detail; horizontal sectioning, relating an author to contemporary, including nonanthropological, figures and ideas; in general, a clear sense of historical context, and of historical problem. In other words: use of more than the "great books" as sources; attention to the interaction between ideas and their verbal embodiment, alertness to find other than present meanings in past usage, more than mere "semantics" in an author's wrestling with his verbal tools; seeing more than the "vertical" dimension of the profession's history that can be viewed as a lineal succession down through time; in general, judgments that are not anachronistic or a priori, but informed by historical relativism that answers to an anthropologist's wariness of ethnocentrism; studies that are more than chronicle.

As one of the papers that had these marks of a truly professional history of anthropology, let me cite that on Tylor and the concept of culture by my colleague in the department of History, George Stocking. When someone writes a paper showing that Matthew Arnold held a position of major importance in the cultural life of the times vis-à-vis that held by Tylor, between which there was an interaction; that Arnold in fact held a conception of culture closer in some respects than Tylor's to our own; and, further, that the changes in the use of the terms "culture" and "civilization" in parallel passages of Boas' earlier and later writings show that when Kroeber and Kluckhohn attributed the modern concept of culture to Tylor's definition, and to Boas an apparent delay of a generation in its subsequent development, they had matters almost exactly turned about—then we are in the presence of a level of scholarship which makes retrospective speculation about our history passé. If we want to talk about it ourselves, we will have to meet similar standards.

As to the second point: each time a major intellectual issue arose—the relationship of science and humanities in anthropology; the comparative method; the place of Boas—an historical topic was converted into a substantive contemporary issue, enlisting arguments and sometimes emotions, among the anthropologists present. A negative lesson is how little ready sense of historical problem in this area most anthropologists have, or at least how difficult they find it to be historical about themselves. On the positive side, however, it shows that our history cannot be a matter of indifference to us, and that one reason for training historians of anthropology is to provide some objective control over our use of our history for legitimation, theory, and controversy. If some of the historians are anthropologists, their value is likely to be increased in these regards, as being sensitive to the relevance of the history to current issues.

Some controversies will dissolve, or at least change their character, when studied historically in an adequate way; and the essential controversies will show in a clearer light. It becomes a little silly to charge Boas with not having solved the social organization of the Kwakiutl, if, as Eggan pointed out at the Conference, the proper concepts to apply to the Kwakiutl were not developed in the field until a few years ago. More historically appropriate issues about Boas can be investigated. Of course historians of science themselves may become personally involved in anthropological controversies. It is not a question of resolving perennial issues by historical study, but of dealing with them on a more worthwhile level.

As to the third point: the scholar with an historian's starting point, and the scholar with an anthropologist's starting point, has each a somewhat different groundsense, a somewhat different predisposition and comfortableness with particular kinds of material. This appeared in the kinds of comments and points of fact contributed to the discussions at the Conference. In my own paper I argued at some length for the contribution which the practicing anthropologist could make to the history of his field, including some historical topics in which he alone is likely to be interested. Obviously, as Raymond Firth stated at the conference, and my preceding paragraphs imply, there is equally an essential contribution which the professional historian can make. But this returns us to the main point, that we need the contributions of both. I should like to close by relating that point to one further consideration.

Anthropology today is flushed with success in the United States; course enrollments increase, and across the board; jobs multiply; sources of funds enlarge. To some extent this material success may be misleading as an index of the future. Not that there may not always be an anthropology, but that besides the indices of quantity, some of quality should be considered. Consider how much has changed in the terms of our competition, as it were, in the ecological niche of other related fields. The major ideological battle that American anthropology has fought in the past generation has been largely won; almost everyone is a cultural relativist now (in the sense in which the term is opposed to parochialism, and ethnocentrism). And our private preserve, the parts of the world no one else much seemed to want to study, is no longer ours. Scholars in almost every field of study today are going to Africa, India, Pakistan, the Philippines, etc. In short, two traits that have been of central importance and have formed much of our present image—cultural relativism, and fieldwork in faraway places—no longer give us an evolutionary advantage.

To a large extent, then, we can maintain our place, not by what we do, but only by the way we do it. Having lost much of what advantage we had in the way of unique outlook and subject of study, we have to look much more to the quality of our work. That statement has many implications. One, I believe, is the deepening of standards of historical scholarship among anthropologists, both for work on special topics and on the history of anthropology. Specialization of some of us in the history of science as it concerns anthropology is one route.

Note

[1] This paper was read in its essentials under the title "The History of Anthropology: SSRC Conference Report" at the 1962 annual meetings of the Kroeber Anthropological Society, meeting jointly with the Southwestern Anthropological Association, in Berkeley, April 13–14. I am indebted to the organizers of the Conference, and the SSRC; and I should like to thank John H. Rowe for much stimulation and encouragement to my own interest in the history of anthropology. The notes on the marks of professional historical papers stem from some comments of his.

References

Papers for the Conference on the History of Anthropology

(In the order in which they were summarized by their authors as topics for discussion. Papers not discussed are as indicated after the title.)

I. *Conceptual Perspectives: General Considerations and Problems.*

A. Irving Hallowell, Anthropology and the History of the Study of Man.

Frederica de Laguna, Folklore in the History of Anthropology. (Briefly discussed in the morning: discussed further in the afternoon when Dr. de Laguna arrived.)

Sol Tax, J. S. Slotkin's Work in the History of Anthropology. (Not discussed.)

II. *External Historical Events and Differential National Developments.*

Harry L. Shapiro, Anthropology and the Age of Discovery.

Robert Heine-Geldern, One Hundred Years of Ethnological Theory in the German Speaking Countries: Some Milestones.

Alfred Metraux, Some French Precursors of South American Anthropology (XVIth to XVIIIth Century).

VIII. *Applications of Anthropology.*

Anthony F. C. Wallace, The Study of Social Problems by American Anthropologists. (Shifted to Friday from Saturday.)

III. *Interrelations with Other Disciplines and Influences.*

John C. Greene, The Role of Anthropology in the Rise of Evolutionary Ideas.

Bernard Barber, Some Relations between Anthropology and Sociology: One Sociologist's Life-History.

IV. *Characteristic Methods and Conceptualisations.*

Kenneth E. Bock, The Comparative Method of Anthropology. (Not discussed.)

Fred Eggan, Some Reflections on the Comparative Method of Anthropology.

David H. French, Anthropological Interpretations of Similarities and Differences.

George W. Stocking, Jr., Matthew Arnold, E. B. Tylor, and the Uses of Invention (with an appendix on Evolutionary Ethnology and the Growth of Cultural Relativism, 1871–1915: From Culture to Cultures).

VI. *The Role of Individuals in the Development of the Field.* (Discussed before V.)

Jacob W. Gruber, Biography as an Instrument for the History of Anthropology.

John F. Freeman, Biography in the History of Anthropology: The Case of Henry Schoolcraft.

Leslie A. White, The Ethnography and Ethnology of Franz Boas.

Nancy O. Lurie, Early Women in American Anthropology.

C. F. Voegelin, Typology of Information for Deciphering Writing.

(Discussed here because of its emphasis on individual personalities, rather than under V where originally listed.)

V. *Sub-divisions of the Field and Special Problems.*

A. *Linguistics.*

Dell H. Hymes, Toward a History of Linguistic Anthropology.

Rulon Wells, Phonemics in the Nineteenth Century, 1876–1900.

B. *Ethnology.*

Melville J. Herskovits, A Genealogy of Ethnological Theory.

C. *Social Anthropology.*

Raymond Firth, History of Modern Social Anthropology.

VII. *Development of Professionalization.*

Edward Lurie, The Origins and Development of the Profession of Anthropology in the United States.

IX. *General Discussion.*

(Joseph Spengler, parallels from the study of history of economics)

(Sol Tax, substantive issues, methods, practical issues, including publication, and follow-up: agenda for another conference?)

Also Present:

Harry Alpert, University of Oregon
Clifford Geertz, University of Chicago (Saturday afternoon only.)
Pendleton Herring, Social Science Research Council
Daniel Lerner, Massachusetts Institute of Technology
Alexander Lesser, Hofstra College
Rowland L. Mitchell, Jr., Social Science Research Council
Thomas A. Sebeok, Indiana University
Richard H. Shryock, American Philosophical Society
Florence M. Voegelin, Indiana University
Harry Woolf, The Johns Hopkins University

Invited but absent:

Kenneth E. Bock, University of California, Berkeley
Donald H. Fleming, Harvard University
Charles C. Gillispie, Princeton University
Robert K. Merton, Columbia University
Ernest Nagel, Columbia University

24. The History of Anthropology as an Anthropological Problem

A. Irving Hallowell

In thinking about the history of anthropology, it is desirable in the first place to focus upon anthropological questions, rather than upon labeled disciplines, or groups of disciplines, as we now find them conventionally defined.[1] By anthropological questions I mean any of those to which we would now seek answers in a professionally recognized tradition: in the literature of physical anthropology, archaeology, cultural or social anthropology and linguistics. For these areas of specialized knowledge only emerged after anthropological questions had been articulated, answers to them consciously pursued, and organized data and concepts embodied in a professionally transmitted tradition. In this respect anthropology is a very recent development in the intellectual history of western culture.

At the same time, the broadly gauged comparative and historical framework of inquiry which we now assume in anthropology has led to a consideration of all kinds of data relevant to man in a universally human perspective. In this frame of reference we may ask: How far did the cultures of non-western peoples provide answers to anthropological questions? Were there any conditions present which motivated a search for answers to them? What observational data were available to the people of these cultures? What quantitative and qualitative differences existed in the kind of anthropological knowledge available? What circumstances and events promoted, or retarded, the accumulation of such knowledge in different cultures? If we were in a position to answer questions of this kind we would be better able to appraise the cultural and historical background of the interest in anthropological questions which became articulated and reached fruition in the organized inquiry with which we are familiar.

From the *Journal of the History of the Behavioral Sciences*, vol. 1, no. 1 (1965), pp. 24–38. Reprinted by permission of Clinical Psychology Publishing Company, Inc., Brandon, Vermont.

The history of anthropology considered as an anthropological problem supplements an exclusive concern with the history of organized inquiries and any attempt to arbitrarily isolate their development from its roots in a wider cultural context. On the contrary, it directs attention to the cultural context and historical circumstances out of which formulations of anthropological questions must have developed and suggests that, at this level, one may find parallels in early western culture to non-western cultures. The history, then, of what is now labeled anthropology in western culture is linked with the study of the sociology of knowledge, "ethnoscience" and the study of man and his behavior from many different points of view, humanistic and scientific, in the modern period of western culture. If we look for the most authoritative answers to anthropological questions in both societies other than our own and in the earliest phase of western culture[2] we are most likely to find them embedded in the cognitive orientation of a people, in their culturally constituted world view, from which they have not been abstracted and articulated. Questions related to man and his nature are an integral part of mythology and religion. The persons most concerned with such matters are priests, theologians, philosophers, or their equivalents. The kind of knowledge possible in this type of tradition is limited by its dogmatic character, in the absence of any motivations which encourage independent or objective inquiry. In western culture we know that radical changes occurred in the course of a few centuries and that this level of knowledge was transcended: A secular view of the world based on independent inquiry arose to challenge the traditionally sanctioned one—"La crise de la conscience européenne" of Paul Hazard. The class of persons to whom one could turn for authoritative answers to anthropological questions began to shift. The criteria for evaluating the reliability of anthropological knowledge became transformed as independent, objective inquiry expanded.

The significance of these historic events, which were only part of the revolutionary intellectual changes which occurred in Europe, are unique in their anthropological implications. For in their total range and sweep, they have no precise parallel in the cultural development of any other society. Western culture, among other things, is distinctive as the theatre of a continuing and accelerating effort by man to obtain increasingly reliable knowledge about his own nature, behavior, his history and varying modes of life, as well as his place in the universe. The labels which ultimately emerged to discriminate varying facets of the professional study of man sometimes obscure the enduring and characteristic intellectual preoccupation with himself that became so ramified, and so persistent in the history of western culture.

Besides this, the concomitant historical events which occurred have a dual interest for anthropology today. On the one hand, they involve on a large scale what have now become familiar problems of inquiry to anthropologists on a smaller scale: cultural changes and radical social readjustments, movements of population; cultural borrowing and the effects of contacts with other cultures; economic transformation and radical changes in value systems. On the other hand, it was during this same period in western culture that new anthropological questions came to the fore, while older ones were more sharply focused.

While in western culture the rise of the conscious pursuit by specialists of answers to anthropological questions is unique, at the same time this only expresses in a highly developed form a universal interest in himself exemplified by man everywhere. For man's capacity for becoming an object to himself and contemplating his existence as a being living in a world conjunctively with beings other than his kind is concomitant with his distinctive mode of cultural adaptation itself.[3] Consequently, it is not surprising to find man's ideas of his own nature reflected in the traditional world views of human societies. All cultures provide answers to some anthropological questions which are considered to be authoritative and final. Traditional knowledge of this kind may be characterized as folk anthropology, i.e., a body of observations, beliefs, and socially sanctioned dogmas which parallel folk knowledge about other aspects of the phenomenal world. What we have in the case of western culture is an opportunity to *document* an intellectual shift from the level of folk anthropology to a level of systematic observations and inquiry detached from traditional beliefs, and inspired by values giving prime emphasis to the search for more reliable knowledge of all aspects of human phenomena.

Unfortunately, the reliability of different areas of folk knowledge has not yet been as carefully studied as it might be. In some areas where direct observation and experience is involved, such as ethnobotany, animal and human anatomy, its level may be much higher than once supposed. Laughlin, e.g., goes so far as to say that:

> "We may consider the likelihood that man was always aware of his affinity with other animals and consequently did not need to 'discover' this obvious relationship any more than he discovered his stomach or eyeballs, or than the female of our species discovered that she was bearing the young. The early apprehension of a working knowledge of anatomy, human and non-human, was indispensable to man's survival. This was crucial in an animal form that was liquidating various physical abilities and instincts in exchange for the use of tools, who had both to defend himself from predators and to hunt and utilize other animals and who required assistance for the birth of his young. . . . Though varying greatly around the world, the anatomical information possessed by most peoples has probably been consistently underestimated."[4]

On the other hand, we know that there were many anthropological questions which could neither be posed nor answered in terms of the personal experience of men cognitively oriented in the provincial traditions of non-literate, or even early literate, cultures. Among the most obvious of these is any knowledge of the total range in the physical types of mankind throughout the world, or the actual antiquity of man. Furthermore, even if we grant that man recognized his anatomical affinities with other animals at a very early period, was this the only kind of affinity recognized or the primary one emphasized? Did animals have "souls," like men, or were they only "machines"? And, in the case of the Greeks, it is said, as Kluckhohn does, that they "saw man as a part of nature and to be naturalistically understood,"[5] can we say that "nature" has an equivalent meaning at all periods of European culture, to say nothing of its meaning in other cultures?[6] The conceptual framework in which observations are ordered and the explanation of phenomena must be considered in their cultural and historical context before significant comparison can be made. To recognize that man has animal-like characteristics had a different meaning in a nineteenth century evolutionary context than it had for the Greeks, or in earlier periods of European culture, or for non-literate people. Further investigation in the area of "ethnoscience" may provide a more satisfactory basis for making detailed comparisons of the limits and range of reliable knowledge possessed by non-European peoples both with respect to its pragmatic aspect, and the way in which such knowledge is classified and ordered in relation to the premises of different world views.[7] It would be interesting to know in how many cultures where close observation of any order of phenomena led to knowledge of more or less immediate pragmatic value this level was transcended and what steps led to this later development.[8] For a very limited knowledge of man may be pragmatically adequate within a particular sociocultural system. There may be no need to question its validity. Incentives stimulating the acquisition of new, or more reliable knowledge, may never arise. Essential anthropological questions, of limited scope, can be answered in meaningful fashion by appeal to traditional and personal experience.

In early western culture the level of knowledge represented in the traditional Christian world view is equivalent to folk anthropology. It was culturally constituted, untested knowledge about man and his world, reinforced by socially sanctioned religious values which gave it the stamp of ultimate truth. This traditional world view of the West is the historical backdrop against which changes in the answers to anthropological questions may be plotted. It is the known cultural base line against which shifts from a level of folk anthropology in the direction of more reliable, objective, tested knowledge about man can be documented. It is in this respect that the culture history of the West provides the record of a unique experience in the history of man's awareness of himself.

Thus an anthropological approach to the history of anthropology in western culture suggests that this history should be set squarely within the cultural context of western civilization. Relationships should be sought between historical events, changing intellectual currents and other factors having a bearing on the kind of anthropological questions that were being asked and the answers that were being sought at successive periods. This would supersede the historical chronicle in which lip service is given to Herodotus as the "father" of anthropology, an oversimplified linear chronology of name-dropping passes for history and a casual leap is made from western culture to that of Greece in the fifth century B.C. The actual historical process is more complicated and devious than can be represented in any straightaway linear scheme of ideas or "influences."[9] Classical writers and the classical tradition do enter the picture, of course, but within the context of the intellectual history of western culture itself as part of its literature. What in anthropological terminology we might call "literary acculturation" was actively promoted, including the attempt to reconcile this pagan heritage with the Bible and the Christian world view. One example of this heritage was Pliny's uncritical collection of material concerning fabulous races and peoples. "If theologians ever doubted these tales," says Hodgen, "they were restrained by a traditional classicism and scholastic logic from refuting their existence. As for man as a whole, the Fathers desired less to know him than to save him."[10] Belief in the existence of fabulous races was actually reinforced: they appeared on maps right up to the discovery of the New World and after.[11] The answers to anthropological questions given by the Greeks themselves, or other peoples of the ancient Near East, would require independent studies. Such investigations would illuminate the differences between the cultural historical situation in these societies as compared with the West in the development and fruition of anthropological ideas.[12]

The first chapter, then, in the history of anthropology may be conceived as a history of the conditions, events, activities and ideas which undermined the provincial folk anthropology of early western culture and, at the same time, laid the groundwork for independent observation and the ultimate accumulation, ordering and interpretation of a body of knowledge which provided more reliable answers to a wide range of anthropological questions. To those of us working in the field today, for example, it seems obvious that anthropology should make use of a comprehensive spatio-temporal frame of reference which embraces all living varieties of *Homo sapiens,* as well as extinct cultures and peoples of the distant past and more ancient hominid types besides. This basic frame of reference is essential to the ordering of our wide-ranging empirical data. The interesting historical question, then, is how this inclusive spatio-temporal "grid" came into being. The answer, I think, is that it only became possible to employ systematically such a conceptual frame of reference after a long and complex series of historical events had occurred in Europe which were, to begin with, quite extraneous to the study of man.

So far as a world-wide geographical perspective is concerned, this could not emerge until the entire globe had been explored. It began, of course, with the great Age of Discovery. And what is significant for the history of anthropology is that this was a unique achievement of the people of western Europe. Even in the absence of organized anthropological inquiry it had a profound impact upon their thought. The broadening of the base thus provided for the direct empirical observation of the physical characteristics, languages and cultures of the living peoples of the world was one of the necessary conditions required for answering vital anthropological questions. It was logically analogous to the broadening of the base of visual observation of objects in outer space after the invention of the telescope. The growing acquaintance with the peoples of distant, almost semi-fabulous lands, through the proliferation of *Narratives, Descriptions* and *Collections* of the reports of travelers of all kinds, brought home to the peoples of Europe the inescapable fact that their own outlook was, after all, extremely parochial. The idea of cultural relativity did not have to await the development of cultural anthropology. "It is perfectly correct to say," writes Hazard, "that all the fundamental concepts, such as Property, Freedom, Justice and so on, were brought under discussion again as a result of the conditions in which they were seen to operate in far-off countries, in the first place because, instead of all differences being referred to one universal archetype, the emphasis was now on the particular, the irreducible, the individual; in the second, because notions hitherto taken for granted could now be checked in the light of facts ascertained by actual experience, facts readily available to all inquiring minds. Proofs, for which an opponent of this dogma or that had laboriously to rummage about in the storehouses of antiquity, were now reinforced by additional ones, brand-new and highly coloured. See them just arrived from abroad, all ready for use!"[13]

In many respects an adequate temporal dimension relevant for the study of man lagged far behind a global geographical perspective. It could not become significant until the traditional view that the whole of creation and man's entire history could be encompassed within the span of 6000 years was displaced. It was contingent upon a reconsideration of the chronology of human history,[14] a revitalization, linked with material evidence, of the Three Age system of man's industrial development, (stone, bronze, iron ages),[15] the periodization of the history of the earth, in terms of geological and paleontological evidence,[16] and the empirical demonstration of man's "prehistory," a term used for the first time in 1851.[17] It will be recalled that John Frere, who sent some flint hand axes to the Secretary of the Society of Antiquaries of London in 1797, remarked in his accompanying letter that the situation in which they were found tempted one "to refer them to a very remote period indeed; *even beyond that of the present world.*" (Italics ours.) But these remarks were ignored. Although modern archaeologists would place these tools in the Lower Paleolithic, no one took Frere's speculations seriously.[18] At this time there was no temporal frame of reference into which they could be fitted. But more than this was involved: there was no archaeological frame of reference, either. As Heizer points out, certain preconditions had to be met, "stone tools had to be admitted as having been made by man. The correction of the idea that flaked and polished stone tools were thunderbolts which fell from the sky came about slowly through the discovery and awareness of savage peoples, particularly those of the New World following its discovery by Columbus, and the realization that these peoples who used stone tools lived in a pre-metal stage and were living as modern man once had lived."[19] In other words, sixteenth century published accounts of the manufacture of stone tools by living American aborigines, circulated as a consequence of the Age of Discovery, provided an initial clue relevant to the question of man's antiquity. These revelations planted the seeds of the classical "comparative method," for in the sixteenth and seventeenth centuries, Montaigne, Hobbes and Locke were already expressing the view that American Indians were existing representatives of an earlier general stage of human cultural development. However tentative and extraneous, at first, to anthropology as we think of it now, this line of thought anticipated the establishment of a firm spatio-temporal framework as a necessary foundation for the orderly investigation and solution of anthropological questions that were to become more and more clearly focused in the future.

While the Age of Discovery and the expansion of European peoples provided an essential condition for the direct, first-hand observation of the living peoples of the world, this was not a sufficient condition for the accumulation of reliable information of a high order. What has not been carefully investigated are the factors that retarded the reliability of observation and the motives, techniques, concepts, and other factors which promoted reliability. What seems to have happened is that for a considerable time the new observational facts concerning man's physical traits, cultures and languages, continued to be rationalized in relation to the persisting tradition of folk anthropology or other concepts. Besides this, European ethnocentrism created fictitious images of native peoples—the image of the Noble Savage on the one hand, and the ignoble or bestial savage on the other. Seen in modern anthropological perspective these images are the kind of phenomena which might be expected to be one of the consequences of superficial contact with, or secondhand knowledge of, exotic peoples prior to any systematic or scholarly study of them.[20] Although lack of written records and pictorial material makes the problem difficult to study, the images of primitive man projected by Europeans are counter-balanced by the images of civilized man and European culture for which we have evidence among some non-literate peoples. Lips published a fascinating collection of photographs of museum specimens in his book, *The Savage Hits Back,* and cargo cults offer interesting material. Like Europeans, non-literate peoples made use of what knowledge they had of other peoples' cultures for their own purposes.

Anthropologists have paid little attention to the images of the "savage" in European culture—possibly because some of the best examples are found in the humanist tradition, in literature and the pictorial arts.[21] Recently Wilcomb Washburn, an historian, referring to the American Indians, has pointed out that "it has become fashionable for twentieth-century critics to ridicule the 'noble savage' presumably 'created' by such writers (as Rousseau), but it is evident that the assumptions of twentieth-century writers about seventeenth—or eighteenth century Indians must be examined as critically as the assumptions of the earliest writers."[22] He has also pointed out that changing images may, in part, prove to be a function of changing power relationships.[23] There is a nice problem here because once anthropology entered the phase of an organized discipline, some of the travel literature that was previously used to create what some have thought to be fictitious images of primitive man became source material in ethnography.

Direct observation of the non-literate peoples of the world did, of course, dispel some ancient fictions of folk anthropology. But the process was sometimes slow. The final disappearance of some of the fabulous races took several centuries. The *monopoli*—with no heads, but with faces in their chests—were included in Pliny's inventory, referred to by John Mandeville in his reputed fourteenth century travels and reported by Sir Walter Raleigh as living in the New World (Guiana) in the sixteenth century, although the latter did not claim to have seen them himself. A picture of one of these individuals, associated with several perfectly decent Indians, is to be found in a plate in Lafitau's *Moeurs des sauvages Amériquains* (1724).[24]

How indeed was it possible to evaluate the reliability of observations on distant races and cultures of the world, particularly when observers sometimes disagreed? John Mandeville's travels were read in eleven languages and for five centuries before it became known that they never took place at all, but were compiled from other authorities back to Pliny. In the sixteenth century it was even thought by some that Mandeville was more reliable than Marco Polo, Columbus and Cortez.[25] Banks and Cook did not find giants in Patagonia. Yet their more reliable observations were not, at the time, considered superior evidence to the testimony of others. One of the interesting factors here is that, in support of the existence of giants, pictorial material had appeared plainly showing the difference in height between Europeans and Patagonians.[26] The question of the validity of observations is of anthropological interest both with respect to the steps by which a higher level of reliability was achieved and the role played by persistent traditions of any kind which retarded the progress of objective knowledge.[27] Even in this century overtones of this old problem—although in a more refined form—are sometimes heard. A decade ago Kluckhohn said: "In cultural anthropology we are still too close to the phase in linguistics when non-European languages were being forcibly recast into the categories of Latin grammar."[28]

Among the positive contributions that emerged from the Age of Discovery was the fact that it became more and more apparent that many of the anthropological observations reported could not be reconciled with traditional folk anthropology. While all the many revolutionary new questions which arose could not be satisfactorily answered or, if they were, do not seem adequately treated to us today, nevertheless, many of them were legitimate anthropological questions: the influence of climate, the diffusion of customs and social and cultural development. We still are faced with many of the same questions today and the answers are controversial. In order to place some of these questions in their historical context, I wish to quote here a passage from an unpublished manuscript of Katherine George who some years ago systematically surveyed the African travel literature from the fifteenth through the eighteenth century.

Among other things, Dr. George points out that "The Age of Discovery not only confronted the travellers with an astonishing array of cultural diversities which seemed to call for explanation, but after these had been considered and somewhat assimilated, it also disclosed the presence of cultural correspondences or parallels; correspondences such as that between a familiar homeland society and one in Africa, between a custom or culture and a similar trait or condition among the Old Testament Hebrews, or between African society and the social life of the classical peoples of European antiquity. Often these parallels, which were recognized as both contemporary and historical, were merely noted but not explained. But occasionally in early reports, and more frequently in later, notation was accompanied by efforts on the part of travellers to place them in broader context of theory. In other words such parallels were accounted for as the outcome of either diffusion or development. The travellers who adopted the diffusionist position emerged with explanations inferring contact at some period in past time; while those who ascribed similarities to a uniformly operative process of social development noted correspondences between existing African custom and earlier cultural conditions among European or other historical peoples. The latter assumed, in short, that the primitive folk encountered in Africa were an early stage of progressive or developmental change like that which was once manifested during the course of the history of some civilized people."[29]

In addition to the posing and answering of anthropological questions which Dr. George documents in the African travel literature, she also notes a radical shift in attitude towards *Africans* in the eighteenth century. The concept of "the bestial African primitive," and "the lawless, promiscuous society peculiarly associated with him," disappears. "The institutions and customs of the African primitive are not merely accepted with a new tolerance by the eighteenth century traveller; they are even fairly often upheld as models to be admired and emulated by the civilized world. For the 'noble savage' is indubitably a personage in these accounts." Admittedly a romanticism which, "in its extremer forms, at least, can and does distort objectivity." George concludes that the errors "to be chalked up against this new positive prejudice in favor of the African primitive are as nothing beside the almost countless errors of commission and omission attributable to the earlier negative prejudice." Consequently, she thinks that the concept of the "noble savage" "became of necessity a friend rather than an enemy to the advance of knowledge about the primitive. A bias it might remain, with capacities to distort . . . , (nevertheless) it introduced a compulsion to go forth and observe." It may have been "a door to objectivity," if not objectivity itself.[30]

So far as genuine anthropological concepts are concerned, there are clearly defined historical links with a past which long antedated the rise of any variety of anthropological discipline. Radcliffe-Brown found that his distinction between ethnology and social anthropology had its roots in seventeenth and eighteenth century writers. These two interests, he says, were clearly recognized by William Robertson in his *History of America* (1777) where this author "gives one of the earliest definitions of the study that later came to be called social anthropology, and distinguished from the investigation of the origins of peoples which we now call ethnology."[31] It was Robertson, it may be added, who explicitly stressed parallel development, rather than migration or historical contacts, as the explanation of cultural similarities.[32] Hoebel, who has also studied Robertson's work, finds that he anticipates Tylorian and Morganian anthropology. More intensive research will no doubt turn up other links with the past which will enable us to appraise current anthropological ideas in better historical perspective.

While a comprehensive temporal frame of reference, although slow in developing, ultimately provided a convenient means of integrating facts about hominid evolution and prehistoric man with human history and events in the natural world, its most vital significance did not lie in its chronological usefulness. It was, rather, because the conception of time characteristic of western culture embodied distinctive qualitative features which made it possible to order the dynamics of human evolution, changes in socio-cultural systems, linguistic forms and other phenomena of change in an orderly linear form. In this temporal frame of reference, too, persistent, enduring, and unchanging properties of phenomena could be distinguished from variable ones. What is significant, then, in that anthropology arose and developed in a culture whose world view embodied the archetype of a conception of human events in time which differed radically from that of the more ancient civilizations. In contrast with Greek culture, for example, where the passage of time was conceived as cyclical and not rectilinear, a number of scholars have pointed out that the Christian world view embodied the notion of a universal history of mankind moving along a linear course between Creation and the Last Judgment.[33] It comprised a unique series of historical events which were irreversible. It now appears that, more and more widely applied and secularized, a linear, rather than a cyclical, conception of time, vital because it was seen as the ground for the generation of novel configurations of events and developmental sequences, eventually became the model in western culture for the interpretation of the dynamics of historical events in all orders of phenomena.

Since cosmogenesis found its explanation in folk cosmogony, physical science (mechanics, astronomy), at first, was not at all concerned with the "history" of the universe. For Newtonian physics the world was the same today as yesterday and in the distant past. Physical science concentrated upon what Simpson has called immanent, or nonhistorical processes and principles, inherent in the very nature of matter-energy (gravity, energy, radiation). However, "the actual state of the universe, or any part of it at a given time, its configuration, is not immanent and is constantly changing. . . . History may be defined as configurational change through time, a sequence of real, individual, but interrelated events."[34] Simpson points out that before the eighteenth century most people thought that the configurational aspects of natural phenomena were likewise unchanging (the hills are "everlasting") both aspects being simply given, "probably by the creative acts of gods."[35] And, since until Darwin living species were thought to be immutable, each occupying its assigned niche in the Great Chain of Being, a time dimension in early observationable and classificatory biology was not of central importance.

What is of special interest historically, and particularly from an anthropological point of view, are the two main sources from which the knowledge and intellectual stimulus came which required an explicit differentiation between immanent and configurational characteristics. These were geology and human history. "No matter what they thought of causes," Simpson points out, "the pioneer geologists learned that the configuration of the earth is constantly changing, that it has a history. Hence it follows that the structure of the earth is constantly changing, that it has a history. Hence it follows that the structure of the earth—and, by an extension quickly made, that of the whole physical universe—is not immanent but is at any moment a transient state within a historical sequence." And, "in the field of human history, change in social structure and the human condition were generally evident, so that a thoroughgoing belief in static configuration was hardly possible to even the earliest historians."[36] Thus a linear conception of a sequence of irreversible events in time more and more deeply permeated the thinking of western man not only in the humanities, but in the physical and biological sciences and the incipient social sciences from the eighteenth century onward.

While there are traces of cyclical theories in the Middle Ages and later, as a consequence of the influence of Arabic and Classical learning, they did not prove viable. In the sixteenth and early seventeenth centuries the belief that a general process of degeneration was taking place had its vogue.[37] But, from the seventeenth century forward, writes Eliade, "linearism and the progressivistic conception of history assert themselves more and more, inaugurating faith in an infinite progress, a faith already proclaimed by Leibniz, predominent in the century of 'enlightenment' and popularized in the nineteenth century by the triumph of the ideas of the evolutionists."[38] It was within the intellectual climate engendered by the early phase of the conceptualization of the history of man as progressive that the cultural data already accumulated in the Age of Discovery began to be fitted into this new frame of universal temporal reference. General stages, or grades, of cultural development were discerned and articulated, notably by the Scots of the eighteenth century, in terms of "conjectural history."[39] Associated with the reconstruction of cultural stages in the development of mankind, without the benefit of prehistoric archaeology, we find the emergence of the "comparative method" in its earliest form.[40] Although used by, and sometimes identified with, nineteenth century anthropologists it was far from being original with them. In fact, Auguste Comte (1798–1857) considered it integral to his positive philosophy and sociological method. A whole constellation of ideas, too, which defined a distinctive level of primitive mentality—a child-like quality, a concrete rather than an abstract mode of thought, a capacity for myth making, with even a tincture of madness—not only antedate organized anthropological inquiry, but date back to the earliest phase of the progressive philosophy of human development.[41]

By the time the question of the mutability of species had been settled by Darwin in the middle of the nineteenth century, all human phenomena could be considered diachronically in a linear scheme of temporal reference. The Biblical age of the World had been transcended and the way was cleared for a more objective approach to anthropogenesis, and an increasing precision in ordering and interpreting human phenomena in time and space.

All I have tried to do here is to give emphasis to the fact that the events and conditions which led up to the period when anthropological questions became the concern of specialists and organized disciplines, require exploration as an anthropological problem—as a significant chapter in man's pursuit of knowledge about himself as part of his cultural adaptation. At the same time, this chapter in man's history in western culture is as much a part of the history of anthropology as the subsequent chapters concerned with the techniques, methodologies, concepts and theories developed. The primary historical question is not when anthropology began but, how did it come about that in western culture thinkers were increasingly motivated, not only to search for more reliable knowledge about their surrounding world, but to intensify their efforts to collect and analyze data that would provide more and more reliable answers to anthropological questions. Even a superficial consideration of this problem directs attention to distinctive features of western culture, to unique historical events, which made the rational and empirical study of man possible in a manner unparalleled in any other culture: the expansion of the European peoples beginning with the Age of Discovery, the development of modern science as a rational approach to the study of phenomena which transcends folk knowledge on all fronts. Furthermore, Butterfield has stressed the fact that "we do not always remember that it [western civilization] is similarly distinguished for its 'historical mindedness'. . . . For a long time we have been coming to realize that we must study the history of science if we wish to understand the character and development of our civilization. We have been much slower in realizing the importance of the history of history."[42] We have been even slower in undertaking the detailed investigation of the history of the study of man. Yet, it has been in western culture that man has become most completely aware of his own unique being and the possibility of making himself the subject of rational objective inquiry. The historical and cultural factors that led to this type of inquiry are an important part of the history of anthropology. However, as Margaret T. Hodgen has observed recently,[43] we have not yet probed far enough, nor deeply enough into the past. Particularly at a time, too, when there is such an upsurge of interest in the history of science, the history of anthropology should not be viewed as antiquarianism, or even marginal to current interests. A historical orientation to the development of anthropological knowledge should provide a point of departure for a sounder appraisal of current trends of thought and further research, as well as clarifying our professional role in relation to other disciplines concerned with the study of man.

Notes

[1] Based upon a paper with the same title read at a Symposium on the History of Anthropology, Annual Meeting, American Anthropological Association (Chicago), November, 1962. A background paper ("Anthropology and the History of the Study of Man"), prepared for the Conference on the History of Anthropology, sponsored by the Social Science Research Council (N.Y.: April, 1962) also has been drawn upon. Since many of the problems alluded to in this paper have not been studied, documentation is chiefly illustrative.

[2] *I.e.*, the period subsequent to the fall of Rome in the West in 476, A.D.

[3] See Hallowell, 1963.

[4] Laughlin, pp. 150, 172.

[5] Kluckhohn, p. 42.

[6] Collingwood.

[7] French and Sturtevant.

[8] Goodenough, *e.g.*, (p. 110) points out that, ". . . practical and empirical in their approach, the Carolinian people belie the frequent assumption that man everywhere is awed by the marvels of nature and, stirred to speculate thereon, seeks to formulate a coherent theory as to the origin and meaning of the cosmos. . . . Rooted in navigation, aimed at determining directions and predicting the weather, native astronomy is perhaps too important for personal safety to permit its being removed from an empirical context."

[9] cf. Butterfield (*Man* . . ., p. 32) who writes: "The history of science could never be adequately reconstructed by a student who confined his attention to the few men of supreme genius. We should produce a misleading diagram of the whole course of things if we merely drew direct lines from one of these mighty peaks to another. The great books are undoubtedly preferable to the reader, more serviceable in education, and more enriching to the mind; but, if we restrict ourselves to these, the result is likely to be a rope of sand; and in any case this is not the way in which to make discoveries in the history of any science. In reality, the technical historian, bent on discovery—proceeding therefore from the known to the unknown—tends to find himself drawn rather in the opposite direction."

[10] Hodgen, p. 50 and Chapter 1, The Classical Heritage.

[11] For further details see Wittkower.

[12] See, e.g., Lutz, who points out that the Sumerians entertained the idea of progressive stages in the cultural development of man. Yet there is no evidence of empirical research. *Cf.* the Three Age concept.

[13] Hazard, p. 10. *Cf.* Butterfield (*Origins* . . . , pp. 183–184), who makes the point that changes in European thought and value towards the end of the seventeenth century were not only due to developments in physical science but were affected by widely read books of travel that reported discoveries in distant lands. See also Shapiro.

[14] Haber recalls (p. 33) that Joseph Justis Scaliger (1540–1609) revolutionized chronology in his *de emendatrione temporum* (1583). "He showed that ancient history was not confined to that of the Greeks and Romans, but should include Persian, Babylonian, Egyptian, and the secular Jewish history. He gathered extant fragments of ancient history, succeeded in reconstructing the lost *Chronicle* of Eusebius . . . and studied the ancient systems of time keeping. He was thus able to compile for the first time in the modern period a sound—though sometimes erroneous—universal chronology of profane history, as distinguished from the uncritical and somewhat mythological sacred history of traditional chronology." The attempt of B. G. Niebuhr (1776–1831) to substitute historical scholarship (in his *History of Rome*, 1811–1832, see Stern, p. 46 *ff.*) for the folk history of Livy, is comparable in principle to the

transcendence of the level of folk anthropology which had scarcely begun. But historical scholarship was not prepared to deal with such large questions as "universal" or "general" history. (See Butterfield, *Man* . . . , chapter 2, "The Rise of the German Historical School"). "In reality," he writes (p. 103), "the work of providing a rational account of man on the earth would seem to have been taken over from the theologians by the general philosophers in the eighteenth century. The need to know how mankind had come from primitive conditions to its existing state would appear to have been felt before the historians were in a condition to supply what was wanted. Man's reflection on the matter marched ahead of his researches; and it was the *philosophes*—the 'general thinkers' as we might call them—who attempted to map out the course of things in time. And this would appear to be the reason why the philosophy of history, as it was called, came to its climax before the study of history had reached its modern form. The Göttingen school resented the facile generalizations which the men of the enlightenment produced without research, and imposed upon human history from the outside." General history, of course, did not include archaeological prehistory; the necessary temporal frame of reference had to be radically expanded.

[15] See Daniel (1943, 1950) and, in particular, Heizer (1962). Also Sanford.

[16] See Gillispie. Charles Lyell (1797–1895) published the first volume of his *Principles of Geology* in 1830. Despite resistance in orthodox circles, by the middle of the next decade the age of the earth had been extended to millions of years. "With Lyell's *Antiquity of Man* [1863] and Lubbock's *Pre-Historic Times* [1865]" says Haber (p. 287), "the last step had been taken in the overthrow of Biblical chronology as an all inclusive time span for the work of creation." For a concrete example of how the Mosaic Time Scale hindered and distorted the development of a temporal framework required for an intelligible interpretation of racial and cultural events, see Mulvaney's discussion of the Australian material.

[17] By Daniel Wilson. See Daniel (1964), p. 9.

[18] See Daniel (1964), pp. 40–41. Heizer (1959) publishes Frere's letter.

[19] Heizer (1962), p. 260.

[20] In the 4th century B.C. Theopompus (born ca. 378), a Greek historian, wrote about the Etruscans in a manner which reminds us of some of the early reports of the people of the South Pacific. According to him sexual promiscuity existed, sexual intercourse sometimes occurred publicly, and children did not know their own parents. For quotation see Hus (pp. 157–158). The first work to present the sexual mores of the people of the South Seas for the English reader was Hawkesworth's *Account of the Voyages . . . in the Southern Hemisphere . . . Drawn up from the Journals which were kept by the Several Commanders* . . . etc. 1773. He was a man of letters and had not been on any of the voyages. As a matter of fact, his book was condemned for inaccuracy and indecency, yet it obtained wide circulation. Boswell met Capt. Cook at dinner in 1776 and asked him about the book. Boswell reports in his *Journal* (p. 308) that Cook said, "Hawkesworth made in his book a general conclusion from a particular fact, and would take as a fact what they had only heard. . . . He said that a disregard of chastity in unmarried women was by no means general at Otaheite, and he said Hawkesworth's story of an *initiation* he had not reason to believe." "Why, Sir," Boswell goes on to say, "Hawkesworth has used your narrative as a London tavern keeper does wine. He has *brewed it* (i.e. mixed other ingredients with it)." Boswell also says (p. 341) that Cook "candidly confessed to me that he and his companions who visited the South Sea Islands could not be certain of any information they got, or supposed they got, except as to objects falling under the observations of the senses, their knowledge of the language was so imperfect they required the aid of their senses, and anything which they learnt about religion, government, or traditions might be quite erroneous."

[21] See Fairchild, Pearce and Smith. An example of how the circulation of pictorial material created confusing and undiscriminating racial images, even relating to the ancestors of Europeans themselves, is the intricate connection between John White's drawings of *Indians* of Roanoke, made on the spot in the late sixteenth century, De Brys' engravings of *Picts* (1590) and "The Portraiture of the Ancient Britaines," published by John Speed in 1611 (see Kendrick, pp. 123–125 and Plates XII–XV). Kendrick comments: "Speed . . . seems to have realized that it was no use quoting classical authors to the effect that the ancient Britons wore few, if any, clothes, and painted themselves, if at the same time one refused to recognize that the picture of a naked and painted person would give some idea of the probable appearance of an Ancient Briton. There was no question of any disgrace here, but rather an occasion for pride; for nakedness implies hardiness, and painting oneself is, after all, art. Where an Ancient Briton was concerned, there could be no doubt that savagery must include the idea of nobility."

[22] Washburn, 1964, p. 415.

[23] Washburn (1957, p. 54): "Perhaps the 'idea of the noble savage' developed its greatest force when the white man was dependent on the Indian for his safety and sustenance (as in the early years of exploration and settlement), perhaps the 'idea of the treacherous savage' represents a period when both groups were powerful and a threat to each other. Finally, the 'idea of the filthy savage' may well have developed its greatest force when the Indian came to be dependent on the will of the White man (as in the late eighteenth century). Frederick J. Dockstader of the Museum of the American Indian in New York has suggested a most recent idea: that of the 'incompetent savage' which he suggests has arisen because of the growing economic rivalry between Indians and Whites in recent years." Smith (p. 244) points out that in the early nineteenth century pictorial material from the South Pacific was used in missionary propaganda to create an image of the ignoble savage.

[24] Reproduced in Hodgen, opposite p. 335.

[25] For information on Mandeville consult Letts and particularly Bennett, *cf.* Hodgen, pp. 69–71.

[26] "Making faithful records of the native peoples of the Pacific proved to be more difficult than making accurate records of plants, animals, or landscapes," writes Smith (pp. 20–21). "There was, for example, the question of size . . . there had accumulated by 1768 a formidable body of evidence that the natives of Patagonia were giants. The Captains, Harrington and Carmen, had come back in 1704 with stories of giants. Byron, in 1764, only four years before Cook sailed in the Endeavor, corroborated their story. . . . Byron's meeting with this chief was illustrated in Hawkesworth's *Voyages,* the chief being made, in accordance with Byron's description, to tower above the Englishman." However, since Byron had no professional artist with him, this was "simply an illustration based on a written statement." Banks, accompanying Cook, did have artists and was anxious to correct misconceptions about the size of the Patagonians. He wrote in his *Journal* that the men were from five feet eight inches to five feet ten inches in height, while the women were smaller, seldom exceeding five feet. Furthermore, Buchan and Parkinson both made drawings of the Fuegians showing them to be normal in height. Nevertheless, a belief in the giantism of the Patagonians persisted. Lord Monboddo claimed that Hawkesworth's summary weighed heavily in this direction and even after the publication of the latter's *Voyages,* there was an English collection which illustrated a giantess and a French collection showing a giant Fuegian receiving Commodore Byron. See Smith (p. 255 and Plates 167, 168, 169 for the transformation wrought after the invention of photography by Daguerre (1789–1851) and the use of instrumentation and modelling. See Smith, too, for example of the articulation of the general need for more precise observation on men by such eighteenth

century writers as Ferguson, Monboddo and Herder, as well as the more detailed and explicit instructions given La Pérouse (1785) as compared with Cook (pp. 100–102).

[27] According to Smith (see pp. 30, 34) the acceptance of the idea of giants in Fuegia probably reflects a long tradition in Europe of *antipodal inversion* i.e., "the long-standing belief that things in the southern hemisphere were somehow inverted or at least governed by laws which differed from those governing the northern parts of the world."

[28] Kluckhohn, 1953, p. 508.

[29] *Social Theory in the early literature of voyage and exploration in Africa.* Doctoral Dissertation, Dept. of Social Institutions, Univ. of California, Berkeley, 1944. Katherine B. Oakes (Mrs. H. C. George).

[30] George (1958), pp. 71–72.

[31] Radcliffe-Brown, p. 146.

[32] See Hallowell, 1960, pp. 13–14.

[33] See, e.g., Brandon, Eliade, Peuch, Haber.

Butterfield (*Man* . . . , Preface ix–x) writes: "Philosophy and religion in many parts of the world, and even in ancient Greece . . . too often led to the depreciation of history—the feeling that time's changes are meaningless, the notion that events move in aimless, ever-recurring cycles. . . . Yet the Christian could not turn his back on history, for his very religion was 'historical': it was essential for him to regard Christ as an actual historical figure. In view of the Incarnation and the Crucifixion, it was impossible for him to take the line that events in time are really of no significance or that history offers the pattern of aimless, repeating cycles. Perhaps it was the pull of the Old Testament which, in the last resort, kept him close to earth—close to history—when he was in danger of moving away from reality. Perhaps it was as a result of the influence of the Old Testament, which began its story of mankind with the Creation, that there developed so remarkably under Christianity the notion of a 'universal history'—that is, a single story of all mankind. . . . Other factors, such as the Scientific Revolution of the seventeenth century . . . affected the course of historical inquiry, and in the subsequent period, the growing currency of the idea of progress seemed to give new point, new meaning, to history itself—new reason for discovering the course of man's development in the antecedent age." Haber (p. 25) says that it was St. Augustine who placed "the conception on a unique, concrete, course of time in the mainstream of Christian eschatology," and if, "in the eighteenth century, the time scale of Biblical chronology became an onerous barrier to scientific progress, it had served an heroic role during the Patristic period in establishing the archetype of progress itself which science so readily borrowed."

[34] Simpson, 1964, p. 122 in chapter 7, "The Historical Factor in Science."

[35] Simpson, 1960, p. 118.

[36] *Ibid.*, p. 118.

[37] See Harris and Hodgen, p. 263 *ff*.

[38] Eliade, pp. 145–146.

[39] See Bryson. The term "conjectural history" was introduced by Dugald Stewart.

[40] For the seventeenth and eighteenth century use of the comparative method see Bock and Teggart (pp. 92 *ff*.).

[41] See Manuel pp. 43–44; 141–142. Fontenelle (1657–1757) "revived the Augustinian analogy between the history of mankind and the development of the child to maturity, and envisioned the historical process as the gradual elimination of puerile myth and its replacement by adult mathematical-physical reasoning. Fontenelle defined primitive mentality, but he did not admire it; this was a stage of human consciousness which mankind was fortunate enough to have outgrown. In comparing the ancients, the savages, the peasants, and the children, Fontenelle allowed them the attributes of

humanity, even a rudimentary capacity to reason, but he regarded them as incapable of exercising those higher powers of abstraction so remarkably concentrated among members of the French academies. For every event, Fontenelle believed, the primitive like the peasant, demanded a concrete specific cause" (p. 44).

[42] Butterfield, *Man* . . . , New Preface, VII.

[43] Foreword, p. 7.

25. A History of the Personality of Anthropology

Alfred L. Kroeber

By personality we mean the totality of the faculties, bent, qualities, and temperament which characterize an individual person.[1]

When the term is applied by transfer to anthropology, it continues to denote characteristic activities and propensities, but propensities now of the current of anthropological inquiry viewed as a unit or whole.

It is thus plain that my title will not allow me to escape the holistic aspects of our chosen branch of science. I will seek to pinpoint the core, but cannot ignore the peripheries; and our peripheries are wide.

Yet in spite of much pervasive homogeneity of the personality of anthropology, I must start, paradoxically, with a duality.

When we put anthropology and sociology side by side, it is astonishing how diverse they are in most of what they specifically do and actually occupy themselves with, and yet how alike they prove to be in their general assumptions and basic theory.

Sociologists and anthropologists agree in dealing with sociocultural phenomena autonomously. Sociocultural data rest on biotic and individual psychic factors, of course, and are therefore limited by them; but they are not in any serious measure derivable, constructively explicable, from them. The analysis and understanding of sociocultural phenomena must be made first of all in terms of sociocultural structure and process. Durkheim called them "social facts"; Spencer, "superorganic effects" which themselves became causes and conditions; Tylor appropriated and defined the term "culture." It is a truism, but also an inescapable fact, that man's societies always exist in association with a culture; his cultures, with a society. Particular studies can abstract from the social aspects of a situation to investigate the cultural aspects, or the reverse, or they can deal with the interaction of the social and cultural aspects. This is common doctrine of the two sciences; and it is in contrast with this postulational basis which they share that sociologists show a strong propensity to

From the *American Anthropologist,* vol. 61, no. 3 (1959), pp. 398–404. Reprinted by permission of the American Anthropological Association.

focus their interest on social data, structure, and process, but anthropologists on cultural.

We can go farther. The basic assumptions and principles shared by sociology and anthropology are virtually the only general theory existing in that area which it has become customary to call "social science." Economics, politics, jurisprudence obviously concern themselves with particular facets of society and culture. They take for granted that there is a larger totality, but scarcely concern themselves with it. Psychology is of course basically oriented toward individuals, much as is biology; social psychology represents a secondary extension, in the development of which sociology was about as important, at least in our own country, as was psychology itself. Classical economic theory was formulated earlier than generic sociocultural theory. This was possible because it applied to only one special part of the sociocultural totality, and because economic phenomena tend in their nature to come more quantified than other behavioral data. The classical economic theory was also a relatively well-insulated model, whose effectiveness rested upon the assumption that economic phenomena could profitably be considered in a virtual vacuum; if other motivations had now and then to be admitted, common-sense psychology was sufficient.

Not only do sociology and anthropology then essentially share their basic theory, but this theory is the only holistic one yet evolved for the sociocultural realm.

In view of this sharing of their basic concepts, it is remarkable how preponderantly sociology and anthropology do not share the areas which they work most actively, do not share the methods by which they work them, or the interests which motivate them.

Most conspicuous, of course, is the virtually total neglect by sociology of several of the fields which between them constitute the majority of the area operated in by anthropology. These fields are: biological anthropology, misnamed physical in days when souls were still maintained to be separate from bodies; archeology and prehistory; linguistics, general, descriptive, and historical; culture history; primitive ethnology; and the folk ethnography of peasantry in civilized countries as it is pursued in Europe. Sociologists do not hesitate to use results obtained by us in these subdisciplines; but they rarely make intrinsic contributions to them, as all anthropologists do in one or more of the fields.

Now it is notable that with one exception—that of primitive ethnography—all these fields are shared by us anthropologists with nonanthropologists of some kind or other. Biological anthropology of course is only a fragment of biology, and whether a worker calls himself anthropologist, anatomist, or human geneticist is largely a matter of his job classification. Archeology inevitably runs into art and classic studies—there even are notable university departments named "Art and Archeology," and our

Archaeological Institute of America was founded and is run by classical scholars. Somewhat similarly, prehistory merges into protohistory and full history. Some general linguists have been recruited from anthropology, but more from the various philologies. Culture history has been pursued also by historians and geographers, and some of the best has come from Sinologists like Laufer and Carter. European folk ethnography is closest to what we in England and America call folklore, and in folkloristic activity the students of English and other current languages of civilization are more numerous than we. The result is that unless anthropologists specialize in primitive ethnography—which no one other than they seems to want to undertake—they share their specialty with collaborators in some natural science or in some humanity and are likely to be outnumbered by them.

What impulse is it that drives anthropologists as a group to participate in so many fields which are already being cultivated by others? It seems to be a two-pronged impulse to apperceive and conceive at once empirically and holistically. We constitute one of the smaller learned professions, but we aim to take in perhaps larger tracts of phenomena than any other discipline. Our total coverage must thus of necessity mostly be somewhat thin. Yet it is rarely either vague or abstruse—we start with concrete facts which we sense to carry an interest, and we stay with them. Perhaps our coverage can fairly be called spotty; though without implication of being random, irrelevant, disconnected. If a whole is steadily envisaged, the relation of its fragments can become significant, provided the known parts are specific and are specifically located within the totality. At any rate, the holistic urge is perhaps what is most distinctive of us as a group.

This is balanced by a love of fact, an attachment to phenomena in themselves, to perceiving them through our own senses. This taproot we share with the humanities. And we also tend strongly here toward the natural history approach. Sociologists have called us "nature lovers" and "bird watchers," Steve Hart and John Bennett say; and from their angle, the epithets stick. They have added another: "antiquarians." There are anthropological museums of tangible objects, but no sociological museums. We are strong on photographs, films, and tapes that reproduce sights and sounds. We write chapters on art in ethnographies and sometimes offer courses in primitive art. How many sociologists would venture that or even hanker to be venturing it?

We insist on fieldwork as an opportunity, a privilege, and a professional cachet. We want the face-to-face experience with our subjects. The anonymity of the sociological questionnaire seems to us bloodless, even though its specificity and quantifiability are obvious assets to which we cannot easily attain by our methods. When the Lynds first went in person to study Middletown-Muncie, it was widely heralded as a taking-over of anthropological technique.

To return to the other prong, the holism, this seems expressed also in our inclination to historical and to comparative treatment. American sociology is certainly neither antihistorical nor anticomparative in principle; but it certainly is primarily interested in the here and now, in our own culture and social structure more often than in foreign, remote, or past ones. Sociology began with a marked ameliorative bent, and with concern for practical matters of utility. Anthropology commenced rather with an interest in the exotic and useless. We did not constitute our Society for Applied Anthropology until 1941. The "action research" of World War II was largely thrust upon us by government and military, and by some it is remembered largely as a sort of spree of forced decision-making on grossly inadequate information.

It is certainly significant that the sharing of anthropological fields is with the natural sciences (I am still including psychology in the natural sciences) and with the humanities. The only active overlap of long standing with any social science is that on theory with sociology, with which we also share some interest in demography. Specific primitive ethnography and perhaps most of the community studies in civilized societies continue to be done by anthropologists, but quantifiable studies of problems in civilized countries by sociologists. The latter tend to define terms more sharply and problems more limitedly. They probably rank next to economists and psychologists in abundance of statistical treatment. We still tend to shy at statistics.

Balancing our virtual agreement on sociocultural theory, there exists a strong drift in sociology to emphasize social structure and social action as compared with cultural product or pattern, and to assume or treat the cultural accompaniments as implicit, contained in, or derivative from the social structure. Anthropologists, at any rate until recently, and going back as far as Tylor, have contrariwise emphasized culture as their special concern. To be sure they have made almost a fetish of the social feature of kinship, and have frequently given close attention to specific aspects of social structure and functioning, ever since the initial days of Morgan and Bachofen. But they tend to look upon society as one part of the total domain of culture, on which one can specialize or not as one can specialize on religion or art or values, or again on subsistence or technology or economic life. This procedure works with us to give consistent results, much as the contrasting sociological assumption and procedures yield effective results in their hands.

However, there is a point which no one appears yet to have thought quite through. Developmentally, evolutionistically, society far antedates and thus underlies culture, as shown by the existence of complex societies, especially among insects, long before any culture existed. In man, who alone of all species on earth possesses culture in substantial measure, this culture invariably coexists with society. In analytic study the two are separable, and in practice, I repeat, one can focus on societies, or on cultures, or try to focus on the interrelations of the two. However, it remains conceptually unclear, at least to me, how the sociologist can successfully treat culture as something embedded in or derivative from social phenomena, and the anthropologist can with equal success treat social structure as only a compartment or sector of culture. There is some legerdemain of words at work here, I feel, which my rational eye is not fast enough to perceive. I must admit I have found few colleagues who were seriously troubled by the contradiction that puzzles me.

I encounter a possibly related blocking of thought when I try to define "social anthropology" as a conscious movement or strand within total anthropology. It has emerged since my own maturity, as a successor to "functionalism," and the present generation of British social anthropologists have been trained by the "functionalists" Malinowski and Radcliffe-Brown. In Britain, where sociology is only recently recognized, anthropologists stress the "social" aspect of their work, and appear to accord primacy to social structure and functioning almost as much as do American sociologists. At the same time they are obviously interested in cultures holistically, much as the rest of us are, even though, also like us, they rarely in a career get around to portraying or dissecting the entire totality of even one culture and society. They certainly are excellent primitive ethnographers, as indeed Malinowski was—and supremely so—when he did not let facile theorizing seduce him away from his superb descriptions of concrete culture functioning. But why the sense of separatism of a limited circle of social anthropologists?

In America social anthropology seems to have become consciously active when Lloyd Warner returned from his association with Radcliffe-Brown in Australia. Warner is interested in the interactions of persons in society, especially our own, and perhaps most of all in social mobility. He uses cultural data skilfully to vivify his findings which basically concern our class structuring.

The British social anthropologists certainly are really still doing old-fashioned ethnography—reporting on promitive cultures—more often than we now are doing it. Also, they start from the phenomena, let these take them where they lead, and are in no sense system mongers. But they seem to be giving their ethnography additional depth, or texture, by socializing it more than when Boas, Lowie, Spier, and I were concentrating on laying bare the skeletal structures of cultures. If this is so, the fact would take social anthropology out of the category of a cult, and would leave it as an endeavor at needed and vital enrichment of long-established basic cultural aims.

In that case "social anthropology" would resemble culture-and-personality, or personality-in-culture, which started out somewhat self-consciously as the revolutionary adding of a new dimension to the view of culture, but which seems now essentially to be contributing to the portrayal of culture a greater depth of personalization than was formerly thought necessary, possible, or meet.

There is another factor which may have impinged on social anthropology, namely, influence from applied anthropology.The period of rapid development of both is the same; and in both movements culture has lost some of its primacy as focus of interest. Not that applied anthropology wants to minimize culture or to bypass it. It recognizes cultural forms and that it must operate with them, since it is by alteration of these forms that it can achieve the end of social welfare, which is the welfare of whole societies or of social groups within them.

The lateness of the beginnings of applied anthropology is really remarkable, when we consider that economics and politics, and largely sociology also, commenced to be studied precisely because they were considered useful, and still are pursued mainly in that belief. True, similar claims were now and then advanced for anthropology as far back as the 19th century, as by Tylor, but they made little impression: they resulted in no organized effort, and long attracted no following. Anthropology continued to be pursued out of curiosity—all the effect on the current of mundane activity hoped for by anthropologists like Powell and Boas and Sapir was an intellectual influence. This fact is not realized by many of our younger colleagues, and has sometimes been forgotten by those not so young, who grew up in, or were early induced to accept, the assumption that anthropology was a social science and must therefore necessarily comprise applied as well as fundamental intellectual activity.

If I do not say more about applied anthropology, it is for lack of personal experience. I have never practiced nor even dabbled in it. I am not trying to deny it a place. We are certainly all of us grateful that the scheme of the universe allows the applied art of scientific medicine to flourish alongside the fundamental sciences of physiology and biochemistry, and engineering beside physics. It is by its fruits that applied anthropology should be appraised. But I would be a poor appraiser. There are some individuals who can in their own person make notable contributions in both approaches: Pasteur, for instance, and Virchow, and our own Margaret Mead. But there are others whose bent is one way or the other, and who can produce more successfully by keeping that bent. I am in this category.

I have said that primitive ethnography is the only field in anthropology which no one else wants to share with us. I might have added that it is also the field for which it has been notoriously most difficult to secure research funds from foundations and academic sources. Our other unique propensity in social science is our holism. It is therefore a natural supposition that the two peculiarities may be connected. I owe to Walter Goldschmidt the suggestion that our early and continued holistic proclivities are derivative from concern with primitive peoples, and that this led also to our emphasis on cultural relativism. I believe that this interpretation must be accepted. Interest in one's self and appanages can never be wholly discarded, but it tends to extend itself outward slowly. Yet once there exists genuine curiosity about the peripheries, these, in conjunction with the ever-present center, imply an interest in the relation of the two foci, and in the whole which the foci encompass or indicate. The history of the origin of grammar in the Mediterranean world illustrates the involved mechanism. The Greeks seem to have developed for themselves, by reasoning more than by substantive analysis, some few rudimentary principles of Greek grammar. But the full structure became recognized only after Alexander's conquests, when Hellenized Cilicians and Thracians were able to view Greek in comparison and contrast to their "barbarous" mother tongues. Much so, the past and contemporary anthropological readiness to deal with the remote, the exotic, even the illiterate and deprived, seems to have led to and promoted holistic approaches and relativistic thinking.

As for relativism, I accept the criticism sometimes made, that as a final conclusion and summating principle it is sterile and a renunciation, as indeed any terminal thinking must be. But as a validated assumption serving as the basis for further inquiry, relativism is both indispensable and productive.

Since personalities are initially determined by their ancestry, it is a relevant fact, if I am right, that anthropology was originally not a social science at all. Its father was natural science; its mother, esthetically tinged humanities. Both parents want to attain reasoned and generalized conclusions; but they both also want to reach them by way of their senses as well as by reasoning. After a brief first childlike decade or two of outright speculation, anthropology settled down to starting directly from experienced phenomena, with a bare minimum of ready-made abstraction and theory, but with a glowing conviction that it was entering new territory and making discovery. Its discovery was consciousness of the world of culture, an enormous product and a vast influence, with forms and patterns of its own, and a validating principle: relativity. There were far boundaries to this demesne, which included in its totality alike our own and the most remote and diverse human productivities. The vision was wide, charged, and stirring. It may perhaps fairly be called romantic: certainly it emerged historically about at the time point when esthetic romanticism was intellectualizing. The pursuit of anthropology must often have seemed strange and useless to many people, but no one has ever called it an arid or a toneless or dismal science.

Now, maturity has stolen upon us. The times and utilitarianism have caught up with us, and we find ourselves classified and assigned to the social sciences. It is a dimmer atmosphere, with the smog of jargon sometimes hanging heavy. Generalizations no longer suffice; we are taught to worship Abstraction; sharp sensory outlines have melted into logicoverbal ones. As our daily bread, we invent hypotheses in order to test them, as we are told is the constant practice of the high tribe of physicists. If at times some of you, like myself, feel somewhat ill at ease in the house of social science, do not wonder: we are changelings therein; our true paternity lies elsewhere.

I do not end on a note of despondency; for the routes of fulfillment are many. And specifically, it is well that with all their differences of habitus, of attitude, of kinds of building stones, sociology and anthropology have emerged with a substantially common basic theory. That should be an encouragement to both, and a rallying point to others. And it will serve as a foundation for all the social sciences to build on.

Notes

[1] A first draft of this paper was read on May 17, 1958, at the second annual meeting in Berkeley of the Kroeber Anthropological Society, under the title: *The Personality of Anthropology*, and has been printed in the Publications of the Society for the fall of 1958.

The present version, further thought out, somewhat enlarged, and revised, is herewith published, with the consent of the Kroeber Anthropological Society, to complete the record of the symposium on the History of Anthropology held in plenary session at the Washington meeting.

26. Anthropological Controversies
Alfred Haddon

Next to geographical discovery, perhaps the most stimulating influence on anthropology has been the succession of controversies in which it has constantly been involved. It has always been regarded as a somewhat anarchical subject, advocating views which might prove dangerous to Church and State; and many are the battles which have raged within and without. Huxley attributed the large audiences which were wont to throng the Anthropological Section of the British Association to the innate bellicose instincts of man, and to the splendid opportunities afforded by anthropology for indulging those propensities.[1]

The discussions of the earlier centuries were focussed round the question of the origin of man, and from this highly debatable problem arose the two antagonistic groups of the monogenists, or orthodox school, deriving all mankind from a single pair, and the polygenists, who believed in a multiple origin. Before the discoveries of prehistoric archæology had advanced sufficiently to show the futility of such discussion, anthropologists were split up into opposing camps by the question of the fixity of species, and became embroiled in one of the fiercest controversies of modern times—that of evolution. A subordinate subject of contention, implicated in the polygenist doctrines, was the place of the Negro in nature, involving the question of slavery.

Origin of Man

Among the ancient philosophers the question of the origin of man was answered in various ways; some, like Pythagoras, Plato, and Aristotle, believed that mankind had always existed, because there never could have been a beginning of things, relying on the scholastic argument that no bird could be born without an egg, and no egg without a bird. Epicurus and Lucretius believed in a "fortuitous cause," a preparation of fat and slimy earth, with a long incubation of water and conjunction of

From Alfred C. Haddon, *History of Anthropology*, 1910. Reprinted by permission of G. P. Putnam's Sons: pp. 57–83.

heavenly and planetary bodies. Others, that men and animals "crawled out of the earth by chance," "like mushrooms or blite."

With the spread of Christianity the Mosaic cosmogony became generally adopted, and monogenism developed into an article of faith. The Church fulminated against those atheists who admitted doubts on the subject of Adam and Eve, or believed in the existence of antipodal man, or that man had existed for more than the 6000 years allotted to him by Scripture. If the censure of the Church did not lead to recantation, the heretic was burnt. A seventeenth-century divine, Dr. Lightfoot, Vice-Chancellor of the University of Cambridge, was even more precise than Archbishop Ussher: he reached the conclusion that "man was created by the Trinity on October 23, 4004 B.C., at nine o'clock in the morning."[2]

The discovery of the New World dealt a severe blow to the authority of the Fathers on matters of science. Antipodal man, whom St. Augustine[3] had extinguished as "excessively absurd," was found to exist, and the Spaniards forthwith excused their barbarities to the American natives on the plea that they were not the descendants of Adam and Eve.

Polygenism and Monogenism

Henceforward the polygenists began to gain ground. Theophrastus Paracelsus (1520) first asserted the plurality of the races of mankind, and explained the Mosaic cosmogony as having been written "theologically—for the weaker brethren." Vanini (1616) mentions a belief, entertained by atheists, that man was descended from or allied to monkeys. In 1655 Isaac de la Peyrère, a Calvinist scholar of Bordeaux, published in Amsterdam his *Præ-Adamitæ*, to prove that Adam and Eve were not the first human beings upon the earth; and his work, being prohibited by authority, became immensely popular.

His theory, though unorthodox, was founded on Scripture, and regarded Adam and Eve as merely a special and much later creation; the Gentiles, who peopled the rest of the earth, having been formed from the dust of the earth, together with the beasts of the field, on the sixth day. The inhabitants of the New World, which, being separate from the Old, could not have been peopled with the same race, were of Gentile origin. This theory was bitterly opposed. The *Parlement* of Paris caused the book to be publicly burned. The Inquisition laid hands on the author, and he was forced to abjure both his Pre-Adamite heresy and his Calvinism. He died in a convent in 1676.

The writings of the Encyclopedists, the freedom of thought claimed by Voltaire and Rousseau, together with the classification of species by Linnæus, emboldened the polygenists. Lord Kames[4] was one of the earliest exponents in England, and he soon found many followers. Two separate lines of antagonism may be distinguished in the controversy. In one—the Anglo-French—Prichard, Cuvier, and de Quatrefages represent the monogenists, and Virey and Bory de Saint-Vincent the polygenists; the other, in which America and the slavery question were implicated, polygenists and anti-abolitionists going hand-in-hand, was represented by Nott and Cliddon in America, Knox and Hunt in England, and Broca in France.

When materials began to accumulate they were detrimental to the polygenist theory. Especially was this the case with regard to the proof of what Broca termed "*eugenesis*"—*i.e.*, that all the *Hominidæ* are, and always have been, fertile with each other. This, which formed a test between species and varieties in botany and zoölogy, was claimed also in anthropology, and the polygenists had to seek for support elsewhere. They found it in linguistics; "language as a test of race" bulked large in ethnological controversy, and is not yet entirely extinct.

At first the monogenists claimed language as supporting their views. All languages were to be traced to three sources—Indo-European, Semitic, and Malay; and these, in their turn, were the offspring of a parent tongue, now entirely lost. But it was soon found impossible to reconcile even Aryan and Semitic, and a common parent for all three languages was inconceivable. The linguistic argument then passed over to the polygenists.

Hovelacque stated that "the ascertained impossibility of reducing a multiplicity of linguistic families to a common centre is for us sufficient proof of the original plurality of the races that have been developed with them." M. Chavée[5] went further. "We might," he says, "put Semitic children and Indo-European children apart, who had been taught by deaf-mutes, and we should find that the former would naturally speak a Semitic language, the latter an Aryan language." F. Müller and others took up this line of argument, holding that distinct stock languages proved the existence of distinct stock races. But, as Professor Keane points out, in his summary of the controversy (1896, chap. vii), *quod nimis probat, nihil probat*—"what proves too much, proves nothing"—and the hundred or more stock languages in America alone, reduced the argument to an absurdity.

Monogenists

Among the monogenists may be included most of the older anthropologists—Linnæus, Buffon, Blumenbach, Camper, Prichard, and Lawrence. Since they held that all mankind was descended from a single pair (the question as to whether this pair were white, black, or red, occasioned a further discussion), they had to account for the subsequent divergence producing the present clearly-recognised varieties; and, in so doing, anticipated the theory of evolution, which was not clearly enunciated until the time of Lamarck.

Linnæus believed in fixity of species, but had doubts about the Biblical account. As a naturalist, he found it difficult to credit the exceptional nature of a country which had supplied the wants of zoölogical species as opposed to one another as the polar bear and the tropical hippopotamus.

Buffon ascribed the variations of man to the influence of climate and diet. Though Prichard and Lawrence both denied the possibility of the transmission of acquired characters, Prichard believed that the transmission of occasional variations might, to some extent, account for the diversities of races.[6] Lawrence wrote more clearly: "Racial differences can be explained only by two principles—namely, the occasional production of an offspring with different characters from those of the parents, as a native or congenital variety; and the propagation of such varieties by generation." He considered that domestication favoured the production of these congenital and transmissible variations, and, anticipating the Eugenic school, deplored the fact that, while so much care and attention was paid to the breeding of domestic animals, the breeding of man was left to the vagaries of his own individual fancy.

Lawrence

Sir William Lawrence (1783–1867) was appointed Professor of Anatomy and Surgery to the Royal College of Surgeons at the early age of thirty-two. His lectures on "Comparative Anatomy, Physiology, Zoölogy, and the Natural History of Man," delivered between 1816 and 1818, raised an immediate outcry; and the author (to use his own words) was charged "with the unworthy design of propagating opinions detrimental to society, and of endeavouring to enforce them for the purpose of loosening those restraints in which the welfare of mankind exists." Lawrence was forced to bow before the storm of abuse, and announce publicly that the volumes had been suppressed, as he was refused copyright. It is interesting to note that these lectures are among those at present recommended for the use of students of anthropology.

Lawrence was far in advance of his time, and much of his teaching may be said to have anticipated the doctrine of evolution. Unfortunately, the theological protest raised by his lectures—published when he was only thirty-five—resulted in his forsaking anthropology altogether, and he henceforward devoted himself entirely to anatomy and surgery.

Lord Monboddo

Another prophet in advance of his times was Lord Monboddo. James Burnett Monboddo (1714–1799) was regarded as one of the most eccentric characters of the eighteenth century, mainly on account of his peculiar views about the origin of society and of language, and his theories as to the relationship of man with the monkeys. He was deeply interested in all the current accounts of "tailed men," thus justifying Dr. Johnson's remark that he was "as jealous of his tail as a squirrel." Later students of his writings are less struck by these eccentricities, which afforded endless jests to the wags of the age, than by his scientific methods of investigation and his acute conclusions. He not only studied man as one of the animals, but he also studied savages with a view to elucidating the origin of civilisation.

Many other pre-Darwinian evolutionists might be mentioned, but Professor Lovejoy's caution must be noted:

> The premature adoption of a hypothesis is a sin against the scientific spirit; and the chance acceptance by some enthusiast of a truth in which, at the time, he has no sound reason for believing, by no means entitles him to any place of honour in the history of science.[7]

The first to enunciate a coherent theory of evolution—that of Transformism or Transmutation—was Lamarck.[8]

Lamarck

Lamarck (1744–1829) believed that species were not fixed, but that the more complex were developed from pre-existent simpler forms. He attributed the change of species mainly to physical conditions of life, to crossing, and especially to use or disuse of organs, which not only resulted in the modification, growth, or atrophy of some, but, under the stress of necessity, led to the formation of new ones. "*La fonction fait l'organe.*" He also held that changes produced in the individual as the result of environment were transmitted to the offspring. Organic life was traced back and back to a small number of primordial germs or monads, the offspring of spontaneous generation. Man formed no exception. He was the result of the slow transformation of certain apes.

Lamarck's views were first published in 1801, and were enlarged in his *Philosophie Zoölogique*, 1809.

Cuvier

Lamarck's chief opponent was Cuvier (1769–1832), Professor of Natural History and of Comparative Anatomy in Paris, who, besides being the recognised authority on zoölogy (his great book, *Le Règne Animal,* was long the standard work on the subject), was even more renowned as an anatomist. He upheld the theory of Catastrophe, of alternate destructions and regenerations, against the new theories of Transformism and Evolution.

According to this widely accepted belief, the universe was subject to violent terrestrial revolutions, involving the destruction of all existing things and the total annihilation of all living beings belonging to the past epoch.

The theory was by no means new; it was current in the East in the thirteenth century. In a book written by Mohamed Kaswini on the wonders of nature, he tells the following tale:

> In passing one day by a very ancient and extremely populous city, I asked of one of the inhabitants who founded their city. He replied to me: "I know not, and our ancestors knew no more than we do on this point." Five hundred years afterwards, passing by the same place, I could not perceive a trace of the city. Inquiring of one of the peasants about the place when it was that the city was destroyed, he answered me: "What an odd question you put to me; this country has never been otherwise than as you see it now." I returned there after another five hundred years, and I found in the place of the country I had seen—a sea. I now asked of the fishermen how long it was since their country became a sea; and he replied that a person like me ought to know that it had always been a sea. I returned again after five hundred years; the sea had disappeared, and it was now dry land. No one knew what had become of the sea, or if such a thing had ever existed. Finally, I returned once more after five hundred years, and I again found a flourishing city. The people told me that the origin of their city was lost in the night of time.[9]

Cuvier's position was supported by the evidence brought to France by Napoleon's scientific expedition to Egypt (1801). Here were seen numbers of mummified animals, probably dating back some three to four thousand years, but showing no appreciable difference from existing types. This was held to demolish the theory of evolution by proving the immutability of species.

Etienne Saint-Hilaire

Etienne Geoffrey Saint-Hilaire (1772–1844), the zoölogist on the Egyptian expedition, interpreted the results differently, and was one of the most brilliant supporters of Lamarck. In 1828 he published his convictions that the same forms have not been perpetuated since the origin of all things, though he did not believe that existing species were undergoing modification. Cuvier returned to the charge, and propounded his doctrine of the periodical revolutions of the earth, of the renewal each time of the flora and fauna, and of the incessant and miraculous intervention of a creative Will. And for a time, owing to his position and authority, he held the field.

Robert Chambers

In 1844 appeared a book which had an enormous influence on the pre-Darwinian history of Evolution. This was an anonymous work entitled *Vestiges of the Natural History of Creation,* the authorship of which was not revealed until the publication of the twelfth edition in 1884. It was the production of Robert Chambers (1802–1871), co-editor with his brother William of *Chambers's Journal,* and author of many books on Scotland and a few on science. He traced the action of general laws throughout the universe as a system of growth and development, and held that the various species of animals and plants had been produced in orderly succession from each other by the action of unknown laws and the influence of external conditions. The *Vestiges* became at once the centre of scientific discussion, denounced by the orthodox, and held "not proven" by most of the men of science of the time. Its supporters were called "Vestigiarian," a term which implied also "unscientific," "sentimental," and "absurd."

The curious point is that in the *Vestiges* we find much of what was subsequently called the Darwinian theory already enunciated. According to Wallace, it clearly formulated the conception of evolution through natural laws, and yet it was denounced by those who soon after were to become the champions of Darwinism. This was partly due to the way in which the doctrine was treated and expressed, partly also to the "needless savagery" of Professor Huxley.

Huxley wrote in 1887: "I must have read the *Vestiges* . . . before 1846; but, if I did, the book made very little impression on me. . . . I confess the book simply irritated me by the prodigious ignorance and thoroughly unscientific habit of mind manifested by the writer." Professor Lovejoy[10] explains the reasons for Huxley's attitude:

> The truth is that Huxley's strongly emotional and highly pugnacious nature was held back by certain wholly non-logical influences from accepting an hypothesis for which the evidence was practically as potent for over a decade before he accepted it as it was at the time of his conversion. The book was written in a somewhat exuberant and rhetorical style. With all its religious heterodoxy, it was characterised by a certain

> pious and edifying tone, and was given to abrupt transitions from scientific reasoning to mystical sentiment. It contained numerous blunders in matters of biological and geological detail; and its author inclined to believe, on the basis of some rather absurd experimental evidence, in the possibility of spontaneous generation. All these things were offensive to the professional standards of an enthusiastic young naturalist, scrupulous about the rigour of the game, intolerant of vagueness and of any mixture of the romantic imagination with scietnific inquiry. . . . He therefore, in 1854, almost outdid the *Edinburgh Review* in the ferocity of his onslaught upon the layman who had ventured to put forward sweeping generalisations upon biological questions while capable of errors upon particular points which were palpable to every competent specialist.

Huxley refers to this review as "the only review I ever have had qualms of conscience about, on the grounds of needless savagery." Darwin more mildly described it as "rather hard on the poor author." Indeed, he confessed to a certain sympathy with the *Vestiges;* while Wallace, in 1845, expressed a very favourable opinion of the book, describing it as "an ingenious hypothesis, strongly supported by some striking facts and analogies."

The strongest testimony to the value of Chambers's work is that of Mr. A. W. Benn, who writes in *Modern England,* 1908, concerning the *Vestiges:*

> Hardly any advance has since been made on Chambers's general arguments, which at the time they appeared would have been accepted as convincing, but for theological truculence and scientific timidity. And Chambers himself only gave unity to thoughts already in wide circulation. . . . Chambers was not a scientific expert, nor altogether an original thinker; but he had studied scientific literature to better purpose than any professor. . . . The considerations that now recommend evolution to popular audiences are no other than those urged in the *Vestiges.*

Herbert Spencer

The next great name among the pre-Darwinian evolutionists is that of Herbert Spencer. About 1850 he wrote:

> The belief in organic evolution had taken deep root (in my mind), and drawn to itself a large amount of evidence—evidence not derived from numerous special instances, but derived from the general aspects of organic nature and from the necessity of accepting the hypothesis of evolution when the hypothesis of special creation had been rejected. The special creation belief had dropped out of any mind many years before, and I could not remain in a suspended state: acceptance of the only possible alternative was imperative.[11]

This suspended state, the *tätige Skepsis* of Goethe, was just what Huxley was enjoying; in his own words, "Reversing the apostolic precept to be all things to all men, I usually defended the tenability of received doctrines, when I had to do with the transmutationists; and stood up for the possibility of transmutation among the orthodox."

Thus, up to the date of the publication of the *Origin of Species,* scientific opinion was roughly divided into two opposing camps; on one side were the classic, orthodox, catastrophic, or creationist party, who believed in the fixity of species, and that each species was the result of special miraculous creation; on the other, the evolutionists or transmutationists, who rejected special creation, and held that all species were derived from other species, by some unknown law.

It was the formulation of this unknown law that makes 1859 an epoch in the history of anthropology.

Charles Darwin

Darwin's work may best be summed up in the words of his loyal and self-effacing co-worker, Alfred Russel Wallace:

> Before Darwin's work appeared the great majority of naturalists, and almost without exception the whole literary and scientific world, held firmly to the belief that species were realities, and had not been derived from other species by any process accessible to use . . . [but] by some totally unknown process so far removed from ordinary reproduction that it was usually spoken of as "special creation." . . . But now all this is changed. The whole scientific and literary world, even the whole educated public, accepts, as a matter of common knowledge, the origin of species from other allied species by the ordinary process of natural birth. The idea of special creation or any altogether exceptional mode of production is absolutely extinct. . . . And this vast, this totally unprecedented, change in public opinion has been the result of the work of one man, and was brought about in the short space of twenty years.

Huxley describes the attitude towards the theory in the year following the publication of the *Origin of Species:* "In the year 1860 there was nothing more volcanic, more shocking, more subversive of everything right and proper, than to put forward the proposition that, as far as physical organisation is concerned, there is less difference between man and the highest apes than there is between the highest apes and the lowest. . . . That question was not a pleasant one to handle." But the "horrible paradoxes of one generation became the commonplaces of schoolboys"; and the "startling proposition" of 1860 was, twenty years later, a "fact that no rational man could dispute."[12]

This question of the difference between man and the apes was embittered by the personal encounter between Huxley and Owen. Professor Owen, in 1857, stated that the *hippocampus minor,* which characterises the hind lobe in each hemisphere in the human brain, is peculiar to the genus *Homo*. This Huxley denied[13]; and, as neither disputant would acknowledge that he was mistaken, the question became "one of personal veracity."

As a possible explanation of this famous dispute, it is interesting to note the discovery announced by Professor D. J. Cunningham of the absence of this cavity on one side of the brain of an orang-outang, with the suggestion that Owen "may in the first instance have been misled by an abnormal brain of this kind."[14]

The further history of the development, expansion, and curtailment of the Darwinian theory as such lies beyond the scope of this little book. The criticisms of sexual selection and of the origin of the higher mental characters of man by Wallace; the denial of the inheritability of acquired characters by August Weismann and others; the orthogenesis theory of Theodore Eimer, the "mutation" theory of Hugo de Vries and Mendel's researches—all opened up lively controversies, and the field of science is still clouded with the smoke of their battles.

The ferment provoked by the publication of Darwin's *Origin of Species* profoundly affected, as was natural, the nascent science of anthropology. At the meeting of the British Association in Nottingham in 1866 Dr. James Hunt read an address before the Anthropological Department to show that "the recent application of Mr. Darwin's hypothesis of 'natural selection' to anthropology by some of Mr. Darwin's disciples is wholly unwarranted either by logic or by facts."[15] In this address he said that he still believed the deduction he had made three years previously—"that there is as good reason for classifying the negro as a distinct species from the European as there is for making the ass a distinct species from the zebra; and if, in classification, we take intelligence into consideration, there is a far greater difference between the negro and the European than between the gorilla and chimpanzee." He insisted that "anthropologists are bound to take the totality of the characteristics of the different types of man into consideration." "It is to be regretted, however," Dr. Hunt continues, "that there are many writers in Germany who have recently written as though the question of man's place in nature were settled"; but he is delighted to find that "Professor Carl Vogt is doing all he can to show the fallacy of the unity hypothesis." He quotes Professor Vogt as saying:

> This much is certain, that each of these anthropoid apes has its peculiar characters by which it approaches man. . . . If, in the different regions of the globe, anthropoid apes may issue from different stocks, we cannot see why these different stocks should be denied further development into the human type, and that only one stock should possess this privilege. The further we go back in history the greater is the contrast between individual types, the more opposed are the characters.

The controversies and discussions of this period were not confined to those who had technical knowledge or scientifically trained minds. All sorts of people joined in the fray, mainly because they fancied that the new ideas were subversive of "revealed religion"; but it would serve no useful purpose to recall the false statements and bitter expressions that were bandied about. Some had merely a sentimental objection to the doctrine of evolution; but at the present day most people would subscribe to the declaration of Broca, who wrote: "Quant à moi, je trouve plus de gloire à monter qu'à descendre et si j'admettais l'intervention des impressions sentimentales dans les sciences, je dirais que j'aimerais mieux être un singe perfectionné qu'un Adam dégénéré."[16]

The Negro's Place in Nature

Another controversy, which, though mainly political in origin, cleft the ranks of the anthropologists, arose from the slavery question. Clarkson had started his agitation for the abolition of the slave trade about 1782, and during the early years of the nineteenth century many unsuccessful attempts were made to bring the system to an end in America. In 1826 over a hundred anti-slavery societies were in existence, mainly in the middle belt of the States, while the Cotton States were equally unanimous and vehement in opposition. Feeling naturally ran high; riots, murders, lynchings, raids, and general lawlessness characterised the agitation on both sides, and added fuel to the flames which finally dissolved the Union in 1860. In England the question was hotly debated, and popular feeling was excited by the speeches of Clarkson and Wilberforce, and, most of all, by the publication of *Uncle Tom's Cabin* (1852). Being mainly a question of race, anthropology was soon implicated, monogenists and polygenists naturally ranked themselves on opposite sides, and the Ethnological Society became a strong partisan of the philanthropists and abolitionists.

In the midst of the excitement James Hunt, Honorary Fellow of the Ethnological Society and President of the newly formed Anthropological Society, read (1863) his paper on "The Negro's Place in Nature."[17] In this he carefully examined all the evidence on the subject, physical and psychical, and arrived at the conclusion that "the negro is intellectually inferior to the European, and that the analogies are far more numerous between the ape and negro than between the ape and the European"; moreover, that "the negro becomes more humanised when in his natural subordination to the European than under any other circumstances," "that the negro race can only be humanised and civilised by Europeans," and "that European civilisation is not suited to the negro's requirements or character." An abstract of the paper was read by Dr. Hunt at the meeting of the British Association at Newcastle, 1863, where the presence of an eloquent coloured speaker enlivened the subsequent discussion.[18] A tremendous outcry greeted the publication of this paper, and tightened the tension on the already strained relations between the two societies. Fierce denunciations from Exeter Hall and the "broad-brimmed school of philanthropists" were matched by equally vehement applause from the opposing camp. When Dr. Hunt died, a few years later, the following obituary notice, extracted from a New York paper, appeared in the *Anthropological Review*,[19] under the heading "Death of the Best Man in England":

> We are pained to hear of the death of Dr. James Hunt, beyond doubt the best, or at all events the most useful, man in England, if not, indeed, in Europe. The man that leads all other men in knowledge essential to human well-being, that thus extends the bounds of human happiness, and best illustrates the wisdom and beneficence of the Almighty Creator to His creatures, is, *per se* and of necessity, the best man of his generation; and such a man was the late Dr. James Hunt of England. . . . Dr. Hunt, in his own clear knowledge and brave enthusiasm, was doing more for humanity, for the welfare of mankind, and for the glory of God, than all the philosophers, humanitarians, philanthropists, statesmen, and, we may say, bishops and clergy of England together. . . . His death at the early age of thirty-six is a great loss to England, to Christendom, to all mankind; for, though there are many others labouring in the same great cause, especially in France and Germany, there was no European of this generation so clear and profound in the science of humanity as Dr. Hunt.

A serious discussion of the anatomical and psychological relation of the Negro to the European is still to the fore, especially in the United States of North America. But even as late as 1900 a book was published in America with the following title, and we have been informed that it has had a very large sale in the Southern States:

> THE NEGRO A BEAST; or, "IN THE IMAGE OF GOD." *The Reasoner of the Age, the Revelator of the Century! The Bible as it is! The Negro and His Relation to the Human Family!* The Negro a beast, but created with articulate speech, and hands, that he may be of service to his master—the White man. *The Negro not the Son of Ham,* neither can it be proven by the Bible, and the argument of the theologian who would claim such, melts to mist before the thunderous and convincing arguments of this masterful book. By Charles Carroll, who has spent fifteen years of his life and $20,000.00 in its compilation. Published by American Book and Bible House, St. Louis, Mo., 1900.

The publishers are "convinced that when this book is read . . . it will be to the minds of the American people like unto the voice of God from the clouds appealing unto Paul on his way to Damascus."

This preposterous book could appeal only to the ignorant and bigoted, and we mention it merely as an extreme instance of the difficulties against which science has sometimes to contend when dealing with burning social questions.

The latest word on this subject is by Professor F. Boas, who believes that the Negro in his physical and mental make-up is not similar to the European. "There is, however, no proof whatever that these differences signify any appreciable degree of inferiority of the negro . . . for these racial differences are much less than the range of variation found in either race considered by itself. . . . The anatomy of the American negro is not well known; and, notwithstanding the oft-repeated assertions regarding the hereditary inferiority of the mulatto, we know hardly anything on the subject."[20] The real problem in America is the mulatto, since "the conditions are such that the persistence of the pure negro type is practically impossible."

Notes

[1] Add. Brit. Ass., Dublin, 1878.

[2] Clodd, *Pioneers of Evolution,* quoting from White, *Warfare of Science with Theology.*

[3] *De Civitate Dei.*

[4] *Sketches on the History of Man,* 1774.

[5] See Topinard, 1878, p. 424.

[6] In an essay entitled "A Remarkable Anticipation of Modern Views on Evolution," Professor E. B. Poulton draws attention to the ideas expressed in the first and second editions of the *Researches,* by Prichard, "one of the most remarkable and clear-sighted of the predecessors of Darwin and Wallace. . . . It is an anomaly that such works as the *Vestiges* should attract attention, while Prichard's keen insight, sound judgment, and balanced reasoning on many aspects of organic evolution, and especially on the scope of heredity, should remain unknown." *Essays on Evolution,* 1908, pp. 175, 192.

[7] *Pop. Sci. Monthly,* 1909, p. 499.

[8] De Maillet and Robinet had already outlined part of the Lamarckian doctrine.

[9] Quoted from R. Knox, *Anth. Rev.*, i., 1863, p. 263.

[10] *Loc. cit.*

[11] Duncan, *Life and Letters of Herbert Spencer,* 1898, ii., p. 317.

[12] Add. Brit. Ass., 1878, Dublin.

[13] "It is not I who seek to base man's dignity upon his great toe, or to insinuate that we are lost if an ape has a *hippocampus minor.*"—*Anth. Rev.*, i., 113.

[14] Cunn. Mem., ii., R.I.A., p. 128.

[15] *Anth. Rev.*, iv., 320.

[16] *Mémoires d'Anthropologie,* iii., p. 146.

[17] *Mem. Anth.*, i., p. 1.

[18] *Anth. Rev.*, i., p. 386.

[19] January, 1870, p. 97.

[20] Franz Boas, "Race Problems in America," *Science,* N. S., xxix., p. 848, 1909.

27. Man and Culture: An Essay in Changing Anthropological Interpretation

Fred W. Voget

Introduction

This paper is an attempt at defining the shifting interpretations of man and culture from 19th century evolutionists to the present.[1] I have not tried to explain why anthropological views of man and culture have shifted, but have confined myself largely to exposition, content to show that when the interpretation of culture has changed, the explanation of man's relation to culture also has moved into line, and vice versa. Finally, I have endeavored to point out some of the significant implications which more recent developments hold for the future of anthropology and for an integrated science of man.

Since anthropology in its scientific aim has been committed to a cumulative unfolding of the human reality, it would be strange indeed if it did not demonstrate periodic shifts in its theoretical conceptions of that reality, defined traditionally as man and his cultural milieu. We might expect, too, that changes in the interpretation of culture would result in shifts in the view of how man relates to culture, and in the very nature of man himself. Anthropologists admittedly have avoided controversy in their own ranks over "man's fundamental nature" and they certainly have never tried to spell it out in detail. Yet, the issue of man's nature—how this primary datum may influence his cultural behavior and how in turn learned social behavior may modify basic nature—hovers in the background and intrudes upon every explanation of culture patterns and how culture changes. As anthropologists groped their way forward to a distinctive reality for their discipline, selecting *culture* as their proper focus and domain, some claimed to have settled the issue of human nature and culture, but more often the issue was dispersed in immediate engage-

From the *American Anthropologist*, vol. 62, no 6 (1960), pp. 943–965. Reprinted by permission of the American Anthropological Association.

ments, such as historicism, culturalism, and functionalism. But the relations of human psychology to learned social behavior are so vital and necessary to anthropological explanation that the problems involved reappeared over and over again. Moreover, the relation between socially learned behavior and human psychology tended to link anthropology firmly to psychology, stimulating a selective borrowing which influenced anthropological theory and method considerably before the rise of social interactionism and new linkages with sociology.

Psychogenic Evolutionism (1860 to 1900)

The so-called cultural evolutionists of the 19th century must be credited with the first conceptualization of man and culture that can be called anthropological. Their basic ideas stemmed from the philosophical rationalism of the 18th century *philosophes* and the scientific positivism of the early 19th century. The political theory of Locke (1956 [1690]), Rousseau (1926 [1762]), and Condorcet (1955 [1795]) carry basic assumptions that were to influence the later cultural evolutionists, including the idea that all men are alike essentially, that in their better natures men are reasoning beings and strive naturally to improve themselves and their conditions by acts of intellect and moral will.[2]

The approach of the evolutionists to man and his culture rested on four basic assumptions. First, they assumed that mankind was a part of nature, operating according to the laws of the universe. Second, they assumed that the natural laws governing development were unchanging through time as exemplified in the geological principle of uniformitarianism. Third, evolutionists accepted the idea that natural processes tended to move progressively from a simplicity to a complexity, from the unorganized to the organized, from something that was lesser to something that was better.[3] Fourth, in the evolutionist view, men throughout the world held similar potentials but differed basically from each other in a quantitative development of intelligence and experience.

When applied to mankind the principle of uniformitarianism committed the evolutionists to the idea that whatever governed man's cultural development in the past governs this development equally today (Tylor 1874, I:32–33; McLennan 1896:26; Spencer 1910, I:434). Further, since man's intelligence accounted for his distinctive quality in relation to the animal world and allowed him to create social institutions and culture, it followed that mankind everywhere shared a common psychic unity. If man in the primitive world differed from his civilized confreres, it was not because of any qualitative differences in his mind, but because in the civilized world man's mental potential, his intelligence, was cultivated and developed in greater degree. In any society a man's intelligence was a product of his experiences, exemplifying the degree to which his intellective faculty could emerge and thrive in that cultural milieu. Yet, as the evolutionists saw it, phylogenetically man's rationality followed an inevitable development, as if it were driven by some inner evolutionary and cosmic force. Men in primordial days, as contemporary savages were witness, began with a limited intelligence, and as mankind moved into the cultural stages of Barbarism and Civilization, the forces of passion and of appetite gave way in progressive steps to the force of reason. Everywhere the natural history of mankind could be described as the inevitable progression from Savagery through Barbarism to Civilization. The dynamic quality of mankind, the fundamental link with universal processes, must be sought in the processes of the human mind, which was never static, but which, ever emergent, moved progressively upward in competition with baser instincts (Bachhofen 1861; Tylor 1937 [1881], II:159–160; Hartland 1909, I:255–256).

From their writings it is clear that the evolution to which the 19th century theorists of man and culture committed themselves was basically psychogenic rather than cultural (Tylor 1874, I:68). Yet cultural forms were vital to the evolutionist position since they held the key to interpreting man's psychic development. From qualitative differences in their cultures it was evident that peoples throughout the world had to be viewed in different stages of mechanical, intellectual, and moral progress. By arranging the institutions of mankind along a mental coordinate—from the least to the most reasoned—a chronological chart of man's intellectual history could be plotted and "index" institutions could be assigned to natural stages, quite like the geological and life charts used by students of the earth and of life forms. Once this intellectual-historical chart was completed, an institution could be readily assigned to it and the intellectual and historical stage of a particular people could be marked accurately and their future progress plotted within predictable limits.

The assumption that illogical and reasonless customs belong to an earlier time, whereas customs in agreement with a measure of reason must be later, allowed the evolutionists to breathe historicity into customs which lay beyond written documents or the dated chronologies unearthed by archeologists. The "doctrine of survivals," as this conceptualization came to be called, was a necessary corollary to the basic assumptions of psychogenic evolution and psychic uniformitarianism (Tylor 1874, I:chpts. 3 and 4; Hodgen 1931; McLennan 1896:17). Now, with the use of analogues from cultures around the world, it would be possible to peel back layer after layer of the psycho-historic strata in man's progress until the very bedrock of man's intellectual beginnings had been reached. With the "doctrine of survivals" the evolutionists apparently were able to clinch their case for a psycho-cultural prehistory and to place their natural history of the mind on a firm scientific footing.

The commitment to a mind emergent also colored the entire evolutionist effort to describe and explain man in relation to his culture. The emphasis on reason did not deprive man of his feeling states. Affect, indeed, was a part of man's being, but it played a far more effective role in his past than in his present civilized state (Hartland 1909, I:255–256; Tylor 1874:30–31). Contemporary savages were more passionate and childlike, and the passage from childhood to adolescence and to adulthood provided an appropriate analogue for the stages of Savagery, Barbarism, and Civilization, each of which rested on a more comprehensive and logically arranged experience than the stage which preceded it. Savage and Civilized men were rational in essence and operated psychologically by laws of association, but in their savage experience primitive men were wont to mis-associate ideas and lacked the exacting technique of critical thinking which could free them from their erroneous associations. For all that, primitive men had achieved some signal triumphs through speculative reason both in technology and in the explanation of the world. In magic he even had attained a conception of causal determinism which was analogous to the determinism of scientific explanation (Frazer 1900, I:61). In the final analysis, man's progressive advances in the early stages, as they are now, derived from the speculative reasoning of "primitive philosophers" who lighted the way for the others. It followed that men, at least the intellective elite, were able to transcend the limitations of their cultural experiences and to advance the accumulation of knowledge which would lead to change and progress.

Since evolutionists had defined the essential process of reality in terms of thought, with man moving from unconscious to conscious processes, their natural history of man found little place for documented chronological history. For evolutionists the history of the events was submerged in the universal process, and while diffusion of forms and ideas was admitted, and also special adaptations to local environments, particulars such as these did not alter the general trend in independent institutional development. Historic events could be—and in practice tended to be—ignored in the interests of the broad comparative effort. So, too, the momentary historic regressions illustrated by the fall of empires were of secondary importance to the march along the road to progress and civilization. In the words of Morgan (1931 [1877]:179–180):

> Out of a few germs of thought, conceived in the early ages, have been evolved all the principal institutions of mankind. Beginning their growth in the period of savagery, fermenting through the period of barbarism, they have continued their advancement through the period of civilization. The evolution of these germs of thought has been guided by a natural logic which formed an essential attribute of the brain itself. So

unerringly has this principle performed its functions in all conditions of experience, and in all periods of time, that its results are uniform, coherent and traceable in their courses. These results alone will in time yield convincing proofs of the unity of origin of mankind. The mental history of the human race, which is revealed in institutions, inventions and discoveries, is presumptively the history of a single species, perpetuated through individuals, and developed through experience. Among the original germs of thought, which have exercised the most powerful influence upon the human mind, and upon human destiny, are those which relate to government, to the family, to language, to religion, and to property. They had a definite beginning far back in savagery, and a logical progress, but can have no final consummation, because they are still progressing, and must ever continue to progress.

Historical "Interactionism" (1900–1925)

The second view of man and culture appears at the century mark when Boas called for repudiation of "metaphysical" presuppositions that "prejudiced" the study of man and culture alike. In place of the psychogenic "history" of the evolutionists he demanded a verified "scientific history." The grand scheme of comparative reconstruction should be abandoned and attention directed to particulars, with the express purpose of seeing how unique events actually were connected in time and space. Perhaps there were laws of culture growth as the evolutionists asserted, but such laws would not be found in universal processes of the human mind. Rather, ". . . the psychological problem . . . [would be] contained in the results of the historical inquiry" (Boas 1940 [1896]:279) since one historic continuity after another could be cited to show how similar culture forms had originated "from unlike causes" (Boas 1887: 485–486). An antecedent cultural fact (i.e., historic event) best explained a succeeding cultural event, each of which was immersed in a complex milieu of biological and ecological factors.

In the new scientific view, the proper study of mankind should focus on specific cultures and their mutual interconnections and unique environmental adaptations in place of the philosophic study of culture-in-general. Obviously, anthropological data seldom presents the investigator with historically documented materials, but in the absence of precise documentation culture forms could be carefully plotted and analyzed to disclose probable connections—then, and only then, could culture forms be explained as independent inventions. Even independent inventions might not yield identical psychic processes which the evolutionists require. Before any form in one area could be equated in all respects with another form in another area and thus be accepted as a parallel form, rigorous analysis must prove that both products are not the result of independent yet convergent psychological processes, or that either or both have diffused from the same or different sources. Before this knowledge can be attained the history of the form must be known through documentation or must be constructed analytically by placing the forms within the context of their interacting culture universes (culture areas, continents, etc.), (see, e.g., Lowie 1916; Spier 1921; Goldenweiser 1910).

The new historical interactionist approach obviously introduced a new conceptualization of the man and culture reality. Causation was not immanent to a structure as the evolutionists had argued but lay outside the structure. A culture, for example, was not the product of internal processes so much as it was a consequence of interactive processes which involved one culture with another. The processes of culture growth were best described by terms like diffusion, adaptation, and interaction rather than by independent origin and parallelism, although these latter could not be wholly ruled out (Boas 1940 [1911]:297; Lowie 1912). As cultures came to be viewed in terms of the history of their forms they were considered to be complicated accumulations of traits and complexes rather than organized systems. And in their ethnographic accounts the historicists stuck to a simple topical coverage of a culture, following the "universal culture pattern" of Wissler (1923). They also were fond of specific and detailed studies of culture complexes, describing and analyzing forms in their temporal and spatial ranges, usually within a region which was homogeneous in geography and culture.

By very definition of the man and culture problem the historical approach to culture could not find much place for the study of cultures as systems nor for the individual as a structured personality. The individual, like the culture to which he belonged, was a product of a complex growth, varying from others (as his culture) by virtue of his unique biology and special (historical) experiences in society. Though subject to the conditions of his cultural environment, which imposed severe limitations on the range of individual choice and action, the person nevertheless interacted with his cultural environment, adapted it selectively, influenced it at times, and even transcended it in deviant ways (Radin 1927:184–185).

In the new historical view the individual was considered subject to habit in much of his daily behavior, despite the conception of the man and culture relationship as a complicated and subtle interaction, a mutual give and take between man and his cultural world. Habituation made for slow change and "cultural inertia was more evident in the change process than active efforts to move in new directions. Habit and feeling were as much a part of man's behavior in civilized as in primitive communities" (Boas 1924:218–219). In the beginning men had not lived in societies where rude appetite and blind instinct governed a limited rational faculty and later succeeded, in gradual stages, to a civilized society in which men enjoyed a state of rational autonomy, freed from the grosser components of the body, and free, too, of cultural habit. In contradiction to the thesis of the movement from unconscious feeling to conscious motivation in the upward march of civilization, the historicists were wont to point out analogies between primitive and civilized behaviors. Modern men had totemistic inclinations in naming fraternities and athletic clubs after animals, and, if primitives made use of talismans to protect themselves, civilized men had their "good luck" charms to tide themselves over dangerous situations. "There is a streak of logic as well as much irrationality in the make-up of the primitive mind; the same holds of the modern mind," wrote Goldenweiser (1933:185) in judging the two "minds."

The historicists, like the evolutionists, seemed to enunciate, "man is one," but they followed it quickly with "civilizations are many" (Goldenweiser 1922:14), since each culture is a product of a unique concatenation of historic events. Actually, the study of processes by the historicists was starting to bear fruit, for, in spite of their historical posture, they were beginning to see the man and culture relationship as a timeless "man-in-culture" process. Both primitive and civilized men thus were subject to the habituative and feeling processes in the cultural context. Perceptual discriminations and behaviors based on reasoning also were present in both primitive and civilized men, as a short glance at the practical knowledge and use of mechanical principles by men in any society would witness. The historicists in a sense were the harbingers of functionalism, but they did not understand it well, and, besides, they were too involved in the historic "accidental" processes to accept the structural (immanent) determinism which full-bodied functionalism implied.

The new scientific view of the man-in-culture process led empirical historicists to reject all efforts to define qualitative differences that would separate primitive from civilized men. There could be no "pre-logical" primitive mentality as Lucien Lévy-Bruhl (1910) argued in contradistinction to a "logical" civilized mentality; for, in the first place, such a distinction did not accord with behavioral process which individuals, civilized or not, revealed, and in the second place, the implied linear developmentalism violated known historic processes (Lowie 1937:220–221; Goldenweiser 1933:179–188).

Since men and their cultures were largely the result of "accidental" historic events and interactive adjustments, "scientific" historicism did not admit any kind of determinism. Man's behavior in any time and clime could not be viewed as biologically-determined, geographically-determined, not culturally-determined. The psychological instinctual determinism of a MacDougall was just as reprehensible as the geographical determinism of a Huntington or a Semple (Wissler 1926). Neither were the historicists willing to accept sociological conceptions of determinism such as the "group mind" or the "cake of custom." Radin (1957 [1927]: 36–39) took special pains to point out that man in the primitive world was a "personalist"—to the point almost of being an anarchist. While this view may be judged extreme, historicists nevertheless remained uncertain and ambivalent in the face of custom. Boas occasionally interspersed his theoretical ruminations with references to the way in which culture molded individual behavior, yet man, in his view, decidedly was not a culturally conditioned automaton. In the words of Goldenweiser (1933:26), man was not "a mere microcosm reproducing the cultural macrocosm."

Culturalism—Functionalism—Holism (1925–1940)

As American historical interactionists came to grips with the man-in-culture process some of them moved to a redefinition of culture and of the individual's relation to his "superorganic" milieu (Kroeber 1915, 1917; Lowie 1917; but cf. Sapir 1917). A part of the problem involved the distinction of culture as the proper field of study for anthropology, and both American and continental anthropologists attempted an evaluation and a discrimination of their discipline's dimensions from psychology and to an extent from sociology. This task of putting anthropology on its cultural feet, together with certain convergences in related fields, probably contributed to the inflated role now assigned to culture as a determinant of human behavior. More than this, culture was held to be an order of distinct reality, a "superorganic" in every way, "explainable only in terms of itself." The ethnologist, as Lowie (1917:66) wrote, must above all "account for a cultural fact by merging it in a group of cultural facts or by demonstrating some other cultural fact out of which it has developed."

The raising of culture from its complex interrelations with other dimensions of the human context to a special and distinct reality operating according to laws of its own being initiated the third view of culture and of the man-in-culture process. Now the individual had no real part in the cultural process and the anthropologist had as little need for psychological processes for explanation as Watsonian Behaviorism had for mind and consciousness. The new interpretation made the members of any society an effect of culture—a veritable image and distinct impression of the cultural process. Attention to culture meant little time for the individual, however, for the individual's behavioral processes were contained in the results of the cultural inquiry (Lowie 1948 [1924]:204). When the individual emerged, he did so only to typify the representative behavior found in a culture pattern.

The new posture assumed with regard to culture represented a further step in the direction of functionalism, since it implied a systemic quality to culture. However, none of those who initiated this step moved to this conclusion, since they still were in the grip of the previous interpretation which insisted that the basic reality of the anthropological science was historic. There was no marked effort to treat cultures as systems, and efforts of Kulturkreislehre to define "historic" culture-systems that diffused as units were roundly criticized. As Lowie (1948: 183–184) put it:

> . . . I prefer to practice the historical method by tracing the distribution in time and space of traits with sharply defined individuality and to establish sequences where the distribution is spatially continuous or rendered plausible by documentary evidence or at least by known ethnographic principles; and the establishment of more ambitious schemes strikes me as distinctly premature.

The new cultural-historical determinists relied on Behaviorism to supply the psychological underpinning of man-in-culture processes. The evidences of conditioning presented by Pavlov were accepted casually as quite congruent with the cultural process, whereas Freudian interpretations that called attention to the reactions of individuals to cultural processes generally were vigorously opposed or ignored (for an exception, see Sapir 1934, 1938; cf. Kroeber 1920, 1939).

Functionalism, as interpreted by Malinowski (1931, 1944) and Radcliffe-Brown (1922, 1935, 1952) broke the historic barrier imposed by the historicists and substituted the primacy of immanent structural processes for the accidental and unique (cf. Boas, 1940 [1930]:269). In the functionalist view, cultures were structured systems and their basic processes were largely maintenance operations. The systemic qualities of cultures and their processes then were more vital to anthropology than the tracing of historic connections and developments. Therefore, the basic processes of culture were not historic, but processes of internal and reciprocating connections. Functionalists would study the religious or political processes and their contributions to the on-goingness of the whole in the same manner as biological specialists might study the digestive processes and how these helped the organism to continue other important processes. As it developed, functionalism divided into two major streams, with Malinowski stressing the relation between common biological needs and culture, while Radcliffe-Brown emphasized the structured interconnections and maintenance processes of the social system.

Both the "biological" and "institutional" branches of functionalism renewed the question of human nature and the nature of human adjustment to the cultural milieu. For Malinowski, man's universal biological needs constituted the basic reality with which anthropologists should begin their study of man-in-culture. In the final analysis culture was no more than a very complicated instrument for the fulfillment of essential survival needs. However, in developing instrumental cultural behaviors in reference to basic needs, men in different societies built up secondary need-motivations connected to these instrumental cultural behaviors. The relation of secondary need-motivations (drives) to the primary survival drives inevitably involved psychological processes and Malinowski early launched himself into this area armed with psychoanalytic tools of interpretation. Thus, in *Sex and Repression in Savage Society* (1927:182–183) he writes:

> It will be my aim to show that the beginning of culture implies the repression of instincts, and that all the essential elements of the Oedipus complex or any other "complex" are necessary by-products in the process of the gradual formation of culture. . . .
>
> To this end I shall try to show that between the human parent and child under conditions of culture there must arise incestuous temptations which are not likely to occur in animal families governed by true instincts. I shall also establish that these temptations have to be met and ruthlessly repressed in mankind, since incest and organized family life are incompatible. Again, culture implies an education which cannot be carried on without coercive authority. This authority in human society is supplied within the family by the father, and the attitude between the father and son gives rise to suppressed hatred and other elements of the complex.

Obviously, need-oriented functionalism challenged the unique and accidental reality of the historicists and seated the basic human reality in man's psychological processes—right where the evolutionists had sought it in the first place. Man, in effect, was a culture-building creature because of the necessities of his inner structure, and culture was designed to sustain this structure in the face of external threats. As will be apparent, the human reality postulated by the functionalists was not the intellective and reformative complex of the evolutionists but a complex of interrelated feeling-states.

Thus, Radcliffe-Brown, in developing institutional functionalism, also engaged psychological problems and processes. However, within the theoretical context of social structure the important psychological operations both for the individual and for the group were derived from social interaction and role expectancies. The individual responded to the demands of the social organism and hardly at all to the primary need-drives which Malinowski considered the foundation for the cultural superstructure. For example, if Malinowski considered anxiety a common human response in the presence of insurmountable obstacles owing to inadequate knowledge and technique and explained the universal presence of magic as an effort to overcome anxiety and to reduce tension, Radcliffe-Brown was inclined to see anxiety arising from stresses accompanying social role performance, and to observe further that in some instances the "Psychological effect of the rite is to create in him a sense of insecurity or danger" (Radcliffe-Brown 1939:39, cited by Homans 1941:169).

Whatever differences Malinowski and Radcliffe-Brown may have had over the "ultimate" sources of the human cultural reality, they were in agreement on one thing—it was grounded in *sentiment.* All cultural behavior is charged and sustained by an emotional configuration. And from this affect base functionalists stepped off into the spacious and controversial domain of system and integration. Malinowski (1944:85–131) seems to have approached a culture system along a number of axes of sentiment, ultimate complex derivatives of the primary needs, which eventuated in the basic institutions. The structured wholeness of any culture then was more a mechanically-reciprocating connection of the parts than a configuration in the accepted sense, although Malinowski had the latter in sight also.

Radcliffe-Brown, on the other hand, saw people in any particular culture engrossed in a basic activity which had an unusual meaning for them, producing a basic configuration of feelings which recurred time and again in their daily routine. From the Andaman study (1922:277) he concluded:

> . . . by far the most important social activity is the getting of food, and it is in connection with food that the social sentiments are most frequently called into action, it is . . . appropriate that it should be through his relation to food that the child should be taught his relation to the society, and thus have those sentiments implanted in him or brought to the necessary degree of strength.

Thus, for the Andamanese, food-getting activities concentrated the sentiments and symbolic behaviors that brought integration to their culture and made the individual aware of his rights and obligations to others in his community. The social value of food also held the proper explanation for ritual abstentions from food and the program of instruction and transition to adulthood imposed upon each individual during adolescence (1922:278–279).

It is apparent that functionalists turned the anthropological stream in the direction of system and integration and laid the groundwork for describing and analyzing cultures as unified structures. Their focus on basic social and psychological processes contributed heavily to the climate of thinking that led to culture and personality studies. Among Americanists, Benedict (1930) signalized the new orientation with her article, "Psychological Types in the Cultures of the Southwest," followed by the analysis (1934) of Dobu, Kwakiutl, and Pueblo cultures in terms of their styles of life. During the same time Mead (1949 [1928]; 1953

[1930]) studied the process of childhood socialization in Samoa and Manus. In their studies both Benedict and Mead accepted an "original" nature for mankind, but considered this universal dimension "so subject to the [cultural] environmental influences that the only way to arrive at any conception of original nature is to study it as modified by different environmental conditions" (Mead 1953:165). For both, too, the "science of custom" (culture) provided the essential psychological understandings, since human behavior was largely conditioned and given direction by "unconscious [cultural] canons of choice" (Benedict:1950). In the homogeneous primitive society as well as in the heterogeneous urban society, culture appears as "a more or less consistent pattern of thought and action"—a unity greater than the sum of its parts (1950:42–43), and the individuals of these societies appear as mirror-copies—true cultured personalities. Culture measured not only the individual's normality, but his abnormality as well (Benedict 1934), and "most people . . . [were] shaped to the form of their culture because of the enormous malleability of their original endowment," temperament alone providing escape to individuality (Benedict 1950:234–235).

The systemic study of cultures, in terms of their institutional structurings and functions, implied and indeed asserted a tightness of fit between the individual and his culture. His sociopsychological processes were grounded in emotional configurations which were largely learned, habituated and automatic if not wholly conditioned and unconscious in their operations. Functionalists, holistic configurationists, and cultural-historical determinists alike were in agreement on this datum of the man-in-culture reality, although they each arrived at this conclusion by different routes. The need-oriented functionalism of Malinowski alone provided a base for individual escape from the culture-press, since these needs were found to be in opposition to most normative specifications. Reactive behaviors based on shared need-structurings thus would allow in theory considerable numbers of individuals to initiate deviant behaviors that might transcend the pattern requirements. However, after defining this position in his early works, Malinowski left it fallow and pursued his man and culture analyses through the study of "institutions."

Synthetic Interactionism and Complexity (1940 to present)

The period beginning with the mid-thirties and enduring to the present is marked by the appearance of outstanding trends and reappraisals in man-in-culture relationships. Developments in new fields, such as acculturation and applied anthropology, and the gradual penetration and acceptance of a tempered Freudian interpretation of personality processes, not only traced new ground but also brought accepted interpretations of man and culture under challenge. The new appraisal generally stressed the complexities of the human situation and of the need for exploring in depth the different dimensions of the human reality. There was also a growing realization that the concepts and techniques of any single social science were inadequate to the task, and that to be successful the attack on understanding and explaining human behavior must be a concerted and cooperative venture by all the social disciplines.

Reappraisals can be agonizing and seldom escape the controversial. The concept of culture which the historicists had labored to place at the focus of anthropology and so to distinguish it as a science began to be searched and was found wanting as an explanatory process for human action in society. The social and psychological cut which functionalism brought to anthropology seated process and reality in role expectancies and in sentiments (sociopsychological processes). At best functionalists admitted a selected aspect of culture to their reality as Murdock (1951) later was to point out. As a matter of fact, Chapple and Coon (1942) demonstrated that social interactionism did not need the concept of culture at all to describe and explain role interaction among members of a society. Wherever individual people were studied in the interactive field situation the concept of culture was found either too vague as an heuristic device (Bennett 1954) or too indeterminant in explaining individual variations in a relatively homogeneous milieu (Hart 1954).

Thus, as anthropologists focused increasingly on the particular—the individual—the stereotype of standardized cultural behavior was cast in doubt. In the hands of culture and personality students, also committed to a dynamic interaction (id-ego-superego), patterning took on the quality of emotional configurations that grew out of reactions to social situations structured in terms of dominance-submission, reward-punishment, frustration-aggression, and insecurity-security processes (Kardiner 1939; DuBois 1944; Honigmann 1954). The impact of culture upon personality no longer was conceived to be direct, a product of conditioned learning, but rather culture's effects were indirect, giving rise to "deutero-learnings" (Bateson 1947 [1942]) and other unanticipated consequences flowing from the way in which the learning situation was structured.

Part of the controversy during reappraisal involved the definition and redefinition of the concept of culture itself. For some, culture still remained "That complex whole [of] . . . knowledge, belief, art, morals, law, custom, and any other capabilities and habits acquired by man as a member of a society" (Tylor 1874, I:1). On the other hand, some prominent anthropologists were asserting that culture was best described as a system of "conventionalized understandings" that lay behind the manifest act (Redfield 1941:132). In this latter view culture would not include the products of man's organized efforts, the tools and furniture of his dwellings, for example, but would apply to man's ideas about what form they should take and how they should be valued and used. As Linton (1940:125–126) pointed out when discussing cultural change:

> . . . We talk glibly of the phenomena of cultural change and are prone to forget that such change consists, in the last analysis, of *changes in the attitudes and habits* of the individuals who compose a society. We do not know, and will not know until the psychologist tells us, how these changes are brought about. . . . As long as the anthropologist is content to describe and analyse cultural phenomena in static terms he can get along without the psychologist. As soon as he turns to dynamic studies he finds himself confronted with a series of problems which cannot be solved without him. (Italics supplied).

The same point was made by Kluckhohn (1943:219) when he observed that the most important contribution the anthropologist could make to the administrator lay in the knowledge that covert patterns of behavior (i.e., the psycho-affect or "unconscious canons of choice") changed but slowly and were retained frequently in the face of visible changes in behavioral form and artifact. In his discovery of an unchanging Ojibwa personality despite two centuries of acculturation, Hallowell (1946) seemingly contributed a striking confirmation of persistence in covert patterns.

Indeed, culture, like personality, had gone processual and psychological. However, the psychology of culture as Linton and Kluckhohn defined it in the early forties still rested on habit-conditioning. In 1943 (p. 230), for example, Linton observed that cultures usually are perpetuated "unconsciously and as a part of the normal processes of individual training and socialization." His definition of a nativistic movement as "any conscious, organized attempt on the part of a society's members to revive or perpetuate selected aspects of its culture" (1943:230) implied a position little different from that of the historicists who insisted on the primacy of prior cultural moments in determining the succeeding cultural moment. In short, the psychological redefinition of culture did not admit the predominance of reactive-constellations such as neo-Freudians insisted were at the background of cultural behavior. Culture patterns and cultures simply were not projections of psycho-affect states ("projective systems") ultimately derived from interpersonal relations in childhood and the basic discipline experiences, as Kardiner (1939, 1945) argued. Culture patterns still were transmitted learnings for the most part.

Nevertheless, there was a growing consensus that the fit between the individuals of any society and their culture was far looser than formerly assumed. Individuals were not conditioned automatons and neither were they simple reactive products of special childhood experiences, such as breastfeeding, swaddling, and toilet-discipline. Individuals in any society were partly this and something more: they were involved in reactive responses to the sociocultural milieu in which they found themselves and moved also to act out of inculcated feeling-states; but they also acted out of deliberation and made thoughtful as well as thought-provoking choices. Recognition of the role of individual leaders in change situations underscored the "particular bias which an individual . . . may give to a cultural event . . . [as a] result of his native ability and his own life history" (Erasmus 1952:54:176; cf. Barnett 1951; Spencer 1958:640–657; Voget 1950:53–63).

In these new assessments of the man-and-culture reality it is apparent that human nature was held to have universal qualities (Kluckhohn and Mowrer 1944). Part of these qualities were rooted in the biological processes and part in psychic potentialities associated with the ego processes of mastery or defense (e.g., Spiro 1954:28). While mankind shared the cognitive process, the basic axes of human response were grounded in emotional and largely unconscious operations (Kluckhohn, Murray, Schneider 1953:7–8). Man acted from bases which were better described by anxiety, hostility, compensation, and the like.

In the view that human action was moved largely by affect states to which the individual was habituated, a thread of continuity was maintained with prior anthropological assessments that man was not predominantly a deliberative actor. Thoughtful action more often followed than preceded the act, as myth rationalized and gave meaning to ritual. However, in giving primacy to affect states, and especially in the place accorded to reactive constellations, contemporary anthropologists carried themselves beyond the traditional anthropological view.

Changes in the conceptualization of how any culture was organized and integrated moved in step with the view that the individual could not be conceived as a tightly integrated mirror for culture (Kluckhohn et al 1953:31). Cultures might in some instances be configurated by a special ethos, but more often they were unified by interacting "themes" which demonstrated recurrent consistencies and inconsistencies. Opler (1945, 1946), who first summarized this new conceptualization, defined a theme as a postulate, expressed or implied, about the nature of the world and of man, of man's relation to man, and of the desirable and the undesirable. Individuals within a society operated with culture patterns that usually embodied these basic assumptions. Studies in the values-base of various cultures also supported the conclusion that cultures were more or less consistently oriented and organized, but not tightly integrated wholes (Goldschmidt 1951; Kluckhohn 1941; Vogt 1951). Moreover, if a value, as Kluckhohn (1952:395) defined it, represented a conceptualization, "explicit, or implicit, distinctive of an individual or characteristic of a group, of the desirable which influences the selection from available modes, means, and ends of action," it is apparent that judgment in human action is admitted and the individual no longer is conceived to be a habituated social unit or subject wholly to unconscious feeling states. The trend moved cautiously in the direction of Grace de Laguna's (1949: 380) assertion that:

> . . . Man's rationality is not a higher faculty added to, or imposed upon, his animal nature. On the contrary, it pervades his whole being and manifests itself in all that he does as well as in what he believes and thinks. Men may rationalize more often than they think objectively, but it is only because they are fundamentally rational beings that they are capable of rationalizing—or feel the need of it. Man is rational in all his acts and attitudes, however unreasonable these may be; he is rational also in his feelings and aspirations, in his unconscious desires and motivations as well as in his conscious purposes, and his rationality shows itself in the very symbolism of his dreams. Men could not act and feel as they do if they could not form concepts and make judgments, but neither could they make use of concepts and engage in the ideal activity of thinking if they had not developed their innate capacity for the "idealized" modes of behavior and feeling characteristic of human beings.

In short, man is a complex of rational-irrational processes (Spiro 1954:23; Barnett 1951:16).

The period of reappraisal also witnessed some advance in the analysis of the nature and structure of culture patterns. The convergent effects of these new developments added up to a loosening of the tightly-knit unity of cultures as previously conceived and limited the impact of culture on the individuals of the society. As Linton observed (1936: 272–274), some patterns are applicable to all, hence "universals," whereas others are "specialities," and still others no more than "alternatives" (cf. Kluckhohn 1941). Greater cognizance was taken of the fact that culture patterns were phrased in two modes, the ideal and the real, and in any society the behavior of individuals might or might not show a close approximation to the ideal specifications. In final analysis, culture patterns were seen to represent a consensus in the case of the ideal pattern and a statistical (modal) construct in the case of the real or behavioral pattern. The anthropological problem was to determine the range of variability and of concentration in any series of individual acts and then proceed to the determination of the modal construct (Linton 1945: 43–47). A statistical approach to patterning in culture of necessity meant that some individuals would not conform and variation and deviancy were expectable.

Studies of cultures in change likewise brought fresh support to efforts at redefining the man-and-culture reality. The contact of peoples of different cultures had always been given a front rank position in the historical interpretation of culture growth and spread. When the problem shifted from plotted culture-traits to specific cultures undergoing first-hand contact, the complexity of the process began to surface. Granted that acculturative situations (defined as persistent and pervasive contact events) were rather special situations, they nevertheless underscored the fact that the human reality is a complex of interacting processes. Cultural homogeneity gave way in the change process and personal conflicts indicated the importance of subjective factors for understanding what was happening. A state of normlessness (anomie) was described for certain individuals, as in the case of "detribalized" Africans (Thurnwald 1935) and "mixed blood" Indians (Barnett 1940). Thus, under conditions of disorganizing contact, individuals were described as virtually stripped of their sociocultural learnings and spurred to the fulfillment of ego-needs. At the same time it became evident that in breaking away from the traditional way of life, people were not at ease in an unpredictable milieu and strove to standardize their behaviors and so to stabilize their expectancies. But, in place of the minor modification of traditional complexes, as commonly interpreted by the historicists, it was now recognized that farreaching changes and reinterpretations of culture forms occurred in the acculturative process. Wallace (1956:265) is clearly emphatic in pointing out that "revitalistic movements" constitute "deliberate, organized, conscious efforts by members of a society to construct a more satisfying culture."

Popular movements aimed at renewing the social and cultural web to life do not always reveal special commitments to maintaining the traditional (Barnett 1957:141–142). Actually, some American Indian movements of reform strongly suggest that a relatively conscious effort is made to disengage the self from the traditional matrix and to bind the self to a sickness-badness—health-goodness configuration, which in turn is linked with the notion that people must change their sinful ways (Voget n.d.). Sanctified by special revelation, a prophet attracts the uneasy and disturbed who would change the self by changing the social and cultural system. Ego-needs thus are a firm part of any causal determinants that might be cited in such acculturative events. Popular efforts of this kind usually demonstrate accommodative and syncretistic processes, and the innovation that results combines forms, meanings, functions, and principles drawn from the traditional culture, the contemporary life, and basic values and patterns of the dominant culture which are beginning to find a wider acceptance (Barnett 1957:143; Voget 1956). There are pervasive and persuasive influences from a number of cultural sources, but no outright determinisms from a single culture source. True, as Barnett (1953:181) reminds, the innovation is "a creation only in the sense that it is a new combination" of "pre-existing components," but traditionally persistent and borrowed forms alike give ground in their original significances to new meanings, uses, and functions. The creative process in innovation thus "is a complex commingling of perception, cognition, recall, and affect" (Barnett 1953:81; cf., Wallace 1956:265).

Summary and Reflections

In our brief historical review, anthropological conceptualizations of the man and culture reality are suggested to be four: 1) psychogenic evolutionism, 2) historical interactionism, 3) culturalism-functionalism-holism, and, 4) synthetic interactionism. In those approaches that have preceded synthetic interactionism, anthropologists of somewhat differing theoretical bases have explored and interpreted the nature of the human reality according to their separate biases. In historical retrospect it can be argued that each measured but a portion of this reality—yet all have considered themselves "scientific."

Devastating criticisms can and have been leveled at each of these approaches, but in the overview, it is possible to see that each has contributed to the enrichment of anthropological awareness in problem, method, and reality. The anthropological reality-universe has been gradually broadened and deepened by the experiences derived from investigations within the narrower confines of evolutionism, historical interactionism, and culturalism, functionalism, and holism. At the moment it does not appear as if anthropologists are out of the woods by any means—they still have much exploring to do, but they now appear to have a firmer grasp on the *complexities of the human reality* and are in a much better position to define problems and to program their explanations. They seem, too, much better prepared to extend their efforts in cooperation with other disciplines. In what follows evidence for these statements is presented in summary fashion.

As a first consideration we can see that the emergence of "interactionism" as constituting the basic processes of the human reality, and as comprising reality itself, is a signal event in the development of anthropology. The interactive process must be considered in a broad way, to include interrelations that are stimulative, contributive, reciprocating, synthesizing, and reactive. Always implicit in the anthropological view, interactionism did not become a cornerstone of anthropological interpretation until the functionalist position became well-established after the thirties. What we see in retrospect is the gradual transference of the principle of interaction from one dimension of the man and culture reality to another until it becomes the most general principle for integrating and explaining human events.

The commitment to interactionism also is notable since it seeks to describe live situations in terms of their actional processes. There is a shift from the static description of special forms (e.g., culture traits and complexes) to the processes that have given rise to these forms, their persistences and changes.

Through process, explanation of the human event, rather than a cultural, "social," "geographical," or "historical," event, turns out to be the essential problem. Realization of this fact explains why some anthropologists gradually have concluded that the concept of culture is inadequate to explain the human reality. It gives context to Kluckhohn's (1951:xii) introductory remarks assessing Vogt's study of Navaho Veterans:

> Perhaps the greatest increment to theory consists in the careful dissection of the *intricate interdependence of personal, social, and cultural factors* in the acceptance or rejection of aspects of a foreign culture. *This examination would not have been possible within the framework of narrowly anthropological concepts.* (italics supplied)

Clarification of the scientific problem in terms of human events and associated processes means that reality is no longer fragmented, and indeed cannot be organized for purposes of explanation into variant hierarchies of autonomous realities. Reality for man is not in one instance biological, in another, geographical, or social, psychological, cultural, historical, functional, or evolutionary. Each event in the human reality rather is an interacting configuration of these several analytical components of reality (cf. Murdock 1954:28–29).

Acceptance of this basic datum (a unified interacting reality linked through time) is an achievement of no mean merit, simple as it may seem, for in attaining to a full awareness of the implications of this conclusion, anthropology has been strengthened in depth and anthropologists have undergone significant transformations. At the moment it is best to describe this acceptance as implicit and ambivalent, for in official publication there is a tendency to view reality as a fit subject for a rational division of scientific labor.

Consider, however, that with a unified reality-universe fully in mind there is no longer any need to discover a special autonomous reality peculiar to anthropology nor to debate whether it is cultural, historico-cultural, sociopsychological, functional, or evolutionary. (See e.g., Bidney 1944, 1946; Kroeber 1948; Lowie 1946; Radcliffe-Brown 1947, 1949; White 1945, 1949, 1959a, 1959b). There seems little necessity either for controversy to continue between anthropology and the other social sciences as to where scientific fences begin and end. To do so would only lead to a perpetuation of biased conceptions and interpretations like those of the blind men when observing and recording their impressions of the elephant.

For some a denial of the autonomy of culture as the unique and distinctive anthropological reality may prove a difficult adjustment since it would appear to be a denial of anthropology itself. However, in its very development anthropology demonstrates the necessity for a complex and interrelated interpretation oriented to a unified human universe rather than one based on a narrow and separate dimension. By holding to culture as the sole reality in the human universe, and by asserting its independence and primacy over the other dimensions, anthropologists actually may have denied themselves what they have held to be the goals of their science,—namely, to view man and his environment as a whole and to "search for a set of principles which governs man's physical and cultural development" (Beals and Hoijer 1959:6).

What then lies ahead? Must anthropology relinquish its own cultural image? In the short term probably not, but in the long-term the answer must be in the affirmative. *All disciplines focusing on man must reorient themselves and surrender something of their self-images.* Each of the humanistic and social disciplines in the past has made important contributions to the understanding of man, but to prolong their autonomy in the interest of *l'amour propre* would be an unjustified and wasteful self-deception in the light of our present understanding. Immediate and helpful cooperation among the several disciplines can lead the way, as it is now doing, but finally, cooperation also must give way to integration—to a social science in which anthropology, sociology, psychology, history, and the like are unified methodologies and not independent contributing specialities.

We may assume that the development of any integrated social science will come slowly, but at no previous time has the basis for this constructive step forward really existed. Today, convergences in the various disciplines are easy to detect, and each science reveals an enrichment that has followed contact and interaction with other fields. More significant, however, are the separate convergences upon the unified human reality, for it is on this common ground of experience that a unified social science can be constructed. Surely it is an oddly assorted and packaged reality which Gibson (1950:151, 152, cited by Hallowell 1954:216) describes when he deplores the inadequacy of theories of social learning and finally threatens:

> If the social psychologist does not formulate a theory of learning, the cultural anthropologist will have to do so—and also the psychiatrist, the clinician, the educator, and the student of child development.

A human reality that can be cut like a pie, according to the "scientific," bias, can hardly further the understanding of man in nature, society, and culture for very long.

Notes

[1] I wish to thank Robert C. Dailey, Professor of Anthropology, University of Toronto, for reading and criticizing this paper. Also, in the interests of publication, documentation in detail, with footnotes, has been abandoned in favor of documentation in illustration.

[2] The only confirmed dissenters to the idea of a reasoned progress at that time were demographers and economists like Malthus (1926 [1798]) and Ricardo (1933 [1817]), who, in the first instance, saw mankind constrained and directed by disproportions in rapid population and lagging productivity in food, and in the second by a disproportionate supply of labor in the face of a limited potential for expanding productivity.

[3] All of these ideas are implicit (sometimes parenthetically introduced) in the evolutionist writings, but only Spencer (1862) developed the evolutionary hypothesis in theoretical depth, grounding it in a movement from a simple unorganized unity to a complex integrated unity.

28. Retrospect and Prospect in History

Margaret Hodgen

The mind's fidelity to the old has left its mark on anthropology as well as on other fields of thought. Modern cultural investigation has taken up its abode in a mansion of organizing ideas already designed, built, and richly furnished with traditional assumptions more closely related to the early levels of Western theology and philosophy than to the data of human history. Nearly all the principles of inquiry employed by recent generations of scholars in Europe and elsewhere are of great age and authority. Were their genealogies consulted, it would become quickly apparent that their antecedents are to be found in the Judeo-Christian Scriptures, in the classics, or in the derivative Christian literature of the Middle Ages. Non-European folk have had no part in their formulation. Buddhist ideas, Muslim ideas, East Indian or Chinese ideas on cultural problems are unrepresented. Moreover, though European field workers, collectors of artifacts, and describers of the nonliterate cultures of the world have done admirable work, their strength has resided less in doctrinal inventiveness than in industrious observation. There have been few Galileos, Newtons, or Einsteins, in anthropology or sociology.

Unquestionably, these long-lived and prescriptive organizing ideas have often been a source of uneasiness to critical minds. Recent years have seen occasional debate over which among them are suited, in a modern European world, for the solution of problems stated in more or less modern terms. Evolutionary doctrine, for example, so long regarded as welcome theory for imposing order upon the array of the world's cultures, has been widely attacked by men such as Graebner, Koppers, Rivers, and others. Diffusionism and functionalism have produced competing schools, a sure sign that a satisfactory procedure in this realm has not yet been reached.

While drift and imitation have abounded during the last three hun-

From Margaret Hodgen, *Early Anthropology in the Sixteenth and Seventeenth Centuries*, © 1965. Reprinted by permission of the University of Pennsylvania Press, Philadelphia, Pennsylvania: pp. 478–501.

dred years, little methodological tension appeared until very late or after the middle of the nineteenth century. It was then that Sir Edward Burnett Tylor fought so successfully to repel a flurry of degenerationism as applied to savagery, which would have wrecked the logical foundations of current development or evolutionary theory—and this, be it noted, not by suggesting some drastically new principle, but by the revival of the seventeenth-century theory of "remainders" or "remnants" in the nineteenth-century terminological dress of "survivals."

Soon after this episode, so triumphant for the maintenance of the *status quo ante*, modernism in ethnology and related subjects became expressed either in the collection of "survivals" in the spirit of Lang or Frazer, William Graham Sumner or Carl Jung; or, with the assistance of "survivals" and similarities, the elaboration of differing hierarchical, developmental, or evolutionary series by Bachofen, Lewis Henry Morgan, Marx and Engels, Herbert Spencer, Sumner and Keller, and countless others, together with borrowings in adjoining fields by current idols such as Freud, Durkheim, and Veblen. "What has greatly influenced anthropology mainly to its damage," declared Alfred Kroeber out of his long experience, has not been Darwinism (actually a later arrival on the intellectual scene), "but the vague idea of evolution. . . . It became a common practice in social anthropology to 'explain' any part of human civilization by arranging its several forms in an evolutionary sequence . . . allowing each successive stage to flow spontaneously from the preceding . . . without cause. At bottom this logical procedure was astonishingly naïve."

No old problem known to sixteenth- or seventeenth-century ethnology, and no old solution, has been wholly abandoned or become obsolete. If not preserved in the very structure of the language, it has passed out of fashion for a while only to return, more acceptable than ever; or more often, a minor idea, split off from its source and refreshed with a new terminology, has temporarily been given the limelight. Whether actively followed, or respectfully laid on the shelf, theories of earlier anthropologists are often presented not as false starts based upon faulty logic or infirm conceptualization, but as "current" schools of thought among which many anthropologists prefer to maintain a tolerant eclecticism. Seldom are such theories subjected to anything more exacting than courteous re-examination or minor modification. If, from time to time, changes have occurred in teaching or research methods, these changes have been temporary, not the products of dramatically original thought. Regrettably, as Agnes Arber has pointed out, "the general intellectual atmosphere of any given moment has an effect" on the choice of problems of investigation and their solution "which is compulsive to a humiliating degree. . . ." Despite advances in biology, physics, and chemistry, students of man have seldom ventured beyond the conceptual schemes of previous generations. They have remained indifferent to the import of the history of ideas in their own fields of study, including its Europocentrism. Seldom, even by scholars of the most elevated philosophical and historical vision, have widely entertained and cherished principles been brought before the bar of conscious and rigorous judgment.

Should these old organizing principles, which seem already to have achieved immortality, be summarized again? Will still another brief statement clarify their influence upon the ethnological thought of the Enlightenment, of the Encyclopedists, and of the Scottish Moral Philosophers, to whom nineteenth- and twentieth-century social thought is so heavily indebted?

Well, whenever and wherever in Europe or around the Mediterranean the collection and description of the manners and customs of mankind have assumed considerable volume, or when new and astonishing types of human behavoir have been called to the attention of Europeans, there and then the arresting problem of cultural diversity, or some one of its subordinate problems, has emerged—not only for the Hebrews, the Greeks, and the Romans, not only for the amateur anthropologists of the sixteenth and seventeenth centuries, but also for the moderns. There and then, an ancient and unexamined European monogenism, an ineradicable belief in the one-time physical and cultural uniformity of mankind has raised the question of how that original uniformity became splintered into existing diversity. This question and its answer were of course traditional. Save for tradition, Scripture, and logic, there is not one scintilla of evidence that the original culture of mankind was ever either uniform or not uniform; or, if uniform, was ever dissevered into the array of existing cultures. Reliable historical evidence begins ages after the primordial uniformity assumed. Nevertheless, diversity is the problem which underlies and qualifies the statement of all other problems in modern anthropology. Old Testament embellishments may have been rejected along the way. The argument may have been almost entirely secularized. But the form of the problem and solution remains recognizably the same as in the Book of Genesis.

More than this, the so-called problem of similarities in its several expressions is both logically and historically dependent upon a prior acknowledgment of that diversity in culture which is believed to have supervened upon an original uniformity. No question having cultural similarities as its subject matter could have been framed at all in absence from an assumption of an anterior onset of diversity after an initial period of uniformity. The recent admirable attempts by such men as Boas, Sapir, and others, to arrive at cultural time sequences by importing a chronology into the undated and undatable distributions of nonliterate similarities share the same logical or traditional background. Their solutions are tied by many threads of argument to earlier solutions of the problem of differences; and in many cases these innovations in method are based upon an "age and area" theory known to and used by seventeenth-century scholars.

During the last four hundred years, from the sixteenth to the twentieth century, anthropological inquiry, as expressed in the Scripturally inspired problem of cultural differences, has formulated or inherited three major types of solutions, each sanctioned by age and authority. With varying degrees of emphasis these solutions have been found along old avenues of diffusionist doctrine, environmental doctrine, or in doctrines of cultural change framed in long banks of time, and enriched with copious illustrations (not proofs) culled from the files of history, or documented with similarities.

Doctrines of social change may in turn be divided into three categories. One, now out of favor but likely to recover its influence with the increasing popularity of cyclical theories of history, is degenerationism. A second, once widely held but now dismissed as a result of the secularization of thought, is providentialism. A third, the official doctrine not only of anthropology but of many other fields of social inquiry, appears under several designations. In its most general sense, it may be referred to simply as progressivism. By some it has been called developmentalism. More recently in the study of society and culture it has been known as social evolutionism. Whatever the differences in nomenclature, however, this theory is to be noted, first, for its dependence upon earlier hierarchical notions of arrangement; and second, upon its inflexible Europocentrism, which has consistently belittled the mentality of the aborigine by installing him at the bottom of some scale of being. As Tylor once said almost a hundred years ago, the educated world of Europe and America has practically settled the matter "by placing its own nations at one end of the social series, and the savage tribes at the other, arranging the rest of mankind between these limits according as they correspond more closely to savage or cultural life."

Obviously, these three theories of cultural change, including evolutionism, have never been more than hypotheses—verbal or conceptual descriptions of purported processes, involving value judgments among peoples and periods of history. And hypotheses they must remain. We have the word of many fine scholars that for them no scrap of confirmatory evidence was, is, or can be forthcoming. From the standpoint of scientific method, the intrusion of moral or ethical judgments into the making of hypotheses renders proof illusory. This scientific blunder has been pointed out again and again with reference to progressionist, developmental, and evolutionary social doctrines. Nevertheless, "proofs" are still tendered, and always take one form: the form of appeals to hierarchical arrangements of cultures, logically rather than historically arrived at. There have been countless constructions and varieties of unilinear cultural series, each differing from all others except in basic model and basic assumptions, and none subject to scientific corroboration. Nor are the diffusionists exempt from the same criticism. Even when the criteria for the historical interpretation of their geographical distributions of traits bear inspection, they have seldom made the transition from the contemplation of these to a general theory of change without resorting to the same errors. They, too, often fall back upon an unverifiable evolutionism inherited from their forefathers.

Meanwhile, certain eighteenth- and nineteenth-century scholars succeeded with considerable adroitness in "harmonizing" these hierarchical, developmental, or evolutionary theories, so ignoring incongruities and expanding "testimonies" collected from Old and New World materials, so modernizing superficial terminologies, as to make old principles appear to be newly minted by original minds. Here one thinks of Voltaire during the French Enlightenment; of Adam Smith, Adam Ferguson, and other Scots; of Herder during the *Aufklärung*, of Engels and Marx in the mid-nineteenth century, and of Veblen in the twentieth. But apart from substituting the idea of progress for that of providence, or using the term development or evolution in place of progress; apart from the important amendment of diffusionist doctrine by the acculturationists, apart from a determined effort to collect and describe the existing customs of existing nonliterate peoples of the world, recent centuries have witnessed little that warrants the title of theoretical innovation.

Lest the above indictment appear too severe, let us review the ethnological work of a few major figures in the eighteenth century, especially those who have exerted a profound influence upon their successors in the nineteenth and twentieth. In partial extenuation of the modern championship of the intellectually old and doubtful, let it be conceded that no investigator can undertake an inquiry *de novo*. He must have somewhere to start in his thinking. Nor can any inquirer lavish all of his working hours on the intricacies of methodological debate. On grounds such as these, organizing principles were, after all, no less necessary to the Enlightenment and to the scientific endeavors of the following two centuries than they were to the Age of Faith. The only question is, what principles were used, those that were old and fallible or those which were new and promising?

Though eighteenth-century thought has often been praised for its skepticism, or for its unwillingness to accept any theory based on Scriptural premises, the ethnology of the period was characterized by the consolidation of old solutions: first, by the environmentalists; second, by some of the diffusionists; and third, by the developmentalists or evolutionists. All of these carried with them to a greater or lesser degree the more imaginative glosses of the Old Testament commentators.

Among the environmentalists of the Enlightenment, the ancient explanation of cultural differences, revived by Bodin during the Renaissance as an alternative to Biblical diffusionism, was again called into service by Sir William Temple in the field of literary criticism, and was soon extended into other fields of social inquiry. Dating back, as a commonplace, to Plato, Aristotle, Hippocrates, Strabo, and Vitruvius, it appeared again in Temple's essay *Of poetry* (1690), to account for the alleged superiority of English comedy. By this critic, the British propensity for humor was explained as the result of the variability of the island climate, the native plenty of British soil, the ease of the King's government, and the liberty of his subjects to profess divergent opinions and factions. Plenty begets wantonness and pride, and wantonness, said Sir William, "is apt to invent and pride scorns to imitate. Liberty begets stomach or heart, and stomach will not be constrained. Thus we have more originals. . . ."

Not long afterwards the Abbé Dubos expressed similar views, and so did Thomas Blackwell, the Greek scholar. According to the Abbé's *Reflexions critiques sur la poésie et sur la peinture,* published in 1719, natural influences controlled the development of the human spirit, either by encouraging or by retarding its expression. According to Blackwell, in his *Enquiry into the life and writings of Homer* (1735), the climate of Asia Minor was one of the favorable environmental features operating to produce the supreme genius of the great epic poet. A few years later, in 1748, the same general theory was given a broader application by Montesquieu in his *Spirit of the laws.* In the discussion of law in its relation to external nature and slavery, servitude, civil or domestic, was said to depend upon climate or soil. "We ought not then to be astonished that the effeminacy of the people in hot climates has almost always rendered them slaves; and that the bravery of those in cold climates has enabled them to maintain their liberties." The goodness of the land in any country, it was said in the latter connection, "naturally establishes subjection and dependence. . . . Thus monarchy is more frequently found in fruitful countries, and a republican government in those which are not so. . . ."

Similar ideas, accompanied with great collections of "proofs," or rather illustrations, were later advanced in every field of social investigation, including ethnology, throughout the nineteenth and twentieth centuries. The materials are massive and persuasive. But the critical literature is also well developed. Consequently, he who seeks in these latter days to gain acceptance for a theory of the geographical determinism of culture has a hard road to travel.

Among those committed to the revival of diffusionism during the Enlightenment, David Hume must be mentioned. Always skeptical of the purported high correlation between the manners of men and their external surroundings, Hume leaned heavily on the efficacy of contact among peoples as an explanation of differences. In his *Essay of national charac-*

ters, published in 1741, several years before the monumental *Spirit of the laws,* his readers were reminded that there were substantial faults in the environmental explanation of human behavior, that there were moral as well as physical antecedents to the appearance of cultural diversity. With reference to those said to be physical, Hume found reason to doubt the universality of their operation. The Greeks and Romans were charged with having mistakenly "confined genius and fine understanding to the more southern climates," whereas Hume took pride in pointing out that his own northern home had produced "as great men, either for action or learning," as the classical empires. Moreover, and this was a formidable obstacle to simonpure environmentalism, it could no longer be denied that while geographical stations remained unmodified, the manners of peoples could change "very considerably from age to age." Was this due to concomitant changes in climate, as some environmentalists wished to insist, or to changes in government and the intermixture of peoples? Hume leaned toward the latter, in effect sending his readers back to one of the theses of Moses. From this Scripturally descended theory of Hume's only the corollary of the degeneration of diffused traits was omitted, the origianl terminology and illustrations being altered. Ararat was no longer considered the center of the effective dispersion. Students were no longer urged to regard movement away from some tribal hearthside as a first step in cultural corruption. On the contrary, "if we run over the globe," said this historian and philosopher, "or revolve the annals of history, we shall discover everywhere signs of sympathy and contagion in manners, none of the influence of air or climate."

Inspired in part by Hume, the theory of diffusion has since been granted a ready hearing among ethnographers, though occasional details in their thinking have more than once suggested the pervasive spell of the evolutionists. Here, for one we may recall Tylor, who tried so hard during his young manhood to deal even-handedly with both bypotheses. Also to be remembered, in the nineteenth and twentieth centuries, are men such as Graebner, Father Schmidt, Koppers, Wissler, Rivers, Elliot Smith, and Perry. Little need be said here to distinguish among their several views, but it may be observed that the theories of the English diffusionists Smith and Perry exhibit in their extreme pan-Egyptianism how any hypothesis of migration from a single center (derivable ultimately from the Mosaic model), can be done to death. The members of the Kulturkreise School, historically trained and historically oriented, are important examples of a more promising treatment.

To some writers, the third theory of cultural change—progressionism, developmentalism or evolutionism—has seemed to emerge, unheralded and without precusory intimations, in eighteenth-century thought as something radically new and different from anything that had gone before. For this reason the men of the Enlightenment have often been fulsomely acclaimed. The late Ernst Cassirer was one who held them in exaggerated esteem. Through the philosophes, he declared, European thought sought hitherto unknown goals; it confronted the world with the fresh joy of courage and discovery, "daily expecting new revelations." A similar tribute has also been paid to the Scots across the Channel. As philosophers, they have been designated as the "founders" of that empirical study of mankind which made economic, social, and institutional relationships definitive fields of inquiry with respect to the operation of natural and moral law. In short, the Enlightenment is often regarded as an extraordinary age in which Nature's laws were first fully explained by the New Philosophy.

But what justification exists for celebrating the accomplishments of this period of Western thought, when, as Basil Willey has it, "biology had as yet revealed no disturbing ancestries, and man was still unassailed by anthropology and psychoanalysis"? How judicious is an evaluation of an era which describes it "as the silver age of the European Renaissance," when "sanity, culture, and civilization had revived; and at last across the vast gulf of the monkish and deluded past, one could salute the ancients from an eminence perhaps as lofty as their own"? Certainly, so far as ethnology was concerned, little that was noteworthy or original was accomplished. Praise of the Enlightenment, if grounded upon purportedly new insights into the manners of man, overlooks the persistent and uncritical use by still another company of learned men of the same old body of doctrine, the same old organizing ideas and principles.

Canon Raven has intimated that the French Encyclopedists were pretty dull fellows, whose best could never be anything more than an imitation of their predecessors. Be that as it may, all scholars at the time, other than the diffusionists, relied upon hierarchical presuppositions known since the Middle Ages. As gifted propagandists, they were engrossed in the exposition and extension of this central organizing doctrine. Professor Cassirer and other uninhibited admirers of the Enlightenment are at least in partial error. They have failed utterly to mark the dependence of their idols upon seventeenth-century ideas of which they were not the authors but the purveyors. Like many an earlier thinker who turned to an unmodified analogy with periods of organic rise and decline, these newer men fell under the influence of progressionism. They either sheared off the declining arm of the cultural cycle, replacing it with an ascending one; or, by underestimating the evidences of human corruption, they allowed this element in an older envisagement of cultural change to go by default. When this was done, Dr. Petty's earlier seventeenth-century view of the place of the savage in the chain of being was readily adoptable.

Logically speaking, if an eighteenth-century progressive or developmental sequence of cultural stages was to withstand criticism, then the theory of Adamic innocence and subsequent degradation, and the classical theory of the noble savage, would have had to be abandoned as acceptable conceptions of human beginnings. It is notable that all of this had already been accomplished before the Encyclopedists or their Scottish colleagues, were born. Neither Purchas in 1613, nor Heylyn in 1620, cherished any admiration for savagery. But both spoke of the natives of America, Africa, and the South Seas as examples of "originall mankind," "naturals," or "first men." Another early and even bolder advocate of the same position was Thomas Hobbes. It was his opinion in 1651 that European mankind had passed from a pre-political to a political condition. Nothing was said in the *Leviathan* about a Fall, recurrent degenerations, or recurrent historical cycles. Humanity had started at the bottom, and the bottom was a brutish condition of *bellum omnium contra omnes,* like that reportedly existing in savage America. Hobbes's influence upon subsequent thought was immense.

To observe the impact of seventeenth-century or earlier ideas upon the supposedly original but actually imitative scholarship of the early Enlightenment, the reader may turn among others, to the jurist Von Pufendorf (1632–1694), the satirist Bernard Mandeville (1670?–1733), the Jesuit missionary Père Lafitau (1670–1746), the statesman Turgot (1727–1781), the historian-philosopher Vico (1694–1724), and to Goguet (1716-1757) and de Brosses (1709–1777). To observe the borrowings of the men of the later Enlightenment from these same sources the reader may refer among the Encyclopedists to Voltaire (1694–1778) and Condorcet (1743–1794); among the Scottish moral philosophers, to Dugald Stewart (1753–1828), Adam Smith (1723–1790), Adam Ferguson (1723–1816), the putative founder of sociology, and Lord Kames (1696–1782); among the Germans, to Kant (1723–1808) and Herder (1744–1803), and many others.

Leaning markedly upon Hobbes, Samuel von Pufendorf in *De jure naturae et gentium* (1672) was one of the more famous seventeenth-century scholars, who asserted that the condition of men in a presocial, savage condition had been deplorable until societies "had been set on foot." With a few notable exceptions this was the common view. "All nations," said Bernard Mandeville in 1714, "must have had mean beginnings." Charles de Brosses in his *Du culte de dieux fétiches* (1760) set forth the theory that fetishism, as exemplified by the West African Negroes, was the fundamental and earliest form of religious worship. This doctrine was not only widely disseminated but became, in the thirties of the nineteenth century the slender "factual" foundation of Auguste Comte's primary, fetishistic, or theological stage in the development of society. As early as 1724 in the Jesuit *Relations* Pére Lafitau testified to the prevalence of the same view of savagery among the clergy. Many of the missionaries who had written upon the manners of their charges had described them as devoid of religion, law, or any form of government. This description, declared Lafitau, was false, if it meant that they were also beasts. His object was to demonstrate that they were merely early and barbarous.

But logic is ever a frail reed against tradition, especially tradition as embedded in Scripture. Though an hierarchical and progressive plan might be wholly acceptable to a collector faced with the simple spatial problem of arranging items on cabinet shelves, it was not quite so easy to accept in a temporal or historical version. The introduction of the existing savage as the first member of a series assumed to be ever advancing toward perfection was not in accord with the events of the Adamic period, the expulsion from Eden, and the onset of corruption. Accordingly, throughout the eighteenth century, when the idea of progress seemed to threaten the authority of other organizing ideas, there were frequent and tortuous efforts both to accept it and at the same time to reject it; to appear secular in secular company, but Scripturally orthodox as occasion seemed to demand. Turgot's was one of these. Disinclined in his *Discourse* at the Sorbonne to question the historicity of the Book of Genesis, he avoided that pitfall by skipping the first few chapters, and taking up the Mosaic story only after the Fall, or at the time of the dispersion after the Deluge. For him, as for others, these older and Biblical conceptions were still to be reckoned with, but sometimes by compromise or suppression. Vico chose suppression, excluding all disturbing Hebrew materials from theoretical consideration in his theory of change. Goguet was less drastic. Not unlike Turgot, he chose compromise, admittng to argument only that part of the account in Genesis which dealt with post-Adamic, post-Deluge events susceptible to a progressionist interpretation.

The *Nuove scienza* (1725) of Giambattista Vico (1668–1744) is very instructive both as an illustration of the problem of handling Biblical tradition and as an essay in the secularization of hierarchical ideas. Essentially a philosophy of history—"an ideal eternal history traversed in time by the histories of all nations"—it stands today as an early and notable attempt to arrive at a statement of a universal historical process by the winnowing of the common in human experience from that which is nonrecurrent and irrelevant. Vico also made a somewhat important departure from the historiographical habits of fellow historians. Adopting the position that the historical process was one whereby human beings built up relatively permanent systems of behavior, called social institutions, he made these institutional systems, rather than the flashy careers of princes and potentates, the subject matter of his inquiry. How had the law, marriage, government, and language, in all their diverse forms, come to be as they were? This was his central question. By virtue of concentrating his attention upon these institutional entities; by trying to form a clear idea of what was actually involved in what he regarded as the historical method; by extending his investigations backward into remote and remoter times; and by comparing histories or periods of history, he became convinced that the sequence of cultural epochs in all historical areas, the destinies of social institutions in all areas, exhibited a similar character and a similar temporal order. "Our New Science," he declared, "must be a history of the form of order," universal and eternal, and bound together by a chain of causes. His science of history was thus "far removed from history itself." The series of social forms possessed for him attenuated but familiar and unavoidable hierarchical and progressive implications.

Incidentally, Vico was conspicuous among the very few students of the cultural hierarchy who ever attempted to recover, not only social origins, but all the members of the developmental series. In so doing he became an advocate of the old-fashioned triadic division of the cultural past, an economical procedure frequently used, and later embodied in Augusts Comte's *Cours,* by which it was transmitted to twentieth-century sociology. But in his *New science,* the rule of three was sometimes carried to ludicrous extremes. It was impressed upon every possible sequence, and upon some that were impossible. "The nations," Vico declared, "will be seen to develop . . . through three kinds of natures. From these natures arise three kinds of customs; and in virtue of these customs three kinds of natural laws of nations are observed; and in consequence of these laws three kinds of civil states or commonwealths are established. And in order that men, having reached the stage of human society, may . . . communicate with each other . . . three kinds of languages and as many characters are formed; and in order that they may on the other hand justify them, three kinds of jurisprudence assisted by three kinds of authority and three kinds of reason in as many judgements." According to the Italian philosopher-historian, there were three poetic characters in Greek mythology, Vulcan, Mars, and Venus; there were three ages of poets before Homer; and fathers could sell their children three times. Not content with this, he preserved the three-fold symmetry of his plan of organization throughout every step of his analysis. A classifier of historico-cultural data rather than a narrative political historian, he observed "that all nations, barbarous as well as civilized, though separately founded because remote from one another in time and space, keep these three human customs: all have some religion, all contract solemn marriages, all bury their dead." A broad law of nations, proceeding through three stages, governed aristocratic commonwealths, popular commonwealths, and monarchies alike.

Of more substantive interest, especially since Vico emphasized the problem of the reconstruction of the earliest and most obscure period of human temporal experience (or the first member of his triads), was his advocacy of what he misconceived as a new form of documentation, the place he allotted in his many three-stage sequences to ancient and existing savagery, and the theoretical relationship thus suggested between savagery, early European man, and the acceptance of progressionist doctrine. Indeed, some of Vico's supposed originality arose from his familiarity with classical literature, and the free use that he made of it, in conjunction with materials on savagery, to illuminate a supposedly primordial condition of culture. As a student of philology and religion, he was sensitively aware of the documentary potentialities of language and myth. The vulgar tongues of European rustics, created in a remote past before refinements had been imposed, were freighted, in his judgment, with potential evidence of what that past had been like. By using philological procedures, especially by examining the speech of country people or the folk, he proposed to recover the kind of life led by all peoples when the world was young, or when the peoples were first forming their languages. The same was true of myth. Mythologies were the civil histories of the first nations. Composed by natural poets, they presented in fragmentary outline the political structures of early societies.

After this, however, Vico adopted a more familiar method. Though it might well be true that whenever men found it difficult to form an idea of ancient and unknown things they judged them by what was familiar and near at hand, that procedure, he felt sure, should be checked with "fact." Hence it is that we find this Italian historian proceeding in the opening decades of the Enlightenment, in a manner already made familiar as early as the sixteenth century. For purposes of proof or documentation, comparisons were made, first, between the early institutional forms recovered or documented by means of language or myth, and with the practices of European tribalism as reported by Caesar, Tacitus, and Procopius; then, second, with the behavior of existing savages, as observed in the Americas by Lescarbot, Oviedo, and Acosta, in Guinea by Van Linshooten, in Siam by Joost Shouten, and in Virginia by Harriot. Over and over again it was said that the rude and simple nations "help us to a much better understanding of the founders of the gentile world." The common, if erroneous, assumption that savages were culturally identical at all times and in all places, was again put to work. For, said Vico, the first of all men, like his nonliterate contemporaries, did their thinking under the "strong impulsion of violent passions, as beasts do"; and we, of the modern European present, possessors now of humane and refined natures, are descendants of the same kind of wild and bloodthirsty creatures.

Biblical history meanwhile was a source of acute embarrassment to Vico. It could neither be woven logically into his secular historico-philosophical system, nor be comfortably left out. In the end, therefore, although there is some treatment of some of the episodes narrated in

Genesis, although in piety he lost no opportunity to adduce proofs from gentile sources of the reliability of Jewish historians, the whole early Hebrew period, together with the irreconcilable episode of the degeneration of Adamic man, was more or less reverently set on one side as irrelevant to generalizations concerning the progressiveness of the remainder of human history. Jewish historical experience, as the outcome of the direct intervention of God, could not be regarded as subject to the laws of secular history, or so Vico made himself believe. Its course was unique. Harmony between the historically sacred and the historically profane was achievable, but only by giving to each a respected place of its own.

As for Vico's role among the progressionists of the eighteenth century, some commentators will have it that he was an adherent of the theory of historical cycles—a claim which can be supported by isolated sentences here and there. In accordance with this theory, it must be acknowledged that for him, as a classifier rather than a narrator of history, certain periods had a general character and an order of appearance which was repeated from place to place and time to time. But decline, that element usually inseparable from cyclical theory, was never stressed. The cyclical movement in the *Nuova scienza,* as Collingwood says, was never a mere rotation; it was a spiral. History never fatuously repeated itself. It was always creating novelties. It came around to each new phase in a form different from any that had appeared before. Hence Vico was a progressionist.

Another eighteenth-century figure, whose work provides an illuminating example of the conflict between the tormented conscience of the believer and the secular philosopher of history, is the French jurist and historian Antoine Yves Goguet (1716–1758). Far less original than Vico's *Nuova scienza,* indeed a potboiler by comparison, this work published a quarter of a century later, in 1758, was described as "un des bons écrits du temps . . . plein d'érudition, de recherches, et d'une critique aussi judicieuse que profonde." Actually commonplace, but widely read and translated, it may be taken as even more instructive concerning the general level of educated European opinion at this time than its Italian predecessor.

Goguet states frankly in his preface that he is interested in recovering the earliest condition of human beings, and in this only. He is one among many scholars who, believing in progressionism, and admitting the desirability of demonstrating it with the reconstruction of the whole progressive series, nevertheless restricted his attention to social origins. The book is entitled *The origin of laws, arts, and sciences, and their progress among the ancient nations,* and is completely orthodox in that it made no effort, such as was made in Vico's work, to exclude Hebrew or Biblical history. Goguet merely insisted with a straight face that since

Moses had chosen to inform posterity only of those grander events which it seemed necessary for mankind to know, and had suppressed all others, "which would have served only to gratify an idle curiosity," he had included too little in Genesis to justify a modern reference to the Adamic or antediluvian period. The book starts, therefore, with the days just following the Flood, "as in some sort the first age and infancy of the world," and proceeds to a consideration of life and knowledge among the ancient historical peoples: the Hebrews, first, the Babylonians, the Assyrians, the Medes, Lydians, Phoenicians, Egyptians, Greeks, and finally the Romans. This constituted for Goguet a progressionist study of origins. All the discoveries made by these peoples "belong entirely to the ages included in this work"; and these discoveries "undoubtedly comprehend the origin of laws, arts, sciences and their first improvements."

Concerning the adequacy of the documentation of the postdiluvian period of social origins, Goguet felt no misgivings. Mankind, he said, is not "condemned to the hard necessity of fluctuating in perpetual doubt, about the principal facts which have been transmitted to us by history and tradition. The most important events, such as the formation of nations, the origins of laws, arts, and sciences, are known." Faithful, therefore, to the common practice, he availed himself of the customary kind of "evidence." When he found himself destitute of hard, dated facts and historical monuments, he turned without hesitation to what had been said by ancient and modern writers on the manners of savage nations. These, too, were "ancient" in the historiographical sense he wished to employ. Like others before him in the sixteenth and seventeenth centuries, or while the earlier explorations to the New World were under way, Goguet felt sure that these descriptive materials could be made to contribute clear and just ideas of the state of the first wandering colonies of the Noachidae, immediately after the confusion of tongues and the dispersion of families. He regarded narratives concerning the American Indians as extremely valuable. We may judge the state of the ancient world, he said, "by the condition of the greatest part of the New World when it was first discovered." He often compared the reports of modern travelers with those of ancient historians, "and mingled their narratives." Like Vico and others both before and since, he declared that they mutually supported one another. They laid a solid foundation for everything he had to say concerning social origins and the progress of the human understanding.

From the second half of the eighteenth century, and well into the nineteenth and twentieth, the same objectives prevailed, except for occasional examinations by way of environmentalism or diffusionism. That half-century was once again a period of reliance upon hierarchical and related ideas, as well as one of secularization. As a result, Genesis, with its accounts of the Creation, the Fall, and the Deluge, was rejected out of hand. Nevertheless, anthropological thought continued to take its inspiration from concepts which were nothing other than disguises of what had been discarded. Moreover, when developmental series of cultures were presented, less and less evidence was produced, even of the commonest and most questionable sort. Less and less time was allotted to the detailed recapitulation of the whole series of stages in the conjectural cultural sequence; and less also to the assemblage of savage materials intended to shore up proposed theories of social and institutional "origins." Where once the hierarchical and evolutionary hypothesis had demanded at least some argument and a solid body of "testimony" to ensure the acceptance of its astonishing inferences, these were now taken for granted. Students dealt no longer with an extremely difficult and unsolved historical problem, but with finding a few illustrations whose attenuation was in itself symbolic. The French Encyclopedists, in some respects so skeptical, constitute one illustration of this perfunctory and naïve type of inquiry which adhered to precarious intellectual positions without intellectual discomfort. The Scottish moral philosophers, with their offspring the sociologists, were another in the nineteenth and twentieth centuries of the many followers of each school.

Caught in a revolutionary situation which played its part in the religious reformation, the Encyclopedists contended that an ancient and powerful clerical tradition had obstructed intellectual advancement. Since the theological postulates of preceding generations were denied intellectual value, assumptions in ethnological reflection thought to stem from them, were considered "sheer error, due to the unscrupulous and calculating hypocrisy" of the priesthood. In attacking this fortress of dogma and superstition, an attempt was made to replace every presupposition recognized as Scriptural or theological with another presumably more in harmony with natural science. For one example, the supernatural mission of the Hebrews was denounced. The true authors of civilization, said these detectors of error, were the Egyptians. Recurring often to a much earlier and ever-attractive hypothesis of the westward or northward diffusion of civilization, French savants insisted that civilized achievement had taken a meandering geographical course, from the cities of the Nile and the coasts of Phoenicia to Greece and Rome, and thence to Northern Europe. Recent discoveries in geology, paleontology, and chronology, in so far as they seemed to possess an anti-Scriptural bias, were also of absorbing interest. By means of these and other borrowings from their predecessors during the Renaissance, the Book of Genesis was thought once and for all to have been laid to rest.

But unfortunately, French intellectuals, their Scottish colleagues and German sympathizers were far less successful in abstaining from an enveloping Scriptural tradition than they fondly supposed. Knowing little of the permeating theological sources of ethnology, they permitted much of the Bible to slip through their fingers and back into their theories. Omitting the more obvious theological principles enunciated by Moses, they unwittingly accepted the less obvious. Among the latter was their wholehearted adoption once more of an hierarchical type of explanation of the phenomenon of cultural diversification, slightly transfigured as the plan of Nature rather than of God. Apart from ideas such as these, the convictions of the Encyclopedists are not easily distinguishable from those of other progressionists. The *Encyclopédie* contains relatively little discussion of the process of cultural change itself. But when it does, the *notions directrices* are the same. There is the same developmental, genetic arrangement of peoples and nations, with the same Europocentrism; there is the same stress upon the description of social origins; and the same use of travelers' reports to substantiate the assumption that existing savagery is representative of the culturally low, brutal, and early.

Belief in the villainy of savagery as a whole, and hence in the propriety of regarding any representative of the nonliterate group of mankind as an acceptable illustration of the first stage of development, became so self-evident that little effort was expended in amassing documentary materials. Not only was savagery seldom defined, but it was assumed without argument to belong on the lowest rung of the cultural ladder; and all the origins of civilized institutions were said to be found in some phase of its deplorable activities.

What else was there to say? What other alternatives were there? There were none.

29. Brixham Cave and the Antiquity of Man

Jacob Gruber

During the past fifteen years, human paleontology has been revitalized by a series of discoveries whose interpretation has produced a new excitement in the search for man's ancestry.[1] New paths of human evolution are replacing those which have become rutted through decades of repetition of the same data and the same theories. The current vigor recalls the new spirit of just a century ago when, during the 1850's and early 1860's, the discoveries of the "cave men" revolutionized the concept of man's past and created for him a previously unbelievable antiquity. Like those discoveries, the finds of our generation, culminating in the evidences from Olduvai Gorge, have led to a reexamination of the bases of human behavior and its development. Hallowell's own stimulating examinations of the nature of the human achievement, of human nature itself, have been instrumental in that redefinition of man's uniqueness which underlies the contemporary search for the human threshold in the evolutionary past. And with the reawakening of studies of human evolution both physically and behaviorally, it is perhaps of some interest to examine those events of an earlier period, in an earlier state of the science, which provided the foundations of both data and concept upon which our present knowledge and interests have been built.

Looking backward to events of a seemingly distant past, James Geikie wrote in 1881 that:

> When the announcement was made some years ago that rude stone implements of undoubted human workmanship had been discovered in certain alluvial deposits in the valley of the river Somme under circumstances which argued for the human race a very high antiquity, geologists generally received the news with incredulity. That the advent of man was an occurrence merely of yesterday, as it were, and a matter to be discussed properly by chronologists and historians alone, most of us until lately were

From Melford E. Spiro, ed., *Context and Meaning in Cultural Anthropology*,

> taught to believe. So ingrained, indeed, had this belief become, that although evidence of the antiquity of our race similar to those subsequent French discoveries, which succeeded at last in routing the skeptical indifference of geologists, had been noted from time to time . . . , yet it was only noted to be explained away, and in point of fact was persistently neglected as of no importance (Geikie: 1881, p. 3).

The events to which Geikie referred were indeed of his own era; they were less than a generation past. It is true that when Geikie wrote with such certitude, there were still a few scattered voices frantically raised in defense of man's recent origins and recent history; but these were the last laments for the loss of the recency of man's creation. Their very shrillness of tone betrayed the weakness of their position. They were the echoes of a past's prevailing theme, reverberating hollowly in the new chamber into which the new science of prehistory had ushered man.

Geikie was writing during a period of calm which followed one of the great intellectual revolutions of the nineteenth century—the discovery of man's past. It was a revolution the more intolerable because it was so personal, because it struck so violently at man's most hallowed conception of himself. After a time, the threads of history become tangled and the individuality of movements and events become confused and compressed into an unreal simplicity confined within the rubric of an *ism*. Old channels of thought—originally separate and distinct—are covered over and lost as the new cuts its way more deeply into the changing landscape of the mind. It is perhaps, of some value to retrace in some fashion these features of an earlier intellectual horizon.

The ideological conquests during the past century of the idea of organic evolution have led to the general acceptance of an intimate association between the concept of man's high antiquity and that of organic evolution. So closely have these two revolutionary concepts come to be related that the former is often thought to have been but an inevitable conceptual and chronological consequence of the latter. Thus, Graham Clark (1957, p. 32) in surveying the growth of prehistory as a science, notes that "It needed a revolution in man's conception of nature and antiquity of man as an organism before the bare notion of primary prehistory could take birth. Such a revolution was wrought by the publication in 1859 of Charles Darwin's *Origin of Species;*" and he goes on to suggest that it was as a result of the *Origin* that the occasional and previously questioned finds of man's antiquity were reexamined and rehabilitated. The fact that these two intellectual revolutions—the idea that all organic species result, through long periods of time, from a natural process of generational modification and that man's demonstrated history is much different from that which any reconciliation with the scriptural record or Mosaic chronology can justify—the fact that these two great events in the history of human thought occurred almost simultaneously has led to the generally held conclusion that it was the statement of an acceptable theory of organic evolution which made man's antiquity both intelligible and defensible. As a matter of historical fact, however, these two concepts as they emerged a century ago, were the products of two quite separate intellectual traditions—that is, separate to the extent that any two movements within the same intellectual milieu can be said to be separate. The elisions of history, however, have subsequently merged these two separate currents into a single intellectual stream.

For much of the nineteenth century, the concept of the antiquity and/or recency of man had two related but quite different meanings. Of somewhat lesser importance, in the absence of any valid means of measurement, was the absolute age of man's earthly existence. Much more important, however, was the relative period of man's emergence or creation as judged by his faunal associations. It was through the analysis of a whole range of such faunal complexes as they revealed themselves in the accumulating body of fossil remains that the geologists had transformed a succession of lithic strata into a chronologically arranged series of organic communities. Within the limits imposed by credulity as well as by a geology-based chronology, it was possible to expand man's history backward in time so long as the relative position of his emergence was not so altered as to make him a comtemporary of fauna foreign to (and therefore assumed to be anterior to) existing forms.

To understand the paramount importance for an interpretation of man's place in nature of this second concept of age based upon faunal association and the significance of its introduction for both the science and the natural theology of a century ago, we must be aware of the accepted synthesis which had emerged from decades of theogeological controversy. It was Cuvier who set the tone for the new science of geology by his insistence on observation and his denigration of speculation. The excellence of his comparative anatomy, the dedication of his empiricism, and the rigor of his logic combined to provide him with that position of authority which directed the thinking of his followers throughout the world long after his death in 1832. Basing his conclusions on his own reconstructions of the strange new mammalian fossils from the Paris basin this "antiquary of a new order" concluded from the obvious evidences, both geological and paleontological, that the earth had been visited by a succession of sudden and cataclysmic revolutions. "Thus we have . . . a series of epochs," he noted (Cuvier: 1817, p. 8), "anterior to the present time, and of which the successive steps may be ascertained with perfect certainty. . . . These epochs form so many fixed points, answering as rules for directing our enquiries respecting the ancient chronology of the earth." And each of these epochs, these "thousands of ages" marching inevitably to the present, bore some characteristic segment of the "thousands of animals" which a succession of revolutions had destroyed. The serious and adventurous efforts of numbers of collectors, following in the path which Cuvier had opened, filled in the outlines of the paleontological past in much the same way and with much the same passion and spirit with which the followers of Linnaeus earlier had expanded beyond prior conception the borders of the living universe. The zeal to observe and to record combined with the tedium surrounding the old controversies to produce a new spirit in geology. "A new school at last arose," wrote Lyell (1855, pp. 58–59) himself one of its most distinguished members, "who professed the strictest neutrality . . . and who resolved diligently to devote their labours to observation. . . . Speculative views were discountenanced. . . . To multiply and record observations, and patiently to await the result at some future period, was the object proposed by them; and it was their favourite maxim that the time was not yet come for a general system of geology, but that all must be content for many years to be exclusively engaged in furnishing materials for future generalizations. By acting up to these principles with consistency, they in a few years disarmed all prejudice, and rescued the science from the imputation of being dangerous, or at best but a visionary pursuit." Nevertheless the very weight of the evidences carved from the superimposed strata of the earth's crust produced a generally accepted theory of its past.

Time—the restricted time of literally interpreted Scripture—was no longer a problem; eons—stretching back beyond the ken of even the most liberal of a prior generation—were there for the asking. And through a large part of that time, living forms had occupied the earth, albeit forms quite different from those now alive. And in this vast new dimension of the organic universe, there was still design and plan and purpose. Although the Noachian deluge, as the one single catastrophe separating the past from the present, had long been abandoned, it had been supplanted by a series of equally destructive forces whose effects could be seen in the tilt of the strata and in the exotic fossils they contained. Although an increasing paleontological sophistication made more subtle the spasms which marked the history of the earth, the idea of catastrophism had both popular and scientific approval. Almost fifty years after Cuvier and just prior to the publication of Darwin's *Origin*, Louis Agassiz, admittedly overly enthusiastic in his catastrophism, but still the most popular American natural scientist, could write:

> Modern science . . . can show in the most satisfactory manner that all finite beings have made their appearance successively and at long intervals, and that each kind of organized beings has existed for a definite period of time in past ages, and that those now living are of comparative recent origin. At the same time, the order of their succession, and their immutability during such cosmic periods, show no causal connection with

> physical agents and the known sphere of action of these agents in nature, but argue in favor of repeated interventions on the part of the Creator (Agassiz: 1859, p. 84).

One could not speak—nor think—of one organic universe, but only of many, each succeeding the other in a changing order of separate creations. Arguing from his uniformitarianism, Lyell might maintain that the succession was not to be equated with progression; but in the face of the fossil evidence, his cry, if heard at all, went unheeded. For most, a designed improvement within the established types, as an improvement in the types themselves, was a self-evident fact both in the societies of man and in the creations of God. So readily did the doctrine of progression permit the acceptance of the high antiquity of the earth that within a generation this heresy of a former time had become reconciled with—indeed, a part of—prevailing theological belief. The effect of the new reconciliation was the onset of a period of intellectual calm during which the findings of geology and the interpretations of Scripture were made to validate each other to the satisfaction of most of the advocates of both.[2]

On one conclusion, however, all were agreed: The most important of these creations was the last, that in which man appeared, that which Genesis described. Thus, through this new system of belief and its acceptance of a past, man was effectively insulated through the maintenance of what was to become a dogma of his own recent creation. Here lay man's uniqueness, his worth, his tie to God. So long as he could feel himself the product of this last, this most recent, of God's works, he could feel that special kinship to his creator which made him man and not brute. The recency of man's creation, so readily admitted and so easily accepted, was adduced as one additional support—in fact, the major one—of the progression of the successive creations of life under divine guidance and within a divine plan. In effect, the system was a self-sustaining one: The paleontological succession afforded evidence of a progressive series; man's position as the most recent of the series supported the view of progression; the separations or breaks in the fossil record, those revolutions for which there was no sufficient natural explanation, implied directive creation; Scripture supported the concept of creation, the idea of progressive succession, and, most important, the terminal creation of man as the apex of the series. The clearest expression of this new synthesis, a synthesis which was used to disprove the charge of atheism in science and to validate the truths which science was unveiling, is reflected in the writings of the Scottish amateur geologist, Hugh Miller, who was himself the most active, the most widely read, and probably the most effective advocate of this view.[3]

Within this general interpretation of the paleontological succession—so easy to reconcile with prevailing belief and so consistent with the known geological facts—geology settled down to a premature old-age, eschewing speculation in its zeal to make more specific the nature of each of God's creations. It was a period, known in the history of every science, of relative calm, of synthesis, of consolidation.

Through these years of intensive collecting, the assumption of the continued absence of any evidence for man's antiquity, that is, for the association of his remains with any of those extinct creatures of the past, was the crucial constant which maintained the faith for most progressionists; so delicately balanced and arranged were the various parts of the ideological structure built upon this synthesis of Scripture, progress, and geology that the alteration of any part threatened to collapse the whole.

The absence of such evidences, however, was in fact a myth, a myth which was nurtured with increasing zeal. Frere's often quoted discoveries and lucid interpretation (Frere: 1800) had occurred in the last years of the eighteenth century; but they came too early to introduce even a jarring note into a system which had not yet been constructed. Thus, unexplainable and unexplained, they remained ignored. With increasing paleontological activity, however, particularly in geological deposits of more recent origin, such evidences occurred at an accelerating and alarming rate.

From the cave earths and from the gravel terraces, those leavings of some prior catastrophe, the remnants of man were exposed. Buckland, one of the most ardent of the new geologists, had examined the remains of a human skeleton in Paviland Cave (Buckland: 1822) but was quick to explain it away as that of a courtesan to the soldiers of a Roman camp nearby. But already as he reviewed the early evidences from the cave explorations of Europe in his *Reliquiae Diluvianae* (Buckland: 1824), he was able to record at least seven additional instances in which human bones had occurred in circumstances suggesting their high antiquity; but their associations with extinct fauna were, he argued, fortuitous: "the human bones are not of the same antiquity with those of the antediluvian animals that occur in the same caves with them" (Buckland: 1824, p. 169).[4]

At Kent's Hole in Devon, Father MacEnery in the 1820's had satisfied himself of the contemporaneity of chipped stone implements and the remains of extinct fauna which he had found together below the stalagmite of the cave floor (MacEnery: 1859; Pengelly: 1869); but Buckland in person and Cuvier by reputation persuaded him that both his observations and his inferences were in error.[5]

In the previously undisturbed deposits of the Belgian caverns near Liége, under circumstances of incredible difficulty, Schmerling in the early 1830's had again uncovered human remains in direct association with what had come to be a predictable cave fauna. Against the attacks and ridicule of his associates, forced to defend his own integrity as an excavator, he could only maintain that time alone would prove the correctness of his assertions that man had existed at the time the caves were filled with the mud and fossils they contained (Schmerling: 1833–34, Vol. II, p. 179). And the similar discoveries of the 1820's by Marcel de Serres, Christol, Tournal, and others in the caves of Southern France were widely quoted only to be questioned and repudiated.[6]

The most famous of these early discoverers of man's antiquity was Boucher de Perthes, who lived long enough to see the vindication of his views. Active in the Société d'Émulation of Abbeville at the mouth of the Somme, Boucher de Perthes became interested in the curious chipped flint implements, "*haches*," which were found in the Somme gravels. These gave promise of proving the reality of an antediluvian human race of whose existence he had been convinced on logical grounds since 1838. "I have glimpsed," he wrote (Boucher de Perthes: 1857), "for a long time that antediluvian race and during all these years have anticipated the joy which I would feel when in these terraces which geology has so often declared to be barren and anterior to man, I would finally find the proof of the existence of that man, or in default of his bones, a trace of his works." From his first discoveries in 1840, Boucher de Perthes pressed his inquiries and his hypothesis with a good-natured tenacity that resisted the defamation and ridicule of his Parisian colleagues. His extensively illustrated *Antiquités Celtiques et Diluviennes,* although covering the whole range of French prehistory, included the first extensive supports for the existence of man as a contemporary of the extinct fauna whose remains were being discovered with an almost monotonous regularity in both the open gravel terraces and in the stalagmite-covered cave earths. Although he was convinced of the validity of his position by concepts which were even then outmoded, the persistence of his advocacy and his own longevity served to cast him in the role of the prophet of man's prehistory.[7]

Properly interpreted, these accumulating data, by thrusting man back into a paleontological past, would have gone far to demolish the carefully raised structure that was British geology in the second quarter of the nineteenth century.

In the excitement following the later documentation of man's antiquity and, I suspect, as a by-product of the attempt to maintain the developing reputation for objectivity and impersonality in science, there was a tendency to regard these earlier discoveries as so obscure as to have gone unnoticed by those who might have interpreted them correctly. This was not the case.

Still a young man with his *Principles of Geology* only recently published, Lyell had visited the Belgian caves in which Schmerling was breaking both his body and heart; but, puzzled himself over the evidences, he could only sympathize with the difficulty of the problem. To

Gideon Mantell, he wrote (Lyell: 1881, Vol. I, pp. 401–402) in 1833: "I saw . . . at Liege the collection of Dr. Schmerling, who in *three years* has, by his own exertions . . . cleared out some twenty caves untouched by any previous searcher, and has filled a truly splendid museum. He numbers already thrice the number of fossil cavern mammalia known when Buckland wrote his 'Idola specus'; . . . But envy him not—you can imagine what he feels at being far from a metropolis which can afford him sympathy; and having not one congenial soul at Liege, and none who take any interest in his discoveries save the priests—and what kind *they* take you may guess more especially *as he has found human remains in breccia, embedded with extinct species, under circumstances far more difficult to get over than I have previously heard of* . . ." (italics mine). The evidences from Kent's Hole were common knowledge as were the discoveries from the French caves and the interpretations placed upon them by their discoverers.

Nor did the discoveries from the Somme Valley (Boucher de Perthes: 1847, 1857) go unnoticed or unchampioned. Boucher de Perthes engaged in an extensive correspondence with geologists and antiquarians throughout Europe; and he took every available opportunity to send copies of his *Antiquités Celtiques et Antediluviennes* to any one to whom it might have the slightest interest.[8] Darwin wrote to Lyell (C. Darwin: 1887, Vol. 3, p. 15) in 1863 that he "had looked at his [Boucher de Perthes'] book many years ago, and am ashamed to think that I concluded the whole was rubbish!" Boucher de Perthes had sent the British Archaeological Association "a quantity of Celtic antiquities in flint discovered by him in the environs of Abbeville . . . some of which he assigns to an antediluvian date." The Association was to have discussed these discoveries, but apparently never did (*Literary Gazette:* 1849). Roach-Smith, a remarkable English archaeologist and one of the more ardent of Boucher de Perthes' supporters in England wrote to him on April 11, 1850 (*Boucher de Perthes Correspondence*) that "Dr. Gideon Mantell, one of our first geologists, sent to me yesterday to borrow your *Antiquités Celtiques* to lecture on or refer to in one of his lectures"; and on November 26, 1851, he wrote "I expect from Dr. Hume of Liverpool a copy of his paper in which he comments favourably on your '*Antiquités Celtiques.*' . . . Dr. Hume has asked me if I thought you would like to be a member of the Lancashire and Cheshire Historical Society. I have written in the affirmative" (*ibid.*).[9] And another English archaeologist, James Yates wrote on February 12, 1850 (*ibid.*) that "I have not seen the Dean of Westminster [Buckland] since I sent him your *Antiquités Celtiques.*" Thus, whatever attitudes particular individuals may have entertained with reference to the work of Boucher de Perthes, both man and his work were known and discussed in England. As was the case with Kent's Hole, however, it was the "amateurs" and the archaeologists who tended to support him and the "professionals" and geologists who opposed him.

It was not therefore that these important data were unknown or information concerning them poorly distributed. Rather they were too well known and their advocates too enthusiastic. Consequently all such evidences were examined with extremes of scientific caution and criticism and unnecessarily rejected as, at best, "not proven." The net effect of such caution, laudable as it may be in any abstract judgment of science as an activity, was that with the authority of Cuvier perpetuated by Buckland, it could be maintained that:

> The only evidence that has yet been collected upon this subject [the antiquity of man] is negative; but as far as this extends, no conclusion is more fully established than the important fact of the total absence of any vestiges of the human species throughout the entire series of geological formations. Had the case been otherwise, there would indeed have been great difficulty in reconciling the early and extended periods which have been assigned to the extinct races of animals with our received chronology. On the other hand, the fact of no human remains having as yet been found in conjunction with those of extinct animals, may be alleged in confirmation of the hypothesis that these animals lived and died before the creation of man (Buckland: 1837, Vol. I, p. 103).

Still later, the world of the 1850's, secure now in it traditional faith in revelation and in its new-found allegiance to science, could echo the heartfelt and poetic expression which Hugh Miller gave of the compatibility between these two sources of truth:

> It may be safely stated . . . that that ancient record in which man is represented as the last born of creation, is opposed by no geological fact; and that if, according to Chalmers, 'the Mosaic writings do not fix the antiquity of the globe,' they at least *do* fix—making allowance, of course, for the varying estimates of the chronologer—'the antiquity of the human species.' The great column of being, with its base set in the sea, and inscribed, like some old triumphal pillar, with many a strange form—at once hieroglyphic and figure—bears, as the ornately sculptured capital, which imparts beauty and finish to the whole, reasoning, responsible man. There is surely a very wonderful harmony manifested in that nice sequence in which the invertebrates—the fishes, the reptiles, the birds, the marsupials, the placental mammals, and last of all, man himself—are so exquisitely arranged[10] (Miller: 1857, pp. 132–133).

Rising above the voices of those whose interests introduced a sometimes strident note into their advocacy of the new palliative was the clear and measured tone of Lyell's authority. Although no progressionist himself, he was firm in his view as he disposed one after another, of the claims for man's antiquity, that "we have every reason to infer that the human race is extremely modern, even when compared to the larger number of species now our contemporaries in this earth" (Lyell: 1855, p. 148). Such recency, stated with such authority and unanimity by those who constituted the professionals of the day, negated any possibility of the contemporaneity of man with any of those exciting forms which had been turning up in the cave deposits and in the gravels of the post-Pliocene and whose existence immediately antedated the last of the earth's great revolutions which sealed off, so to speak, the human epoch and its occupants from the organic events of the past.

Without reference to the scientific merits of the question or the evidences adduced for the support of its solution, this response to the problem of man's past—as well as to his relationship with the organic world as a whole—in a world that had quite suddenly become almost inconceivably old as man's last refuge in the search for his uniqueness and the best hope for the maintenance of his divinity.[11] The defenses constructed to protect his own dignity were sufficient to repel for half a century the occasional assaults of questionable associations of human implements with extinct mammalia; but they fell, at last and in some disorder, before the force of the unanticipated evidences from Brixham Cave.

The men immediately responsible for the discoveries at Brixham Cave, discoveries which were to initiate a revolution, were Hugh Falconer, trained in medicine but active as both botanist and paleontologist, William Pengelly, a provincial school teacher, and Joseph Prestwich, wine merchant. These men themselves are interesting symbols of the ferment which was altering the whole substance of nineteenth-century natural science.[12] Pengelly and Prestwich were both amateurs in the sense that, like most of their co-workers, they lacked formal training in science and were able to "geologize" only during those scant hours stolen from their more mundane pursuits.[13] They formed part of that large and enthusiastic body for whose works John Herschel (1830, pp. 15–16) had written the justification: "The highest degrees of worldly prosperity, are so far from being incompatible with them [scientific researches] that they supply additional advantages for their pursuits. . . . They may be enjoyed, too, in the intervals of the most active business; and the calm and dispassionate interest with which they fill the mind renders them a most delightful retreat from the agitations and dissensions of the world, and from the conflict of passions, prejudices, and interests in which the man of business finds himself continually involved." Their heroes were, during these maturing decades of natural science, the leaders of geology—the Lyells, the Murchisons, the Owens, and the Bucklands—whose extensive publications and commanding positions provided them with the authority of intellectual command. Although Pengelly and Prestwich were exceptional in their command of the field, there were many of their kind whose primarily descriptive articles fill the geological journals of the period.

These were initially collectors and observers whose more limited contributions provided the factual bases for the broader syntheses of their leaders. Diffident and often practical, they were in tune wtih their times; and in their caution they were often led to a conservatism which maintained theoretical views whose fashion had faded under the weight of new evidences and of the theories to which they gave rise.[14] When they did speculate, it was often on the basis of insufficient or provincially circumscribed data or upon general assumptions no longer valid.

Falconer was, however, another sort. Like many of the period, he had been led to a career in natural science through the comparative anatomy of a medical background and through the scientific spirit still perceptible at the Edinburgh University where he had trained. He was one of the new men of nineteenth-century natural science for whom observation was more important than theorizing but who saw in a revived empiricism a virgin field for the collection of the data which would eventually disclose the secrets of nature. He was more a romantic than a rationalist and he approached his work more often with the zeal of the former than the cold logic of the latter. Each new discovery moved him with an excitement to pass on so that he was never able to complete the work he continuously projected for himself.

The literature of Brixham Cave is relatively scant. Death, timidity and delay so postponed the publication of the results of the year-long excavation that by the time the final report at last appeared (Prestwich: 1873), this parent of prehistory had already been devoured, both in interest and in importance, by its more spectacular offspring. Nevertheless the public bickerings over priority of discovery and Pengelly's invaluable manuscript journal of the excavations[15] make it possible to reconstruct the short history during which man's antiquity was for the first time substantiated beyond serious doubt or question through the unlooked for discovery of a few flint implements in direct and indisputable association with the bones of the great extinct mammalia of the Pleistocene.

Like most significant clues to man's past, the cavern on Windmill Hill, at Brixham, overlooking Torquay in South Devon, England, was discovered accidentally. And, significantly for the history of archaeology, it was explored by *geologists* with a view toward the solution of certain *geological* problems. There is no evidence from the contemporary documents that its signficance for the "man question" was at all anticipated. As Falconer pointed out, in his request for support from the Geological Society of London, scientific interest in cavern researches had virtually disappeared since the excitement which followed Buckland's publication of his *Reliquiae Diluvianae*. So thorough and so comprehensive had been Buckland's researches and so conclusive and authoritative his conclusions that it seemed nothing more could be added beyond what was contained in that scientific *tour de force*. The results of Buckland's influence were that all caves were

> . . . popularly regarded as containing the debris of the same mammalian fauna, and as having been overlaid with their ochreous loam by the same common agency at the same period. The contents of the different caverns were thus considered as being in a great measure duplicates of one another, and the exceptional presence of certain forms in one case, and their absence in another, were regarded more in the light of local accidents than as significant for any general source of difference. Hence it followed that more attention was paid to the extrication of the bones, and to securing good specimens, than to a record of their relative association and the order of succession in which they occurred. The remains have been, in some instances, huddled together in provincial collections—the contents of five or six distinct caves, without a discriminative mark to indicate out of which particular cavern they came. Another consequence has been, that being regarded in the light of duplicates, the contents of some of the most important and classical English caverns have been dispersed piecemeal; and so far as regards them the evil is beyond remedy (Falconer: 1868, Vol. II, pp. 487–488).

During the 1850's, however, with the increasing anatomical discrimination of the expanded number of mammalian species and with the developing awareness of the subtle differences which separated organic types both in time and space, Falconer had become interested in the construction of the temporal and geographical distribution patterns of the cave fauna which might fill in the details of the late, little known and generally neglected period of earth history whose deposits overlay the Pliocene strata; and he felt that controlled investigations of undisturbed cave deposits gave the best promise, through cross-correlation and stratigraphic analysis, for a more comprehensive understanding of the Glacial Age and its faunal variations.

In the course of reconnaissance of the limestone caves in the west of England during the spring of 1858, Falconer stopped off at Torquay, famous for its sporadically plundered Kent's Hole. He had probably been induced to make the detour through a notice in the *Western Times* of April 10 regarding the discovery of Brixham Cave.

The cave itself had been opened, during quarrying operations, by its proprietor, John Philp, on January 15, 1858; and, a short time later, it had been called to the attention of William Pengelly of Torquay, a part-time geologist, and moving force of the Torquay Natural History Society. Pengelly visited the cave as soon as possible, saw some of the fossil material which Philp had hastily dug up for commercial exploitation, noted (Pengelly: 1860, Vol. 1, p. 6) particularly "at 75 feet from the entrance . . . [a] fine antler of some kind of deer lying *on* the stalagmite, attached to, but not imbedded in it"; and immediately discovered (*ibid.*, Vol. 1, p. 7) that the proprietor was "not disinclined to dispose of the Cavern or rather the right of working it to any person prepared to pay him well for it."

Excited at the possibilities of securing specimens for the Torquay Museum, Pengelly, on March 29, called a meeting of a Committee of the Society, the result of which were instructions that a local cave committee should "make such arrangements as they may think desirable for securing specimens for the Museum from the recently discovered Bone Cavern at Brixham (*Ibid.*, Vol. 1, p. 8). Insofar as Pengelly was concerned, the cave was to be one more source of specimens. Philp, it was found, demanded a rental of one hundred pounds, an exorbitant price and far beyond the means of either the Museum or the society which supported it.

It was just at this point that Falconer dropped in, in the midst of his own excitement over the cave researches that had occupied him almost exclusively for five years. After visiting the cave, Falconer met with Pengelly to discuss possibilities. "We were unanimous," Pengelly noted (*ibid.*, Vol. 1, p. 10) in his journal "as to the probability that the cavern was likely to be of importance and also that it was not to be left in Philp's hand, as we had some reason to doubt his veracity. In fact, we had, separately, detected in his glass case, skulls, etc. of animals probably not dead a week, certainly not dead a long time; but which he at first affirmed were found by him in his cavern; subsequently . . . he confessed that they were forgeries, and that he had smeared them with cave earth to give them the requisite colour."

While Pengelly continued to hope that some means might be found to secure the scientific and controlled excavation of this virgin cavern, Falconer had himself been active. Upon his return to London, he addressed a fervent letter to the Council of the Geological Society of London requesting that some means be found to insure the excavation. By the middle of May, the Geological Society had appointed a top-level Brixham Cave Committee, consisting of Sir Charles Lyell, Richard Owen, Joseph Prestwich, A. C. Ramsay, Pengelly, and Falconer; and had obtained a grant of one hundred pounds from the Royal Society. A friend of Pengelly's contributed another fifty pounds. For the next two months, there were lengthy negotiations to secure the lease, to hire the laborer and collector[16] who would do the actual excavation, and to establish the mode of procedures as well as the relations which were to exist between the controlling committee in London and the local enthusiasts at Torquay.

As is not unusual in such situations even today, the local amateurs, excited by the possibility of specimens for local collections fought for the rights of local interests and suggested excavation methods which would most readily and speedily produce the largest number of such specimens without regard to the problems of spatial and temporal relationships whose solution was uppermost in the minds of the members of the London Committee. Pengelly and Falconer were agreed that in order to solve the geological problems involved, the utmost care would have to be exercised in the excavations. "The plan of operations laid down," went the minutes of an early meeting of the London Committee (*ibid.*, Vol. 5, p. 4) "was to break up the stalagmite floor throughout, and explore the first bed beneath it leaving any inferior beds for subsequent examination;—in this manner the exact extent of the cavern would be ascertained, and the true succession of the beds and the precise position and association of the organic remains would be clearly determined."[17] Thus each bed or stratum would be excavated separately so that there could be no confusion with respect to the actual location of any fossil nor could there be any occasion for the common accusation of the accidental intermingling of specimens through careless cuts through the strata. While the disagreements between the local collectors and the "scientists" in London with respect to this technique were never satisfactorily resolved, it was the latter who were dominant; and despite a developing bitterness among the members of the local committee, the excavations proceeded along the path originally charted.

Fortunately, if accidentally, the excavations were initiated at the original entrance of the cave; consequently, as the overlying stalagmitic covering was taken off, a rich bone bed was exposed below. Each succeeding day of the excavations was excitingly productive so that after a month's work over 1500 bones had been removed.

Within two weeks of the start of operations, the first flint implement was found in the midst of the fossils of the cave earth which underlay the seal of stalagmite. At the end of July, Pengelly noted (*ibid.*, Vol. 4, p. 2): "Bones have been found every day since my last entry. A flint implement was found today about 74 feet from the entrance, just under the spot where the antler lay. It was about 9 inches deep in the 3rd (i.e., bone) bed, and the bed was covered with a cake of stalagmite 3 inches thick. A flint (probably) implement had been found near the same place on the previous day but was not so well formed as that just mentioned." This initial discovery of human implements was followed by other such finds until by the close of the excavations a year later, thirty-six pieces of flint "all more or less white and having a porcellaneous aspect, and, at least some of which are believed to be *human implements*, were met with in various parts of the cavern" (Pengelly: 1874, p. 828). The stratigraphic situation of these implements was such as to leave no doubt that whatever the origin of the contents of the cave, these implements of human manufacture were at least as old as the mammalian remains. And there could be no doubt about the latter. The bone bed in which the flints were found contained the remains of the tichorine rhinoceros, cave bear, and cave hyena. Most significantly, however, both bones and implements lay together, under and sealed off by stalagmite on the surface of which was imbedded "a fine horn of rein-deer nearly perfect, from the basal 'bur' to the terminal branches of the beam," a discovery which indicated to Falconer that the "Rein-deer continued to be an inhabitant of Britain after the appearance of man in the island" (Pengelly: 1860, Vol. 8, p. 6).

The significance of these discoveries was quickly recognized; and, in Falconer's mind at least, took precedence over the paleontological questions whose hoped for solutions had provided the initial motivation for Brixham's excavation. The discovery of human implements intensified both questions of methodology and interpretation. Falconer wrote (*ibid.*, Vol. 4, p. 11) Pengelly on August 18: "Lyell has written me from Germany that he had shown to him at Maestricht, 'a fossil human skeleton *imbedded in the matrix* dug out of the Loess and that it was stated to resemble the type found by Schmerling at Liege.' We must therefore conduct our Brixham exploration in a careful and guarded manner, keeping an accurate record of the succession of the remains and their association." And upon Pengelly's request that he be permitted to read a paper on the Cave at the up-coming meetings of the British Association in September, 1858 the London Committee "Resolved, that Mr. Pengelly's application . . . be sanctioned; but that in the present early stage of the investigation it is not considered expedient to enter into any discussion or account of the organic or other remains that have been met with" (*ibid.*, Vol. 5, p. 5).

Pengelly's paper which, at his request, appeared only by title in the published proceedings of the Association was cautiously descriptive; but he could not resist the temptation of mentioning the flint implements in order to stress the importance of the excavation. He concluded:

> I cannot take leave of this subject without asking shall the explorations which have been carried on with more than encouraging results be continued or abandoned? Is the Cavern to be fully and systematically investigated, or as in too many cases, partially only? Shall we succeed in exhuming nearly 2,000 bones in about nine weeks, discover previously unsuspected galleries and chambers, disclose new beds of unknown depth, find human industrial remains with the bones of extinct animals, catch a ray of light on this question and that sufficient to stimulate but not to satisfy and prematurely abandon the work? This question resolves itself into one of Ways and Means only. There is the work to be done and there are the men able and willing to do it; but though the Committee are desirous of acknowledging both the public and private liberality which has enabled them to do so much, and though they are most anxious to

> observe all economy, they cannot conceal from themselves the fact that a very few weeks will exhaust the means now at their disposal (Pengelly: 1860, Vol. 8, pp. 19–20).

While Pengelly could but allude indirectly to the human material, the Committee's own "Report of Progress in Brixham Cave," read to the same meeting immediately afterward was much more direct. Prepared by Falconer, signed by him, Pengelly, and Ramsay, and made public over the protests of the more cautious Prestwich, the Report concluded (Pengelly: 1860, Vol. 8, p. 6; Falconer: 1868, Vol. II, pp. 495–496) with a section entitled *"Human? Industrial? Remains."* Despite the inclusion of the question marks, the text leaves little doubt as to the author's certainty:

> Several well marked specimens of the objects called 'Flint Knives,' and generally accepted at the present day as the early product of Keltic or pre-Keltic industry, have been exhumed from different parts of the cavern, mixed in the ocherous earth with remains of *Rhinoceros, Hyaena,* and other extinct forms. One of these so-called 'Flint Knives' was brought up from the deposit No. 2 from a depth of 30 inches below the superficial stalagmite No. 1. We failed in detecting evidence that these so-called flint knives were of different age as regards the period of their introduction from the bones of the extinct animals occurring in the same stratum of cave earth, or that they were introduced into the cavern by different agencies.

Referring to similar discoveries already known from the Continent and the rejection of these evidences because of alleged faulty excavation techniques, the Report further notes that:

> The attention of Mr. Pengelly has been closely directed to a careful and minute observation of the circumstances of the association in Brixham Cavern. The results of the exploration of each day are carefully put aside and labelled; and it may be anticipated that data will be arrived at for settling the disputed question of the contemporaneous introduction, or otherwise, of the supposed human industrial objects into the cavern along with the remains of the extinct mammalia.

Both reports were received by the crowded meeting with excitement, enthusiasm, and some feeling of incredulity. To his wife, Pengelly wrote (H. Pengelly: 1897, p. 80) from the meetings: "I have read my paper [on Brixham Cave] to a crowded house, all the great geologists came in apparently. Owen followed in very eulogistic strains, characterizing exploration of the Cavern, as the only satisfactory and good attempt of the kind that ever had been made. I was very much complimented at the close by sundry persons . . ." There is no evidence, however, that Richard Owen, whose authoritative anatomical investigations for over a generation had corroborated the geological proofs of man's recent creation, was convinced by the Brixham data. Although a gracious endorsement of Pengelly's excavations, his comments were designed to stress the fact that "no discoveries had been made up to this time calculated to show that man is of higher antiquity than has commonly been supposed" (Pengelly: 1860, Vol. 8, p. 9). Whatever the opinion of the various spokesmen, however, for the first time in at least a decade, serious discussion was now entertained—both among professional geologists and in the popular scientific press—on the subject of man's antiquity.[18]

With a continuing grant from the Royal Society, completion of the Brixham excavation could now be expected, and it was the sense of the Committee that no final interpretive report should be published until the work had been done. But although further implements and bones were discovered in diminished frequencies, none equaled in importance those of the first six weeks, which for the less skeptical at least, had gone so far to establish beyond reasonable doubt the fact of man's contemporaneity with the extinct fauna of the Glacial Period and thus, by presumption, his high antiquity.

Following the Leeds meeting of the British Association, Falconer prepared to leave England for the winter—both for reasons of health and in order to examine at firsthand the cave collections in the south of France and some newly discovered fossiliferous caverns in Sicily. In the few weeks prior to his departure, he was almost completely occupied with the Brixham "flint implements"—comparing them with artifacts in the British Museum, arguing for their authenticity against the "hard sceptics" on his Committee, and, in one case, joining two fragments together to form a relatively complete tool. This preoccupation is evident in a letter to Pengelly, written a week before his departure:

> You will see that the matter of the association of the 'Flint Knives' *under* the Reindeer's antlers, and mixed in the same cave ochre with teeth of extinct animals is now assuming an aspect of grave and serious importance. A part of the case has been adduced before, but the conditions had been so carelessly observed that suspicion was very properly cast on the accuracy of the observations, and the results were considered worthless either as proof of the antiquity or reverse. In the case of our cavern, we had taken the stand that the phenomena would be observed and recorded with a severe fidelity which would place them above suspicion. Trust not, I intreat of you, to Keeping. He is, I have no doubt, a good worthy man of honest intentions, but he is liable like us all to error, and a check ought to be held over him. Tell him, with my love, that if he makes any more mistakes about the exact position of the Flint Knives, etc., he will be handed down with execrations to the remotest posterity. If this does not touch him, he must have the feelings of a rhinoceros. . . . If not making too great a demand on your valuable time I would suggest that you went over the details of position of every one of the flint knives in

such a way that we could give an affidavit to them . . . (*ibid.*, Vol. 9, p. 6).

And in order to emphasize the importance of the exact location of the flints whose authenticity and uniqueness had been affirmed by the authorities of the British Museum, Falconer wrote again a few days later (*ibid.*, Vol. 10, p. 2) that "incredulity is rife about the position of the 'Flint Knives' and every damaging hypothesis that can be thought of will be launched against them," not the least of which was that of forgery. The "incredulity" was occasioned as much by the reluctance of some to recognize man's antiquity as it was by the fact that there were also those who saw in the evidences from Brixham Cave the substantiation of the long-discredited Noachian Flood.[19]

It was with a mind full of the flint knives that Falconer left for the Continent. Remembering an earlier meeting with Boucher de Perthes whose figures in the *Antiquités Celtiques et Diluviennes* he had used to identify the Brixham specimens (Falconer: 1868, Vol. II, p. 593), Falconer decided to break his trip at Abbeville. "Next Saturday," he wrote (*Boucher de Perthes Correspondence*) "I shall be en route to Paris when I shall stop at Abbeville for two hours in the hope that I shall find you there. During the past three months we have found in English ossiferous caves some flint knives probably of very high antiquity."

As always Boucher de Perthes was gracious to his guest; and Falconer, in turn, was tremendously impressed with the mass of materials which the Somme gravels had yielded. After leaving Abbeville, he wrote (Pengelly: 1860, Vol. 11, pp. 6–7) to Pengelly from Avignon: "You remember the book on Celtic Antiquities (Flint knives, etc.) which I took down with me to Torquay. I made a journey to Abbeville purposely to see Mons'r Boucher de Perthes' collection. He showed me very rude flint knives which had been dug up by his own hands mingled in gravel with molars, which I saw, of the Mammoth. I got evidence of the same kind from Professor Jourdain of Lyons. I am now within a few hours distance of the famous caves of Limel-viel near Montpellier, which I shall visit in a couple of days." Earlier, while still at Abbeville and in the flush of excitement which Boucher de Perthes had aroused, he wrote to Prestwich, who was still not fully convinced, still "hesitating" to accept Falconer's conclusions without additional "unmistakable corroboration" (Prestwich: 1899, p. 117). "As the weather continued fine," Falconer wrote:

> I determined on coming here to see Boucher de Perthes' collection. I advised him of my intention from London, and my note luckily found him in the neighborhood. He good-naturedly came in to receive me, and I have been richly rewarded. His collection of wrought flint implements

> and of the objects of every description associated with them far exceeds anything I expected to have seen, especially from a single locality. He had made great additions, since the publication of his first volume, in the second—which I have now by me. He showed me "flint" hatchets which *he had dug up with his own hands* mixed *indiscriminately* with the molars of *E. primigenius.* I examined and identified *plates* of the molars—and the flint objects, which were got along with them. Abbeville is an out-of-the-way place, very little visited, and the French *savants* who meet him in Paris laugh at Monsieur de Perthes and his researches. But after devoting the greater part of a day to his vast collection, I am perfectly satisfied that there is a great deal of fair presumptive evidence in favour of many of his speculations regarding the remote antiquity of these industrial objects, and their association with animals now extinct. . . . If, during next summer, you should happen to be paying a visit to France, let me strongly recommend you to come to Abbeville. . . . I am sure you would be richly rewarded. You are the only English geologist I know of who would go into the subject *con amore.* I am satisfied that English Geologists are much behind the indications of the materials now in existence relative to this walk of post-glacial geology, and you are the man to bring up the leeway. . . . What I have seen here gives me still greater impulse to persevere in our Brixham exploration (*ibid.*, pp. 119–120).

Stimulated by Falconer's enthusiasm, Prestwich arranged for a group of geologists to visit Abbeville during the Easter holiday of 1859. Of those invited, only John Evans, paper manufacturer, numismatist, and antiquary, came. Upon his return, he described the trip in his journal:

> . . . to Abbeyville, where I found Prestwich waiting for me at the Station and very glad to see me. . . . We went straight to bed and soon after 7 the next morning M. Boucher de Perthes, the first discoverer of the stone axes we were in pursuit of, came to take us to some of the gravel pits from whence his collection had been derived. A. M. Marotte, the Curator of the Museum, accompanied us but we did not succeed in finding anything. We then adjourned to the house of M. de Perthes . . . with a wonderful collection of flint axes and implements found among the beds of gravel and evidently deposited at the same time with them—in fact the remains of a race of men who existed at the time when the deluge or whatever was the origin of these gravel beds took place. One of the most remarkable features of the case is that nearly all if not quite all of the animals whose bones are found in the same beds as the axes are extinct. There is the mammoth, the rhinoceros, the Urus—a tiger, etc. etc. . . . Of course our object was if possible to ascertain that these axes had been actually deposited with the gravel, and not subsequently introduced; and we had received intelligence from Amiens that in one of the gravelpits there an axe was to be seen in its original position, which made us set off at once. . . . We proceeded to the pit where sure enough the edge of an axe was visible in an entirely undisturbed bed of gravel and eleven feet

from the surface. We had a photographer with us to take a view of it so as to corroborate our testimony . . . (Joan Evans: 1943, pp. 101–102).

At Abbeville and Amiens, Prestwich had "worked on the ground" as he had desired and his caution had been overcome by the "unmistakable corroboration" which he required. The trip to Abbeville, spurred on by his responsibility for Brixham and by the excitement of Falconer, marked his conversion. Upon their return from Abbeville, both Prestwich and Evans immediately began to prepare separate papers on their observations. Prestwich's paper read before the Royal Society on May 26, 1859 (Prestwich: 1859) dealt primarily with the geological features of the Somme Valley and the specific associations of the flint implements. Whatever general conclusions might be drawn, he affirmed, upon his position as the foremost student of the post-Pliocene deposits, that the implements were of human manufacture; that they were found in undisturbed ground; that they were associated with the remains of extinct mammalia; and that the deposits themselves were laid down in a late geological period but one anterior to the surface assuming its present outline.[20]

To the Society of Antiquaries a week later, Evans reported more specificially on the implements themselves and the archaeological implications of their discovery. After summarizing Prestwich's geological findings, he demonstrated the human workmanship of the implements and emphasized their distinctness from previously known objects of the so-called "Stone" period. On the basis of his typological separation, Evans hoped that his audience would "be prepared to receive with less distrust the evidence . . . that they are found under circumstances which show that, in all probability, the race of men who fashioned them must have passed away long before this portion of the earth was occupied by the primitive tribes by whom the more polished forms of stone weapons were fabricated, in what we have hitherto regarded as remote antiquity" (Evans: 1859, pp. 293–294). And after predicting that "before many years have elapsed . . . the existence of man upon the earth previously to the formation of these drift deposits will be regarded by all as a recognized fact," Evans concluded his paper with a positive summary designed to stress upon his archaeological colleagues the significance of the discoveries in the Somme gravels:

> This much appears to be established beyond a doubt; that in a period of antiquity, remote beyond any of which we have hitherto found traces, this porition of the globe was peopled by man; and that mankind has here witnessed some of those geological changes by which these so-called diluvial beds were deposited. Whether they were the result of some violent rush of waters such as may have taken place when 'the fountains of the great deep were broken up, and the windows of heaven were opened,' or whether of a more gradual action, similar in character to some

of those now in operation along the course of our brooks, streams, and rivers, may be a matter of dispute. Under any circumstances this great fact remains indisputable, that at Amiens land which is now one hundred and sixty feet above the sea, and ninety feet above the Somme, has since the existence of man been submerged under fresh water, and an aqueous deposit from twenty or thirty feet in thickness, a portion of which at all events must have subsided from tranquil water, has been formed upon it; and this too has taken place in a country the level of which is now stationary, and the face of which has been but little altered since the days when the Gauls and the Romans constructed their sepulchres in the soil overlying the drift which contains these relics of a far earlier race of man (*ibid.*, p. 306).

The addresses of Evans and Prestwich, directed to the two Societies most vitally concerned, resurrected in the most forceful fashion the question of man's antiquity. The significance of their conclusions was the greater not only because of the new evidence brought forward but even more because of the acknowledged conservatism and authority of both authors. Falconer's announcement (Falconer: 1859) immediately following, of corroborative evidence from the Sicilian caves only served to emphasize the weight of the evidence pressing man, however resistant, backward into time. In a letter to his wife, Pengelly suggests the growing excitement. "The last *Athenaeum* is worth looking at," he wrote (H. Pengelly: 1897, p. 87). "There is an interesting letter, by Wright the antiquary, on the papers by Prestwich and Evans on their Flint Implements in the drift. In the list of meetings for the ensuing week there is an 'Extraordinary Meeting of the Geological Society at 8 P.M. (yesterday)' to hear 'Further Observations on the Occurrence of Human Art in the Bone Breccia in the Caves near Palermo,' by Dr. Falconer, and 'Reports on the Exploration of the Cave at Brixham,' by Dr. Falconer, also 'On Flint Implements recently obtained from the Gravel near Amiens,' by Flower. Flints are to the fore . . ."

Almost immediately, the excitement infected the whole community of geologists and antiquaries, amateurs and professionals. From Canterbury, one of the members of the Society of Antiquaries wrote the secretary a month after Evans' paper (*Society of Antiquaries Correspondence*): "I feel so much interested by the controversy in respect to the stone axes, arrowheads, etc. found in the Drift, that I feel almost tempted to run up to town to inspect them, but as I fear I cannot leave home for a week or ten days could you inform me how long they will remain in the Library."

Two months later, Sir Charles Lyell—the most eminent geologist of the century and, for the public, the court of last appeal on such matters—having himself made the pilgrimage to Abbeville, announced (Lyell: 1859) his own conversion in his presidential address before a packed meeting of the Geological Section of the British Association for the Advancement of Science at Aberdeen. His address was, according to Pengelly, "a masterpiece of ability and frankness"; and it started Lyell on his three-year search for the materials which formed the substance of the last of his great contributions to science (Lyell: 1863). In Lyell's view, "the facts recently brought to light during the systematic investigation, as reported on by Falconer, of the Brixham Cave, must, I think, have prepared you to admit that scepticism in regard to the cave-evidence in favour of the antiquity of man had previously been pushed to an extreme" (Lyell: 1859, p. 93).

Lyell's address represents something of a watershed in the history of man's conception of his own past. There was still strong opposition at the Aberdeen meeting to the new idea of man's antiquity, but it was even there strongly opposed by the logic of the geological evidence. Pengelly described the reaction to his wife:

> Yesterday was a good day here; . . . The fourth paper was by Rev. Dr. Anderson . . . 'On Human Remains in the Superficial Drift,' in which he attacked all the evidence which has recently been produced of 'Man among the Mammoths,' and a very great deal which no one ever regarded as bearing on the question. After wading through a great amount of rubbish, he boldly attempted to castigate Lyell for his opening address; next he ridiculed Horner's argument of the pottery, etc. in the silt of the Nile . . . Then he ran off to Germany to cudgel Bunsen, then back again, pitched me into Brixham Cave, and did his best to bury the Cave and myself in ridicule, and finally he gave us a yard or two of bad pulpit. There was a considerable amount of orthodoxy in the room, and he got a very undue share of applause. And now *per contra.* Lyell handled him as a gentleman and a philosopher alone can do it. Next Phillips, having rubbed his hands in oil, smoothed him down, but in such a way as to scarify him; then Ramsay seized him by the button-hole, and informed him of a fact or two connected with caverns, and finally handed him over to me upon which I seized him by the collar, dragged him in Brixham Cave, and showed him its facts and their whereabouts. Then came Symonds and pulpited him . . . (H. Pengelly: 1897, p. 90).

The intellectual explosion which had dispersed this skepticism now expanded the corridor of man's past backward into geological time; and, perhaps more significantly, for the studies that were to follow, it made the study of this past a part of a geology which had become not only historical but also developmental.

All of these events occurred prior to the publication of Darwin's *Origin* and without reference to the thesis it expounded; in fact, the critical discoveries of Brixham occurred within so short a time of the first reading of the abstract that it is impossible to see any connection between the two events at all. What is surprising—if not disturbing—is the complete absence in any of Darwin's published correspondence of any reference to the Brixham discoveries which so clearly eased the last and most significant line marking the limits of putative separate creations. Whatever the effect on Darwin, however, the significance of Brixham could not have been lost on a knowing public, a public which had been nourished on the concept of a series of distinct and progressive creations with that of man the last and finest of the series. It was a concept which had had, until Brixham, the force of both logic and observation for its support. Cannon has recently shown (Cannon: 1960a) the sufficiency of the logic and of the evidence as both were marshaled in favor of the progressionism of the catastrophists by the dialectical skill of Whewell, the philosopher of the new science. So long as the discontinuity separating man as a culture-bearing animal from the earlier creations could be supported in the geological record, the defense of the successive creations could be successfully maintained both as a matter of logic and of science. The discoveries at Brixham and the care exercised in their documentation constituted, however, a crushing blow to the defense. With the merging of man's past into creations long gone, with the knowledge of glacial man and the optimistic promise of Tertiary man, evolution, once suggested, must include man. Into the intellectual vacuum made necessary by the demonstration of a continuity, progressionist perhaps, even through man's creation itself, Darwinian evolution was quick to move. For those who could read the evidence of Brixham, Darwin's evolution applied to man with a violence; and for those who still had to maintain man's dignity through the uniqueness of his divinity by virtue of the uniqueness of his creation, such application had to be rejected. With the evidence of man's newly established antiquity, it could be rejected only through a rejection of Darwinian evolution itself.

As an intellectual event, the work of Falconer, Prestwich, and Pengelly at Brixham Cave was rapidly absorbed in the more intensive ferment which accompanied the publication of the *Origin* and the more spectacular discoveries from the caves of France. So ignored, in fact, was the catalytic role of Brixham Cave in the rehabilitation of Boucher de Perthes and his predecessors, so intense the desire to do justice to that aged prophet of man's past, that Brixham Cave was virtually dropped from history.[21] The circumstances of its discovery and excavation demand, however, some re-creation, for the value of which Falconer himself provided the justification when, in writing of some other half-forgotten event in the history of science, he noted that:

> The same kind of retrospect which from time to time we cast on the material facts [of science], justice demands of us to apply also to the history of discovery in science. Facts which are now fused in the common mass may have exercised a powerful influence when first brought to light.

> The impartial historian will regard them in this light, and not merely as they now appear. He will also be scrupulously careful to award to the first observers fairly what is their due; for, a part from the abstract consideration of justice, the only guarantee which we have that our own labours shall be respected in the future is the fairness with which we ourselves deal with the labours of our contemporaries and of those who have gone before us (Falconer: 1868, Vol. I, p. 310).

The establishment of man's geological antiquity was, however, of even greater importance to the emergence of anthropology. I have stressed the role of geology and geologists in the establishment of man's antiquity because it was through that role that prehistory as a discipline—and I believe, by extension, the subsequent synthesis that was to become anthropology—achieved its methodology, its point of view and, most significantly at the time, its status as a science.[22] Even more, much as evolution provided the core around which the several separate biological disciplines were to relate themselves as *Biology*, so prehistory served as the focus at which the already specialized efforts of archaeologists, culture historians, human biologists, and ethnographers could be related as a redefined *Anthropology*. For the varied students of man, already specialized in both techniques and concepts, the ideological world of the mid-nineteenth century was already cramping; the breakthrough into the past provided them with both the opportunity and the materials to build a new science. It was this new dimension to man's existence which provided the stimulus and the meaning for the search for the fossil remains of the past as it did for ordering of the relics of the present.

Notes

[1] Much of the material upon which this paper is based was gathered during the course of a sabbatical leave granted by Temple University and with the aid of a fellowship from the National Science Foundation and a grant from the American Council of Learned Societies; to these institutions I wish to express both acknowledgment of and gratitude for the aid given. I wish to express particularly my appreciation to Mr. Wilfrid T. Wiatt and to the Torquay Natural History Society of which he is honorary secretary for the cooperation in making available to me the Pengelly manuscripts in the possession of the Society; to the Secretary of the Society of Antiquaries at London; and to Mlle. Lecat, librarian of the Bibliothèque Communal d'Abbeville for making available the correspondence to Boucher de Perthes. In addition, I am grateful to Dr. Walter F. Cannon, Dr. John Cotter, and Dr. John C. Greene for reading earlier versions of this paper and for the liberality of their comments. The inclusion of this paper in this volume cannot, however, pass without my acknowledgment to Dr. Hallowell for the invaluable stimulation of his many conversations with me.

[2] For stimulating, authoritative, although not necessarily compatible accounts of the developments of geology through the first half of the nineteenth century, see Cannon (1960a and b); Eiseley (1958); Gillispie (1951); and Greene (1959).

[3] See particularly Miller (1841, 1857). See also the "popular" presentations of Gideon Mantell (1844).

[4] For the significance of Buckland's cave researches, which caused something of a sensation at the time of their publication, see *Edinburgh Review* (1828) and North (1942).

[5] Kent's Hole or Cavern, at Torquay, is perhaps the most famous of the fossil-bearing caves in England and it had long been known and sporadically plundered (Pengelly: 1868). Moreover, it did supply evidence to support the view of man's contemporaneity with extinct fauna. MacEnery, the most persistent and careful of the early workers at Kent's Hole, did suggest such an associaetion but was never able to commit himself fully to such a view in the face of Buckland's caution regarding the possibilities of excavation errors and/or later intrusions. His conclusions, therefore, as posthumously published by Vivian (MacEnery: 1859) and Pengelly (Pengelly: 1869) were equivocal and do not support the martyrdom granted him by his later admirers. For an interesting controversy over MacEnery's role, see Howorth (1901, 1902); Hunt (1902); and Watson (1902).

[6] While the data were widely known, the interpretations followed the pattern established by Buckland in his *Reliqiae* (Buckland: 1824) of disassociating for one reason or another the human materials from the fossils with which they were associated. See, for example, *Edinburgh New Philosophical Journal* (1834), for a rebuttal of de Serres' claims for the antiquity of man in France.

[7] As is the case with MacEnery, subsequent events and commentators tended to distort the actual relationship of Boucher de Perthes' work to the times. There can be no doubt as to the value of the tenacity with which he pressed the claims to antiquity of his implements and of the men who made them. His conclusions as well as the discoveries upon which they were based were closely related to his own wide-ranging antiquarian interests, the work of the French cave-explorers of the 1820's and 1830's, and the diluvial concepts which they tended to support (see Aufrere: 1936, 1940; Meunier: 1875).

[8] Thus a letter dated December 9, 1857, from Robert Fitch to Ackerman, the secretary of the Society of Antiquaries (*Society of Antiquaries Correspondence*): "I have received a letter from my friend Mr. C. Roach Smith, informing me that M. Boucher de Perthes, was about sending some copies of two antiquarian works to your care, one of which he had kindly presented to the Norfolk & Norwich Archaeological Society . . ."

[9] A note from Roach-Smith, dated January 31, 1852, says (*ibid.*) "The people of Liverpool will elect you into their Society." A footnote in Boucher de Perthes (1857), suggests that Dr. A. Hume published in Liverpool in 1851 a memoir entitled *Stone Period* "where a part of the work of M. Boucher de Perthes 1847 was translated and his figures reproduced." The British Museum does not have a record of this publication nor have I been able to trace it elsewhere. The clustering of these events in the years immediately after 1849 and the inclusion of a slip in my volume of Boucher de Perthes (1847) which reads "Cet ouvrage, inprimé en 1847, n'a pu, en raison des circonstances, être publié qu'en 1849" indicate that despite the date of 1847 on the title page, this volume was not distributed until 1849; its publication date should therefore be the later date.

[10] The chapter from which this portion is quoted was delivered as a lecture before the Edinburgh Philosophical Institution in 1853. Miller committed suicide on Christmas Eve, 1856.

[11] It should be noted, that by the 1840's and 1850's comparative anatomy was making it increasingly difficult to draw clear-cut and unmistakable distinctions between species which had heretofore seemed to occupy discrete steps on the progressionist scale of being. It is highly possible that it was the threat of the elimination of clear-cut distinctions, particularly between man and the anthropoid apes which led Richard

Owen (Owen: 1859) to stress man's uniqueness as the occupant of the mammalian subclass *Archencephala.* Because I am concerned here with the geological path which led to the recognition of man's antiquity, I do not refer to the interesting developments in comparative anatomy in particular and in zoology in general which tended to destroy the concept of man's biological separateness and uniqueness, a line of development which culminated in T. H. Huxley's *Essay on Man's Place in Nature* (1863) whose significance in the area of man's biological affinities matched that of Brixham Cave in the area of his temporal or paleontological relations. It must be realized, however, that the two paths were, for the most part, quite separate, converging only occasionally. Within the scientific milieu of the period, the problem of man's antiquity in a geological sense could be and was quite separate from that of man's zoological place in nature. It was the destruction of this kind of separatism—in the whole domain of natural history—that was one of the primary contributions of "Darwinism."

[12] All three men have been memorialized in a fashion. Both Prestwich and Pengelly are the subjects of the typical nineteenth-century biographical memoir: Pengelly's by his daughter (H. Pengelly: 1897) and Prestwich's by his wife (Prestwich: 1899). Both are long tributes which conceal more than they inform. Falconer's biographical legacy, unfortunately for so interesting a figure in the history of nineteenth-century science, is a collection of his works, most of them previously unpublished, prefaced by a brief biographical notice, a respectful and judicious treatment which adds little to the knowledge of the man (Falconer: 1868).

[13] In 1874, however, Prestwich, at 62, was appointed Professor of Geology at Oxford; but this was little more than an honorary post.

[14] Thus, Boucher de Perthes, often regarded as a pioneer in if not the founder of prehistoric studies, interpreted his evidences from the Somme gravels within a diluvial theory which had been completely rejected—and on sufficient grounds—by the "professional" geologists of his time.

[15] Now in the possession of the Museum of the Torquay Natural History Society, to whose generosity I am indebted for making the manuscript available through its secretary Mr. Wilfrid T. Wiatt. It is impossible to say when this "journal" was written. It is in Pengelly's handwriting and fills thirteen composition books, of which the second is missing. On the basis of internal evidence, I do not think that it represents a running account written during the actual operations nor is it a series of field notes. Rather, it appears to be the occasional collection and, perhaps abstraction of field journal notes and the letters relating to the excavations combined into one connected narrative. While some of the parts appear to have been written while the researches were in progress, the whole seems to have been completed several months after the conclusion of the excavations. Part of the inspiration for the journal was undoubtedly the already developing, in 1860, conflicts over priority of discovery; and, in part, Pengelly hoped to use this edited version of his notes as the basis for his final report to the Royal Society of London.

[16] Henry Keeping who had done a considerable amount of fossil hunting, especially on the Isle of Wight, was hired to do the actual excavation under Pengelly's almost daily supervision and instruction.

[17] It was this technique, so productively utilized at Brixham, which formed the pattern for the later, more highly publicized and better financed but less significant excavations conducted by Pengelly from 1864 to 1880 at Kent's Cavern (Pengelly: 1884). And it was these latter which a half century later provided the model and impetus for the early controlled archaeology in the United States (Woodbury: 1960).

[18] See for instance the report of the meeting in the newly established *Geologist* for December, 1858 (1, 538):

> The communications of Mr. W. P. Pengelly and Professor Ramsay, on the ossiferous cavern at Brixham in Devonshire, gave an indication of what we may expect when the details of the cave shall be fully worked out. . . .
> In the paper read by Mr. Pengelly . . . it was stated that upwards of 2000 mammalian bones had already been exhumed, amongst which were mingled flint knives and other objects, evidently the work of a primitive race of men.
> M. Boucher de Perthes, of Abbeville, the well-known French antiquary, several years ago pointed out the existence of flint weapons and other such artificial objects in the gravel drifts around that town, and with admirable perseverance that gentleman has accumulated, from various and distant localities, a magnificent suite of these objects. . . .
> For many years past, too, we have had accounts of human remains, from gravel and other deposits, which have been too commonly regarded as apocryphal or as the result of a careless commingling of the contents of proximate strata of very different ages. . . .

[19] Interestingly enough, the "liberal" position, held by the majority of "professionals" was based upon the rejection of the flood as a geological agent, an hypothesis which had already been abandoned for a generation, and the acceptance of the progressionist system which regarded man as the terminal creation. The "conservatives," still following Buckland's original thesis from which he had been converted in the late 1830's, maintained the diluvial hypothesis; and they saw in the evidences from Brixham Cave both the proofs of the existence of antediluvial man and the deluge which had destroyed him. See, for example, Vivian (1858).

[20] It is important to note here that Prestwich was not convinced of nor was he necessarily arguing for a high *chronological* antiquity of man. What struck him as significant and that to which he was testifying as a geologist was a stratigraphically earlier position of man than that generally recognized, i.e., the contemporaneity of man with an earlier—and conceivably separate—geological and palaeontological horizon.

[21] The French, understandably, have always seen Boucher de Perthes as the great pioneer; see Mortillet (1865, pp. 11–12); Breuil (1945); and Boule and Vallois (1957, p. 15) where, incidentally J. W. Flower, the archaeologist who did visit Boucher de Perthes is confused with J. H. Flower, the anatomist, who did not. However, the same pattern is evident in the English literature; see, for example, Peake (1940) and Brace (1868, p. 333), who, even at that early date, could write: "These discoveries of M. de Perthes at length aroused the attention of English men of science, and during 1859, a number of eminent gentlemen . . . visited M. Perthes' collection and saw the flints *in situ*." See also Joan Evans (1949).

[22] See Daniel (1950, pp. 57–67) for a different view.

30. Some Problems in the Understanding of Nineteenth Century Cultural Evolutionism

George W. Stocking, Jr.

As is so often the case with historians, systematic work in one period led me back into the period which preceded it.[1] In the process of research on Franz Boas and turn-of-the-century American thought on race and culture, I of course had done a fair amount of reading and thinking about nineteenth century anthropology; but it is only since the publication of *Race, Culture, and Evolution* (Stocking 1968a) that I have attempted a more systematic inquiry. That inquiry is still in process, and has in fact changed its character somewhat since the ideas of this essay were first formulated. What follows, then, is not only programmatic; it is a program much of which someone else may have to realize. Hopefully, however, this may add to rather than detract from its historiographical utility; and in any case, it suggests certain general interpretive themes which may subsequently be elaborated (cf. Stocking 1969, 1971, 1973).

If my interest in evolutionism grew out of my research on Boas, it was given a sharper definition when I had occasion to review a volume of the translated writings of Johann Bachofen, whom Robert Lowie once described as "an evolutionist of the old school" (Stocking 1968b; cf. Lowie 1937: 41). If we remember Bachofen at all today, it is as the father of "motherright" and of a scheme of "unilinear" evolutionary stages in the development of the family. And indeed he was. But his "evolutionism" was of a very different sort than, for instance, that of E. B. Tylor—although one of Tylor's classic papers explicitly defended arguments first advanced in 1861 in Bachofen's "great treatise" *Das Mutterrecht* (Tylor 1888: 255). Bachofen's "evolutionism" was rooted not in ethnography but in the classics; not in English empiricism or Comtean positivism, but in German romantic historicism and Hegelian idealism. It was embodied not in a cumulative growth of human reason, but in a *Weltgeist* whose "stages" were manifestations of different aspects of human spiritual

Printed by permission of the author.

nature, of underlying "ideas" which "unfolded and flowered" at specific points in time and space—but which were encompassed within a general sexual dialectic leading man gradually from "nature" to "culture," from the dominance of the materialistic, earth-oriented, Oriental maternal principle to the dominance of the spiritual, heaven-oriented, Occidental paternal principle (Bachofen 1967: passim).

Bachofen's method was myth analysis. Myth was the "exegesis of the symbol" unfolding "in a series of outwardly connected actions what the symbol embodies in a unity" (Bachofen 1967: 48). With the passage of time myth obscured "the original intuition" of the unifying symbol, as men rationalized those elements of the myth which clashed with the changing forms of their cultural life. Through myth analysis, however, one could recapture history—not on the basis of euphemerist assumptions, but because behind the *form* of ostensible events lay the content of the underlying idea, in whose vestiges and transformations were embodied the collective memory of a prior cultural state. In contrast to Tylor, whose methodology required a fragmentary review of culture (Stocking 1968c), Bachofen's approach was methodologically grounded on an integrative and holistic view of human cultural life. It was because social organization, religious belief, and cosmic conceptions were all integrated as the expressions in each cultural stage of a single symbol or idea that one could hope to reconstruct that stage. Thus if Bachofen's conception of "vestiges" is similar to the Tylorian doctrine of "survivals," his emphasis was not on the functional anomaly of the "survival" in the present, but on its integration in the coherent symbolic framework that had gone before (Bachofen 1967: 220).

In this context, what is most striking is that Bachofen, despite his "evolutionism," was clearly a part of the same romantic, historicist intellectual tradition in which Franz Boas also had deep roots, and towards which Tylor was basically antagonistic (Stocking 1968a). Thus Bachofen insisted that in addition to the approach to knowledge in terms of "rational combination" there was another in terms of the "imagination," which—"aroused by direct contact with the ancient remains"—grasped "the truth at one stroke." And like Boas, he placed great emphasis on understanding each cultural phenomenon in its own context and in its own terms, without the blinders of ethnocentric preconception.

It is of course true that Bachofen argued that the stages of hetaerism, Amazonism and matriarchy—with all the implications of its etymology—were "universal phenomena," stages in a general historical movement toward the patriarchal family (Bachofen 1967: 93). But even here it is worth noting some differences between Bachofen and our conception of "classical evolutionism." Bachofen seems to have been little interested in "independent invention" or the "parallelism" of human development. His use of the "comparative method" was much closer than Tylor's to that of comparative linguistics. It was largely directed to the establishment of *historical connections* of migration and kinship. Thus *The Myth of Tanaquil,* his last major work, was devoted to demonstrating the existence of an underlying oriental and matriarchal cultural stratum in Italy (Bachofen 1967: 211).

All of which is to argue that the idea of "classical" or "unilinear" evolutionism is an umbrella term which has too long sheltered viewpoints which were actually quite diverse. There may be a level at which "evolutionism" may be regarded as a more or less coherent "paradigm," but the adequate definition of this synthetic view will I think require first a more differentiated and systematic investigation into the varieties of evolutionary argument.

The problem may perhaps be illuminated by a brief review of the historiography of cultural evolutionism—schematized quite frankly from the point of view of its effect on my own perception of the present historiographical problem. In the first place, there is a tradition which may be identified with the Boasian critique of evolutionism, although it is not unrelated to viewpoints in intellectual history which subsume most of the late nineteenth century evolutionary thought under the umbrella category "social Darwinism" (cf. Halliday 1971). This tradition may be traced to Boas' own account of "The History of Anthropology," in which he suggested that evolutionism in anthropology was the result of "Darwin's powerful influence" (Boas 1904). Boas' own picture of late nineteenth century anthropology—perhaps because he himself was a product of it and had a participant's sense of the diversity of its currents—was still rather variegated. But among his students—for whom the battle against evolutionism was the starting point of their own training and of a truly "scientific" viewpoint—one can find fairly well elaborated the picture of the "old school of evolutionism" which conditions informal scholarly opinion even today. Thus on several occasions Goldenweiser summarized the orientation of the school: it was founded on the doctrine of the psychic unity of mankind, which responded to similar environmental situations by creating (by independent invention) similar cultural phenomena. Beyond this, certain assumptions were made about the laws of cultural development: it was uniform (or parallel); it was gradual; it was progressive. Furthermore, a similar unilinear development took place in relation to each of the aspects of culture, all of which were correlated in regular cultural stages. The method of reconstructing these was "the comparative method," supplemented by the "doctrine of survivals." It is important to note that Goldenweiser and Lowie—who were still fairly well-read in the literature of late nineteenth century anthropology—were aware that not all evolutionists fit the model perfectly. Thus Goldenweiser argued that "in his better moments, the evolutionist was, of course, aware of the presence of cultural diffusion"—though he did not fit diffusion into his theories (Goldenweiser 1925: 220). Similarly, Lowie, in his treatment of individual writers—as opposed to his comments on evolutionism as a whole—was by no means insensitive to individual variation (Lowie 1937). But this was always against the implicit model of "the evolutionist of the old school," whose dominance covered the whole thirty-five year period from Darwin to Boas.

A second important line of historical interpretation, which also emerged in the period of the counter-evolutionary reaction, is that of Frederick J. Teggart and his students. On the one hand, they explicated some of the underlying presuppositions of "the comparative method" (Teggart 1925; Hodgen 1936). On the other, they attacked the notion that cultural evolution derived from Darwin by tracing its roots proximately to the writers of the French and Scottish Enlightenments, and ultimately to the Greeks (Bock 1956; Bryson 1945; Hodgen 1964). But if Teggart and his students attacked the assumptions of "conjectural history" based on the comparative method, their historiography unfortunately suffered itself from a somewhat conjectural character—and it was particularly weak in tracing what happened to evolutionism between the Enlightenment and its reemergence in 1860.

In this context, the problem of the causes of the decline and reemergence of evolutionism has been taken up by a more serious historical scholar than either the Boasians or the followers of Teggart: J. W. Burrow, whose *Evolution and Society* appeared several years ago. Burrow explains the decline in terms of the general eclipse of Scottish thought by an a-historical utilitarianism. He sees the reemergence not as an emulation of the achievements of biology, geology and philology, but "as a reaction against the collapse of systematic utilitarianism and the weakening of traditional religious belief." Various early nineteenth century intellectual currents had undercut the basis for the utilitarian assumption of a common human nature, and the "specific attraction" of evolutionism was that it "offered a way of reformulating the essential unity of mankind, while avoiding the current objections to the older theories of a human nature everywhere essentially the same. Mankind was one not because it was everywhere the same, but because the differences represented different stages in the same process" (Burrow 1966: 97–101).

All of which has doubtless advanced our understanding of the emergence of evolutionism around 1860—though there are I think still unanswered questions on this point, as well as on the issue of its earlier decline (cf. Stocking 1973). At the same time, recent scholarship has dispelled certain traditional notions about the character of the old school of evolution. Thus Marvin Harris has been at some pains to refute the "myths" that evolutionists saw the developmental process as unilinear, that they denied diffusion, and that they rejected racial determinism

(Harris 1968: 148–216); and my own work has dealt with these same issues in a somewhat different manner, but to a similar point (Stocking 1968a).

If, however, the result has been to qualify our picture of the "classical evolutionist," all of the writers I have mentioned still tend to assume the existence of some such undifferentiated model. No one has to my knowledge systematically followed up Sol Tax's suggestion of a distinction between "historical" and "psychological" or "scientific" evolutionists (Tax 1937). I would like to suggest that this is largely due to the narrowness of the empirical basis of our conception of the classical evolutionist. As my previous remarks imply, this narrowness is in part the end product of a process. The Boasians tended to subsume a diverse literature within a single polemical model; but where Lowie and Goldenweiser had direct contact with the literature, subsequent anthropologists have only the model, given flesh perhaps by reading a few major figures. At the same time, this narrowing has been reinforced by the prevailing style of intellectual history, which still tends to focus on a few major thinkers rather than on systematic recreation of intellectual milieu. But for whatever reason, the fact is that our present conception of classical evolutionism is based for the most part on Morgan, Tylor, and Spencer; to a much lesser extent on McLennan, Lubbock, and Maine; and in a very marginal way, on Bachofen and Bastian.

I was particularly struck with this recently when I came across a two-volume work entitled *Prehistoric Man* which appeared in 1862 and was written by Daniel Wilson, a Scot who had migrated in 1853 to become professor of history in Toronto, and who was still active in the late 1880's in the British Association Committee under which Franz Boas did his field work in British Columbia. Wilson's work is suggestive in a number of ways of the process by which evolutionism emerged, and yet I do not recall it being mentioned in any history of anthropology (Trigger 1966a, 1966b). Similarly, in studying nineteenth century ideas on the evolution of the family, I have come across the titles of various works which are similarly overlooked. The point is simply that if we want to get a more adequate picture of the "classical evolutionist," we will have to consider a much larger group of writers than the traditional big three or even the big three plus five: among them Pitt-Rivers and Wake in England, Brinton and Powell in the United States, Letourneau and Giraud-Toulon in France, and Post and Andree in Germany, as well as the much larger number of men who wrote in the anthropological journals of the period.

But the narrowness of the empirical base is only part of the problem. There is also the issue of how the evolutionists have been read and analyzed. In general they have been approached in terms of present theoretical concerns: the work of each has been viewed as an undifferentiated whole; that whole has been considered in its relation to the present, or to the assumed model, rather than in detailed comparison to the writings of other evolutionists. This is true to some extent even of Burrow, whose underlying purpose is to explain why functionalism was so late in developing in British anthropology. I do not mean to imply that Burrow's treatment of this problem is not suggestive, nor that the problem itself is not worth investigation—rather that our answer to it, and to other questions relating to the counter-evolutionary reaction around 1900, would be more satisfying if we had a picture of evolutionism more adequately grounded in a systematic analysis of content of evolutionary thought in its own terms; in terms of the questions which motivated the evolutionists' inquiry; the logic and data of their arguments in contemporary context; and their development over time. In developing this analysis, I think it will be particularly important to pay systematic attention to a number of dimensions of differentiation within the much broader group of writers it will be necessary to examine, not simply by noting ways in which they depart from an assumed model, but in order to find uniformities and differences among them which may provide the basis for a more adequate model.

In the remainder of this essay, I would like to suggest and briefly to illustrate some of the dimensions of such a more differentiated view of evolutionism. On this basis, it may be possible to suggest something about the nature of the evolutionary paradigm—to the extent that such a term may be appropriate (cf. Kuhn 1962)—about how it developed in time, about its relation to other currents in late nineteenth century anthropology, and about the subsequent reaction to evolutionism. To provide a context, however, it may help to offer first a brief and frankly schematic picture of the development of anthropology before 1860.

Let me start by offering what might serve someday as a first line for a comprehensive history of anthropology: "In the beginning of anthropology was the word, and the word was genesis; in the beginning of anthropology was the act, and the act was discovery." If one can speak of paradigms in anthropology—and it will be evident as we go along that I am drawn to the notion as a kind of heuristic metaphor, even though the discipline may be in Kuhn's terms "pre-paradigmatic"—then it is I think useful to regard the Bible as the first paradigm in anthropology in the sense that it generated, in the context of the data of discovery, a series of questions about man, and provided a framework of assumption for their answer. Unlike Marvin Harris, who sees the Bible as incipiently evolutionary (Harris 1968: 25), I see it as offering a quite different model of investigation: an *historical* model, if you will, rather than a *scientific* one, one which emphasizes unique events that permanently alter the subsequent course of things, rather than repeated events that can be explained in terms of lawful processes regularly producing the same effects from the same causes. The most important of these unique events were the Creation, the Noachian flood, and the destruction of the Tower of Babel. In the context of these divine interventions, mankind was differentiated out of an original unity in a very limited time span. Insofar as regular processes enter implicitly into the biblical model, they are processes of migration, diffusion, and environmental modification. Furthermore, these processes are largely viewed as degenerative rather than progressive: mankind in general, and especially savage non-Christian man, has *fallen* from a prior state of fullness, grace and harmony, rather than *rising* from a state of nature. Represented pictorially, the model is that of a series of branchings all of which can be traced to a single root: a tree, if you will—perhaps with some drooping branches to allow for the notion of degeneration (cf. Stocking 1973).

Against this model can be posed the evolutionary one which the Teggart school has traced to the Greeks, and which developed as a serious alternative to the biblical view of the 18th century. Its character should already be evident by way of contrast: it is, if you will, scientific rather than historical; it emphasizes repeated, regular, gradual, progressive change out of a uniform natural state. For present purposes it can be represented not as a tree, but simply as a series of parallel lines pointing upward.

Despite Burrow's work, the decline of this evolutionary model in the early nineteenth century has not been adequately investigated. That period still remains the Dark Ages of the historiography of anthropological ideas (cf. Stocking 1973). Several things are fairly evident, however. While the evolutionist model does not disappear completely (witness the line from Condorcet to Comte and thence to Tylor), the religious historical model is strongly reasserted. Both models, moreover, were affected by the emergence of physical anthropology and by the general cultural preoccupation with race, which called into question both the common human nature prerequisite to evolutionary regularity and the unity of origin assumed by religion (cf. Stanton 1960). Furthermore, in the context of racial debate and religious revival, theories of degeneration came to the fore. No one has looked systematically at the various manifestations of degenerationist thought in this period, but from the point of view of anthropology it is worth noting that they appear in physical anthropology, archaeology, and linguistics as well as in ethnography (cf. Freeman 1965). In physical anthropology, degenerationism provided an alternative to a developing notion of multiple human origins—as for instance in Blumenbach's view of the degeneration of the major races from a Caucasian original (Blumenbach 1865). In archaeology, degenerationism was a corollary to the discovery of the remains of once great civilizations (Carpenter 1950). In early comparative linguistics, degeneration is the process by which modern European languages emerged out of an original more perfect Sanskrit (Hymes: in press). I do not mean to suggest that the notion of progress in civilization disappeared in this period. Quite the contrary. But it did tend to be viewed by many men in historical terms; its development was much more problematic and providential; and it was increasingly limited to one major racial group.

Granted all this is grossly oversimplified, it does I think help to define the anthropological significance of contemporary savagery in the period before about 1860. Degenerative offshoot rather than part of the mainline of human development, the savage tended to be of primarily descriptive antiquarian or humanitarian interest—as the journals of the early Ethnological Societies suggest (Stocking 1971). Insofar as savagery had broader theoretical significance, it was in terms of what may be called "the ethnological problem"—which is I think crucial to the understanding of nineteenth century anthropology. Derived from the biblical paradigm, the ethnological problem, in the words of J. C. Prichard, the leading ethnologist of his age, was an attempt to trace "the history of human families from the most remote periods that are within the reach of investigation," to discover "their mutual relations," and to arrive at conclusions "as to their affinity or diversity of origin" (Prichard 1848: 302). Now it is important to note that the primary thrust of the ethnological problem was historical—it was a matter of tracing diffusion and migration and racial affinity in the context of environmental modification and the relatively short biblical time span. However, there was also an implicit thrust toward scientific classification of groups existing in the present, and this increasingly in biological terms which saw man as part of the animal realm. Within this framework, the emerging studies of comparative linguistics and physical anthropology tended to be seen as competing methods for the solution of the single ethnological problem, rather than as equally valid approaches to the study of different aspects of human variation.

It is in this context that one must view the controversy between the monogenists and the polygenists which preoccupied the ethnologists of the 1840's and 1850's (Stanton 1960; Stocking 1973). Although the lines are not always clear-cut, the monogenists are the religiously orthodox advocates of linguistic solutions to the ethnological problem, which they define in essentially historical terms on the assumption of an original Adamic unity of origin. The polygenists are the partisans of science, who emphasize a biological approach to a problem which they redefined in classificatory terms as the systematic definition of the primordially diverse races of man. The contrast is evident in the titles of certain major works: on the one hand, Prichard's *Natural History of Man* (1843); on the other, Nott and Gliddon's polygenist compendium, *Types of Mankind* (1854). Pictorially, monogenism can still be seen in terms of the tree; polygenism, however, is perhaps best represented in terms of the parallel lines, unequal in length and arranged in a pyramid. By the end of the 1850's the polygenist view was on the verge of carrying the day, and the emergence of a new set of scientific societies called "anthropological" in fact symbolizes the legitimation of a scientific approach to man in biological—although not yet in Darwinian—terms (Stocking 1971; Gruber 1967).

In the meantime, however, the problem of the significance of savagery was radically redefined by discoveries in prehistoric archaeology, whose significance for the emergence of cultural evolutionism has been convincingly argued by Jacob Gruber (1965)—and incidentally treated by Burrow in an article which came out after his book (1967). The evidence of a greatly lengthened time span for the existence of man (particularly in Europe) defined a new problem. Perhaps better, it placed a problem which was already of interest both inside and outside of ethnology—that of the origin of European civilization—into a new framework. But if archaeology brought to the fore and redefined the problem of European origins, it did not, except in relation to the material aspects of civilization, really begin to offer an adequate solution. It provided little evidence on the development of religion or the family, of the social and ideational order generally. In this context, the data of ethnology, of contemporary savagery, could take on a very different meaning. The change is reflected in the titles of many of the important anthropological works of the 1860's: perhaps archetypically, Lubbock's *Prehistoric Times as Illustrated by Ancient Remains and the Manners and Customs of Modern Savages* (1865). Suddenly, the manners and customs of modern savages had a new significance: they could be used to fill in the great developmental gaps in the prehistoric archaeological record.

So far, I have argued (to some extent in criticism of Burrow) the need to consider the immediate anthropological (as opposed to the general philosophical) context of social evolutionism. But in taking this line, I do not wish to deny the Teggart school's argument that evolutionism had deeper historical roots. Quite the contrary, I suspect that further investigation will establish that the men who developed the evolutionist argument in the 1860's still had various ties to the Scottish and French Enlightenments, as well as to more recent expressions of the older developmental tradition. Furthermore, I suspect that the tendency of both the Teggart school and Burrow to minimize the impact of Darwin will require some modification. To argue the impact of prehistoric archaeology is already in fact to suggest that cultural evolution was closely linked to the Darwinian revolution, broadly viewed. Beyond this, it seems clear that the social and cultural evolutionists were quite consciously trying to explain the natural development of the peculiarly human qualities of language, religion, science, and the family, and in this sense were answering questions that had been raised by Darwinism (cf. Stocking 1969).

Having defined, schematically, the historical context, let me now suggest briefly nine dimensions of differentiation among the group of writers usually lumped within the rubric "classical evolutionist."[2]

1. As my remarks on Tylor and Bachofen have already indicated, there are important differences of intellectual lineage. At a gross level, one may pose the Anglo-French against the German tradition: the one rationalistic, empirical, atomistic and positivistic; the other romantic, idealist, holistic and historicist; the one seeing the evolutionary process as the accumulation of human reason, the other as the organic unfolding of human potentiality. The national lines, however, are not clear-cut. In England Maine drew on both traditions; whereas Tylor is clearly in the former. At a less general level, there is the question of ties to certain specific traditions of intellectual inquiry: on the one hand, one may group the writers such as Tylor, Lubbock, and Morgan who had important ties to the ethnological tradition as redefined by prehistoric archaeology; on the other, those such as Maine and Bachofen, whose ties were primarily to jurisprudence, social theory, comparative Indo-European philology, and classical studies.

2. There is a further dimension of differentiation in terms of principle motivating problems. All of the evolutionists shared a concern with the origin of European civilization—indeed this is perhaps the basic qualification for group membership. However, those whose work grew out of ethnology can be distinguished from those whose work was rooted in jurisprudence or classical studies. The former tend to be much concerned—at least in certain stages of their work—with two questions which have significance in relation to the ethnological tradition I have described: on the one hand, the problem of the unity of the human race; on the other, the issue of degeneration versus progress, which had special methodological significance if one attempted to fill the archaeological time gap with the data of contemporary savagery. Tylor was preoccupied with both of these issues; Morgan, with the unity question; Maine and Bachofen were little concerned with either. Finally, there was among cultural evolutionists a general concern with legitimizing their study in broad methodological terms, although this took different forms. With some—Tylor is an example—the issue tends to be posed in terms of positive science versus religious tradition and antiquarian descriptive ethnology. Both Tylor and McLennan were concerned lest the greatly increased time gap be filled, as Dugald Stewart had feared a half century or more before, with religious speculation rather than developmental law. Others, however, were less concerned with the conflict of science and religion. Both Morgan and Wilson, whom I mentioned earlier, in fact

concluded by rationalizing the two. Others are concerned with broad methodological issues at a somewhat different level. Thus Maine and Bachofen talked about science, but they are fundamentally historical: Maine was concerned with the establishment of a "scientific" (which is to say an historical) jurisprudence; Bachofen with a more "scientific" history, which in fact tends to be seen in terms of the special character of the *geistes* as opposed to the *naturwissenschaften.*

3. There are also differences relating to methodological issues and assumptions of a more specific sort. Not all of the so-called evolutionists operate in terms of the same time scale. At least in their early work, Maine and Bachofen wrote essentially within a time span limited to the historic record; others started from the greatly enlarged time span of prehistoric archaeology. There are also differences in the conception of human psychic unity, which as I have already suggested, Tylor saw in terms of a unilinear accumulation of rationality, but which Bachofen saw as an unfolding of different aspects of human psychic nature. They differ also in the degree to which they adopted a functionalist or an holistic view of cultural phenomena. Tylor tended toward atomism; Morgan at points saw his stages in more integrated terms; Bachofen approached even more closely the modern concept of culture as an integrated, holistic, ideational phenomenon. Finally, they seem to me to differ in their conception of "the comparative method."

This is a point which I would like to elaborate, since it is important to the argument I will develop later. Various writers have suggested that the proximate source of the comparative method in evolutionary ethnology is in the comparative linguistics of the early nineteenth century (e.g. Eggan 1965). However, it seems to me that the comparative method as used in comparative linguistics is not in all respects based on the same assumptions as it is in evolutionary ethnology—a point which has been implied, but not I think adequately elaborated, by Burrow. Because the history of the comparative method in linguistics—and of the specific assumptions it involved—has not itself been fully explored, I am a bit hesitant in venturing on this question—especially since there is evidence that these specific assumptions changed over time, and that *genealogical* comparison and *typological* comparison involve different assumptions (cf. Hymes: in press). Insofar as mid-nineteenth century comparative linguistics was genealogical, however, it involved a different procedure than that of the social evolutionists. It was based on the comparison of languages which were, or which there was reason to believe were, genetically related: i.e. the members of the Indo-European family. Furthermore, the comparative method of genealogical linguistics was buttressed by historical documentation, and its laws of development were based largely on verifiable historical sequences of cause and effect. The comparative method of evolutionary ethnology differed in each of these respects. Its data were taken from the world over, and were intended to recreate typological stages rather than specific historical relations; its very conception was designed to circumvent the lack of documentary data; and its laws were based—as Franz Boas later noted (1896)—not on the comparison of verified sequences of cause and effect, but on the assumption that once a given effect could be in principle adequately explained in terms of some hypothesized cause, and a certain amount of data could be randomly collected to justify the existence of the assumed causal process, then all instances of that effect could, by an inversion of reasoning, be explained in terms of the hypothesized cause—a procedure archetypically represented in McLennan's *Primitive Marriage.*

That at least some contemporaries were in fact aware of some such difference in methodological assumption among the practitioners of "*the* comparative method" is evident in Maine's criticisms of McLennan; and perhaps most specifically in a long review of McLennan's last book that appeared in the *Quarterly Review* in 1886–and which has been attributed to Maine. Arguing along lines that I have just indicated, the reviewer maintained that McLennan's method was not at all that of comparative linguistics, but was rather derived from that of the biologist's reconstruction of ancient animal forms. The passage in fact raises the problem of survivals or vestiges, and I have already suggested that this, too, was an aspect of method in terms of which the evolutionists may be differentiated.

4. The evolutionists also differed in terms of subject matter—although the issue is not quite so clear-cut as Sol Tax's suggestion (1937) that the historical evolutionists were interested in marriage forms and social structure, and the psychological or scientific evolutionists in religion: McLennan and Tylor (in his well-known article of 1888) are examples of "scientific" evolutionists concerned with the former problem.

5. The evolutionists differed also in their conceptions of evolutionary "stages." Some developed elaborate sequences with precisely defined stages, like Morgan; others, like Tylor, distinguished only rough lines of development in specific institutions. Some were more insistently "unilinear"—although in general the "unilinearity" of social evolutionism has been too much insisted on.

6. The evolutionists differed in their treatment of issues of evolutionary process. As I have already suggested, Tylor was much concerned with the alternatives of diffusion and independent invention, which were of little concern to Bachofen. There was also among the evolutionists in general a tension between process in purely ideational terms and process in terms of material causation. It is not enough to dismiss them all as essentially idealists (cf. Harris 1968). The tension in Morgan between a development in terms of regular response to the necessities of similar

external conditions and an unfolding of a "few primary germs of thought" is evident in other writers as well.

7. One can see, too, important differences in attitude toward the evolutionary process and the phenomena evolving. Thus one might arrange Bachofen, Maine, Tylor and Morgan on a continuum in terms of their orientations toward the past and the future—Bachofen at points clearly sensing the loss of a prior harmony; Maine accepting the movement from familial holism to individualistic atomism without a qualm; Tylor quite satisfied with the present if it be purged of animistic survivals; Morgan, at least in some passages, looking to a future more democratic society.

8. There are also important differences of historical context. This problem is of course crucial to our whole historical understanding of evolutionism, and begins to carry us outside the rather internal intellectual framework which I have used so far. Burrow's argument that evolutionary anthropology was a response to the collapse of utilitarianism and the weakening of religious belief is of course a major step in this direction, but by no means the last word on the subject. Some writers were clearly affected by the revolutionary movements of 1848; others by the changes taking place in the middle-class family (cf. Stocking 1971). Here, too, there are clearly differences in terms of national tradition. One notes the reflection of concern with class in Tylor and other English writers, and Morgan's characteristically American view of evolutionary process as man's "working himself up." Or consider Morgan's ambivalent attitudes toward the American Indian, expressed in a kind of cyclical drama of the American continent—the primitive red American democrat incapable of raising himself above barbarism, his destiny in a sense fulfilled at a higher level by the civilized white American democrat.

9. As a final dimension of differentiation, I would suggest the temporal. As I have argued elsewhere (Stocking 1968a), there is a movement in Tylor's three major works *from* history *to* evolutionism, a shift marked by increasing emphasis on the evolutionary comparative method and the regularity of evolutionary development—and this movement can also be found in other writers.

So much for dimensions of differentiation. No doubt these could be elaborated, but I would prefer here to suggest, rather tentatively, the possibilities of their reintegration in a more adequate synthetic view of evolutionism. I suspect that it will be useful to begin at a rather general level. Quite independently of Darwinism, in the context of emerging political stability and prosperity symbolized in England by the Crystal Palace Exposition, there was in the 1850's a general and rather diffuse preoccupation with the development of European civilization which expressed itself in a variety of writings, some of which we do not now see as specifically cultural evolutionist. This generalized preoccupation involved certain assumptions about the primitive mind, about the process by which civilization developed, about the role of race in that process, and about the civilization that had emerged. At the broadest level, this generalized preoccupation—which continued for some time after 1859—may be viewed as a kind of retrospective validation of the ideal concept of Victorian man, and of the contemporary relations of the civilized and the "noncivilized" world. From the early 1860's on, however, in the context of a greatly increased time scale, there was within this generalized evolutionary preoccupation a thrust from the historical toward the evolutionary, or toward classical evolutionism as we have traditionally conceived it: from the tracing of historical relations to the recreation of evolutionary stages, and toward a redefinition of the comparative method. In the case of McLennan, there is a clear discontinuity (Stocking 1969), but in general the development is in terms of an overlay upon traditional approaches, which by no means disappear completely. Many of the more elaborate manifestations of what may be called the specifically evolutionary viewpoint tend to appear quite late, and it is against these later elaborations, indeed against a kind of extrapolation of the logic of the argument itself, that the sharpest reaction against evolutionism takes place—although in the context of a general cultural reaction against the more diffuse evolutionary viewpoint.

To provide a kind of documentation for this interpretation, I would like to look more closely, albeit still tentatively, at the development of one evolutionist—Lewis Henry Morgan—over time. As a simple heuristic device let us compare the opening lines of Morgan's three major works. *The League of the Ho-de-no-sau-nee* (1851) opens with the sentence:

> To encourage a kinder feeling toward the Indian, founded upon a truer knowledge of his civil and domestic institutions, and of his capabilities for future elevation, is the motive in which this work originated.

Systems of Consanguinity and Affinity (1871) opens as follows:

> Philology has proved itself an admirable instrument for the classification of nations into families upon the basis of linguistic affinities. A comparison of . . . certain languages has shown them to be dialects of a common speech; and these dialects, under a common name, have thus been restored to their original unity as a family of languages.

Ancient Society (1877) opens:

> The great antiquity of mankind upon the earth has been conclusively established. . . . This knowledge changes materially the views which have prevailed respecting the relations of savages to barbarians, and of barbarians to civilized men.

The *League* was published in 1851 and although one can find in it numerous evidences of a progressivist view of civilization, its predominant character seems to me that of descriptive and humanitarian ethnology within an essentially historical framework. On the other hand, *Systems*, which was conceived in the 1850's and accepted for publication in 1868, is a volume in which one can trace the emergence of a specifically evolutionary viewpoint out of the ethnological controversies of the 1850's. Aside from the interest of the data of the classificatory system of kinship itself, the major issue motivating Morgan's inquiry is the quite traditional one of the origin of the American Indians in the specific context of the debate between the monogenists and the polygenists. His whole argument, which is based explicitly on a comparative philological model, is an attempt to establish the Asian origin of the Indians and to refute the notion that they are an aboriginally distinct species—as the polygenists had argued. Pictorially, the model is still that of the tree, not that of parallel development. However, Morgan was already operating in terms of a time span and a body of data which made historical inquiry extremely tenuous, and his attempt to trace historical diffusion left him with problems which impelled him toward what we now call "classical" evolutionism. Specifically, his friend McIlvaine raised the question as to how the classificatory system had developed in the first place (Resek 1960: 94). The answer McIlvaine proposed—a hypothesized state of primitive promiscuity—was the basis for Morgan's elaboration of a sequence of 15 stages of marriage forms and kinship systems. From another point of view, this evolutionary sequence may be regarded as a response to the problem of polygenism: the spread of the classificatory system linked most of the populations of the earth, but the dichotomy between it and the descriptive system still remained as a barrier to human unity. By placing both in one evolutionary sequence, Morgan was able to bring all men again within a unified framework. In terms of the development of the comparative method, however, it is necessary to note that Morgan was still at great pains to reject the notion that the classificatory system had been independently invented on more than one occasion: it emerged only *once* in history and was thenceforth diffused, not by borrowing, but in the very blood of migrating racial groups (Morgan 1871: 467–506).

The opening lines of *Ancient Society* (1877) signalize a further considerable shift in orientation: the problem is now explicitly that created by the expansion of human chronology; the focus is now not on establishing specific historical relationships, but on recreating generalized evolutionary stages; comparative linguistics recedes into the background; the assumptions of "the comparative method of ethnology" seem much more in evidence. And yet the older viewpoint has not been shed entirely. It is in this framework, among others, that one must see the persisting tension in *Ancient Society* between evolutionism (in the specific sense) and diffusionism, between progressive and unfolding relations, between the similar operation of the human mind in similar environmental situations and the development of major institutions out of germs or ideas which emerged only once in history and were subsequently diffused. The evolutionary model has been overlaid on a diffusionary ethnological one. Pictorially, the result is neither the tree nor the ascending parallel lines, but a combination of the two. The parallel lines are there, although within a pyramidal outline, since the development of European civilization is ultimately for Morgan the unique contribution of the Aryan race. However, these lines are connected by a network of diffusionary linkages, thicker at the center, sparse at the edges, which represent the isolated survivals of a prior savage stage.

A similar thrust to that I have found in Morgan toward a stricter evolutionism and a redefinition of the comparative method in the context of a greatly increased time span can I think be found in the work of two other writers who come from a quite different tradition—that of jurisprudence and classical studies rather than that of ethnology: Maine and Bachofen. Although they were led to quite different conclusions as to the character of the primitive family (Maine arguing the priority of patriarchy and Bachofen of matriarchy) both men worked originally within a limited time span in terms of bodies of source material of verifiable antiquity. Over time, however, both became dissatisfied with the historical material available to them, which seemed inadequate for the resolution both of the general problem and of the critical case of the nature of the Roman *gens*. Morgan's *Ancient Society* treated the Roman gens in context of a comparison with the Iroquois, and in the late 1870's both Maine and Bachofen exchanged letters with Morgan over the issues involved. Prior to the publication of Morgan's book, Maine had already drawn an explicit distinction between Morgan's method and his own: the former was based on the observation of contemporary savages; the latter on "ancient institutions which I can more or less distinctly connect with Modern ideas." Maine felt, however, that "the two lines of inquiry promise more and more to connect themselves together" (LHMP 7/30/1876) and in a subsequent letter in response to *Ancient Society* he suggested a point of specific contact in the problem of the nature of the Roman gens, which he then went on to discuss in terms of the possible light cast on it by Morgan's Iroquois data (LHMP 4/30/1878). Bachofen, too, moved in the same direction, and in relation to the same issue. After 25 years or more of study, he had concluded that "the classical sources are insufficient to bring us to a result more than hypothetical" as to "the origin and nature of the Italian gens," and that this "period of human existence must be studied by the observation of nations still existing, as you have done it in so instructive a manner and with so brilliant success" (LHMP 2/24/1879). Bachofen later suggested that his own most recent work—which was interrupted by his death—had been an attempt to place "the phenomena of the so-called classical antiquity in parallel with other corresponding phenomena, whether of decayed peoples of civilization or of still existing barbarian races, and (to) endeavor through the latter to explain and render understandable whatever is seen in the former that is obscure" (LHMP 10/29/1880).

But if one can find in various writers a thrust from history toward evolutionism and a redefinition of the comparative method, it is also true that the older ethnological orientation never disappeared entirely. There were, as it were, different levels of ethnological concern, both in the discipline in general and in the work of individual ethnologists. On the one hand, an analysis of the contents of the *Journal* of the Anthropological Institute of Great Britain in the last thirty years of the nineteenth century—the traditional heyday of classical evolutionism—suggests that the specifically evolutionary content was somewhat limited. More often, the articles expressed a kind of mixed interest in ethnic origins that involved certain generalized evolutionary assumptions about the nature of savagery or the progress of civilization within a framework of quite traditional concern with the ethnological problem of diffusion, migration, and historical ethnic relationships—and indeed many of the articles were almost wholly in the latter framework. Similarly, one can find this duality expressed in the works of specific anthropologists: Tylor continued to write diffusionary studies into the 1890's (Friere-Marreco 1907); Alexander Gatschet, who was quite evolutionary in some of his assumptions about the development of human language (Stocking: in press) was capable of writing a study of the migration legend of the Creek Indians which is much within the older ethnological tradition (Gatschet 1884). Even in the Bureau of American Ethnology itself—the stronghold of that arch-evolutionary J. W. Powell—much of the actual ethnological work was quite within the older tradition. Finally, there were some influential anthropologists like F. W. Putnam, in whom the overlay never really took place, and who remain throughout the period quite skeptical of the specifically evolutionary viewpoint. Indeed, one of the more interesting documents of nineteenth century anthropology is an unsigned typescript in the Putnam papers in which the author (presumably Putnam) alleged that his friend Morgan retreated from his evolutionary extremism just prior to his death (FWPP n.d.). Nor is this the only evidence that a major evolutionist might have begun to have second thoughts. Elsewhere (Stocking 1968a: 211) I have quoted a letter from Tylor to Franz Boas suggesting in 1896 that "the logical screw" of anthropology was very much in need of tightening.

There were other men, however, who had no apparent qualms. Indeed, one can find (at least in the United States) some of the more extreme evolutionist positions coming very late in the period. Daniel Garrison Brinton and John Wesley Powell were taking rather rigidly anti-diffusionist positions in the mid-1890's. Brinton, quoting Steinmetz, argued that similar customs should be explained by historical diffusion "only when there are special, known and controlling reasons indicating this"—otherwise the presumption was always in favor of psychic unity, common cultural stage, and similarity of environment (Brinton 1895: 247). Powell published a series of rococco "pentalogic" elaborations of evolutionary stages in every area of human existence (e.g. Powell 1899). And in England, J. G. Frazer carried forward the basic assumptions of "classical" evolutionism until well into the twentieth century—albeit in rather a-theoretical and eclectic style.

All of this raises interesting questions about the dynamics of intellectual development in nineteenth century anthropology. As I have already suggested, much of this history seems to me illuminated metaphorically by Thomas Kuhn's ideas about how the natural sciences develop (Kuhn 1962). The transitions at both ends of the evolutionary period, from Prichardian ethnology to evolutionism after 1860 (Stocking 1973), and the counter-evolutionary reaction around 1900 (Stocking 1968a), both resemble in certain respects Kuhn's scientific revolutions. For the evolutionary period itself, one can argue that evolutionism functioned to some extent as a scientific paradigm. Thus, in some cases at least, it directed ethnographic research toward problems which were in a sense generated by the paradigm—perhaps most clearly in the case of "primitive promiscuity." Once this hypothetical state had been defined as part of the evolutionary model of the development of the family, field ethnographers began to search for evidence to establish it empirically. The correspondence of Lorimer Fison and E. B. Tylor (EBTP) over the last two decades of the century may be read as an increasingly disillusioned search for this will-o'-the-wisp, which actually existed only as a "stage" of evolutionary theory—and perhaps also as a fantasy in the collective conscience of sexually repressed Victorians.

This last possibility may make one pause before pushing "paradigms" too far. Certainly, the continuity of the older diffusionary ethnological viewpoint during the evolutionary period would suggest that we may have to do rather with enduring alternatives in a pre- or non-paradigmatic inquiry. Even so, Kuhn's model seems to me metaphorically illuminative—perhaps because there is a tendency for development in scient*ist*ic areas of humanistic inquiry to follow developmental patterns in the natural sciences; perhaps because Kuhn has in fact said something about the processes of intellectual development generally. The dialectics of certain types of intellectual discourse may in various ways impel thought toward the kind of systematization within and discontinuity between viewpoints that the paradigm idea implies. I think in this context of Burrow's distinction between a man's "view" and his "theories" (Burrow 1966: 32)—which I would explicate (and extend) as the distinction between what all that a man unites and what he really thinks, between cautious qualification and secret certainty, between the recognition of alternatives and the unified logical extrapolation, between the variegation suggested by my dimensions of differentiation and the stereotype of the classical evolutionist of the old school. Both are historical realities. There were in fact diffusionary currents within evolutionary thought, and no adequate historical picture can neglect them. But in another sense these were not what evolutionism was all about, and from this point of view the Boasian critics of Morgan were right in directing their criticism toward a stereotype. That sort of extrapolation is in fact inherent in intellectual discourse. But from the historian's point of view, all of these phenomena—the variegation, and the tendency to consistency, both in the intellectual current itself, and in the minds of its protagonists—are aspects of the dynamics of intellectual development, and therefore equally the subject of his inquiry. He must sort out historical phenomena in such a way as to recapture their actual diversity, and yet not lose the unifying tendencies that are in a sense no less real.

Notes

[1] Revised version of a lecture given January 30, 1969 to the Department of Anthropology, University of Minnesota. The bibliographic references were added much later, and are not intended to be exhaustive. Documents were consulted from Lewis Henry Morgan papers, Rush Rhrees Library, Rochester, New York; Papers of Edward B. Tylor, Pitt Rivers Museum, Oxford; and Frederick Ward Putnam Papers, Harvard University Archives.

[2] In what follows, I will draw without specific citation on the following works: Bachofen 1967; Lubbock 1865, 1870; McLennan 1865; Maine 1861; Morgan 1870, 1877; Spencer 1850, 1877; Tylor 1865, 1871.

31. Social Anthropology at Cambridge Since 1900

Meyer Fortes

An Inaugural Lecture is a fit occasion for taking stock. The Chair I am privileged to hold was established twenty years ago with the help of a bequest from Mr William Wyse, whose name is commemorated in its title, and on the initiative of the Master, Fellows and Scholars of Trinity College. We think nothing nowadays of asking for a Chair to be established to put a neglected branch of scholarship and research on the academic map. It was not so in the past. Anthropology had to show that it was able to survive, and grow, before the dignity, respectability and security symbolized in a Chair were conferred on it. To-day we can regard the future of anthropological studies in Cambridge with some optimism; but this is due above all to the small band of undaunted Victorians who kept them alive here and elsewhere in the years between 1890 and 1930.

The cause in which they were engaged concerned not only Cambridge, but all the great centres of learning in this country; and not anthropological studies alone, but all the related disciplines and interests. For as they insistently taught, anthropological studies cannot flourish in isolation, either in one place or in one academic compartment. The circulation of men and of ideas between universities, between different branches of science and scholarship, between the world of learning and the world of practical affairs, between different *countries*, has been vital for their development. If it had not been for Bronislaw Malinowski, an expatriate Pole who chose to make England his home, British social anthropology would to-day be in a parlous state.

The men who created modern anthropology came from many walks of scholarship and of public life, and for them anthropology was as large as life itself. So they had no hesitation in borrowing methods and data, theories and speculations from any promising source. As Haddon remarked in 1905:[1] Psychology and theology, history and sociology, all

From Meyer Fortes, *Social Anthropology at Cambridge Since 1900*, 1953. Reprinted by permission of Cambridge University Press: pp. 1–30.

overlap in the area in which 'the anthropologist prowls'. He could safely have added geography, linguistics, classical studies, jurisprudence and the arts of government. The borrowing was reciprocal and the process goes on. For advances in anthropological knowledge are inseparable from advances in related human sciences.

It is characteristic and important that anthropological studies owe a great deal to enthusiasts from outside the academic world, to officers of the Crown, to missionaries, traders and travellers. Anthropology at Cambridge owes a very special debt to them. It was Sir Richard Temple, equally noted in his day as an administrator in India and as an Orientalist, who gave what might be called the first inaugural lecture on anthropology in Cambridge. This was on 17 November 1904, forty-eight years ago, when he gave an address to welcome the establishment of the Board of Anthropological Studies. But I am thinking more particularly of the fact that both the first William Wyse Professor, Professor T. C. Hodson, and his successor and my predecessor, Professor J. H. Hutton, were authorities on the ethnology of India, who came to the Chair after distinguished service in the I.C.S. Building on the heritage of Haddon, they made our Tripos what it is to-day. And in this connexion I wish also to pay a tribute to the work done for Cambridge anthropology by another ex-administrator, the late Mr J. H. Driberg.

In his address Sir Richard Temple laid great stress on the importance of anthropology for those whose work lies in distant lands. The necessary knowledge, he said, could not be acquired by simply living among a people of different culture. It needed a habit of intelligently examining them; and the cultivation of such a habit as well as the accumulation of scientific knowledge was what he hoped would be encouraged in the University.

In this he was echoing Haddon and other anthropologists and administrators of the time. They all believed that anthropological studies had what Haddon called 'a practical value'. They often quoted examples of the price paid for ignorance and the gain reaped from knowledge of the customs and institutions of the peoples of India, Africa and Oceania; for the 'practical' meant for them what could be used for the benefit of the native peoples, and not solely for the advantage of the European rulers. It was due to this that various Colonial governments encouraged and assisted important anthropological researches which would not otherwise have been possible. The flood of government largesse we have had since the war (now, alas, coming to an end) could never have been foreseen in 1939, let alone 1904. It behoves us to remember with all the more gratitude the support given to anthropological studies by governments of British overseas territories in the past. They helped to make a concern with the practical value of our research a characteristic of British anthropology. This is now so much part of our tradition that it is perfectly respectable to pretend to be indifferent to it! Professor Hutton spoke at length on this subject in his Inaugural Lecture in 1937, and I need therefore say no more about it.

What lay behind this faith of Haddon and his colleagues in the practical usefulness of their work? No doubt the ethics common to all who considered themselves to be enlightened in that period of liberal thought had something to do with it. But most of all, it stemmed directly from the theory of organic evolution, the theory which gave birth to modern anthropology. Tylor had not hesitated to end his great book on *Primitive Culture*, published in 1871, with the bold slogan: 'The science of culture is essentially a reformer's science.' This meant for him chiefly the battle against what he called 'the usurpation of intellectual authority by a sacerdotal caste', which his generation of Darwinian evolutionists had to fight. But it also had the wider meaning implied in Haddon's notion of practical anthropology. The essential premiss of evolutionary anthropology is expressed in Westermarck's dictum[2] that the path which can lead to truth is 'open to him alone who regards organic nature as one continued chain the last and most perfect link of which is man'.

Thus anthropology was defined as an omnibus subject. It was thought of, in Seligman's words,[3] as 'the science of man and of his culture at various levels of development . . . the study of the human frame, of racial distinctions, of civilization, of social structures, of man's mental reactions to his environment'. But the heart of this study was the uniquely human attribute of *Homo sapiens* which Tylor called Culture, and defined as 'that complex whole which includes knowledge, belief, art, morals, law, custom and any other capabilities and habits acquired by man as a member of society.' Before Darwin these attributes of mankind had been commonly regarded as standing outside the realm of nature, subject primarily to divine law, and symbolized in man's being the only creature with an immortal soul. The cold light of the evolutionary theory showed man, even in his most spiritual aspect, to be part of the same process of nature as had produced the physical universe. So it was not just a specious analogy when Herbert Spencer extended the notion of the organism to human social life. Nor did it seem unreasonable to seek in the habits acquired by man as a member of society the expression of the biological laws of variation, selection, survival, adaptation and progressive improvement. Evolution was the key to the uniformities previously only guessed at but now demonstrated in the great variety of human physique, custom and social life, past and present, which had been brought to light by archaeologists and explorers. From it promised to come 'the general laws which have regulated human history in the past, and which, if nature is really uniform, may be expected to regulate it in the future,' as Frazer put it in 1908.[4]

There was grandeur in this conception, for it included *all* mankind and *all* man's works—not only the extinct cave-dwellers and the naked foodgatherers of the Australian desert, but the men who propounded it as well. So it emphasized the unity of all mankind. But it also brought out their differences and the obvious supremacy of European civilization; and this required a notion of grades of culture which, in the evolutionary context, meant a concept of progress.

The idea of progress regarded as a fact, as a law of social development and as an ethical ideal, was the germ of the belief in the practical value of anthropology. A primitive culture had value in its own right as a stage in human development. Progress was not to be thrust upon it. Drastic imposition of European economic devices or religious beliefs, followed as they often were by new diseases, might destroy the tribe, as Rivers showed. The right way was by adaptation based on knowledge of the native life. To build up this knowledge was a scientific task; more than that, it was a moral duty, for these savage ways of life were rapidly disappearing. If we do not record them, said Frazer, repeating the plea reiterated day in and day out by his fellow anthropologists, 'how shall we . . . look when we stand at the bar of posterity arraigned on a charge of high treason to our race'.

Half a century ago, then, the evolutionary idea was not only a scientific hypothesis but a creed and a scale of worth for those engaged in anthropological studies. In accordance with the spirit of the times, they believed in the method of natural science as the royal road to the explanation and regulation of human affairs. The most uncompromising of them looked forward to the final triumph of an understanding of nature—human nature included—based on the discoveries of science and no longer on the dogmas of religion; and they thought therefore, as Frazer declared,[5] that 'every obstacle placed in the way of scientific discovery is a wrong to humanity'.

We see this in the most typical, perhaps greatest anthropological monument of this period, Frazer's *The Golden Bough*. Its scarcely veiled contempt for the magical and religious customs so vividly described, and its complacent self-righteousness, spring from impatience with beliefs that might thwart scientific discovery. Jane Harrison's exclamation,[6] 'But I abhor obscurantism', is in the same spirit.

Most noteworthy, though, is the place the evolutionary theory gave to anthropology in the intellectual life of the first twenty years of this century. It brought about that circulation of men and of ideas to which I have referred. For evolution was the ruling fashion of thought in all branches of scholarship and science concerned with man's life and history, and the works of anthropologists were eagerly culled for comparisons and explanations. It is hardly necessary to remind a Cambridge audience of the close ties anthropology had with classical scholarship when we have just celebrated the centenary of Jane Harrison's birth.

Frazer's classical erudition was the rock on which his vast researches were founded. Perhaps the latest representative of this alliance is Professor Arnold Toynbee's *Study of History*. There is some excellent anthropology in it and his combination of a genetical and a comparative method is reminiscent of evolutionary anthropology. Political philosophers have, of course, used—and abused—ethnological information ever since the discovery of the New World. 'Comparative jurisprudence', said Vinogradoff in 1920,[7] 'has almost become synonymous with the study of primitive societies.' Last, but from the anthropologist's point of view most important of all, are the mutual links with archaeology, sociology and psychology created at that time. I must repeat that it was a two-way traffic, for anthropologists borrowed as freely as they gave.

In this way anthropological studies came to have close ties with both the natural sciences and the humanities, as well as with the world of practical affairs; and they had a considerable vogue also with the educated public. This was connected with the expanding geographical horizon that came with the final opening up of Africa and the Orient, and the wider historical horizon due to new discoveries about ancient civilizations. There was also the obvious relevance of anthropology to controversies about the bearing of scientific discoveries on the doctrines of religion.

This is, I think, a fair outline of the status of anthropology in England about the time of the first World War. But I fear it may give too rosy an impression. For in spite of the wide interest commanded by their writings, and the recognition, by learned societies as well as the public, of the intellectual eminence of leading anthropologists, the fact remains that anthropological studies were in a precarious state. 'Our Cinderella science' was Haddon's rueful description of anthropology in 1903 after a visit to the United States,[8] where he had found it already a well-staffed and flourishing subject of university teaching and research. 'I must confess . . . a not inconsiderable amount of envy', he added, when he compared this with the 'apathy which pervades our own country'. In 1908 Ridgeway, as President of the Royal Anthropological Institute, initiated a proposal for an Imperial Bureau of Anthropology. But when the Government of India offered a contribution of a hundred pounds a year, and the governments of British East Africa fifty pounds a year, towards the scheme, the Home ministers refused to sanction this. Ridgeway's proposal was several times revived in the next forty years, always to no avail. No doubt the money will be found one day, when the time comes for a memorial to an archaic political system that was once fittingly called 'imperial'.

What was the position in the universities? In 1923 Haddon circulated a note on the History of Anthropology at Cambridge. Only the London School of Economics had a Chair in the subject at that date. Oxford had a Reader in Social Anthropology and a Lecturer in Physical Anthropology. Here Haddon, getting on for seventy, still held the Readership in Ethnology conferred on him in 1909, and carried most of the burden of teaching. A Diploma had been instituted in 1908, a Tripos in Archaeology and Anthropology in 1919; and Colonial and Indian Probationers later attended courses as a part of their training. 'It has been a long and hard struggle to create a new department of studies in the University', says Haddon in this memorandum. Indeed it had been, as anyone can see from Mrs Quiggin's inimitable story of his life.[9] It applied, however, not to Cambridge alone, but to all our universities.

At almost every meeting of the British Association between 1900 and 1930, the needs of anthropology were brought to public notice, and especially the need for trained observers. Nor did the demand come only from academical anthropologists. Crooke, speaking with the authority of long years of ethnological research in the Indian Civil Service, made it the theme of his presidential address to Section H of the British Association in 1910. 'Anthropology', he said, was 'in danger of being submerged by a flood of amateurism'. Observers trained in scientific methods were now urgently needed. Ten years later, Karl Pearson, in his Presidential Address to Section H, went further. He pleaded for the creation of professional posts in anthropology, and for the setting up of anthropological institutes in at least three universities; for trained observers could not be produced without adequate teaching facilities, nor employed without funds for research.

But the long struggle was not without avail. The first rewards were an extra professorship at the London School of Economics for Malinowski (1928), and the foundation of Chairs here and at Oxford, in 1932 and 1937. The number of professional anthropologists still came to only a handful though, at the outbreak of the war in 1939. There were perhaps twenty in the whole of the British Commonwealth, and only four or five of these had received their undergraduate education in British universities. I do not, incidentally, want to suggest that anthropology was alone in these trials, for all the social sciences were in the same boat.

But let us not jump to conclusions. One of the benefits of an anthropological education is that one learns to regard with respect, if not always with approval, collective judgments which are casually attributed to tradition, bias, or even malice. Leaving aside the wider issues of policy and habit, was the cautious response of the universities to such pleas as those of Karl Pearson entirely unjustified? I think not. For the hard truth is that anthropology was not yet a subject, in the sense that anatomy or philology, for instance, is one. Anthropologists had a magnificent field of enquiry; but even though it was limited to what they called the lower stages of civilization, it had no intrinsic unity. There was no discipline, in the sense that an anatomist's or philologist's procedures and concepts make up a discipline that is common to the general body of the profession and can be taught to those entering it. A discipline must be specific to a subject matter and must have a framework of theory. Conformity to the rules of logic and zealous collection of facts do not make one.

At the stage of development it had reached in 1920, anthropology, both in this country and elsewhere, was a bundle-subject, its data gathered, so to speak, from the same forest but otherwise heterogeneous and tied together only by the evolutionary theory. This is seen in some of the ethnological works of the time, where cranial measurements, descriptions of tools and implements, accounts of ceremonies and beliefs, vocabularies, and anything else that might occur to the author, are indiscriminately bundled together. Without discipline and theory there can be no criteria of significance, and it is not surprising to find much that is trivial and irrelevant in these writings. Elliott Smith's fantastic doctrine of the origin of all civilization in ancient Egypt and its distribution by the mysterious 'Children of the Sun' could not have been foisted on a well-grounded scientific discipline.

The foundation of the William Wyse Chair in 1932 was a sign that Haddon's faith and tenacity of purpose had prevailed. But equally important was the recognition this implied that anthropology had become a subject. Moreover, a definite organization of anthropological studies was implied. It could only mean that social anthropology, the science of culture as Tylor had called it, was accepted as the central theme of anthropology in Cambridge as in other universities which had already legitimatized it as an academic study.

This was a natural development. Among the bundle of interests held together by the evolutionary frame of thought, the interest in cultures, that is, the facts of custom and social organization, among primitive peoples, had always been paramount. Haddon and Seligman, for example, like Boas in America, made notable contributions to physical anthropology, but these were all subordinate to the main purpose of tracing relations between human groups in terms of their artefacts, social customs, art forms, religious beliefs and so on—in short, their cultures. Prehistoric archaeology was therefore of interest because of its connexion with human palaeontology and with the study of the evolution and spread of culture. These studies, focused on the geographical distribution and interrelations of the material, social and ritual elements of culture, and on their putative movements from one area to another, constituted what Haddon called ethnology. By social anthropology he meant the study of culture in its own right by sociological and psychological methods. Thus, by 1932, the evolutionary bundle had fallen to pieces, and of the scattered members social anthropology had emerged as the basic discipline concerned with custom and social organization in the simpler societies. Physical anthropology was becoming even more specialized as the study of the comparative biology of man, and ethnology appeared as the bridge between the other two interests.

The main credit for this belongs to a movement which had grown directly out of evolutionary anthropology but in opposition to it. The functionalist movement, as it came to be called, is associated mainly with the names of A. R. Radcliffe-Brown and the late Professor B. Malinowski. The steps by which it has become the generally accepted basis of theory and research in British social anthropology have often been discussed.[10] But the chief innovation for which it stands was a contribution of the Cambridge School of Anthropology. This is the principle of 'the intensive study of limited areas' as Haddon described it. He claimed this as the distinctive teaching of the Cambridge School, and coupled with his plea for the saving of vanishing data, it became almost a slogan with him. It meant for him the study and analysis of a living community in its native habitat with reference to its total social life. It meant making of social anthropology an empirical discipline based on direct observation by professional students and not, as in the past, on reports of amateurs and travellers. Hence, like most anthropologists of his day, he thought of social anthropology as a branch of natural science.

The first serious attempt to carry out an intensive study was made by his and Rivers's pupil, A. R. Radcliff-Brown of Trinity, among the Andaman islanders in 1908. But the full demonstration of its possibilities did not come till 1922, when both Radcliffe-Brown's book on the Andaman Islanders and Malinowski's famous *Argonauts of the Western Pacific* were published. They introduced field-work of a kind that can only be carried out by trained investigators. What Crooke foresaw in 1910 has come to pass, and it is no longer possible for the amateur, however gifted, to make a contribution of theoretical value to social anthropology.

Here I would like to interpolate a personal note. The tradition of field-work created by Haddon, Rivers and Seligman has only just entered its third generation; but it has already led to widely acclaimed advances in social anthropology. This is due in no small degree to a common heritage of theory and method, built up in an unusual comradeship of masters and pupils, and transmitted in a direct line. In a very real sense, most of the social anthropologists now holding senior teaching and research positions in this country and the Commonwealth, as well as some leading American anthropologists, are the heirs of Haddon and his comrades of the Cambridge School. For all of us are the pupils of either Malinowski, himself the pupil of Haddon's life-long friend and admirer C. G. Seligman, or of Radcliffe-Brown; and some of us were even fortunate enough to have been taught also by Haddon himself, or as in my own case, by Seligman.[11]

Intensive field work was the experience that transformed social anthropology in the first thirty years of this century. But a technique of investigation does not, by itself, make a scholarly or scientific discipline. It is the body of theory that grew up, as I have mentioned, with intensive field-work that gives functional social anthropology a basis of discipline.

This theory drew inspiration from many sources. Here I will only mention the new psychology of William James, McDougall and later Freud, which had a great influence. Thus the emphasis on the part played by emotion and sentiment in social life, as opposed to the association of ideas and the faculty of reasoning which dominated Tylor and Frazer, is one of the main contrasts between modern and prefunctionalist social anthropology.

But the essential change it meant is better seen if we consider the evolutionary concept again. This is a blend of two concepts, as Darwin appreciated, that of historical succession, and that of scientific law or causation. The evolutionary anthropologists arrived at the idea of stages in the development of social life on the assumption that, as Tylor said, the institutions of man are as distinctly stratified as the earth on which he lives.

By the 1920's ethnologists with field experience, like Haddon, Seligman and Boas, had dropped the notion of fixed evolutionary stages, though not the concept itself. They had seen alleged stages coexisting as the result of the borrowing of customs and institutions by one people from another. But there was still confusion over the concept of history in anthropological theory. So insidious, so apparently self-evident is the belief that the only satisfactory way of explaining social institutions is by some kind of history, that the most acute thinkers succumb to it. It has been a stumbling-block to clear thinking in the anthropological sciences for a century.

There are two possibilities, as the Greeks saw long ago, of explaining similarities and differences of custom. They can be traced to common or different sources. This is history if the steps in the transmission can be documented; and where the evolutionists failed was in their disregard of this elementary rule. But these similarities and differences may also be due to the presence or absence of common causes or common factors, and these have usually been sought either in the physical environment or in what is loosely called human nature. It is on this principle that Tylor, Frazer and their followers deduced psychological 'origins'; for example, Frazer's far-fetched explanation of Australian totemism as the work of some 'inventive genius' who deliberately imposed it in order to prevent close kin from marrying.

This confusion of what might be called causal origins and historical origins was not due to lack of acumen but to the presuppositions of evolutionary historicism. It was so general that Rivers, in a famous paper of 1911,[12] chastized British anthropologists for assuming that similarities of custom 'are due to independent origin and development' resulting from 'the fundamental similarity of the working of the human mind'. He plumped for an alternative version of conjectural history, not recognizing the even greater absurdities this led to. And so we get his reconstructions of earlier forms of marriage, which are as untenable in the light of even his own field observations as they are logically nonsensical. The truth is he could do no other. For he was enslaved to the same assumptions as those whom he criticized, and limited by the same quality and amount of field data. Yet he came to the very brink of the new field discoveries and of the radical shift in theory represented by functional anthropology.

Stripped of its evolutionary implications and therefore of its pseudo-historical bias, ethnology as the study of cultural distributions and movements has an important place among anthropological studies, and great advances have been made in it since 1911, particularly in America. Its chief importance, however, lies not in the historical reconstructions attempted, but in the evidence it gives of the autonomy of human social organization and culture in relation to environment and race. Thus defined, ethnology is an indispensable adjunct to social anthropology but, as Haddon well understood, the two are different in aim and method.

This is obvious if we look at the scientific aspect of evolution. The distinction is well stated by Julian Huxley.[13] There are, he points out, 'three separate fields of discourse . . . of fundamentally different natures' in the study of evolution. 'Palaeontology deals with the *historical* course of evolution. The machinery for the transmission of hereditary factors, together with any differential survival or reproduction of individuals of different types, constitutes the *mechanism* of the process. The adaptation of species or evolutionary lines, and the reasons for their spread or extinction, constitute the *functional* aspect' (my italics). And he goes on to remark about 'the illegitimacy of using data on the course of evolution to make assertions as to its mechanism' and vice versa.

Mechanism and function, to use Huxley's terms, are discovered by scientific observation and experiment upon living things. They are used to provide explanatory hypotheses for the sequences found in the palaeontological record. It is by invoking the laws of mechanism and function observed to be operating among living organisms that the development of species is accounted for.

No reputable social anthropologist now commits the error of confusing history with speculative evolutionary stages, or believes it possible to reconstruct the origins of social institutions in the absence of records. This is due largely to the exposure of these fallacies by the functionalists. But this is incidental; for their main achievement is the transformation of social anthropology into a discipline concerned, in Huxley's words, with mechanism and function. It has meant a shift from speculation to observation as the test of hypothesis; but, more significantly, it has meant a radical change of interest, a change to the kind of questions investigated by the sciences from which the biological, as opposed to the historical, elements of the evolutionary concept are derived.

This shift owes most to the influence of Emil Durkheim and his sociological school.

It is a striking symptom of the state of sociological and psychological studies here and in America before the first World War that Durkheim's ideas, like Freud's, were received with scepticism, if not contempt. Terminology was part of the trouble. But the main reason was the implied challenge to some of the most cherished nineteenth-century myths—the myth, for instance, that society is no more than an assemblage of individuals held together by rational social and political arrangements, and the myth that human motives are either of instinctive origin or consciously knowable. Anthropologists, however, have had to take note of Durkheim, if only because so much of his theoretical work was based on ethnographic data. Perhaps it is easier for them because they know that men have so many different ways of living and so many extraordinary beliefs, that universal norms of a rational social life cannot be found.

Durkheim's influence on functional anthropology is writ large in the work of Radcliffe-Brown, Malinowski, and all their pupils. His vital contribution, however, lay in his general postulates of method. His basic theses, that social facts are real in their own right, are collective possessions invested with moral constraint for the individual, and are to be explained primarily by their functions, that is the social ends they serve in maintaining a social order, formed the starting point of functional theory. Curiously enough, this point of view was in some ways anticipated by Tylor, and that may have made it more easily assimilable by social anthropology. Its effect was revolutionary. It enabled social anthropology to throw off the bonds of evolutionary historicism, and to recognize itself, once and for all, as a separate discipline concerned with 'mechanism and function'.

The essentials of functionalist theory are summed up in a well known paper by Radcliffe-Brown published in 1935.[14] It holds, he said, 'that a social system (the total social structure of a society together with the totality of social usages in which that structure appears and on which it depends for its continued existence) has a certain kind of unity which we may speak of as functional unity. We may define it as a condition in which all parts of the social system work together with a sufficient degree of harmony or internal consistency. . . .' It is a theory peculiarly adapted to the needs of intensive field-work and to the relatively small, culturally homogeneous, and institutionally undifferentiated societies commonly studied by anthropologists. Its ideal unit of reference is a single and entire social system. To see its unity, the parts of such a system must be seen working together contemporaneously, as is possible in intensive field studies in primitive societies. This is what Radcliffe-Brown calls 'synchronic study' by analogy with linguistics. Historians also carry out synchronic studies when they deal with a total society during a limited period. But synchronic studies in living communities provide data which no records or relics of past human activity can furnish. To see customs and social institutions in action is something different from reconstructing their actuality from records.

Functional research investigates either the part played by institutions and customs in operating and maintaining the total structure of a society or of a type of society; or conversely, it seeks to analyse the action upon one set of institutions of the other parts of the social system.

As the crucial method of study is by direct observation in living communities social anthropology is often described in America as a 'behavioural science'. With this emphasis on contemporary social relations and custom, attention has necessarily been given to the changes going on in primitive societies as a result of European influence. Thus we find the interest of Haddon and his generation in the practical value of anthropology continued in a new framework of theory.

Superficially it might seem that there has been mainly a change of emphasis in the development from nineteenth-century social anthropology to functionalist theory. But the change is, in fact, fundamental. This is best seen from the kind of hypotheses we now investigate. Following Malinowski, we look for the meaning of a myth in its value as a charter of belief and action. Frazer's generation thought that myths were corrupt historical records or representations of the animistic beliefs distinctive of savagery. We can see the change from diffusely historical to specifically functional hypotheses better still in another field. Our greatest advances in the past twenty years have been made in the study of primitive family and kinship institutions. British research on this subject began with Rivers, and there was genius in some of his work. But his basic hypotheses were absurd. Radcliffe-Brown supplanted them with more economic and more specific hypotheses that are capable of being verified by field observation. Rivers recorded the special relationship that usually exists between mother's brother and sister's son in a patrilineal kinship system. He accepted the improbable hypothesis that it was a survival of mother-right because this fitted his preconceived ideas. Less than ten years later, Radcliffe-Brown, applying functionalist theory, showed this relationship to be a regular feature of segmentary social structures with patrilineal descent, and a means by which a moral tie of crucial importance is maintained with the mother's kin.[15] This is one of a series of verifiable generalizations about mechanism and function in family and kinship systems that has been built up in the past twenty-five years. By an irony of fate, Rivers's theories now survive mainly among Marxist anthropologists, who derive them, as he did, from L. H. Morgan, and among the so-called historical school of Pater W. Schmidt.

At its present stage of rapid and exciting growth, the most pressing task of social anthropology is ethnographic field research. Now good ethnography must be local, particular, and circumstantial. It must, as Malinowski[16] wrote, take in 'the imponderabilia of actual life and typical behaviour.' The master-economist, said Lord Keynes,[17] must have 'a rare combination of gifts. . . . He must contemplate the particular in terms of the general, and touch abstract and concrete in the same flight of thought.' He works with an 'amalgam of logic and intuition and a wide knowledge of facts most of which are not precise'. A good ethnographer is a humbler version of this kind of economist. He has grown up as a member of society and he will, consciously or not, draw on his life experience to sharpen his insight. All students of man and society do this. But intuitive knowledge also plays a very large part in physical and biological sciences. The first paragraph of *The Origin of Species* reminds us of this. It is the subsequent work of demonstration by facts open to general observation that turns intuition into discovery and so into the data of science. In ethnography this intuitive element creates the false impression that our model is literary or historical description. This is one reason why anthropologists get trapped into disputing whether their studies belong to science or to history. But it is a dispute that also has roots in our evolutionary heritage and in nineteenth-century controversies about historical method. Some of the best minds in anthropology have made a false dilemma of this.

The functionalist point of view has always been precise and consistent. It was stated in 1931 by Radcliffe-Brown,[18] when he declared that the aim of social anthropology is the discovery of 'general laws or tendencies' of human social life. It was often affirmed by Malinowski, and has been repeated by most of their pupils in a variety of contexts. It can be summed up as follows: leaving aside the blind alley of conjectural history, we must distinguish between two roads in the study of social life. The true historical method, applicable where there are documents and records, seeks to explain customs and institutions by tracing their antecedents in the past and the chronological steps by which they came to be what they are where they are. In doing this historians commonly use theories taken from the social sciences. For as Professor Hancock says[19] 'historians who have no theory fill the vacuum with their prejudices.' Sociological method, on the other hand, seeks explanations of contemporaneously interdependent customs and institutions, the significant connexions being those that reveal the functions of an institution in relation to the whole social system. Whereas history aims at establishing particular sequences and combinations, social anthropology aims at discovering verifiable 'general laws or tendencies' in the particular case. The two are not opposed but complementary, and essential to each other. All the same they must be distinguished so as to avoid confusion. For social anthropology, like other theoretical social sciences, tries to establish generalizations that hold *irrespective* of period and place and to test them by empirical study in living communities; whereas history is the description of past social life in its local and chronological setting.

Notes

1 In his Presidential Address to Section H of the British Association for the Advancement of Science.

2 *History of Human Marriage* (abridged ed.), p. 9.

3 *Encyclopaedia Britannica*, 13th ed., s.v. Anthropology.

4 In his Inaugural Lecture, 'The Scope of Social Anthropology,' given at Liverpool, and reprinted in *The Devil's Advocate*, 1927.

5 *Loc. cit.*

6 In the Introduction to *Themis.*

7 *Historical Jurisprudence*, vol. I, p. 138.

8 In his Presidential Address, 'Anthropology, Its Position and Needs,' *Journal of the Royal Anthropological Institute*, vol. L.

9 A. Hingston Quiggin, *Haddon the Head-Hunter*, 1942.

10 Cf. E. E. Evans-Pritchard, *Social Anthropology*, 1951.

11 Cf. Evans-Pritchard, *op. cit.*

12 His Presidential Address to Section H of the British Association for the Advancement of Science.

13 *Evolution: the Modern Synthesis*, p. 41.

14 'On the concept of function in social science,' reprinted now in A. R. Radcliffe-Brown, *Structure and Function in Primitive Society*, 1952.

15 See A. R. Radcliffe-Brown, *op. cit.* ch. 1.

16 Introduction, *Argonauts of the Western Pacific.*

17 *Essays in Biography* (new ed.), p. 141, and p. 158n., in speaking of Alfred Marshall.

18 In his Presidential Address to Section H of the British Association for the Advancement of Science.

19 *Economic History at Oxford*, Inaugural Lecture, 1946.

References Cited

The bibliography from all articles cited is reproduced here together with bibliography from the introductory material for each section. It is not, therefore, a complete bibliography of the history of anthropology. It is very detailed in areas covered by particular articles and has obvious gaps in other areas. The general introductions, however, attempt to give references for further study throughout the range of the history of anthropology. Some references are incomplete for the style used here; they are reproduced as presented by the authors of original selections.

Aberle, David

1957 The influence of linguistics on early culture and personality theory. In Gertrude Dole and Robert Carneiro (eds.), *Essays in the Science of Culture*. New York: T. Y. Crowell, pp. 1–29.

Achelis, T.

1889 *Die Entwicklung der Modernen Ethnologie*. Berlin: E. S. Mittler und Sohn.

Agassiz, L.

1859 *An Essay in Classification*. London: Longmans. First published as an introduction to *Contributions to the Natural History of the United States* (1857).

Anghiera, Pietro Martire d'

1912 *De orbe novo; the eight Decades of Peter Martyr d'Anghiera*. Translated from the Latin with notes and introduction by Francis Augustus MacNutt. New York and London: Putnam. 2 vols.

Ashmole, Bernard

1956 Cyriac of Ancona and the Temple of Hadrian at Cyzicus. In *Journal of the Warburg and Courtauld Institutes*, 19, nos. 3–4: 179–191. London.

Aufrere, L.

1936 Essai sur les premiers decouvertes de Boucher de Perthes et les origines de l'archaeologie primitive 1838–1844. Paris: Staude.

1940 Figures de prehistoriens: J. Boucher de Perthes. In *Prehistoire*, 7: 7–134. Paris: Staude.

Bachofen, J. J.

1861 *Das Mutterrecht*. Stuttgart.

1967 *Myth, Religion and Mother Right: Selected Writings of J. J. Bachofen*. Bollingen Series LXXXN. Princeton: Princeton University Press.

Bacon, Roger

1900 *The Opus majus of Roger Bacon*. Edited, with introduction and analytical table, by John Henry Bridges. London, Edinburgh and Oxford: Williams and Norgate. 3 vols.

Baker, Herschel
1947 *The Image of Man: A Study of the Idea of Human Dignity in Classical Antiquity, the Middle Ages, and the Renaissance.* Cambridge: Harvard University Press.

Barbeau, Marius C.
1950 Indian captivities. In *Proceedings of the American Philosophical Society,* 94: 522–548.

Barnes, J. A.
1960 Anthropology in Britain before and after Darwin. In *Mankind,* 5: 369–385.

Barnett, Homer G.
1940 Culture processes. In *American Anthropologist,* 42: 21–48.
1953 *Innovation.* New York: McGraw-Hill.
1957 *Indian Shakers, A Messianic Cult of the Pacific Northwest.* Carbondale: Southern Illinois University Press.

Bartlett, John Russell
1847 *The Progress of Ethnology.* New York: American Ethnological Society.

Bastian, Adolph
1881 Die Vorgeschichte der Ethnologie. In *Deutschland Denk Freunden Gewidrnet für eine Mussestunde.* Berlin: F. Dummler.

Bateson, Gregory
1947 Social planning and the concept of deutero-learning. In *Science. Philosophy and Religion, Second Symposium,* Conference on Science, Philosophy and Religion, New York.

Beals, Ralph, and Harry Hoijer
1959 *An Introduction to Anthropology.* 2nd ed. New York: Macmillan.

Bearce, C. D.
1961 *British Attitudes Toward India, 1784–1858.* Oxford: Oxford University Press.

Beattie, John
1955 Contemporary trends in British social anthropology. In *Sociologus,* 5: 1–14.

Bender, Donald
1965 The development of French anthropology. In *Journal of the History of the Behavioral Sciences,* I: 139–151.

Bendyshe, T.
1865 The history of anthropology. In *Memoirs Read Before the Anthropological Society of London,* I: 335–360.

Benedict, Ruth
1930 Psychological types in the cultures of the Southwest. In *Proceed-*

ings of the Twenty-third International Congress of Americanists. (1928) New York.
1934 Anthropology and the abnormal. In *Journal of General Psychology,* 10: 59–80.
1950 *Patterns of Culture.* New York: Mentor.
Bennett, John W.
1954 Interdisciplinary research and the concept of culture. In *American Anthropologist,* 56: 169–179.
Bennett, Josephine W.
1954 *The Rediscovery of Sir John Mandeville.* New Association of America.
Bernal, J. D.
1954 *Science in History.* London: Watts.
Bidney, David
1944 On the concept of culture and some cultural fallacies. In *American Anthropologist,* 46: 30–44.
1946 On the so-called anti-evolutionist fallacy: a reply to Leslie A. White. In *American Anthropologist,* 48: 293–297.
Biondo, Flavio
1927 Scritti inediti e rari di Biondo Flavio, con introduzione di Bartolomeo Nogara. In *Studi e Testi,* 48. Roma: Tipografia Poliglotta Vaticana.
Blumenbach, J. F.
1865 *The Anthropological Treatise of J. F. Blumenbach.* London: Longmans.
Boas, Franz
1887 The occurrence of similar inventions in areas widely apart. In *Science,* 9: 485–486.
1896 The limitations of the comparative method of anthropology. In *Science,* N.S., 4: 901–908. Reprinted in *Race, Language and Culture.*
1904 The history of anthropology. In *Science,* 20: 513–524.
1911 Review of *Methode der Ethnologie,* by F. Graebner. In *Science,* N.S., 34: 804–810. Reprinted in *Race, Language and Culture.*
1924 *The Mind of Primitive Man.* New York: Macmillan.
1930 Some problems of methodology in the social sciences. In Leonard D. White (ed.), *The New Social Sciences.* Chicago: University of Chicago Press. Reprinted in *Race, Language and Culture.*
1936 History and science in anthropology: a reply. In *American Anthropologist,* 38: 137–141.
1940 *Race, Language, and Culture.* New York: Macmillan.
Bock, Kenneth E.
1956 The acceptance of histories. In *University of California Publications in Sociology and Social Institutions,* 3: 1–132.

Bodnar, Edward W.
1960 Cyriacus of Ancona and Athens. In *Collection Latomus,* Vol. XLIII. Bruxelles-Berchem.
Bolgar, R. R.
1954 *The Classical Heritage and Its Beneficiaries: From the Carolingean Age to the End of the Renaissance.* New York: Harper & Row.
Bormann, Eugen, and Wilhelm Henzen
1876 Inscriptiones urbis Romae Latinae. Pars primia. In *Corpus Inscriptionum Latinarum,* 6: 1. Berlin: Georg Reimer.
Boswell, James
1963 *The ominous years, 1774–1776.* Edited by C. Ryskaup and F. A. Pottle. New York: McGraw-Hill.
Boucher de Perthes, J.
Correspondence to Boucher de Perthes (MS 682, Bibliotheque Communal d'Abbeville).
1847, 1857, 1864 *Antiquites Celtiques et Diluviennes.* Paris: Treuttel et Wurtz. 3 vols.
Boule, M., and H. V. Vallois
1957 *Fossil Men.* Translated by M. Bullock. New York: Dryden Press.
Brace, C. L.
1868 *A Manual of Ethnology; or the Races of the Old World.* 2nd ed. London: Murray.
Brandon, Samuel G. F.
1951 *Time and Mankind, An Historical and Philosophical Study of Mankind's Attitude to the Phenomena of Change.* London: Hutchinson.
Breuil, H.
1945 The discovery of the antiquity of man. In *Journal of the Royal Anthropological Society of Great Britain and Ireland,* 75: 21–32.
Brew, J. O.
1968 *One Hundred Years of Anthropology.* Cambridge: Harvard University Press.
Brinton, Daniel G.
1890 American languages and why we should study them. In *Essays of an Americanist.* Philadelphia: David McKay.
1892 Anthropology as a science and as a branch of university education in the United States. Philadelphia.
1895 The aims of anthropology. In *Science,* 2: 241–252.
Broca, Paul
1869 Histoire des progrés des études anthropologiques depuis la fondation de la société en 1859. In *Memoires Société d' Anthropologie de Paris,* 3: cvii–cviii.
Browne, Edward G.
1906 Columbus, Ramon Pane and the beginnings of American anthro-

pology. In *Proceedings of the American Antiquarian Society*, 16: 310–340.

Bryson, Gladys

1945 *Man and Society: the Scottish Inquiry of the Eighteenth Century*. Princeton: Princton University Press.

Buckland, W.

1822 Account of an assemblage of fossil teeth and bones discovered in a cave at Kirkdale, Yorkshire, in the year 1821. In *Philosophical Transactions of the Royal Society of London*, pp. 171–236.

1824 *Reliquiae Diluvianae*. 2nd ed. London: Murray.

1837 *Geology and Mineralogy Considered with Reference to Natural Theology*. 2nd ed. London: Pickering. 2 vols.

Buettner-Janusch, J.

1957 Boas and Mason: Particularision vs. generalization. In *American Anthropologist*, 59: 318–324.

Burn, Andrew Robert

1962 *Persia and the Greeks; the Defence of the West, c. 546–478* B.C. New York: St. Martin's Press.

Burnet, James

1967 *Of the Origin and Progress of Language*. Menston, England: Scholar Press.

Burrow, J. W.

1966 *Evolution and Society: a Study in Victorian Social Theory*. London: Cambridge University Press.

1967 The uses of philology in Victorian England. In R. Robson (ed.), *Ideas and Institutions of Victorian Britain*. London: Bell.

Butterfield, Herbert

1960a *The Origins of Modern Science*. New York: Macmillan.

1960b Man on his past. In *The Study of the History of Historical Scholarship*. Boston: Beacon Press.

Ca'da Mosto, Alvise

1937 *The Voyages of Cadamosto and Other Documents on Western Africa in the Second Half of the Fifteenth Century*. Translated and edited by G. R. Crone. Works issued by the Hakluyt Society, second series, no. LXXX. London.

Calverton, V. F. (ed.)

1931 *The Making of Man; An Outline of Anthropology*. New York: Modern Library (Random House).

Cannon, W. F.

1960a The uniformitarian-catastrophist debate. In *Isis*, 51: 38–55.

1960b The problem of miracles in the 1830's. In *Victorian Studies*, 4: 5–32.

Carpenter, E. S.

1950 The role of archeology in the nineteenth century controversy between developmentalism and degeneration. In *Pennsylvania Archeologist,* 20: 5–18.

Cary, M., and E. H. Warmington
1929 *The Ancient Explorers.* Baltimore: Penguin Books.

Chapple, Elliot D., and Carleton S. Coon
1942 *Principles of Anthropology.* New York: Holt, Rinehart & Winston.

Clark, G.
1957 *Archaeology and Society.* 3rd ed. Cambridge: Harvard University Press.

Clark, Terry
1968 Emile Durkheim and the institutionalization of sociology in the French university system. In *European Journal of Sociology,* 9: 37–91.

Cole, Fay-Cooper
1952 Eminent personalities of the half-century. In *American Anthropologist,* 54: 157–167.

Collingwood, R. G.
1945 *The Idea of Nature.* Oxford: Clarendon Press.

Condorcet, Marie J.
1955 Sketch for a Historical Picture of the Progress of the Human Mind. Translated by June Barraclough. London: Weidenfeld and Nicolson.

Cornelius, Paul
1965 *Languages in Seventeenth and Early Eighteenth Century Imaginary Voyages.* Geneve: Libraire Droz.

Cosenza, Mario Emilio
1962 *Biographical and Bibliographical Dictionary of the Italian Humanists and of the World of Classical Scholarship in Italy, 1300–1800.* Boston: G. K. Hall. 5 vols.

Cull, R.
1852 Recent progress of ethnology. In *Journal of the Ethnological Society of London,* 3: 165–177.

Cunningham, J. D.
1908 Anthropology in the eighteenth century. In *Journal of the Royal Anthropological Institute,* 38: 10–35.

Curtin, Philip
1964 *The Image of Africa: British Ideas and Action, 1780–1850.* Madison: University of Wisconsin Press.

Cuvier, G.
1817 *Essay on the Theory of the Earth.* Translated by Robert Jameson. 3rd ed. Edinburgh: Blackwood.

Daniel, Glyn E.
1943 *The Three Ages.* Cambridge, England: The University Press.
1950 *A Hundred Years of Archaeology.* London: Duckworth.

1962 *The Idea of Prehistory*. London: Watts.
Daniel, Norman
1966 *Islam, Europe and Empire*. Edinburgh: Edinburgh University Press.
Darnell, Regna
1967 *Daniel Garrison Brinton: An Intellectual Biography*. (M.A. thesis, University of Pennsylvania).
1969 *The Development of American Anthropology, 1880–1920: From the Bureau of American Ethnology to Franz Boas*. (Ph.D. dissertation, University of Pennsylvania.)
1970 The emergence of academic anthropology at the University of Pennsylvania. In *Journal of the History of the Behavioral Sciences*, 6: 80–92.
1971a The professionalization of American anthropology. In *Social Science Information*, 10: 83–103.
1971b The Powell classification of American Indian languages. In *Papers in Linguistics*, 4: 71–110.
1971c The revision of the Powell classification. In *Papers in Linguistics*, 4: 233–257.
In press Introduction to James Burnet, *On the Origin and Progress of Language*. New York: AMS Press, Inc.
Darwin, F. (ed.)
1887 *The Life and Letters of Charles Darwin*. London: Murray. 3 vols.
Dawson, Christopher Henry
1955 *The Mongol Mission. Narratives and Letters of the Franciscan Missionaries in Mongolia and China in the Thirteenth and Fourteenth Centuries*. Translated by a nun of Stanbrook Abbey. Edited with an introduction by Christopher Dawson. London and New York: Sheed & Ward.
Degérando, Joseph-Marie
1969 *The Observation of Savage Peoples*. Translated and edited by F. G. T. Moore. London: Routledge and Kegan Paul.
de Laguna, Grace
1949 Culture and rationality. In *American Anthropologist*, 51: 379–391.
Dexter, Ralph
1966 Putnam's problems popularizing anthropology. In *American Scientist*, 54: 315–332.
Diamond, Stanley
In press *The Nature and Function of Anthropological Traditions*. Philadelphia: University of Pennsylvania Press.
Diaz, Bernal
1963 *The Conquest of New Spain*. Translated by J. M. Cohen. Baltimore: Penguin.

Diels, Hermann
1959 *Die fragmente der Vorsokratiker.* Neunte Auflage heraugegeben von Walther Kranz. Berlin-Charlottenburg: Weidmannsche Verlagsbuchhandlung. 2 vols.

Dieserud, Jules
1908 *The Scope and Content of the Science of Anthropology.* La Salle, Ill.: Open Court.

Dixon, Roland
1912 Maidu texts. *American Ethnological Society Publication,* 4.
1930 Anthropology 1866–1929. In Samuel Eliot Morrison (ed.), *The Development of Harvard University since the Inauguration of President Eliot, 1869–1929.* Boston: Harvard University Press, pp. 205–215.

Dorsey, George A.
1896 The History of the Study of Anthropology in Harvard University in *Denison Quarterly* (Granville, Ohio).

Du Bois, Cora
1944 *The People of Alor.* Minneapolis: University of Minnesota Press.

Dupree, A. Hunter
1957 *Science in the Federal Government: A History of Policies and Activities to 1940.* New York: Harper & Row.

Easton, Stewart C.
1952 *Roger Bacon and His Search for a Universal Science; A Reconsideration of the Life and Work of Roger Bacon in the Light of His Own Stated Purposes.* New York: Columbia University Press.

Edgerton, Franklin
1943 Notes on early American work in linguistics. In *Proceedings of the American Philosophical Society,* 87: 25–34.

Edinburgh New Philosophical Journal
1834 Proofs that the human bones and works of art found in the caves in the south of France are more recent than the antediluvian bones in those caves, 16: 302–310.

Edinburgh Review
1823 Geology of the deluge, 39: 196–234.

Eggan, Fred
1965 Some reflections on comparative method in anthropology. In Melford Spiro (ed.), *Context and Meaning in Cultural Anthropology.* New York: Free Press, pp. 357–372.

Eiseley, L. C.
1958 *Darwin's Century.* New York: Doubleday.

Eliade, Mircea
1959 *Cosmos and History, the Myth of the Eternal Return.* New York: Harper & Row (Torchbooks).

Engels, Frederick
1884 *The Origin of the Family, Private Property and the State.* New York: International Publishers, 1942.

Erasmus, Charles J.

1952 The leader vs. tradition: a case study. In *American Anthropologist*, 54: 168–178.

1953 *Los Dimensions de la Cultura: Historia de la Ethnología en los Estados Unidos entre 1900 y 1950.* Bogota: Editorial Iqueirna.

1967 Cultural anthropology in the United States since 1900: a quantitative analysis. In *Southwestern Journal of Anthropology*, 23: 111–140.

Essen, Carel Claudius Van

1958 *I Commentaria di Ciriaco d'Ancona. Il Mondo Antico nel Rinascimento; Atti del Convegno Internazionale di Studi sul Rinascimento,* Firenze–Palazzo Strozzi, 2 Settembre 1956. Firenze: Instituto Nazionale di Studi sul Rinascimento, pp. 191–194.

Essling, Victor Massena, Prince d', and Eugène Müntz

1902 *Pétrarque; Ses Études d'Art; Son Influence sur les Artistes; Ses Portraits et Ceux de Laure; l'Illustration de Ses Écrits.* Paris: Gazette des Beaux-Arts.

Estienne, Henri

1566 *Apologia pro Herodoto, siue Herodoti Historia Fabulositatis Accusta. Herodoti Halicarnassei Historiae lib. IX and De Vita Homeri Libellus* . . . ab Henr. Stephan, Recognita, pp. (ix–xxxii). Geneva.

Evans, J.

1859 On the occurrence of flint implements in undisturbed beds of gravel, sands, and clay. In *Archaeologia*, 38: 280–307.

1943 *Time and Chance: The Story of Arthur Evans and his Forebears.* London: Longmans.

1949 Ninety years ago. In *Antiquity*, 23: 115–125.

Fairchild, Hoxie N.

1928 *The Noble Savage, A Study in Romantic Naturalism.* New York: Columbia University Press.

Falconer, H.

1859 On the Ossiferous Grotta di Maccagnone, near Palermo. In *Palaeontological Memoirs*, 2: 543–563. (Originally communicated to the Geological Society of London, May 4 and June 22, 1859.)

1868 *Palaeontological Memoirs and Notes of the Late Hugh Falconer, A.M., M.D.* Compiled and edited by Charles Murchison. London: Hardwicke. 2 vols.

Ferguson, Wallace Klippert

1948 *The Renaissance in Historical Thought; Five Centuries of Interpretation.* Cambridge: Houghton Mifflin Company, The Riverside Press.

Fernández de Oviedo y Valdés, Gonzalo

1851–55 *Historia General y Natural de las Indias, Islas y Tierra-firme del Mar Océano.* Madrid: Real Academia de la Historia. 4 vols.

Firth, Raymond

1951 Contemporary British social anthropology. In *American Anthropologist*, 53: 474–490.

1957 *Man and Culture: An Evaluation of the Work of Bronislaw Malinowski.* London: Routledge and Kegan Paul.

Fitzgerald, C. P.

1964 *The Chinese View of Their Place in the World.* London: Oxford University Press.

Fontana, Bernard L.

1963 Pioneers in ideas: three early southwestern ethnologists. In *Journal of the Arizona Academy of Sciences,* 2: 124–129.

Fortes, Meyer

1953 *Social Anthropology at Cambridge since 1900: An Inaugural Lecture.* Cambridge, England: Cambridge University Press.

1969 *Kinship and the Social Order: The Legacy of Lewis Henry Morgan.* Chicago: Aldine.

Frazer, James G.

1900 *The Golden Bough, A Study in Magic and Religion.* London: Macmillan. 3 vols.

Freeman, John Finley

1965a Religion and personality in the anthropology of Henry Schoolcraft. In *Journal of the History of Behavioral Sciences,* 1: 301–313.

1965b University anthropology: early departments in the United States. In *Kroeber Anthropological Society Papers,* 32: 78–90.

1967 The American Philosophical Society in American anthropology. In Jacob Gruber (ed.), *The Philadelphia Anthropological Society.* New York: Columbia University Press.

French, David

1963 The relationship of anthropology to studies in perception and cognition. In Sigmund Koch (ed.), *Psychology: A Study of a Science.* Vol. 6: *Investigations of Man as Socius.* New York: McGraw-Hill, pp. 388–428.

Frere, J.

1800 Account of flint weapons discovered at Hoxne in Suffolk. In *Archaeologia,* 13: 204–205.

Fried, Morton

1972 *The Study of Anthropology.* New York: T. Y. Crowell.

Friere-Marreco, B.

1907 A bibliography of E. B. Tylor. In H. Balfour, et al., *Anthropological Essays Presented to E. B. Tylor.* Oxford: Clarendon Press.

Gaeta, Franco

1955 Lorenzo Valla; filologia e storia nell' umanesimo italiano. In *Istituto Italiano per gli Studi Storici,* Pubblicazione 8. Napoli.

Gatschet, A. S.

1884 *A Migration Legend of the Creek Indians.* Philadelphia: Brinton.

Gay, Peter

1966 *The Enlightenment: An Interpretation; the Rise of Modern Paganism.* New York: Knopf.

Geikie, J.
1881 *Prehistoric Europe.* London: Stanford.
Gellius, Aulus
1927–28 *The Attic Nights of Aulus Gellius.* English translation by John C. Rolfe. Loeb Classical Library. London: William Heinemann; New York: Putnam. 3 vols.
George, Katherine
1958 The civilized west looks at primitive Africa: 1400–1800; a study in ethnocentrism. In *Isis,* 40: 62–72.
Gibbs, George
1863 Instructions for research relative to the ethnology and philology of America. In *Smithsonian Miscellaneous Collections,* 160: 13–17.
Gibson, James
1950 The implications of learning theory for social psychology. In M. J. G. Miller (ed.), *Experiments in Social Process: A Symposium on Social Psychology.* New York: McGraw-Hill.
Gillin, John (ed.)
1954 *For a Science of Social Man; Convergences in Anthropology, Psychology, and Sociology.* New York: Macmillan.
Gillispie, Charles C.
1951 *Genesis and Geology: The Impact of Scientific Discovery upon Religious Beliefs in the Decades before Darwin.* Cambridge: Harvard University Press.
1959 *Genesis and Geology: A Study in the Relations of Scientific Thought, Natural Theology, and Social Opinion in Great Britain, 1790–1850.* New York: Harper & Row.
Glacken, Clarence J.
1967 *Traces on the Rhodian Shore: Nature and Culture in Western Thought from Ancient Times to the End of the Eighteenth Century.* Berkeley: University of California Press.
Glover, Terrot Reaveley
1924 *Herodotus.* Sather Classical Lectures, Vol. 3. Berkeley: University of California Press.
Goldenweiser, Alexander A.
1910 Totemism, an analytical study. In *Journal of American Folklore,* 23: 179–293.
1922 *Early Civilization.* New York: Knopf.
1925 Cultural anthropology. In H. E. Barnes (ed.), *The History and Prospects of the Social Sciences.* New York: Knopf, pp. 210–255.
1933 *History, Psychology, and Culture.* New York: Knopf.
Goldschmidt, Walter
1951 Ethics and the structure of society: an ethnological contribution to the sociology of knowledge. In *American Anthropologist,* 53: 506–524.

Goldschmidt, Walter (ed.)
1959 The anthropology of Franz Boas. In *American Anthropological Association, Memoir* 89: 61–75.
Goodenough, Ward H.
1951 Native astronomy in Micronesia: A rudimentary science. In *Scientific Monthly* (August).
Gossett, T. F.
1963 *Race: The History of an Idea in America.* Dallas: Southern Methodist University Press.
Graebner, Fritz
1911 *Methode der Ethnologie.* Heidelberg: C. Winter.
Granatino, Giovanni Leone
1957 Jean-Léon l'Africain. Description de l'Afrique. Nouvelle édition traduite de l'italien par A. Epaulard et annotée par A. Epaulard, Th. Monod, H. Lhote et R. Mauny. In *Institut des Hautes Etudes Marocaines,* Publication 61. Paris: Librairie d'Amérique et d'Orient Adrien Maisonneuve. 2 vols.
Greene, J. C.
1959 *The Death of Adam.* Ames, Iowa: Iowa State University Press.
1961 *Darwin and the Modern World View.* Baton Rouge: Louisiana State University Press.
Gruber, Jacob
1965 Brixham Cave and the antiquity of man. In Melford E. Spiro (ed.), *Context and Meaning in Cultural Anthropology.* New York: Free Press, pp. 373–402.
1967 Horatio Hale and the development of American anthropology. In *Proceedings of the American Philosophical Society,* III: 5–37.
Guy, B.
1963 The French image of China before and after Voltaire. In Theodore Besterman (ed.), *Studies on Voltaire and the Eighteenth Century.*
Haber, Francis C.
1959 *The Ages of the World—Moses to Darwin.* Baltimore: Johns Hopkins Press.
Haddon, Alfred C.
1910 *History of Anthropology.* New York: Putnam.
1934 *History of Anthropology.* London: Watts.
Halliday, R. J.
1971 Social Darwinism: a definition. In *Victorian Studies,* 14: 389–405.
Hallowell, A. Irving
1946 Some psychological characteristics of the Northeastern Indians. In Frederick Johnson (ed.), *Man in Northeastern North America.*
1954 Psychology and anthropology. In John Gillin (ed.), *For a Science of Social Man; Convergences in Anthropology, Psychology, and Sociology.*

1955 *Culture and Experience.* Philadelphia: University of Pennsylvania Press.
1957 The impact of the American Indian on American culture. In *American Anthropologist,* 59: 201–217.
1960 The beginnings of anthropology in America. In Frederica de Laguna (ed.), *Selected Readings from the American Anthropologist, 1888–1920.* New York: Harper & Row, pp. 1–90.
1963 Personality, culture and society in behavioral evolution. In Sigmund Koch (ed.), *Psychology: A Study of a Science.* Vol. 6: *Investigations of Man as Socius.* New York: McGraw-Hill, pp. 429–509.
1965 The history of anthropology as an anthropological problem. In *Journal of the History of the Behavioral Sciences,* I: 24–38.

Hanzeli, Victor Egon
1969 *Missionary Linguistics in New France: A Study of Seventeenth and Eighteenth Century Descriptions of American Indian Languages.* The Hague: Mouton.

Harding, T., and E. Leacock
1964 Morgan and materialism: a reply to Professor Opler. In *Current Anthropology,* 5: 109–110.

Harris, Marvin
1968 *The Rise of Anthropological Theory.* New York: T. Y. Crowell.

Harris, Marvin, et al.
1968 CA Review: the rise of anthropological theory. In *Current Anthropology,* 9: 519–533.

Harris, Victor
1949 *All Coherence Gone.* Chicago: University of Chicago Press.

Harris, Zellig
1952 Review of David Mandelbaum (ed.), The *Selected Writings of Edward Sapir.* In *Language,* 27: 288–333.

Hart, C. W. W.
1954 The sons of Turimpi. In *American Anthropologist,* 56: 242–261.

Hartland, E. Sidney
1909–10 *Primitive Paternity.* London: D. Nutt. 2 vols.

Haven, Samuel
1856 Archaeology of the United States: sketches, historical and bibliographical, of the progress of information and opinion concerning the vestiges of antiquity in the United States. In *Smithsonian Contributions to Knowledge,* 8: 140–159.

Hazard, Paul
1953 *La Crise de la Conscience Européenne.* Paris: Boiven and Cie, 1935. Translated later as *The European Mind. The Critical Years (1680–1715).* New Haven: Yale University Press.

Heine-Geldern, Robert
1960 Recent developments in ethnological theory in Europe. In A. Wallace (ed.), *Selected Papers of the Fifth International Congress*

of Anthropological Sciences. Philadelphia: University of Pennsylvania Press, pp. 49–53.

Heitz, Emil

1869 *Fragmenta Aristotelis.* Paris: Editore Ambrosio Firmin-Didot.

Heizer, Robert F.

1959 *The Archaeologist at Work.* New York: Harper & Row.

1962 The background of Thomsen's three-age system. In *Technology and Culture,* 3: 259–266.

Hellman, Geoffrey

1968 *Bankers, Bones and Beetles: The First Century of the American Museum of Natural History.* New York: Natural History Press.

Helm, June (ed.)

1966 Pioneers of American anthropology. *American Ethnological Society.* Seattle: University of Washington Press.

Helton, Tinsley (ed.)

1961 *The Renaissance; a Reconsideration of the Theories and Interpretations of the Age.* Madison: University of Wisconsin Press.

Herodotus

1921–38 *Herodotus.* English translation by A. D. Godley. Loeb Classical Library. London: William Heinemann Ltd.; Cambridge: Harvard University Press. 4 vols.

1954 *The Histories.* Baltimore: Penguin Books.

Herschel, J. F. W.

1830 *Preliminary Discourse on the Study of Natural Philosophy.* London: Longmans.

Herskovits, Melville

1953 *Franz Boas: The Man in the Making.* New York: Scribner.

Hodge, Frederick Webb

1932 Biographical sketch and bibliography of Adolphe Francis Alphonse Bandelier. In *New Mexico Historical Review,* 7: 353–370.

Hodgen, Margaret T.

1931 The doctrine of survivals. In *American Anthropologist,* 33: 307–324.

1964 *Early Anthropology in the Sixteenth and Seventeenth Centuries.* Philadelphia: University of Pennsylvania Press.

Hodgkin, T.

1848 The progress of ethnology. In *Journal of the Ethnological Society of London,* I: 27–45.

Hoebel, E. Adamson

1960 William Robertson: an 18th century anthropologist-historian. In *American Anthropologist,* 62: 648–655.

Hofstadter, Richard

1944 *Social Darwinism in American Thought, 1860–1915.* Philadelphia: University of Pennsylvania Press.

Homans, George C.
1941 Anxiety and ritual: the theories of Malinowski and Radcliffe-Brown. In *American Anthropologist*, 43: 164–172.
Honigmann, John J.
1954 *Culture and Personality*. New York: Harper & Row.
Hortis, Attilio
1879 *Studi Sulle Opere Latine del Boccaccio, con Particolare Riguardo Alla Storia della Erudizione nel Medio Evo e Alle Letterature Straniere.* Trieste: Libreria Julius Dase Editrice.
Howorth, H. H.
1901 The earliest traces of man. In *Geological Magazine*, N.S., 8: 337–344.
1902 The origin and progress of the modern theory of the antiquity of man. In *Geological Magazine*, N.S., 8: 16–27.
Hunt, A. R.
1863 Introductory address on the study of anthropology. In *Anthropological Review*, I: 1–20.
1902 On Kent's cavern with reference to Buckland and his detractors. In *Geological Magazine*, N.S., 9: 114–118.
Hus, Alain
1961 *The Etruscans*. New York: Grove Press.
Hyman, Stanley Edgar
1954 Freud and Boas: secular rabbis? In *Commentary*, 17: 264–267.
Hymes, Dell
1961 Alfred Louis Kroeber. In *Language*, 37: 1–28.
1962 On studying the history of anthropology. In *Kroeber Anthropological Society Papers*, 26: 81–86.
1971 Morris Swadesh: from the first Yale School to world prehistory. In *Morris Swadesh, the Origin and Diversification of Language*. Chicago: Aldine, pp. 228–270.
in press *Traditions and Paradigms: Studies in the History of Linguistics*. Bloomington: Indiana University Press.
Jacoby, Felix
1926–30 *Die Fragmente der Griechischen Historiker (F Gr Hist); Zweiter Teil, Zeitgeschichte*. Berlin: Weidmannsche Buchhandlung. 2 vols. in 6 parts.
Jefferson, Thomas
1964 *Notes on the State of Virginia* (1785). New York: Harper & Row.
Johnson, Frederick (ed.)
1946 Man in northeastern North America. In *Papers of the R. S. Peabody Foundation for Archeology*, 3. Andover: Phillips Academy, the Foundation.
Judd, Neil
1967 *The Bureau of American Ethnology: A Partial History*. Norman: University of Oklahoma Press.

Kardiner, Abram
1939 *The Individual and His Society.* New York: Columbia University Press.
1945 *The Psychological Frontiers of Society.* New York: Columbia University Press.
Kardiner, Abram, and Preble, Edward
1961 *They Studied Man.* New York: Mentor.
Kendrick, T. D.
1950 *British Antiquity.* London: Methuen.
Khaldûn, Ibn
1958 *The Muqaddimah: An Introduction to History.* Translated by Franz Rosenthal. New York: Pantheon.
Kluckhohn, Clyde
1941 Patterning as exemplified in Navaho culture. In Leslie Spier (ed.), *Language, Culture and Personality.*
1943 Covert culture and administrative problems. In *American Anthropologist,* 45: 213–29.
1944 Culture and personality: a conceptual scheme. In *American Anthropologist,* 46: 1–29.
1951 Introduction. In Evon Z. Vogt, *Navaho Veterans, a Study of Changing Values.*
1952 Values and value-orientations. In Talcott Parsons and E. A. Shils (eds.), *Toward a General Theory of Action.*
1953 Universal categories of culture. In *Anthropology Today.* Prepared under the chairmanship of A. L. Kroeber. Chicago: University of Chicago Press.
1961 *Anthropology and the Classics.* Providence: Brown University Press.
Kluckhohn, Clyde, Henry A. Murray, and David Schneider
1953 *Personality in Nature, Society, and Culture.* New York: Knopf.
Kroeber, A. L.
1915 Eighteen professions. In *American Anthropologist,* 17: 283–288.
1917 The superorganic. In *American Anthropologist,* 19: 163–213.
1920 Totem and taboo; an ethnologic psychoanalysis. In *American Anthropologist,* 22: 48–55.
1939 Totem and taboo in retrospect. In *American Journal of Sociology,* 45: 446–451.
1948 White's view of culture. In *American Anthropologist,* 50: 405–415.
1950 A half century of anthropology. In *The Nature of Culture.* Chicago: University of Chicago Press.
1956 The place of Boas in anthropology. In *American Anthropologist,* 58: 151–159.
1959 A history of the personality of anthropology. In *American Anthropologist,* 61: 398–404.

Kroeber, A. L., et al.
1943 Franz Boas, 1858–1942. In *American Anthropological Association Memoir,* 61.
Kroeber, A. L., and Clyde Kluckhohn
1952 Culture: a critical review of concepts and definitions. In *Papers of the Peabody Museum of American Archaeology and Ethnology,* 47. Harvard University.
Kroeber, Theodora
1970 *Alfred Kroeber: a Personal Configuration.* Berkeley: University of California Press.
Kuhn, Thomas
1962 *The Structure of Scientific Revolutions.* Chicago: University of Chicago Press.
Lamb, Daniel
1906 The story of the Anthropological Society of Washington. In *American Anthropologist,* 8: 564–579.
Laughlin, William S.
1961 Acquisition of anatomical knowledge by ancient man. In Sherwood L. Washburn (ed.), *Social Life of Early Man.* New York: Viking Fund Publications in Anthropology, 31 (Wenner-Gren Foundation for Anthropological Research).
Leach, Edmund
1966 On the "founding fathers." In *Current Anthropology,* 7: 560–567.
Lebrija, Elio Antonio de
1926 *Nebrija, Grammatica de la Lengua Castellana (Salamanca, 1492), Muestra de la Istoria de las Antiguedades de Espana, Reglas de Orthographia en la Lengua Castellana.* Edited with an introduction and notes by Ig. González-Llubera. London: Humphrey Milford, Oxford University Press.
1946 *Grammatica Castellana.* Texto establecido sobre la ed. "princeps" de 1492 por Pascual Galindo Romeo y Luís Ortiz Muñoz, con una introducción, notas y facsímil. Madrid: Junta del Centenario. 2 vols.
1951 Vocabulario español-latino por Elio Antonio de Nebrija (Salamanca 1495?). In *Real Academia Española,* Facsimiles, serie II, no. IV. Madrid.
Legrand, Philippe Ernest
1932 De la "malignité" d'Hérodote. In *Mélanges Gustave Glotz,* 2: 535–547. Paris: Les Presses Universitaires de France.
Lehmann, Hartleben Karl
1943 Cyriacus of Ancona, Aristotle and Teiresias in Samothrace. *Hesperia* XII: 115–134.
Letts, Malcolm
1949 *Sir John Mandeville; the Man and His Book.* London: Batchworth.

Lévy-Bruhl, Lucien

1910 *Les Fonctions Mentales dans les Sociétés Inférieures.* Paris: F. Alcan.

Linton, Adelaide, and Charles Wagley

1971 *Ralph Linton.* New York: Columbia University Press.

Linton, Ralph

1936 *The Study of Man.* New York: Appleton.

1940 (ed.) *Acculturation in Seven American Indian Tribes.* New York: Appleton.

1943 Nativistic movements. In *American Anthropologist,* 45: 230–240.

1945 *The Cultural Background of Personality.* New York: Appleton.

Lips, Julius E.

1937 *The Savage Hits Back.* With an introduction by Bronislaw Malinowski. New Haven: Yale University Press.

Literary Gazette

1849 Notice of the meeting of the British Archaeological Association. In *The Literary Gazette and Journal of Belles Lettres, Arts, Sciences,* etc., April 28 and May 5.

Locke, John

1956 *Two Treatises of Government.* Hafner Library of Classics, 2. New York: Hafner Publishing Company.

Lovejoy, Arthur O.

1933 Monboddo and Rousseau. In *Modern Philology,* 30: 275–296.

Lowie, Robert H.

1912 On the principle of convergence in ethnology. In *Journal of American Folklore,* 25: 24–43.

1916 Plains Indian age-societies: historical and comparative summary. In *American Museum of Natural History Anthropological Papers,* 2: 877–992.

1929 *Culture and Ethnology.* New York: P. Smith.

1936 Lewis H. Morgan in historical perspective. In *Essays in Anthropology Presented to A. L. Kroeber.* Berkeley: University of California Press, pp. 169–181.

1937 *The History of Ethnological Theory.* New York: Holt, Rinehart and Winston.

1946 Evolution in cultural anthropology: a reply to Leslie White. In *American Anthropologist,* 48: 223–243.

1948 *Primitive Religion.* New York: Liveright.

1956a Boas once more. In *American Anthropologist,* 58: 159–163.

1956b Reminiscences of anthropological currents in America half a century ago. In *American Anthropologist,* 58: 995–1015.

1959 *Robert H. Lowie: Ethnologist.* Berkeley: University of California Press.

Lubbock, John
1865 *Prehistoric Times*. London: Williams and Norgate.
1870 *The Origin of Civilization*. London: Williams and Norgate.
Lucretius
1951 *On the Nature of the Universe*. Translated by Ronald Latham. Baltimore: Penguin Books.
Lutz, Henry F.
1927 The Sumerian and anthropology. In *American Anthropologist*, 29: 202–209.
Lyell, C.
1855 *Principles of Geology; or the Modern Changes of the Earth and Its Inhabitants*. 9th ed. London: Murray.
1859 On the occurrence of works of human art in post-Pliocene deposits. In *Report of the British Association for Advancement of Science*, 29: 93–95.
1863 *The Geological Evidences of the Antiquity of Man*. London: Murray.
Lyell, K.
1881 *Life, Letters and Journals of Sir Charles Lyell, Bart*. London: Murray. 2 vols.
Lyon, Patricia
1969 Anthropological activity in the United States, 1865–1879. In *Kroeber Anthropological Society Papers*, 40: 8–37.
MacCurdy, George Grant
1899 The extent of instruction in anthropology in Europe and the United States. In *Science*, 10: 910–917.
1902a The teaching of anthropology in the United States. In *Science*, 15: 211–216.
1902b Twenty years of Section H, Anthropology. In *Science*, 15: 532–534.
MacEnery, J.
1859 *Cavern Researches, Discoveries of Organic Remains and of British and Roman Reliques in the Caves of Kent's Hole, Anstis Cave, Chudleigh and Berry Head*. Edited from manuscript notes by E. Vivian. London: Simkin, Marshall.
Mahdi, Muhsin
1957 *Ibn Khaldûn's Philosophy of History*. Chicago: University of Chicago Press.
Maine, Henry
1861 *Ancient Law*. London: Murray.
Malinowski, Bronislaw
1927 *Sex and Repression in Savage Society*. London: Kegan Paul.
1931 Culture. In *Encyclopedia of the Social Sciences*, 4: 621–645. New York: Macmillan.

1944 *A Scientific Theory of Culture and Other Essays*. Chapel Hill: University of North Carolina Press.
1967 *A Diary in the Strict Sense of the Term*. New York: Harcourt Brace Jovanovich.

Malthus, Thomas R.
1926 *First Essay on Population, 1798*. London: Macmillan.

Mancini, Girolamo
1891 *Vita di Lorenzo Valla*. Firenze: G. C. Sansoni, Editore.

Mantell, G. A.
1844 *The Medals of Creation: or First Lessons in Geology and in the Study of Organic Remains*. London: Bohn. 2 vols.

Manuel, Frank E.
1959 *The Eighteenth Century Confronts the Gods*. Cambridge: Harvard University Press.
1962 *The Prophets of Paris*. New York: Harper & Row.

McCown, Theodore
1961 Alfred Louis Kroeber, 1876–1960. In *Robert H. Lowie Museum of Anthropology Annual Report*. Berkeley, Calif., pp. 29–37.

McCrindle, John Watson
1877 *Ancient India as Described by Megasthenes and Arrian*. With introduction, notes and map of ancient India. Calcutta: Thacker, Spink; Bombay: Thacker; London: Trubner.

McGee, W J [sic]
1897 The Bureau of American Ethnology. In G. Brown Goode (ed.), *The Smithsonian Institution, 1846–1896: The History of Its First Half-Century*. Washington: Devine Press, pp. 367–396.
1901 Man's place in nature. In *American Anthropologist*, 3: 1–13.

McLennan, J. F.
1865 *Primitive Marriage*. London: Macmillan.
1896 *Studies in Ancient History*. London: Macmillan.

Mead, Margaret
1949 *Coming of Age in Samoa*. New York: New American Library.
1950 *Sex and Temperament in Three Primitive Societies*. New York: New American Library.
1953 *Growing Up in New Guinea*. New York: New American Library.
1959 *An Anthropologist at Work: The Writings of Ruth Benedict*. Boston: Houghton Mifflin.
1972 *Blackberry Winter: My Earlier Years*. New York: William Morrow.

Mead, Margaret, and Ruth Bunzel (eds.)
1960 *The Golden Age of Anthropology*. New York: Braziller.

Mercier, P.
1966 *Histoire de l'Anthropologie*. Paris: Presses Universitaires de France.

Meunier, V.
1875 *Les Ancêtres d'Adam: Histoire de l'Homme Fossile.* Paris: J. Rothschild.
Meyer, Eduard
1953–56 *Geschichte des Altertums; Fünfte Auflage.* Basel: Benno and Company. (First published 1884–1902.) 4 vols. in 7 parts.
Millcr, II.
1841 *The Old Red Sandstone: or New Walks in an Old Field.* Edinburgh: Constable.
1857 *Testimony of the Rocks: or Geology in Its Bearings on the Two Theologies, Natural and Revealed.* Boston: Gould and Lincoln.
Miller, M. J. G. (ed.)
1950 *Experiments in Social Process: A Symposium on Social Psychology.* New York: McGraw-Hill.
Mitra, Panchanan
1933 *A History of American Anthropology.* Calcutta: University of Calcutta Press.
Momigliano, Arnaldo
1955 Ancient history and the antiquarian. In *Contributo Alla Storia Degli Studi Classici, Storia e Letteratura,* 47: 67–106. Roma.
1960 The place of Herodotus in the history of historiography. In *Secondo Contributo Alla Storia Degli Studi Classici, Storia e Letteratura,* 77: 29–44. Roma.
Mommsen, Theodor Ernst (ed.)
1957 *Petrarch's Testament.* Edited and translated, with an introduction. Ithaca: Cornell University Press.
Montaigne, Michel de
1958 *Essays.* Translated by J. M. Cohen. Baltimore: Penguin Books.
Montesquieu, Baron de
1949 *The Spirit of the Laws.* Translated by Thomas Nugent. New York: Hafner, pp. 221–234.
Moraux, Paul
1951 Les listes anciennes des ouvrages d'Aristot. Préface par Augustin Mansion. Aristote; Traductions et Etudes. In *Collection Publiée par l'Institut Supérieur de Philosophie de l'Université de Louvain.* Louvain.
Morgan, Lewis H.
1851 *League of the Ho-de-no-sau-nee.* New Haven: Behavioral Science Reprints (1944).
1871 *Systems of Consanguinity and Affinity of the Human Family.* Washington: Smithsonian Institution.
1877 *Ancient Society.* New York: Holt, Rinehart & Winston.
1931 Organization of society upon the basis of sex. In V. F. Calverton (ed.), *The Making of Man; an Outline of Anthropology.*
Mortillet, G. de
1865 *Matériaux pour L'Histoire Positive et Philosophique de*

L'Homme. Première Année, September 1864, à Août 1865. Paris: Edouard Blot.

Muller, Carl Wilhelm Ludwig
1874–83 *Fragmenta Historicorum Graecorum*. Paris: Editore Ambrosio Firmin-Didot.

Mulvaney, D. J.
1958 The Australian Aborigines, 1606–1929. In *Historical Studies: Australia and New Zealand*, 8: 150–151.

Murdock, George P.
1951 British social anthropology. In *American Anthropologist*, 53: 465–573.
1954 Sociology and anthropology. In John Gillin (ed.), *For a Science of Social Man; Convergences in Anthropology, Psychology, and Sociology*.

Murphree, I.
1961 The evolutionary anthropologists: the progress of mankind. In *Proceedings of the American Philosophical Society*, 105: 265–300.

Murphy, Robert
1972 *Robert Lowie*. New York: Columbia University Press.

Myres, J. L.
1906 The influence of anthropology on the course of political thought. In *Nature*, 31: 379–384.
1908 Herodotus and anthropology. In R. R. Marett (ed.), *Anthropology and the Classics*. Six lectures delivered before the University of Oxford. Oxford: Clarendon Press, pp. 121–168.
1953 *Herodotus, Father of History*. Oxford: Clarendon Press.

Nagel, Ernst
1961 *The Structure of Science: Problems in the Logic of Scientific Explanation*. London: Routledge.

Nasr, Seyyed Hassein
1968 *Science and Civilization in Islam*. New York: New American Library.

Newcomb, T. H., and E. L. Hartley (eds.)
1947 *Readings in Social Psychology*. New York: Holt, Rinehart & Winston.

Nolhac, Pierre de
1907 *Pétrarque et l'Humanisme*. Nouvelle édition, remaniée et augmentée. Bibliotheque Littéraire de la Renaissance, N.S., tomes I–II. Paris: Librairie Honoré Champion, Editeur. 2 vols.

Norden, Eduard
1922 *Die Germanische Urgeschichte in Tacitus Germania*. Zweiter Abdruck mit Ergänzungen. Leipzig, Berlin: Verlag von B. G. Teubner.

North, F. J.
1942 Paviland Cave, the "Red Lady," the Deluge, and William Buckland. In *Annals of Science*, 5: 91–128.

Nott, J. C., and George Gliddon
1854 *Types of Mankind.* Philadelphia: Lippincott.
Olschki, Leonardo
1960 *Marco Polo's Asia; an Introduction to his "Description of the World" called "Il milione."* Berkeley and Los Angeles: University of California Press.
Opler, Morris Edward
1945 Themes as dynamic forces in culture. In *American Journal of Sociology,* 51: 198–206.
1946 Cultural anthropology: an application of the theory of themes in culture. In *Journal of the Washington Academy of Sciences,* 36: 137–166.
1962 Integration, evolution and Morgan. In *Current Anthropology,* 3: 478–479.
1964 Cause, process and dynamics in the evolution of E. B. Tylor. In *Southwestern Journal of Anthropology,* 20: 123–145.
Oviedo, Gonzalo Fernández de
1959 *Natural History of the West Indies.* Translated by Sterling A. Stoudemire. Chapel Hill: University of North Carolina.
Owen, R.
1859 *On the Classification and Geographical Distribution of the Mammalia.* London: Parker.
Panofsky, Erwin
1960 Renaissance and renascences in Western art. In *The Gottesman Lectures, Uppsala University,* VII. Stockholm: Almqvist and Wiksell. 2 vols.
1962 Artist, scientist, genius: notes on the "Renaissance-Dämmerung." In *The Renaissance; Six Essays.* New York: Harper & Row, The Academy Library, pp. 123–182.
Parsons, Talcott, and E. A. Shils (eds.)
1951 *Toward a General Theory of Action.* Cambridge: Harvard University Press.
Peake, H. J. E.
1940 The study of prehistoric times. In *Journal of the Royal Anthropological Institute,* 70: 103–146.
Pearce, Roy H.
1953 *The Savages of America; a Study of the Indian and the Idea of Civilization.* Baltimore: Johns Hopkins Press.
Pengelly, H.
1897 *A Memoir of William Pengelly of Torquay, F.R.S. Geologist.* London: Murray.
Pengelly, W.
1860 *Journal of the Excavations at Brixham Cave,* ms. in possession of Torquay Natural History Society. Torquay, England. 13 vols.
1868 The literature of Kent's Cavern, Torquay, prior to 1859. In

Transactions of the Devonshire Association for the Advancement of Science, Literature, and Art, 2: 470–522.
1869 The literature of Kent's Cavern. Part 2, in *Transactions of the Devonshire Association for the Advancement of Science, Literature, and Art*, 3: 191–482.
1874 The Cavern discovered in 1858 in Windmill Hill, Brixham, South Devon. In *Transactions of the Devonshire Association for the Advancement of Science, Literature, and Art*, 6: 775–856.
1884 The literature of Kent's Cavern. Part 5, in *Transactions of the Devonshire Association for the Advancement of Science, Literature, and Art*, 16: 189–434.

Penniman, T. K.
1965 *A Hundred Years of Anthropology*. London: Gerald Duckworth.

Peuch, Henri-Charles
1957 Gnosis and time. In *Man and Time, Papers from the Eranos Yearbooks*. New York: Pantheon.

Pizzicolli, Ciriaco de'
1742 *Kyriaci Anconitani Itinerarium nunc primum ex ms. cod. in lucem erutum* . . . Editionem reconsuit . . . nonnullisque ejusdem Kyriaci epistolis . . . locupletavit Laurentius Mehus. Firenze: Giovanni Paolo Giovannelli.

Plinius Secundus, Caius
1938–63 *Pliny, Natural History*. English translation by H. Rackham, W. H. S. Jones, and D. E. Eichholz. Loeb Classical Library. London: William Heinemann; Cambridge: Harvard University Press. 10 vols.

Polo, Marco
1938 *Marco Polo, the Description of the World*. Edited by A. C. Moule and Paul Pelliot. London: Routledge. 2 vols.

Powell, John Wesley
1877 *Introduction to the Study of Indian Languages*. Washington: Smithsonian Institution.
1891 Indian linguistic families of America north of Mexico. In *Annual Report of the Bureau of American Ethnology*, 7.
1899 Sociology, or the science of institutions. In *American Anthropologist*, 1: 457–509, 695–745.

Pratt, Peter P.
1971 Peter Duponceau's contributions to anthropolgy. In *Ethnohistory*, 18: 147–158.

Prestwich, G. A.
1899 *Life and Letters of Sir Joseph Prestwich*. Edinburgh: Blackwood.

Prestwich, J.
1859 On the occurrence of flint implements, associated with the remains of animals of extinct species in beds of a late geological period in France, at Amiens and Abbeville, and in England at Hoxne. Abstract

in *Proceedings of the Royal Society,* 10: 50–59; *Philosophical Transactions of the Royal Society, 1860–61,* pp. 277–318.
1873 Report on the exploration of Brixham Cave, conducted by a committee of the Geological Society. In *Philosophical Transactions of the Royal Society of London,* 163: 471–572.
Prichard, J. C.
1843 *The Natural History of Man.* London: Bailliere.
1848 On the relations of ethnology. In *Journal of the Ethnological Society of London,* 1: 301–329.
Putnam, Frederick Ward
1895 The history, aims and importance of the American Association for the Advancement of Science. In *Science,* 2: 171–174.
Quatrefages, Armand de
1867 *Rapport sur les Progrès de l'Anthropologie.* Paris: Imprimérie Imperal.
Radcliffe-Brown, A. R.
1922 *The Andaman Islanders.* Cambridge, England: The University Press.
1935 On the concept of function in social science. In *American Anthropologist,* 37: 394–402.
1939 *Taboo* (Frazer lecture for 1939). Cambridge, England: The University Press.
1947 Evolution, social or cultural? In *American Anthropologist,* 49: 78–83.
1949 White's view of a science of culture. In *American Anthropologist,* 51: 503–512.
1952a Historical note on British social anthropology. In *American Anthropologist,* 54: 275–277.
1952b *Structure and Function in Primitive Society.* Glencoe: The Free Press.
1958 M. N. Srinivas (ed.), *Method in Social Anthropology: Selected Essays.* Chicago: University of Chicago Press.
Radin, Paul
1933 *The Method and Theory of Ethnology.* New York: McGraw-Hill.
1957 *Primitive Man as a Philosopher.* New York: Dover.
Ray, Verne F., and Nancy O. Lurie
1954 The contributions of Lewis and Clark to ethnography. In *Journal of the Washington Anthropological Society,* 44: 358–370.
Read, C. H.
1906 Anthropology at the universities. In *Man,* 6: 56–59.
Redfield, Robert
1941 *The Folk Culture of Yucatan.* Chicago: University of Chicago Press.
Reimann, Eugen
1895 Quo ex fonte fluxerit Nicolai Damasceni paradoxōn ethōn syna-

gōgē. In *Philologus,* 54. Band (N.F., 8 Band), No. 4: 654–709. Göttingen.

Resek, Carl
1960 *Lewis Henry Morgan: American Scholar.* Chicago: University of Chicago Press.

Ricardo, David
1933 *Principles of Political Economy and Taxation.* London: Dent (Everyman's Library).

Robertson, William
1777 *The History of America.* Edinburgh: J. Robertson, pp. v–xiv.

Robertson-Smith, W.
1914 *The Religion of the Semites.* London: Adam and Charles Black, pp. 15–27.

Rohner, Ronald P. (ed.)
1969 *The Ethnography of Franz Boas: Letters and Diaries of Franz Boas Written on the Northwest Coast from 1886 to 1931.* Chicago: University of Chicago Press.

Rousseau, Jean J.
1913 *The Social Contract and Discourses.* London: Dent (Everyman's Library).

Rowe, John Howland
1962 Alfred Louis Kroeber 1876–1960. In *American Antiquity,* 27: 395–415.
1964 Ethnography and ethnology in the sixteenth century. In *Kroeber Anthropological Society Papers,* 30: 1–19.
1965 The Renaissance foundations of anthropology. In *American Anthropologist,* 67: 1–20.

Sabbadini, Remigio
1888 *Inscriptiones Christianae Urbis Romae Septimo Saeculo Antiquiores.* Edidit Ioannes Bapt. de Ross. Vol. 2, pt. 1. Roma: Libreria Filippo Cuggiani.
1905–14 *Le Scoperte Dei Codici Latini e Greci ne' Secoli XIV e XV.* Firenz: G. C. Sansoni, Editore. 2 vols.

Salas, Alberto Mario
1959 *Tres Cronistas de Indias; Pedro Mártir de Anglería, Gonzalo Fernández de Oviedo, Fray Bartolomé de las Casas.* México: Fondo de Cultura Económica.

Sanford, Eva M.
1944 The study of ancient history in the Middle Ages. In *Journal of History of Ideas,* 5: 21–43.

Sapir, Edward
1917 Do we need a "superorganic?" In *American Anthropologist,* 19: 441–447.
1934 The emergence of the concept of personality in a study of culture. In *Journal of Social Psychology,* 5: 408–415.

1938 Why cultural anthropology needs the psychiatrist. In *Psychiatry*, 1: 7–12.
1965 *Letters from Edward Sapir to Robert H. Lowie*. Berkeley: University of California Press.

Sarton, George
1948 Introduction to the history of science. In *Science and Learning in the Fourteenth Century*, part II. *Carnegie Institution of Washington Publication*, 376, vol. III. Baltimore: Williams and Wilkins (reprinted 1953).
1959 *A History of Science: Hellenistic Science and Culture in the Last Three Centuries* B.C. New York: Wiley.

Scalamonti, Francesco
1792 Vita di Ciriaco Anconitano. In *Della Antichita Picene dell' Abate Giuseppe Colucci*, 15: i–cly. Fermo: Dai torche dell' autore. (Text in Latin).

Schmerling, P. C.
1833–34 *Recherches sur les Ossemens Fossiles Découverts dans les Cavernes de la Province de Liege*. Liege: Collardin. 2 vols.

Schneider, Louis (ed.)
1967 *The Scottish Moralists on Human Nature and Society*. Chicago: University of Chicago Press.

Schroeder, Walter Alfred
1921 *De Ethnographiae Antiquae Locis Quibusdam Communibus Observationes*. (Dissertatio inauguralis . . . in Academia Fridericiana Halensi . . . Halle, Karras, Kroeber and Nietschmann.)

Sebeok, Thomas (ed.)
1963 *Portraits of Linguists: A Biographical Sourcebook for the History of Western Linguistics, 1746–1963*. Bloomington: University of Indiana Press.

Shapiro, Harry L.
1964 Anthropology and the age of discovery. In R. A. Manners (ed.), *Process and Pattern in Culture, Essays in Honor of Julian H. Steward*. Chicago: Aldine, pp. 337–348.

Sikes, Edward Ernest
1914 *The Anthropology of the Greeks*. London: David Nutt.

Simpson, George Gaylord
1960 The history of life. In Sol Tax (ed.), *Evolution after Darwin*. Volume 1: *The Evolution of Life*. Chicago: University of Chicago Press, pp. 117–180.
1964 *This View of Life; the World of an Evolutionist*. New York: Harcourt Brace Jovanovich.

Slotkin, James Sidney
1965 *Readings in Early Anthropology*. Chicago: University of Chicago Press.

Smith, Bernard
1960 *European Vision and the South Pacific, 1768–1850; a Study in the History of Art and Ideas.* Oxford: Oxford University Press.
Smith, Henry Nash
1950 *Virgin Land: the American West as Symbol and Myth.* New York: Vintage.
Smith, Marian
1943 Centenary of the American Ethnological Society: forward and brief history. In *American Anthropologist,* 45: 181–184.
Society of Antiquaries Correspondence
In possession of Society of Antiquaries of London. London: Burlington House.
Spencer, Herbert
1851 *Social Statics.* London: Williams and Norgate.
1862 *First Principles.* London: Williams and Norgate.
1877 *The Principles of Sociology.* New York: Appleton.
Spencer, Robert F.
1958 Culture process and intellectual current: Durkheim and Ataturk. In *American Anthropologist,* 60: 640–657.
Spiegelberg, Wilhelm
1927 *The Credibility of Herodotus' Account of Egypt in the Light of the Egyptian Monuments.* With a few additional notes by the translator, Aylward M. Blackman. Oxford: Blackwell.
Spier, Leslie
1921 The sun dance of the plains Indians; its development and diffusion. In *American Museum of Natural History Anthropological Papers,* 16: 451–527.
1941 (ed.) *Language, Culture, and Personality; Essays in Memory of Edward Sapir.* Menasha: George Banta.
1943 Franz Boas and some of his views. In *Sobretiro de Acta Americana,* 1: 108–127.
Spiro, Melford E.
1954 Human nature in its psychological dimensions. In *American Anthropologist,* 56: 19–30.
Stanton, William
1960 *The Leopard's Spots. Scientific Attitudes toward Race in America, 1815–1859.* Chicago: University of Chicago Press.
Stark, Karl Bernhard
1880 *Systematik und Geschichte der Archäologie der Kunst.* Handbuch der Archäologie der Kunst, erste Abteilung. Leipzig: Verlag von Wilhelm Engelmann.
Starr, Frederick
1892 Anthropological work in America. In *Popular Science Monthly,* pp. 289–307.

Stein, Otto

1931 (Megasthenes 2) Griechischer Ethnograph Indiens, im 4/3. Jhdt. v. Chr. *Paulys Real-Encyclopädie der Classsischen Altertumswissenschaft, neue Bearbeitung begonnen von Georg Wissowa,* 29. Halbband. Stuttgart: J. B. Metzlersche Verlagsbuchhandlung, pp. 230–326.

Stegner, Wallace

1954 *Beyond the Hundredth Meridian: John Wesley Powell and the Second Opening of the West.* Boston: Houghton Mifflin.

Stern, Bernard J.

1931 *Lewis Henry Morgan: Social Evolutionist.* New York: Russell and Russell.

Stern, Fritz (ed.)

1956 *The Varieties of History. From Voltaire to the Present.* New York: Meridian.

Steward, Julian

1961 Alfred Louis Kroeber, 1876–1960. In *American Anthropologist,* 63: 1038–1060.

Stocking, George W., Jr.

1960 *American Social Scientists and Race Theory: 1890–1915.* (Unpublished Ph.D. dissertation, University of Pennsylvania).

1966 The history of anthropology: where, whence, whither? In *Journal of the History of the Behavioral Sciences,* 2: 281–290.

1968a Empathy and antipathy in the heart of darkness. In *Journal of the History of the Behavioral Sciences,* 4: 189–194.

1968b *Race, Culture and Evolution: Essays in the History of Anthropology.* New York: Free Press.

1968c Review of *Myth, Religion and Mother Right: Selected Writings of J. J. Bachofen.* In *American Anthropologist,* 70: 1188–1190.

1968d Edward Burnett Tylor. In *International Encyclopedia of the Social Sciences,* 16: 170–177. New York: Macmillan.

1969 *John Ferguson McLennan: Ontogeny and Phylogeny.* (Paper to King's College Seminar in Science and History, Cambridge, England.)

1971 What's in a name? The origins of Royal Anthropological Institute (1837–1871). In *Man,* 6: 369–390.

1973 From chronology to ethnology: J. C. Prichard and British anthropology, 1800–1850. In Introduction to J. C. Prichard, *Researches into the Physical History of Man.* Chicago: University of Chicago Press.

In press The Boas Plan for American Indian linguistics: a preliminary examination of the historical evidence. In Dell Hymes (ed.), *Traditions and Paradigms: Studies in the History of Linguistics.* Bloomington: Indiana University Press.

Strabo

1917–32 *The Geography of Strabo,* with an English translation by

Horace Leonard Jones. Loeb Classical Library. London: William Heinemann; Cambridge: Harvard University Press. 8 vols.

Sturtevant, William C.

1958 The authorship of the Powell Classification. In *International Journal of American Linguistics,* 25: 196–199.

1964 Studies in ethnoscience. In *American Anthropologist,* 66, no. 3, part 2, Special Publication 1, pp. 99–131.

Swadesh, Morris

1951 Diffusional cumulation and archaic residue as historical explanations. In *Southwestern Journal of Anthropology,* 7: 1–21.

1961 The culture historic implications of Sapir's linguistic classification. In A. William Cameron Townsend, et al., *Vigesimoquinto Aniversario del Instituto Linguistico de Verano,* Mexico, D.F.

Swanton, John

1911 Indian tribes of the lower Mississippi valley and adjacent coast of the Gulf of Mexico. In *Bureau of American Ethnology Bulletin,* 43: 9–26.

MS Autobiography. In National Anthropological Archives, Smithsonian Institution.

Syme, Ronald

1958 *Tacitus.* Oxford: Clarendon Press. 2 vols.

Symonds, John Addington

1888 *Renaissance in Italy; the Revival of Learning.* New York: Holt, Rinehart & Winston.

Tacitus, Cornelius

1938 *De Origine et Situ Germanorum.* Edited by J. G. C. Anderson. Oxford: Clarendon Press.

Tax, Sol

1955 From Lafitau to Radcliffe-Brown: a short history of the study of social organization. In Fred Eggan (ed.), *Social Anthropology of North American Tribes.* Chicago: University of Chicago Press, pp. 445–481.

Taylor, Alfred Edward

1911 The Dissoi logoi. Varia Socratica, first series. In *St. Andrews University Publications,* 9: 91–128. Oxford: James Parker.

Teggart, F. J.

1925 *Theory of History.* New Haven: Yale University Press.

1945 *Theory and Process of History.* Berkeley: University of California Press.

Thompson, Stith

1968 Reminiscences of an octogenarian folklorist. In Hari S. Upadhyaya (ed.), *Asian Folklore Studies,* 27: 1–65.

Thurnwald, Richard

1935 *Black and White in East Africa.* London: Routledge.

Tolstoy, P.
1952 Morgan and Soviet anthropological thought. In *American Anthropologist,* 54: 8–17.
Toulmin, Stephen, and June Goodfield
1965 *The Discovery of Time.* New York: Harper & Row.
Trigger, Bruce G.
1966a Sir Daniel Wilson: Canada's first anthropologist. In *Anthropologica,* 8: 3–28.
1966b Sir John William Dawson: a faithful anthropologist. In *Anthropologica,* 8: 351–359.
Trüdinger, Karl
1918 *Studien zur Geschichte der griechisch-römischen Ethnographie.* Inaugural Dissertation . . . Basel. Basel: E. Birkhauser.
Tyler, David B.
1968 The Wilkes Expedition: the first United States exploring expedition, 1838–1842. In *American Philosophical Society Memoir,* 73.
Tylor, Edward B.
1874 *Primitive Culture.* Boston: Estes and Lauriat. 2 vols.
1884 American aspects of anthropology. In *Popular Science Monthly,* 26: 152–168.
1888 On a method of investigating the development of institutions: applied to laws of marriage and descent. In *Journal of the Royal Anthropological Institute,* 18: 245–269.
1937 *Anthropology.* 2nd ed. The Thinker's Library. London: Watts. 2 vols.
Untersteiner, Mario
1954 *The Sophists.* Translated from the Italian by Kathleen Freeman. Oxford: Blackwell.
Valla, Lorenzo
1922 *The Treatise of Lorenzo Valla on the Donation of Constantine.* Text and translation into English by Christopher B. Coleman. New Haven: Yale University Press.
1962 *Laurentius Valla, Opera omnia,* con una premesa di Eugenio Garin. Monumenta Politica et Philosophica Rariora, Series I, nos. 5–6. Torino, Bottega d'Erasmo. 2 vols.
Venturi, Lionello
1929 *La Critica d'Arte e Francesco Petrarca; Pretesti di critica.* Minano: Ulrico Hoepli Editore, pp. 37–51.
Vivian, E.
1858 The Brixham Cavern. In *Torquay Register* (September 29).
Voegelin, Carl F.
1952 The Boas Plan for the presentation of American Indian languages. In *Proceedings of the American Philosophical Society,* 96: 439–451.

Voget, Fred W.
1950 A Shoshone innovator. In *American Anthropologist,* 52: 53–63.
1956 The American Indian in transition: reformation and accommodation. In *American Anthropologist,* 58: 249–263.
no date *The Role of Reformation in the Accculturative Process* (manuscript).
1960 Man and culture: an essay in changing anthropological interpretation. In *American Anthropologist,* 62: 943–965.
1967 Process, science, history and evolution in eighteenth and nineteenth century anthropology. In *Journal of the History of the Behavioral Sciences,* 3: 132–155.
1968 Anthropology in the age of Enlightenment: progress and utopian functionalism. In *Southwestern Journal of Anthropology,* 24: 321–345.

Vogt, Evon Z.
1951 Navaho veterans, a study of changing values. In *Papers of the Peabody Museum of American Archaeology and Ethnology,* 41, no. 1. Harvard University.

Voigt, Georg
1894 *Pétraque, Boccace et les Débuts de l'Humanisme en Italie, d'apres la Wiederbelebung des Classischen Alterthums de George Voigt.* Traduit sur la 3e édition allemande par M. A. LeMonnier. Paris: H. Welter, Editeur.

Wacholder, Ben Zion
1962 Nicolaus of Damascus. In *University of California Publications in History,* vol. 75. Berkeley and Los Angeles: University of California Press.

Wagner, Henry Raup
1947 Peter Martyr and his works. In *Proceedings of the American Antiquarian Society,* 56, pt, 2: 239–288. Worcester, Mass.

Wallace, Anthony F. C.
1956 Revitalization movements. In *American Anthropologist,* 58: 264–281.

Wallis, Wilson
1957 Anthropology in England early in the present century. In *American Anthropologist,* 59: 781–790.

Walser, Gerold
1951 *Rom, das Reich und die fremden Völker in der Geschichtsschreibung der früher Kaiserzeit; Studien zur Glaubwürdigkeit des Tacitus.* Baden-Baden: Verlag für Kunst und Wissenschaft.

Washburn, Wilcomb E.
1957 A moral history of Indian-White relations: needs and opportunities for study. In *Ethnohistory,* 4: 47–61.
1964 *The Indian and the White Man.* (ed.) In Documents in American Civilization Series. New York: Doubleday.

Watson, J. A.
1902 Dean Buckland and MacEnery. In *Geological Magazine,* N.S., 9: 85–86.
Wax, Murray
1956 The limitations of Boas' anthropology. In *American Anthropologist,* 58: 63–74.
Wells, G. A.
1959 *Herder and After: A Study of the Development of Sociology.* The Hague: Mouton.
Wells, Joseph
1923 The Persian friends of Herodotus. In *Studies in Herodotus.* Oxford: Basil Blackwell, pp. 95–111.
White, Leslie A.
1945 Diffusion vs. evolution: an anti-evolutionist fallacy. In *American Anthropologist,* 47: 339–356.
1947 Evolutionism in cultural anthropology: a rejoinder. In *American Anthropologist,* 49: 400–411.
1949 *The Science of Culture.* New York: Farrar, Straus & Giroux.
1959a The concept of culture. In *American Anthropologist,* 61: 227–251.
1959b *The Evolution of Culture.* New York: McGraw-Hill.
1963 The ethnology and ethnography of Franz Boas. In *Bulletin of the Texas Memorial Museum,* 6. Austin.
1966 The social organization of ethnological theory. In *Rice University Studies,* 52: 1–66.
Wilkins, Ernest Hatch
1927 *The University of Chicago Manuscript of the Genealogia Deorum Gentilium of Boccacio.* Chicago: University of Chicago Press.
Williams, J. L.
1936 Boas and American ethnologists. In *Thought,* 11: 194–209.
Wilson, Daniel
1862 *Prehistoric Man.* London: Macmillan.
Wissler, Clark
1923 *Man and Culture.* New York: T. Y. Crowell.
1926 *The Relaxation of Nature to Man in Aboriginal America.* New York and London: Oxford University Press.
1942 The American Indian and the American Philosophical Society. In *Proceedings of the American Philosophical Society,* 86: 189–204.
Wittkower, Rudolph.
1942 Marvels of the East: a study in the history of monsters. In *Journal of the Warburg and Courtauld Institutes,* 5: 159–191. London.
Wolfart, H. Christoph
1967 Notes on the early history of American Indian linguistics. In *Folia Linguistica,* 1: 153–171.

Woodbury, R. B.
1960 Nels C. Nelson and chronological archaeology. In *American Antiquity*, 25: 400–401.
Wyngaert, Anastaas Van Den
1929 *Itinera et Relationes Fratrum Minorum Saeculi XIII et XIV*, collegit, ad fidem codicum redigit et adnotavit P. Anastasius van den Wyngaert, O.F.M. Sinica Franciscana, Vol. I. Quaracchi-Firenze.

Index